DATE DUE

DEMCO 38-296

ruth crawford seeger

ruth crawford seeger

A Composer's

Search for

American

Music

JUDITH TICK

New York   Oxford
Oxford University Press
1997

Oxford University Press

Oxford   New York
ınd   Bangkok   Bogota   Bombay   Buenos Aires
                    Dar es Salaam   Delhi   Florence   Hong Kong
Istanbul   Karachi   Kuala Lumpur   Madras   Madrid   Melbourne
Mexico City   Nairobi   Paris   Singapore   Taipei   Tokyo   Toronto   Warsaw

and associated companies in
Berlin   Ibadan

Copyright © 1997 by Judith Tick

Published by Oxford University Press, Inc.,
198 Madison Avenue, New York, New York 10016

Oxford is a registered trademark of Oxford University Press

Library of Congress Cataloging-in-Publication Data
Tick, Judith.
Ruth Crawford Seeger : a composer's search
for American music / Judith Tick.
p.   cm.
"Chronological checklist of works"
Includes bibliographical references and index.
ISBN 0-19-506509-3
1. Seeger, Ruth Crawford, 1901–1953.
2. Composers—United States—Biography.
I. Title.
ML410.S4446T5   1997
780'.92—dc20   95-30085
[B]

Portions of this work were first published in somewhat different
form in the following articles: "Dissonant Counterpoint Revisited: The First
Movement of Ruth Crawford's String Quartet 1931," in A Celebration
of Words and Music in Honor of H. Wiley Hitchcock, ed. Richard Crawford, R.
Allen Lott, and Carol J. Oja (Ann Arbor: University of Michigan Press,
1990): 405–22; "Ruth Crawford's 'Spiritual Concept,': The Sound Ideals of
an Early American Modernist," Journal of the American Musicological Society 44
(Summer 1991): 221–61; "Ruth Crawford—Modernist Pioneer," in
Ruth Crawford, Two Chamber Compostions. Music in the United States, Vol. 1
(Ann Arbor: A-R Editions, 1993); "Some Notes of a Biographer," American
Women Composers News/Forum 11 (Spring/Summer 1993): 4–5; "Ruth
Crawford's Proletarian Ricercari," Sonus: A Journal of Music Theory 15
(Spring 1995): 54–79.

Frontsipiece: photograph of Ruth Crawford
by Fernand de Gueldre

1 2 3 4 5 6 7 8 9
Printed in the United States of America
on acid-free paper

To
Stephen Howes Oleskey,
a loving husband,
and
Mike Seeger,
a loving son

preface

I first saw the name of Ruth Crawford Seeger on the blue and orange cover of a CRI record while browsing in a store on Telegraph Avenue in Berkeley, California, in 1970. I immediately bought this curiosity, for I had never encountered music by a female composer, never mind an American woman, on a classical record before. My teachers in graduate school had filled my ears with preclassic symphonies and medieval motets; orthodox musicologists studied the European past. It would be years before I could hear the dissonant harmonies of Ruth Crawford's Preludes for Piano with aesthetic empathy.

Like so many other young women in those awakening years, I began to investigate women's history in my field. I wrote an article about "sexual aesthetics" and a letter in 1971 to Ruth Crawford's husband, Charles Seeger, for information about two obscure pieces whose titles sounded "political." Three years later he answered me that "Sacco, Vanzetti" and "Chinaman, Laundryman" were "declamations of tremendous power" and not in print.

To his friends he wrote, "Have you seen notices of Ruth's music? She would be very pleased at their 'renaissance.'" Slowly, works like the String Quartet 1931 and the Three Sandburg Songs won acclaim from modern audiences and critics. Simultaneously, this obscure American modernist became a symbol of light and dark—for at the same time that the process of recognition started in earnest, so did questions about unfulfilled promise and silence.

I began this project obliquely, not with the intention of writing a biography but with the goal of publishing music still in manuscript. In 1982 I went to Washington, D.C., for the first performance in over fifty years of the Sonata for Violin and Piano. Apparently, there was no autograph among the composer's estate; at that time I did not suspect the significance of this omission. A score given as a gift had been lost and then found again by Ruth Crawford's pupil and friend, the distinguished composer Vivian Fine; she had heard its performance in Chicago in 1928. Now she and Ida Kavafian were playing it in the Coolidge Auditorium at the Library of Congress. The emotional explicitness of the sonata's four movement markings in the program—"vibrant, agitated," "buoyant," "mystic, intense," and "allegro with ardor"—piqued my curiosity. Fierce dissonances and passionate themes swept through the hall. At a post-concert reception in a living room the size of a soccer field, Vivian Fine stood talking animatedly to a slight, long-haired man, whose boyish dress and speech resonated with a country twang. I thus met Crawford's son, Mike Seeger, with whom I had exchanged one letter, and was immediately swept into the vortex of their dialogue; they discussed my many questions that were on my mind: "Why did Ruth stop composing?" "Was there room in the house for two points of view?" Did she "waste her time" on folksong? Each knew little of the other's world.

The next day I hunted up music manuscripts as I had planned and read diaries as I had not. At twenty-six years old, Crawford wrote, "One can draw a kind of rhythmic or dynamic pleasure from the very smallest things." A piece of scrap paper "rustling across the sidewalk created a perfect scherzo of rhythmic variety and subtlety." As composers are wont to do, she experienced the world through sound. Her earnest transcendentalism touched me. The "voice"—that abstract concept that allows us to translate musical expression into human content—became a person.

I rifled through scrapheaps of papers, delightedly discovering a proper bit of documentary musicological evidence—a scruffy piece of paper on which Ruth Crawford Seeger had scrawled some corrections for the score of the String Quartet 1931, her greatest work. In the margin of this document she had scrawled reminders about household chores in code, the proverbial "laundry list" for biographical zealots.

"What does that have to do with her music?" a musician friend scowled at me. She had been harassed out of a conducting class at a noted conservatory and, futilely denying the direction of her considerable natural gifts, was trying to become a singer, that most feminine of musical careers. Perhaps as a kind of reparatory act for her own history, she reasserted the formalist creed of autonomous art, reproaching me for any hint of collusion with those persecuting forces that made gender relevant to a musician's ambitions. Yet for me a list of daily trivialities opened a window into a world where a composer was not historicized either through augmentation or diminution as a figure engaged in epic struggle, a male archetype. This composer was my kind of heroine—a modern woman whom I could understand as well as admire—someone who was living with messiness and gray patches of confusion and responsibility that afforded some relief from the starkness of dichotomies. The juxtaposition of the two concerns, one the creative self and the other the relational, embodied the fundamental forces that are so unwisely seen as rivals when in fact they are twins—work and love.

W hich side are you on? That early conversation between Mike Seeger and Vivian Fine had rattled me. Sometimes I thought about my subject as Ruth Crawford, other times, Ruth Seeger. Who claimed my loyalties, the composer or the "matriarch"—a term she would have resisted—of a legendary family in the urban folk revival movement that began in the 1930s, with three generations of professional musicians in its family tree? At the apex of the family's fame and influence stands Ruth's stepson Pete Seeger. "Hey Jim-along, Jim-along Josie," Pete sang in a Folkways record album inspired by her work, changing his banjo licks to suit "Jump Jim-along," "Run Jim-along," "Hop-Jim-along," "Skip Jim-along" just as she did in her piano accompaniment in her book *American Folk Songs for Children*. Because folk music had never been part of my professional training, I shared the innocence of discovery that so shaped her folk revival work in the 1930s. Preparing to teach a course on American music, I stumbled across Clarence Ashley and the Carter Family in Harry Smith's *Anthology of American Folk Music* and Gid Tanner and the Skillet Lickers on *Smoky Mountain Ballads*. I fell in love with old-time genius while browsing through a library on Flatbush Avenue.

The integration of these two worlds Ruth Crawford Seeger once described as "stratosphere" and "well-traveled highway" slowly emerged as a major theme of this biography. At first I saw her life through the lens of cultural politics—that is, as a metaphor for a rite of passage for a crucial American cultural moment, when the high individualism of the avant-garde in the 1920s was supplanted by a new populist ethos of accessibility. Because she was so influenced by radical politics, I wondered if Communist rhetoric against elitist art had undermined her. An eminent American composer who admired Crawford Seeger's music had once warily suggested this to me. Indeed, for her—as for later generations of folk revival musicians—the folk revival initially empowered the culture of an outsider class of rural poor.

As I traced the process of cultural mediation that engrossed Ruth Crawford Seeger, which she described as building bridges between country folk, who "came by it natural," and city people, who deserved to know their national legacy, another theme took shape. Because she remained first and foremost a composer, no matter what she did, all of her various activities as transcriber, editor, and arranger of folk materials reflected that sensibility. I began to see how she understood tradition through a modernist perspective, finding affinities that linked the very old with the very new. An ideology of opposition pervaded her work. Just as modernism flouted conventional practice, so did tradition. Just as modernism rejected Romantic excess, so did tradition. Decoding the ways opposition as a value informed her musical choices integrated the two parts of her musical identity.

It also took much pondering to separate issues of loss and choice from arguments about the relative merit of two profoundly important types of musical expression, the individual and the collective. How did nursery school children reinventing lyrics and movement "make a sort of composition"? On the surface, the arena in which she moved within folk revival circles seemed so conveniently conforming to conventional roles for women. Crawford Seeger herself wondered about "going back to her own music" too often while delighting in her resumption of it just before her death for us to assume that one kind of music substituted for the other.

In the end Ruth Crawford Seeger's struggles with her own multiple and divided selves did not dissolve through ideas. Eventually, I accepted this as an enabling rather than constraining force in the writing of her life. She was the "straddler of two worlds," the "bridge builder," the "runner of a four-ring circus," the "liver of too many lives at once." She acted out the tensions in the paradoxical modernist idiom of dissonant counterpoint that so engrossed her as a young woman—"sounding together while sounding apart." That phrase from art turned into a leitmotif of her humanity as a woman, whose genius transformed all the musics where she found a home.

A Note on Names

In the literature about the subject of this book, "Ruth Crawford Seeger" is the most commonly found name. For most of her life she used the surname Crawford on the scores of her original composition. After her marriage, she added the name Seeger to hers. There were other permutations along the way as well, as the reader shall see. Even Charles Seeger occasionally referred to "my wife, Ruth Crawford." I use Crawford as her surname throughout this book for the sake of clarity and literary convenience.

Northeastern University, Boston   J.T.
July 1996

acknowledgments

As my family, friends, and even acquaintances know, I have been involved with this book for more years than I ever expected to be. I have received many different kinds of help along the way. Those who have shared primary sources and privately held material are listed in the Selected Bibliography. I would like first and formost to thank the Seeger family—in particular, Barbara, Mike, Peggy, and Pete—for their generosity of spirit and the interest they took in this project.

For answers to all kinds of questions I am indebted to Cyrilla Barr, Alan Buechner, Barry Chametzky, Dena Epstein, Pozzi Escot, Sorrel Hays, James R. Heintze, Erika Kronshage, Caroline Lake, Roberta Lukes, Charles Miller, Eric Montenyohl, Bruno Nettl, Nancy L. Parker, Vivian Perlis, Nolan Porterfield, Nancy Reich, Eva Riegger, Irene Shere, Cynthia Stover, Elizabeth Vercoe, Barry Wiener, and Ray Wilding-White. I owe a special debt of gratitude to Judith Rosen, a tenacious bicoastal researcher. I also relied on the professional skills of a number of librarians and archivists, among them Wayne Shirley, Music Division, Library of Congress; Lynn R. Beideck-Porn, University of Nebraska, Lincoln; Jeff Driggers, Jacksonville Public Library; Peggy Harmon, Mars Hill College; Priscilla Hewetson, Ohio Historical Society; Joe Hickerson, Archive of Folk Culture, Library of Congress; Brenda Nelson-Strauss, Director of Archives, Chicago Symphony Orchestra; Judith Tierney, Korson Archives, King's College; Nancy Turner, Ball State University; and Esperanza B. Varona, University of Miami.

I am deeply appreciative of the support this book has received from the National Endowment for the Humanities, the Rockefeller Foundation, the

City University of New York, the American Council of Learned Societies, and Northeastern University.

Thank you also to Karen Burnham and Janet McMorrow for assistance with transcriptions; and to the many who helped me in the last stages of manuscript preparation: in particular, Laurie Blunsom; also Liane Curtis, Roger Golde, Jennifer Stinson, Ingerlene Voosen, Eleanore Weiss; Marilyn Bliss for her comprehensive index; and especially Nancy Hoagland at Oxford University Press.

Biographers need loyal listeners and friendly critics. I am indebted to Paul Beaudoin, Adrienne Fried Block, Frances Burke, Virginia Eskin, Ann E. Feldman, Karen Jacobs, Murray Melbin, Barbara Schectman, Joan Stein, Mark Tucker, Mae Rockland Tupa, and Elizabeth Wood. A number of friends and colleagues who read parts of this book in draft improved it with their suggestions: in particular, Wayne Shirley; also Martin Brody, Sandra Buechler, Richard Crawford, Archie Green, Bess Lomax Hawes, Jane Holtz Kay, Alan Lomax, Carol J. Oja, Nancy Reich, Wayne Schneider, Kay Kaufmann Shelemay, Joseph Strauss, and the members of my biographers group in Boston—Joyce Antler, Frances Malino, Megan Marshall, Susan Quinn, and Lois Rudnick.

I am thankful for the love and encouragement I have received from my parents, William and Miriam Tick, my brothers Jim and David, and my sister Beth. To my family—Stephen, Allison, Erica, and Max—who lived through the travails of this book with immeasurable patience and love, I owe a special debt of heartfelt gratitude.

contents

Part I

e
a
r
l
y

y
e
a
r
s

1901–1920

a m i n i s t e r ' s
d a u g h t e r

Some time around 1927 or 1928—it was hard for Martha Beck to remember just exactly when—Ruth Crawford stood in the doorway of Beck's studio at the American Conservatory of Music in Chicago and wondered, "How does one ever write work without a reminiscence of something that has been written before!" That modernist fantasy merged patriotic pride with personal ambition. Ruth Crawford's "before" encompassed the past of European tradition. Her present glowed with the promise of her own youth. Born in 1901, she believed that the late 1920s were a time when American music sounded richer and more compelling than ever before. Even if she had discovered her musical calling as a composer just a few years earlier, she placed herself among a small band of "moderns" whom the critic Paul Rosenfeld praised as pioneer voices of national autonomy, starting "to represent the forces of American life, to interpret them in a large way."[1]

By 1927 Ruth Crawford had publicly joined them. As one of six "members of the young generation," she—along with Aaron Copland and Marc Blitzstein—had been featured in a concert on February 26, sponsored by the League of Composers in New York, where her Sonata for Violin and Piano, written in 1926, received its world premiere. *Musical America* touted the event as "American Youth to Have Its Fling," printing photographs of the two women included on the program. Crawford's showed a handsome serious woman, whose dark bob framed a round face, the pensive tilt of her head contradicting the resolute set of her mouth. Reviews conceded her a future by granting dispensation from the weaknesses of sentimentality and conservatism historically stigmatizing the "woman composer"; they implied she composed like a man. One critic praised the sonata as the "most masculine in quality the afternoon brought forth with the exception of the Copland"; another wrote how the sonata was "boldly energetic and virile."[2]

About a year later the violin sonata received its local premiere in Chicago, Crawford's musical home town, at a gala concert inaugurating the second American chapter of the International Society of Contemporary Music. The hall at the Cliff Dwellers Club included several local critics, who turned Miss Crawford into a musical athlete. One said she could "sling dissonances as mean as any of them," while another made her into an "intrepid, fearless swimmer in a sea of notes."[3]

If others made her work into a representation of gender and modernity, Ruth Crawford resisted such confinements by finding more spacious images of identity, which she expressed in a poem from 1925: "Spirit of me, dear rollicking far-gazing straddler of two worlds, message carrier from real to unreal. Vagrant wanderer thro cycles and universes, Biding a while to travel my small ways." The incongruous juxtaposition of "universes" with "small ways" hints at the vulnerability of the young woman, who sat among Chicago's musical elite, eating her two-dollar banquet dinner, waiting for music by Milhaud and Stravinsky to pass by. Finally, she heard her own piece receive enthusiastic applause. Should she stand and take a bow?

Watching her hesitate, Frederick Stock, the ISCM chapter president and the esteemed conductor of the Chicago Symphony Orchestra, took action. Crawford wrote how he "came to my seat, led me to the front, gripped my hand several times, saying 'very beautiful.' " She inked the date in her diary in dark bold letters while understating the moment as an occurrence to be "set down for memory's sake." Even though there would be other triumphs, she never forgot this one, which made the violin sonata an emblem of ambition and success for the rest of her life.[4]

Clara Crawford, Ruth's mother, sat next to her daughter in the Cliff Dwellers Club audience, for it was "ladies night," permitting women as guests for this special event. She knew what the performance meant for her daughter's career, and wrote her son a few days later acknowledging the double context of the achievement: "Four new compositions by well-known men and Ruth's. The sonata was beautifully played by two Chicago artists with critics' comments in several morning papers. Very thrilling."[5]

The musical bond between mother and daughter exceeded ordinary maternal pride because it was based on reparation and unfulfilled dreams. A memoir Ruth wrote long after her mother's death begins with an account of her sixth birthday that captures Clara Crawford's intention to rear her daughter within the rules of conventional domesticity and at the same time give her opportunities she had been denied:

> On my sixth birthday my mother did two things. She took me out on the front porch with great mystery, brought out her sewing basket, and gave me my first lesson in darning socks. Later she took my hand to lead me down the street to

another surprise. This she did [in] a sort of mixture of solemnity and triumph, for it represented something she had wanted and been deprived of all during her childhood. She took me to my first piano lesson.[6]

Crawford linked the lack of music in her mother's youth to the rules for social and artistic abstinence that characterized fundamentalist Methodism in the nineteenth century, for Clara Crawford was a minister's daughter whose parents were born-again Christians. Clara's father, the Reverend William Plummer Graves, converted to Methodism in 1838, when it was the fastest growing Protestant denomination in the country. In 1847 the Reverend married Mary Fletcher, a member of a prominent New England family, who could trace her lineage back to 1630. Mary Fletcher's conversion to Methodism at fifteen and her willingness to endure the itinerancy of a Methodist minister's family capture the extraordinary appeal of this young Protestant denomination, as it grew from a small sect in 1800 to a religious body so numerous that its "web of preaching circuits crisscrossed the frontier." After several years in Vermont, Reverend Graves was rewarded by his conference (a regional district of churches) with a pastorate in Victoria, in central Illinois, where Ruth's mother Clara Graves was born in 1858, the third of six children.[7]

The memorabilia of Clara Graves's youth (a diary and family letters) reveal a feisty young woman who felt psychologically and physically displaced as a Methodist minister's daughter. She took no comfort in the rewards of what a southern female writer once called the "candlelit drama of salvation"—eulogizing women who helped bring the gospel to the rural poor. Suffering a nomadic existence as her father took on a new parish every two years, she dismissed one small town as "totally insipid, dead, flat, uninteresting, demoralized etc. etc."[8]

Clara would later complain to her daughter Ruth about the "Graves way" of ordering life. Ruth in turn condensed the reverend's mentality in one telling phrase: he "forbade superfluities." Clara told stories of a cramped childhood, where as a young girl, she had to lock herself in a closet to do the "superfluity" of woodcarving. The reverend's zeal invaded every corner of home life, controlling large and small details. No "useless" flowers cluttered the Graves kitchen garden. His granddaughter Ruth satirized such thinking by parodying his rhetoric: "Grandmother wasn't allowed to grow flowers because you couldn't eat them." Although he later paid for Clara to have a year at Northwestern University in the early 1880s, when few women attended college, the reverend disapproved of decorative accomplishments like music for the same reason he disapproved of flowers.[9]

He feared that Clara might become what the critic James Huneker called "a piano girl . . . chained to the keyboard" to advance "social display." The stereotype of the "piano girl" epitomized the confusion between social constructions of gender and class on the one hand, and the act of performance on the other. Often trivialized as a social grace or "accomplishment," cultivated music in late nineteenth-century America served as a parlor skill for a young lady. The doctrinal Methodist point of view added further constraints, seeing social music outside of hymn singing as a secular vanity. In the Graves household Clara's piano lessons were withheld throughout Clara's youth. She began at seventeen, and even then, duty came first.[10]

When she was "kept away from her beloved Chickering [piano]" and forced to skip a lesson so that she could "sew a bias ruffle on Allie's dress," she rebelled: "When will we learn that the cultivation and enlightenment of the mind (ahem!) is infinitely of more importance?" Her own daughter would later adopt the mannerism of writing out little "ahems" as reminders to lighten the sermonizing that had been ingrained in them both. Clara Graves's hyperliterary sensibilities searched for alternatives to life as a "bundle of *duties*, great and small." Her longings to escape once turned a cow pasture into a poetic English countryside, where an impressionable young girl heard a "thousand soft voices floating in the air, bringing pleasure to my music-loving ear." From this came the subversive thought that "Nature seems to appeal to Man's soul of *pleasure* not *duty*."[11]

Clara's musical soul—her aural response to other aspects of daily life—appears in even humbler moments, when she analyzed a toddler's pre-verbal vocalizing as a series of "many variations on the first vowel and uttered in all the different tones from high to low A." Such primary sensory apprehension of the world through sound is a characteristic trait of the musician, and one that Ruth inherited. Yet for all of Clara's responsive nature, she remained a seventeen-year-old who advised a more daring girlfriend not to ice-skate in daylight but "to wait until dark and not make her sprawling motions quite as public." If Ruth later blamed her upbringing for her own conflicts about sexuality, she internalized her mother's codes sufficiently to call menstruation "womanly manifestations," duly passing on that verbal relic to her oldest daughter in the 1940s.[12]

Nevertheless, for her time and place, Clara Crawford was a feminist, as it was understood in the late nineteenth century, when the "New Woman" in all her contradictions was discovered by the American public. Determined to achieve emotional and financial independence before she married, and eager for adventure, Clara refused two offers of marriage at twenty-five and three years later left home with her brother to prove a claim in Monte Vista, Colorado, where the state was selling land to encourage the growth of timber on the western prairies. She took such pride in that act of daring that Ruth once said she "heard about Monte Vista enough so that the place seemed like an old friend," and later wrote about her mother as a frontier heroine.[13]

After that, Clara Graves taught school and then switched careers again in the 1890s. Ruth would later describe her mother as "one of those first female stenographers"—a pioneer once more. As a working woman in a labor force that was less than 20 percent female, Clara Crawford achieved the economic autonomy so crucial to feminist goals at the turn of the century.[14]

This was the period that Charlotte Perkins Gilman would later describe as "Women's Evolution from Economic Dependence: . . . the increasing desire of young girls to be independent, to have a career of their own, at least for a little while." Gilman's predictions of "altered family relations" fit the Graves household. Clara told her brother how "very hard [it was] to be looked upon as a 'dependent.'" She would later try to channel Ruth's musical gifts into a practical career path, worrying about the poor prospects of composers. A list detailing the tiniest expenses on a tourist excursion testifies to Clara's respect for money, a trait that turned into frugality in her daughter. The first thing Clara bought was a Sohmer upright piano, which she paid off over three years: the certificate of purchase was saved in the family archives and passed from daughter to granddaughter.[15]

In accounts of her mother Ruth gave her an identity that is totally consistent with Clara's own words. Her sympathy for her mother later contributed to her own rejection of religion. It also forged a bond between them, for the daughter grew up under the shadow of contrasting privilege. Even if music entered the lives of so many American girls as a social accomplishment, for Clara and Ruth, it was a bond of reparation. Ruth practiced on the Sohmer, hardwon symbol of independence. At night her mother played Schumann's *Träumerei*, Mozart sonatas, and Wagner's *Bridal March* at Ruth's bedtime.[16]

After joining her parents in Pasadena, California, following their retirement, perhaps no one was more surprised than Clara when she met and fell in love with Clark Crawford in 1894; their engagement was announced within the year. "I am only today sufficiently recovered from my astonishment to attempt a letter," a relative wrote in response to the news. For in the end the rebellious Clara chose a man outwardly just like her father. "That he should be a minister seemed improbable, but that he should be a Methodist minister seemed *impossible*." The fact that Clark Crawford made three times the salary of her father helped his suit, as did his advanced education. Clara wrote back that he was "very much of a student—has a fine mind with a will, energy and courage that will carry through anything possibly undertaken." Even so, she confessed to her brother that "his work in life was a hard thing for me to make up my mind to be willing to share—not that I think the amount of work would be too much for me to endure—but the *kind* of work has always been distasteful to me. . . . I must think a good deal of the Minister or I wouldn't be willing to undertake it."[17]

Born in 1854 in Cabin Creek, West Virginia, Clark Crawford felt the call into service when he was eighteen and became licensed to preach a year later. With their quotations from Pascal and Milton, Crawford's sermons show a literary cast of mind. A graduate of Ohio Wesleyan University in 1883, the reverend did not conform to the stereotype of the fire-and-brimstone Methodist exhorter, treating such themes as "The Value of Man" and "Social Christianity" through philosophical abstractions in a literary style more suited to urban Methodist churches than the frontier circuit-rider pastorates where he had begun his career. In 1885 Crawford was appointed pastor of the First Methodist Church in Pasadena, California, where at forty-one he met Clara Graves (then thirty-five) and quickly fell in love. During their first year of marriage, Clara gave birth to their first child, a son they named Carl Fletcher Crawford. In a move that cannot have been easy for Clara Crawford, the family was asked to leave sunny southern California in 1898 to relocate in East Liverpool, Ohio, a bleak mill town of about 17,000, just west of Pittsburgh. (Bordered by the foothills and ridges of the Appalachians on one side and the Ohio River on the other, East Liverpool was known nationally for its production of art pottery and dishware since the mid-1800s.) Two years later, on July 3, 1901, the Crawfords' second child was born—a daughter named Ruth Porter Crawford.[18]

The names the Crawfords chose for their children allow us to glimpse the balance of power in their marriage. Carl was an anagram of their own shared letters; his middle name came from Clara's mother's family. Ruth received the middle name of Clark's mother's family, and a first name with import for both parents. The biblical heroine Ruth was a convert (as was Clark) whose familial line eventually led to Christ, and therefore demonstrated the possibility of salvation through choice so basic to evangelical work. Ruth also represented the power of an exceptional version of a mother-daughter bond, again forged through choice. The story of a young widow and Jewish convert, who, when entreated by her mother-in-law to return to her own kind, pleads for the right to embrace a new way of life, was told repeatedly to Ruth Crawford. She remembered how "father used to stop in front of me as I sat playing and let off a long nonsense jargon, including some Bible history linking me with Ruth the Moabite."[19]

Ruth the Moabite's pledge—"Whither thou goest, I shall go"—was the reality of a Methodist minister's family life. In 1902 the Crawfords moved to Akron, about seventy miles away; in 1904 to St. Louis, Missouri; and in 1906 to Muncie, Indiana, where they lived from 1906 through 1910. Although she would later move twice more with her father and spend all her adolescent years in Jacksonville, Florida, Ruth clung to the memories of her four or five "very happy" years in Muncie as the locus of her childhood and her sense of home for the rest of her life. The move to Muncie (later studied as the sociological model for "Middletown") was a promotion for the Reverend Crawford. In a town of 35,000 that supported thirty Protestant churches, his High Street Church was the fourth largest Methodist congregation in the United States.[20]

Religious observance governed the general tempo of Ruth's childhood, with religious school and two services on Sunday (mid-morning and evening) and family prayer hour at home. She memorized portions of the Bible each week and sang hymns. Associated with an affluent church, the Crawfords lived well, and even late in life, when she was known for her indifference to her appearance, Ruth still relished the memory of the "pink hair ribbons and pink stockings and a white dress with black velvet running through the beading" that she wore to Sunday church services. A photograph of the family in their Sunday best in front of the parsonage in Muncie places the Reverend Crawford standing behind his wife and daughter. Their six-year-old daughter sports an oversized bow in her hair.[21]

When Ruth wrote about her childhood in Muncie, she offered snapshots of past times in the style of a vernacular idyll—Sunday school picnics and "playing games . . . around the church and schoolyard in summer twilight." Although such nostalgic scenes breathe an American innocence and wholesomeness that characterized a part of Ruth's personality throughout her life, they imply a small-town history that does not quite fit the case. The Crawfords did not stay in one place long enough to accumulate the generational past that is the hallmark of small-town life; nobody knew her family beyond its most immediate nuclear self. And that family was on public display. Ruth accepted how "the pastor's family [was] an example for the whole church," and she endured the prohibitions against secular pleasures such as theater and dancing. At eighteen, she wrote down the date in her diary when "I danced a little for the first time." In her early childhood, even the circus was beyond reach.[22]

How she longed to see the "Greatest Show on Earth," which came to Muncie every spring. At fifteen Ruth based a high-school English theme on a childhood memory of temptation and wonder as a grand circus parade passed by her house: "She would sit on our porch and wait for the wonders of it all": the spectacle of animal wagons, clowns, and the "pony cart . . . carrying the sweetest, fairest princess, who would wave and kiss her hand to the children," Ruth wrote effusively. "This was not an important event? He does not know the heart of a child who so declares." Her father had done so four years earlier, extracting insincerities from his dutiful daughter in a letter, where she wrote: "You told me about the show that was in town. You said you were not a bit interested in the parade. Well, now, what do you think? I just feel like you do. Isn't that strange for a little girl like me to feel *that* way?" The circus thus became a lifelong symbol of pleasure and spectacle in a world where imagination and play could triumph over duty.[23]

In 1912 Clark Crawford became seriously ill, undergoing a series of operations in his last years. When he spent one summer at the Mayo Clinic in Rochester, Minnesota, eleven-year-old Ruth wrote to him regularly. Her letters are marked with the meticulous conscientiousness that dominated her character. In one she counted the number of people ("about 247") at Sunday School in Bluffton, Indiana, the parish that had followed Muncie in 1910, and reviewed the substitute preachers. Above all, she assured him that she prayed for him every night and that, since he was sick, she "put more into it, my dear Papa."[24]

The following fall Crawford refused a major appointment to Syracuse, New York, because of his ill health, asking for a less demanding climate. He was placed in Jacksonville, Florida, at Snyder Memorial Methodist Church. The family moved into a comfortable parsonage, and Crawford plunged into serious evangelizing, organizing Jacksonville's first house-to-house Methodist canvass, receiving 92 new members and founding two mission churches in other neighborhoods. Ruth was twelve when her father died of tuberculosis at fifty-nine. Two newspaper articles, one a front-page obituary and the other a long account of his funeral, testify to his community stature.[25]

Clark Crawford's death left a void in Ruth's life. Idolizing a father she knew only as a child marked her with a great, perhaps exaggerated respect for missionary fervor. Her admiration for his sermons heard constantly in church and read for their "literary merit" at home accustomed her to the power of the word as public performance and persuasion and to the voice of masculine authority. But she could use it herself and often spoke from a metaphorical pulpit in her high school essays. The sober fifteen-year-old echoed her father's warnings that God "would be displeased to see us spend our time entirely in pleasure seeking . . . we should count every second, every minute, and not let them pass in idleness; for idleness is evil. . . . We each have our mission in this life. There is something designed for each of us which can be done by no one else. So, if we do not perform our task, it will go undone, and our life will have been useless." Often in her diaries she addressed herself in second-person syntax to give agency to her conscience, reinforcing her father's themes. "And listen to me, Ruth," she instructed her sixteen-year-old self: "You will never make a success of yourself in this world, unless you learn to exercise your will power . . . Buckle to!!" The perfectionism that she herself would later try to temper exploited these traditional Methodist values of hard labor and perseverance as a way to order life.[26]

Clark Crawford's death ended Ruth's "fairly normal childhood." The Crawford family was homeless within the year: the parsonage at 120 West Monroe Street had to be vacated for the new minister and his family. Since the token pension from the Methodist Conference provided around five dollars per year of service, less than $200 per year, the responsibility of supporting herself and her daughter fell on Ruth's mother, Clara, a widow at fifty-five. Mrs. Crawford rented a large three-story house at 305 West Duval Street, a few blocks away from the church, and opened a rooming house which was Ruth's home for the next six years. Carl summed up the social fall from grace: "Mrs. Crawford—the minister's wife" became "the landlady." And a minister's daughter became a boarding-house child, living among the ebb and flow of strangers. Ruth suffered a loss that she would attempt to repair as an adult when reestablishing a sense of place for herself. One of her closest women friends from her adult life would later mark the "transcendental importance" that Ruth attached to her own home, which has its roots in this period of mourning and displacement.[27]

As in many areas of Florida, unregulated real estate development produced boom-and-bust cycles. Although the population would almost double in a decade (from 58,000 in 1910 to 91,000 in 1920), just when Clara Crawford opened her boarding house, the city suffered a serious depression, and Hemming Park, across from the church, was filled with unemployed and homeless men.[28] But somehow the family scraped by. Carl at nineteen turned down a Harvard acceptance and went to work at Armours department store. Occasional shipments of food and clothes from Methodist relief offices helped, and their boarders paid $7 a week. Ruth described a difficult Christmas in her 1917 diary: "money is scarce, Mama is downcast, and the holiday is not as 'merry' as it used to be." She wished for "plenty of money. . . . What wouldn't

I do. And Mama should not have a bit of work to do. And I should have pretty dresses. And we could help people and make them happy."

Clara Crawford carried on, keeping up the manners of the middle class. She managed to send Ruth to school in a smart outfit on the first day of Ruth's senior year in 1914, described in detail by her daughter: "I wore my honeycomb skirt, blue and white striped shirtwaist, pink tie, white corduroy coat, pink hat, sport high-top shoes and silk stockings." In scrapbooks Ruth kept souvenirs of rare treats by pasting chocolate candy wrappers and wads of gum into ruler-lined notebooks, with each item neatly labeled in ink, as if it were a scientific specimen.[29]

Ruth applied scientific observation to herself as well. "I will introduce you, my diary, to me. I am an ugly girl of thirteen years," she wrote in 1915. She took too much perverse pride in self-deprecating honesty. A photograph of Ruth shows that she was not ugly, just younger than most of her class in Duval High School, still round with baby fat, still wearing large bows in her hair. Carl later recalled her as overly serious and shy and he attempted to lighten her mien. In the few early letters that survive between brother and sister, Carl's expansive sociability contrasts sharply with his sister's introspection. One time he dispensed the advice of the entrepreneur he eventually became:

> Yes, Ruth, if you want to be popular with the boys, you've got to get some pep! Be vivacious, and lively & a good sport. Meet people every chance you get, make acquaintances with girls who know all about such things. You've got to advertise, Ruth. You can't just sit in your corner, and sew, & expect them all to come to you. You've got to be interesting, so interesting that they'll *want* to come & see you.

In effect, Carl restated socially accepted feminine norms in the language of masculine capitalism. Lucky Carl, whose temperament fit the energies of the early 1900s so naturally. (He would later earn a considerable fortune in construction, and Ruth leaned on him for financial support many times in her adult life.) His intellectual sister accepted his "good advice" and wrote it down "to have it in black and white, and follow it as best I can."[30]

Clara also watched Ruth sit on the front porch and brood, and like most mothers of self-conscious adolescent girls, she tried to help by combining her list of virtues with hints for social survival. Ruth duly recorded "Mama's Advice":

1. Learn to disguise unkindly feelings.
2. Be proud that you are bashful, but try to overcome it to the extent of being comfortable, enjoying yourself and making others enjoy themselves in social affairs.
3. Let your neighbor's business take care of itself. You have enough to do to take care of your own.
4. Pretty is as pretty does.
5. We live for others. Let us not grudge any little act, tho' it may cause us a little trouble, which will make another happy. M.E. [Methodist Episcopal]
6. Be very thoughtful of others' feelings.[31]

Clara was training Ruth to be a good Christian woman, and she succeeded in raising her daughter to be loving and generous. Yet, "Mama's Advice" represented the one-sidedness of a female subculture, whose imperatives of nurturance and altruism were insufficiently balanced by ideals of self-realization and autonomy, particularly crucial for the development of an artist. Even if Ruth Crawford would rarely doubt her moral compass, the acts she would later label "selfish" testify to the code she accepted at an early age, operating at full strength even during adolescence. Thus her conscience, already fortified through her identification with her father, occasionally tyrannized her. Too many diary entries from these years offer examples of minor weaknesses furnishing occasions for morbid self-reproach. One unusual long entry broods about "a sort of burning, irritating, impatient feeling" in her "heartside." Ruth named her faults—"listlessness, neglect of duty as to sewing, . . . bent to putting off unpleasant tasks: are these faults not enough to make a person dislike herself[?]" Her ever-active superego urged her to "mend your ways." In a high school essay on the theme of "The Model Girl," Ruth wrote that the goal was "to keep everything out of your heart which is bad."[32]

Ruth's need to inscribe such values both privately in her diary and publicly as academic themes shows how the process functioned as a means of psychological discipline. Her persona of a Methodist preacher urged her onward and upward in self-improvement. At the same time, the writer honed her skills in observation by recording conversations of friends and family and providing short sketches of boarders.

Other literary energies found more formal outlets in verse, for Ruth began to write poetry at a very young age and by sixteen had "filled two books with over two hundred 'poems,' one of them in 800 rhymed couplets." At eleven she had some verse published in magazines, and two years later she "published" her first collection of writings for her family. She wrote in her diary: "Now I tell you what I want to be. I want, oh so bad to be an authoress or poetess . . . I am making a history of the . . . Life of Ruth Crawford, Great American Authoress, Ahem!" At Duval High School she frequently published stories and poems in the school literary magazine, *The Oracle*. She and a few girlfriends also started a rival journal to circulate their work. They called themselves the "Wrens" and titled their magazine the "Chirps of the Wrens." Such a humble persona for budding writers, awkwardly warding off charges of ostentatious self-display. Ruth Crawford, aspiring world-class authoress, was content to label her work the slightly comical "chirps." Ambition collided with feminine propriety, and modesty prevailed.[33]

A poem Ruth wrote when she was thirteen predicted her great American future:

Fireside Fancies

When I sit by the side of the blazing fire
    On a cold December night,
And gaze at the leaping and rollicking flames
    As they cast their flickering light

I see what I would be in future years,
    If my wishes and hopes came true,

And the flames form pictures of things that I dream,
  Of the deeds that I hope to do.

One tall yellow flame darts above all the rest,
  And I see myself famed and renowned,
A poetess I, and a novelist too,
  Who is honored the whole world around.

That flame then grows dim, which to me seems to say,
  That my first hope must soon die away,
Then another one darts on a great opera stage,
  The most exquisite music I play.

And then, after many flames rise, and die down,
  The first burns even and slow,
And I see myself singing to children my own,
  On the porch of a small bungalow.

Oh, I dream, and I dream, until slowly the fire
  Burns lower, grows smaller, less bright,
Till the last tiny spark has completely gone out,
  And my dreams are wrapt up in the night.

Ruth possessed an unusual prescience about her gifts and a high degree of self-awareness. In this script of love and work, she was too innocent to anticipate conflicts between artistic ambition and her equally strong desire for home and children. Just at the time a new generation of feminist sociologists were doing research on women trying to balance "the world of women, of esthetics, of nurturance . . . and the world of men, of rationalism, of personal achievement," a thirteen-year-old projected multiple citizenship: poetess, keyboard diva, singing mother. At thirteen, she wanted it all.[34]

By Ruth's senior year the United States had entered World War I. At the same time that her future husband was fired from the University of California for his pacifistic socialism, a patriotic Ruth was writing anti-Kaiser poems and lyrics for high school rallies and listening to Jane Addams advise girls at Duval High School on how they could help the war effort at home. Ruth's brother Carl was training for the air force in Atlanta and Texas, and she recorded the outcome of battles in her diary. At school the issue of German music was discussed: should it be played during the war? She mulled over and rejected the possibility of writing her senior thesis on the lives of great German composers. She continued to do her church activities, recording her success as "special superintendent" for "Girls' Day" at Snyder Memorial Church on July 28, 1918. A month later she, along with other girls from a local WCTU chapter, ran a musicale for the Seaman's Institute, which tried to provide wholesome recreation for sailors in port.

As her high school years drew to a close, Ruth Crawford had made her mark in her class more as a writer than musician. When she graduated from Duval High School in the class of 1918 with eighty others, *The Oracle* yearbook staff proclaimed the rather vague goal of "poetic diction" as her chief aim and she was chosen class poet. Ruth also served as class treasurer, a stage assistant for the senior play, class historian, and a contributing editor for *The Oracle*. Her "pet expression" was "let me think." The caption under her senior picture read, "Knowledge Is Power." But this is not typically the case among adolescents, who tax the smartest among them, and Ruth later wrote how "high school was lonely." Her "book title" assigned in another senior class feature was "Not like Other Girls." Perhaps inadvertently, the cliché foretold her future: she would be labeled an exception-to-the-rule throughout her life.[35]

What might a "poetess" do after graduation? A number of Ruth's classmates (girls as well as boys) planned for college. But the Crawfords could not afford that, and during Ruth's junior year, Clara had asked Ruth to transfer out of the college preparatory track into the "normal" course, which trained teachers for elementary and secondary public schools.

But Ruth managed a bit more for herself. Even though her writer's talents had won her a place in high school, her piano lessons claimed more and more of her interest. By her junior year she found a mentor in Bertha Foster, one of her first piano teachers and the founder of a music school in Jacksonville. Miss Foster had intervened with Mrs. Crawford just in time to allow Ruth to finish the college course. She also promised Ruth a job. After high school graduation in June, 1918, Ruth went to work immediately as a junior music teacher at Foster's School of Musical Art.

an "american woman pianist"

*Almost before we realized it the native-born, and
in some instances, native-trained, pianist arose in our midst,
and we discovered the American woman pianist.*

—Harriette Brower, 1918[1]

Bertha Foster hired Ruth Crawford because she had already invested in her protegée for three years. Ruth began lessons with her in 1913, and after Clark Crawford's death in 1914, when Clara Crawford could no longer afford the weekly $1.50 for lessons, Foster had permanently waived the fee. In June 1918, Ruth took Miss Foster's ten-week teacher-training course where she read Trumbull's *Child Training* as part of her work. By August, Ruth had eleven pupils in the smaller South Jacksonville branch of the school, earning enough to liberate her mother from the hated rooming-house business. In January 1919 Clara Crawford sold her house on West Duval Street ("Hurrah! $1600 cash," Ruth wrote), and they moved to a bungalow on Van Wert Street, near Riverside Avenue on the outskirts of town.[2]

Channeling Ruth into music teaching made good sense to her mother and teacher. They had witnessed the enormous growth in the field and its opportunities for women, who were working outside the home in greater numbers than ever before. Between 1880 and 1910, while the population of the United States almost doubled, the number of musicians and music teachers increased almost five times. During this period classical music established itself as a cultural industry in the United States: orchestras and conservatories were founded, and classical-music journalism flourished through a multitude of nationally distributed magazines such as *Musical Courier* (founded in 1880), *Musical America* (1898), *Etude* (1896), and the *Musical Leader* (1907), with their networks of local correspondents fanning out to report on events in the burgeoning cities. Middle- and upper-class women emerged as the "chief promoters of culture," the majority of conservatory students, and—within the workplace—the rank and file of new music teachers. The percentage of women in the field rose from 42 percent in 1880 to 61 percent in 1910. Even after dropping slightly in the 1920 census, music and music teaching, at 56 percent female, still ranked third (after nursing and school teaching) among the most highly "feminized" professional occupations in the United States.[3]

Thus as a music teacher of young children, Ruth assumed a most conventional post. The influx of women into music teaching was indebted partially to the nineteenth-century tradition of feminine accomplishment, and it did not inherently challenge prevailing Victorian ideologies about the proper role of women. Since musical "accomplishment" filled domestic space in the parlor, in a sense, part-time teachers, traveling around to pupils' homes or receiving them in their own, had not moved so very far from it. Female musicians clustered around the lower-status lower-paying rungs of the professional ladder. "Music teacher"—an umbrella term that could cover the lady around the corner who gave lessons in her home to the teacher with her own studio—was one thing, while "musician" another, and when the census distinguished between them, the distribution clarified the differences between private and public space. The great majority of musicians out in the world, on stage as performers, in print as composers, were men.[4]

Yet Ruth Crawford's luck held when she found Bertha Foster, who was not a conventional "lady musician." Born a generation later than Ruth's mother, Bertha Foster (1880–1968) did not have to battle quite so fiercely the stereotype of the decorative Victorian "piano girl." She began her career teaching organ and music theory in a fledgling music department at the Florida Female College in Tallahassee. (Renamed the Florida State College for Women the next year, the school eventually grew into the coeducational Florida State University, now supporting one of the largest music schools in the country.) In contrast to the large number of female pianists, women organists were a relatively new breed, with the opening up of major church jobs and professional concert opportunities starting around the turn of the century. Thus Bertha Foster represented another version of the "New Woman." Even though it was widely understood that unmarried women like Foster had been "pressed into self support," the "New Woman" could choose from occupations now considered appropriate. Along with other professional women making their "advent" —such as women dentists, lawyers, clergy, physicians, scientists—were the "woman composer," the "woman organist," and the "woman pianist."[5]

Foster moved to Jacksonville in 1908 to found the School of Musical Art at 818 Laura Street, around the corner from the Snyder Memorial Church parsonage, where the Crawford family would later live. It was a sensible choice. Although no longer enjoying the cultural boom of its earlier fin-de-siècle tourist decades, Jacksonville supported a lively if limited musical life. In order to satisfy northern tourists, who had demanded city music, the larger hotels had traditionally imported dance orchestras of northern musicians, some of whom remained down South. Educated local women had organized the Ladies Friday Musicale, which grew from a small private club into the "oldest and best-known musical organization in the state," sponsoring annual series of international virtuoso singers and pianists. (The 1915 roster included Nellie Melba, Lillian Nordica, Fanny Bloomfield-Zeisler, Alma Gluck, Augusta Cottlow, Olive Fremstadt, Maud Powell, Ernestine Schumann-Heink, David Bispham, and Harold Bauer.) In 1875 Jacksonville had boasted that it had more pianos per capita than any other city of its size, about thirty thousand people. Whether or not that was true, the fact that the *Florida Times Union* printed a simplified keyboard course in 1906 shows the market for amateur music. One conservatory had been established in 1889 during the peak of the city's popularity as a winter playground; Foster's was the second.[6]

Foster made a grand success of her school, offering courses in harmony, counterpoint and composition, the history of music and languages, as well as performance in organ, piano, and voice. In its seventh season the school offered diplomas in music for the first time. In 1916–17, three additional staff piano teachers taught beginners at the main school and Foster had opened a branch site in South Jacksonville.[7]

Ruth saved newspaper clippings about her school and Miss Foster. In 1911 Foster accompanied the three hundred-person Jacksonville Choral Society when Walter Damrosch and the New York Philharmonic Orchestra were imported south as part of the Choral Society's third spring festival. Notices of faculty concerts and elaborate student recitals in spring ran routinely in the *Florida Times Union* and in the nationally distributed *Musical America*. Bertha Foster, a dynamic administrator, would leave Jacksonville in 1921 to start another conservatory in Miami; to merge it with the University of Miami, becoming its first dean of a school of music in 1925; to establish one of the first retirement homes for musicians in 1939; to be honored repeatedly as a leading force in Miami's musical life; and finally to sponsor Pete Seeger at a concert "way back in the frightened '50s," he recalled in 1982. "[W]e were picketed by the American Legion, [a]nd she stood up to them. . . . 'Any time you want me to go on a picket line with you, Pete Seeger, just let me know,' and at the same time, she let me know that 'you know, Ruth Crawford was one of my students.'"[8]

Bertha Foster was one of Ruth's first heroines. In her diary, she took a verbal snapshot: "Miss Foster. Radiates happiness, joy and life wherever she goes. Quick, 'sweet,' pleasant, lover of children, nervous, beautiful auburn hair."[9]

After Ruth had been at the school for three years, Foster assigned Ruth to the best piano teacher in her school, Valborg Collett. Ruth described the musician who would prove to be her most formative influence in her youth as "warm-hearted, generous, sympathetic, impulsive." At the first lesson Madame Collett received Ruth "with open arms, saying, 'Hello darling, is this you?'" Ruth recorded her reply: "And I said it was." Sometimes Madame's florid style overwhelmed her.[10]

But the "darlings" quickly yielded to stern judgment:

> She said I played like a baby, that *her* pupils did not play like babies, *they* played like little artists, which hurt my feelings a bit. I am not saying I did not need & deserve this criticism: I am saying it hurt my feelings a bit, as I think it would anyone's. And I do not feel mad at her, at all.

Well, when I got to Staccato Caprice, my fingering caused commotion. My fingering, it was unheard of. But my other teachers had seldom said anything to me about fingering, I did not consider myself much to blame. At 4:50 I left— Oh, I forgot to say that we took up the 9th Concerto of Bevot, the accompaniment which I was to play with Elizabeth.

Madame judged without mercy, but Ruth reacted with characteristic fortitude. Like the ten-year-old girl who wrote to her father that she did not miss seeing the circus, Ruth said she did not "feel mad" at Madame Collett "at all." Instead, intimidated by the prospect of failure, she turned her humiliation inward. She "came home feeling very dejected . . . I remember I wished on the way home, that somehow I could lose consciousness—die or something, to forget the responsibility of having to practise as Mme. Collett had told me to." At a period in her life when poetry vied with music for her loyalty, Ruth coped with the blow to her ego by recreating herself as a literary heroine, investing fiction with the power of resolution. In three short stories about her musical coming of age, she baptized herself "Mary Marshall" and Madame Collett became "Madame Zielinsky." Madame Zielinsky fit Ruth's stereotype of the snobbish European musician. Speaking to the American Ruth/Mary "from her height of foreign superiority," she

> pours a torrent of high-toned invective on the head of poor little Miss Marshall. . . . "You have no understanding! no knowletch of piano-blaying! You blay like a baby!"—"Ach! In Europe they do not bley so! Such finkering! Such hants! Ach! It is terrible! My bupils they do not blay so! Dey play like artists, Ach!"

Fiction enabled Ruth to bypass conscience and admit her anger. Madame Collett, whom as an adult Ruth later described as "very fine and beloved, but much-feared," turned into a vaudeville dialect act. Resentments against "foreign superiority" would later find their constructive integration into Crawford's ambition for and insistence on an American voice in modernist composition.[11]

Madame Collett began to weed out what she labeled "trash, bash, mush" from Ruth's repertory. She had studied with two outstanding Norwegian musicians, Johan Svendsen (rival of Edvard Grieg) and Agathe Backer-Grondahl (1847–1907); she attended the Leipzig Conservatory, taught for twenty years in Oslo (then called Christiania) and taught at Hamburg as well. When she joined Bertha Foster's school in 1910, the catalogue promoted her as "one of the finest teachers of piano in the United States."[12]

The next three years saw Ruth learning nineteenth-century Romantic repertoire—Mendelssohn's "Songs Without Words," Moscheles etudes, Chopin preludes, an unidentified Beethoven sonata, and Brahms waltzes. Madame Collett also assigned Heller etudes and, as her recital piece, Chopin's Variations Brillantes in B flat Major, op. 12. This was Ruth's big piece. Not much more than "Gallic eau sucrée," in the estimation of James Huneker, a famous critic of the period, but the summit of Crawford's training in her youth. In 1918, she played it at the School of Musical Art on May 18, at a benefit concert for St. Vincent's Hospital on May 31, and, most important, at the public recital for the School of Musical Art's "advanced students" in Duval Theater on June 20.[13]

"Am scared of recital in Duval Theater. I do not know my piece very well," Ruth worried two days earlier. Duval Theater, decorated with thousands of shasta daisies, was filled with a "large and most enthusiastic audience" (it seated about thirteen hundred people) assembled in spite of the heat. This was "testifying most forcibly to the fact that Jacksonville people . . . are anxious to give encouragement and countenance to all proper musical effort," according to the review in the *Florida Times-Union* the next day. Ruth's brother Carl recalled the recital as "somewhat of a significant event in Ruth's early period." One of three pianists among the fourteen soloists, even Ruth was satisfied with herself. "Recital over. Everyone says I did splendid. I did not tremble a bit but controlled myself. Almost forgot the audience."[14]

A few months later Ruth objectified this moment in her life in a second story of Mary Marshall and Madame Zielinsky:

> Mary forgot the audience—the lights—everything—absorbed in putting her whole soul and heart into the music. Melody, each note like a pearl, so perfect and so beautiful. The audience was entranced. It listened as one in a dream.[15]

As the expression of her idealized self and a channel for her adolescent narcissism, Ruth's fiction permitted a freer, more passionate side of her personality to be expressed. Invoking the subversive potential of the woman as Romantic artist, Ruth as author sanctions ambition and ego for her alter-ego Mary, whose emerging subjectivity overwhelms the constrictions of gentility.

At the same time that Ruth liberated "Mary", she invented "Stuart," a complementary musician-hero, to live out her dream of harmony between love and work. Embodying both father-figure and artist-partner, he ministers to her by "praying for Mary Marshall while she is on stage," and calling her his "little girl."

Even though fifteen years later, Crawford described her fiction as "tales of romantic dreamings spread out over the years," the image of a partnership persisted as a recurrent construction of her identity. The more music empowered her in real life, the more Ruth Crawford polished herself in print, defining herself as a young "American woman pianist" through musical act and literary construction.[16]

She was hardly alone. Along with the American "woman composer," the "American woman pianist" came into focus in the early twentieth century, both through the achievements of actual performers and through the cultural discourse that objectified them. Following the trail blazed by Teresa Carreno, a nineteenth-century prodigy and international virtuosa, performers like Augusta Cottlow, Olga Samaroff, and Fanny Bloomfield-Zeisler won considerable fame. These women inspired the rank and file of female pianists and piano teachers, whose entrance into the profession had so altered its statistics. Catering to their consumers—that is to say their heavily female readerships—the national magazines produced a huge literature on the role of women in music. As a barometer of gender ideology, this transient literature reflects its broad spectrum of beliefs and values, touching on identity and commitment (the process through which one becomes a composer), professionalization (the socio-economic choice of occupation), and aesthetics (the relationship between gender and musical performance or composition).[17]

Writ large over this diverse literature are the tensions that typically accompany shifts in power; it acknowledged the visibility of the "American woman pianist," on the one hand, and her marginality, on the other, in language that mediated her status in the marketplace of classical music. Indeed, the whole notion of an "American woman pianist" or "Woman's Work in Music" reflects the ambiguities associated with the metaphor of a "separate sphere" of gender-determined activity and identity in American society. As the historian Linda Kerber has pointed out, this metaphor relies on a loose nexus of meanings, including an "ideology imposed on women, a culture created by women, a set of boundaries expected to be observed by women."[18]

All three meanings come into play in the early part of the century. How much economic viability did the "American woman pianist" have? W. S. B. Mathews on "The Young Woman Pianist and Her Business Prospects" forecast gloomy prospects for success but painted an endearing portrait of the "virtuoso who does not wear her heart upon her sleeve, a generally uncommunicative person with no end of grit . . . and a warm heart inside her, who if given a warm atmosphere to play in, will astonish you now and then." What kind of repertory should she play? In his article "Some of the World's Greatest Women Pianists," James M. Tracey disclaimed sexual equality in music, for "women did not possess the physical strength necessary to carry them through the immense amount of work" demanded by a professional career; and those that did lacked "sufficient talent, temperament, perseverance and concentration." Even Ethel Leginska, a rising young musician around World War I, occasionally expressed disappointment in her sex. In an interview titled "Are Women Men's Equals as Pianists?" she answered in the negative, for women lacked "unity of purpose and the strength to carry it out." Should the American woman musician leave home and go abroad to study? What advice could be gleaned from concert stars, past and present? Read "American Women Pianists: Their Views and Achievements. Back from Drudgery Abroad. Our Artists Need Encouragement and Support of Their Countrymen—Careers of Prominent Native Artists and Jottings from Their Conversations." Thus the commercial classical musical press made issues of gender and music topical. Within the classical music workplace, the status of the American woman musician was in flux, her equality in doubt; but attention was paid, and a domain within music was constructed both *for* and *by* women—a negotiated cultural space resounding with the contradictions that marks periods of significant social change.[19]

October 12, 1918: "*Etude* came today," Ruth wrote in her diary. "Read it all morning." To some American male musicians, chafed by their marginality in the masculine world of commerce and gazing longingly at their European counterparts, these magazines epitomized the evils of a capitalist culture. The puff pieces of publicity for touring virtuosi, the advertisements that turned concerts into commodities grated on Charles Ives, for example; he reproached "the commercial monopolists" for the "Prostitution of Art," catering to the "ladies' smiles," he said, feminizing, in a gesture of vengeful contempt, the hostile male critics who spurned his music. Ruth Crawford's future husband, Charles Seeger, might have concurred. In 1912, just beginning his career as professor of music at the University of California, Seeger banished *Etude* and its sister magazines from his academic milieu in one of his first acts in his new post. In the waiting room for prospective students at the summer session for music teachers, he saw the magazines prominently displayed by his assistant. Miss Sweesey proudly told him that the magazines constituted "one of the most valuable assets of our work." Seeger then ordered their removal. "Please see that by tomorrow morning there's not a sign of any of them in this room," Charles said, the imperial dialogue recounted to an interviewer fifty years later. "You can imagine the consternation," he recalled, "but there were no more of them."[20]

But Ruth, like the hapless Miss Sweesey and many other young American women musicians and music teachers, needed *Etude* as a window into the world of art. When years later she laughed at a woman she saw reading *Etude* in New York, she was attempting to transcend the provincial feminine in her past. "I didn't know anybody outside of Squeehonk read that!" she said. Yet in Jacksonville she read the November 1918 issue of *Etude* devoted to "Women's Work in Music" (the third in a series spanning 1901 to 1929), with articles by the noted composer Amy Beach on "The Girl Who Wants to Compose," the great singer Ernestine Schumann-Heink on "The Mother's Part in Musical Training of the Child," the progressive educator Francis Clarke on "Music as a Vocation for Women," and for the young "American woman pianist," an unsigned article on "Small Hands and Their Extraordinary Possibilities."[21]

A fter the recital in 1918, which coincided with her graduation from Duval High School, Crawford made her way into the musical life of Jacksonville. Madame Collett had waited for the time when her star pupil could begin to practice four and five hours a day; Ruth's diary charts her varying degrees of diligence — small segments of 45- and 50-minutes sessions duly listed along with the whole mornings or afternoons at the keyboard. In addition, she served as a social pianist in a variety of ways, accompanying various students and teachers in their recitals and playing at local hospital benefits, women's clubs, and the Jacksonville Tourist Club. Because of mobilization for the war, Jacksonville was filled with soldiers. Ruth often organized lunches for them at her church, "played piano part time, helped serve part time." Notices of a few public performances of more than casual entertainment are scattered through these years. On New Year's Day, 1919, she played at the YWCA and then on February 4 and February 24 for the Woman's Club. Although Madame Collett tried to arrange a concert for her at the Jacksonville Ladies Friday Musicale, it is not clear whether Ruth's appearance before them on Oc-

tober 24, 1918, mentioned as scheduled in her diary two weeks earlier, actually occurred. Madame Collett proposed her for the opening concert of the
Ladies Friday Musicale in January 1919, but without success. "Just missed a
chance," Ruth said. "Madame Collett certainly 'praised me up.'"[22]

On the whole, Crawford's familiarity with serious professional music-
making was fairly limited. Years later she recalled the very few concerts by se-
rious concert artists she had been able to afford: "one concert each of [Percy]
Grainger, Paderewski, and Hoffman [Josef Hofmann]"; she forgot Leopold
Godowsky (billed as the "World's Greatest Pianist") and the violinist Mischa
Elman, whose programs she saved.[23]

Crawford's other musical experiences amounted to very little. In 1915 the
Ladies Friday Musicale helped a local violinist, George Orner, found a youth
orchestra; Ruth, who was still in high school, had joined with great enthusiasm. She had previously served as the alternate pianist for a pick-up orchestra
at Snyder Methodist Memorial Church, but her friend Althea Stevens had
first claim on the job. How Ruth fretted over that—even though the orchestra comprised an undisciplined group of amateurs, and concerts were given
with whatever instruments were at hand. At one church service an orchestra
of four violins and a drum played a "Song Without Words"! When Althea
missed a rehearsal, the conductor suggested that Ruth become an alternate.
Even this modicum of assertion provoked Mrs. Crawford. She told Ruth it
would be a "great piece of indelicacy . . . to speak about a thing, a change, to
Althea, which is going to benefit me." Ruth kept silent and wrote, "Just to
think I can not go to practice any more. I *do* want to. I *wanted* to stay." Later
on in her career, when her professional advancement and her emotional well-
being would have benefited from less anxiety over ambition, she had already
internalized her mother's warnings against egotism.[24]

Between 1917 and 1921 Crawford became known as an excellent piano
teacher for children in the community. Her day book entries for the year 1919
trail off from her earlier careful accounts into lists of names of pupils. She routinely scanned beginners' literature to select suitable music for her many
pupils, going downtown to Cohen's Department Store to look through pieces
and sending off requests for "approval music" to music publishers.[25]

Ruth Crawford found her way to composition through the routine of playing through music for her small pupils. A few notations in her diary outline
the steps. On December 18, 1918, Ruth "looked over more music [for teach-
ing] and improvised some." January 3, 1919: "Have made up another piano
piece—the 2nd one," she wrote, adding, "Love to do it!" She showed her
compositions to a Mr. Pierce, who perceived talent and decided to teach her
some theory. He gave her what she later belittled as "four dry lessons from
Chadwick's harmony book"; but on January 17, she wrote in her diary that she
was "crazy about harmony." Two piano pieces, "Whirligig" and "The Elf
Dance," date from this period. "The Elf Dance" was pronounced "real cunning" by Mrs. Doe, a teacher at the School of Musical Art, and a "cute thing"
by Madame Collett. Mr. Ward—perhaps the same Mr. Ward who taught
Frederick Delius composition many years earlier—"gave her several good sug-

gestions." A few years later the head of composition at a major conservatory would praise "Elf Dance" as having a "certain perfection about it." As an adult Ruth would dismiss the now lost scores as a "few little bits of piano music."[26]

Did she stumble into her self? The air of serendipity recounting Ruth Crawford's debut as a composer typifies the lack of self-consciousness about composing at this point in her life. She had no sense that a professional path had opened, little comprehension of her gift. Instead, her ambition remained focused on the concert stage.

In 1918 the war was over and a sense of opportunity was in the air. "Carl is home, *Carl home!*" Ruth wrote, when her brother returned in December, a month after the armistice was signed. On April 22, 1919, she heard a concert by the American pianist Beryl Rubinstein, a prodigy who had studied with Busoni in Berlin. She pronounced him "perfectly wonderful. His technique is marvelous. Scales like pearls." That summer she apparently took some lessons with him when he returned to Jacksonville to give master classes. But more change was thrust upon her. In 1921 Bertha Foster announced that she would relocate her school, which by 1920 had a student body of 750 and a faculty of 35, to Miami in 1921.[27]

Ruth decided to make her move as well and to leave Jacksonville. Carl remembered several decades later how his sister had the "ability, the initiative and the consuming desire to follow her music, and so it was worked out that she would go." That decision caused all of them "considerable sacrifice" during a post-war period when "things were not too prosperous." Carl had already moved to Orlando. Even though Mrs. Crawford would be left alone, Ruth persisted, and word traveled among her family that she wanted to leave. A cousin—Nellie Graves—offered to finance a year.[28]

The plan was for one year's study with a famous pianist, but exactly where and with whom remained in doubt. Europe was out of the question, for Mrs. Crawford refused to consider study abroad. She had read Amy Fay's *Music Study in Germany*. She disapproved of "how lessons were given over there. . . . Mrs. Taylor told me all big foreign musicians are what we would call immoral. . . . No daughter of mine with my consent would ever leave our own shores for music."[29]

Mrs. Doe, who was running the School of Musical Art in Bertha Foster's absence, had already suggested that Ruth go to New York or Chicago the next summer to study with Harold Bauer or Leopold Godowsky and then come back and "get a big price for lessons." Ruth wrote to the Polish pianist Sigismond Stojowsky, who had headed the piano department at the Institute of Musical Art (forerunner of the Juilliard School) in New York and was still teaching privately in the city. He replied on May 14, 1921, that he would accept her as a pupil. (Stojowski's later pupils included Guiomar Novaes and Oscar Levant.) But both Bertha Foster and Clara Crawford had ties to the Midwest, and either one might have suggested the American Conservatory of Music in Chicago, which Ruth eventually chose. Founded in 1886, the American Conservatory had a solid national reputation as a very good teaching institution. Madame Collett vouched for the reputation of Heniot Levy, head of its piano department, and Miss Foster wrote Ruth a letter of recommendation. Ruth planned to take the one-year degree program leading to a teachers' certificate.[30]

In the fall of 1921 Ruth Crawford "achieved" Chicago. She left on September 6 from the newly constructed Union Terminal train station to take the 36-hour train ride north.[31] The *Florida Times-Union* wrote in its fanciest alliteration the next day:

MISS RUTH CRAWFORD WILL PERFECT HERSELF IN
PIANO STUDIES UNDER PEDAGOGUE

Miss Ruth Crawford left yesterday for Chicago, where she expects to spend the winter. Miss Crawford leaves a gap in musical circles here, for in the past few years she has become well and favorably known for her teaching and has come to be recognized as one of the best teachers of piano in the city. . . . She is a brilliant performer, reflecting credit upon Madame Collett, her teacher. . . . In Chicago, she will continue her studies under the well known pedagogue Henriot [sic] Levy. . . . All of Miss Crawford's friends and admirers are predicting for her a brilliant career.

In one of her first letters home Ruth protested to her mother that she felt "humiliated" by the "exaggerations" of this article. "It . . . sounded almost like a take-off. All the people for whose opinions I care know that I am not a *brilliant* player. I know Mrs. Gamble wrote it."[32]

Clara Crawford had her own ideas about her daughter's future. The separation was temporary, for Ruth had money enough for one year to meet tuition expenses of about $175 and room and board of some $36 per month. The sacrifice would be worth it, for her daughter would redeem the promises of her own youth. Clara imagined a future in which womanhood complimented art. She held up her ideal to her daughter. It was the pianist Augusta Cottlow whom Clara praised as the "beautiful finished American lady artist," and "charming to watch, American trained. Nothing bohemian about her. . . . I would be proud to have you like her." Clara wanted Ruth to become a "real lady musician, with nice manners and poise and self-confidence and pretty clothes."[33]

A triumphant Ruth would return home sounding and looking "different," looking the "new Chicago way." Then she would join the ranks of the elite circles in Jacksonville, list her Conservatory certificate and "pupil of" on her business cards, and start her own piano studio as Clara Crawford's apostle of success and independence: the American woman pianist.[34]

Part II

c
h
i
c
a
g
o

1921–1929

the "wonder city"

*I wrote a few phrases of a symphony in my sleep the other night,
heard the clarinets and oboes coming in and the violins etc.*

—Ruth Crawford, March 1923

Crawford arrived in Chicago on September 8, 1921, to make her musical fortune. Just as her mother had homesteaded the hills of Colorado fifty years earlier, she would prove her own claim in the third largest city in the world. With a population of about three million, the "Metropolis of the West" was six times larger than Jacksonville. Clara called Chicago "advanced."[1]

The routines of a music student's life marked off the boundaries of Ruth's territory: where she practiced, took classes, and attended concerts. At Wabash Avenue and Jackson Boulevard, the American Conservatory occupied three of the sixteen floors in the new Kimball building, Chicago's counterpart to Carnegie Hall. In the Auditorium Building on South Michigan Avenue, the Chicago Opera performed in a hall seating 4,700 people—larger than the Metropolitan Opera in New York. Orchestra Hall nearby housed the Chicago Symphony. All of these buildings lay near or on the central artery of Michigan Avenue, an elegant street lined with Chicago's famous department stores. Ruth wrote home to her mother about the windows of Marshall Field. She walked to the nearby Art Institute and watched the changing moods of Lake Michigan. "It was so beautiful on a clear day."[2]

She settled in at the YWCA on 830 South Michigan Avenue. The Y housed about four hundred young women and, since it was recommended by the Conservatory, its entire ninth floor was given over to music students, who paid $9.50 for board and room and $1.25 for piano rental per week. Generations of women, new to city life, had found a home there. Its central location helped them tolerate what literary pioneer Margaret Anderson remembered (in 1912) as the Y's bad food, uncomfortable beds, and sap-green walls—

"it smelled like a laundry," she wrote. Crawford's letters home minimized every discomfort and lavished approval on new acquaintances, mostly other aspiring young women. She shared a small room with another musician —"so nice, without any of that slang and jazz about her," she wrote her mother. She observed, with provincial optimism, the lives from which Midwest writers like Sinclair Lewis and Willa Cather fashioned their fictional heroines.[3]

So Ruth Crawford did not immediately bob her hair or hear a Russian Jewess sing the "Internationale," like the librarian Carol Kennicott in Lewis's *Main Street*. Instead, she adapted to the cloistered culture of the "American": who were "star pupils" of various teachers; who had "won Commencement" (the winner played a solo concerto at graduation). The conservatory's student body was about 85 percent female and its top-ranking performance faculty was 85 percent male—proportions that prevailed generally in the United States in the 1920s. Within days Ruth heard typical conservatory gossip. One student related an ill-fated teacher-student romance. Ruth imprudently told her mother that "the consensus of opinion of other girls here seems to be that 'they would not marry a musician on a bet.' 'If their wives knew all that happens at a lesson!'" She appended some comfort: "I have heard this only of violin teachers, however. Let us hope!" She reiterated her vows: "I am here to practice, not to fall in love." And so were most of her Y compatriots, whose overloaded schedules of outside jobs, practice hours, and lessons impressed her. By October she marveled at the ease of her adjustment: "Sometimes it seems so strange to me that I am actually in Chicago. I take everything for granted . . . the L (elevated), the busyness of it, the soot(!), the store windows, and forget that I am actually in Chicago, the wonder city and a thousand miles from home."[4]

Crawford's "wonder city" enjoyed so much classical music that a later critic would recall the opulent 1920s as "the years of splendor." They were gilded by a brilliant Chicago Opera and the Chicago Symphony Orchestra, both in their prime; four conservatories of national stature—the American Conservatory of Music (founded 1887), the Chicago Music College, the Chicago Conservatory, and the Bush Conservatory; a prominent musical publishing company, Clayton F. Summy, Inc., noted for educational materials; and a nationally distributed magazine, the *Musical Leader*. When describing Chicago's 1921–22 season, *Musical America* paid the city's arts the supreme compliment by equating their growth to that of its city's industries. Five music critics, some with national reputations, issued daily judgments in Chicago newspapers.[5]

To Ruth Crawford, whose only exposure to live classical music had been solo recitals, Chicago offered a series of revelations. Having never attended a symphony or opera performance (and she had heard only one concert by a "traveling chamber music group"), she started catching up and relishing every minute of it. The opera season of 1921–22 was particularly brilliant. Mary Garden in her one year as "directa" (her term) mounted an extravagant season of twenty-nine operas. Ruth bought a Thursday night subscription, writing enthusiastic accounts to her mother of *Tannhäuser* (sung in German for the first time since the war) and *La Bohème*, in which Claire Dux made her debut: "they were both so *very* wonderful." She witnessed the celebrated soprano Edith Mason open her long career in Chicago in *Madama Butterfly*, telling her mother how much she loved Puccini's operas.[6]

She also faithfully attended concerts by the Chicago Symphony Orchestra, led by Frederick Stock, standing at "the great center of everything in the city." At her first concert, she asked a friend to point out the different instruments by name. She heard the symphonic repertory for the first time—Beethoven, Schumann, and Schubert, for example—often attending each concert twice, once with and once without a score. She was profoundly moved, and as composers often do, she transformed the musical work from object to subject. Beethoven's Pastoral Symphony became her friend and she "longed to hear it again, as one longs to meet again a friend one loves."[7]

In effect, Crawford was learning the old and the new at the same time. In 1921, Chicago taste considered Debussy quite modern. In spite of the city's skeptical conservatism about new work, Stock programmed an eclectic range of European and American contemporary music, so that the Chicago Symphony Orchestra's repertory was more extensive and more diverse than that of any other major American orchestra in the period. The 1921–22 season included local premieres of Debussy's "Printemps," Ravel's "La Valse," Franz Schreker's "Ekkehard," and Stravinsky's "Petrouchka." During the following season Crawford remarked on performances of Mahler's Seventh Symphony and Scriabin's "Divine Poem," the latter one of Stock's favorites. Ruth climbed 120 steps to the gallery, counting the orchestra as one of her blessings in the city.[8]

Yet the divinities of Crawford's world still remained the legendary giants of an Olympian age of pianism—Josef Hofmann, Ossip Gabrilowitsch, Sergei Rachmaninoff, Harold Bauer, Artur Rubinstein, and Leopold Godowsky—all booked for concerts during Ruth's first year. When Serge Prokofiev came to Chicago in 1921 for the world premiere of his opera *The Love of Three Oranges* on December 30—a performance later recalled by the Chicago critic Alfred Frankenstein as "one of the most beautiful and thrilling things I have ever sat through"—Crawford did not mention the event in her letters home. Instead, she described Prokofiev as a concert artist who was "[Annette] Essipoff's pupil" and therefore in the Lescheitizky sphere of pianistic influence.[9]

She wrote about visiting virtuosi in the voice of a worshipful acolyte, using the sensuous sublimations of Romantic aesthetics that eroticized a pianist's tone and touch. She described "finger[s] like velvet," the "soft tones so soft they seemed heavenly, and yet full and round, penetrating the stillness of the hall with their magic daintiness." The playing of the "classicist" aristocratic Gabrilowitsch sent her into an emotional tailspin—"I almost could not remain still—cry, laugh, dance, something to form an outlet for my feelings!" Outwardly reserved, Crawford engaged and released her freest and deepest emotional expression and sexual energies through her performer's persona. To Charles Ives, hissing ridicule at Gabrilowitsch by caricaturing his name as "Ossssssip," the "sissy" typified a musician who was spoiled by too much adulation:

Ives pronounced him a "poor musician." To Ruth Crawford, Gabrilowitsch was "an artist, a painter of pictures, a weaver of fancies and dreams, a master."[10]

At the American Conservatory Crawford was surrounded by well-known artist-teachers: Heniot Levy and Silvio Scionti in piano; Jacques Gordon and Adolf Weidig, violin; and Wilhelm Middelschulte, organ. Master classes by Josef Lhevinne, Percy Grainger, and Chicago's own Fanny Bloomfield-Zeisler were scheduled routinely as well. The atmosphere fostered intense competition; Ruth vied with many gifted students for recital opportunities, doled out as rewards. She was starting at the bottom of the ladder, enrolled in the one-year licentiate certificate program in the "Normal" department, which would certify her has a teacher for students "up to the middle grades." (The conservatory also offered collegiate diplomas after three years of study; a postgraduate degree program, granting the bachelor of music and master of music.) She began her first of four terms, each ten weeks long, taking one private half-hour lesson per week, and four class courses for harmony, music history and pedagogy, and "normal" training. She practiced seven or eight hours a day. As one of sixty piano pupils studying with her teacher, she waited for Heniot Levy to notice her.[11]

Born in Warsaw and educated primarily in Berlin, Heniot Levy (1879–1946) had "concertized extensively throughout Europe" before joining the American Conservatory of Music in 1904. Occasional appearances with the Chicago Symphony and annual recitals, at which he often played a group of his own compositions, along with his post as head of the forty-member piano department, made him a musician of high repute in the community. "He was a good pianist," according to the composer Otto Luening, and an "excellent teacher" according to Levy's former pupil, the composer Radie Britain.[12]

Within a month Levy commanded Crawford to switch from the one-year licentiate certificate program into the associate certificate track. The former required only a moderate technique and modest repertory: "all major and minor scales, simple broken chords and arpeggios; octaves; a limited number of etudes by standard composers; sonatas of moderate difficulty by Haydn and Mozart; easier sonata movements by Beethoven; compositions of moderate difficulty by Mendelssohn, Schubert, Schumann, Chopin, Weber, Grieg and others; and representative works by modern standard composers." The associate certificate program required selections from etudes by Czerny, Cramer, and Chopin; Bach three-part inventions; more extended works by Chopin and Liszt. By December Levy had assigned her the most difficult music in her experience—a Bach French Suite, Beethoven's op. 31, no. 3, and Chopin's Fantasie Polonaise in A Flat. In her Christmas letter to her "dear darling Ruth," her old teacher Madame Collett reacted to this news with words that added and subtracted at the same time: she was "astonished" and "stupefied"; she thought the Chopin "dreadful difficult—musically difficult! Mr. Levy must surely have found out something about you! You ought to be very proud! I am!"[13]

Despite her sprint from the starting line, the year did not go well. Crawford paid a price for her success. Overwork pushed her to the brink of nervous collapse, and in the spring of 1922 anxiety made her "shake all over" with chills and chattering teeth as she walked down the hall of the Y near a practice room. Far more serious was the severe case of muscular neuritis in her left arm she developed not long after. She wrote home to her mother that "I cannot practice! My left arm has gone on strike!" She suffered from what was then named "occupational neuritis," and as recalled by a fellow student at the conservatory, it was considered a "fatal thing." She curtailed her long hours at the keyboard and, under a doctor's care, began taking long walks daily. Clara vacillated between urging Ruth to come home and giving her practical advice on staying the course.[14]

Levy's indifference to Ruth's problems disappointed her. Slowly she decided that more than overwork had produced the mess, and she began to suspect him. It was no small matter to switch teachers at the conservatory, where one's teacher determined one's identity. Yet other Levy pupils were plagued by similar symptoms. Was he the "killer" that another conservatory student recalled? Ruth had mixed feelings. It took two years before she could admit to her mother, "Mr. Levy's interest was so impersonal"; that "he cared not a whit whether I came back or whether I didn't"; he was "reticent, quiet, undemonstrative" until toward the last.[15]

Nevertheless, Crawford placed among the top five students among a class of eighty or ninety at year's end. She was invited to compete for prizes at a student recital in Kimball Hall. That achievement guaranteed her a gold medal for the year; and even though her performance of the Chopin Fantasie Polonaise placed her fourth, she was thrilled. She wrote, "I am the only one of Mr. Levy's pupils in the Certificate class who gets a medal! I keep saying to myself, how can it be, how can it be?" After the concert she reveled in her new status: "A week ago I was nobody, and now I am somebody."[16]

The gold medal allayed the concerns of both Mrs. Crawford and Ruth's brother Carl. But in a sense the physical crisis only unmasked a shift of focus already underway. Soon after her arrival, Ruth began taking the first two quarters of harmony simultaneously in order to meet the associate certificate requirements. She wrote her mother how

> it seems so wonderful each lesson to discover some new chord which will make more variety; and it is so interesting, the composing of one's own melodies, I just love it. Orchestration and composition would come next year,—one composes fugues, sonatas, barcarolles, etc.—small ones, of course. But think, how *extremely* interesting.[17]

Another time she rhapsodized "at some new effects I could get because of something Mr. Palmer told me Tuesday that I danced around the room singing 'I am so happy, I am so glad.'" Here, at the beginning of the road, even the rudiments of harmony yielded minor epiphanies.[18]

Perhaps such letters were designed to assuage her mother's doubt. But Clara was skeptical, asking what purpose such theoretical work served:

> You will be judged when you come home by what you can show *when you play*, and not by what you know of the science of music composition. And moreover

Mrs. T[aylor] says when you teach you do not teach harmony etc. to your pupils.
They go to a harmony class for that. You are not supposed to give that to them,
for you will be encroaching on the profession of the harmony teacher.[19]

She had a point. But in her own way Clara Crawford unconsciously carried on
the old Graves sanctions against "superfluities."

Ruth held her ground. She continued to address her letters to "dearest
Mummy," and sign them "your little girl," but within months she planned for
a second year because of her new priorities. "You *do* know I feel that I cannot
leave my *harmony* work," she wrote. Capitulating, Clara Crawford responded
with practical advice. Ruth would need a job to stay on. She encouraged Ruth
to confide in her teachers. When necessity demanded it, Clara summoned up
the courage of her youth. "Push yourself into people's notice. When you want
a thing, ask for it," she wrote in a fierce letter later that spring.[20]

On June 20, 1922, among a group of seventy-three women and five men,
Crawford received her associate teachers' certificate in piano, pedagogy, and
harmony, with an honorable mention in counterpoint and composition, a
special honorable mention in history of music, and a silver medal in the Normal Department. After a summer in Jacksonville, she returned in the fall of
1922 without any savings or stipend from a rich relative. Desperate for work,
she was grateful when Levy recommended her to the Hamilton Park Studio as
a teacher for young children. The business arrangements were brutal: she was
given a list of 100 names of prospective pupils to canvass and from that she
acquired five; one-third of her fee of $1.25 per lesson went to the studio; to
one of the homes she "rode an hour and a quarter through the stock-yard district and an hour and a quarter back again."[21]

In addition, Crawford, who had never seen a professionally produced play,
took a job as an usher and hat-check girl at several of Chicago's twenty legit-
imate theaters, working most steadily at the Studebaker. The opportunities to
see such plays as *Anna Christie*, *A Bill of Divorcement*, *Porgy*, and the *Dybbuk*
compensated for the dreary work and a boss who aroused resentments which
she funneled into her small-town anti-Semitism. "He is so amusing, this Jew,"
she wrote. "Amusing did I say? Maddening. He talks to you as if you were six
years old and a criminal already—when you are twenty-one and a minister's
daughter." To her mother she wrote how "it often strikes me as one of life's
queer tricks that Papa's daughter, brought up to avoid the theater and anything connected with it, now *ushers* in one! It would have sounded very dramatic and would have finished nicely the preceding sentence to continue 'and
feels as much at home in [a theater] as in a church.'" The thought that had
obviously sprung into her head had to be denied. "May I never be able truth-
fully to make that statement," she lied. For the theater was a revelatory world
which touched her deeply. Some of her most romantic fantasies about love
and art were written on the back of theater programs. On one, she wrote a
love letter to an imaginary beloved in a fairy tale of her future:

I do not know you. I have never seen you. I have never heard your voice. Yet
you are part of my heart, part of my life—all of my thought. . . . You are mine.

I shall recognize you when we meet. You will know me. It will be as thou our
souls have talked and felt together since time was. And we shall be one during
all eternity. When wilt thou come?[22]

On another the awakening composer spoke:

I am full of music tonight. I feel as tho I shall burst. Not concrete music, but
abstract. In other words, I am in a receptive more than creative mood. I said
to Agnes as we walked along Michigan tonight that I felt like composing or
loving, one of the two. But I believe I am wrong. Tomorrow night, perhaps
will bring forth the results of tonight's mood. Now, I must feel, and dream and
long and be at once sad and happy; tomorrow—let it be put on paper if it
will.[23]

Crawford gave up on Heniot Levy in her second year. Still plagued by neuritis, in December 1922 she transferred to a new piano teacher, Louise Robyn,
(pronounced Roe-bine), who ranked as the "most prominent among the conservatory's women instructors" and the only woman who had "real standing
among the men." Robyn's roster of students included some of the best in the
school: Marion Roberts, the leading "big name" among the students in the
1920s; the child prodigy Storm Bull; Irwin Fischer, a composer destined for
the conservatory's faculty; and Robert Fizdale, who later found success as part
of a piano duo (Gold and Fizdale). Professionally, Robyn was well known in
the field of children's piano pedagogy (her course books included *Technic Tales*
and *Keyboard Town*). At the conservatory she had become an eminence,
whose connection to children's art was "almost mystical." Crawford adored
Louise Robyn, much as she had Bertha Foster, and the mix of children and
music made for a "fireside fancy" once again. She joked with her mother that
she would "never marry a man who will not promise to live in Chicago, so
that I can start every one of my thirty-five children in Miss Robyn's class!"[24]

Crawford entered into the community of the conservatory in a new way
because of Louise Robyn. She formalized her decision to become a musician
first and a performer second by writing her mother about the "apprenticeship
which I now accept at twenty-one." The word "apprenticeship," which sounds
old-fashioned to contemporary ears, implied an integrated musical education,
in which theory, keyboard skills, performance, and music literature—so often
compartmentalized today—were treated as contingent, interdependent aspects of the totality of music. The very word "music" now embraced craft, art,
and humility. One learned musical rudiments the way one learned a language.
And as one alumna remembers, the earlier apprenticeship began, the better.
She envied Robyn's students their knowledge of harmony, and she wondered
if she could ever catch up to the star Marion Roberts with so many years lost:
"I was spending my teens in blissful ignorance even of dominant seventh
chords." (To Edith Borroff, whose training with her mother Marie Bergerson,
another American Conservatory "star," had begun when Edith was three years
old, it was "incredible" that Ruth could do it.)[25]

The demands of apprenticeship anchored Crawford's work at the conservatory, allowing her to rationalize her study even as a concert career slipped

away from her: "What am I here for?" Ruth asked both herself and her mother after she left Levy. "Would I not better have taken Mama's usually best advice and stayed at home?" "What am I gaining that is worth it all?" . . . "The knowledge that I am to blame for making my mother suffer is ever present with me, even more than it was last year." . . . "I think and think—Am I doing wrong to stay up here? . . ." She answered her own question:

> Again and again the debate has raged and always peace and contentment come in the answer: my theoretical work. Yes, even it alone is worth my being here. I feel myself broadening; my ear—the inner ear whose good judgment and training is of infinite value to composers—is hearing better than it did last year.[26]

As the vision of Ruth in her own studio in Jacksonville dimmed, Clara Crawford balked at this change in plans. On the basis of an "inner ear," how could Ruth justify another year's stay? Through letters between mother and daughter from the academic year 1922–23—ten- and twelve-page tomes written two and three times a week—one senses the fragility of the enterprise. One can hardly view Ruth Crawford's switch from performer to composer as unique, but few such prolific and intimate records exist of this rite of passage through the eyes and ears of an American woman, so innocent at the start, and so candid about the journey. Many letters chronicle the small triumphs that constituted the signposts along the way. Some praise, or a successful performance of her work in an ensemble class, or even a period of unencumbered composing—all these moments eventually gathered enough momentum to convince her that she could stay the course.

Much depended upon the judgment of Crawford's teacher Adolf Weidig (1867–1931), head of the composition faculty. Weidig commanded a great deal of respect in Chicago's musical life. Born and trained in Hamburg, he had studied with Hugo Riemann, the most influential German theorist of the late nineteenth century. Initially a violinist with the Chicago Symphony Orchestra from 1892 to 1896 (under Theodore Thomas), Weidig joined the faculty of the American Conservatory in 1893. His solid reputation as theorist, performer, composer (with works premiered by the Chicago Symphony throughout his career) is summed up in Otto Luening's description of him as the "Old Master." Weidig's father had apprenticed to Brahms and remained within his circle as a copyist. When Weidig began his sentences with the phrase "As Brahms said," Crawford knew she was hearing the truth.[27]

Weidig was not easy to please. Ruth rarely criticized anyone except herself in print, but one allusion to "sarcastic roly-poly Weidig" shows that the ruder side of his teaching manners affected her. "He must have eaten sour kraut" the night before one class, she told her mother. In fact, as a former student recalled some sixty years later, Weidig could be "extremely tactless, or perhaps it would be truthful to refer to it as cruelty . . . seeming to take pleasure in reducing students to tears." To a nun in one of his classes he is reputed to have said, "Just because you wear those black rags should give you no reasons to submit stuff like this to me." To a pianist, who inquired what other music she should "take," he replied "'poison'—and left the room." With such a sense of humor, Weidig came to class with "his pockets stuffed with white handker-chiefs, which he would . . . hand over to students who broke down under his cruel remarks." Yet because his tactlessness was in part related to his extremely high and uncompromising standards, and because he would "go all out" for a person who he thought was talented and hard-working, he was not only tol-erated but admired.[28]

Over the course of the year (1922–23), Crawford wrote several composi-tions without any "definite help" from Weidig. He was impressed but cautious, initially qualifying his compliments. She "had something to say" in her sec-ond piece, a Nocturne for Violin and Piano (1923); its ideas were "refined and modernistic." But whether they were "spontaneous or studied" would be dis-covered the following year with private lessons. A set of theme and variations (1923) was "gold in the rough."[29]

Her work accrued more praise as the year passed. "Every time you come, . . . you bring me renewed proof of the fact that there is something in you," he told her in March. By spring 1923 Ruth wrote her mother of the outcome of her trial: Weidig "knows," and her other teachers concurred:

> Can they be wrong? Perhaps they have overestimated, can it be that Weidig knows? Yet surely he must. He has been cautious enough about giving his final verdict; from October til March he has waited for final proof. If you remember, when he said nice things, there was a string tied always. . . . Now he pronounces the verdict: now he knows.[30]

If he knew, so could she. Crawford grew into the implications of her gifts, running the race far more swiftly than she had dreamed possible. A charac-teristic understatement summed up her success: "I had always imagined that Mr. Weidig's composition class would be full of budding composers, possessors of more technique in writing, more talent, more ability, than I; it seems not." Her confidence grew. "I have written a gem of a little song" (left unnamed), she told her mother in March 1923. Within months she had matured enough to separate her own personality from that of her teacher. For she strained at the tonal leash from the very beginning of her work with Adolf Weidig. She had not yet officially begun composition when she wrote a song that turned into a piece for violin; its second theme was in a key entirely unrelated to the first (I in A minor, II in E-flat major). It was a measure of her growing confi-dence that she deflected the anticipated criticism from Adolf as "trite."[31]

Such success with Weidig helped her combat inner accusations of selfish-ness threatening to undermine her resolve. "Why can't a girl get an education without having to make her mother pay, not in cash but in embittering lone-liness," she cried. She wrestled with guilt, and in order to rationalize the an-swer, she turned her question into a moral dilemma. "I think and think—Am I doing wrong to stay up here? To whom is my duty greater—my mother or what talent I possess?" she wrote in early February 1923. When her mother asked her about plans for a third year in Chicago, Crawford framed her deci-sion as an external imperative:

If I am to be that which Weidig intends, I must. Two friends are leaving for home, Irene and Edith. Then suddenly the thought came to me: why can't I go? Nothing but composition and two pupils hold me. Asking Miss Robyn for her opinion, Miss Robyn says "If it were just your piano, I should say 'Go.' But *composition* . . . Why just now Mr. Weidig came in with almost tears in his eyes and talked about you. You have arrived at the crucial point: it might be fatal for you to leave. The next ten weeks will mean more to you than you could ever regain."

Given this model,

it would be impossible . . . to approach her [Miss Robyn] again on the subject of leaving. It would mean lack of interest, and almost defiance. Our plans for three months together, oh isn't it a shame. I sometimes wish I had no talent, and could be like Agnes, carefree, with no feeling of responsibility continually weighing on me.[32]

She had internalized the apprenticeship model of music as a way of life. Weidig's "almost mystical" dedication to art resonated inside of her. Thus, Crawford issued her own verdict: not only would she return for a third year, but she would stay in Chicago to study composition. She refused to go home even for the summer, resolving her dilemma by asking her mother to consider moving to Chicago instead.

Had not Robert Schumann, coming late to his career as she was, similarly reconciled music and duty? she asked herself. That summer Crawford read his letters, after digesting the two-volume biography of Clara Schumann by Bertold Litzmann during the fall and winter of 1922–23. She suggested that her own mother read Robert's letters in order to divine the loving inner thoughts of her "spirit-child" daughter. But her mother could not be won over through sentimentality, which she had resisted even in her own youth. Why model one's life after either of the Schumanns? Had not Ruth noticed just how "Robert had become the boss after marriage"?[33]

Clara Crawford vacillated over the course of the year, reaffirming and at the same time withholding. She wanted her daughter to redeem the dreams of her own youth, but as they assumed their own enigmatic shapes, Clara found it hard to relinquish her authority, to recast the bond of reciprocity that music had created between them. She expected gratitude, resisted the mores of a new generation, cleaved to her old anxieties. Yet when her daughter needed her, she rallied to Ruth's cause, even as she staked her claims to Ruth's success.

You certainly give very interesting accounts of your encounters with Adolf. I surely think there is no doubt of his interest in your ability and there is no reason why he should not be sincere. He has nothing to gain by deceiving. There is no reason why you should not have discovered in yourself a talent for some phase of music. Your mother loved it and tried to implant a love for it in you, and you have taken at least a lesson a week since you were six years old! Why should you not have absorbed enough to begin to give it out? Just take it for granted you ought to and are going to and stop worrying about it. What man has done (Schumann) woman can do (Crawford). What will your stage name be?[34]

Clara compensated for Ruth's humility, issuing a declaration of creative equality for a new composer, even while she continued to play the theme of financial independence. Ruth should try to be her own "boss" somewhere, and she questioned Ruth closely about the financial prospects for composers. When listening to Ruth's accounts of the "brilliant future ahead" for Stella and Marion Roberts—"Weidig considers the Roberts girls [to] have the biggest talent of them all" Ruth reported—Clara wrote:

> You speak of the Roberts girl in Weidig's class being so brilliant and having a great future ahead. What does she plan to *do*? Someway I can't just see what the talent at composition leads to. Education to be practical should have some definite object in view, for money must be earned and a living made. Will she compose and sell the products of talent, or expect to fill a position as teacher of harmony etc.—or what IS meant by the expression "a brilliant future?"[35]

Ruth reacted to the thrust by parrying with a list of her achievements and a reassertion of purpose:

> You speak of my not having accomplished so much this year, with having to work to earn my way. Truly, I do not think I could have done more if I had been a lady of leisure—sore arms are sore arms—and ushering and teaching have taken me out in the fresh air when I should never have done so otherwise. . . . But has this year meant less to me than last? In piano technique, yes. In brain expansion, emphatically no. When you remember that at this time last year I had no more idea how to write a composition than you have, and that now with almost no definite help from Mr. Weidig (that will come next year) I have written the things I have, when you remember that, and have heard them this summer, I believe you will agree that along a different and less tangible line I have developed so much. . . . Financially, what will come of it? Ultimately I suppose I shall publish. Songs are always in demand if they are good. Children's teaching pieces are saleable. But I am not thinking much about that yet, excepting that I reached the state of feeling you advised: I take it for granted that some day I shall be able to send you Summy Editions of my compositions.[36]

Her own words used to confound her, Clara Crawford reached a decision. Ruth had urged her mother to move to Chicago during the year; "If I could only have my mother here, I should be happy," she wrote at the end of her third year, while at the same time, her mother was writing how "Chicago is no place to live permanently." But finally Clara left her Jacksonville bungalow. She had hoped Ruth would be willing to relocate in Orlando, where her son Carl was in business; the Florida land boom was on, and Carl, a housing contractor, could build them both a home. Instead, by November 1923, she and Ruth had taken an apartment at 4515 Lake Park in a drab neighborhood way out near Pulaski and Grand boulevards. They lived frugally. Ruth's finances improved, and during 1923–24, her fourth year in Chicago, she supported them both by making $13 to $15 a week through private teaching. Carl sent supplementary sums now and then.[37]

That victory altered the relationship between mother and daughter permanently. Its outward sign could not have been clearer. "So you have bobbed your hair!!!!!!" Carl wrote his sister. "I'm not sorry, for from your picture I really believe it improves your appearance and it must be a lot less trouble, but I am surprised you secured Mother's consent." Clara Crawford's opinion was not really the issue. What would Adolf Weidig think of this daring act? Several years later Ruth confessed to Charles Seeger that "as for roly-poly Weidig, the second year I studied with him I was afraid to bob my hair because I thought his opinion of me would fall fifty degrees—crazy child I was."[38]

Perhaps too much attention was being paid to the judgment of the master. Yet within the protective world of the American Conservatory, Weidig defended standards of excellence that enabled Crawford and other talented women to flourish. He expected, indeed insisted, that she and the other women rise above conventional feminine behavior, blaming their social conditioning for producing false modesty which crippled their development. Ruth told her mother how he contemptuously discussed the "poses" of his women students, specifying the "pose" of "humble professions of ignorance and disparagement of one's own work. "He contends that surface modesty is simply the cover for an under strata of conceit. He will not stand for false humility." Indeed he attacked her for just that fault: "I get so discouraged sometimes," she told him. "No, that's a pose," he replied. "It is not," she retorted, amazing herself at her boldness, preferring to admit weakness rather than hypocrisy.[39]

Nevertheless, she strove for originality as an artistic goal from the start. Even before she had written any serious work, Crawford told her mother she "was hoping to be able to compose compositions which will be *different*."[40]

The direction Ruth Crawford's "difference" naturally followed is apparent in those compositions written between 1922 and 1924, whose manuscripts she saved, although she later excluded them from the catalogue of her serious work. Among them are two pieces for violin and piano, two sets of theme and variations, a one-movement sonata for piano, three songs, and several elementary piano pieces for children.

Her first surviving work, a "Little Waltz" for piano (1922), a modest but skillful intermediate-level piece intended for the commercial teaching market, already has the fingerprints of her compositional personality in its opening section. A foreshadowing of her subversive harmonic nature presents itself in the very first phrase, where Crawford implies and then thwarts the conventional harmonic gesture: the D flat in m. 7, coloring the IV, is respelled as C sharp in the bass at m. 9 to propel a second phrase that cuts short any simple consequent to the first. As she rushes head-on into a climactic diminished seventh in m. 15, we sense her intensity and harmonic fervor. Even here in a children's piece, the tonal boundaries are extended beyond one key, for the second section moves from A minor to A flat major and back again (Ex. 3-1).

Composition as taught by Weidig depended upon the absorption and emulation of models from the "old masters" more than following the prescrip-

Example 3-1   "Little Waltz," mm.1–22. Used by permission of the Seeger estate.

tions of a textbook. In some of her student works Crawford's models are easy
to spot. Beethoven is imitated in the sonata, for example, and Chopin in the
Nocturne for Violin and Piano and in the first theme and variations for piano.
Bach's *Art of the Fugue* hovers in the background of some dutiful but crude
counterpoint exercises written between 1923 and 1924.

Crawford sensed the limits of Weidig's receptivity to modernism, even
though he did not fit the stereotype of the German academician. As a composer, Weidig was fairly conservative, rooted in Brahms and reaching out only
late in his career to Debussy. (The indebtedness to the Brahmsian model
could hardly be clearer than in Weidig's Symphonic Suite, op. 46, premiered

in Chicago in 1914, which begins with a passacaglia in E minor that recalls the last movement of Brahms's Symphony no. 4.) However, in some of his works written after World War I, Weidig responded positively to newer influences. "Whole-tone harmonies," he wrote, "were enchanting and effective ingredients for the harmonic palette of every modern composer." Weidig's textbook, *Harmonic Materials and Their Uses*, published during Crawford's second year at the conservatory, further displays a wide range of knowledge of contemporary music literature, citing music by Schoenberg and Hauer, for example. One meets Weidig's name in unexpected places such as Horace Miller's *Modern Harmonic Practices* (1930), where a set of examples of "four-note fourth chords" includes along with Holst, Scriabin, and Ravel a "Weidig chord" (G F B E flat A flat).[41]

Crawford composed a few songs around 1922 and 1923 to texts by popular female poets, among them Louise C. Moulton and Sara Teasdale. In such poems as Moulton's "To Night" and Teasdale's "To One Away," "Joy," and "The Return," Crawford responded to sincerely dramatized female experience, Teasdale's strength. She praised Teasdale's "restless movement," which lifted her work out of conventional "smugness" to the realm of "bird-flights," "power," and "defiance." Here was a counterpart for her own musical temperament.[42]

For Crawford cultivated an idiom rich in coloristic dissonance and tonal ambiguity, and even as a second-year composition student, she developed a bold harmonic language as fast as possible. She soon learned to handle chromatic chords, leaning heavily on augmented sixths for expressive effects and adding whole-tone formations, both through chords and linear patterns, to her idiom by 1923. Confirming her growing confidence, "Kaleidoscopic Changes on an Original Theme, Ending with a Fugue" (1924) is the outstanding piece from her early years. "What do you think of the name!!!" she wrote on a program booklet. Three exclamation points predicted its rich harmonic colors and tonal surprises.[43]

Written in D flat major and traversing several keys, the piece opens with augmented triads in a four-bar vamp setting up a languorous tune Duke Ellington would have liked. Within moments, however, Crawford shatters the mood by turning the melodic E natural into a harmonic goal (E major, m. 14), a precipice from which she can descend through chromatic figures to return to solid earth. Here is a signature in Crawford's earliest work: a theme that abruptly shifts away from conventional closure into remote tonal areas. That gesture yields material for six variations, including a fugue (Ex. 3-2).

One can see the fresh treatment of ideas throughout. The first variation in A major reimagines the tune as a scherzo with little chromatic bass line patterns filling in the melodic skips. The second variation treats the theme contrapuntally in the right hand, its exposed tritones an acerbic contrast to the lush bluesy chords that follow. Although the fifth variation preceding the fugue, which recycles a "scherzando" section from an earlier set of variations (1923), seems awkward here, the syncopated figure that opens the fugue foreshadows Crawford's later love of rhythmically adventurous ostinati; the coun-

Example 3-2 "Kaleidoscopic Changes on an Original Theme, Ending with a Fugue," theme, mm. 1–15. Used by permission of the Seeger estate.

tersubject developed from the theme foreshadows her intense chromatic language as well (Ex. 3-3).

Kaleidoscopic Changes" was the last work that Crawford composed as an undergraduate at the conservatory. In June 1924 she received her bachelor's degree in music, specializing in music theory, harmony, and orchestration. Shortly before graduation, Weidig held his annual recital of composi-

Example 3-3   "Kaleidoscopic Changes on an Original Theme, Ending with a Fugue," variation 6, fugue, mm. 1–9. Used by permission of the Seeger estate.

tions by advanced students, which was noteworthy enough to be written up in the *Musical Leader*. One of thirteen composers (nine women and four men) whose works were showcased that evening, Crawford regarded the concert as an honor and opportunity. She had long hoped to take part, telling her mother the year before that Weidig's advanced student concert was "an event of the year, attended, if hearsay is correct, by publishers as well as other well-known people."[44]

Now her mother was able to share her daughter's moment of glory in Chicago, and she wrote her son in Orlando, Florida, about it: "I don't remember whether I mentioned the concert at which Ruth played her own composition. She played it masterfully—not a missed note. As an original composition it has been very much praised and especially by the 'great' Adolf. He told a pupil it was the equal of anything ever turned in by a member of his composition class."[45]

Crawford had charted out a daring and advanced path. The harmonic language of her "Kaleidoscopic Changes" had its share of influences—Chopin, perhaps even Gershwin—and its moments of originality in its striking dissonance, harmonic boldness, and unpredictable shifts in mood and figure.

Where would this path lead? "Ruth was a little ahead of herself," a fellow student recollected disapprovingly. Weidig could offer little explicit guidance; his virtue was his ability to "bring out the creative instinct . . . to inspire his students to work," and according to Stella Roberts, a fellow student and longtime teacher at the conservatory, he was "somewhat baffled by the newness of Crawford's idiom."[46]

Thus many things had not quite settled yet, even as Crawford entered the master's degree program in the fall of 1924. Clara Crawford's old dreams of her daughter's career as a concert pianist persisted as well. She confided to Carl that "Ruth's improvement in her piano work, in spite of the trouble with her arms, has been good. This next year, she must have the best teacher to be found—perhaps it will not be in the American Conservatory. I think it will probably be a private teacher." Perhaps this teacher could redress the balance between performance and theoretical work so that her daughter might return to the fold of the "lady musician." Never was Clara Crawford more wrong. In the fall of 1924 Ruth began piano lessons with Djane Lavoie Herz. Like a Chicago wind gathering force as it blows across Lake Michigan, Madame Herz swept her off her feet.[47]

new ways of
knowing

R uth and Clara picked Djane (Dee-ann) Lavoie Herz as the "best teacher
to be found" because of the success of her pupil, Gitta Gradova, at brilliant recitals in New York and Chicago in 1923 and 1924. The Crawfords undoubtedly read the superlative reviews that mentioned Herz by name as the
artistic force behind the bravura pianist's "virility and great power." If the
young Gradova was being touted as the "greatest interpreter" of Scriabin, then
surely her teacher deserved some of the credit.[1]

Djane Herz (1888–1982) was more than a teacher with authentic artistic
ties to the late Russian master; she was a disciple of his esoteric aesthetic mysticism. Coming back to Toronto (her birthplace) in 1914, after two years in
Brussels among Scriabin's circle, Herz wrote that she was "initiated in his philosophy of life, which his music so perfectly expresses, a philosophy which
could satisfy the most advanced thinker,"—which she believed she was. Not
only did she dedicate herself to promoting Scriabin's music, she and her husband followed his religion of theosophy.[2]

Their move to Chicago in 1918 had allowed the Herzes to join a new community of believers, as Chicago in the early 1900s was fairly congenial to
theosophy, then enjoying a vogue among intellectuals. Far from being an exclusively European sect, theosophy as a spiritual movement had been born on
American soil in the 1870s, and by the 1920s, American chapters claimed
7,000 of the world total of about 45,000 members. Theosophists hoped to
spread the ideas of Eastern religions as an alternative to Christianity. Ever
since Swami Vivekananda addressed the World Congress of Religions at the
Chicago World's Fair in 1893, inaugurating the "missionary movement to the

West," the city became more receptive to esoteric philosophy and had (as did New York and Los Angeles) an active chapter of the Theosophical Society. In 1926, with great fanfare, Chicago hosted the 40th annual International Convention of Theosophy, attended by the movement's leader, English political activist Annie Besant and her young protégé, Krishnamurti.[3]

Scriabin's music found enthusiastic advocates in Chicago throughout the 1920s, even while his reputation declined in eastern cities. Frederick Stock, the conductor of the Chicago Symphony Orchestra and Chicago's preeminent musical leader, programmed Scriabin's *Divine Poem* almost annually for nineteen years between 1922 and 1941.[4]

Crawford became a double disciple, bonded twice over, reacting to Djane Herz's world as if she had landed in a Wagnerian ashram in the middle of Chicago. In a way she had. The Herz apartment on Grand Boulevard (on the South Side, not far from the University of Chicago) was furnished with Chinese and Indian paintings and sculpture and an extensive library of books on philosophy and occultism. Djane's husband, Siegfried, published an article about Scriabin in *Etude* magazine, and around 1924 he organized a study group on Nietzsche. A four-foot sculpture of a Tibetan Buddha presided over Madame Herz's piano studio, where Crawford took her weekly lessons and later gave theory lessons to the Herzes' young son, whom they had named Tristan. Incense scented the air. A Hindu named Shandra, wearing a white turban, greeted the Herzes' numerous guests, for there were many that imbibed an atmosphere that was "redolent of mystery." Because Siegfried worked for Arthur Judson, the most powerful agent in the period, the Herzes "knew everybody"—all the famous celebrity soloists and conductors and composers.[5]

Madame Herz's influence on Crawford grew steadily in the mid-1920s. Not adopting theosophical aesthetics quite as much as Gradova, who described music by Bach and Scriabin as a "soul experience" and "music of the astral body," Crawford nevertheless ranked both composers as "the greatest spirits in music" in 1927. She read Madame Blavatsky's *The Secret Doctrine* and described herself as "especially interested in Eastern philosophy" and "mysticism," familiar with the *Bhagavad Gita* and Lao Tse.[6]

Crawford quoted chapter and verse from her new bibles when needed. She recited an aphorism to Martha Beck's brother from the *Bhagavad Gita* about the purposes of art: "That man who sees inaction in action and action in inaction is wise among men." Raised with the idea that idle hands do the devil's work, Crawford rebelliously embraced Taoist values of passive receptivity as sources of wisdom. Convinced that Madame Herz's "knowledge of philosophy and other subjects is phenomenal," she inscribed in her diary Madame Herz's various dicta from 1927 to 1928, among them this: the "distinction between the artist and the mystic is that the latter is simply farther along the road which the former is travelling; he has gone beyond the need for expression." That equation made Ruth all the more eager to cultivate both art and mysticism in herself. As Methodism receded into her past, a new aesthetic theology filled its place.[7]

Crawford joined Djane Herz's community of pupils. Herz told a reporter for the *Musical Leader* how she "made a study of each pupil" when he or she began work with her. She encouraged an unusual practice among them—the reporter called it a "charming element of companionship"—where students were permitted to listen to all lessons. Few people were indifferent to Madame Herz. She was a small woman (about five feet tall) with jet black hair cut in a short bob, who dressed for teaching in elegant caftans that trailed behind her as she strode magisterially around her piano studio, gesturing forcefully to her students, giving them the idea of the "grand sound, the big sound that you needed to project a piece." Didactic intensity heightened the sense of drama that she cultivated. To some, she was artificial; to others she was dynamic and charismatic. The composer Dane Rudhyar, who knew her well, thought her a sensitive musician, and a "typical French-Canadian—the very positive and at times ebullient and slightly dramatic kind."[8]

Crawford was overwhelmed by a temperament that contrasted so powerfully with her own, and she fell, not exactly "in love," but into a kind of adolescent adoration that she recognized in other instances as the "parts of her that were still sixteen." She portrayed Lavoie Herz as a

> nature that responds instantly to impressions; it is as tho the pores of her consciousness were ever open to breathe in, unconsciously, with no effort, thoughts, sensations, artistic feeling, which I must stab at awkwardly with a fork, chew long on, swallow with a gulp, and digest with great effort. She is much further in the evolution of her self.[9]

On other occasions, such emotional attachment to Djane Herz made her jealous. When her teacher's picture appeared in a publicity story in the *Musical Leader*, Ruth resented that "any others outside her very closest circle of friends should be permitted a kodak picture of her." After one evening in Madame Herz's studio, Ruth admitted how "I always feel awkward and know nothing worth saying. What a cold person I am. I believe that even my often spontaneous, free, lively moments are only froth. I am afraid I have no great depth of feeling. Have I capacity for really great friendship? Do I love Madame Herz? I curse myself for my English reserve. The Latin temperament is perhaps harder to live with, more painful at times,—yet possessing such warmth and life and capacity for loving."[10]

Crawford's emotional gullibility turned Djane Herz into an "idol [that] gripped [her] five years." Even though she worshipped with her soul rather than her body, her sexual energies—or rather her "sexual suppression" that a friend later remarked on—added fuel to the fire. If, according to an admirer, Herz taught music by "rousing the flame of creative power within the pupil," then Crawford was burning with desire. Two poems from this period illustrate the passion that spilled over into her music. "Shades of Dead Planets" (1927) exalts the "soul that shall soar in the face of suns": "To burn . . . ecstasy of pain. . . . Even to burn/To touch flame, creator, destroyer . . ./To fold unto me space, time, rhythm, form. . . . In my veins the liquid fire of all suns." "Creator" (1925) asserts the supremacy of composer, suggesting Crawford's unconscious competition with the star pupil. Even if Gradova's performance of Scriabin's Fourth Sonata "spoke universes," she—the composer—created them:

> You are the lover of the creations of God,
>   The buds and green things;
> You will water them and love them into growing . . .
>   But I,
> I shall myself be a god,
> I shall create trees of sound and color
> Whose branches reach up
>   In masses of power . . .
> Out of the great love of my heart shall be born
> Flowers for others to caress
> And warm into greater beauty
>   Than perhaps I dreamt of . . .
>   For you are the sun,
> But I am the creator of suns.

A young woman, newly empowered by dubious metaphysics, triumphs over self-doubt. In 1928 Crawford dedicated her set of piano preludes to "Djane, my inspiration."[11]

Like Ruth, Gitta Gradova was "under Djane Herz's spell. We all were," Gradova said. At least she was for a few years, until her technique collapsed around 1929 and she blamed "Madame Schmerz" as she bitterly called her, for her plight. But Madame's influence had stayed with her more than she knew, for in 1986 the score of Scriabin's Fourth Sonata stood on the grand piano in Gradova's lavish Lake Shore Drive apartment in Chicago, decorated with Chinese and Indian paintings. Gitta Gradova at seventy-five could only dimly recall Ruth as a "nice girl . . . a nice clean wholesome girl, . . . such a direct person that I couldn't identify with her. . . . I was more at home with cultured Europeans than with Americans from the Midwest." Like most contemporary compositions Crawford's music "meant so little" to her in her youth.[12]

Yet the two had been united in a common project by their teacher. Crawford had written five piano preludes—two in the fall of 1924, three more in the following spring—that had impressed Djane Herz so much that she urged Gradova to program at least one of them in forthcoming concerts. Gradova's performance of Crawford's second prelude at a recital in New York at Aeolian Hall on December 13, 1925, marked Crawford's professional debut outside of Chicago. Gradova lavished praise on Madame Herz's discovery. In one interview she said that "Ruth Crawford, a young Chicago girl, has composed several remarkable preludes in an entirely modern idiom. . . . She has broken through the shell of tradition, and is affirming herself as one of the most promising of our young American composers." In another interview Gradova claimed that Crawford's "several preludes for piano reveal a nature of exquisite sensitiveness as well as great intensity." Crawford had already played four preludes (as "Four Short Sketches") in a recital of works by Weidig's composition students that May, when they had been received as "charming" in the local press. Now at least one of them was allowed a deeper, less gender-bound range of emotive content through Gradova's performance. Crawford's prelude, "sensational, pugnacious, curt," was preceded by a formidable group of works, among them Stravinsky's "Chez Petrouchka"; Henry Cowell's "Episode"; Dane Rudhyar's "Stars," from *Moments*, op. 17; Bartók's "Allegro Barbaro"; and "The Tug" by Eugene Goossens. In retrospect, one marvels that this two-minute work was even noticed amidst so much bravura. Gradova repeated the prelude at another recital in Chicago on November 26, 1926. The composers surrounding the Crawford miniature had shifted to Scriabin, Bloch, and Ibert; yet again the prelude stood out from the crowd, according to the critic for the *Musical Leader* (perhaps rooting for the local artist), who wrote that the "most daringly modern of the group was undoubtedly the charmingly impertinent little Prelude by Ruth Crawford, a young Chicago composer of great promise."[13]

Djane Herz had insisted that Gradova also learn music by two other composers she counted as friends—Henry Cowell and Dane Rudhyar. They occasionally visited her as they crossed the country from California to New York in the 1920s. At a time when little American avant-garde music was performed in Chicago, the Herz home was an informal salon for new work—perhaps outpost is a better word—and "the six and a half people interested in it . . . a kind of Mecca for visiting contemporary musicians, of which there weren't many in those days."[14]

In the winter of 1925 Ruth Crawford met the "ethereal" Dane Rudhyar, who proved to be a catalytic influence for the next few years. Not much older than Ruth, Rudhyar (1895–1985) already had twice her experience. A French émigré, intellectually reborn through his discovery of Hindu philosophy, the composer came to the United States in 1914 as penniless as a Buddhist monk. A serendipitous meeting with Djane Herz in New York in 1918 yielded an invitation to stay with her family in Toronto, an act of hospitality that a grateful Rudhyar remembered years later as "saving my life."[15]

Rudhyar adopted Scriabin as his new ideal, hailing his music as a "magical force used by the spiritual Will to produce ecstasy, that is, communion with the Soul!" By 1921 his writing settled into a tone of cosmic authority that would characterize him for the rest of his life. His "Surge of Fire," a tone poem for orchestra and three pianos, was delivered as a "record, by means of instrumental tones, of subjective experiences lived by the author, a record of inner happenings." His work began to attract support from the small circle of radical modernist composers that lived in New York in the early 1920s, among them Carl Ruggles, Henry Cowell, and even Charles Ives.[16]

In 1925 Rudhyar stayed at Djane Herz's apartment in Chicago for a few months, writing an article for the *Musical Observer* about her "regeneration of piano teaching" in her example of an "unselfish and sacrificing life devoted to Art as to a religion. . . ." He also worked on a set of piano preludes that represented a new stage in his compositional development. *Moments* (later revised as *Tetragrams*) was a set of fifteen tone poems dedicated to Djane Lavoie Herz "as a[n] homage of gratitude"; its publication was underwritten in part by her husband. According to Rudhyar, Crawford heard some of these pieces, after which, he later said, she "composed the first interesting music she wrote." In fact two of her preludes had been written before they met.[17]

To Crawford, Rudhyar was a messianic figure, whose passionate espousal of utopian modernism affected her deeply. The elevation of the artist to priest-hood, which the leading Theosophist architect Claude Bragdon described as the salvation of the modern world, intrigued her. Like Bragdon, Rudhyar championed a new crusade of beauty. She installed Rudhyar as a second "idol" in her private temple of art; she was "immersed" in him. After hearing him read poetry one night at Djane's, she began "to feel his beauty as never before. Previously when he was here I have admired and stood afar worshipping vaguely, you might say intellectually, because I was dazzled by his erudition. Now I begin to 'feel' his greatness. Some part of the film has been lifted from my eyes, there is a rift in the clouds which before were so dense." The lapsed Methodist searched for true communication from the "soul world" which reigned supreme as the highest reality. As the kind of person who pushed her-self to epiphanies, Crawford was frequently "beginning to see" this or that idea or concept, or "preparing for a discovery." In 1927 she "suddenly realized" what in fact she had been writing poems about for two years: "the close rela-tion of the artistic and the religious emotion," and like Rudhyar and Djane Herz, she embraced the prototype of the artist/priest/mystic.[18]

In Rudhyar's creationist myth of the origins of harmonic practice, conso-nance was "tribal"—and therefore inferior—because it represented the prim-itive expression of provincial habits. Dissonance, on the other hand, was "universal" because it symbolized the inclusiveness of the theosophical "Uni-versal Brotherhood." In effect, he equated social emancipation with the emancipation of the total chromatic. Impressed by Rudhyar's utopian disso-nance, Crawford quoted long excerpts of his lecture for the Chicago chapter of the Pro Musica Society in November 1928. She was impressed by Rudhyar's vision of the brotherhood of man, which "blends all as human beings, despite slight exteriors which are discordant. To bring together in harmony far-related objects is a glorious achievement."[19] Crawford's artistic quest had a pur-pose that was similar to psychoanalysis. In effect, theosophy, mysticism, and spiritualism were pre-Freudian ways to approach the subconscious. Undoubt-edly these led Rudhyar to suggest alternative approaches to composition. Like the philosophies of the eighteenth century and early French modernists, he attacked Western musical practice as decadent and overintellectualized; he rejected the traditional structural forms of tonality and the techniques of counterpoint as rationalistic rather than intuitive. In a revealing offhand comment made some years later, Crawford said that she "scorned counter-point for two years" because of him. This reaction against "ossified formal pro-scriptions" of musical practice characterized early modernism, yet few besides Rudhyar practiced what he preached, since he described composing as a process controlled by a higher power than the intellect.[20]

"The mind did not have to guide the formation of a composition," he told both Ruth and her friend Martha Beck. "When the hands fell at random— that was the composition." Martha Beck, who thought him a "bit of a phony," told him that theoretically the hands of a five-year-old child could also compose as he did. Rudhyar agreed with her, "but added that the hands of a five-year-old would not fall where Dane Rudhyar's hands fell. . . . "[21]

Despite—or perhaps because of—the intellectual rejection of reason, Crawford found Rudhyar's ideas about compositional process liberating. Just as conscience could encumber psychological spontaneity, so rationality could suppress creative inspiration. At least, that proposition seems to be the underlying motive for Crawford's willingness to legitimize Rudhyar. "I like to wonder about things," Crawford once wrote, "rather than know about them," and she told Martha Beck that "contact with [Rudhyar] has given me quite a bit of freedom."[22]

Rudhyar was one of the first composers of the 1920s whose works were performed, published, and promoted almost exclusively through a young American avant-garde movement, developed specifically through the efforts of the California composer/pianist Henry Cowell and his various enterprises for new music. In the 1920s they were known as the "ultra-moderns," and Ruth Crawford joined them after Cowell discovered her.[23]

They met at Djane Herz's studio when Cowell came to Chicago on a recital tour in 1925. Cowell was twenty-eight years old, just at the threshold of a career as composer, pianist, and prime mover in the radical wing of American composition. One year earlier Cowell had founded his New Music Society, intended to support concert series at which recent works would be played exclusively. At his debut recital in Chicago on February 28, 1924, he treated the piano as if it were a wild bull and he, the matador of the keys. Whatever one's point of view, Cowell made great copy—a "pale young man, languid and blasé, quite at ease but indifferent to surroundings," who had come to Chicago to show its pianists "how to crush all the keys at once." Gitta Gradova seditiously called him a pianist from the school of Hart, Schaeffner and Marx, referring to the men's clothing store because of the way Cowell's coatsleeves brushed the keyboard, and she begrudgingly played his "Episode for Piano" at her New York recital in December 1925. To Ruth Crawford, Cowell was a kindred spirit.[24]

Cowell was so impressed by Crawford's music that within months of their first meeting, he invited her to join the non-resident Board of Outside Advisors for the New Music Society. By 1926 she was on his letterhead, supporting Cowell's goal of presenting "musical works embodying the most progressive tendencies of this age and to disseminate the new musical ideas." That same year Cowell included her in his lecture series on modern music in San Francisco and Carmel, California, surveying music by "Goossens, Honegger, Malipiero, Béla Bartók, Leo Ornstein, Ruth Crawford, Edgard Varèse and other important modern composers, showing the trend which is indicated by their music."[25]

Henry Cowell considered Ruth Crawford to be an amazing discovery for two reasons. Not only was she a "completely natural dissonant composer," but she was also that minor miracle: a woman who could actually write his kind of new music. He praised her Sonata for Violin and Piano as "vital . . . with none of the undesirable sentimentality which often destroys the creative efforts of women composers." For the magazine *Musicalia*, he wrote, "Her work of deep beauty is at the level of high accomplishment that men realize. She is the only female composer, that I know of, of which I can say this." By this time Cowell had seen a set of four more piano preludes, written between 1927 and 1928, which he published in the fifth issue of the *New Music Quarterly* in October 1928. This turned out to be the only music from her Chicago period that was published in her lifetime. More than any other musician, not only in the 1920s but throughout their enduring friendship, Henry Cowell supported Ruth Crawford, the composer. All subsequent publications of her music and the one recording of her work in her lifetime came under his sponsorship or through the organizations which he had founded.[26]

In summing up her own development Crawford paid tribute to Herz, Rudhyar, and Cowell and then listed the other important musical experiences that influenced the course of her composition, immediately staking out her relationship to the European modernist composers who dominated the scene — in 1925 Scriabin and Stravinsky, then later Schoenberg and Hindemith. American modernism in music was still too young and too unarticulated as a cultural phenomenon for American composers not to assess themselves in relation to the Europeans.

Opportunities to hear new music in Chicago were somewhat limited. Moreover, "new" does not necessarily mean "avant-garde," and the now obscure names of composers programmed by Stock and other groups outnumber those composers that today form the modernist mainstream. Still, many noteworthy performances occurred and Crawford took advantage of them. On November 7, 1924, with the Chicago Symphony Orchestra, Stock conducted the Chicago premiere of Stravinsky's *Rite of Spring* — the same year it was first played in both New York and Boston. On February 21 and 22, 1925, Stravinsky himself, during his first American tour, conducted *The Rite of Spring*, as well as *The Firebird Suite*. And in January 1926 the orchestra gave a rare evening of Schoenberg's music, playing *Transfigured Night*, the suite from the tone poem *Pelleas and Melisande*, and Five Pieces for Orchestra, op. 16. That same month Stock appeared with the music and dance ensemble Chicago Allied Arts, headed by Eric De Lamarter and the dancer Adolph Bolm, to conduct the Chicago premiere of Schoenberg's *Pierrot lunaire*, with Mina Hager as soloist (January 3, 1926); it was the work's second performance in the United States, three years after its American premiere in New York.[27]

The impact of these events is hard to recapture today, when recordings have made such music easily accessible. One can overestimate the significance of a world premiere even half a century ago by failing to consider how local such events were. Later performances in other places could be just as crucial to the vitality and dissemination of modernism. In American music there was no historical equivalent of, say, the 1913 Armory show, a watershed for American painting. Rather than through any single decisive event, the techniques and effects of musical modernism accumulated through discrete performances given over a wide span of time. Chicago was slowly catching up with European modernism in the 1920s. And Ruth Crawford found these events formative for her development: "I discovered Scriabine at this time; the music of Schoenberg and Hindemith I did not hear until later; Stravinsky's *Sacre* and *L'Oiseau de Feu* came to me too about this time [1925]."[28]

When her friend Alfred Frankenstein returned from a trip to Europe in 1924 with recordings of music still unavailable in the United States, Crawford went over to his apartment to hear new works by Milhaud, Hindemith, Stravinsky, and Vaughan Williams. "These recordings were very hard to get in Europe [and] almost impossible to get in this country," he said. "And I know that Ruth was very much interested in those things." They had met by 1925 or 1926, and they were neighbors on the South Side.[29]

Frankenstein (1906–81), who would later become a respected music and art critic, was at that time a young musician and writer eagerly immersing himself in Chicago's musical life. At twenty-one he had already written a small perceptive book of music criticism called *Syncopating Saxophones*. Brash and occasionally "myopically local," Frankenstein wrote about contemporary music with a journalistic brio indebted to both Ben Hecht and Carl Sandburg. One essay described Stravinsky rehearsing the Chicago Symphony Orchestra in 1925, directing "in four languages at once. . . . At the climax of the [*Firebird*] Suite . . . Stravinsky jumps a foot into the air." "The Latest Lively Art" proclaimed that "anyone in the profession of tone who does not believe in jazz is considered either slightly demented, or else as some sort of rare antique or fossil. . . ."[30]

Frankenstein exemplified the progressive Chicago stance toward the musical style emerging from its dance halls, blues clubs, and cabarets on the South Side. A now legendary jazz scene (home to such great musicians as "King" Oliver, Alberta Hunter, and Louis Armstrong) had a powerful impact on classical musicians. One of Chicago's leading composers, John Alden Carpenter, had integrated jazz idioms into concert music long before Gershwin composed *Rhapsody in Blue*, which Paul Whiteman brought to Chicago in October 1924. Frankenstein played clarinet with Eric De Lamarter's Civic Orchestra and in a jazz combo at a cabaret on the South Side. Whether he took Ruth to the "black and tan" blues clubs where the races mixed socially is not known, but she surely knew jazz, perhaps because of him.

Very occasionally, amidst theosophical talk of fire and the spirit world, Crawford invoked a vernacular image—"a little jazz dance" of a piece of paper hopping along the ground or gnats doing the "shimmy" or the "little uneven bricks in the sidewalks with a syncopated tune that sounded very much like jazz." In 1929 under the pseudonym Fred Karlan, she wrote a pleasant though not outstanding popular song, "Lollipop-a-Papa," with blues harmonies and old-fashioned vaudeville ragtime rhythms (Ex. 4-1). Perhaps the jazz-like rhythms and syncopations of the clarinet solo in the Suite No. 1 for Woodwinds and Piano (1927) are an oblique tribute to her clarinetist friend, for she and Alfred occasionally played chamber music together.[31]

Alfred fell in love with Ruth, courting her for three years to no avail. She

Example 4-1 "Lollipop-a-Papa," opening of refrain. Used by permission of the Seeger estate.

"liked Alfred very much" and for a short time even entertained the idea that more could come of it, but nothing did. Later she told her friend Alice Burrow that she felt "repressed" around him, that he "did not seem to enjoy jolly joking," which she needed from her friends. It is a measure of their incompatibility that for his part, Alfred felt he could not break through the "little reserve" with a woman he described as "a Methodist minister's daughter." Perhaps the difference in their cultural backgrounds misled him; as he once said, "I don't know quite how to put it. One just assumed and understood that she was a lady and slightly on a pedestal."[32]

Ruth took him around to Madame Herz's studio, Alfred later reported. There he heard some of her work, and met Cowell and Rudhyar as well. Cowell, catalytic for so many, eventually helped Frankenstein land a job at the *San Francisco Chronicle*, where he did "everything [he] could to keep the situation open for contemporary composers" for the next forty-one years, writing enthusiastically about Ives, Ruggles, and of course Crawford. He in turn changed her life by introducing her to Carl Sandburg, Chicago's leading poet and man of letters, who was looking for a suitable piano teacher for his three daughters.[33]

"The skill did not take," said Helga Sandburg, who was about seven or eight years old at the time, and her sister Janet could not carry a tune, said the oldest daughter Margaret. But "we all loved Ruth. We were very attached to her. . . . I can see her the way she was in Elmhurst. She had black bobbed hair, a sort of round face, very smiling, always good humored. She was very modern to me." The Sandburg children were "boisterous," Ruth said. She was impressed by their mother's patience, lavishing mystical compliments on "Mrs. Sandburg's peace in the midst of turmoil—her imperturbable *yet* paradoxically *sparkling* calm gave me a sense of certain passages of Laotze's Tao." She described Carl Sandburg as "ethereal"—high praise for men during these years. After one visit, "he comes, takes my hand in his strong grip, and draws me to him in a sweet kind of fatherly embrace. I am touched, of course. 'You're one of the kids,' he says. 'Now the family is all here.'"[34]

As a "sort of added informal unadopted daughter" (Sandburg's words), Crawford dropped the persona of the piano teacher. She found the "spontaneity of a child within her" that had "woke late," remembering a time at the Indiana dunes when she "ran like a young animal over and down the desolate sand-wastes, something in the desert-like stretches, the rough lake, the wildness, setting the child free." This athletic "romping" side, which Sandburg released, is captured in a snapshot taken near his home in Harbert, Michigan: Ruth, dressed in knickers, poses with an axe in front of a huge felled tree. Standing off to the side, Carl Sandburg stretches out his arm to show off the girl wonder. It could be captioned, Pete Seeger later said, as a believe-it-or-not photo—"see this Amazon is going to chop this huge trunk in two." As her mentor, Sandburg kept a lifelong fondness for this young woman with the "Chinese face"—his favorite phrase for her round nose and round jaw and bobbed dark hair. His observations of Crawford with his children would later surface in a letter of recommendation written to the Guggenheim Foundation on December 5, 1929, when he spoke of "her traits of character and gifts of personality that cannot easily be incorporated in a report such as this. Her letters, her talk, her ways with children show a range of expression which is extraordinary in originality."[35]

That Sandburg's influence on Ruth Crawford would eventually involve her "extraordinary ways with children" remained in the distant future when Ruth Seeger would write, "My first appreciation of and affection for American stuff came through you." "You got me started." For by happenstance she got involved in the most commercially successful anthology of folk music to be published in the 1920s—Sandburg's *The American Songbag* (1927).[36]

Sandburg's anthology spoke to the cultural moment. Even if the viability of American folk songs would continue to be debated by intellectuals for the next decade as well, the "steadily increasing interest in the study of American folk songs" that Edmund Wilson remarked in 1926 gathered momentum throughout the 1920s. Sandburg contributed his populist charm, as the "people's troubadour," combining folk singing with poetry reading on the literary lecture circuit. For *The American Songbag* Sandburg hired Crawford's friend Alfred Frankenstein to notate tunes from his singing in a process described euphemistically as "constructive memory." The first limited edition in 1926 consisted of melodies alone in a small print run of about six hundred copies; then the publisher decreed that the basic structure be changed from tune book to a sing-around-the-piano anthology by providing each melody with a substantive piano accompaniment. Away in Europe at the time, Franken-stein reacted angrily to the decision: "Who in hell is the flathead that got the brilliant idea to harmonize those songs? There isn't the slightest reason for publishing them so, and there are a million reasons against it." When his ob-jections were not heeded, he refused to allow his name to be used as the tran-scriber. Sandburg scrambled around for music arrangers, and Crawford was one of sixteen composers enlisted for the project.[37]

Her arrangements, filled with brooding Romantic harmonies, reflect her emotional response to the material as personal rather than social document. Once she described Sandburg as sitting "there in the lamplight singing song after song, simply, sometimes wildly, sometimes mournfully, his understanding voice winding in and out among the irregular nuances, and accompanied by stray chords on the guitar." And her arrangements express that lonesome in-troversion as well. Crawford contributed four: "There Was an Old Soldier," a Civil War tune; "Lonesome Road," which Sandburg described as a southern mountain song of "self-pity"; "Ten Thousand Miles Away from Home"; and "Those Gambler's Blues," a version of "St. James Infirmary." That was Craw-ford's favorite, and she played and sang it for friends at the MacDowell Colony a few years later (Ex. 4-2).[38]

Her work falls into the category of "concert folk song," a genre whose im-petus had come from Europe and became increasingly popular in the United States in the early decades of this century. Black spirituals, for example, which typically had been arranged for choral concert performance, were being han-dled as solo songs by great artists like Roland Hayes and Paul Robeson for the first time. If the "concert spiritual" with its own aesthetic traditions is but one manifestation of the larger genre, then Crawford's "concert folk songs" shared its potential and its weaknesses. Technique does not burden "Those Gambler's Blues," while it distorts "Lonesome Road" with overly chromatic chords. She continued working in the genre briefly, in 1928–29, setting Louis Unter-meyer's "Jewish Lullaby" (which she retitled "Russian Lullaby") in an impres-sionistic style that fell somewhere between her Sandburg arrangements and her modernist idiom.[39]

The American Songbag loomed large in Crawford's subsequent narrative re-constructions of her life as her initiation into the field, memories occasionally tinged with conscience. In the 1930s and 1940s, as an advocate of "authen-ticity," she would regret "having set them as she had [because] the folk song element got lost"; she later remarked to a friend that at the time, "my mind wasn't on folk songs; my mind was on the fact that I was going to have a com-position in print." But "authenticity" was not the point in the 1920s, a period when the style and context of folk-song arrangements were indebted to Dvořák and an aesthetic of Romantic nationalism; when as Michael Kammen has described it, "the emotional discovery of America" overshadowed docu-

Example 4-2 "Those Gambler's Blues," last two lines. From Carl Sandburg's *The American Songbag,* © 1927. By Harcourt Brace & Company and renewed 1955 by Carl Sandburg. Reprinted by permission of the publisher.

mentary impulses. As a populist poet, Sandburg bestowed a powerful dignity on what the '20s called the "American scene" in a book he called a "ragbag of strips, stripes and streaks of color from nearly all ends of the earth . . . rich with the diversity of the United States." Reviewed widely in journals ranging from the *New Masses* to *Modern Music, The American Songbag* influenced a number of American musicians. Pete Seeger, who calls it a "landmark," saw it "almost as soon as it came out." The composer Elie Siegmeister took it to Paris with him in 1927, and he and his wife Hannah "were always singing those songs. That was home. That was where we belonged."[40]

A s important as *The American Songbag* was, Carl Sandburg as poet influ- enced Ruth more at the time. She set several of his poems to music, one group (Five Songs on Sandburg Poems) written in 1929 and the second set (Three Songs) in 1930–32. In the literary world Sandburg would soon come to represent an alternative version of modernism, one whose vernacular alle- giances got pushed to the sidelines by T. S. Eliot and the new formalism; but in Chicago and the Midwest—even in the 1920s—his point of view retained its authority. Crawford's admiration for Sandburg was shared by many artists of the period, among them Langston Hughes and Virgil Thomson. Diary en- tries and poems from the period suggest how Crawford assimilated the imagi- native vision of Sandburg, and she even approved of his populism as well, writing how he was "right to search among down and outers for underlying poetry," for he was "ten times more likely to find it there than in more polite circles."[41]

Crawford adopted Sandburg's imagistic idioms in several poems she wrote in the late 1920s. She anointed the Tribune Tower a "sedate priest, star-gazer, gray-robed mystic among skyscrapers"; she heard the "grumbling steel-song of train wheels" and "voices of men and songs of engines, Of the whirring crescendos of autos, and the shrieking of brakes,—And the somnolent drawl of a drunkard huddled on the low curb."[42]

Sandburg, moreover, stood on the shoulders of writers whom she perhaps loved even more: Emerson, Thoreau, and Whitman. Crawford opened her 1927 diary with a quotation from *Walden Pond*, underlining Thoreau's admo- nition to "probe the universe in a myriad points." She alluded to Whitman frequently. One diary entry recounts a telling incident at Djane Herz's studio: "I pick up *Leaves of Grass* and find a good many of the first verses of 'Song of Myself' underlined. I feel at home." Whitman's cosmic metaphysics inspired her. "His constant reiteration of the oneness of himself with all other crea- tures—a sense of bigness" was an article of faith in her aesthetic theology.[43]

Sandburg and Whitman also represented the democratizing of creativity that marks Crawford's aesthetic. Unlike German expressionists, who searched for artistic truth in the neurotic and inspiration in the subconscious, Crawford meditated on the ordinary, crediting the humblest elements in nature with creative power. "One can draw a kind of dramatic or rhythmic or dynamic pleasure from the very smallest things," she believed, and her diary often reads like a set of exercises in sensory awareness, with its descriptions of bus rides and traffic light patterns or leisurely walks through Jackson Park. She had the zeal of a transcendental convert, who would rather watch gnats undulate in the wind than the great ballerina Pavlova dance. She whimsically wrote how they "seem to have the original of the chorus girl shake, these gnats, a kind of angular 'shimmy'. . . . But what joy they give me." Such rich transformations could be won from the most ordinary moments:

> Last spring an inflated empty envelope cut such capers when the wind found its cup, first rushing across the sidewalk, then sidling enticingly, slowly, as tho doing a bit of quiet flirting, then suddenly turning most unladylike somersets into a grass plot, where it lay discontented till it could creep stealthily back to the sidewalk for more acrobatics,—created such a perfect scherzo of rhythmic variety and subtlety that I laughed right out loud.[44]

Here is where Crawford's female sensibility turned gnats into chorus girls and the unruly envelope a seductive unladylike acrobat. In her poem, "Filling the Lake," she merges herself with the lake, "dreaming, feeling . . . her life-pores open." Sitting by an ocean, watching the waves ripple sea grass, Crawford wrote how "Earth will not let her hair be combed." In reading nature as female, Crawford constructed a bridge between sensory experience and art.[45]

Sandburg inspired many Chicago artists with images which embodied their midwestern experience of modernity. Among Chicago composers those images were often transformed into music that integrated jazz and popular music. Crawford resisted this trend. Instead, she tracked a path between two seemingly incompatible figures, Scriabin and Sandburg, by inheriting and then reworking a legacy of ideas and values that had been linked together in American life from the early 1900s as the basis of her spiritual aesthetics. In this eclectic transcendental modernism Emerson, Thoreau, Whitman, and Sandburg coexisted with Lao Tse, Madame Blavatsky, and the *Bhagavad Gita*.

Humor was part of this world, offering necessary relief from spiritual solemnities. Once Crawford playfully asked, "Sandburg: has he convictions? His spirit goes swooping into byways, pinching a piece of dust and asking 'Are you a fact or fancy? Have you a little dust-soul somewhere? Where are you going and what for?'"—questions she continually posed to herself during these years.[46]

Crawford reaped the harvest of her hard work during her last five years in Chicago. The American Conservatory hired her for the regular piano staff and the children's department in the fall of 1924, a post she kept for five years. She and her mother moved to a new apartment, having found what was described to Carl as a very nice and attractive place on 4517 Oakenwald Street, by themselves at last, no longer needing to sublet their extra rooms to make ends meet. In 1925 Mrs. Crawford sent Carl the catalogue of the American Conservatory of Music. Carl replied, "I am very proud of her, and the number of pupils you mention also savor of considerable accomplishment so that from now on she will no doubt begin to receive some financial remuneration from the years of hard work." In 1928–29, she was appointed to the harmony faculty as well. Crawford supplemented this income by teaching piano and harmony at the School of Music at Elmhurst College from 1926 through 1929 and by taking on private students, supporting herself and her mother with some help from Carl. Carl sent $100 a month for 1925 to 1926, and then reduced that to $50 when the real estate market in Florida crashed in 1927. "The teaching had mushroomed," Crawford wrote; for the first time in many years, "finances were very easy." Indeed, one diary entry refers to a twelve-hour Saturday with twenty pupils.[47]

Crawford found pupils among the social circles of her new friends, particularly that of Djane Lavoie Herz. The Herzes moved among the upper-class German-Jewish community in Chicago (the crowd that knew the families of Leopold and Loeb) and names like Sulzberger and Bloch appear in her diary. Ruth wrote to her brother about her new connections to the rich and pointed out "with pride . . . Mrs. Bloch's impressive mansion on Greenwood . . . [as] the home of one of her pupils" to her friends; predictably, she later reproached herself for that small snobbery, "disgusted" with herself for being a "braggart." She would tell the Guggenheim Foundation in her application for a fellowship that she had been "compelled to teach intensively to earn my living, and this left me little consecutive time or strength for composing," doing most of it "at night and on Sundays."[48]

She occasionally bewailed the fact that she had sold away her composing time for money, and then rebuked herself for "selfish thoughts." Despite the declaration of power symbolized by her earlier poem "Creator," her sense of entitlement as a composer was fragile. She struck her friend Alfred Frankenstein as "extremely modest" about her composition. The margins for women to be "selfish" were so thin that when a pupil expressed a preference for one lesson time over another, Crawford was "annoyed" at the student's display of ego. Then she decided that this young girl "did not mean to be selfish," that there was no "intentional unpleasantness." Yet teaching had its own rewards, as she herself often acknowledged.[49]

Through Djane Herz, Crawford acquired her outstanding pupil Vivian Fine, who became a lifelong friend and a distinguished composer. In the fall of 1924 Herz had proposed a barter scheme to help Ruth pay for her own private lessons: in exchange for piano lessons, Ruth would tutor one of Djane's piano students in harmony and theory. Herz sent along eleven-year-old Vivian, who would study with Crawford for five years and whose career in composition she initiated. "One day she asked me to write a piece of music," Fine recalled. And I was twelve years old. Nobody had asked me to write a piece before. And so I wrote a piece . . . and I remember how she listened to it. When I turned around and looked at her, she was looking very thoughtful . . . and her response to it played a critical role in my life. She listened to it very carefully; I could tell she was really paying attention. I think this was a critical experience for me — to have somebody respond to something I did. She liked it very much. The piece was rather unconventional and had its own shape. . . . I really believe it's possible I would never have composed, or composed much later if I hadn't been asked then. . . . You do need a role model, someone who says to you, 'You too can compose.'"[50]

Crawford treated Vivian Fine as a protégée, whose "summer output of original compositions" in 1927 impressed her with "their profuseness, force, depth, breadth of conception. . . . [They] seem remarkable at thirteen," she reflected. As she had compared herself to Robyn's students several years earlier, she again was reminded "how very late was my own musical, or rather compositional development compared with hers." Crawford played her own music for Vivian as well, who in turn performed some of them at concerts. Sometime between 1927 and 1929 Crawford gave her a full autograph score of the Sonata for Violin and Piano, a work which Fine recorded more than fifty years later.[51]

Crawford wrote the Sonata for Violin and Piano in early 1926. The first performance of what proved to be the most important composition from her Chicago years may have been an inconspicuous concert on April 13, 1926, as part of the Composers' Night for the musical honor society, Sigma Alpha Iota. The following month she played it again at the annual recital of Weidig's composition students. Still satisfied with Weidig as a composition teacher, Ruth remained his student through 1929.[52]

In 1926 Crawford won an extension scholarship in composition from the Institute of Musical Art, which had just been taken over by the Juilliard Musical Foundation (preparing the way for an eventual merger of the institute and the Juilliard Graduate School). Crawford submitted both the Sonata for Violin and Piano and Music for Small Orchestra, a two-movement suite, which was her first work for more than two instruments. Perhaps she was also motivated to try orchestral writing through her acquaintance with conductor Eric De Lamarter. As a percussion player in De Lamarter's Chicago Civic Orchestra in its 1926-27 season, she gained some needed experience with the inner workings of an orchestra, adorning "the percussion section . . . for part of [the 1926–27] season, counting, not too successfully, measures by the hundred behind a triangle." De Lamarter called the concert series he conducted for Chicago Allied Arts—an innovative music and dance collaborative started in 1924—"Music for Small Orchestra," the very name Crawford used for her own composition.[53]

Despite her success, 1926 was a difficult year. One diary entry refers to 1926 as a "nightmare," with a darker reference to one "bitter, irritable day" in which "more sensitive morbid people become suicides. My wretchedness comes from the returning to my eyes of last year's pulling, wracking strain, which makes practice and composing hard." Little else is known about this crisis of nerves and health, or about an operation that Ruth had in the fall of 1925 to alleviate these symptoms. They abated but did not disappear entirely, and could trigger what Crawford described as spells of "depression."[54]

Crawford held the Juilliard Extension Scholarship for three years. In 1927 she received her master's degree summa cum laude in musical theory, composition, and orchestration; in 1928 she won the conservatory's highest honor in composition—the Weidig gold medal. That fall she completed a Suite for Piano and Winds, and between 1927 and 1928, five more preludes for piano.

While she wrote in a style that she knew had little commercial viability, Crawford reached out toward the commercial piano-teaching market as well. The Crawfords always had an enterprising streak in their family, and her brother Carl reminded her of the market. "Does Ruth ever get in on a radio program? If so, let me know ahead of time and we will tune in. If she could get in on a program now and then, it would help her greatly from an advertising standpoint," Carl wrote his mother.[55]

And his sister thought about the market as well. During these years she composed several kinds of teaching pieces. In 1925 she had been accepted into Sigma Alpha Iota; the following year she won the national prize in the SAI composition contest not only for Five Preludes for Piano but for her most ambitious teaching piece, the piano suite "The Adventures of Tom Thumb." Modeled after Louise Robyn's "picture suites" for children (Robyn published "A Peter Pan Picture Suite" for the piano in 1927), where each movement was accompanied by captions from a well-known children's story, "The Adventures of Tom Thumb" used material from the Grimm brothers' fairy tale in each of its six sections. Crawford was fond of this work, playing it at the SAI concert on April 13 and at Djane Herz's—the only work Alfred Frankenstein remembered hearing—and trying to get it published in 1951. She also wrote several smaller piano pieces, among them "Whirligig"—a title from her very first piece; "A Little Study in Short Trills: Mr. Crow and Miss Wren Go for a Walk"; "Jumping the Rope"; "Little Lullaby"; "Playtime"; and "We Dance Together." She even self-published the last of these pieces, with an old-fashioned couple on a cover designed by one of her friends.

Despite all of this hard work, Crawford enjoyed life and her different circles of friends and colleagues, who brought out different parts of her personality. Among the "girls" at the conservatory or at SAI meetings, as she called them, she could be a light-hearted spontaneous person who took swims in the lake at Jackson Park and played tennis in the summer. Martha Beck remembers her as blessed with a "sunny disposition. . . . She was not a melancholy person by any means . . . and she had a sense of humor." She could laugh at herself as well. Even while fretting over her stocky shape, she wrote that neither her face nor her weight of 130 pounds suited her "'childish' ways," and that she would never be "the thin wiry modernist."[56]

Another circle of friends at the conservatory included Weidig's advanced students, who would meet regularly for lunch. Among was them Elwind Bull, leading a double life as a professional mechanical engineer and a composer, reserving lunch times for his "younger friends in music," including among its regulars for many years, Crawford, Stella Roberts, and Irwin Fischer, a pianist-composer later on the faculty at the American in the 1940s. Ruth was also close to other younger teachers at the conservatory, including Martha Beck, Pearl Appel, who played some of Crawford's preludes in 1929, and Alice Burrow, an actress and singer. Burrow, as Vivian Fine recalled, was "imbued with some sort of religious intensity. . . . Ruth admired Alice a great deal and . . . she once brought Alice to sing for Madame Herz, who was not too impressed."[57]

Through Djane Herz, with her wide contacts among Chicago's intelligentsia, Crawford gained an entrée into Chicago's elite intellectual set. It took her a few years to get over her self-consciousness among these people, and several diary entries express her hesitancy among them, her lack of "ability to get out of my coat of steel." Yet evenings at various study groups with the Herzes, professors from the University of Chicago, Ben Hecht, and Clarence Darrow made for memorable occasions. The artist Carl Bohnen, well known in Chicago at this time, was another friend, doing a small pencil sketch of Ruth in 1928 that she later used in publicity material.[58]

Recognition accumulated in the last years of the 1920s, as Chicago itself became more open to new music. Crawford had never participated in Rue (Mrs. John) Alden Carpenter's Arts Club, which had prompted interest in modern art and music since 1916 by sponsoring lectures and recitals by visiting European artists and composers. However, when some alternatives to this exclusive coterie emerged, she took part. She was on the board of a local chapter of the Pro Musica Society (1927) when that winter it sponsored a lecture recital by the French composer Darius Milhaud, and later evenings with Bartók and Ravel. The Pro Musica Society, originally the Franco American Musical Society, began in 1920 and continued through 1932. In 1928 Crawford also was one of the founding members (along with Cowell and Rudhyar) of the Pan American Association of Composers, a group based largely in New York.[59]

The most important milestone for her Chicago reputation happened that same year—1928—when Chicago musicians formed a local chapter of the International Society for Contemporary Music (ISCM). Initially founded in Europe in 1922 as a postwar cultural reconstruction effort. New York hosted the first American chapter in 1923; five years later the Chicago movement, "sponsored by all the leading musicians of Chicago," aspired to present new music to Chicagoans. Crawford was chosen to represent the local scene at the first concert of the ISCM on February 8, 1928, when Amy Neill, violin, and Lee Pattison, piano, performed the Sonata for Violin and Piano at the Cliff Dwellers Club. The event was regarded as a watershed for the city's modernist musicians. Edward Moore, the city's preeminent critic, wrote in the *Chicago Daily Tribune*, "There is now a full fledged Chicago chapter of the ISCM. The first concert was last night. There is every reason to say it got off to a good start. At least it brought tidings of great joy to some in the audience, and of great distress to others, and nothing could be more in its favor than that."[60]

Crawford's selection by the music committee was surprising in view of her anomalous relationship to Chicago's compositional traditions. Two of its more prominent composers, John Alden Carpenter and Leo Sowerby, worked with vernacular materials (one with jazz and the other with traditional folk melodies), and both were invested in tonal traditions. Crawford's music was far more radical, already atonal and highly dissonant. As the *Musical Leader* would describe her in 1929, she was "already widely known for the startling modernity of her style." Perhaps Frederick Stock's appreciation of Scriabin and her similarly spiritual expressionistic thrust accounted for her selection by the music committee, which he chaired. Vivian Fine overheard him discussing how "very talented" Crawford was that evening. The favorable critical response to the formal debut of the work in New York the previous year could have played some role as well. The League of Composers, turning their attention to American talent after several seasons of sponsoring European premieres, had featured her, along with Copland, Marc Blitzstein, and a few others, in a concert featuring young American composers. The first in the league's series of concerts of "New Music by Young Americans," it, along with the founding of Chicago's ISCM chapter, represented a renewed surge of interest in new American music in the late 1920s.[61]

Just a few months later, Crawford received another significant New York performance. On May 6, 1928, the well-known pianist Richard Buhlig performed her two Preludes for Piano at a "Copland-Sessions Concert of Contemporary Music," an event that got a great deal of critical notice. The two composers were producing their first season of concerts devoted to new American music. Overall, the concert was a success, playing to an almost full house, with both Copland and Sessions there (Copland, in fact, performing, and Sessions eager to hear the debut of part of his First Sonata). Whether Crawford went to New York is not known.[62]

Nor is it clear just how Crawford's preludes came to be programmed. Copland's note to Sessions stated only that "Buhlig is playing at our second concert nine pieces by Rudhyar (Three Paeans), Adolph Weiss, a pupil of Schoenberg's and Ruth Crawford, a girl who lives in Chicago." Copland had heard her Sonata for Violin and Piano at that point; he would speak about Crawford as a admirer of Scriabin in his lectures on "Masterpieces of Modern Music" written around this time. Although he had outgrown his youthful worship of Scriabin, some respect for the "anarchist . . . démodé to the present-day composer" nevertheless emerges, for Scriabin could "at moments, touch secret springs." It seems likely that Richard Buhlig was engaged to play a group of modern pieces and that he himself chose the repertory, for several works reappeared in his recital for Cowell's New Music Society in San Francisco later that fall. For this concert he chose Crawford's fifth and eight preludes (1925 and 1928).[63]

Richard Buhlig (1880–1952) was a fine pianist and a tall, elegant man, whom Charles Seeger would later describe as "very charming, rather presentable, with a leonine face and magnificent curly hair . . . who could only sleep in violet silk pajamas." As a "composer's pianist" he had pioneered performances of the European modernists Bartók, Kodály, Schoenberg, and Debussy before the war; and in the 1920s he began to play for Cowell and his circle. Buhlig had probably met Ruth in Chicago during 1927 or 1928 at Djane Herz's, and she responded gratefully to his interest, dedicating her last prelude (spring 1928) to him. They met again later that year, for a diary entry from December 9, 1928, says simply "with Buhlig all day." Buhlig later programmed one of Crawford's preludes in a new format, including them in his lecture-recital series "Landmarks of Five Centuries of Keyboard Literature."[64]

Reviews of the preludes from Buhlig's two concerts of 1928 were mixed. Comparisons were made with Debussy, Chopin, Scriabin, and Schoenberg—none to fellow Americans. The best reviews praised Crawford's "individuality" and her unique "strange sonorities." One hostile review in the *New York Telegraph* suggested that she was "running a race" with Adolph Weiss to see "which could be more erotic." Rudhyar fared even worse: the *New York Sun* described him as as "naked and unashamed . . . . one of the cave men of modernism."[65] Those who liked her work distinguished her from the stereotype of lady composer. Nicolas Slonimsky praised Crawford as "anything but feminine in the rough-and-tumble of her 'Lento, tempo rubato' and 'Leggiero.'" A critic who would later condescend to some female musicians in his various reference works, Slonimsky interpreted her dissonant harmonies, which she described in images of mystical primal power, as "rough-and-tumble" boyish pugnacity. He also rebuked her for "musical manners" that were "slightly out-of-date. . . . Perhaps had she known the East . . . she would have realized this. Otherwise, she seems to be not without perspicacity, and there may be a chance for her in the future."[66]

Crawford thought over her "chances for the future" as an issue of identity. Talking about her "self" rather than her music, she asked, "How much of myself can I claim, and how truly my personality can be likened to Joseph's coat of many colors: just how much of the cloth is of my own substance and how much is simply a matter of very skillful weaving in of foreign materials which please my fancy?" Did the composer wear Joseph's coat of many colors as well? In mulling over the new music she was hearing, Crawford asked, "Do I know what I do like? *What* do I like? . . . Would I think much of my own music if someone else had written it? What would my criticism be?"[67]

She trusted her own growth enough to live those questions. Even if she occasionally resorted to the overheated prose of the theosophical novitiate, she propelled herself toward a state of grace. Her reward for such relentless self-interrogation was the insight to rework aesthetics into compassion:

> What an inconceivably beautiful thing is this soul world, and that the thought that existence among people, which I sometimes deplore as banal and boring, could be a glorious experience if one could speak to the soul and not to the brain. . . . I feel in different people a thing I could not feel a year ago. It must be that my inner growth enables me to feel the beauties in others. I am growing more and more in love with my self, with a kind of flowering joy that seems to have, lately, a more or less permanent blooming inside me, and becoming more and more sensitive to beauty within myself, I begin to comprehend its presence in others.[68]

"trees of sound and color"

music, 1924–1929

I shall create trees of sound and color
Whose branches reach up
In masses of power. . . .

—Ruth Crawford, 1925

Crawford's music written between 1924 and 1929 constitutes her first distinctive style period. Her "trees of sound and color"—her magical phrase for her own music—stood in a dense forest of early American modernism, where new idioms crowded in on one another, competing for their place in the sun.

The stylistic context for her work might be termed "post-tonal pluralism": post-tonal in that she regarded tonality as an option rather than a premise; and pluralistic because, like many American composers, she was catching up with European modernism after the hiatus caused by World War I. Without compromising her determination to be original, Crawford was enthusiastic and curious about Scriabin, Schoenberg, Stravinsky, Honegger, Rieti and Hindemith, to name a few.

Such pluralism, or the "eclectic tendency," to use Paul Rosenfeld's phrase, that came easily to Crawford during her years in Chicago, may well have been encouraged by America's relative isolation from European cultural politics. Crawford, after all, encountered the works of many important European composers long after those works were written. Thus she heard such music in a relatively neutral context, removed from the contention among the "isms" and intellectual stances that marked their reception in Europe. She had no nationalistic commitment to Stravinsky or Schoenberg, or intimacy with such trends as prewar primitivism, futurism, and expressionism or with postwar trends such as the German "Neue Sachlichkeit" ("New Objectivity") or French neoclassicism. When Edgard Varèse issued his rejection of artistic ideology in the manifesto that gave birth to the International Composers Guild, he invited a pluralistic approach: "the International Composers Guild disapproved of all 'isms,'" and "denied the existence of schools, recognizes only the individual." Her assimilation of practices widespread in the early twentieth century included ostinato layering, part writing based on dissonant motives, chords constructed from fourths, and asymmetric rhythms and meters.[1]

Was tonality a natural law of music or a cultural construction? In the 1920s the question was generally framed as a choice between revolutionary atonality (symbolized by Schoenberg) or reconstructed tonality (symbolized by Stravinsky). Even though the question was less politically charged for American composers than for their European colleagues, and was even overshadowed in the mid-years of the 1920s by the indigenous controversy over the merits of symphonic jazz, most mainstream American modernists chose to follow Stravinsky's course. Crawford joined the dissenters. Occupying a somewhat anomalous position within early American modernism, she followed neither Stravinsky nor Schoenberg, and instead took Scriabin (particularly his late music) as her point of entry into radical modernism. Although she claimed to adhere to "tonal centricity," her music abandons the semiotic framework of keys and key signatures after 1924. The hallmark of her individuality was her harmonic language and the extent to which she saturated her work with dissonance. This carried her far along the trajectory of radical sound. She concentrated on creating enigmatic, often abrasive dissonances and generating a context in which they sounded coherent. The "profundity of her strange sonorities" attracted Cowell from the onset. Crawford's praise for the "sublime, strident dissonances" of Carl Ruggles mirrors her ambitions for herself.[2]

The Five Preludes for Piano, miniatures that range from about one minute to almost three minutes in length, are mood pieces, where ruminative introspections are often interrupted by whimsical humor and playfulness. Scriabin's influence shows itself in relation to harmony and meter. Crawford's typical chords are built from tritones, fifths, and perfect fourths. A sense of suspended animation comes from slow tempos combined with varied compound meters: 12/8 is her equivalent of common time, with frequent interpolations of other metric schemes. Prelude no. 3 is one case in point, using a meter of 21/8 for its first four measures, then fluctuating between 15/8, 12/8, 9/8, and 18/8. Scriabin's Poeme, op. 52, no. 1, a work with similar metric vagaries, may have been one model, for Gitta Gradova was performing it in 1925 just at the time these works were being written.

The first prelude gives us a whiff of the world to come. Written on three systems to accommodate a wide register span, the piece fleshes out its desultory melodic line with streams of augmented chords and parallel triads stabilized only by pedal tones in the bass line. The shift from this languor to the faster triplets climbing upward in crescendo in three stages to the fortissimo climax of the piece in the highest registers of the keyboard is characteristic. Each time the line is arrested by a slightly different highly dissonant six-note chord that is a variation of Scriabin's "mystic chord" pitch complex (Ex. 5-1).

Example 5-1 Prelude for Piano no. 1, mm. 1–6. © 1993. Throughout these preludes, accidentals affect only individual notes before which they occur. Used by permission of Cassia Publishing Company.

[a) Before beginning, depress these notes silently and depress sostenuto pedal. Release in bar 4.]

The effect is quixotic and brittle, her sonorities relentlessly dark despite the whimsical figuration. When the opening melody returns, it rounds out the piece with a simple formal clarity that is typical of all of these preludes—a trait that distinguishes her piano music from the through-composed *Moments* of Rudhyar.

Crawford indicated that the second prelude, described by a critic as "sensational, pugnacious, curt," be played "with subtle sparkling humor." We are in her world of wry smiles at scraps of paper tossing in the wind. Interlocking perfect fifths provide the signature sonority for this prelude. The passage in Example 5-2 shows some characteristic idioms, as the second phrase cadences through arabesques that land on the rim of a harmonic volcano. The "burlesco" theme suddenly plunges us to the lower depths with a huge opening jump of a ninth and a concluding leap of a tritone, its grotesque shape foiled by impudent delicate roulades in the upper registers. It is an inspired moment.

The fifth prelude is in some ways the most radical of the set. Unrelieved by flashes of humor, the germinal idea of interlocking fifths used in Prelude no. 2 are reconceived as the darker sonority of interlocking tritones. The opening measures lodge this sound in our ears as a pedal point, shifting away chromatically for only brief respites. A typical climb on a chromatic melodic ladder to a dissonant climax is accompanied by reminders of the earth below in the tritone clusters. The pianissimo ending of Crawford's interlocking tritones, gnarled further by chromatic clusters, is intense and extreme.

Crawford followed this set of miniatures with one of her longest most expansive works from these years —the Sonata for Violin and Piano (1926). Crawford cast the sonata in a traditional four-movement plan: the first with the underpinnings of a conventional sonata form movement (one of the autographs contains thematic labels—"Principal Theme," "Subsidiary Theme"), the second movement an exercise in double counterpoint, the third a slow movement, the fourth a kind of rondo, ending in a return of material from the first movement.

The violin sonata expands beyond the two moods of the preludes into the high drama of expressionist intensity. The violin sweeps through free-ranging lines in which leaps of sevenths, octaves, and ninths abound. In the other movements certain signature formal characteristics appear, among them the use of an ostinato containing some compelling syncopated or dotted rhythm and an exposed dissonant interval. The left-hand ostinato which opens the second movement uses sevenths and tritones as points of congruence between the lines (Ex. 5-3). The last movement relies on cyclic thematic references, recalling elements from previous movements. (This technique will reappear in later chamber music.) Here the theme from the third movement is reworked for a slow section of the finale. Just before the end, the introductory dissonant chord complexes from the first movement return to emerge as a ritornello for the piece as a whole.

The Sonata for Violin and Piano also contains several passages in which Crawford uses the esoteric indication "mystic" as an expressive direction. To

Example 5-2   Prelude for Piano no. 2, mm. 12–20. © 1993. Used by permission of
Cassia Publishing Company.

Example 5-3   Sonata for Violin and Piano, second movement, mm. 4–6. © 1984,
New Music Edition. Used by permission of Theodore Presser Co.

understand the two "mystic" events in the sonata, a few comments about the
harmonic language are in order. In the first movement, the introduction and
the first theme employ a series of chord complexes of six and seven different
pitch classes at one time (Ex. 5-4). If one arranges the pitches linearly, their
common construction from chromatic segments is clear, as is their interrelationship: each includes a six-note segment of four half steps followed by a
minor third. Although there are many simpler harmonies in the piece, these
are characteristic formations, where Crawford includes chromatic aggregates
within her chords. In this respect her harmonic palette is darker than Rudh-

Example 5-4   Sonata for Violin and Piano, first movement, mm. 1–2. © 1984, New Music Edition. Used by permission of Theodore Presser Co.

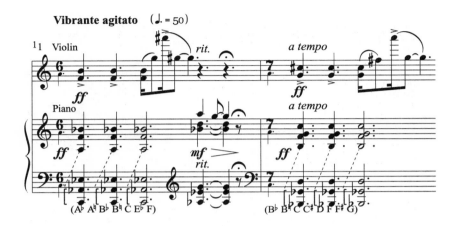

Example 5-5   Sonata for Violin and Piano, first movement, mm. 29–31. © 1984, New Music Edition. Used by permission of Theodore Presser Co.

yar's. He tends to use massive pile-ups of perfect fourths and perfect fifths, the melodic lines less inflected with chromaticism.

One "mystic" event placed in the closing section of this movement (mm. 29–31) stands out precisely because it departs from these vertical sonorities (Ex. 5-5). Crawford's "mystic chord" in m. 29 re-ordered in fourths (C F sharp B flat E flat A D) is similar to Scriabin's famous sonority. The structural function of this "mystic" moment is linked to the value of spontaneity or unpredictability, which Rudhyar linked to intuitive compositional process. These two measures, occurring directly after a climactic passage and an arrival on a fortississimo chord, derail the momentum of the drive toward the final cadential phrase. The fluid compound meter allows languid gestures

Example 5-6   Sonata for Violin and Piano, first movement, mm. 7–8. © 1984, New Music Edition. Used by permission of Theodore Presser Co.

unimpeded by metric downbeats. As if to emphasize its interpolative quality even further, the passage is followed by another fortissimo section, which restates thematic material from the introduction.

The earlier "mystic" passage (mm. 7–8) is somewhat different (Ex. 5-6). The chord is a carefully voiced chromatic hexachord. Yet the term "mistico" applies to more than the harmony, appearing first over the single tone G sharp. Such a gesture seems disingenuous: how can one tone convey a mystic mood? The answer lies most likely in Rudhyar's theory of the symbolic content of the single tone, which he took from non-Western music. It was a leit-motif in his thought at the time. Crawford noted a few years later, "I heard much of the 'single tone,'" as did her student Vivian Fine, who recalled how "we wrote low notes with the word mystic over them" in this period. Among Rudhyar's published explanations of its meaning is this passage from *The Rebirth of Hindu Music*, which Rudhyar claimed Crawford "must have read":[3]

> A tone is a living cell. It is composed of organic matter. It has the power of assimilation, of reproduction, of making exchanges, of growing. It is a microcosmos reflecting faithfully the macrocosmos, its laws, its cycles, its centre. Concentrate on a cell, and the mysteries of the universe may be revealed to you therein. Concentrate on a tone and in it, you may discover the secret of being and find Ishwara, the Christ within.[4]

Thus Crawford's association of "mystic" with a single tone was intended to alter the performer's mentality, changing the nature of the concentration that would somehow be communicated through touch.

That Crawford's single "mystic" note was not a capricious gesture is demonstrated in later works, albeit in a less explicit context. A single repeated tone opens the chamber suite, Music for Small Orchestra, a work composed the same year. The symbolism of the single tone was apparently used semantically by other composers in the Herz circle. Crawford's Music for Small Orchestra also carries the imprint of her spiritual aesthetics. Marked "slow, pensive," and exuding a mood of hushed intensity, the first movement opens with a signature gesture that can be "decoded" through several associations. A single tone (F') is reiterated nine times in off-beat patterns in the piano, (mm. 1–2), then haloed by a carefully scored ninth chord on G in strings, clarinet, and bassoon (m.3). The single tone perseveres as a nonconforming element in the fabric, demanding attention through the first several measures of the work. Sharing the same aesthetic convictions as the Sonata for Violin and Piano and composed the same year, Music for Small Orchestra nevertheless expands into new artistic territory. Written in two movements each about four minutes long (half the length of the violin sonata), it brings more of Crawford's individuality as a composer into the light. Had Rosenfeld known this work, he may not have treated Crawford as a member of a faction led by others. The scoring is fresh and the part writing significantly different from previous work; the competing polyrhythms and layering of harmonically unrelated ostinati foreshadow the issues Crawford would argue in later works.[5]

Music for Small Orchestra, scored for an ensemble of flute, clarinet, bassoon, four violin parts, two cello parts, and piano, is Crawford's first work for more than two instruments. Even in this first orchestral essay, Crawford's scoring is individual, perhaps even unique. No other piece written for this ensemble—with its unusual omission of both oboe and viola—comes to mind. In fact, the piece frequently sounds in the alto range. Moreover, Crawford often uses instruments in the extremities of their registers, sensitive to the different tone colors and levels of intensity that are produced: the high bassoon (recalling Stravinsky's *Rite of Spring*) above the low flute (mm. 10–16), the cellos playing higher than violins (mm. 26ff), and the low violin trills (mm. 19–27). So little doubling occurs that when the four violin parts and one of the two cello parts (in treble clef) play a "solo espressivo" melody in unison (mm. 61–65), the weight and power of the moment contrast with the restrained string colors in the rest of the piece. At another point Crawford reaches for an eccentric string effect at the understated end of the string color spectrum, asking one violin to play harmonics and the second to use mute for an otherworldly "tranquillo" moment (m. 69). From the piano, treated strictly as an ensemble instrument, she requires both murky bass chords, placed so low they sound like muffled gongs, and the hypnotic ostinati that are also heard in other instruments. The opening pedal ostinato of a tritone plus perfect fourth heard in the piano (related to Scriabin) becomes a harmonic fingerprint in her music.

The pitch organization of the first movement relies on vestigial features of tonality. The movement's tripartite division into introduction (mm. 1–5), A (6–41), B (42–66), A1 (66–95) is underlined by chromatic transpositions of both chords in the bass and of the principal five-note ostinato that appears first in the cello (m. 6). The bass harmonies that open all three sections emphasize G chords—not triads to be sure, but nevertheless chords built on fourths functioning analogously. That Crawford slides away from G to end the work on its tritone (D flat arrives in m. 77) qualifies but does not destroy the play with pitch centricity on G. Both the organization of timbre and the control of ostinato patterns further support the form, with woodwinds used primarily as melodic instruments in the A sections and strings functioning in a similar fashion in the middle section.

Above the bass float ostinati in increasingly complex cross rhythms and harmonies. At mm. 25ff, for example, rhythmic patterns of duplets through sextuplets (all contained as subdivisions of a single measure) appear simultaneously (Ex. 5-7). Crawford's plan calls for each section to begin with one, perhaps two ostinati in place and then slowly increase the density of the texture.

Although the rhythmic and tonal diversity among the various strata is impressive, the cohesiveness of the movement depends upon shared intervallic motives. The motive of the oscillating half step, set in place in the introduction (mm. 3–4), is one germinal idea in the movement; another, the ubiquitous tritone, exposed in the various transpositions of the five-note ostinato (first appearing in m. 6) and in melodic lines (flute, mm. 25, 67; violins 1, 2 m. 47). If one reorders the pitches in the five-note ostinato m. 6 (D sharp, E, C, B flat, G flat reordered as C, D sharp, E, G flat, B flat), then that exposes the structural importance of both major and minor thirds as well. That much of the melodic material is shaped through chains of thirds and half steps (bassoon, mm. 10–17; clarinet, mm. 30–33) helps pull the various strata of the piece into an organic whole.

Crawford once remarked that she preferred the paintings of Corot to those of Monet, who used "light, all light," that in a great painting "one must find the balance between shadow and sun . . . so that not only does the light illuminate the darkness but by its contrast the *darkness irradiates the light.*" This observation supplies a metaphor for the primary expressive technique of the movement, with its interplay between the "darkness" of texture and the "light" of lyrical line.[6]

The solemn first movement is followed by a contrasting second movement "in roguish humor." Here ostinati come more conventionally into play, with the division of labor clearly articulated between theme (initially in flute and clarinet marked "solo") and accompaniment—a double layer of ostinati in bassoon, cello, and piano. Perhaps the ostinato structure is a bit too mechanistic; one might wish that the joints were less exposed. Nevertheless, the second movement of this work illustrates Crawford's sense of humor, no small part of her gift as a composer. This scherzo resembles the second movement of the Sonata for Violin and Piano marked "buoyant." But there the ostinato was irregular and reckless; here the ostinati are the "straight men" and the theme is the "rogue," adding triplets—a favorite scherzo fingerprint—to the regular duple rhythmic mix and moving in chromatic arabesques. Something of the perpetuum mobile pervades this movement, which achieves its climaxes by the familiar trick of setting parts consecutively in motion.

In contrast to the Sonata for Violin and Piano, which by 1929 was Crawford's best-known composition, Music for Small Orchestra was never performed in Crawford's lifetime, at least according to Crawford's own records.

Example 5-7   Music for Small Orchestra, first movement, mm. 25–28. © 1993, American Musicological Society. Used by permission of A-R Editions.

Its first performance was in 1969 in Canyon, Texas, at West Texas State University, initiated by Matilda Gaume, Crawford's first biographer. Recognition followed its professional premieres in both New York and Boston several years later.

The release in 1975 of the first recording of Music for Small Orchestra afforded Crawford's old friend, the music and art critic Alfred Frankenstein, the opportunity to reminisce about the creative milieu in which this "beautifully made and admirably expressive" work emerged. According to Frankenstein, the piece was "strongly influenced by Ives," whose music "was the property only of a secret cult" led by Henry Cowell. Frankenstein credits Cowell via Crawford for first bringing him into contact with Ives and his world, and he cites the

> "Ivesian" influence in their thoroughgoing polytonality. They are unIvesian in that the tonality in each line of the dissonant web is completely perceptible. The slightly folksy thematic material is also in the Ives tradition. . . . It has been given a superb performance.

Frankenstein may have been wrong in asserting Crawford's debt to Ives. Both Vivian Fine and Charles Seeger believe that Crawford knew Ives's music only after her arrival in New York in 1929. "I would swear to it," Fine said stoutly.[7]

The following year Crawford composed another set of Preludes for Piano and the Suite no. 1 for Five Wind Instruments and Piano. The preludes explore the same kind of expressive world as the first set, but in more advanced language. The association between mysticism and post-tonal harmony is explored further in the sixth prelude for piano (1927), marked "Andante Mystico" and dedicated "with deep love and gratitude to Djane, My Inspiration." Here Crawford's thick resonating chords are deconstructed into intervallic components. A cyclic ostinato pattern appears in the right hand as the upper line, presenting eight ascending dyads which contain all twelve notes of the scale. The high range of the right hand most probably symbolizes celestial regions and the spirituality Crawford associated with Herz. The extraordinary pedal markings, demanding unusual constant sostenuto in the left hand and damper effects in the right, produce what the pianist Eugene Flemm, who made a study of these pieces, calls a "continuous sound": the damper pedal "controls the upper voice duet . . . while the sostenuto pedal 'sustains' the melody and lower arabesque figures . . . [rarely] do the pedals move simultaneously . . . the regular 'breathing' of the sustaining pedal is always covered by the slower moving sostenuto pedal. . . .The pedaling is unique in piano repertoire." Crawford was probably influenced here by Rudhyar's proselytizing for "the paramount importance of the pedals" in "blending chords."[8]

Despite the symbolism at work in several of Crawford's pieces, she maintained a certain distance from it by refusing to use titles on any of her works. In contrast, Scriabin gave his works elaborate titles and even occasionally affixed his own poetry to them in the best traditions of nineteenth-century program music. Similarly, Rudhyar's evocative titles were mythopoetic, as if he were emulating D. H. Lawrence: "Daughters of Men," "Breath of Fire," "Salutation to the Depths," "The Gift of Blood." Crawford both embraced and denied the existence of program procedures in her music, seeking inspiration for specific works in extramusical sources, but publicly severing the impulse from its consequence. One entry in her diary is the only clue to the hidden meaning of the ninth piano prelude, dedicated to the pianist Richard Buhlig. Apparently moved by a conversation to disclose its program, Crawford revealed that it was inspired by her beloved Lao Tse and the ideal of calm. A friend remarked that "it was very difficult to express meditative 'calm' in music." Crawford asked herself

> if that is not true since music is supposed to be an e-motive [*sic*] experience, an effort to send forth out of one's self certain strong feelings that cannot stay inside. But Norman replies, and I am quite moved by it, "No; I would say rather that music is an effort to gain calm."[9]

Unlike Ives, whose literary sensibility flooded his music with titles, quotations, and programs, constantly directing the listener to representational reception, Crawford separated process from finished work of art, once describing herself as a "scorner of titles." She might reveal a program in private, but she would not direct a performer or a listener in a certain path. Thus there is no indication of this program in the score for the ninth prelude, and its expressive mark of "tranquillo" is hardly sufficient to interpret the work as a spiritual statement. It was not a case of believing in music as absolute or "pure" in the nineteenth-century sense of the term, but rather a matter of her "English reserve," taking the form of reticence about spiritual belief and the role of the composer in controlling the interpretation. As her own commitment to Methodism waned by the late 1920s, she disparaged the "personal element" and the "too material and literal" attitudes she associated with mainstream religion. Why should she reject the literal and the personal element in Methodism only to replace it with the literal in mysticism?[10]

A program, as she saw it, was a point of departure for the composer, rather than a representational guidepost for the listener, and her love of the abstract surface that hid private references was typical of her modernism. When she heard a performance of Ives's *Three Places in New England*, her reaction was revealing: "Ives is probably much greater I realize. But the middle movement, sounding like a band concert and a prayer meeting hymn fest prejudices me violently."[11]

Crawford preferred the paradoxical aphorisms of Eastern mysticism to Ivesian quotation. Although we do not know which aphorism from the *Tao* inspired the ninth piano prelude, the clue about "calm" in the diary entry may refer to the "wise passiveness" Crawford quoted from the *Bhagavad Gita* as well. For Lao Tse the Tao (or Divine Principle) reveals itself in the doctrine of "eternal reversion" from activity of motion to passivity or emptiness as organizing principles of wisdom.[12]

The opening section of Crawford's prelude (Ex. 5-8) suggests the cosmic nature of tranquility through a number of techniques. One is the enormous musical space bounded by the two interval fields associated with the lower and upper registers, evoking the earth below and the sky above. In the left hand a tetrachord, almost at the bottom of the keyboard, oscillates between two major seconds that define the lower and upper limits of a whole-tone scale; its murky sonorities are blurred even further through its extreme softness ("ppp") and the pedaling, which enhances its resonance in Rudhyar's manner. In the right hand, more than five octaves away, an arc of parallel

Example 5-8   Prelude for Piano no. 9, mm. 1–9. © 1928, New Music Edition. Used by permission of Theodore Presser Co.

sevenths descends from B flat/A in m. 4 to its lower axis F/E in m. 7, climbing back up in a quasi-retrograde. Underneath the activity of the opening eight measures are five pairs of sevenths that chromatically fill in the tritone from E to B flat. Here is another example of the association between meditative stasis, which was called "mystical" in the Sonata for Violin and Piano, and the structural reliance on dissonance controlled through a chromatic pitch-collection.

Crawford's handling of rhythm supports the mood of complex tranquility as well. The left-hand ostinato is never presented in the same rhythmic proportions, although it is repeated seven times in nine measures. Similarly in the right hand, the phrases are of irregular length, rarely coinciding with the downbeat of the barely perceptible meter. The steady stream of quarter notes that rises and falls in tidal motion is echoed in miniature by the left-hand ostinatos.

Some of the spiritually evocative idioms Crawford developed in her second set of Preludes for Piano reappear in a group of songs she wrote in 1929. Spending the summer at the MacDowell Colony in New Hampshire, Crawford picked five Sandburg poems from four different collections of poetry to set as songs for contralto and piano: "Joy" from *Chicago Poems* (1916); "White Moon" (originally titled "Baby Face") and "Loam" from *Cornhuskers* (1918); "Home Thoughts," from *Smoke and Steel* (1920); and "Sunsets," from *Good Morning, America* (1928). Crawford wrote them as a group rather than as a formal cycle, establishing an order in her final autograph that differed slightly from their strict chronology. "Sunsets" was written first, "Loam" second. By July she had written a third song, although it is not clear which it was, either "White Moon" or "Home Thoughts." In August, she set "Joy." Crawford had created an opportunity to lavish her style of dissonant music on poetry whose aesthetic she had internalized. Setting Sandburg's words to chromatically saturated, highly angular melody, she employed her dissonant fourth chords for the harmonic framework. She succeeded best in "White Moon," which became the most popular of the set in the 1930s, and in "Loam." Passages in both of these songs illustrate characteristics of the set as a whole.

Crawford's setting of "Baby Face," which she retitled "White Moon," captures the poet's imagistic treatment of moonbeams and light initially through a filigree of an interval chain of sevenths in the high registers of the keyboard, not unlike what she used in her sixth prelude. Beneath the surface of "flimmering shafts" and "silver shadows" Sandburg suggests the erotic scene of a woman in a bedroom, waiting perhaps for her lover, and Crawford responds to that subtext by setting the climactic last verse virtually without piano. To conclude the song, Crawford brings back the ethereal opening to set off the last line with its beautifully tender final cadence.

"Loam" is as bound to the earth as "White Moon" is to the sky. Reflecting Crawford's symbiotic identification with Sandburg's prairie mysticism, the piano opens with a chord whose pitches almost match Scriabin's "Mystic Chord" (the only difference is her E flat as opposed to his E natural). The monotone melody for the first line evokes primal chant and Rudhyar's spiritualized low register (Ex. 5-9). Crawford herself wrote about a mystical experience in Elmhurst where the Sandburgs lived. Walking on grass in a park, Crawford remembered a feeling of "awe": "I have a sudden illuminating sense of the inconceivable depth, massive, solid, that stretches beneath my feet. I feel it is a kind of sacred thing . . . that my feet are beating out in regular rhythm a kind of hymn to the earth." "Loam" translated that moment into music.[13]

Within a few months of the Sandburg songs, Crawford completed two large compositions—the Suite no. 1 for Five Wind Instruments and Piano, begun in 1927 and now revised, and a new work, the Suite no. 2 for Four Strings and Piano. Both are unusual pieces, the first suite not as successful as

Example 5-9   "Loam," mm. 5–9, from *Five Songs for Contralto and Piano*. © 1990. Used by permission of C.F. Peters Corp.

the second, but vital and engaging in several ways. The work is in three movements—Adagio religioso/Giocoso-allegro non troppo, Andante tristo, and Allegro con brio. That the spiritual sign of the enigmatic single tone—this time in the plaintive French horn—should open a movement marked "Adagio religioso" should not surprise us.

The playfulness of the scherzo-like first movement is indebted to her transcendentalist view of humor as part of spiritual consciousness. Here in the juxtaposition of solemnity and play are the expressive parameters of Crawford's first set of piano preludes, now reaching fruition in a larger, more risk-taking venture. This sprawling movement, filled with sharp sectional contrasts, vacillates between cyclic form and a more defined theme-and-variations scheme. The opening "burlesco" clarinet melody has a jazzlike ambience to it, grounded by a plodding ostinato in the piano. Then comes a discrete brilliant "piano solo" section, reinterpreting the clarinet theme in a flashy texture of rapid octave work at the loudest possible level—its expression mark "fuocoso" another version of a scherzo mood. The appearance of material from the introduction as a concluding gesture indicates Crawford's affinity for cyclic ritornello schemes in this period. The second movement, which opens with a duet for oboe and piano, later uses dissonant chords based on Crawford's ubiquitous fourths. The melody begins with a long oboe solo, motivically derived from the introduction and indebted to tritones and fourths. Underneath this, the piano elaborates with brittle vertical counterparts of the same intervals.

After the fanfare flourish that opens the third movement, Crawford sets up an irregular rhythmic pattern dividing 13 beats into 6 plus 4 plus 3 in the flute and oboe (Stravinsky and his ostinato techniques echoed here). The piano and bassoon offer a jazzy syncopated melody throughout this exuberant, reckless finale. Crawford was confronting issues of form when she first composed the suite in 1927, and her ambitions to create larger, freer works were frustrated, she believed, by problems in thematic development. A later revision did not help much. Still, the other side of its diffuseness is its energy and ambition. Like Music for Small Orchestra, the Suite no. 1 for Five Wind Instruments and Piano was never performed in Crawford's lifetime. (A few performances since 1975 and a recording in 1994 have given it some exposure, although it remains one of Crawford's few unpublished works.)

Crawford surmounted the structural problems of the first suite in her subsequent Suite no. 2 for Four Strings and Piano, which is one of her finest works. The three-movement plan (Lento-Cantando, Leggiero, Allegro energico) projects a sense of cyclic unity on the largest level by bringing the opening nine measures back in later movements and, at a smaller level, by generating its musical material from a few key motives. The first movement begins so softly ("ppp") and in such a low range that it is barely audible, its chromatic ostinati in the piano and low strings supporting five brief, disjointed thematic gestures in the two violins. Again Crawford's understated opening—this time without the single-tone sign—suggests a reference to earlier spiritual roots (Ex. 5-10). In addition to serving as the opening, this fragmentary material occurs in varied repetitions at the end of the second movement and then again at the end of the entire piece. The placement of the two repetitions at such crucial points in the form suggests that the three movements may also be considered two larger parallel statements. The first two movements, the Lento-Cantando and the Leggiero, though varied in character, are concentrated and brief, lasting together about five minutes, while the third, Allegro energico, lasts as long as the first two put together. The final movement is bold, improvisatory, and quixotic, with many changes of mood and tempo. By restating the opening material as a concluding refrain, Crawford reins in its bravado, reasserting the primacy of the beginning's more serious mood.

Ties between this suite and her earlier chamber works, Music for Small Orchestra and Suite no. 1 for Five Wind Instruments and Piano, are clearly evident. An anecdote suggests the lingering ghost of Stravinsky, for the chromatic writing in the cello (Suite, first movement, mm. 1–3) not only recalls the cello ostinato in Music for Small Orchestra but may be the echo of *The Firebird* that Crawford acknowledged to a fellow student. In this exchange the friend "asked her if *that* [unidentified] was from *Firebird* when she played me the opening on the piano, and she said, yes it was." (Crawford uses four of the

Example 5-10 Suite no. 2 for Four Strings and Piano, first movement, mm. 1–5.
© 1993, American Musicological Society. Used by permission of A-R Editions.

same pitches, as well as similar intervals and the same low string timbre, that Stravinsky does in the opening of *Firebird*.)[14]

Other links between the two chamber suites are even more pronounced. Irregular metric play controls large sections of both works. In the "Brillante" section of the third movement of Suite no. 1, a 13/16 meter divides into 6 plus 4 plus 3. In Suite no. 2, the leggiero movement exploits alternations between 6 and 5. And their scherzo themes tell the same joke: the "burlesco" clarinet theme in the "giocoso" section of the Suite for Five Wind Instruments and Piano resembles the acrobatic main theme of the third movement in Suite no. 2. The latter theme appears first as one line for the piano, to be played "with vibrant energy" as it lurches about the lower regions of the keyboard (m. 10). Later it serves as the basis for a discrete "giocoso" quasi-fugal section (mm. 56ff). Both underscore Crawford's sensitivity to the scherzo potentialities of mercurial movement. Such connections between the two suites are hardly surprising, since the first was being revised while the second was being written (November 1929).

Crawford's Suite no. 2 for Four Strings and Piano shows a considerable advance in her handling of thematic development, an issue she found problematic in much modern music. The ostinato layers, often exposed in Music for Small Orchestra, yield to a more authoritative handling of textures: to finely argued and organically unified part writing, powerful and extended thematic statements, and more skillful use of imitative polyphony.[15]

Crawford's heightened interest in counterpoint indicates new compositional priorities in which linear exploration replaced the harmonic preoccupations of her earlier music. Her earlier disinterest in counterpoint (later attributed to Rudhyar's influence) was overcome when she "literally fell for Hindemith," the apostle of the new counterpoint, and her admiration augured more concern for traditional craftsmanship. In addition, Crawford's self-scrutiny as a composer urged her to seek occasional advice from teachers outside the conservatory, which in one case put her on a short-lived diet of species counterpoint. Through Henry Cowell and Carl Ruggles, she began to head toward an American modernist solution to the problem of thematic development: dissonant counterpoint.[16]

Mentioned often in musical writing of the period, "dissonant counterpoint" was viewed as one of the hallmarks of the new music of the 1920s. The term was applied to such diverse composers as Hindemith, with his neoclassic models, and Carl Ruggles, with atonality as his goal. Given Cowell's enthusiasm for Ruggles, Crawford was exposed to dissonant counterpoint even before her years in New York.[17]

Crawford's knowledge of Ruggles's style was grounded in music rather than in theory. She knew his orchestral piece *Men and Mountains*, which had been published in the *New Music Quarterly*, as well as other works that Cowell shared with her personally. At about the time Crawford was revising one suite and composing the other, she met Carl Ruggles. She noted that she had shown Ruggles a score, unidentified, and that he gave her "valuable hints on dissonant counterpoint."[18]

One unmistakable source of the surer technique of the Suite no. 2 for Four Strings and Piano is Crawford's command of dissonant counterpoint as handled by Cowell, her mentor in Chicago, and Ruggles. She wrote the "dissonated" melody that they favored, relying on sevenths and seconds to radicalize the line and avoiding tonal implications—"shifting the center of gravity from consonance to dissonance," as Cowell described it. The cantando section of the first movement shows Crawford's use of seconds and sevenths as vertical congruents. As with Music for Small Orchestra, in both the first and third movements of the suite, one line designated "solo" carries melodic primacy in the fabric. Yet the other parts are more than mere accompaniment; they are independent voices, generated from motives with a plasticity that avoids periodic phrase structure. The memorable homophonic moment in the first movement of the suite (m. 22) stands out not only because C is the highest pitch used to that point, but also because it brings textural relaxation for the first time.

Crawford also experimented with controlling pitch repetition in Ruggles's manner, sounding seven to ten pitches before repeating one. The powerful climax in the third movement of the Suite no. 2, mm. 25ff, shows Crawford's assimilation of Ruggles's technique, for throughout this section eight pitches sound before one repeats. Moreover, this section, both in the prose structure of its themes and in the intense dialogue between piano and strings, projects her own version of the "sublime, strident dissonance" she admired in Ruggles's work, *Portals*.[19]

In sum, Crawford integrated some of the techniques of dissonant counterpoint into the framework of an already established style. Motoric rhythms and metric play are essential to her rhythmic sensibility. Ostinati often govern bass lines. In addition, Crawford's harmonic need for some references to pitch centrality, although freed from Scriabinesque fourth chords, asserts itself often in organized bass-line motion and other forms of pitch repetition. Idiomatic while eclectic, the Suite no. 2 for Four Strings and Piano is a mature, fully formed work, its combination of spirituality, exuberance, and visionary musical idioms summarizing Crawford's early style.

"a career or life?"

During the years that Ruth Crawford reflected on the soul of sound, Charles Ives wrote that a "good dissonance is like a man." Was it by accident or design that Crawford's spiritual concept of dissonance eluded the sexual aesthetics he and many others presumed? She began her career in music at a time when American writers decried the "feminization" of classical music, spoke approvingly of a "distinguishing virility" as a hallmark of achievement for her generation, continued to debate the potential of the "woman composer," and entertained the possibility that the "emotional life of Woman" was "antagonistic to the creative process in music."[1]

Perhaps the egalitarian atmosphere of the American Conservatory of Music enabled Crawford to become a composer in the first place. As the composer Edith Borroff recalls, the "attitude at the American Conservatory about masculinism and feminism was a middle-western attitude . . . seen as yang and yin, needed by everyone; virtuosity [in the outside world] of course, was viewed as masculine, but at the American Conservatory, virtuosity was yang-yin, made of both elements. There was no feeling about women's lack of anything." In her composition classes, where most of the students were women, her teacher Weidig called excessive modesty a feminine "pose" and insisted on the male-identified values of ambition and achievement. In a sense the school had the ethos of a women's college, offering support and opportunities not necessarily duplicated outside its walls. Did Crawford notice that the competition for the Prix de Rome fellowships in composition—won by a teacher at the conservatory in 1922—was open only to unmarried men?[2]

Crawford never left any document that used the phrase "woman composer" to describe herself or any of her female colleagues. "We didn't think of ourselves that way," said her pupil, Vivian Fine, who would later be described as "very thick-skinned," one who "never bothered" to be blown off course by the prevailing winds of prejudice much later in her career. "I don't like being put in a category as a composer," stated Martha Beck, Crawford's colleague; "I don't know whether Ruth thought anything about it, but for me it wasn't an issue."[3]

To ignore is to resist: the more one acknowledged gender as an "issue," the less one felt a full citizen in the world of art. Moving to Chicago two years after the suffrage amendment had been passed, Crawford belonged to a post-enfranchised generation who, now that the right to vote had been won and a new civic identity secured, transferred the ideal of political parity to other parts of their lives. In such challenging times, she and her friends enfranchised themselves as composers by rejecting claims about female creativity grounded in biological determinism. She would later be described by her husband as an "ardent feminist" precisely because of her belief in intellectual parity between the sexes. "You'd be in trouble if you tried to argue with her about the case," he said.[4]

Yet she was also a woman who never called herself a feminist in her youth. Like many young women in the 1920s, Crawford resisted the strategies of her Progressive predecessors, refusing to join the sisterhood of women's clubs and societies. Even while she pressed her claims that one contemporary writer assigned to the "modern young woman"—the right to economic independence and the combination of marriage and career—she behaved as if there were no need for collective political action to improve women's status or their opportunities.[5]

Other women within the world of classical music built professional networks among themselves, supporting a variety of alternative institutions, such as societies of women composers and all-women orchestras. Crawford's affiliations in such groups began and ended with her membership in the musical sorority Sigma Alpha Iota, which she had joined in 1926. She did not belong to the Society of American Women Composers, formed in 1924 for the "production and advancement of compositions by American women." Another factor may have been the stylistic gulf between her and its membership, who generally wrote tonal music.[6]

Chicago offered Crawford other similar opportunities that she apparently ignored as well. The Musicians Club of Women, which sponsored concerts by famous visiting artists and programmed pieces by its membership, numbered about 600—including the Roberts sisters from the American Conservatory of Music. Both Crawford and her friend Martha Beck declined invitations to join. Martha explained that "it would have meant attending the monthly meetings and I could not add any more involvements, and I am sure that Ruth would have felt the same way." Chicago also hosted the Women's Symphony Orchestra, founded in 1924 and by 1929 recognized as the most important of many such groups; its conductor, Ethel Leginska, was the "first woman to put herself forward as a conductor of leading symphony orchestras." No documents have yet been uncovered that tie Crawford to this group either.[7]

Even so, Crawford recorded private resentments about the limitations of womanhood. In the summer of 1927, she "vented her spleen on the fact of being a woman," provoked by "the fact that beastly men, not satisfied with their own freedom, encroach on that of women, and procure in them a kind of necessitous fear which binds them about." The composer who thrived on enigma wanted to roam about the city streets in the "mysterious and delightful night, when shadows are deep and silent, and the occasional whirrings of cars make swift crescendos and diminuendos in the night symphony." Fear cloistered her at home.[8]

Her longing for space expanded into dreams of flight from responsibilities of family and duty. Only men had the freedom "to work one's way around the world, a poet-tramp, stoker, bell-boy, deck-hand, finding, probing into the essences of the roots of living. . . . Or [becoming] a recluse for a few years like Thoreau, building a hut off in the deep woods, feeling in his pulse a great freedom. . . . " She decided bleakly that "for all the talk of advancement for women, for all that they have gained greater independence . . . men have that which women will never have."[9]

Little did Crawford know that while camping out at Walden Pond, Thoreau ate at least one meal a day with his mother—as she herself did. Ruth and Clara were still sharing an apartment at 4736 Woodlawn Avenue, a three-story brick apartment complex in Hyde Park, where they had lived since 1925. Dependencies had shifted over the years, and occasionally Ruth mused about a place of her own. During the summer of 1927 she and Clara had rented a small cabin on Dewey Lake, Michigan, taking a rare and much treasured vacation from the harried schedule that Ruth kept in Chicago. Most of the time they lived amiably together, but occasionally tensions surfaced, each judging and being judged by the other.

To Ruth, Clara seemed old-fashioned and pedestrian, particularly in comparison to her new heroine, Djane Herz. Trying to become sophisticated, Ruth made herself less conventional by making her mother more so. She "thought her mother a bit too earthy and lacking in spiritual insight because she once in a while mourned being away from her things and set down in an indifferent Chicago apartment." Clara read "trivial news" in the newspaper, and she herself, "tho ashamed of the fact, like to pause a few minutes over gruesome 'human interest' stories." But that spiritual paragon Madame Herz did not. Occasionally Ruth's need to separate herself from her mother took the perilous form of contempt for women in general. Ruth had shown her mother a sketch for the Suite for Five Wind Instruments and Piano, which she was working on at Dewey Lake in the summer of 1927. Her mother could be merciless; this does not sound "inspired," Clara had said. At that Ruth rightly "bristled," deciding to retaliate with a "patronizing smile." In the mirror of honest introspection, Ruth's smile inverted to a frown. Even though her mother had wounded her, Ruth acknowledged that her own aggressive posture was unfair: "how much of a type of the superior, blustering, impatient at feminine-foibles, fount-of-knowledge *man* I am becoming with mother," she wrote. She had appropriated a "truly remarkable masculinely withering tone and look at mother's problems. . . . Why, a man-hating feminist author could almost write me up as a type." Perhaps she was absorbing the misogyny of the culture.[10]

At once critical of men and critical of women who criticized them, Crawford was living through the "contradictions within feminism," described by the historian Linda Gordon as the place where "female and feminist consciousness stand in complex relation to each other: clearly they overlap, for the female is the basis of the feminist, yet the feminist arises also out of a desire to escape the female." About six months later those contradictions cast a shadow over an important professional moment of Crawford's career—the evening on February 7, 1928, at which the Sonata for Violin and Piano was first played in Chicago.[11]

During the reception after the concert, Crawford's colleague Stella Roberts had approached her to offer congratulations. The two had known each other for several years, moving among the elect circle of Weidig's advanced students without becoming friends. At the end of the evening, Stella surprised her with an unexpected gesture of intimacy. Ruth wrote how "Stella, the dignified, the aloof, awe-inspiring, drew me to her, put her cheek against mine, and told me how much she had been moved by the Sonata." As Ruth well knew, it was not just her music that had prompted Stella's unusual warmth. It sprang also from a profound grief and sense of irreplaceable loss, for Stella Roberts was in mourning for her sister Marion, whom Ruth had admired for several years, and who had died several months earlier. The terrible circumstances of Marion's death had shattered the community of teachers and students at the American Conservatory. In the mid-1920s their star pianist had been living in Paris, studying piano with Alfred Cortot. At twenty-five she was "on the threshold of an extraordinary musical career," according to the conservatory's president, John Hattstedt, but her private life was a series of emotional disasters. In Paris she had fallen in love with a married man, who had subsequently divorced his wife, expecting to marry Marion when she returned from a visit to Chicago in April 1927. The volatile young woman had changed her mind, perhaps even becoming engaged to someone else before returning to Paris and breaking off with her former lover a few days after their reunion. In reaction the man shot her and a few hours later killed himself. The story made even more grisly by its headlines—"Kills Chicago Girl and Self in Paris Tryst" and "Paris Tragedy Laid to Broken Troth"—ran on the front pages of both the *New York Times* and the *Chicago Tribune*. All of this was in Crawford's mind on the evening of the concert several months later.[12]

She "sensed at once of course . . . the underlying tragic strain of Stella Roberts's thought in regard to beautiful Marion." Later in the evening Stella Roberts uttered her warning.

> She said with terrible seriousness which only a person knowing the deeply tragic circumstances could understand—"Ruth, you must not let anything interrupt you; you must go on and on—There are things which can stop you—You must not let them." And knowing I understood, and with tears gathering in her eyes, she disappeared.[13]

The surviving sister conjured up a ghost to deliver the message that passion brings destruction for the woman/artist, that Marion was somehow responsible for her fate. "What wild fury ruins us," Euridice asks Orpheus as his gaze banishes her to a second death.

Instead of basking in the warmth of a professional triumph, Crawford spent the next day "gripped by the occurrence" and was "brought several times to the verge of tears: I have felt almost ill from it." She wrote about "what great beautiful work Marion might have accomplished," and how Stella's "simple caress, so beautifully sincere coming from so undemonstrative a person, she has passed on to me a bit of Marion herself, and that she has also placed on me a double responsibility by those last words borne up out of a great sorrow. And I feel like one who has found a new friend to love." In fact, she and Stella Roberts never did become friends.[14]

Yet Crawford understood the implications of fulfilling Marion's artistic destiny as well as her own, for her own narrative style in telling the tale evokes the literary tradition of the female artist/heroine. Here was the renunciation scene in which the artist/woman confronts the Great Choice: love or work. In 1921 Ruth wrote to her mother that she wanted thirty-five children to populate one of Louise Robyn's music education classes. By 1927, according to a fellow student at the conservatory, she had decided not to marry but to concentrate on her career, accepting the false dichotomy that demanded sacrifice. Now she received Stella's double embrace as if she were a nun taking vows.

A month later, Crawford was shaken by another crisis involving a woman in love. A scandal broke out around Djane Herz, whose husband had discovered that his wife was having an affair with a mysterious "Count Von B." He was "a baron who had saber marks on his cheeks," Vivian Fine recalled, "a much younger man" than Madame Herz. Djane ran off "precipitously" with him, leaving behind Mr. Herz and her thirteen-year-old son, Tristan.[15]

It all seemed "incredible and impossible," so much so that Crawford was living a "nightmare" for two weeks following. "She was very upset," Fine remembers, "and she would call my mother on the phone to talk about it." For Crawford was shocked and "extremely depressed" by the Herzes' separation, her own emotional gullibility exaggerated by her lack of sexual experience. "Such a thing had never occurred to me as possible. I had thought of the [Herzes'] life together as ideal." Slowly she rationalized the circumstances. Since she loved the party who had wounded, she refused to "take sides"; she pronounced Mr. Herz's position as "tragic." He told Ruth "there is only one side and that is Tristan's," but she reminded herself that the boy spent most of the year at boarding school and so he would not miss his mother at home unduly. When Djane Herz's portrait painted by the prominent Chicago artist Weisenborn was placed up for auction—an act of public humiliation by a man whose "amour propre" had been damaged—Ruth reacted as if Djane were being stripped naked in public. She wrote, "Any man who would do such a thing as that must have made life miserable for any woman and Djane was more than justified in leaving. . . . It is incredible. . . . I am very happy that my love for Djane and my sense of justice begin to follow the same path."[16]

Crawford received a twenty-page letter from Djane Herz, describing the nature of her marriage almost as an "arrangement" without passion, and she begged Ruth to "love me as you always have. I have not changed." Sympathy and perhaps Crawford's innocence washed away any skepticism and brought in its wake a new balance of power in their relationship. The personage Ruth called "Madame" became an ordinary mortal whom she could address by her first name, an intimacy Ruth had "longed for" and which "now became possible through pain."[17]

Herz's relationship with Count Von B. lasted a few months, its demise induced by her husband's engineering a choice between lover and son. Eventually she reconciled with her husband and moved to New York with him, but gossip about the affair destroyed her reputation, and she was no longer "received in social circles anymore." Even Clara Crawford initially had retracted normal hospitality. Djane came to dinner anyway, according to Ruth's sister-in-law, who was staying in Chicago the summer of 1928, primarily to help care for Ruth's mother.[18]

At sixty-eight, Clara Crawford was dying from cancer, diagnosed early in 1928. After an operation in June proved futile, Ruth's brother Carl and his wife Catherine, along with their two young children, moved to Chicago to help nurse Clara in the last days of her life. They rented a house at 7610 Constance Avenue near Jackson Park, where the entire family could be together. As Carl remembers it, Ruth lived there, but "was out most of the time with her teaching."[19]

Already guilt-stricken about her relative neglect of her mother in the last few years because of her work, Ruth had planned acts of contrition to make it up to her, "to read, sing, play to her, be with her, give her some sense of the companionship she has missed." By July Clara was too sick to care, and her daughter reproached herself for her selfishness. Ruth decided to keep a literary vigil of Clara's last weeks of life to compensate for the loss.

She spared herself nothing, recording details of her mother's hallucinations, the loss of body functions, the amount of morphine being doled out each day, the nursing routines of baths and enemas, and even the bile that poured out of Clara Crawford's body. On August 1 Ruth wrote, "Tonight, suffering more deeply than she has yet, I believe Mother said, 'O Christ, Christ, did you suffer so?' Then, to Carl, 'Go ask him, Carl. O pain, pain, just plain pain. . . . Must die.'"[20]

What impulse led Crawford to preserve such graphic accounts of misery? Perhaps some remnant of her former religiosity tied her to the ordeal in unexpected ways, as she again became the minister's daughter, offering up her own version of last rites.

Clara Crawford slipped into a coma a few days before her death on August 14. In the last diary entry Ruth's own sense of loss finally tempered her journalistic fever, as she began to grieve.

> I find myself often thinking of something I want to tell or ask Mother. Can it be that I shall never be able to talk to her again? It seems incredible. How little I realized how close she was to me, and what a child I still was, and how very much

her interest and love and thoughts for my music were woven into my life! I feel stifled to think she will never again be there to hear and sympathize; I look forward through the years, and feel tragically alone. I begin to wonder how I can live. And to think that I had been feeling during the past year or two a desire to live alone, never dreaming how painfully soon Fate would answer my misplaced and erroneous desire. . . . How pitifully small was my realization of my love and *need* for Mother. . . . I sit here by her bedside and though she breathes and I feel comfort just in holding her hand on my knee, yet my heart aches and I feel like one in prison, for I can tell her nothing, and if I could, she could not answer.[21]

After her mother's death, Crawford changed little in her outer patterns of work, but she entered a new stage in her life. She took a flat in a three-story apartment building at 4433 Greenwood Avenue in a marginally middle-class neighborhood and began to explore both a solitude and a freedom of movement that were new to her. "I am getting to be a more social person," she wrote in November 1928. She started off that day by visiting Alfred Frankenstein for breakfast and a session of playing clarinet and piano music together; then lunch with Dane Rudhyar, who was in Chicago for several weeks; then an afternoon musicale at the Eisendraths, a prominent family in Chicago's Jewish upper class; at 8:30 Ruth and friends left for Djane's apartment for more talk and music; and after the friends left, more talk about Djane's love life until 3:30 in the morning.[22]

In the 1928–29 season Crawford's professional life as a composer lagged, with few performances of her music taking place. The second group of Preludes appeared in the October issue of Cowell's *New Music Quarterly*. Performances by Richard Buhlig; Keith Corelli, another Cowell stalwart; Dane Rudhyar; and Imre Weisshaus, another discovery of Cowell's, took place in the fall and winter of 1928–29. Other than that, it was a fallow year. When the time came for a recital of Weidig's advanced students a year later in June 1929, Crawford had to use three Preludes as her latest work. They were played by a fellow student—a measure of her distance from professional performance at this time.[23]

Crawford filled this compositional vacuum with introspections about artistic process and craft. Perhaps the depression that hovered over her that fall came from the loss of her mother, her strongest musical supporter and toughest critic. Flashes of relief alternated with declarations of fear. Adopting the process of gestation and birth to explain the dynamic of an anxious time, she wrote about her woman's body as if it were her soul. Describing the womb as the cradle of art, a "mother-heart" as a composer's core, and stillborn thoughts as the symbol of artistic failures, Crawford merged woman and artist in a remarkable and disquieting poem (1928):

Unborn words

Stirring in my womb of thought . . .
Pressing, stretching your little bodies
    Against the narrow walls . . .

How your warmth glows within me!
From my mother-heart to you,
Into the very center of your being
Flows a liquid stream of fire
    Fire of love
Love, that your souls may feel burning
And break into a flame-song within me.
Reverent I seek you.
Children of my womb of thought . . .
    I probe into the depths,
My eyes strain into the deep chasm,
I long passionately for your voice . . .
Sudden in panic I seem to feel the still dumbness
    Of death within me . . .

    O my unborn
In the great hour of your coming forth
        Will I
bending over your lifeless form
Hear only a sighing from a far distance?

In Crawford's real life a "mother-heart" had died and, in turn, some part of the child in the daughter had died as well. The potential for repairing that loss was in art, where she herself could become a mother. The poem speaks to a stage in Ruth's mourning, but it has implications beyond that. Even here, in the contemplation of failure, we see how Crawford's identity as a composer drew on a personal vision of creativity as female: in the world of "unborn thoughts" the phrase "woman composer" is redundant.

Crawford's anxiety reflected in metaphors of stillbirth emerged around the time that she embarked on a new set of compositional priorities. While writing the Suite for Piano and Winds, she had been dissatisfied with her compositional technique—her "lack of skillful development" and her feeling of "great limitations in the conception of large sections." In 1927 she belittled herself as a "dressmaker who sews on the buttons before deciding the style and cutting the goods," the feminine analogy hinting at insecurities about the musical intellect of the "woman composer."[24]

Then too Crawford perceived the limits of her previous training. Weidig had his shortcomings. Adolph Weiss, one of his former students, believed his training with Weidig lacked "discipline." In addition, Weidig's great virtue of leaving his "modernistic" students alone, and sanctioning their experimental forays into dissonance, had its flip side. To be sure, Crawford appreciated his "great musicianship" and "the fact that though belonging to a generation which almost without exception puts hands over ears for modern music, yet he is even more than tolerant—he is appreciative and willing to learn, unusually so." But then, who was teaching whom?[25]

Some time after her mother's death, Crawford decided more drastic action was needed. Alfred Frankenstein found the atmosphere in Chicago too complacent. Her strongest supporter, Henry Cowell, thought she was treading water as a composer in Chicago. Another conservatory was out of the question, at least in the view of Cowell, who believed that Crawford's originality would best flourish with the teacher who had helped him start his own career, a man whom he admired tremendously—Charles Seeger. In California, Cowell had been sent to Seeger when he was sixteen years old, an untutored prodigy, who put his Opus 108 on the piano ledger at the first lesson. Seeger had handled him with tact and skill, letting the "autodidact," as he called him, go his own way: he accepted Cowell's tone clusters and plucked string-piano sounds with equanimity and at the same time exposed him to Scriabin and early Schoenberg. Some years later, the two had become fast friends in New York. Now Cowell offered Crawford the same opportunity for artistic exploration, and he even arranged board and room at the home of his friend Blanche Walton.[26]

Crawford wrote, "[W]hen an offer of a summer scholarship at the Mac-Dowell Colony came along simultaneously with an offer of a year's stay in the home of a New York patron of modern music, I gambled—for there was no capital anywhere, and came east." She left a milieu in which she was established as a teacher and composer to brave New York without any money or prospects of earning any. With her mother gone, she had no personal ties to hold her, and as she would later describe it, she gloried in a "feeling of owning myself . . . to be guarded like a crown jewel." She said goodbye to Chicago at the end of June, arranging for her upright piano to be stored with a friend, then spent a farewell holiday at Harbert, Michigan, with Carl Sandburg and his family.[27]

On July 1, 1929, Crawford arrived at the MacDowell Colony in Peterborough, New Hampshire. Spread out on hundreds of acres of woods and clover fields that were dotted with small cabins, the colony dispensed rural tranquility for American artists. Its ruling presence, Marian MacDowell, had established the colony in 1907 in memory of her husband, Edward. The application process worked rather informally in those days, and after Mrs. Mac-Dowell met Crawford in Chicago and heard some of her work, she offered her a three-month stay. Meeting Mrs. MacDowell again that summer, Ruth described her in her adolescent shorthand as another heroine: "Mrs. MacDowell! Energy seems to leap from her. She thrills me. I feel like weeping because of the beauty she expresses."[28]

In early July Crawford moved into a "studio, a dear, among the pines" and settled into the colony routine. After so many years of taking care of herself, and still recovering from the recent ordeal of nursing her mother that previous summer, she delighted in her carefree existence. Up early for tennis games, working hard in the morning, she took breakfast and dinner at Colony Hall with the other residents; lunch appeared in a picnic basket on the doorstep of her studio at about 1 o'clock. Nobody asked questions about her progress. "Power in any sphere is pleasant," Crawford once wrote, after winning a tennis match. Once or twice a week the group gathered at the Regina Watson studio, where the musicians played for them. At one session Crawford played her "Tom Thumb" suite and a few preludes: "The latter are liked to my delight more than the former."[29]

In the summer of 1929 writers outnumbered artists and musicians, and Crawford shared evening conversation with some of the colony's regulars. Among them were the distinguished poet Edwin Arlington Robinson, whom she described as "present in silence every morning and evening, once in a while treating the table of talkers to spicy brief remarks";[30] the novelist and playwright Thornton Wilder, who had won a Pulitzer Prize for *The Bridge of San Luis Rey* the year before; and Edward Dahlberg, a "grand caustic joker," who had just finished his novel, *Bottom Dogs*.

The composer list for July included Carl Buchman and the New York pianist Charles Haubiel. Although other composers, among them Marion Bauer, Mary Howe, and Ethel Glenn Hier, were scheduled to arrive later that summer, Crawford was the only female musician in residence in July—an unusual occurrence at the colony, where Amy Cheney Beach and Mabel Daniels were regulars.[31]

Perhaps it was just as well, for their style was much more conservative than her own. A small encounter measures the generational gulf. In July, Crawford heard an evening concert played by Rose and Ottilie Sutro, sisters in a well-known duo piano team. Earlier that season they had presented a "salon recital" devoted to Beach's music in Washington. What they played at Mac-Dowell is not known, but someone dismissed them as the "sewing-machine sisters," and Crawford said nothing in retort. She herself pronounced the evening "unbearable."[32]

The MacDowell Colony began to work its magic. On July 1, 1929, Crawford wrote that her practicing session was her "first work for months." The next day she declared it was "glorious to be working again, to feel the swing and begin to know the power. It has been *years* since I worked consecutively." She began setting Carl Sandburg's poem "Sunsets" for voice and piano as the first of a group of five. In contrast to the Suite for Five Wind Instruments and Piano, which had caused her so much anxiety, the songs flowed easily, with only a few patches of discouragement. In contrast to the self-criticism that appears in her diaries of 1927 and 1928, the MacDowell journal contains refreshing instances of self-praise, including additional mentions of "more power" and a note about beautiful work on the song "Loam," on which she "worked with great enthusiasm, talking to myself, telling myself how nice certain sections are." By July 23, she had written three songs, judging "Loam" as "the best poem of the three" and the "most genuine song."[33]

The serenity of hills and woods inspired her: "The entire setting is painfully idyllic," she wrote in a long letter to her friend Alice Burrow. She recounted her "strange rhapsody" of impressions.

> It hurts with its rich beauty. One gets drunk on sensations: the richness of the dark forest, the soft contour of the firs, so sensuous in twilight that one's spirit fondles them as the hand would a rich fabric. Moonlight over the fields, yel-

low moonlight, silver moonlight, clear, clouded, lucid, mysterious, silhouetted through dark pines, through gray birch branches, exquisite birches, bark of silver and black, saying to the dusky pines, "The moon and I, we know many thoughts together."[34]

In such a place summer romances were inevitable. But Mrs. MacDowell "had no intention of allowing her Spartan commune to decay into a free-love society," Edward Dahlberg wrote in his memoirs of that summer; she "viewed the artist as a celibate, a kind of MacDowell Essene, and she did not approve of members of her tribe wandering about and gaping at a birch, or strolling with one of the female practitioners at the colony. There were no overt laws that forbade meandering during eight hours of the sun or squandering the time of a woman in the midst of her masterpiece, but if one did either of these things, he knew he would have to muster up courage enough to stand before the reticent obsidian face of Mrs. MacDowell." Dahlberg made a shallow pass at Ruth but got nowhere.[35]

"The environment here is romantic to the point of being unhealthy," Crawford told Alice Burrow. Within five days of her arrival at the Colony, she came down with a classic case of infatuation, pursued ardently by still another younger colonist, a journalist and poet from Arkansas named Cecil "Gene" Shuford. Within eight days, this new relationship "became more serious"; two weeks more and she decided she had fallen in love. "Don't be disgusted with me, Alice," she pleaded. "I am not disgusted with myself. . . . I joked with Djane about falling in love here. Told her certainly I intended to. I never dreamed I would." Three months earlier, she had decided "to let her romantic tendencies remain mental and purely aesthetic dream experiences." Now she was not so sure.[36]

Neither Gene nor Ruth were unencumbered lovers. Back in Chicago, Alfred Frankenstein remained the importuning suitor. "He was mad for her," Vivian Fine said, "but Ruth didn't care about him." Yet apparently before she left for MacDowell Colony, she had convinced herself that perhaps she "liked him very much," and even though she "wanted freedom," plans were made for them to travel to Cape Cod, New York, and Washington for the Coolidge Festival the following September. Gene Shuford had more serious ties, for at twenty-two, he was engaged to a young woman back in Chicago.[37]

Ruth described Gene as if he were a combination of a French faun, an English poet, and an American cowboy. "The dear boy seems a kind of Shelley. . . . He is charmingly poetic and in his personal attitudes, free as an animal is free . . . young, an idealist, though he admits to keeping his feet close to the ground, eager, a lovable boy, . . . singing folksongs from the Ozarks, his equivalent of Sandburg's Illinois and Chicago." Gene Shuford recalled Ruth many years later more discreetly as a "nice person—six years older than he was, with her hair cut just like a man's, not a stylish boyish bob." ("She didn't want to spend any time on it," Martha Beck said.) Perhaps that midwestern plainness reassured him, for he not only liked her "geniality" and her athletic zest for the outdoors, but he also praised Ruth for being "real," in contrast to most of the other easterner colonists, who were too sophisticated for him.[38]

A snapshot of Crawford dressed in knickers shows a sturdy young woman, standing in front of a large glacial boulder that dwarfs the backdrop of trees; a wide grin lights up her face. Her outward appearance camouflaged a poetic sensibility that could transport her from solid rock to mystical vision. That summer she wrote, "Always I like to sink down on one of the rocks, to dream, to feel, alone, still soaking up the silent answers of earth to sun, sun to earth. Not thinking much, just feeling, sensing."[39]

If she could hear the dialogue between earth and sun, then as an artist Crawford played the role of "message carrier from real to unreal," which as a line from one of her verses written from this period encapsulates her mediating personality. "Spirit of me . . . Dear rollicking far-gazing straddler of two worlds/Message-carrier from real to unreal. . . . " This straddler is no Colossus of Rhodes, who stands masterfully astride two worlds, but a feminine "dear" who "rollicks." To straddle—to stand with one's legs wide apart in two places at the same time—is to be vulnerable, especially for a woman. Typically candid about her vulnerability and at the same time embracing duality, Crawford chose the metaphor of the straddler as her artistic persona. The promise lay in her sense of identity as a bridge-builder; the threat lay in the self-defeating tendency toward psychic splits. Crawford's relationship with Gene Shuford tested both aspects of the straddler's persona.

Confessing her love for "dear Gene, who is a poet in every movement, every action, every look, every thought," Ruth wavered between recklessness and prudence. Their romance had to be kept secret from Mrs. MacDowell, and once when strolling with Gene's arm about her, a friend "whistled carelessly" to warn them they would be seen. Another time they wandered too close to the road and "were filled with real fear" that in one of the passing cars Marian MacDowell was peering out the window, rounding up mavericks. Hoping for a nighttime rendezvous, Gene had notched the trunks of the trees between their two studios to mark a path in the woods. Yet, as Ruth wrote to Alice, she would not commit "rash acting without thinking," and she did not know how to respond to his pressure to make love with him.[40]

Crawford had imposed virginity upon herself throughout her twenties. Even now she was unwilling to commit herself to this man, perhaps to any man, she thought. While she touted modern values of women's freedom—choice and pleasure in both work and love—she retreated from premarital sex, as did most women of her generation. With Gene she knew enough to be cautious. The tensions of the relationship unwound themselves in talk about sex, for attitudes toward female sexuality had liberalized enough in the 1920s so that lack of desire had to be explained. Ruth duly acknowledged how her "puritanical upbringing in which a kiss was a duty performed once or twice a year" might be responsible for her "revulsion against physical attraction." It couldn't be Gene's fault, in any case. "I cannot sincerely give him what he wants," Ruth wrote in the last few days together. "It seems to have been left out of my make-up. I have not the craving." When Gene left at the end of the month, she was still a virgin.[41]

All that talk about sex spurred other revelations. Ruth spoke more frankly about the toll exacted upon her by an overbearing superego. She told Gene about a "second self" who shadowed her like an ominous secret censor, "looking on, taking notes," "telling me I am a queer person, a very queer person. This second self used to be so ever present that I could not say anything, make any remark without his jeering immediately, 'what a dumbbell you are.'" Plagued by recurrent insecurities, Ruth would later name this creature the "gnome."[42]

The aftershocks of the romance with Gene upset Ruth for the first two weeks in August. This time another woman, also a composer, helped restore her equilibrium, providing a shoulder to cry on and some sensible advice. About two days after Shuford left to return to his fiancée in Chicago (whom he would not marry either), Marion Bauer arrived at the MacDowell Colony. Very quickly the two women struck up a friendship. Crawford confided the details of her summer romance one evening after a concert where she played her piano preludes. She wondered "if I shall ever want intercourse, and that is one question in my mind to be decided. I tell her I seem not to be warm and not to desire it." Bauer tried to reassure her that there was nothing wrong with her resistance to a sexual involvement—especially before marriage.[43]

Each struggled to be a "new 1920s woman" in her own way. In a time when the wealthy arts patron and bohemian Mabel Dodge Luhan might pronounce the "sex act . . . as the cornerstone of any life, and its chief reality," Marion told Ruth that her sexual reticence proved nothing about her essential womanliness, that "anyone who writes music like [hers] must be warm, and will want it when the time comes." "No," Ruth replied, "unless the point would be a matter of importance, involving a question as to whether the one person could ever want what the other person wants very badly." Marion Bauer, who never married, assured her, "You will want it."

Still unconvinced, Crawford responded to Bauer with yet another counterargument: "But I continue, I have always before argued that one does not need physical intercourse. I have argued that it can become a spiritual thing, coming forth in one's music or one's art."[44]

Here is the straddler of two worlds, real and unreal, merging sexuality and spirituality with the artist's quest, sacrificing the woman for the artist. Her spirituality was both a retreat from and an outlet for sexuality, a way to reaffirm her female voice but to escape from its biological implications.

Crawford rationalized her celibacy on many levels. Her own strict Methodist upbringing disdained sex outside of reproduction, and in an unusually bitter mood, she reproached men for "abusing" sex by thinking of it primarily as pleasure. Her conversations with Bauer and the few other confessions about sexuality occasionally resonate with the heroic solemnity of one of E. M. Forster's heroines:

> "Sublimation—you are right, you can sublimate," Marion Bauer says. "I had a beautiful friend who taught me that. But the physical act can be accomplished in a beautiful way, as a symbol."

Later she added a plaintive note of healthy curiosity, mulling over the words of a lesbian poet at the colony who was after her to begin an affair. "You have to know what you are experiencing before you can sublimate it," she wrote, but she decided not to know.[45]

Bauer's relationship with Crawford opens a window into Bauer's personality, otherwise little known. Some male colleagues would later dismiss her as a "Hokinson woman," comparing her to the stereotype of suburban matron made famous in *New Yorker* cartoons in the 1930s. For Gene, Ruth immediately turned her into a heroine: "Marion Bauer. You would find her real. She is human. She is sincere. Her humility . . . that is one of the things I love in you. And yet she has great confidence too. Genuine. She has suffered. She has loved and has suffered, and she is radiant."[46]

Fourteen years older than Crawford, Bauer (1887–1955) was already established as a professional composer in New York. Before the war, she went to Paris and became Nadia Boulanger's first American pupil and an admirer of French modernism. Bauer began composing songs, piano pieces, chamber music, and orchestral works in the 1920s. The consummate colleague, she advocated for modern music from several positions, among them a faculty post at New York University and board memberships in the Society for the Publication of American Music and the League of Composers. She worked for the Chicago-based *Musical Leader* as New York correspondent. Unlike Crawford, Bauer did not shy away from affiliations with other women, and she readily joined the Society of American Women Composers in 1927 and took advantage of the Women's Club Circuit to gain audiences for her work.[47]

Bauer had adopted other survival tactics. Often the only woman among men in professional music circles, Bauer armed herself with an "early aspiration . . . not to listen to the sly remarks of intolerant men regarding women composers." She protested publicly against the low number of commissions awarded to women by the League of Composers (one out of eighty). When her String Quartet (1925) was played in New York, a respected critic said she wrote like a man. Just as Crawford's preludes were "anything but feminine" for Nicolas Slonimsky, Bauer's String Quartet was "anything but ladylike" to William J. Henderson of the *New York Sun*, who added, "this does not mean that it is rude, impolite or vulgar, but merely that it has a masculine stride and the sort of confidence which is associated in one's mind with adventurous youth in trousers." Bauer was thirty-eight at the time.[48]

At the MacDowell Colony, Bauer was working on her set of Four Piano Pieces (op. 21), eventually dedicating no. 3, "Toccata," to Crawford. Each recognized "affinities" in the other's music despite their stylistic differences. Their intimacy grew quickly. One evening after a concert, Crawford went to the chair beside Marion Bauer. "She draws me very close to her and kisses me . . . my head is on Marion Bauer's shoulder and her arm is about me and her hand on my arm, and my hand in hers. I have found a beautiful, a sincere, a warm friend. I am deeply stirred."[49]

After Gene left, Ruth could not work. She endured a "final week of torture when I decide I have no talent, no fire, no feeling, no ear, no fire, no poetry. Nothing. I am a shell. I am ice that isn't even sensitive enough to melt." Urging Crawford to get back to work, Bauer danced with the straddler: "Courage, Marion Bauer tells me. Work! You have a great talent. You *must* go ahead. I don't mean that you must not marry. But you *must* not drop your work."[50]

In a scene reverberating with memories of Marion Roberts, Bauer's sensible message brought "such relief," Crawford wrote, that her fears subsided. "Marion Bauer has freed me," she told Gene, who had sent her a memento copy of *Cornhuskers*, Sandburg's book of poetry. "I am writing again. Glory and vision and poetry have come back. And I can make songs." Crawford completed the last group of five Sandburg songs that month.[51]

One of the set, "White Moon," contains the most sensual melody Crawford ever wrote. Sandburg's subtle eroticism matched her mood, and even if she changed the title of the poem from "Baby Face" to "White Moon," Crawford identified with the restless woman "by the window tonight."

But the straddler could hear Bauer's message about work only in a limited way. Love and work vied with each other that summer. On her last evening with Gene Shuford, Crawford had been in a compromising mood. Now that she had considered the possibility of married life with a nonmusician, she admitted to "worry about her career." Immediately sensing her train of thought, Gene had interrupted in youthful idealism that "he would not respect her if she gave it up." "It is not a question of giving it up," Ruth had replied:

> It is a question of *how much* of it I would be giving up. I shall always write wherever I am. I can write songs, piano pieces, small works. But if one expects to write large works, orchestral works—I feel my life would have to be given only to that. . . . I must discover for myself whether it is a "career" or life that I want. I can have a career and life too, but even though the former will be enriched by the latter, there must be sacrifices. I am beginning to think life is what I want. That it is richer.[52]

Crawford danced around the edge of this false dichotomy, behaving as if love and work were rivals rather than twins, and turning one into the other. Perhaps she thought she was being sensible, but in fact, she had fallen ill with the virus of "separate spheres" for female and male creativity, resigning herself to the "smaller forms" if married, abdicating higher forms of symphonic music to the men and nun/composers, again talking religious rhetoric of "sacrifices." The years of work and self-reinvention had not immunized her, and she modified the stereotype of the "lady composer" to fit the newer agenda of "wife/mother—composer."

So much for Ruth Crawford's membership in a generation of "princesses of feminism," as progressive sociologist Lorine Pruette described the middle- and upper-middle-class women of the 1920s; "they thought that nothing was impossible—a family and a career, love and work." As the number of working women increased to about 40 percent at the end of the 1920s (with "perceptible growth in the twenty- to thirty-five-year-old age group") how women would and should juggle both a career and family—a question known as the "woman's dilemma"—was debated endlessly in the press, the progressive "work and marriage" advocates proposing pragmatic solutions.[53]

To abandon orchestral composition amounted to professional retreat. Only the year before, the Victor company had funded a competition offering the spectacular sum of $25,000 for the "best work of symphonic type"—a symbol of American cultural aspirations.[54]

For female composers, it symbolized creative equality in the larger forms of composition. Indeed, in 1929 no American woman had yet matched Amy Cheney Beach's achievement of composing a symphony (1896). Had Crawford been zealous on this point, however, she might have found encouragement in the examples of orchestral achievement which abounded in Chicago. As the historian Laurine Elkins-Marlow has written, "The 1920s and early 1930s were a pivotal period during which many women composers began to change their orientation: they continued to write overtures, tone poems and descriptive pieces, but also showed some interest in larger longer works of symphonic scope." Radie Britain, a student at the American Conservatory of Music—Crawford's school—already had a Symphonic Intermezzo played by the Women's Symphony Orchestra of Chicago in 1928. And in 1932 Florence Price would have her Symphony in E Minor premiered there as well. It is a measure of Crawford's vulnerability that the romance with Gene Shuford pushed her into such a compromising mode.[55]

"All the poetic romantic sweet and sad picture-fancies of my dream world," she wrote to Alice, "have come crowding in" on the decision to remain single and focused on her career. Crawford returned to the issues more obliquely in a letter written to Gene after he had been gone for about a week.

> I do believe that we have an exquisite sympathy between us. I think we could be artists in love, as you said one evening. I think we could each find our own creative pattern and yet together make a poem out of living. . . . I love you. I am trying to know in what way I love you. Why did I not want to give you what you wanted? Why did I not want it? . . . We are suddenly alone. There is something in each of us that can never meet, fuse, with another person . . . a sacred island. Isn't this very feeling of aloneness that makes us reach out for love? And isn't this longing that can never be quite satisfied an indication of some kind of continuing after death? A spiritual fusing never reached physically. All of us groping, wanting, reaching out.[56]

Here was Crawford's own resolution to the much-touted woman's dilemma of the 1920s. She and Gene would be "artists in love," merging love and work in an ideal partnership. She translated the "dilemma" into poetic language, calling work a "creative pattern" and marriage a "poem out of living." The obstacle to this dream was her own sexual confusion. Was she sexually damaged? She despaired of knowing.

Crawford left for New York at the end of August, and in September she met Gene in Orlando, Florida, and introduced him to her brother Carl; then she went to Auburn, Georgia, where Gene was teaching at the University of Georgia.

Returning to New York in late September, she spent a tranquil autumn weekend at Blanche Walton's country house near Westport, Connecticut. "New England has an intimacy of landscape, a mellowness all its own," Craw- ford wrote, as she mulled over the past and anticipated the future. Walking along a rocky beach, she watched restless gulls circle the shores of Long Island Sound. The beauty of the moment, with the smell of salt air, "white sails on the horizon," and the vast blueness of the ocean, stirred her eager sensibility, as she infused the scene of natural harmony with desire:

> I am the gull skimming the water. I lie under a tree on grass. But I am the gull. I pull a straight course six inches above water, long long, to where other gulls gossip raucous on a sand bar. I am the gull skimming and I feel the water under my body, the soothing cradling water inviting me. And I like to know the water is there, and to deny myself. I like to feel the pain of wanting it. At last I yield to it. I am lulled. But I am a gull. My blood is unrest. My blood is fire. I cry out with the burning. I rise from the water, calling. Endless water, endless fire. Where is it,—what am I seeking?[57]

A month later she promised the Guggenheim Foundation a symphony as her new work.

Part III

n
e
w

y
o
r
k

1929–1930

o n e   w e s t   6 8 t h
s t r e e t

The crowd, the meeting of friends and rivals, the
ice cream and the prohibition wine! My affairs draw
all the best of the composers and musicians in New York.

—Blanche Walton

On September 5, 1929, Crawford arrived in New York and moved into
Blanche Walton's spacious corner flat in a small apartment building on
1 West 68th Street. The guest bedroom overlooked Central Park, where beyond the grove of trees and shrubs bordering the avenue lay the green expanse
of the Sheep Meadow, outlined by the hazy skyline of the East Side. The
weather was pleasantly warm; indoors it was quiet unless there was music or
talk about music. A new Steinway "Model B" ruled the sitting room.[1]

New York was at its most beguiling in early September, still tranquil from
the summer heat but humming with anticipation of the coming year. Another
brilliant season of music was planned for the city the Russian pianist Sergei
Rachmaninoff named "undoubtedly the musical center of the world . . . [even]
outranking Berlin." Crawford now lived in walking distance of Carnegie Hall
on West 57th Street, and within easy access to the Metropolitan Opera House
at Broadway and 39th Street. In their shadows various galleries and smaller
halls hosted events for new music, most of them organized by groups that had
started in the 1920s, among them the League of Composers, founded in 1924
and planning seven events; Cowell's New Music Society; the smaller Copland-Sessions Concert Series, founded in 1927, with two to four concerts; the
very new Pan American Association of Composers, begun in 1928; and the
Pro Musica Society, originally named the Franco-American Musical Society
in 1920. The last two groups would perform new works of Crawford's in the
spring.[2]

Thus Crawford had arrived at the epicenter of the American modernist
earthquake, whose shock waves transformed music across the categories. Bril-

liant urbanity vibrated from the symphonic jazz of Aaron Copland and George Gershwin; the tone poems of Edgard Varèse; the irreverent keyboard idioms of Henry Cowell; and the blues ironies of Duke Ellington and Bessie Smith. In several daily newspapers and a host of small magazines, skeptics and advocates debated and celebrated modernity, among them Edmund Wilson, who wrote about "The Problem of the Higher Jazz" for *The New Republic*, and Otto Ortman, who answered the question, "What Is Wrong with Modern Music?" in the pages of H.L. Mencken's *American Mercury*. Even if hostile reviews far outnumbered good ones, enough attention was paid by champions writing in *The Dial* or *Vanity Fair* or Minna Lederman's *Modern Music* so that the critic Paul Rosenfeld could, in the last year of the decade, tout:

> an American music: . . . a body of sonorous work, not jazz, made by persons associated with the American community, to be grouped without impertinence with classic European works. . . . As a whole, the musical movement is still slighter and of less importance than either the pictorial or the literary, in proportion to its comparative recency. But it exists; it swells.[3]

Now Crawford had a chance to "get into the big life," to stop "wasting time in that vacant lot in Chicago"—as the man she came to study with would later say, with typical New York arrogance.[4]

Crawford spent most of September "bopping in and out of the city," she told Vivian Fine. When there, eyestrain plagued her so she could not work; meanwhile the tourist took in the sights. Her friend Alfred Frankenstein, now in graduate school at Yale, drove down from New Haven in his new car and on weekends they visited what she called the "cool tombs" of Wall Street. Marion Bauer introduced her to friends. On September 12, Bauer took her to the Beethoven Associaton to meet Gustave Reese, then an assistant editor at G. Schirmer's Music Publishing Company, his career as a preeminent musicologist some years away. Later, at Reese's apartment, she was "awed by his huge library of Victrola records," from which he chose some eighteenth-century piano pieces that she described as "startlingly impressionistic and Debussy-esque."[5]

That little musicological outing was followed by a grand expedition to the Elizabeth Sprague Coolidge Festival of Music in Washington, D.C., on October 7, 8, and 9. Ruth and Alfred motored down from the city, arriving at 3:30 in the morning after twelve hours on the road. Then in its twelfth season, the festival mixed premieres of new music with older repertory. Ruth summed up her reactions quickly in a letter to a Chicago friend: Hindemith's Concerto for Organ and Chamber Orchestra was "disappointing in comparison to the Concerto Grosso [she had] heard in Chicago," but a violin sonata by Ernest Bloch was "very fine, beautiful, with an exquisite slow movement." For the American premiere of a new arrangement of Bach's *Art of the Fugue* for chamber orchestra, she wrote, "Alice, I feel like borrowing Gawsh. It is so full of punch . . . a satisfying mouthful, and that is what Bach's 'Art of Fugue' is. . . . The work is tremendous, at times thrilling, at times so boring that you are almost hypnotized. An experience I shall never forget. Unique."[6]

Another "fascinating" Gawsh was an unusual concert of American vernacular music. On October 8 Crawford heard "spiritual singing and jazz," with "Negro exultations and Kentucky Mountain Songs" collected and sung by John Jacob Niles, who stood at the threshold of a long career in the folk revival movement, and Nathaniel Shilkret and His Chamber Orchestra, performing "St. Louis Blues" and a "Paraphrase of Three Negro Spirituals." Twenty years later, in her book *American Folksongs for Children*, Crawford included a spiritual she heard perhaps for the first time that evening: "Who Built the Ark? Noah, Noah." She and Alfred sang "Ah got wings, you got wings, All God's chillen got wings" as they drove to see George Washington's home at Mount Vernon. "Get to Mount Vernon, gonna put on my wings, An' float all ovah Mount Vernon." They arrived too late to see "even the shade of a pickaninny" over the walls, Ruth wrote, as if she still lived in Stephen Foster's world of plantation melodies.[7]

In between Coolidge Festival concerts, Marion Bauer introduced Crawford to the "influentials," as she dubbed them. At one concert she met the pianist Harold Bauer and the harpist-composer Carlos Salzedo; at a reception given by Mary Howe, a Washington composer, she found Winthrop Tryon, critic of the *Christian Science Monitor*, "gentle and kind with a dormant twinkle in his eye," and Ernest Hutcheson of Juilliard. Bauer wangled an invitation for Crawford to a lunch hosted by Alma Morgenthau Wertheim, an active patron of New York's League of Composers, who that previous February had founded Cos-Cob Press for new American music. Lunch at the Occidental Hotel was in a room whose walls, Ruth told Alice, "are plastered with celebrities." It was an intoxicating foretaste of the coming year.[8]

Ruth and Marion took the train back to New York, where Djane Lavoie Herz was waiting with an offer to underwrite a week's vacation for her in Chicago. Ruth accepted this gift and then was just as glad the plans fell through. By mid-October she settled down, her relationship with Marion Bauer anchoring her to New York in the first few months.

"My dear wonderful Marion Bauer . . . Our Peterboro friendship has grown more and more beautiful. We feel like sisters. She has been a marvelous friend to me," Crawford wrote. They had met at points of vulnerability for them both, each confiding the details of romantic crises. Looking back on the relationship some time later, Ruth acknowledged how it was "like mad falling in love," and that in New York their "close constant friendship could not continue in the intensity in which it began." In Washington, she believed (although Marion denied) that the two had come close to its sexual expression, retreating each in her own way from what Crawford called the "Lesbian subject." Instead, she cast their feelings into the safer molds of mother and daughter or sisters. "I am Marion's child," she wrote, perhaps missing her mother who had died eighteen months earlier. "I constantly marvel at her sisterly-motherly love for me."[9]

New York's concert halls replaced New Hampshire woods as the backdrop of Bauer's devotion. She showered Crawford with free tickets and engineered introductions to New York composers. Ruth tallied up her blitz: "In the fourteen days since I came back finally to New York—eleven concerts. In nine days, eight concerts. One Sunday, we went to three. And no pennies spilled from my pocket into the ticket office. . . ." On October 20, the two women heard the Russian Symphonic Choir. They visited the studio of its conductor for "two hours of quarter, eighth, and sixteenth-tone music [played by] an ensemble of one cello, one voice, ocarina, trumpet, and zither" of Julian Carillo's experimental compositions, finding it all "very fascinating and moving [with] the remarkable singer [giving] quarter tones . . . more exactness and pitch than many give halves." Crawford planned a later visit to the composer Hans Barth, whose Quartertone Concerto for Piano and Orchestra was to be premiered on March 28, 1930, with Stokowski and the Philadelphia Orchestra at Carnegie Hall. "It would be interesting to experiment in writing" for his quarter-tone piano, Crawford mused, heady with the rush of possibilities.[10]

Marion Bauer was only one player in the cast of Crawford's new life. What she could not give, Ruth's host Blanche Walton could and did. Crawford was ostensibly living on $10 a week, but she was enjoying a kind of luxury and comfort that she had never known. Through Walton's connections, she heard Arturo Toscanini conduct the New York Philharmonic Orchestra in the second program of the season from the most prestigious location in Carnegie Hall:

> We walk down to the concert. Fast and intense, tho we are early. She leads me to the box floor. I am surprised. She is not sure about the right box. If they are Italians. . . . Yes, they are Italians. We are in the right one. Our hostess comes in late. I am introduced. Signora Toscanini. The conductor's wife. I am sitting in the Toscanini box. One of the men insists on my taking his front seat. Watching Toscanini conduct from Toscanini's box.

Toscanini, in the second year of his tenure in New York, did not disappoint her. After the Brahms Third Symphony, "played too slowly until the last movement, which is swept along in thrilling, daring manner," she was "carried away by the Wagner *Götterdämmerung*. By the glorious music and glorious conducting, by his tremendously expressive face. A warm face, rich, powerful, a mobile face."[11]

The link between Toscanini and Blanche Walton was their mutual friend, the Italian violist Ugo Ara. Walton knew Ara because her deceased husband had worked for his patron, Edward de Coppet, a New York investment banker. Ara was part of de Coppet's celebrated Flonzaley Quartet—one of the most important string quartets in the first part of the century—formed by de Coppet to play at his summer estate in Switzerland.[12]

Married at twenty-two and widowed at twenty-eight—when her husband died in a freak train accident—Blanche Walton was left with two small daughters to raise alone and very little else to do. She slowly reconstructed her life through the avocation of musical patronage, drawing on her own training as a pianist. As a young girl from a prominent Philadelphia family, Blanche Wetherill had studied piano with the composer Edward MacDowell. "Mother played very beautifully," her daughter Marion recalled, "but she had not been expected to become a professional musician. I don't think that a lady, and I mean with a capital L, which anybody of the Wetherill family then was, imagined that she would actually be a complete artist. . . . But I never heard her say that she really wanted to be a concert artist; whether she could have been or not, I'm not equipped to know."[13]

Through Walton's connections, Crawford met the members of the Flonzaley Quartet. Since Ugo Ara was visiting New York and staying at 1 West 68th Street, on November 22 Blanche hosted an elegant party for the widow of his patron. Ruth replayed the evening for her friend Alice Burrow: "Gala evening for Pauline de Coppet, . . . to whom her husband, Blanche says, did not leave the bulk of his fortune. The bulk went to [her son] André, who is here tonight too, and she has only eight hundred thousand a year." At dinner Ruth was seated next to the Flonzaley's first violinist, "dear European [Adolfo] Betti, gentle quiet, of the old—the very old—school, musically. . . . He talks . . . about Beethoven's sketch books, even about Schoenberg. It is bright and gay." Desserts were four ice cream cats: three playing violins, one a cello. Ruth warmed to the playful elegance, but when Ara left for Italy the next morning, she breathed a sigh of relief. "Ara stands in the middle of ten or twelve suitcases, packages and bundles. . . . Goodbye to our chivalrous Ara. Now we can talk modern music without fear."[14]

Talking modern music had become the core of Blanche Walton's life over the course of the 1920s, after she met that great proselytizer Henry Cowell around 1918–19. Perhaps, as her daughter suggests, "she was tired of the pretty sounds" of conventional music. "Dear Henry" and his friends turned her Bronxville livingroom into a "salon." One of its habitués, Charles Seeger, would later recall how Mrs. Walton moved to Manhattan a few years later just so "they could forgather a little more conveniently."[15]

"The one contribution I could make," Blanche Walton later wrote, "to the gifted and struggling pioneer composer was to turn my apartment on Central Park West into a meeting place." By 1924 the ultra-moderns found a Manhattan-based salon. The two key figures, Cowell and Seeger, had renewed their friendship around 1918 after Seeger moved to New York. When Seeger met the composer Carl Ruggles, they too became fast friends. Other regulars included Dane Rudhyar, Edgard Varèse, the Russian composer Leon Theremin (the "ether-machine" inventor), and the theorists Joseph Yasser and Joseph Schillinger.[16]

At 1 West 68th, two guest bedrooms near the servants' quarters were often occupied by guest composers. Cowell was one; Béla Bartók, making an American tour in 1927, was another. And now Ruth Crawford—the artist in residence at the home of one of the most important patrons of new music in the city.

Friendship between the two women grew quickly. Walton was fifty-seven, a tiny lady with "greying wisps of hair and light blue eyes . . . and a lovely really very simple manner" that camouflaged purpose and an "advanced" spirit. According to her daughter Marion,

> Mother looked like a little reconstructed Victorian lady, but was really much more modern than that. Mother was warm and she always wanted to help, especially if they [the musicians] were young and talented, but she could be very critical if they bored her. Mother's real admiration for Ruth was her devotion to what she was doing, and that she liked her compositions. . . . Ruth was totally concentrated on her work. That is the impression I got not only through Ruth, partly through her personality, partly from what she talked about, but also from Mother. She was very very serious about her work.[17]

Portraits of Schoenberg, Ruggles, Bartók, and Varèse stood on the mantel of Walton's fireplace. In this context Blanche Walton later evaluated Ruth Crawford as a "young woman whose work held its own with the men." Ruth wrote how "I told her [Blanche] once that one of my dear friends had asked me to thank her for being so kind to me. 'Tell her I'm doing it for Art,' Blanche replied. Then, a twinkle in her eye. And she added, 'And if you don't write good music, then I'm wasting my time!' We both liked that, and laughed delighted."[18]

That fall, at the instigation of her friend Rudhyar, Crawford set her sights on a big prize—a Guggenheim Fellowship in composition, a program of support for artists that had started five years earlier, with the stipulation that its recipients spend their time in Europe rather than the United States. Rudhyar had suggested Crawford to Henry Allen Moe, the director of the awards program, "without knowing quite why it came into my head that he consider a woman composer for the award." "Is there such an animal?" Moe asked.[19]

Crawford asked Carl Sandburg for a letter of recommendation. She detailed her project for the year. What ambitious plans she had, among them various chamber works and a "major work of the general magnitude of a symphony, for full orchestra." Away from the colluding woods of New Hampshire, her ardor for Gene Shuford had dimmed, her flirtation with compromises about "smaller forms" left behind her. Even though her friend Alice heard news about "rare" Gene in the winter, she had already "begun work on a composition for full orchestra, and [had] written part of the first draft of what would be the first movement, except that the entire work may be developed as a single whole, somewhat in the nature of a symphonic poem."[20] New York was acting like a tonic to her artistic optimism, for she followed this tantalizing account of a draft that is no longer extant with plans for other, smaller, instrumental chamber works as well. With one year of freedom barely under way, she reached for another.

A more pressing deadline followed on the heels of the grant application. On November 15 Ruth had to deliver parts for several compositions to musicians preparing for her musicale planned for December 12 at West 68th Street. By mid-October Crawford was hard at work. She revised the Suite no. 1 for Five Wind Instruments and Piano, deciding "to make some drastic changes and insert a few climaxes here and there." At the same time Crawford completed the Suite no. 2 for Four Strings and Piano, getting "some valuable hints on dissonant counterpoint" from Carl Ruggles.[21]

Crawford had previously known of Ruggles only through reviews or musical scores. She described him as a "short, bald" man in his early fifties, "with a beaked nose, blue points of eyes, and a lower lip that extends a challenge. A rough voice with big curves in it. . . . He hasn't many teeth. And only a clown's circlet of hair on a small head that comes to a bit of a point toward the forehead."[22]

An expert raconteur, Ruggles cultivated the persona of the flinty New England eccentric, who, as his biographer has written, "tried very hard to invent his own family background" and damned those who did not fit his mythology. So Crawford tolerated his dirty jokes as the "rough sea bite in his language" and transcribed Ruggles singing what MacDonald Smith Moore has dubbed the "Yankee Blues"—fear that Anglo-Saxon hegemony was threatened by immigration from non-English-speaking countries. Crawford challenged his notorious "New England prejudices." "I'm proud of em," Ruggles said, when he cursed out the "god-damned Ellis Islanders" and questioned the right of composers of non-British descent like Louis Gruenberg or Dane Rudhyar to call themselves "American." She retorted, "You are American if you're American in spirit. . . . Amalgamation will be a great thing. Out of all the races will spring the true American." Her liberal philosophy of inclusiveness, through the "melting pot" ideal, which she would put to such good purposes many years later, was already in place.[23]

Ruggles was in town to oversee the performance of his piece, *Portals*, by the Conductorless Orchestra in Carnegie Hall on October 26, 1929. In its second season, the ensemble, formed to emulate the radical practices of a Soviet group, had made two more radical decisions by deciding to premiere ultramodern music and to hire women for regular posts in its string sections; the manager said they "could bob their hair or not, as they like," in response to baiting questions from reporters.[24]

Crawford assessed *Portals* as

> an astounding work. It comes closer to greatness than any other American work I have heard. It has a transcendental quality. Carl Ruggles swears in every sentence he speaks, and makes an art of telling worse stories than any one else dares tell. But his music soars in rarefied atmosphere. No one can ever forget the ending of *Portals*, with each new group entering a quarter note later on a rising scale of dissonance.[25]

At West 68th Street Crawford heard shop talk between Carl Ruggles and his intimate friend, Charles Seeger, who had long served as his most important critic. One time Ruth recorded their improvising on the subject of the orchestra. Ruggles said:

> Too many strings. We should have a complete set of all wind instruments. Whole family of oboes, clarinets. The beautiful bass oboe. How glorious this would be! The glory of a piece for orchestra in which the instruments would not stop and enter, stop and enter, but instead continue all the time, the whole

orchestra forming a web, out of which now one instrument would rise into prominence, now another; each, when its period of prominence is over, falling back in the web, but not stopping.[26]

Crawford would use the image of a continuous stream of sound in the slow movement of her String Quartet 1931 and "the web of sound" in a piece for women's chorus.

She celebrated the performance of *Portals* in high style. She wore a "grandly glorious black panvelvet evening dress, if you please," bemused by her new glamorous self:

> Yes, indeed, and so stylish that I look like my grandmother. Of this more later, in detail. It is very full, very long, in the back, missing the floor by about eight or ten inches. At the waist tight. . . . Just to show you I am growing up, I won't tell you where I got it, or how much I didn't pay for it.[27]

Ruggles returned in early December for Crawford's musicale at West 68th Street. Its preamble had been tense. Perhaps because the rehearsals were "belated and hectic," Ruth worried that Blanche was going to be "ashamed of her." As she revised the suite for winds and piano in the weeks before the concert, she became "terribly depressed."[28]

Blanche prepared the event carefully, sending out invitations which listed the program and performers. Marian MacDowell declined with an especially gracious note: "How I wish I might have been with you if only to thank you for your great kindness to Miss Crawford, but that I can partly do on paper. I am sure of her talent, and you are doing a fine thing in helping her to live under such lovely conditions." The double doors between the dining room and the sitting room were opened to accommodate the eighty-four rented folding chairs, while a few others stood in the halls. All told, Blanche and Ruth counted one hundred and twenty of the right people. "The crowd, the meeting of friends and rivals, the ice cream and the prohibition wine! My affairs draw all the best of the composers and musicians in New York," Blanche wrote to Ruth the following year, and Ruth's affair was no exception.[29]

Crawford recorded many names in her account of this special evening. In addition to the regulars Carl Ruggles and Charles Seeger, and other composers (Louis Gruenberg, Marion Bauer), "the entire group of dancers interested in modern art, were here. I won't name them except for Martha Graham, who is remarkable." (Graham had just arranged to choreograph Ruggles's *Portals* for the newly formed Dance Repertory Theater and would dance the role of the sacrificial virgin in Stravinsky's *Rite of Spring* in April.) At West 68th the critics could be introduced to a new musical personality without having to make public comment. Paul Rosenfeld "seemed enthusiastic," she wrote. "Observers said he looked as tho he were enjoying himself."[30]

The program featured Crawford's latest work. Ruth herself played the Four Preludes for Piano, but everything else was a premiere: the Suite no. 1 for Five Wind Instruments and Piano was played by the Pan American Ensemble; Five Songs on Poems of Carl Sandburg were sung beautifully by Radiana Pazmor, a singer who specialized in contemporary music; and the Suite no. 2 for Four Strings and Piano was done by the New World Quartet, with Colin McPhee at the piano. Charles Seeger remembered the audience as "very receptive," later remarking "there's one thing that can be said about the atmosphere of those days. The prejudice against women's compositions didn't seem to exist in this small group."[31]

Marion Bauer generously reviewed the private evening for the *Musical Leader* as if it were a public concert. She described Ruth Crawford as a "brilliantly talented young composer"; the Four Preludes for Piano demonstrated her "sympathetic and imaginative understanding of ultra-modern problems in tonality, rhythm, melody and form. . . . Radiana Pazmor made a deep impression as interpreter of Five Songs of poems by Carl Sandburg. . . . Here again was found a sensitive, imaginative and poetic composer."[32]

Crawford was overwhelmed by her success. She paid tribute to Blanche Walton in the prose style she reserved for her heroines: "The reception. Our reception. Blanche's and mine. Dear beautiful Blanche. Rare and beautiful. Exquisite, understanding. Idealism. Devotion to a cause."[33]

Ten days later Crawford had her first public New York performance of the year. On December 16, Fernanda Doria sang "White Moon" at the season's first concert of the Women's University Glee Club, a well-known and excellent chorus comprised of graduates from the eastern women's colleges. Their conductor, Gerald Reynolds, specialized in contemporary music, actively commissioning new work from American composers, among them Copland and Randall Thompson. At a concert devoted to music written by women, Ruth took her bows amidst three generations of American composers: Mary Turner Salter, Marion Bauer, and Louise Talma, five years younger than Crawford and already known as a pupil of Nadia Boulanger. None of the reviews except that in the *Musical Leader* did more than recapitulate the program, or, like the *Times*, nod gallantly at the "ever-growing interest of women in musical composition." It was a nice opportunity for Crawford, who received a commission for some choral music from Reynolds as a result.[34]

Crawford was both exhilarated from and exhausted by the rush that shaped the first half of her year. The stock market crash at the end of October seemed to have no impact on her circle in general or on Blanche Walton. They were all still living the flush life. As the writer Malcolm Cowley noted, "The 1920s didn't end with the Wall Street crash . . . or the last day of December 1929. The moral atmosphere of the boom continued after the boom had ended and the whole year 1930 belonged to the preceding period."[35]

Still, Ruth Crawford lived closer to the edge. Although she adored her "grand and glorious" life in New York, she admitted how tenuous was her claim on it. "Only God and my creditors know how poor I am," she wrote. At the end of December she went to Jacksonville for Christmas to visit her brother Carl and his family. She told Vivian Fine in her Christmas card that she did "expect soon to settle down to some degree of peace." To Alice Burrow she explained how her musicale had already faded from memory because she was "busy on counterpoint. Very much thrilled with it, for it is dissonant counterpoint, and breathtaking. As full of discipline as the old, and plus that, imagination. Charles Seeger has evolved this, and it is with him that I am having the luck to be working."[36]

Charles "is tall, aristocratic, ultra-refined, a bit cold," Ruth wrote as her first impression of Charles Louis Seeger, Jr., whose biographer would label him "the quintessential nineteenth-century New England gentleman." At forty-three (born in 1886), Seeger was fifteen years older than Crawford, more deeply affected by Victorian mores, more comfortable with their public formality. Brown hair receding from a high forehead set off light blue eyes, which looked out at the world over small spectacles set on a long aquiline nose. Among musicians, he talked constantly about music and philosophy, casually juggling ideas across several disciplines. After a few more meetings made him a bit less forbidding, she still mocked his intellectual self-absorption at the same time she took a closer look at this "handsome" man: "he wears a correct mustache, correct glasses and an encyclopedic air."[37]

Even before November 14, when formal lessons in dissonant counterpoint began, Ruth had encountered Charles at West 68th Street. He often came to dinner and escorted Blanche to concerts; his own upper-class background, whose values he once described as a mixture of "German education, French manners, and English clothes and diction," made him thoroughly at home in the Waltons' social circle. So "amusing, aristocratic and attractive," said Blanche's daughter, Marion.[38]

Charles Seeger grew up on Wagner operas played on the piano by a father who was an accomplished amateur pianist. In Boston, while at Harvard (1904–8), Seeger began to carve out his own musical destiny, struggling against his father's insistence that he go into business and actively seeking out contemporary music by the new moderns, Debussy and Strauss. His senior thesis, an orchestral overture to the mystical poem-play, "The Shadowy Waters" by William Butler Yeats, captures a young post-Victorian's yearnings for artistic liberation. The young composer who quoted Shelley and Keats was drawn to this Tristan-like symbolist tale from his "hyperidealism" about music and love as the reality he preferred to the bourgeois world. Its performance by the Boston Pops Orchestra in June 1908 foretold a successful career. Seeger's time in Europe (1908–11) confirmed his artistic direction— French impressionism. His Seven Songs for High Voice and Pianoforte, published in 1911, set texts of Wilde, Shelley, and Keats in a progressive French-influenced style and has many points of individuality and real moments of passion.[39]

In 1911 the University of California at Berkeley hired Seeger, who as its youngest full professor flourished there for the next several years. It was a productive period for an acquisitive intellectual. Contact with colleagues in philosophy and social science spurred his own interest in the young discipline of musicology, and his course on that subject marks a formative moment for the field. Seeger also continued an active life as a musician, mounting and conducting operas, accompanying singers, and composing. This last creative effort proved the most difficult to sustain for several reasons.[40]

Intellectually, he could keep up with the European post-tonal avant-garde whose music he championed as a pioneer modernist. Similarly, his own heuristic intellect had already led him to experiment with various pedagogical innovations to prepare students as new musicians for a new age. Seeger's students worked through what he called "dissonant counterpoint": various reformulations of species counterpoint to "purify the style . . . to get the sentimentality out of it; [to] get the full use of consonance out of it." In that sense Seeger realized the implications of the musical revolution at hand.[41]

Still, in such isolated circumstances, he was unable to absorb the trauma of disjuncture between modernist atonality and the great tradition of tonal music. Years later Seeger summarized his dilemma into a characteristic conundrum whose word-play concealed considerable angst: "I reached a point where I had found out so much about the composition of Schoenberg, Stravinsky, Scriabin, that—and Charles Ives and Ruggles—I realized I couldn't admire the music that moved me and I couldn't be moved by music I admired." The fissure proved disastrous for him as a composer, becoming a metaphor for a disintegrating identity and perhaps for the conflicts of a post-Victorian who could never fully liberate himself from the values of his youth. While he flouted conventions of his class in many ways, he still retained the characteristic Victorian intellectual mentality, described succinctly by the historian Daniel Singal as a "tendency to view the world in polar terms."[42]

Because of his opposition to the war, Seeger left Berkeley as a political pariah and returned to New York in 1918. Recovery from his subsequent emotional breakdown was stalled by his persisting intellectual identity crisis. He continued to be plagued by his own dichotomies, and paralyzed by the din emanating from the "musical Tower of Babel": an "overemphasis on the unique in contrast to the universal . . . instead of one great style, many manners, each one so different from the other as to be nearly unintelligible to any but its special devotees." Although the analysis was prescient, it did little to sustain his own artistic well-being. One composition symbolizes his efforts at reintegrating the various creative forces of intellect and art: his setting of Psalm 137 in his own unique idiom of dissonated melody; the line "How can I sing a song in a strange land?" seems autobiographical.[43]

It could have also reflected his growing sense of professional disappointment. When he met Crawford, he was suffering a low point in his career, later calling the 1920s a "matter of abysmal disappointment," a period when he was in the "depths of despond," living a hermetical life without much professional status or income. As a part-time non-performer faculty member at the Institute of Musical Art (the forerunner of the Juilliard School), he was shuttled into the periphery of the curriculum, teaching accompaniment, general musicianship, and then, later music history and pedagogy. This could hardly match his brilliant years at Berkeley.[44]

In the 1920s Seeger wavered between composing and not composing, although in 1923 he believed that his "literary work [was] largely preparation for a return to composition." In fact, he continued to write prose rather than music. The "encyclopedic air" that Seeger exuded, at least according to Crawford, came from his ardent embrace of the young field of musicology from both historical and systematic perspectives. Disappointed in himself and in the state of modern music in the 1920s, Seeger channeled his intellect into a quest for a science of music. Although the role for his kind of intellectual inquiry remained unfocused, and his own temperament made him more gadfly than seer to many of his colleagues, Seeger believed that musicology could best evolve by developing a scientifically rigorous vocabulary (modeled in part on earlier philosophers like Bertrand Russell, Frederick Taggert, and Ralph Barton Perry) to express its fundamental concepts. He published important journal articles in the 1920s, often behaving as an agent provocateur. "Music is essentially a discipline—or a dissipation," Seeger wrote in 1923.[45]

In the 1920s a disgruntled Charles Seeger did not suspect the influence that his abandoned work on dissonant counterpoint would have. Yet precisely because of the implications of his call to order in composition (paralleling his quest for systematice musicology), Seeger initiated what contemporary theorist David Nicholls describes as a "new more systematic experimentalism," a new praxis, kept vital through Seeger's association with Cowell and Ruggles, each of whom met its challenges in his own way. Cowell felt that it was Crawford's turn to be exposed to his former teacher, whom he admired as an extraordinary musical explorer (the greatest America has produced, he would later write)—if Seeger could be persuaded to take her on.[46]

For Charles, like so many American male musicians of the time, was skeptical about "women composers" and often said so. His "not-very-high" opinions were "based mostly upon the absence of mention of them in the histories of music." He therefore balked at Henry's suggestion for a new pupil.[47]

> Henry said, "You know, really this girl Crawford, she's really got something." I said, oh, nonsense, it's just improvisation on paper. She has no conception of where she's going when she starts in. There's no form to the thing and it is just rehashing one of the materials produced by the little bypath. Anybody can do it. You can sit down and write it as fast as you can write notes.

He did not tell Cowell how he believed "that's what Henry Cowell actually did, himself" as well.[48]

In September 1929, Crawford had received a tactless letter from Seeger in which he told her his opinions of women composers in general and his low expectations of her in particular. To limit the ordeal, he proposed a trial period of six lessons, after which Miss Crawford was free to seek another teacher, should she wish. It was understood that he was equally free to drop her. Her reactions survive in only one terse comment to Charles about a year later: "After your . . . letter, . . . your reputation needed healing-salve." Given this inauspicious prelude, she approached their first lesson armed with determination to prove him very wrong. It was to become part of the Seeger family romance that Ruth Crawford "was so furious that she said she was going to New York just to tell that man what she thought of him."[49]

A less tenacious, more wary woman might have held herself in check and waited in her room in order to make a considered entrance. On the afternoon of their first session Ruth stood in the foyer, ready to greet Charles at the door. That November afternoon she appeared to him as a "buxom red-cheeked woman of about twenty-nine with bright sparkling eyes and black hair, and dressed in the atrocious flapper costumes of that day."[50]

Hovering on the sidelines, Blanche Walton had invited Charles to stay to dinner. She protectively forewarned Ruth that Charles "would appear cold but really wasn't." "In fact, Ruth told Charles a year later, "you were a decided anti-climax!" Ruth was not.[51]

The first lesson was a great success. The two immediately hit it off, becoming so absorbed in music that they were oblivious to time and to the dinner due at seven. They ignored Blanche Walton's crescendo of knocks at the door. Finally, her "genteel Philadelphian voice called through a crack in the door, "'The dinner is spoiling.' . . . So we came out."[52]

Crawford confronted Seeger's brutal evaluation of her earlier music from the outset. After he explained his "critique of European and American composition up to the year 1930," Seeger criticized her style as "too diffuse," having too much reliance upon Scriabinian harmony . . . imitative—the curse of the woman composer, always to follow, never to lead." He had criticized the Suite no. 1 for Five Wind Instruments and Piano very severely, and some of his suggestions had influenced Crawford's final version. As far as he was concerned, she "came to him definitely as an amateur composer."[53]

Another musician might have recoiled at Seeger's analysis of her earlier work; Crawford took it perhaps with too much equanimity. As Ann Pescatello, Seeger's biographer, states, his hypercriticality had a destructive edge: "Henry Cowell had already noted the debilitating effects of the growing self-criticism that blocked Seeger's creativity. According to Cowell, Seeger discarded music that 'almost any composer in the world would have been proud of because of some infinitesimal fault.'" Small wonder then that to Charles Seeger so many living composers were amateurs. In 1921 Charles Ives had sent him his privately printed edition of his 114 songs; "they didn't particularly move me," Seeger later said, and Cowell had to convince him of Ives's merits. Varèse in his opinion was a "very poor composer"; and "when Gershwin crossed the boundary between popular and fine art music," Seeger said "he was a flop . . . a fake." Even his closest friend, Carl Ruggles, had borne the scathing epithet of being "almost hopelessly amateurish" and "very disappointing." "Carl knows [*Men and Mountains*] is not a good piece," Charles once wrote. As for Cowell, his "'Sinfonietta' proved once again that [he] excelled only in his piano music."[54]

Yet, as Crawford was the first to admit, there was some truth in Seeger's criticisms of her work. Back in Chicago, when she and her conservatory friend Martha Beck had discussed the need for intensive study of the traditional musical forms, she weighed it against her musical instincts—would it make her "freer . . . or less original?"—and at that moment even allowed that she had a "not very bad sense for [form] in writing." When at the MacDowell Colony

Crawford discussed her compositional habits with a fellow composer, she disclosed that she had no "pattern or outline ahead of time," and that she composed very slowly. Now she was ready to scrap that way of working, in which spontaneity and inspiration counted for so much, in order to attain greater productivity and control.[55]

In Chicago Crawford had already learned "bits" about Seeger's method from Henry Cowell. She also had seen Ruggles's scores in manuscript as well as the orchestral work *Men and Mountains* in *New Music Quarterly* in 1928. The Suite no. 2 for Four Strings and Piano had already demonstrated her new mastery of motivic development and contrapuntal technique. She knew enough about Seeger's views on the topic to tell Vivian Fine that he had "gone much deeper into the subject since Cowell worked with him" in 1914–16. She revealed her own motivation in her next question: "Would you not be intrigued by the idea of writing counterpoint, not in an idiom which you will never use, but in an idiom which seems to be your spontaneous mode of expression?" Here lay the clue to her own rhapsodic pronouncements about dissonant counterpoint for herself.[56]

Crawford's earliest work with Seeger in the winter of 1930 yielded a group of "diaphonic suites." She began (but left unfinished) the Diaphonic Suite for Two Cellos in February and completed the Diaphonic Suite for Two Clarinets the next month, for on March 15 Crawford wrote to Vivian Fine that she had been "trying to get hold of two clarinetists and two cellists to try some small suites I have been writing and I am hoping to be able to get them here on the same night.") She followed this with a Diaphonic Suite for Solo Oboe or Flute in April. These small studies, consisting of a series of very short movements, each lasting about three or four minutes in total, reflect the shift in her new sound world: from density to austerity; from congested dissonant homophony to animated line. Seeger later summed up the virtues of her new aesthetic in his praise for the Diaphonic Suite for Solo Flute at its premiere, finding a "breath of joy" in "the shortness of the movements, their freshness and spirited friskiness . . . the clean-ness and lean-ness . . . its nice balance and un-balance."[57]

For all of Seeger's influence, Crawford continued to learn from other composers and theorists as well. A letter to Vivian Fine discussing "off-accents" in rhythmic counterpoint advises her to read Cowell's *New Musical Resources*. Schoenberg's new serial music also challenged her.[58]

While in Chicago Crawford had heard some of Schoenberg's early work—Five Pieces for Orchestra and *Pierrot lunaire*—and she knew his Third String Quartet as well. Then she repeated a common reaction of the period by criticizing that work as having "too much pattern, too cerebral." In New York she continued to follow Schoenberg's work with interest. On October 22, 1930, Crawford heard Leopold Stokowski conduct the American premiere of Schoenberg's Variations for Orchestra, op. 31, where the work "had the dis-

tinction of being hissed in Carnegie Hall—as it had been in Berlin as well."
In the winter of 1929–30 she and Seeger studied Schoenberg's early and most
recent music. She analyzed processes of motivic development in Schoenberg's
Second String Quartet, relating its construction from "small motives" to
Brahms and even, curiously enough, to César Franck.[59]

More important, Crawford studied Schoenberg's Piano Suite, op. 25, and
the Wind Quintet, op. 26, as early examples of twelve-tone composition. The
Piano Suite was making the rounds of the ultra-moderns, provoking their be-
grudging admiration. "We discover that the Gavotte in Schoenberg's Opus 25
is like a cactus," Ruth wrote that winter, "and Henry suggests that we insinu-
ate that name onto the poor gavotte. I think Cactic Suite would title well!
Henry adds Cactylclysm." For her taste, Schoenberg had "grown too many
geometric pages" in his music.[60]

Although the published literature on this new music was scanty, Crawford knew Adolph Weiss, Schoenberg's devoted American pupil, because he
was part of Cowell's circle. (Weiss's article, "The Lyceum of Schoenberg,"
appeared in *Modern Music* that winter.) But within the group of New York
theorists who met regularly at Blanche Walton's apartment—among them
Joseph Schillinger, Joseph Yasser, Henry Cowell, and of course, Charles
Seeger—Crawford encountered more criticism of Schoenberg. Absent from
the meeting at which Weiss presented a paper on the "Comprehensive View
of the Schoenbergian Technic," she received a report from Seeger that captures the resistance to Schoenberg's project among these New York theorists, each of whom proposed competing post-tonal theories of modern
composition. Seeger told her how Weiss was "roundly criticized" and "Schillinger is right. . . . [Schoenberg's] 'uncompromising duocoupleness' was
nothing more than "almost pure fantasy," although Seeger readily acknowledged how "Schoenberg's innate musical feeling makes often a work of art
where his organizing head has proposed to execute an utterly diffuse
chaos."[61]

So Crawford learned Charles Seeger's logic instead. The weekly lessons,
which began in November and continued through the beginning of May, consisted largely of "assignments" or "prescriptions for compositions." As Crawford produced real music from these abstract starting points, her teacher took
pleasure in how her work "showed my point very clearly"; at the same time, he
acknowledged her free handling of his method. He would comment later
more than once on Crawford's way of "departing from the assignment" by "always putting in a quirk of her own," which made the music reflect her own
"musical character." At that time, delighted with the results, Seeger wrote to
Carl Ruggles that "Ruth Crawford is doing some very nice work and soon we
shall mail you some stuff with request for a criticism."[62]

Their work brought both of them an extraordinary sense of discovery and
revitalization. In February Vivian Fine received news from Crawford that
"Charles Seeger's dissonant counterpoint is interesting and arresting. He
opens visions to endless new fields yet scarcely touched. He is a brilliant per-

son, a musicologist with imagination as well as knowledge." She urged Fine to come to New York just to study with "this man of vision." The following year she told Seeger again how he enabled her to have "airplane views." It assuaged her doubts about writing works of symphonic scope: "Sitting there at the piano and you with your far vision getting excited over dissonant counterpoint and I feeling that while you were there, I could write symphonies. Always after a lesson I felt a new power flowing."[63]

That winter of 1929–30, Ruth Crawford fastened on her own artistic growth through Seeger's passionate intellect as the core of their relationship. If there were any other grounds of attraction between them, she couldn't see it, oblivious to the appeal she might have for an older man, or perhaps saving her eyes for the more important kind of vision she so ardently pursued. The man who struck others as "five feet of ice and ten feet of books" revealed a warmer side of himself to Crawford. She could see how Seeger's "cold almost chilling exterior . . . [covered] a rich emotional personality," Ruth told Vivian Fine. One evening after a counterpoint lesson in February, Blanche noticed that Charles's hands were trembling and he couldn't eat much dinner. Had Ruth seen that? Yes, she had, and it convinced her that she understood him:

> Anyone who can be as excited as Charlie was last week over,—a counterpoint lesson . . . Anyone who can be so emotionally upset that he can't eat and his hands are trembling and his whole evening is a flare of sparks,—all because of a so-called abstract thing as a bit of new music . . . they call him cold?[64]

If Seeger would recollect this time as "one of the most exciting winters of his life," it was because Crawford rescued him from the haunts of failure and disillusionment. She renewed his faith in the value of his theoretical work, and therefore in himself. The quality of her new music helped him bridge the gap between his modernist intellect and his Romantic heart. He "could almost say that I could like what I approved and approve what I liked."[65]

Both Crawford and Seeger were sensitive to the boundaries that guarded her artistic autonomy. The following year she acknowledged "my realization of your selfless attitude toward me during our lessons and all our work, of your conscious building up of my own confidence in myself, of your teaching me to help myself." He believed he respected the limits of his role: "she never took all my suggestions, and I never expected her to. I would have been disturbed if she had." But the extent to which he was willing to abjure his role of authority fluctuated with the temperature of his own professional ego. On the one hand, he wanted her to be independent; on the other, he behaved as if that were in his power to grant, one way or the other. As for his role as teacher, how much credit he wished to claim for her work vacillated over time. Were his prescriptions for pieces vague or explicit? The two sides of the equation were unstable. On more than one occasion, shades of Pygmalion power come through. Toward the end of his life, Seeger stressed his role in the 1930s by condescending to Crawford's earlier work. He believed she was an "imitator" until "she had studied with Charles Seeger and she had form." From one point of view, Seeger was entitled to his paternal pride. "There is no doubt that Ruth wrote all of this interesting music after she met Charlie," said Vivian Fine. Generous and sincere with his support and enthusiasm at a crucial moment in Crawford's career, Seeger overstated his role in such pronouncements. Did Crawford's artistic achievement provoke anxiety? Pride mingles with envy in Seeger's pronouncements on what was given. How much credit was due to his prodigious originality as a theorist as opposed to her superior gifts as a composer?[66]

It would prove to be a delicate issue for them both at various points in their lives. At the time Crawford had no trouble sorting herself out from him. In her most deliberate retrospective statement, written in a dispassionate tone for outside readers in 1933, Crawford summed up the results of her study with Seeger. Contrasting it to her first encounters with Djane Herz and Henry Cowell, she said her work with Seeger was a second more important "turning point." He

> shared with me his conception of the aspects, and yet untried possibilities, both in form and content, of a new music, and his views as to various means of bringing some organic coordination out of the too often chaotic superabundance of materials in use at present. As a result of this study, my work began at last to take a "handleable" shape, and to present itself in some sort of intelligible continuity.[67]

Her choice of verb—"sharing"—minimized the hierarchical aspects of the teacher-student relationship. Seeger's discipline of dissonant counterpoint was a means to a beginning, not an end in itself.

Teacher, pupil—father, daughter—lovers. Charles would later describe Ruth as "this young immigrant from the wilds of Chicago . . . incredibly naive with a trust of human beings that passed all reason. Anyone who was kind to her was a wonderful person." "You told me that I had to grow up," Ruth recalled. Still, their relationship slid into romance as Ruth and Charles began to fall in love in February. And then she fell out of it by the end of the month as Seeger's prejudices against women alienated her once again.[68]

The incident involved the newly formed New York Musicological Society, which Seeger had helped found. The "small group of men interested in the rapprochement of music and science" who attended its first meeting in January included Joseph Yasser, whose work on the "supra-scale" gained favor in the 1920s, only to fall into complete obscurity a few years later; Joseph Schillinger, whose *Method of Composition* would make him one of the most successful composition teachers in New York; and Henry Cowell, whose *New Musical Resources* had just been published.[69]

For Seeger it was out of the question that Crawford be invited to join, or even be allowed in the room when the second meeting took place on February 22, 1930, in Blanche Walton's apartment. Crucial to Seeger's ambitions was that the society "not be confused with a Women's Club," "because only women's clubs talked about music in the United States at that time, and we wanted to make it perfectly clear that we were men, and that we had to talk about music and women weren't in on it." His arrogance, undoubtedly buttressed by his personal conflicts with his father over his choice of career, also reflected on the routine hand-wringing over the "feminization" of musical culture in America. Thus, excluding women meant claiming more male prerogatives for himself. As the historian Linda Kerber has written, "we live in a world in which authority has traditionally validated itself by its distance from the feminine and from what is understood to be effeminate." Charles allowed Ruth to sit outside the doors that he agreed to leave ajar so that she could listen without technically being in the room. Joining her were two other women—May DeForest, Seeger's student from the Institute of Musical Art, and her roommate, Mona Dunlop; the latter was an "expert stenographer and was supposed to take minutes" as best she could from that post.[70]

When Crawford arrived at her station, she found the door shut tight. Now she fastened on the smaller snub as just cause for indignation and became "irate" with Seeger. "I turn my head toward the closed door and quietly but forcibly say, 'Damn you,' then go in my room and read Yasser's article. Later, my chair close to the door, I hear some of the discussion."[71]

When the meeting was over, Ruth resolutely informed Charles of the curse through the door. Adding insult to injury, he replied that she "might as well have been present since [John] Redfield brought two men who knew little." The sparring continued. Ruth answered "in cocky style" that she "thought she knew more about the subject than several present." When Charles left Blanche Walton's apartment after the meeting, he said to Henry that "Ruth hasn't forgiven me yet." A chastened Seeger later admitted to Ruth, "your integrity compelled my admiration." That evening, Blanche and Ruth gravely discussed the incident. "Charlie should have remembered you. . . . He is the most utterly hopelessly selfish man [I] have ever met." Then Blanche relented a bit: "There are intense beauties in Charlie. There are exquisite finenesses of feeling. Can you feel that you are fond of him, Ruth?" "Yes I can, Blanche."[72]

The situation improved soon after. As a "guest" rather than a "member" (and the only woman among fifteen such guests that first season) Crawford attended and benefited from subsequent meetings of the New York Musicological Society. Even if today, we rarely acknowledge the pioneering enthusiasms of this small group of theorists, Crawford's own eager welcome of alternatives to European models reminds us of their importance for her sense of American experimental independence. She heard Theremin, Schillinger, and in particular, Yasser, whose work meant a great deal to her at this time. She told Vivian Fine to get his article on new scales. His "plan seemed logical and intriguing." His "supra scale . . . thrills me. Also his feeling that atonality is bad because it gives no center."[73]

The incident in February made Ruth distance herself from Charles for the next several weeks, during which time he had an unexpected love affair with

Mona Dunlop, a "very charming English girl" who was twenty-five years old. "All my life I have been the slave of love," Charles later wrote Ruth, contrasting the "hysteria" and "vehemence" of his affair with Mona Dunlop to the comradely platonic serenity that he shared with Ruth. His own marital status was ambiguous; over the course of several years, his "marriage had practically evaporated," but he had been separated from his wife Constance formally only just that fall. The affair with Mona Dunlop was serious enough for Charles to ask Constance for a divorce, which she refused to grant.[74]

Ruth withdrew to the sidelines. There was so much else to occupy her: concerts, receptions, new friends, the sound of applause as her own music was heard. That giddy journey from outsider to insider swept her off her feet, as she became "en famille" in New York's small group of musicians, critics, and patrons that formed the nucleus of the modern music movement. She dashed about to concerts, partied after them in the salons of their rich patrons, argued passionately about this or that new work at concerts attended mostly by the same set of people, and watched the competition as performers and composers pushed themselves forward and jostled for work and recognition.

In late January and February Crawford attended an important set of concerts hosted by the New York chapter of the International Society for Contemporary Music in order to select the American delegates to the international festival scheduled for the fall of 1930 in Liège, Belgium. As she wrote to Vivian Fine on February 7, the composer Louis "Gruenberg has secured a sum of money to cover costs of rehearsals, many works are being given performance in private for the board of judges and a few outsiders. This amounts almost to a little festival of our own. . . . No work of mine is being considered, so I can listen entirely free from worry." Crawford had kind words for many composers; not only her friends like Cowell, Ruggles, Dane Rudhyar, and Marion Bauer, but also for Wallingford Riegger's Study in Sonority for Ten Strings, an "interesting experiment . . . in investigating the effects gained by throwing one range of the same instrument against the other." She herself would try out a similar kind of timbral experiment in the third movement of the String Quartet 1931. Crawford also appreciated Bernard Wagenaar's somewhat conservative Sinfonietta, "frank and boisterous, reminding one a little of the Holst humor. Middle movement, French impressionism, Boulanger sighing through the stringed sweetness." Ruggles would later describe this piece as "fat, filthy and unclean . . . by that louse of a Wagnerian," when it superseded his own *Portals* as the final selection of the European jury of the ISCM. The ISCM rehearsal concerts also included the premiere of Charles Ives's "Three Places in New England," conducted by Nicolas Slonimsky with the Chamber Orchestra of Boston. "Ives is possibly much greater than I realize," she wrote, even though she did not like the middle movement.[75]

The round of receptions continued at 1 West 68th Street. Blanche Walton hosted Henry Cowell on February 8 on his return from a concert tour of the Soviet Union—the first American composer to be invited by the new government. Crawford mingled among the crowd, flitting from one conversation to another, and writing a captivating account of the evening in her journal. There on the couch was the composer Adolph Weiss and "his quiet German frau"; nearby was the contralto Radiana Pazmor, the favorite choice of American composers. At about six feet tall Radiana seemed like an "amazon towering above the pigmies," and she pulled Ruth into a corner to share her joy that "engagements are falling into her lap"—among them the premiere of Crawford's own set of Five Songs to Poems of Carl Sandburg set for April 6. "Radiana has a huge heart and a gorgeous voice," Ruth wrote of a singer whose penetrating interpretation of Ives's "General William Booth Enters into Heaven" made that one of Ives's first important successes and secured her a niche in American music history.[76]

Later Crawford happened on a conversation between the rivals Henry Cowell and Aaron Copland, who with Joseph Achron, were debating the merits of Stravinsky's *Oedipus Rex*. While Crawford sided with Cowell, regarding neoclassicism as a dubious strategy, she decided to worry right at that moment that she was "swallowing opinions whole" and "berating neoclassicism when I know few examples of it." The next day she ran to the library to "deluge her soul" with other Stravinsky scores. The ground stayed firm and she stuck by her contemptuous evaluation of the latest Copland-Sessions concert sent in a letter to Vivian Fine the day before. "Have you heard about neoclassicism, Stravinsky's latest plaything?" Ruth asked Vivian, panning the concert on February 9 as "a dismal shocking example. Sugar-and-water, cambric tea, soup saltless. It is the style, to mix C major triads with dissonances, juggle them in your trickster derby hat, and spill them out at random like so many scared rabbits."[77]

Converted to the cause of radical modernism, Crawford, like many of her cohorts, disparaged and resented the success of competing trends. They were convinced of their own historical centricity, and if occasionally deafened by the voices of their own egos, they believed in their artistic mission. Crawford propitiated the Gods of Ultra-modernism by offering up her Chicago work as a sacrifice. When Claire Reis, the compiler of the biographical dictionary *American Composers Today*, asked Crawford for a works list, the response was summarily brief—the Suite for Four Strings and Piano and Three Songs for Contralto, Oboe, Piano and Percussion.

Yet all these factions could unite on common ground to redress the public's apathy toward new music and still even greater skepticism about American composers. Decency generally prevailed, keeping animosities and jealousies within manageable bounds. Even though Copland's growing stature could rankle, that did not prevent Crawford from talking up Vivian Fine's music to him, and he offered some suggestions on how to improve the seventeen-year-old's latest work.

Crawford's ears were full of Henry Cowell's ferocious Concerto for Piano and Orchestra, which he was practicing at 1 West 68th Street in preparation for its premiere with the Conductorless Orchestra in April. Blanche Walton's Steinway was being martyred for the cause. Turning the nineteenth-century instrument into a "string piano"—Cowell's term for a work in which the sounding board was plucked by hand—he induced what Ruth described as "a season of distress" for Blanche. She "loves the instrument. She has always longed to have a beautiful-toned piano. Two years ago she achieved it. Now the tone is growing brassy, steely, losing its mellowness. Henry. Henry does not care about the instrument. A man of one purpose."[78]

The spring of 1930 proved to be a dramatic finale to the year. At the beginning of March Crawford learned that she had indeed won a Guggenheim Fellowship in musical composition. Such a triumph and opportunity! Now she could look forward to a second year of freedom to compose, underwritten by the $2,500 prize. She wrote Carl Sandburg to thank him for his

> beautiful Guggenheim letter [of recommendation]. I treasure it. I also treasure the result of it. Yesterday Mister Moe smiled and shook my hand when I came to get my manuscript and said, "I think it's all jake. You'll hear from me in the morning!" So it's Berlin and Paris, and I cried on Blanche's shoulders last night because I didn't want to go.

Crawford adored New York and would have been quite content to continue arrangements as they were. But the terms of the award stipulated study abroad for American composers presumed to need the finish of a European grand tour. Even though she was "mournful" about leaving the city, laughing at herself, she thanked Sandburg "for helping to give me this grand chance to be mournful."[79]

Ruth Crawford was the first woman to win a Guggenheim Fellowship in composition (and would remain the only female recipient for the next fifteen years). The honor was duly written up in Chicago's *Musical Leader* on April 3 with a caption below a picture of Adolf Weidig: "Honors Awarded Chicago Student of Adolf Weidig." Carl Ruggles wrote to Blanche, "Glad Ruth won the G-Prize. Give her my love and congratulations."

Three performances of Crawford's music took place in March and April— an impressive record for a young composer. A favorable review greeted the public premiere of Suite no. 2 for Four Strings and Piano, played on March 9 by the New World Quartet with Colin McPhee at the piano at a Pro Musica concert devoted to new American composition. "It was attractive, modern and interesting," according to the critic for the *Musical Courier*. The critic for the *New York Evening Post* gerrymandered a double review as a contest between old and new: "Philharmonic Presents Beethoven and Pro Musica Does Not."

> The capacity audience was most enthusiastic. Some members of it looked sane and some did not, but they all appeared to like what they heard. To us it was mostly a succession of hideous sounds and all of a character too close to suicide for comfort. These children of misery adored it. They will probably revel in the new linguistic medium of James Joyce and care for the new art that is given to taking whiskey bottles, cactus and a pair of dice as a subject for a still life painting and to drawing a view of water tanks and tenement roofs for a landscape.[80]

April brought two more performances of Crawford's newer work. Making a rare appearance as a pianist at a League of Composers' Concert on April 6 at the Art Center, Crawford accompanied Radiana Pazmor, who sang four of the Five Songs on Poems by Carl Sandburg ("Sunsets," "Home Thoughts," "Joy," and "White Moon"). The program included premieres of Roy Harris's Sonata for Piano; Marion Bauer's set of piano preludes, op. 21, the second of which was dedicated to Crawford; Marc Blitzstein's settings of three poems by e. e. cummings (Songs from "is 5"), also sung by Pazmor; and Leo Ornstein's String Quartet, op. 99. Crawford's songs did not attract much attention from the critics; instead all the composers were condemned en masse for writing music that was "entirely tuneless—the conscious, derivative, intellectualized writing, the kind that leads nowhere." Pazmor kept the Sandburg songs in her repertoire, settling on "White Moon" as her favorite. "I do love it," she wrote Crawford some years later after a performance in Los Angeles in 1935.[81]

Crawford's final bow for the New York season introduced her new idiom of dissonant counterpoint for the first time in a mischievous caper of a song finished just the month before. On April 21, Radiana Pazmor sang Crawford's new setting of Carl Sandburg's poem "Rat Riddles" in a concert at Carnegie Chamber Hall sponsored by the Pan American Association of Composers. "Rat Riddles" was the crowning achievement of her year's work.[82]

"Rat Riddles" is a bit of dialogue between nonchalant poet ("Hello rat, I said") and a green-eyed rat-gargoyle, who spouts wise surrealistic riddles from his "gray rat's rathole." The declamatory style of melody that weighted down the earlier Five Songs works far better here in a context of sardonic whimsy. In an inspired stroke, Crawford used an almost orchestral battery of instruments for the accompaniment: piano, oboe, and an array of percussion instruments that play a central role. The imagery of rat behavior (its "green eyes blinked" and its tail "whipped") allow the piano and oboe to "chase each other in the most surprising arabesques to a percussion accompaniment," as Charles Seeger later described this much-admired work.

In spite of a bizarre request on the program asking the audience to refrain from "demonstrativeness," "Rat Riddles" was applauded. Crawford would later give "The Rat," as she called it, two siblings to form a distinguished group of Three Songs; some versions of all three were finished by fall 1930, although revisions would follow the next year. "Rat Riddles" appeared in an event sponsored by the Pan American Association of Composers in their first season. The group, risen from the ashes of the International Composers Guild (1921–26), devoted itself to world or American premieres, and included Varèse (away in Paris) as president; Cowell as acting president, Ruggles and Carlos Chavez as vice-presidents, and Ruth Crawford as a "composer member" along with an interesting mix of other ultra-modern stalwarts (Ives, Salzedo, Rudhyar, Weiss) and Latin Americans (Alejandro Caturla, Silvestre Revueltas, Amadeo Roldan). The concert allowed twelve different composers to be heard, among them Ives, Chavez, Cowell, Weiss, Weisshaus, and Antheil. Weisshaus, a Hungarian composer-pianist who hardly qualified under the rubric of North or South American, was a Cowell discovery who was in town to perform at a Copland-Sessions concert. The review notices were slight, including some mildly favorable comments in *Musical America* and a general dismissal of the whole affair in *Musical Courier*, which characterized the evening's music as "very extreme, occult, cryptic in meaning, dissonant, amorphous."[83]

"Quite a good audience . . . minus [newspaper] critics, however, so I have no notices to send you," Crawford wrote to Vivian Fine two days later, on April 23. Impressed by Fine's progress, she had arranged a performance of her student's "Solo for Oboe," and passed along comments from Cowell, Seeger, and Copland. She reassured her friend not to worry about "influences. Of course we must have them, and not be afraid of them. Scriabine his Chopin, Strauss his Wagner."[84]

And Crawford, her Seeger. The aristocratic professor with the arctic air, who drawled out his polysyllables in an upper-class Yankee twang, supplanted her previous heroes. The mystical Rudhyar, who had meant so much to her in the past, fell off his pedestal; she decided he was not as much of a saint as she had thought (could anyone have been?) and more than capable of "playing the game as human beings do play in New York." She was influenced by Seeger, who disparaged Rudhyar's theoretical diffuseness, having sparred with him in print several years earlier about the nature of Carl Ruggles's dissonant counterpoint. When Crawford played her new "triple passacaglia perpetuo mobile" movement (not named but clearly the third movement of the Diaphonic Suite for Solo Flute or Oboe), Rudhyar

> was not excited. He turns it off with "Of course perpetuo mobile types are not in my line." "But Rudhyar, I reply, If you want to be cosmic, isn't the world and every other planet and everything in the universe doing a perpetuo mobile?" Later he says, "Of course I do not believe much in melodic line, I believe in the single tone." I remind him of line in other arts and add, "If again you wish to become cosmic, what of the melodic line created by the various reincarnations of a soul? The modulations, the rising, the falling, the mountainous leaps?" And I am thrilled at last, in his own field, to have found a reasonable counter-argument for Rudhyar.[85]

Crawford rallied to her own self-defense against what she now perceived as sophistry. Weighing the old Ruth Crawford against the new, Rudhyar would later lament the direction her music had taken. "It was too intentioned, too determined" for his soul-world aesthetic.[86]

N ew York has been a glorious series of experience," Crawford had written to Carl Sandburg in March. And now it was drawing to a close. She had settled her plans for the summer in March, planning to decamp for Blanche's Westport summer cottage in May. Following that she planned not one but three months at the MacDowell Colony, having received a second generous invitation from Mrs. MacDowell in the winter (who also offered to underwrite the cost of transportation to and from New York). In August Crawford was scheduled to sail for Europe. A brief story with her photograph in *Musi-*

cal America gave details: "she would attend the international modern music festival in Liège, after which she will be in Berlin for the greater part of the year. She also plans to spend some time in Paris and Budapest."[87]

Crawford's work with Charles Seeger would come to an end as well, even though "neither of them liked the idea of stopping lessons." Besides, Charles had obligations to his three sons home from boarding school for the summer's vacation; he planned to spend it with them at his parents' farm in Patterson, New York.

But the scenario shifted unexpectedly after Charles offered her the chance to work with him over the summer as his assistant. He had the "very brilliant idea" of making his work with Ruth more concrete by "dictating a résumé of the lessons" to produce a book. That winter, perhaps goaded by the appearance of Cowell's *New Musical Resources* and inspired by his "teaching of Ruth that drew his ideas together," he wrote a miniature manifesto for the new polyphony ("On Dissonant Counterpoint") for *Modern Music*, "very tentatively outlining" his ideas, without undercutting the eventual publication of his larger project. By the end of March Ruth decided she was willing to sacrifice a month at the MacDowell Colony to help him. She would still have July and August for her own music. Instead of heading out to Westport, she packed her suitcase for what she expected would be a month's stay in the country at Patterson, New York, and a finale to a relationship she characterized as merely two grand friends who had spent some profitable months together getting excited over dissonant counterpoint.[88]

Clark Crawford and Clara Graves Crawford, wedding photograph, 1895

Ruth with her parents in
Muncie, Indiana, ca. 1907

Ruth, in backyard of parish
home in Muncie, ca. 1910

Ruth, ca. 1909–10

Ruth and her brother Carl,
ca. 1914

Ruth as a member of the freshman *Oracle* staff, Duval High School,
Jacksonville, Florida, 1915

Ruth, graduation photo for Duval High School, 1918

Bertha M. Foster, Director, School of
Musical Art, ca. 1916–17

Ruth's piano teacher, Valborg Collett,
ca. 1916–17

School of Musical Art, Jacksonville, Florida,
1916-17

Program from the concert presented by the School
of Musical Art, Duval Theater, June 20, 1918

Program

1. Concerto for Two Violins . . . . *Bach*
   MISS SARA OSSINSKY AND MR. J. B. LUCY, JR.

2. Piano—Variations Brilliante in B Major . . . . . *Chopin*
   MISS RUTH CRAWFORD

3. Violin—Sonata in A . . . . *Handel*
   MISS SARA OSSINSKY

4. Vocal—Aria from La Tosca . . . . *Puccini*
   MISS MILDRED SERRA

5. Violin—Elegy . . . . *Ernst*
   MISS BELLE FINKELSTEIN

6. Piano—(a) Etude in F Major . . . . *Neupert*
   —(b) Waltz Caprice . . . . *Newland*
   MISS ETHEL MOUSER

7. Violin—(a) Serenade . . . . *Kocian*
   —(b) Obertass . . . . *Wieniawski*
   MRS. FRED BROOKS

8. Violin—The Bee . . . . *Bohm*
   MISS NADIA RICHARDSON

9. Vocal—(a) The Wind Song . . . . *Rogers*
   —(b) Villanelle . . . . *Del' Aqua*
   MISS ANNIE DEMPSTER

10. Violin—Air Varie No. 22 . . . . . . *Vieuxtemps*
    MISS ELIZABETH LARSEN

11. Violin—Ciaccona . . . . *Vitali*
    MISS MARJORIE HOGG

12. Piano—(a) Etude Melodique . . . . *Raff*
    —(b) Rigaudon . . . . *Raff*
    MISS JOAN RUSSELL

13. Violin—Reverie . . . . *Vieuxtemps*
    MR. J. B. LUCY, JR.

14. Vocal—Aria from Cavalleria Rusticana . . . . *Mascagni*
    MISS EMMA SCOTT

15. Violin Ensemble . . . . The Star Spangled Banner

MISS MARCELLA LA BARRE	MISS NADIA RICHARDSON
MISS SARA OSSINSKY	MISS ELIZABETH LARSEN
MISS BELLE FINKELSTEIN	MISS LILLIAN CARLSON
MISS RUTH MOREY	MISS MARTHA LAUDERBACK
MISS LESLIE GRAY	MISS FRANCES ROBINSON
MISS MARY LANDON	MISS MARGARET DAVIS
MISS ELIZABETH KENDLE	MRS. FRED BROOKS
MISS MARJORIE HOGG	MRS. HARRY DOZIER

MR. J. B. LUCY, JR.
MR. JOHN WADSWORTH
MR. T. J. COOPER
MR. RAMSDELL
MR. FRANK WHITE
MR. FLOYD DURRANCE
MR. RICHARD ZIPPE
MR. RALPH COOPER
MR. JOE DURKEE
MR. FELIX MEYER

BERTHA FOSTER, ACCOMPANIST

American Conservatory of Music,
Kimball Building, Chicago, 1921

Adolf Weidig, Ruth's composition teacher
at the American Conservatory of Music

Louise Robyn, Ruth's piano and music
pedagogy teacher at the American
Conservatory of Music

Ruth, ca. 1924

Ruth and Djane Lavoie Herz, near
Lake Michigan, Chicago, ca. 1925

Program from the concert of the
International Society for Contemporary
Music, Chicago Chapter,
February 8, 1928

THE CLIFF DWELLERS
CHICAGO

CONCERT
BY
INTERNATIONAL SOCIETY FOR CONTEMPORARY MUSIC
CHICAGO CHAPTER
WEDNESDAY EVENING, FEBRUARY 8, 1928

PROGRAM

1 Quartet No. 6, in G (1922) · · · · · · *Milhaud*
   Souple et animé
   Tres lent
   Tres vif et rythmé
     THE GORDON STRING QUARTET
   JACQUES GORDON, 1st Violin   CLARENCE EVANS, Viola
   JOHN WEICHER, JR., 2nd Violin   RICHARD WAGNER, 'Cello

2 Serenade in A · · · · · · · *Igor Stravinsky*
   Hymne
   Rondoletto
     EDWARD COLLINS

3 Sonata for Violin and Piano · · · · *Ruth Crawford*
   Agitated—Vibrant
   Buoyant
   Mystic—Intense
   Fast, with bold energy
     AMY NEILL AND LEE PATTISON

4 "Alt Wien" (Rapsodia Viennese) for two pianos *Castelnuovo-Tedesco*
   Alt Wien (Valzer)
   Nacht-Musik (Barcarolle)
   Memento Mori (Fox-Trot Tragico)
     EDWARD COLLINS AND RUDOLPH REUTER

5 Four Indiscretions, Opus 20 (1924) · · · *Louis Gruenberg*
   Allegro con spirito
   Lento sostenuto e espressivo
   Moderato grazioso e delicato
   Allegro giocoso
     THE GORDON STRING QUARTET

MASON AND HAMLIN PIANO KINDLY FURNISHED BY THE CABLE CO.

Henry Cowell, ca. 1934.
Used by permission of the
H.W. Wilson Co., New York

Dane Rudhyar, ca. 1934.
Used by permission of the
H.W. Wilson Co., New York

Gitta Gradova, in the late 1920s

Marion Bauer, (in the middle, with large hat and pearls), 1922

Carl Sandburg and Ruth Crawford at the dunes, ca. 1929

Vivian Fine, ca. 1928

Program for the concert
of the Pan American
Association of
Composers, Inc.,
April 21, 1930

THE PAN AMERICAN ASSOCIATION OF COMPOSERS, Inc.

113 WEST 57TH ST., NEW YORK CITY

EDGAR VARESE
PRESIDENT
HENRY COWELL
ACTING PRESIDENT
EMERSON WHITHORNE
VICE-PRESIDENT
CARLOS CHAVEZ
VICE-PRESIDENT
CARL RUGGLES
VICE-PRESIDENT
THERESA ARMITAGE
TREASURER
WALTER ANDERSON
SECRETARY

COMPOSER MEMBERS
JOSE ANDRE
JOHN J. BECKER
ALEJANDRO CATURLA
ACARIO COTAPOS
RUTH CRAWFORD
F. F. FABINI
HOWARD HANSON
CHARLES IVES
HECTOR VILLA-LOBOS
COLIN McPHEE
RAUL PANIAGUA
SYLVESTRE REVUELTAS
AMADEO ROLDAN
D. RUDHYAR
CARLOS SALZEDO
PEDRO SANJUAN
WILLIAM GRANT STILL
ADOLPH WEISS

PRESENTS A CONCERT OF WORKS BY COMPOSERS OF
MEXICO, CUBA AND UNITED STATES
CARNEGIE CHAMBER HALL
MONDAY EVENING, APRIL 21st, 1930
AT EIGHT-THIRTY O'CLOCK

SOLOISTS: RADIANA PAZMOR, CONTRALTO; IMRE WEISSHAUS,
COMPOSER-PIANIST; D. DESARNO, OBOEIST; HARRY FREISTADT,
TRUMPETER; STEPHANIE SCHEHATOWITSCH, PIANIST; JEROME
GOLDSTEIN, VIOLINIST.

PROGRAM

I.

SONATINA FOR VIOLIN AND PIANO	CARLOS CHAVEZ
SOLO FOR VIOLIN	HENRY COWELL

MR. GOLDSTEIN AND MR. WEISSHAUS

II.

SUITE FOR PIANO	IMRE WEISSHAUS

IN THREE MOVEMENTS
THE COMPOSER

III.

SOLO FOR OBOE	VIVIAN FINE

MR. DESARNO

THE NEW RIVER		
THE INDIANS	(FOR TRUMPET AND PIANO)	CHARLES IVES
ANN STREET		

MR. FREISTADT AND MR. WEISSHAUS

INTERMISSION

IV.

SIX PIECES FOR SOLO VOICE	IMRE WEISSHAUS
TWO AFRO-CUBAN SONGS	ALEJANDRO CATURLA

MISS PAZMOR AND MR. WEISSHAUS

V.

TWO "MOMENTS"	D. RUDHYAR
TWO PIECES FOR PIANO	GERALD STRANG
TWO SARABANDES	HENRY BRANT
PRELUDE	ADOLPH WEISS
SECOND PIANO SONATE	GEORGE ANTHEIL

MR. WEISSHAUS

VI.

"RAT RIDDLES" (FOR VOICE, OBOE, PIANO AND PERCUSSION)	
	RUTH CRAWFORD

MISS PAZMOR, MISS SCHEHATOWITSCH, MR. DESARNO
AND MR. WEISSHAUS

Charles Seeger, 1932

From left to right: Charles Seeger, Charlott Eisler,
Ruth Crawford Seeger, Hanns Eisler, New York, ca. 1935

Ruth, Ben Botkin,
and Charles,
Washington D.C.,
ca. early 1940s

Ruth, Charles, Michael, and Peggy, ca. 1937

7 West Kirke Street,
Chevy Chase,
Maryland

Ruth Crawford Seeger's music room, 7 West Kirke Street, Chevy Chase, Maryland

Title page,
*American Folk Songs
for Children,*
1948

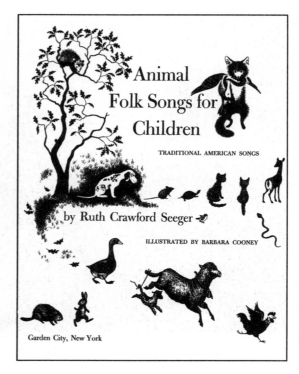

Title page,
*Animal Folk Songs
for Children,*
1950

Ruth Crawford Seeger, with children from Silver Spring
Cooperative Nursery School, ca. 1949

Ruth Crawford Seeger with Burl Ives, Library of Congress,
Washington D.C., ca. 1949

Ruth Crawford Seeger,
ca. 1949–50

The Seeger family, Barbara, Peggy, Michael, Penny,
Charlie, and Ruth, ca. 1949–50

Michael, Barbara, Penny,
and Peggy, ca. 1952

Back row: Tony Seeger, Mike, Peggy, Pete, Penny;
front row: Mika, Toshi Seeger with Tinya, and Danny,
ca. 1960

"the curves in our friendship"

Suddenly Ruth Crawford's world was filled with Seegers, three generations of them living together and apart at Fairlea, a farm estate of fifty acres of hills, meadow, woods, and streams on the outskirts of Patterson, a small village about sixty miles from New York City between Brewster and Pawling.

Charles's parents, Charles Louis Seeger, Sr., and his wife, Elsie Adams Seeger, both approaching seventy, lived in the main house; its ten rooms (plus servants' quarters) were laid out in the classic New England style on two floors, with double drawing rooms, fireplaces throughout, high ceilings, and beautifully carved woodwork: a "fine old mansion," Charles Seeger, Sr., wrote. Lush-leaved elms and maples lined the road.[1]

Ruth began to learn about Charles Seeger in a different way. The Seegers were socially formidable people, listed in the New York Social Register. Their money was new, but their New England "stock" was "good," as Elsie said often to her three children; her first-born, Charles Jr.—even in his nineties—could reel off the eleven surnames in his mother's genealogical chart, ending with the requisite Mayflower ancestor. Born in Mexico and spending much of his youth there, where his father had run a highly successful import business under the reign of Porfirio Díaz, Charles Jr. ("Carlos Luis") had been nicknamed "Don Carlito" or "Don." Charles's aristocratic ease and personal elegance, perhaps even his ironic intellectual detachment from class—so knowledgeable about its privileges and faults—bore the imprint of wealth and entitlement.[2]

Despite his own love for and accomplishments in music, Charles's father had discouraged it as a profession for his son, just as he had opposed poetry for

Charles's brother, Alan. The elder Seeger was a self-made businessman. According to Charles, when he heard that his son wanted to be a musician, he said, "But Don, gentlemen are not musicians." Were there reproaches to be endured in 1918 when Charles's tenure at Berkeley ended? Perhaps not, for Charles's pacifist politics in World War I struck at their own family tragedy, with their brilliant aesthete son Alan, a soldier-poet of the war, becoming one of the first Americans to be killed in France; Alan's poem "I have a rendezvous with Death" served as an epitaph for his generation. Over the course of the summer Ruth witnessed Charles in new roles within his family, his character as son and father emerging at the place that symbolized stability and continuity to him. Never comfortable scrutinizing relationships, Charles had not confided much about his past to Ruth over the course of the year. Even if Blanche Walton acted as an erstwhile advisor about his marital situation, Ruth stayed on the periphery of those conversations. Now at Patterson Ruth experienced the peculiarly subjective yet formal world of Seeger family culture. Charles Seeger had been raised with an outlook appropriate to Mr. Darcy in *Pride and Prejudice*, with the "general feeling that the world was composed of three classes of people: the Seegers, the friends of the Seegers, and the rest of the world." To Charles's parents, Ruth fit in as a friend of a Seeger, but given her background, commanded no social deference.[3]

The figure of Charles's wife Constance gained more substance that summer as well. In the aftermath of a deep depression and breakdown he suffered in 1918, and during the '20s, when his career was in limbo, their marriage slowly disintegrated in a period "marked by a series of separations and reconciliations." An excellent violinist with family ties to New York's musical uppercrust, Constance Edson Seeger had barely endured the years after Berkeley, her ties to her husband crumbling in the face of his retreat from conventional professional success. In 1921 both had been placed on the faculty of the Institute of Musical Art by her adoptive "uncle," Frank Damrosch, its president. The more determined she became to mark out her own career, the more desultory Charles appeared to her. "Since [1921], I have earned a meagre living by teaching a few hours a week, enjoying the leisure that most men only promise themselves after sixty," Charles would later write candidly in 1933. Subsequently, he and his wife renegotiated family responsibilities through different kinds of living arrangements and patterns of schooling and care-taking for their children, including a stint at a Yoga Colony in Nyack, New York. They could no longer afford the servants who had taken such good care of the family in Berkeley. Both retreated from their disappointments and demands of a lesser life in different ways: Constance by announcing in 1927 that she could not or would not take care of their three children; and Charles by withdrawing from her and meeting his needs for companionship with new friends and new intellectual interests that kept him out of the house. Thus summers at Patterson meant the longest family reunion of the year. Some years Charles and the boys came with Constance; after 1924, they came without her. They were attending three different boarding schools, but at Patterson Charles "cooked for them and tended them when they were sick and dressed them up in white trousers and sailor suits to go have dinner with my mother and father at stated times."[4]

Ruth met Charles's three children for the first time—Charles III, seventeen, who looked very much like his father; John, fifteen; and Peter, ten. She was introduced to them as "father's assistant," accepted matter-of-factly by the oldest boy as "just one of Father's students who wanted to work there in the summer with him" and by Pete "as a friend who was a secretary and going to help Father get a book written."[5]

The book controlled its makers, demanding and receiving a room of its own in the large barn where Charles and his boys lived for the summer. Exactly when Grandfather and Grandmother Seeger decided to reclaim their quiet is not clear, but by the time Ruth Crawford arrived, the main house was private, and one of the outbuildings on the estate, a large cow barn, served as casual living quarters; some former hay lofts had been converted into rudimentary bedrooms. For the summer of the book, a study had been set up in another section of the barn, with a rented piano and some makeshift desks.[6]

Walking over from the room that had been arranged for her in a farmer's house about a mile down the road, Ruth came directly to the barn, and she and Charles went to work each morning, for "four hours straight," Pete recalled. Ruth typed as Charles talked, her role as secretary flowing effortlessly into the role of editor and collaborator, as she willingly pressed her own intellect into service. Charles later said, "she put her creative energy in on that book."[7]

Crawford worked on what she described to Vivian Fine as a "Manual of Composition and Dissonant Counterpoint," planned as the second part of Seeger's treatise, "Tradition and Experiment in Twentieth-Century Composition." Some of it recapitulated the ideas of the previous winter, and the invented vocabulary of Seeger's theory became second nature to her. "Neumes"— Seeger's word for melodic elements of two or three pitches—and their "continuants" surfaced in conversation, as did the "dissonant scales" with their dichord and trichord construction that Seeger later claimed foreshadowed Schillinger's work.[8]

Ruth threw herself into Charles's project. There was nothing that Charles Seeger liked more than an eager cohort in the world of his ideas. Here was a woman he respected, if not exactly as his equal, then as his worthy partner; and he could barely contain his delight at finding a match for his playful and prodigiously hyperactive intellect.

Ruth helped so much that the idea of co-authorship did not seem implausible to her. Once when Charles referred to the book as "our magnum opus," she mistakenly assumed that the "our" meant "including my name on the cover":

> Before another word gets said, I must say this which has had such a hard time finding words and meant to get said long ago. . . . You speak of getting a move on toward our future good (in letter 5, concerning the book). If the "our" means including my name on the cover—that must not be done. In an intangible sense—you spoke of our intellectual liaison—it *is our* book, our child. And I

am "unhumilitious" enough to say that I know I helped, and even that I helped a great deal—and what fun it was to watch it all grow and to watch certain sections expand when you protested that there was nothing to say! And to be part of exciting new discoveries and to feel I had my finger quite much in a fascinating pie! But, nevertheless, you are the writer of "our" book and yours the vision, and the ideas, and the pacing up and down a goat-house expressing them, and the fifteen years previous thinking about them. It is your book. So! That's said!

To a woman beleaguered by conflicts between love and work, what could be more wonderful than to cast a book as a child? However much Charles could acknowledge the "creative energy" she put into his work, he never seriously entertained joint authorship—as his private dedication makes clear: "To Ruth Crawford, of whose studies these pages are a record and without whose collaboration and inspiration they would not have been written." Years later Seeger revealed the same ambivalence, referring infrequently to a "book that he and Ruth had written," but more often to a book "dictated to her." Back then he told her that she "gave him enough for a lifetime."[9]

It did not take long for Crawford to realize that the book could not be finished by July, when she was supposed to leave for the MacDowell Colony. She felt discouraged leaving the task undone, and in a black mood, she wrote to Blanche Walton, who in turn responded sympathetically:

> You have given up so much for the book and have put such an immense amount of toil and energy and *yourself* into it, to be thwarted in your effort to complete it in the short time you have to devote to it is harrowing and maddening. I was thankful to see that a happier state of mind followed and I hope that can last—, tho' you really must expect some times of depression. There never yet was a masterpiece brought forth without suffering, and I have *such* faith in this book. It will be a *great* achievement and will startle the musical and scientific world as never before. I don't doubt it for a minute really![10]

Neither did Ruth. She searched for a solution. As Alfred Frankenstein remembered it, "She and Charlie had proposed going to the MacDowell Colony each separately, but to collaborate . . . to work together in the daytime." That was summarily rejected, and "Ruth told me with considerable indignation, that Mrs. MacDowell wouldn't have any of it because they weren't married."[11]

"Are you giving up Peterboro [the MacDowell Colony] altogether?" Blanche Walton asked Ruth. "That is noble indeed!" Although she had planned to write the pieces for women's chorus that Gerald Reynolds had commissioned in the spring, Crawford decided that Seeger's book was more important, and that they could finish before she left for Europe. So her decision to stay on at Patterson was presented to herself and to others as a decision about work.[12]

But could any summer be only about work, even the summer of the book? "I remember that summer of 1930," Pete Seeger recalled. "Father and Ruth would be in the corner of the barn for hours, gales of laughter coming out."

Ruth had won the boys over with her naturalness, and they liked her. As her father's younger assistant, much less beautiful than the graceful Constance, constantly talking about "compositions," as John recalls it, or the book, Ruth did not pose any threat to them or evoke any sense of betrayal toward their mother. She was "earnest, very straight and direct . . . with a good sense of humor." And from the Seeger point of view, perhaps nurtured by their strong sense of family identity, this somewhat awkward shy person was the one who had to fit in. As Pete recalled,

> She'd joined a family of agnostics. We'd strip to the buff and pour pailfuls of water over ourselves. We didn't have running water in the barn . . . and so she'd strip to the buff and pour pailfuls of water over her as well . . . she'd left behind all the small town Methodist life she'd known as a child.[13]

Sometimes after a meal Ruth would join the family in an evening of song:

> we would open up two huge barn doors . . . sit on a settee covered with a huge mattress and lean against a lot of pillows and Father would get out his guitar and we'd sing . . . school songs, better-known folk songs, popular songs of the day, and we harmonized every one of them, so that it was a normal thing to develop a very good rich harmony.[14]

The collective music-making that Ruth Crawford and Pete Seeger would later celebrate so profoundly took root in these experiences.

In this idyllic setting Ruth watched Charles at his best as a father. "Such a lovely two months, last summer," Ruth would later write of this magical interlude in their lives. "You *do* give your boys very much of something that no one else can give them. . . . I constantly marvelled at your keeping of peace and your way of getting things done always with a smile, or a kind tone of voice, or as a joke." Just as she had managed to become part of Carl Sandburg's family, at ease with his daughters, Ruth now became "one of the boys," which is how she thought Charles regarded her, within their "natural kind of family life" together that summer.[15]

As beautiful as Patterson was, they moved down to the Connecticut shore in August. Charles would later mention vaguely that the "restrictions of life at my father's place were a little bit onerous." (Perhaps this referred to a need for greater living amenities.) He borrowed a friend's car to drive to Westport and settled his family in with his friend Helen Finck. Several miles away Ruth stayed with Blanche Walton, happy for her company. Ruth was scheduled to leave for Europe in two weeks, and work on the book continued more intensively than ever in Blanche's small studio. "During those four months we worked all day every day and sometimes into the night—it was a large task for so short a time, but it was almost finished before I left," Ruth would later tell Vivian Fine. "I hope it can soon be printed, for I know it will be very helpful to you."[16]

As much as they talked about music, so little did they talk about themselves. Blanche hovered about, pleased to have some part in the production of what she believed would be a theoretical landmark for their musical cause, taking care of "two foot-sore but triumphant pilgrims [who] at last saw the

Holy Land before them," and loving them both. Mona, Charles's supposed passion from the spring, came to visit and left confused and worried. The contrast between Ruth and Mona could not have been greater, for Mona, like Constance Seeger, had more professional ambition for Charles than he had for himself and seemed "possessive" to him in ways that he resisted.[17]

Plans were made for Blanche and Charles to drive Ruth up to Quebec to meet her ship in the middle of August. The Walton-Seeger-Crawford triangle was straining at its joints, and Blanche discreetly decided to stay home. "You knew, and you *know* now that I understood and understand. Why else should I have refused to go to Quebec to see you off!" Charles said, "Ruth let me take her up [to Quebec] with the idea that we were just good friends and she would go abroad for a year and we would keep in touch with each other and if she stayed there one year, two years, three years, we'd always have a close relationship through our music." Blanche lent them her old Ford runabout with canvas curtains for windows and off they went in the pouring rain, headed first for Carl and Charlotte Ruggles's place in Arlington, Vermont.[18]

It was on this trip that the two of them finally acknowledged what everybody else suspected. Little did Charles know that he would be the one to tell and retell this story:

> We stopped on the bridge there at Arlington and looked at the beautiful river that tumbles down from the high mountains and goes on over to the Hudson through the gap at Cambridge. And all of a sudden, I realized I was in love with her.[19]

Later he told her, "Do you know that all of a sudden on that night you appeared to me as an entirely new person. I remember, the next day, having to reconnect the two Ruths—the old, boyish one and the new, ever so delicate flower just peeping out from a great rock that had almost buried it. It was quite a job!"[20]

He "couldn't face taking her up to Canada. I didn't know what would happen to me if I put her in that boat and sent her away. So I just told her so. Well, she'd arrived at the same point and we had four perfectly extraordinary days." As Ruth wrote a few days later aboard ship, "it seemed like a separate cycle of time set apart just for us—Wotan set us up on a high rock and spread mist and piled clouds around us."[21]

For the rest of their lives Ruth and Charles would draw on the four days in August 1930 as a high point of their love. References to the bridge at Arlington and a bed-and-breakfast on Grand Isle were part of their code of intimacy; a transcription of a birdcall they heard served as a musical signature for love letters the next year.

Ruth was overwhelmed. She had been in and out of love with Charles Seeger for months, dreaming about him in the spring at the same time that he had begun his affair with Mona and successfully hiding her emotions under the rock of friendship most of the time. During that summer his children had braked the sexual aspect of their relationship as well; at the same time they allowed Ruth and Charles to play at being "en famille." Meanwhile, they forged their musical bond ever stronger, containing their emotions within the framework of music-making and talk about music.

Whether or not Ruth was the "first woman friend that Charles had whom he respected," as one of his sons later remarked, his relationship with her was unlike anything he had experienced before because it was built on friendship. "Our intellects and hearts raced along so wonderfully together in pursuit of fascinating ideas and words," Charles wrote to her. Its tempo suited him in the wake of his frustrating marriage and his "hysterical" relationship with Mona. This time his head and heart, so split in his musical life, came together. Any qualms he might have had about entering into another relationship with a younger woman were assuaged.[22]

The tempo suited Ruth for the opposite reasons. At the end of August Ruth had told Charles about Gene Shuford, but she knew how little that really meant. Now her imposing virginity had ended and in her view she had crossed that divide between ignorance and experience, between an image of herself as a "crazy child" and a woman "proud to look men in the eyes," as she later wrote. A "unique experience ours," Ruth said a few months later, "the bread and butter first, then the rhapsody." Her confusions and fears about sex disappeared through her trust in Charles. She was "so deeply thankful," as she told him, "You . . . led me with patience and poetry and . . . artistic understanding to what had been actually repulsive to me—and to what could have been given so differently."[23]

The acknowledgment of love, so reciprocal and so deeply bound up with art and work, changed Ruth's image of herself in profound ways. The dichotomy of life versus a career she had offered up to Gene Shuford receded, for she craved, indeed hungered, for their symbiotic merger. Her solution to the "woman's dilemma" of love and work was to compress their vitality into a single essence. She told Charles that "you and I . . . have . . . been waiting through the years for years for this unseparateable mixture of work and love which made one summer beg more. . . ."[24]

So the union with Charles cured her chronic anxiety about her capacity for love. In November Ruth wrote him a letter that expressed her new identity as self-revelation in spiritual terms. The woman who liked to "wonder" wrote of "blessed knowing," using the verb in the biblical sense:

> During past years I used to despair of knowing. Vague pictures of myself asking what love is anyway, and how one *knows* it when it does come . . . persuading myself quite firmly (but always with a begging hope that I was wrong) that I was not capable of loving anyone, that I was doomed to stand by knowing what it ought to be and with an "artistic" conception of what it must feel like, but myself a cold unfeeling anomaly capable of lukewarm affection but not much more. And being this cold unfeeling anomaly, of course I could not recognize love if it *did* come—how could I *know* when I couldn't *feel?* . . . How blessed now this knowing![25]

R uth was scheduled to leave on August 19 from Quebec, and nothing suggests that she ever considered not going. Two months at MacDowell was one thing, but a year abroad quite another. For Charles his strength to see Ruth off and not try to hold her back was a heroic act—proof that he adhered to what he called "my fundamental principle in all my relations with you— what I might do must not interfere with your career. Yet there I was wanting to smash your career to bits just for the pain of our parting. The only thing to do was to see the plan through and think over the consequences at leisure." He actually told her that she should not regard their love as an "end in itself." What "enabled him to let her go" was the memory of her "as a person, all through the winter, . . . with a serenity beyond anything I have ever seen." It was the "thought of that look of you" that embodied "some value higher than the happy days we might have had, had you stayed or I gone," he wrote a few weeks later.[26]

Yet Charles understood the extent to which their love relationship was built on work and collegiality tested over time. The boat had hardly left the shore when he wrote another one of his heartfelt wordplays: that "the long curve of our lovely friendship (or friendly loveship) . . . is the thing I care most about."[27]

Then a few weeks later, this admission of his need for her: "Do you realise we met for work, grew together while we worked and parted for the sake of work— and I, of all people who almost hates work, except when you make me love it." The patterns of mutual dependency emerge more clearly in this statement than in Charles's assumptions about Ruth's intentions to go or stay. If indeed he and a student had fallen in love, the romance was the aftermath of a stronger, more enduring tie than sex. He told his friend Helen upon returning to Westport that it was a "kind of hopelessly romantic attachment" on the surface but that would endure because it was based on a musical friendship "between two of a small circle of a dozen people interested vitally in one thing—it will exist as long as we live." The "one thing" was more than dissonant counterpoint; it was the whole cause of an American voice in modernist music.[28]

Ruth would later embellish Charles's linear metaphor of a single curve into her own version of dissonant counterpoint. In her response, there are two curves, two personalities who created the points of identification:

> O Charlie dear, do you still feel a oneness between us? I do. And do you still feel that our understanding of each other is quite rare and not often to be found? That our two personalities intertwine and touch at many points as really few do? Do you still hold close to you the strangeness when the curves in our friendship brought these points to meeting?[29]

At the time he felt more like a lover than a teacher, as he attempted to re-gain his balance. "Ruth, dear child," he wrote, "I waved to you until the ship went out of sight—long after the little dot I loved was blurred by tears. . . . I am a bit lightning-struck. I don't know just what *has* happened. . . . which one of us is most miserably happy or happily miserable?"[30]

Ruth suffered less. In the defended manner of those who are leaving, she was already partially gone even before the little boat carrying the visitors saying goodbye had left the ship to return to shore. She was "comparatively calm." Later, when she was far lonelier, she reproached herself. Was she like a child lacking imagination that would enable her to see what it all meant? Was she "partly in a daze"? No, she told Charles, she had to admit how she was already looking forward rather than back, grabbed by "a selfish restless thrill" about the adventure at hand and the enormous privilege it represented. When she was a child she had been denied the magic and wonder of the circus. That image of loss returned, as anticipation and adventure awaited ahead of her. Never mind the circuses a Methodist minister's daughter had missed; now she could cross the Atlantic on the S.S. *Empress of Scotland*, to "a new circus around the corner."[31]

Part IV

e
u
r
o
p
e

1 9 3 0 – 1 9 3 1

"in europe one can work!"

It is true that in Europe one can work! I think true particularly of Berlin. I have never worked so steadily nor accomplished relatively so much as I have these last months.

—Ruth Crawford, January 1931

Crawford arrived at Southampton, England, on August 26, 1930, after an uneventful passage across the Atlantic. In London she visited Curwen Publishers, who looked at her scores but did not commit. Then off she went to Liège, Belgium, for the eighth International Festival of Contemporary Music, running from September 1 to 6.

There she encountered Marion Bauer, who surprised her by having already booked a room for them to share. Ruth wavered between resentment and guilt, for at that intoxicated stage in a love affair, if she could not be with Charles, then she wanted to be alone. Now a steady stream of talk interrupted her own inner dialogue. Poor Marion wanted to recapture the intimacy of the previous summer at MacDowell, but Ruth could only answer with her silence, not wanting to divulge her relationship with a still legally married man. In the end, Marion Bauer "stepped heavily into our secret," Ruth wrote to Charles, still bristling months later, having "asked, almost ordered, her [Marion] not to tell a soul."[1]

Through Marion, who had spent much time in France, Ruth met several French musicians, whom she would later see in Paris. Among them was Yves Tinayre, a singer of early music, there to give concerts at the annual meetings of the International Musicological Society being held concurrently with ISCM. His recitals of "exquisite songs" of fourteenth- and fifteenth-century French composers, "Gombaert [sic] and Machaut among them, some unaccompanied, some with one, two or three instruments," delighted her. Like so many modernists, she found archaic isorhythmic techniques fascinating, and she incorporated their techniques in several works composed later that year:

the Ars Nova of the past pleased Ruth more than the Ars Nova of the present. That was terrible, she told Charles; the "innocuous" chamber music concerts and the "discouraging" evenings of orchestral works heightened her disappointment. Touted as a high point of the festival, the orchestral pieces

consisted of a series of !!!!!!!!!!!! with little continuity or (so far as I could see) reason for being. They left most of the audience either in a worried state of ???????? as to the trend of modern music . . . or worse, in a state of numbed torpitude which wanted nothing more than a bed, Mon Dieu, and SILENCE.[2]

Works drenched in this shower of punctuation included the Soviet composer Alexander Mossolov's tone poem, *The Steel Foundry*, which added a steel metal sheet to the orchestra, and William Walton's Viola Concerto. (The works by Mossolov and Walton, along with Stravinsky's Symphony of Winds and Roussel's Trio for Flute, Viola and Harp, are the only works from this festival that are still played.) Other critics echoed Ruth, one calling the festival a "fiasco." Henry Cowell pronounced it "one of the poorest" festivals yet.[3]

In spite of the presence "of trends not sympathetic" to her, Crawford heard music by the two European composers whom she came to admire most—Berg and Bartók. A concert performance of *Wozzeck* moved her, and she described it to Charlie as "deeply felt, sincere, lines and colors and entire conception really pointed toward an artistic whole." Charlie would have to wait several months more for its American premiere.[4]

She also "liked *tremendously*" the Pro Arte Quartet's premiere of Bartók's "very fine" new Fourth String Quartet, a work that many would later claim influenced her own quartet. One movement (no doubt the second) reminded her of Cowell's piano piece "The Banshee" because of its "glissandos on the strings very artistically used . . . But with more rhythmic interest and subtlety." (In fact, Bartók had written to Cowell in the early 1920s asking for permission to use his technique of tone clusters.)[5]

After a few weeks of sightseeing, Ruth boarded the train for Berlin. "Breathless" with anticipation, she wrote Charles that the sound of the wheels along the track was in 5/8, projecting her nerves onto its rhythms. What awaited her in this hub of European modernism, "overflowing with the flood of new music"?[6]

Little did she anticipate the turning tide. Berlin's renown had depended in part upon the dramatic economic recovery of the young Weimar Republic. But by 1927 it was over. Repercussions from the collapse of the American stock market dried up foreign capital, loans were called in, the "carnival of public spending" shut down, and severe unemployment took its place.[7]

Germany's political life mirrored the economic chaos. National elections on September 14, 1930, gave the Nazi Party its first great electoral victory; its increase from 12 to 105 seats in the Reichstag made it the second most powerful political party in Germany. Bruno Walter, who conducted the State Opera, listened to the returns on the radio with the cellist Emanuel Feuermann. About three in the morning, "Feuermann, usually so gay, left us with the words, 'It's all over with Germany; all over with Europe.'" An unsuspecting Ruth Crawford arrived ten days later, on September 24, at the beginning of the end of "the great days of Berlin."[8]

Crawford moved into a room in the eastern section of the city, at the Pension Frau Schmolke, 65 Nürnbergerstrasse, which served as home away from home for Henry Cowell and his friends. She let herself be charmed by its "dear inevitable flowers, at all the windows" and "plenty of artistic people," including a former pupil of the great violinist Joachim, trying to rekindle her career, and a young unnamed English music critic. For the next few weeks Crawford rode the foreigner's roller-coaster of emotions, up in the "sunshine and morning and glorious autumn in the Tiergarten," where she walked before breakfast, and then down, crying, "Is there any place in Germany where the sky doesn't bear down on you like lead? . . . O I hate it HATE it. It is a damnably horrid heavy depressed heavy-hearted place." Did she react so because of the "lead in me"? she asked Seeger. Perhaps, for she did not allude to external causes, like the chronic strikes or street demonstrations. When the Reichstag opened on October 13, SS brownshirts smashed the windows of Wertheims, a Jewish-owned department store in Alexanderplatz, a main square in the city.[9]

Just before Crawford's departure Seeger had given her advice, "anxious for her not to get too mixed up with European teachers." He and his fellow ultramoderns believed that independence was crucial, for "the United States was giving birth to its own compositional style" that could only be undermined by European influences. Of all the people she was to avoid especially were Schoenberg, who would lead her down the twelve-tone row, and Boulanger, espousing neoclassicism—another threat to modern dissonant music.[10]

This strategy of detachment worked poorly in Berlin. Who *was* she studying with, Berliners routinely asked, wanting some clue to the identity and status of this American—a woman no less—who was improbably armed with a Guggenheim Fellowship. Where did she fit among the younger generation of European composers who flocked to Berlin after the war? The roster boasted Ernst Krenek, Karol Rathaus, Ernst Toch, Hanns Eisler, and Alois Haba from Vienna; Vladimir Vogel and Boris Blacher from the Soviet Union (part of a brilliant émigré colony that included the writer Vladimir Nabokov); and George Antheil, Marc Blitzstein, Adolph Weiss, Aaron Copland, and Edgard Varèse from the United States. Impressing order on this surfeit of émigrés and visitors, the Germans constructed family trees of Berlin's famous composer-teachers (Arnold Schoenberg, Paul Hindemith, Franz Schreker) and their pupils, who then begat the next generation of "pupils of" as well. But Crawford defied their legitimacy test.

> At present I feel very much against the idea of studying with anyone. To work alone: I am convinced this is what I should do, to discover what I really want, to digest last year's work (some of it) alone. When people say, "O, you will study with Schoenberg," and I reply as I have several times that I studied counterpoint in New York with a man whose ideas have the disciplinary advantages of

Schoenberg's but with a vision and a vista that reaches *far* beyond, that *leads* somewhere etc.—they look a little doubtful that such a phenomenon could come from America, and no doubt think me prejudiced. It is difficult for a German to believe that an American upstart will come to Berlin and sit down in a little room without a teacher.[11]

She *was* prejudiced. However, her decision rested not just on judgment clouded by loyalty to Seeger nor even on nationalistic anxiety, but also on the need to clear some ground in her own mind. After four arduous months on Charles's book, she brimmed with "ideas" for new work that she "wanted to work out in as undisturbed a fashion as possible."[12]

Crawford immediately began work on her commission from Gerald Reynolds, who, for his Women's University Glee Club, had scheduled a concert of works written for the group "by holders of Guggenheim Fellowships" for December 18, 1930. A deadline of October 20 glared at her. She had already chosen daring premises for the choral work plan that would draw on her longstanding fascination with mysticism and Eastern religion: her idiom would be chant; her text, the *Bhagavad Gita*. Apparently Crawford revealed her intentions to Reynolds before she left for Europe, for in October he sent her choral music by the English composer Gustav Holst, a devoted theosophist. (The pieces, not identified in the correspondence, were doubtless the second and third set of *Choral Hymns from the Rig Veda*, which Reynolds had performed some years earlier.) Crawford thanked Reynolds: Holst's music was "a help." But she imagined chants of a different order—a still vague but haunting "Oriental" sound—experimental, dissonant, and transcendental all at the same time. The microtonal music of the Mexican composer Julian Carrillo, which she had heard in New York—"extremely Oriental, Hindu in effect"—was still in her ears. And that previous winter, Ruth, along with Charles and Henry Cowell, had seen a performance of the Chinese actor Mei Lan-fang. Mei's voice had transported her to "another world . . . on another planet." Through Cowell, who would later give a lecture on "newly discovered Oriental principles" based on Russian choral music as part of his course "A World Survey of Contemporary Music" at the New School, she learned "a few things about Chinese singing."[13]

Crawford initially planned four chants as two pairs of opposites: "To an Unkind God, to a Kind God; To a Gargoyle, to an Angel." Pressure and solitude enabled three of the four (without "To a Gargoyle") to get written between October 6 and November 10, two finished in ten days. The least known—two received their world premieres more than sixty years later—and perhaps the most problematic of her vocal music, the chants repay our attention because of their experimental bravura.

Even though using excerpts from the *Gita* proved impossible—after five days of trying to find an English translation of a Sanskrit text in a German city, Ruth gave up—she took an even more adventurous step, what she "had wanted to do for years": "making my own . . . syllables, both consonants and vowels." To evoke "Eastern sound . . . not words," she appropriated syllables, both consonants and vowels, from German and English. Nasal dipthongs of "ng" and "ny," harder "k" and "d," the softer "ch" and "sh" and the liquid "l," combine with shifting vowels. Thus, "To an Unkind God" opens with sopranos singing "NG-YE YE-U E YET NAH YU." Within three measures the second part enters in textual counterpoint: "DRU AH KU YA KO LYU NGO CHYAH."[14]

During the month of close work on the chants, Ruth sent scores home and Charles proffered comment, although it took two weeks by mail. She wondered "what you will think of it. I am trying to forget that I wonder what you will think—and really think I have succeeded quite passably well in making myself send you away." For "there are many things not according to *A Manual of Dissonant Counterpoint.*"[15]

"To an Unkind God," written for a core group of three choral parts (SSA) and a floating soprano solo, shifts erratically from one texture to another. Little appoggiaturas approximate the Oriental "hooks" and "slides" that so intrigued Crawford. A haze of dissonant pedal points, interrupted by an unexpected unison climax, act as a foil. "To an Angel" is completely different. Serene and monochromatic, with its "white tone" contributing to its etherealness, a soprano soloist sings Crawford's invented syllables against a backdrop of two-part choral humming. Crawford could not make up her mind about this piece, shifting

> between an objective viewing of it as bad, impressionistic and worthless, and a secret liking for its simplicity and a slightly fascinated interest in the fact that the second part wanders about naively in its own tonality (which was not planned) while the effect is dissonant vertically.[16]

Seeger could not resist getting more involved. After praising much and criticizing one or two moments in the first chant, he sent a long vivid description of Eastern chant based on rare recordings, further suggesting an ostinato for a three-part texture based on the "pranava" "Om," stretched into "or-uu-mm" with various proportions for each syllable, including one in the "dissonant rhythm" of 2-3-4. In the monasteries, each one chanted on his own pitch, disregarding those around him:

> Each voice, however, has a tendency to rise in inflection at the end of each breath (very long breath of course, a kind of hum), and as the repetitions go on, the pitch gradually gets lower and lower. If kept on long enough—say twenty minutes—the men's voices especially (but the women's also), attain an almost incredible impression of depth and the whole body vibrates to the sound as if in an electric shock machine. If you wanted to make a complex dissonant veil of sound for the chanting voice to cut through, this idea would be suited.[17]

His imagery of an "electric shock machine" and a "complex dissonant veil of sound" inspired the third and most radical chant of all, "To a Kind God." Here Crawford used a "kind of new composite mass-pitch" constructed from the "massing of half-steps." To realize the choral mantra of "Om," Crawford wrote out twelve different parts, each on a different pitch, each chanting different irregular rhythms and texts in the proportions of 2 : 3 : 4. Perhaps her old fascination with Rudhyar's ideals of universal dissonance urged this

display of the total chromatic all at once. As David Nicholls remarks, "nothing else like . . . this pulsating cluster . . . occurs in Western music until the
1960s."[18]

Crawford tried to make the piece work for Reynolds by including a chart
showing standing positions for the twelve singers, which might help them to
sustain their pitch-mantras all the way through. The "chanting done in far-
eastern monasteries" had inspired this "complex veil of sound," she told
Reynolds, borrowing words from Seeger's letter, probably hoping to diminish
Reynolds's shock. After she mailed the chant, Ruth confided to Charles that
"I may be crazy, it may not be possible or sound as I think it will. . . . My heart
was a bit in my throat." She asked him to help Reynolds at rehearsal. Still, it
proved to be impossible for the conductor to program the work for the concert
in December. Receiving the manuscripts late, probably about six weeks before
the scheduled concert, he postponed performance until his final concert in
May. Emboldened by the radical daring of the chants, Crawford simultaneously explored the most sensitive issues in her relationship with Charles
Seeger in several probing letters written in October and November. Just after
arriving in Berlin, she realized how strong she was and paid him a generous
tribute:

> how much easier the writing comes, how much less fear there is, how much
> more clearly I feel what I want. The book, on top of last year's work, has given
> me more than . . . O dearest Charlie, you . . . it has also given me myself.[19]

She followed that with an extraordinary "new declaration of independence
signed in Berlin":

> Please give me as unmerciless a criticism as you think I need. I have felt so
> much the need of showing you things. . . . At any rate, I am nursing and beg-
> ging and persuading to stay with me this growing lack of fear as to what I write:
> the sudden realization that even great composers have made mistakes and have
> written bad music as well as good, so why should I worry. . . . In other words I
> shall write what I like, whether I think it corresponds to what my friends like
> or not!![20]

Lest her teacher-lover interpret this as rejection, she explained herself further a few days later:

> You know very well what lies behind my recent declaration of independence in
> two of my letters: your opinion of what I do means so much to me that I only
> want to be sure it is not too closely in my consciousness as I write. No one can
> understand that better than you, who were so careful last year to keep me as in-
> dependent as possible, to try not to impose your musical personality on mine. I
> think my method of procedure might be as follows: an hour or two of counter-
> point every day, following closely some of the many myriad ideas from last year
> and this summer (I am longing to get at them), and then in other writing to let
> myself go, say Charlie (and the world) be damned, and then after a revision and
> listening to be sure I have really pleased *myself*, send the result to you and hope
> intensely that you will be pleased too.[21]

So Crawford arrived once again at a juncture in her life as a woman and an artist, trying to loosen ties of dependence in work at the same time that she strengthened bonds of love.

> So often I have asked myself, just from a musical standpoint, why I am away from you—you, who I feel knows what is best for me more than anyone else can. Perhaps it is better—we can't possibly know. I so often feel the need of you, but it may be a quite necessary experience for me to stand on my own feet and be (even disastrously, perhaps) daring, as in the last chant—unable to ask, having to answer my own questions, often perhaps miscalculating effects, making mistakes, but nevertheless striking ahead with a new sense of fearlessness.[22]

Crawford approached her next tasks with the same confident energy, and between November 24 and December 24 she finished sketches and exercises from her last year's work with ease. These included the Diaphonic Suite for Two Celli and the Piano Study in Mixed Accents, which she sent home as a Christmas present for Blanche Walton. Blanche answered warmly,

> My dear dear Ruth,
> Your letter of December 14 came with the splendid Xmas gift of the "Piano Study"—it's too glorious of you and I'm simply delighted to have it and shall show it proudly round you may be sure. I can't begin to play it as you know but am waiting for Charlie's return to give me an idea of what it's all about! . . . Thank you a thousand times dear Ruth. May masterpieces continue to flow from your pen for years to come is the heartfelt wish of your ancient friend B.W.W.[23]

Seeger told her almost immediately that Henry Cowell wanted to print it in *New Music Quarterly*. She produced other work as well, including a Diaphonic Suite for Oboe and Cello and, most important, a second song to partner "Rat Riddles," which had been asked for by the New Music Society of San Francisco. The new song, "In Tall Grass" (occasionally nicknamed "The Bee"), would receive some finishing touches in January, but was more or less written by December 24, by which time she had started working on a third song ("Prayers of Steel"). In January she wrote Carl Sandburg for permission to set the texts and translate them into German for possible performance there: "'In Tall Grass' has long been one of my favorite Sandburg poems." "Prayers of Steel" she "was anxious to complete . . . but I like the poem so much that I am always tense with a fear of not doing it justice." She sent off copies to Seeger, who wrote back that he was "tremendously impressed with the Suites—the last I shall go over carefully so as I understand the construction."[24]

All this work made fall in Berlin an enormously productive period, of which she was duly proud. But how much did Crawford owe to the city in which these proto-serial works were written? By December she still had not made any effort to meet Arnold Schoenberg. After hearing his Suite for Chamber Orchestra, op. 29, at a concert sponsored by the local chapter of the International Society for Contemporary Music, Crawford reported her mixed reactions: "like his Variations for Orchestra, a long succession of small motives, with very interesting tone colors and effects. . . . In me, the same longing for a line, for even a weak piece of string to lead me out of the mass of rootless treeless leaves." She was treating Schoenberg just like many of his Berlin colleagues did in 1930.[25]

More honored for "the spiritual force of his personality" than his "solitary" art, Schoenberg watched his pre-war expressionist style labeled as "dangerous subjectivity" and his new twelve-tone method called "abstruse." His own temperament more Hapsburg than Weimar, he later candidly admitted that "the unanimity of the rebuke" from the younger generation in Germany in the 1920s was "frightening." He suffered the rise of his rival Paul Hindemith, who espoused "Gebrauchsmusik" ("music for common use") and social criticism.[26]

Crawford had little praise for "Gebrauchsmusik," scorning its low standards, although her dislike made her feel "snobbish." She more readily dismissed Hindemith's neoclassicism. In contrast to Otto Klemperer, who described Hindemith's music as "fresh air and no more pathos," Crawford heard it as stale and empty.[27]

She attended Klemperer's revival of Hindemith's *Zeitoper* (or "topical opera") *Neues vom Tage* ("News of the Day") at the Kroll Opera. With a satirical libretto by the revue writer Marcellus Schiffer, *Neues vom Tage*'s score mixed cabaret, bel canto opera, and jazz with neoclassical polyphony. Crawford echoed the hostility of Berlin critics, when she demeaned the work as "a sophisticated pekinese tied to a libretto that in itself was an impossible crossbreed of a dachshund and a chattering monkey."

Despite Hindemith's "awe-inspiring waves of technique," its "plicking, plucking and pattering" sounded like endless "machinations." Hindemith's melodies did not "lead anywhere," and he could "go to America for a teacher."[28]

Neues vom Tage, with its sensational "bathtub" arioso denounced by Goebbels, was removed from the Kroll Opera repertory in 1930 because of rightwing pressure. On November 6 came the announcement that the Kroll itself was doomed. Although this prompted some political protests from Stravinsky and Kurt Weill, as well as Hindemith, Crawford remarked on none of this in her letters home.[29]

There were oases of experimentalism still to be found in Berlin, among them a concert on November 11 featuring a new electronic instrument, the "trautonium," invented by Friedrich Trautwein. That aroused Crawford's curiosity (as it did other composers, among them Richard Strauss and Hindemith). As she mused about its possibilities for her own work, she was cheered by Trautwein's braving the new world of electronically processed sound: "Imagine a kind of glissando, starting from the low beat-tones, keeping the same speed of beats per second, but rising in pitch to a high xylophone. The xylophone through the entire huge range. Or, starting again with the percussion effect, rising, and modulating in a wide sweep into a cantabile of a cello! . . . I am wondering if the modulation from the percussion to the cello (and a myriad other effects) can be notated and played: I feel tempted to attempt a composition for it!"[30]

Then came another disappointment after an evening of new music sponsored by the "Novembergruppe," the well-known collective for radical artists
who had adopted the name of the month that was synonymous with the 1918
German revolution. Crawford raged about it in a long diatribe:

> Someone said, "Yes, now modern music has become pure and clear." Yes, this
> music was so clear it was like an empty plate; there was nothing to digest. Is this
> the music of the future? The music of the future must grow out of the past—
> that is an unquestionable truth: you should learn from older times. But it is not
> necessary to don the dusty clothes of the period of the great Bach because one
> is in awe of his music. I believe that the modern composer wanders through the
> modern world as if he were a participant at a costume ball; He is a sleepwalker;
> a phantom with eyes in the back of his head. And he clothes his music like a
> lout: a little patch of Bach, a piece of Chopin, a scrap of the sentimental red
> rose of Strauss, and perhaps, circumspectly, a tiny piece of Stravinsky. . . . [31]

More despairing accounts of concerts reached Seeger as she assessed the
viability of their style of "dissonant music." In December she tallied up her
concert-going for Seeger as a series of debits. After dismissing Rathaus's *Der
fremde Erde* and Milhaud's *Christophe Columbe*, she added:

> Perhaps sometime I can tell you in more detail how these two new operas af-
> fected me. I often feel quite pessimistic about the future of "our" modern music,
> though it is impossible for me to lose my feeling that surely such a dead thing
> as Neo-Classicism cannot permanently grip either the people or composers. It is
> incredible to hear such a concert as that of the Novembergruppe: representa-
> tive, or supposed to be, of the modern trend. I could scarcely believe my ears.
> Such sickening sweet inanity. [32]

She greeted concerts of Stravinsky's music with more generosity. Even though
she labeled the octet (which she heard in January) as "inane," she enjoyed
Pulcinella's "great fun tricks." And on February 20, 1931, the conductor Otto
Klemperer's legendary Berlin premiere of *Symphony of Psalms* finally moved
this anti-neoclassicist to admit that she "liked it far better" than any recent
work of his: "He uses close over-lapping dissonances in the voices, especially
in the first section, in a way which I liked very much. It is a mixed work, like
other late works of his. There is very much triad writing, yet also many extremely interesting uses of dissonance." [33]

Although Crawford did not sort out the factionalist underpinnings of the
various political tendencies affecting German music in the final years of the
Weimar Republic, she sensed the onset of reaction. The critics stated baldly
that "the numbers of those committed to modernism decrease daily." The controversy surrounding *Die Massnahme* ("The Measures Taken"), the controversial didactic Communist theater piece by Bertold Brecht and Hanns Eisler
that premiered in December 1930—to no comment by Crawford—marked
the battlegrounds between radical left and right. It would take just a few years
for Eisler to become the heroic model for the American radical left; in Berlin
she did not take note. [34]

At the end of December, Crawford talked musical politics with Edgar

Ansel Mowrer, the noted foreign correspondent for the *Chicago Daily News*. "He is a droll person and reminds me much of Sandburg," Ruth wrote several months later. Perhaps they talked general politics as well, for Mowrer was already well known for his outspoken pessimistic predictions about Hitler, a minority view at that time. His article "Germany Puts the Clock Back," written in spring 1930, would later be expanded into a book of the same title in 1933, earning him both expulsion from Germany and a Pulitzer Prize in one year.[35]

That night Mowrer confessed that after years of sincere listening, "his interest in dissonant music is dead." Crawford answered "her personal convictions" opposed the rising tide of German neoclassicism. Her passionate letter written to Seeger a few days later makes no mention of the state of emergency declared in all of Germany a few days earlier, but rather says, "the poor sick Cause [of Dissonant Music]" needed "valiant fighters." Even before this, Charles had tried to comfort her without much success: "As to the future of dissonant writing—don't be downhearted! Of course we have shot far beyond the level to which things will settle by 1950. But the farther beyond we go, the higher that level will be—so cheer up."[36]

The Hungarian pianist and composer Imre Weisshaus stood in the battlefields with her. A protégé of Cowell, Weisshaus had met Crawford earlier in New York, when he was completing a cross-country lecture-recital tour. Unlike Ruth, he recognized the links between politics and art at that moment and would later join the Resistance against the Nazis in the following years; he wrote a grim, politically astute letter to Vivian Fine shortly after his arrival. "Life over here is very hard," he said in somewhat idiosyncratic English, "and mixed with political tendencies . . . and at the present about 200,000 people are striking here. . . . And nothing seems worse than the future." He explained the disintegration of a musical focus as competition among different factions which left his kind of modernism in the dust:

> At the end there is a small group, not even a group any more, only here and there one poor individual, who say that music must go farther and they are the condemned, the old-fashioned, the conservative, because they are the progressives![37]

Minimizing the threat Hitler posed, Crawford concentrated on cultural politics, writing an extraordinary letter to Vivian Fine that stands as a manifesto for her work. It denounced neoclassicism in familiar terms:

> The Europeans seem to feel more and more that they have passed through a kind of poisonous gas belt of dissonance, that now they can . . . sit down again in easy chairs to *enjoy* music instead of perspiring over it.

She continued in a visionary vein unlike any other letter that she wrote that year, mediating her personal idiom with a more inclusive hope for a stylistic messiah—the "great composer" who could embrace and integrate oppositions:

> Though it is increasingly easy to becomes depressed by this strong tendency, my feeling (I think not blinded by having gotten in a "rut" of dissonance) is

still unshaken: that dissonant music, having rushed to an extreme of dissonance as a reaction from romanticism, will yet find the great composer who
will mold from a *mixture* of consonance and dissonance a great music which is
not only dryly intellectual, as most dissonant music has been so far, but carrying also a deep simplicity—emotion, if we want to use the word—which will
link it with the *people* as with the intellectuals. This may happen very far in the
future. But I can't believe, as many do, that a medium in which so few of the
possibilities have been touched, can be lost, dropped, after fifteen years of
trial.[38]

This revitalizing synthesis for contemporary music still challenges contemporary composers. The underscored word "people," which would surface
prominently in American discourse in the coming years, probably reflects her
awareness of the left-wing musical politics of Weisshaus and his anti-fascist
friends. In the 1930s both Crawford and Weisshaus would search for the "people" in different ways and share similar ironies: she in New York, and he, after
hair-raising escapes from the Nazis and a stint in the French underground, in
Paris (where he was reborn as Paul Arma). Each would try to create new directions for reasons not unlike those defining Berlin's crisis; each would attempt to bridge the gulf between modernism and radical politics; and each
would lose one way to be progressive and find another.

Back then the two dissidents found solace in each other. Crawford moved
to the suburb Charlottenburg to be near Imre and his American wife Virginia,
taking rooms at Joachim Friedrich Strasse 50 with a Frau Von Borckeand. She
wrote Charles that Imre was "always in touch with the worth-while happenings in modern music." As the organizer of concerts at the Bauhaus in Dessau,
in December he introduced Ruth to the great architect Moholy-Nagy, who
was staging both Hindemith's *Hin und Zurück* and Puccini's *Madama Butterfly* for the Kroll Opera's final season that year. She made a pilgrimage to the
Bauhaus in April, writing to Charles about its spiritual aura: "It is the most
optimistic place in feeling (I mean, the architecture, the space-feeling, the
light), a tremendous contrast to Berlin. I felt released, freed."[39]

January 1931 brought with it New Year's resolutions from Crawford to "come
out of her hermit existence for a while." How could an American composer
on a Guggenheim Fellowship come to a modernist mecca pulsating with
manic energy and not meet anyone? She had done just that. Now ready to
"make some of the connections [she] should have made months ago," Ruth
mounted a small campaign. She tried to settle the matter of her studying with
Schoenberg once again with Adolph Weiss:

> So far I have studied with no-one here. My work with Seeger last summer on his
> counterpoint book was very intense, and I felt it impossible to take in any new
> ideas until I had digested some of those already sketched. Thank you very much
> for the long detailed letter to Schoenberg; you were very kind to write so much.
> Unfortunately, it will be difficult or impossible to use, because I do not expect
> to study with him. . . . Even at the time when we talked together last spring, you

and I . . . have become convinced that it is, at least for awhile, necessary for me to work alone. Also . . . I feel that Seeger has given me such a myriad of ideas to work out—extremely interesting ones—that it would be a great mistake to work with anyone else before some of them are carried out in music. . . . It would be of great interest to me to meet Schoenberg, talk with him, and if he wished, to show him some of my work. Would it be too much to ask, that you write a few words for me to use as an introduction to him? I would appreciate this immensely.

Still, Crawford did not call, instead making preliminary contacts with other people whose names and addresses Weiss and Cowell had given her. And she began to like Berlin more.[40]

In January 1931 she met Cowell's Soviet friend, the scientist and avid amateur musican Ernst Chain, and through him, the composer Mieczwslaw Kolinski, whose theories on consonance and dissonance interested her. They played music by Feinberg and Stantschinsky, which got her "tremendously excited." Its "bold vigorous contrapuntability" resurrected her old plan of going to the Soviet Union. In addition, she decided to ask the Guggenheim Foundation for a year's extension, writing a long letter to Henry Moe about her progress. She was willing to stay longer, perhaps, as she told Charles, for six months, as Aaron Copland had. Seeger raised this option as early as November and in March she asked him to write a letter of reference, in part to justify her using three months of the fellowship to work on his book.[41]

Adopting the formal tone appropriate for fellowship committees, Seeger explained how the summer had not been wasted because it allowed her to "consolidate her winter's learning"; he now felt that she could leave for Europe

"on her own feet," no longer a student in the narrow sense of the term. Her entry into the musical life of Berlin and the compositions she has sent me since October prove this is so. I hope your committee will extend her term another year. It will be interesting to see what she accomplishes.

Had the Guggenheim Fellowship committee considered her a "student in the narrow sense of the term," they would never have awarded her the first year abroad. Charles asked Ruth to "forgive the unbearable snottiness [of his letter]. I think it is more impressive, though my very heart goes with it."[42]

In another spurt of ambition, Crawford, with some help from Imre Weisshaus, helped Cowell lay the groundwork for a series of concerts of American music for Berlin, Paris, and Vienna in the summer and fall of 1931. Transatlantic conferences by letter discussed the program and details, with this summation by Charles a few months later: "Henry says most emphatically that you are in charge." (This most likely referred to practical arrangements, not programming.) Ruth expected Slonimsky to conduct her new songs in Berlin, which happened in March 1932, on his historic tour.[43]

The concert aimed at combating the "false impression" that American music was "trivial" by performing "serious" American works, Cowell wrote to potential patrons. Toward that same end, he had published three "reports from America" in the German magazine *Melos*. One report reiterated the widely held view that jazz, although received by most Europeans as the quintessential American music, was in fact outsider art: "Negro Music seen through the eyes of Tin Pan Alley Jews." Repudiating the claims of composers like Copland and Gershwin, who had "pretensions of writing the authentic American music," Cowell proclaimed the "true Americans as the Anglo Saxon Charles Ives and Carl Ruggles." Did these judgments mask resentment at the success of his rivals? Colliding definitions of American identity ill served his larger purpose and, in hindsight, expose a man that most people cherished for his open-mindedness to charges of anti-Semitism. (Years later his wife bristled at them, asking Seeger to explain. He suggested that they were not typical of the man that he knew, although typical of the times, for perhaps Cowell "might have succumbed to the rather prevalent feeling [of anti-Semitism] among composers in the 20s and 30s on account of his not having clicked with Aaron Copland.")[44]

Crawford occasionally transgressed along those lines as well. She had grown up with enough prejudice to expect her Jewish employer at the Chicago theater where she worked in the early 1920s to cheat her. Even though in New York she had stoutly reproached Carl Ruggles for his bigotry, she too occasionally hinted at prevailing resentments against Jewish composers being aided by Jewish patrons. "If I had a Hebrew grandmother," then New York opportunities might be greater, she told Charles that year. Perhaps the climate in Berlin made her more introspective about this fault, for she confessed further how she occasionally reacted to Jews as if they were "Uriah Heep" characters—and hated that about herself. Cowell could hardly have known how his writing foreshadowed German reaction, as the Nazis would later (independently) use the caricature of an African American jazz musician wearing a Star of David on his lapel as a symbol of "Degenerate Music."[45]

In December Crawford found herself mentioned in a second "report from America" in *Melos*. Cowell wrote what he had said to Seeger and to others: that this "young woman from Chicago has at her disposal a better style and more originality than any other woman composer, whose works I am familiar with." His evaluation was based on knowledge of her Chicago work and its rich evocative harmonic language:

> One perceives that she follows the same course as men, although she does not have the ambition to become masculine in her music, in other ways a strong idiom leaves traces of feminine feeling. Her music belongs to no group. The basis of her originality lies in this fact: in the richly complex use of chords, which are not conventional even among modernists. She has found a tone-palette that is off the beaten path from most general harmonic practices.[46]

In contrast to Seeger, who disparaged her Chicago style, Cowell admired it, albeit in highly gendered terms that once again emphasized her exceptional status. More important, Cowell provided her with some additional visibility in Berlin.

Recouping her energies after the December push, Crawford returned to composition. Yet, in spite of enthusiasm conveyed to Henry Moe, she could not start the crucial orchestral project; efforts to work in that genre precipitated bouts of insecurity. She mulled over the possibility of seeking advice in orchestration (Schreker or Hindemith? she asked Charles), chided herself about being "a little lazy in seeking out the right person," and said she was

> a little afraid too of disgracing not only myself but America with my slow ways and the small amount of score-reading I have done and my not-great knowledge (or memory if I have known) of the classics.[47]

At just this moment of vulnerability, she began having difficulties with her friend Imre Weisshaus, plunging her further into a quagmire of doubt. Crawford began to chafe at Weisshaus's air of superiority toward both her and his wife. He "tried to dominate," she said. He in turn accused her of leaning on his ideas too much, that her "inferiority complex" made her appropriate other people's ideas. She was engulfed in a swamp of self-doubt:

> Am I not inclined to take hold of someone else's idea—many of yours, two of Imre's—and call them mine? Of course, the music that comes out is different from what you would have written, or what Imre writes—I have noticed that, and am thankful for at least this sign of individuality. But is the appropriating of the idea condonable, even though the result projects a personality which is myself and not someone else?[48]

This question, ostensibly about Weisshaus, also touched on her relationship with Seeger. If the answer were yes, then perhaps more separation should and would follow. Perhaps her ideal of love and work merging into one contained this fatal flaw. But Charles reassured her as fast as possible. He regarded the need for artistic originality as a contemporary curse, sharing an alternative model of creativity with Ruth at this crucial moment. All the words defining instants along the continuum of creative interplay—copying, influencing, appropriating, borrowing, collaborating, stealing—only underscored the true relational essence of art. What mattered was not originality but identity—the stamp of personality and expressiveness that each artist imparted to a work as a medium or a technique was absorbed and assimilated, reinvented and reimagined. On February 7 he wrote:

> Appropriate all you can. All may not be fair in love or war—but in art it is; if you can take another person's idea the situation is very easy to evaluate. The originator's presentation and the appropriator's stand eventually side by side. The best is the best. Who should bother about the origin? How can we tell that the "originator" did not swipe somebody else's idea anyway? Oh I could punch Imre in the solar plexus. Bah. The idea of patenting musical ideas. Naturally I feel badly when Henry almost goes out of his way to omit my name from the list of those to whom he owes much of his stuff—even the titles, form and character of definite works. But he acknowledges it even more by concealing it.[49]

(The issue of credit with respect to Cowell bothered him for years.)

Ruth was grateful. She honored Charles with the tribute that this and his previous letter were the finest, dearest, most helpful letters you have blessed me with. . . . Dearest, if you knew how these letters helped me. Dear, dear, they were like a new life living in me. I had been dead.[50]

Her Guggeheim promise to write an orchestral work weighed heavily on her shoulders, and after two frustrating weeks, she abandoned the project altogether. In early winter Seeger proposed that she write an orchestral work building on the chamber music idiom of "Rat Riddles," returning a month later to his "suggestion that instead of starting in on a composition for full orchestra, you might make a try at some half- or third-way stage?"[51]

Crawford had already launched herself on a new project. Acting against his advice to stay away from writing for strings—as it might lead to Romantic habits—she decided on a string quartet. Although Crawford had wanted to write one in the spring of 1930, Seeger had discouraged her. Now "in spite of year-old warnings," she was fulfilling this wish in a genre that had no "haunts" of orchestral anxiety hanging over it. She described her emergence from depression in detail.

> That morning, before they [the letters] came, I had again tried to write, and had again found myself tied in knots. Then in disgust I sat on the radiator, and prompted by a restless hurt over a happening with Imre that morning which was making myself ask again as I have often the last few weeks what kind of a friend I am. I began to write down all my fears and was rather appalled. Fear of people, fear of what they will think, fear of not being equal to a friendship, fear of having nothing to say musically, fear of not being able to say it, fear, fear, a whole web of it. To be constructive, I decided to find out what I am *not* afraid of, but didn't get very far. I did see more clearly though, how foolish this fear of people is. And I did too see how Imre and Virginia, while helping me very much in certain ways, have yet for the time being tied me too.[52]

What courage she showed in facing her own demons. Although this letter may seem like more self-reproach, in fact, it marked a stage of freedom from debilitating ambivalence, played out in her vacillations between rebelliousness and submissiveness. When freed from this enervating battle, the truer part of her—the composer—could emerge, releasing the strength of her gifts:

> I went to the piano and began a one-voiced something in metric form and was rather pleased with it. . . . The next day I took the little monody, which is lyric, and gave it a leggiero pal with a bass voice, and it insisted on becoming a string quartet. I have been wanting to write one for months—you tried to dissuade me last Spring, but the desire has come again many times this fall, so I might as well get it out. And the music came more easily, and after these six months of almost complete silence, it is such a relief. You did it. You pulled me up. You freed me.[53]

Two weeks later Crawford returned to the same theme. The quartet was going well and now that it was launched, she told Seeger more about it:

> Dear . . . your idea about a bridge on the way to something for large orchestra did help me though I forgot to tell you. It enabled me to put away the orchestral

sketch to begin with. I wanted to tackle something which had no haunts hanging over it, also something which would have as little to do with tone-color as possible, enabling me to be as abstract as I wished. I am so thankful to be writing again. There was so much responsibility attached to even a work for small orchestra that I was—afraid![54]

It is hard to fathom this fear from a composer who had already written a suite for chamber orchestra several years earlier. Perhaps the block had deeper roots in her own psychic conflicts about a career and a life as she contemplated writing in a male-identified genre. Earlier in the letter, she wrote:

It was strange. It simply wouldn't go. I moped a while, worked on the quartet awhile, then went to the vegetarian restaurant with German-French grammar. . . . Home again, more work on the quartet, but not very satisfactory. It needs you. You're very dear, assuring me on page 3 of this last letter that "you are not interfering or disciplining me." I am no longer afraid of that, and you needn't be. My little fling at "independence" is past, and my worry about it, and autonomy etc. . . . Smile at your child who in the fall and winter cried for independence. And how my music longs for you, knowing well that you know how to guide it, to inspire, to send it like a sky-rocket exiting, and yet, let it find its own path.[55]

In her letters to Seeger throughout the year, Crawford wavered between pronouncements of independence and reaffirmations of its opposite. One month a "declaration of independence," the next month a cri de coeur for advice from "dear idol Charlie." On one level it is easy to understand her. If she did not need him, would he still love her; if she needed him too much, could she still compose?

Both the student/teacher and child/father models disarmed the gods of competitiveness. Her ability to read the best into Seeger's words and discard the worst boded well for their union. Still, the pattern of vacillation—irrespective of the particulars—undermined her own energy to nurture the best in herself. This time she surmounted its debilitating effects. On March 12 she wrote how "the new movement just beginning is an experiment." By April there was "one movement finished, another thwarted, and the third waiting for the second to decide what to do." These were most likely the third and fourth movements, since they are referred to as "the last two movements" in another letter later in June.[56]

Charles wrote enthusiastically about the new piece:

I am so glad the quartet is going well. There are several things I never had time to tell you about string writing. You probably know them anyway but one easily forgets, especially if one has been brought up by the piano.[57]

It mattered not in the least. To be sure, she did not then write the orchestral work about which she was so equivocal. But despite her claims and protestations about how much she needed Charlie, she wrote her best work without him, in a genre that he said was not right for her at the time. Although Seeger would later describe the last two movements (which are based on dissonant-counterpoint theory) as "assignments," they could have been such only in the most abstract sense. Perhaps the couple heard foghorns at New Year's, as he once claimed, and that suggested dissonant dynamics; perhaps she had started the fourth movement in two-part counterpoint as some sort of diaphonic exercise. However, in contrast to so many of her earlier exercises—the Diaphonic Suites she called "ours," the orchestral sketch labeled an ersatz "child" —she never indicated anything of the sort in relation to the String Quartet 1931.

Spring in Berlin found Crawford more actively engaged in the city's musical life and more optimistic in general. She was cheered by news of a performance of the Diaphonic Suite for Flute that Marion Bauer had programmed for a League of Composers Concert on March 1. And Seeger had duly helped with the details. "I have told her [Marion Bauer] that I would take charge of the rehearsing of the Diaphony if they wish to do it. . . . I don't know how reliable M.B. is or whether she can speak legitimately in so authoritative a way. But she does seem to be a good friend of yours and I am trying to be nice to her." Despite his "disfavor of female composers," Colin McPhee had some kind words for Crawford in a review for *Modern Music*, saying that the "calm and enigmatic" flute solo stood out in his memory after the evening. And on March 9 Mina Hager sang one from the 1929 group of Five Songs on Sandburg texts for a concert in Chicago to weak reviews.[58]

In March Crawford had to weather a serious blow to her plans. Renewals of Guggenheim Fellowships were often granted without too much formality, but in this case she was refused. Even though the lists came out in late March without her name, both she and Seeger let themselves believe in a remote possibility that since only two composers (Cowell and Luening) had received grants, perhaps the lists were incomplete. Throughout the rest of the spring and even early summer, Crawford continued to write to Moe and sent him scores in June making her case.[59]

In April Crawford was busy with her first professional event of her year: a concert of American music in Berlin sponsored jointly by the Pan American Association of Composers (planned by Cowell) and the Novembergruppe. Through Weisshaus, whose music was also to be featured on the evening, she approached Vladimir Vogel, a prominent composer in Berlin. Charles had heard and liked his Toccata for Piano at a League of Composers Concert.[60]

In late March Vogel invited Crawford to a "Musikabend" to play her piano preludes. This was just the kind of invitation she needed. Even though the critic Hans Stuckenschmidt, who was known for his open-mindedness about American music, arrived too late to hear her play, she chalked up a few celebrities: "it was a rather imposing party . . . quite a few celebrities—Hans Gutmann of the cold Egyptian face," Wiener, an important man in radio; Balan, the music publisher of Schoenberg and Hindemith. Some issues of *New Music Quarterly* "were passed about, off and on, during the entire evening and seemed to cause interest. Balan talks about wishing to be the Berlin Vertreter." When Ruth took her work to Balan's office in early April, however, he turned her down. She was upset, particularly because Jerzy Fitelberg, whose music she disliked, was there at the time and treated her with condescension. "He whipped the pages of my rat and my suites, looking around the room between whips, turning a page every two seconds. . . . He has a hand whose touch to a page of manuscript is sacrilegious." Typically self-conscious when being un-nice, she added a postscript: "Jealousy from Ruth Crawford Composerin."[61]

Crawford proposed her latest Diaphonic Suite for Viola (or Oboe) and Cello for the Pan American/Novembergruppe concert, scheduled for April 8. Al-though prospects for a credible performance looked good, as the concert drew closer, things fell apart. When, to her dismay, the viola player quit at the last moment, Vogel delayed in finding a replacement until the day before the con-cert. After two "terribly painful" hours of rehearsal with the new player, Craw-ford reluctantly suggested that the last movement not be played. The morning of the concert she arrived at the hall to find no arrangements made for set-up; no piano; no critics invited personally, even though news releases were sent out. She blamed these and other unspecified "unpleasantnesses" on Vogel.[62]

But the concert went "passably well," considering. The Kunststube was full; Weisshaus's position at the Bauhaus also attracted "quite a number of Berlin well-knowns" in the audience, including the architect Moholy-Nagy and the Regisseur of the opera (probably Curjel). The program was balanced between American composers associated with either *New Music Quarterly* or the PAAC and composers who had lived and worked in Berlin. It included Cow-ell's wild "Banshee"; the "Airplane Sonata" by George Antheil, already well known in Germany; and works by the Cuban composer Alejandro Garcia Caturla and Adolph Weiss. Weisshaus played his own sprawling eleven-minute piano study, which Crawford had heard in New York, and two other works, including a piece for solo flute.[63]

For her efforts, Crawford ended up with two minutes' worth of music, no-tably less than Imre's fifteen-minute display. Even Imre's wife, Ruth com-mented, "asked me why another work of mine was not done instead of three of Imre's." Seeger was furious:

> What made me mad was that Imre's flute piece was played instead of Ruth's. I am shaking you because you did not insist upon *your* work being played by Draber and I am criticizing Imre for not seeing that his name appeared once too often on the program and for not being enough of a gentleman to insist upon your work being done. . . . Otherwise, I await with interest the account of things.[64]

Ruth then made her excuses, explaining to Charles that the insulting choice had been Vogel's doing, not Imre's. And then the Methodistical girl is-sued further pronouncements of martyrdom. Instead of annoyance, she was "really glad—almost jubilant" about Imre's share of the program because he had been depressed, and she was "very anxious to hear the violin solo done since it interested me as an experiment in glissando"; besides, their relation-ship was beginning to get twisted and she was anxious to avoid "any further ir-ritations." In his old age, some fifty years later, Imre recalled Ruth as a "very sweet" person, with a gentleness or sweetness that was worthwhile, but in some way lacking in ambition.[65]

Crawford's music fared poorly among German critics. The *Berliner Morgen Post* dismissed her in one sentence: "The work of a lady, Diaphonic Suite for Viola and Cello by Ruth Crawford seemed so bloodless because completely insignificant musical material was so overworked." But two unexpected events saved the day for her. Her friend Edgar Mowrer gave her a long review in the *Chicago Daily News*, casting the evening as a triumph for her.

> Antheil's second sonata and Ruth Crawford's Diaphonic Suite were the most interesting of the evening's dishes. Miss Crawford allows a viola and a cello to talk simultaneously, with the effect of hearing two telephone voices at once. At the end of the second movement the two speakers begin to coalesce. Her aim, as she stated, was to achieve new effects in atonal music and her success was apparent. Perhaps it is necessary for her to plunge ever more deeply into "visible music"—meant to be read rather than heard—before again realizing that the ultimate criterion must be the ear.[66]

"It was interesting reading the amusing clipping of Mowrer," Crawford wrote, after receiving a copy from Vivian Fine a few months later. She was heartened more by an invitation from the head of the Hamburg chapter of the International Society of Contemporary Music to submit her scores for a concert of "Frauen als Komponisten" (Women as Composers) that was to be held the following year. Crawford followed through with a copy of "Rat Riddles" and a work by Vivian Fine as well. (The result was to be a second performance of the Diaphonic Suite for Viola (or Oboe) and Cello in Hamburg on December 8, 1931.)[67]

The rest of April passed in frenetic activity, as Crawford planned to leave or not leave Berlin. She saw the memorable production of *Fidelio* at the Kroll, adorned with the spectacular sets of Moholy-Nagy. On April 10 she went to a concert conducted by Otto Klemperer, in a rare appearance for the local chapter of the International Society for Contemporary Music, where Webern's Symphony Op. 21 elicited the same kind of scorn that it had in New York in 1929.[68]

At the very end of her stay in Berlin Crawford tried to cram in visits with composers and potential publishers. In the last two weeks she called Adolph Mersmann, an editor of *Melos*, and visited the music publisher Peter Limbach. She arranged a reading of the Diaphonic Suites for Two Clarinets. And at last she approached Schoenberg and Hindemith only when the thought of leaving the deed undone was more painful than its doing. When she finally called Schoenberg at the end of March, he was irritable and abrupt, putting her off for a week. A still further week's procrastination on her part ruled out their meeting, for having suffered from influenza during the unusually raw winter, Schoenberg left early for the country. She bemoaned the fact to Charles. "Through my own carelessness, partly, I am missing Schoenberg; he is now *verreist*" (gone away on a journey). Unbeknownst to her, he had been expecting to hear from her earlier. She explained the matter grumpily:

> Only accidentally the evening before I left, did I hear from [Josef] Rufer about Weiss, the well-meaning little rascal, having written to Schoenberg about me. . . .

> So I get in touch with Schoenberg, not knowing this. . . . It naturally didn't set very
> well that the prospective pupil gets in touch with him only on leaving Berlin.[69]

Crawford arranged to talk with Rufer (Schoenberg's assistant) instead. At first Rufer was "frightfully rude" to her but eventually they had two days of "wonderful talks." He became "extraordinarily sympathetic," and he showed her the manuscript for his book on Schoenberg's counterpoint which Ruth had mentioned to Charles in January. (She had urged Charles to "do his durndest," as his "book SHOULD NOT come out later.") To their rival, Rufer, Crawford broached her American alternative to Schoenberg's theories, suggesting that traditional counterpoint might be bypassed because "a discipline should be experienced in the medium in which the composer will finally compose." Considering that Schoenberg spent his class time discussing one tonal piece for four hours a week, twice a week for fourteen weeks, bringing in his own twelve-tone compositions only at the last class meeting, how could his amanuensis Rufer countenance the discarding of traditional training? On that point Crawford doubted that Rufer would ever agree with them. He did not look at her music.[70]

Nothing redeemed Crawford's encounter with Hindemith, whom she described as "cocksure." She was left with "a bad taste," thinking she "should not have gone," that the "psychology was bad." Putting the best face on it, she wrote to Seeger that given her dislike of Hindemith's recent music, perhaps it was just as well. A performance of his Concert Music for Brass, Piano and Two Harps, op. 49 (commissioned by Elizabeth Sprague Coolidge and premiered at the Coolidge Festival in Chicago, October 12, 1930), had its Berlin premiere on April 25, with Walter Gieseking at the piano and Otto Klemperer conducting; she disliked it sufficiently to salvage her wounded pride, for even Hindemith's elegant orchestration did not compensate for his archaicizing technique. The Chopinesque third movement was too sweet for her taste and "unusually bad . . . something is happening all the time, it warbles on, an unending rivulet, or sometimes stops in a Watteau landscape and sentimentalizes Chopin-Field."[71]

As she planned to leave Berlin, Crawford reflected on the experience, trying to understand her own behavior as a factor in repeated rejections. There was no question she had been wounded. Too few people had bothered to look at her music; Vogel had slighted her; Rufer and Hindemith had been rude; Balan had turned down her work; the Novembergruppe concert had been disappointing. She resented Teutonic superiority and what George Antheil labeled an "incomprehensibility that 'true music' could possibly be composed outside the borders of Germany-Austria-Hungary." Crawford told Seeger that "Germans simply can't stand the hurt of having to admit that there is anything someone else can understand better than they."[72]

Still, she had to bear some of the responsibility. Other American composers fared better than she. Cowell, for example, managed a relationship with Schoenberg even though he had disparaged Schoenberg's "inexorable equations and formulas" in the December 1930 issue of *Melos*. After meeting

Schoenberg (apparently on the courts of the Berlin Tennis Club), Cowell was invited to play some of his works before Schoenberg's composition class and occasionally participate in the class as a guest. Roger Sessions, not yet an established composer, was befriended by Otto Klemperer in 1931; Aaron Copland, who had more of a reputation than Sessions, followed in his footsteps in May, deciding rather quickly to arrange a concert of new American music for December when he perceived how little his generation was known. Crawford met a contented Copland in passing at a concert in May, then wondered about the possibility of her own complicity in her unhappy experience.[73]

> It is strange—there is a certain psychology in me in wanting to hurt Berlin and people in Berlin because she too has hurt me. I meet Hindemith two days before leaving though I've been here six months. . . . I've discovered in myself a delight in showing the German people that I can get on without them.

Her relationship with Seeger served as her defense. She

> had gone through the months here, looking Germany straight in the face and not giving a damn what she [Germany] said or thought—or only a very small damn—because, more important, you love me, trust me, want me. Naturally I was glad if I were liked or my music liked—all the more then to take to you. But if I weren't, it didn't hurt as it would have. . . . You have lifted me beyond my normal bravery and self-confidence and independence.[74]

A few months later she cast it all in still a different light. Blaming herself more rather than less, she admitted her reclusiveness in Berlin. Her successful networking in Paris demonstrated the path she might have followed in Berlin rather than "hiding in my shell."[75]

But even so, the general atmosphere, outside of cultured circles, disturbed her. The inner core of the city looked normal; one could have coffee at the American Restaurant on Unter den Linden, soak up the sun coming through the trees, walk in the Tiergarten, attend opera constantly. But in the outskirts, the sprawling slums and squalor of life made the city seem ominous. On Easter Sunday she painted a portrait of grimness stalking the holiday:

> I walked along the old cemetery full of heavy black tombstones that seemed to me just one more typical symbol of the heavy German spirit. . . . Everywhere today the German family was abroad intact. Papa, Mama oder Kinder. . . . Yet none of them seemed very happy. No one rollicks here; is it only the hard times?[76]

"She should have gone to Vienna. Berlin was a mistake," Charles Seeger said fifty years after the fact. Certainly her letters from her week's stay in Vienna radiate a new contentment and more welcoming encounters with musicians. Even an inauspicious interview in May with Emil Hertzka, the powerful director of Universal Editions and perhaps the most progressive music publisher in Europe, did not deflate her. She found him a

> pleasant kind person. But no chance for publishing I'm afraid, although he showed me a terrible sonata from an American who is studying with Krenek,

just published. One thing he said made me rather boil, tho all I did outwardly was to ask him what he meant. The thing he said was that of course it would be particularly hard for a woman to get anything published. What is this for reasoning? He didn't see my music. He had lost money in publishing the music of Ethel Smyth.[77]

The publisher of Bartók, Schoenberg, and Weill, noted for his advocacy of experimental music and young composers, told her that she could send on her music "without hope."

The incident impressed upon her the consequences of her prior isolation in Berlin. Hertzka had asked her for a letter from Wilhelm Gross, a Krenek pupil. Had she been known as Krenek's pupil or Hindemith's pupil, or even as a pupil of a pupil, she told Seeger, then perhaps it would have been a different story.[78]

Crawford recovered her professional aplomb the next day, turning her five-day stay in Vienna into one of the highpoints of the year. Rather than reproaching herself for not writing courteous letters of intent to a check-list of composers—as Imre had urged her to do—she decided that she would rather meet people spontaneously. With her Guggenheim letter in tow, and without any advance notice, Crawford dropped in on Alban Berg at 6:30 in the evening, handed him the letter through the crack in the door and waited. "He opened the door a peek" and Ruth "added Berg to Klemperer" on her list of attractive men: "A huge six-foot mensch in a brown bathrobe, a shock of dark hair, a kind big-featured hospitable face and sympathetic voice."[79]

Berg put off this stranger by suggesting that she call the next day to see if a lesson could be arranged and then refused to see her; he was leaving town in two days. Crawford "cried a bit in St. Stephens Cathedral." Then in a burst of determination so different from her behavior in Berlin, she persisted. She returned to Berg's house only to retrieve the Guggenheim letter from the maid, and then went back and rang the bell a third time. Her nerve was rewarded. Berg answered the door and was trapped: a Thursday appointment was arranged.

The meeting with Berg ranged from a discussion of trends in German music to specific work with some of her compositions. Crawford surprised Berg with her ideas about dissonant counterpoint, a "direction" he did not associate with American music, and one to which he was "sympathetic." She played two early preludes and showed him the choruses for women's voices, probably her least contrapuntal compositions. They "worked them over for quite a while—one wishes that Crawford had been more specific here—and then Berg summed up her style as "too harmonic, too homophonic." Even though she showed him her Diaphonic Suites, he insisted that her polyphony "was still not contrapuntal in his sense of the word." Unfortunately, she had forgotten to bring the quartet movement (probably the first), "which has crabs, canons, contraries, and everything German (I didn't say that!)."[80]

The meeting concluded with some sparring about trends in new music. Contrary to Crawford's own opposition to neoclassicism, or as she corrected him, "Neo-Romanticism," Berg did not see it as "going backward." She then boldly pressed on, venturing a controversial comment that "Schoenberg's work until op. 25 pleases me more than his later work. . . . I am trying to develop (polite) frankness," Crawford wrote Seeger, "and make myself lose my fear of expressing an opinion." One marvels at Crawford's quiet phrase "polite frankness" to describe the manner in which she, an unknown American, criticized Schoenberg to one of his disciples. It soured the encounter somewhat. "Berg was really very sympathetic but not so much so as I'd had hoped. He is more German and more Schoenberg worshipper than I would have thought." She left with an impression of a "towering personality."[81]

Crawford had made better plans for Budapest, asking Imre Weisshaus to write letters ahead to Béla Bartók, Paul Kadosa, and a few others. "He has been so kind and terribly interested in helping me make decisions," Ruth wrote. "The coals of old irritations aren't completely dead, but we try to be careful not to fan them." Beyond a charming reception and a willingness to look at her music, Egon Wellesz said little. Josef Hauer, on the other hand, as a competitive inventor of a post-tonal system, had his views weighed as for or against hers and Seeger's. Crawford's total conviction about the merits of her training with Seeger made these contacts turn into "comparative tests of their ideas" against those prevailing in Europe. Like them, she told Seeger, Hauer espoused "unity, something to hold the structure together, a new system to replace the old, instead of a chaotic overthrowing of all laws." Like them he avowed tonal centricity, and Crawford showed him her Diaphonic Suite for Two Clarinets as a work in which E is taken as the tonality—"as proof that what he says regarding my music and all the rest, Schoenberg, Hindemith and everyone else is not true—that we are seeking for a center, a unity." Defending herself against his charge of tonality, Crawford hazarded a comment about Hauer's own opera: parts were "tonalitous too!"[82]

In early May Crawford traveled to Budapest for "three wild days," cramming in visits with Kadosa and László Lajtha, from whom she learned with envy that "Mrs. Coolidge had ordered a quartet from him."

She even managed a visit with Béla Bartók at the Academy, for only a few minutes because he had a performance in Vienna the next day. Again she had dropped in unannounced the previous morning, handing him her Guggenheim letter as an introduction. At this visit "he was very kind and quite interested too." Later that day Crawford went to his house to retrieve her letter and was granted more time.

> Childlike he showed me his Arabian and Hungarian flutes, and other things. Turned his back, told me not to look and asked me to guess while he played a Jew's Harp. From the subject of overtones, I excitedly branched to undertones and told him what I also forgot to tell you—that Imre and I with a tuning fork on the edge of a piece of paper got the undertones as far as the 7th. He was surprised, said he had understood they were only theoretical and I was inside "tickled" to be able to tell him something. He is a dear quiet shy little person, isn't he![83]

But she did not have time to show him her music. Had she written ahead, he would have been glad to see it.

After Vienna and Budapest Crawford returned to Germany to attend the Festival of Modern Music in Munich under the aegis of Hermann Scherchen. Her letters mention a quarter-tone opera by Haba, but not Stravinsky's *Oedipus Rex*, one of the main works presented. Meanwhile, she received news from home through Seeger.

On May 7 Gerald Reynolds conducted the simplest of her Three Chants, "To an Angel," in a performance that Seeger could find no kinder word for than "adequate." The tempo dragged, he wrote, and the sevenths occasionally slid into octaves. Reynolds was "nervous" and if criticized in rehearsal might just have put the whole thing off. "It is a lovely conception," Charles said, but Reynolds "had no idea of what it should sound like." The review in the *Musical Leader* praised the way she used the "timbre of the voices in a new and fascinating manner." Most other papers ignored it, and the *Brooklyn Eagle* found it worthless. It was the only performance of any of the chants in Crawford's lifetime. Crawford enlisted Reynolds in her campaign to extend the Guggenheim Fellowship and he wrote Moe that the "piece was entitled to hang in any good salon according to Russell Bennett." He himself reserved judgment.[84]

Plans for Ruth's reunion with Charles occupied them both in May. They wanted to spend the summer in Paris. What awaited them? Because of their intense correspondence over the year, they both believed they were different people, coming together in a different relationship. Their letters were a "long coda," she told him, adding "it is time for the second movement to begin instead." And it would—in beautiful Paris. "I didn't dream then of all that was going to happen in letters."[85]

"dear superwoman"

Perhaps had they been together, less might have been said. Ruth believed that "we have 4000 miles to thank for telling us things we might not have known: the discovery of sympathies and often incredible one-pathedness in thoughts and reactions across an ocean does certainly preclude proximity as an inter-influence." They typed and numbered their letters because they did not trust transatlantic mail, following the shipping news of arrivals and departures of the ships *Europa* and *Bremen* more closely than the weather. Over the year the voluminous correspondence totaled about a hundred letters from Ruth and fifty from Charles. In fact, they had produced a diary of their relationship.[1]

That fall of 1930 neither of them was quite sure of much except their shared commitment to dissonant music. "I don't know just what *has* happened," Charles told her. "Even if we never marry or meet again, we should always be related to one another in a lasting bond—a bond that started with friendship and was just sublimated by love." He then contradicted himself by declaring his passionate attachment to her.[2]

Ruth was overwhelmed. As a young girl in Chicago she had written sentimental fantasies to a perfect love, where "it will be as though our souls have talked and felt together since time was." In subsequent years how often had she wondered about her own ability to love. Now secure in new knowledge of herself and dizzy with joy, she wrote out an inspired confession:

Last night there came suddenly to me with definiteness of as something seen ahead out of the future, with a blessed richness it came—had I not known it before subconsciously, and now only it rises to let me touch it thankfully and with love—that you will always be for me the one great love. That you are the elusive mystery I had been waiting for.[3]

Few mortals could sustain that plane of intimate revelation all the time. In spite of such impassioned declarations, the two moderns also discussed sexual fidelity at length. They scorned bourgeois "possessiveness" and debated whether they should "save their bodies for each other."[4]

Theoretically, the answer to that explosive question should have been no. Initially they tried to practice what they preached by extending permission of sorts to the other to go ahead with affairs, and at the same time, disclaiming that desire for themselves. Amidst such principled martyrdom, things occasionally went awry. After Ruth revealed an innocuous flirtation with an English music critic staying at her pension, Charles responded in a text that reads like a theatrical set-piece:

> Like an ache in my heart is the feeling that I am sorry for your sake that you could not have the lovely adventure with the young Englishman complete with all its possible benefit to you, without a thought that it would interfere in any way with our love for each other. I feel I ought to tell you it would make no difference to me—that it would be a test for both of us to know that although you had this affair going on you would drop it as a matter of course as soon as we had a chance to be together again. No, not that it made no difference to me, but that I must urge you to do it in order to prove to yourself and to me that you and I do love each other as we say we do. . . . And I have to answer, I cannot bear to do it. . . . And your sad perturbation says you cannot do it. . . . In spite of our modern heads, our hearts still speak for constancy.[5]

Charles wrote of plans for their summer reunion, that he was arranging to lead a tour to Europe to defray expenses, that Constance would keep the two younger boys if he would plant a garden at Patterson, and then this final burst of emotion:

> I have a kind of trust in you that I have never experienced before. Whatever you do, I think I should feel was right for you to do. And I am tough as they make them and quite open-minded. . . . Such a gift of the gods you are, sometimes I can't help feeling a bit undeserving.[6]

Ruth responded in the same mercurial way. Describing her flirtatious side as her "gnome," she baited and then reassured Charles with details of the last stages of this ephemeral Berlin romance:

> Shall I be feminine and let the little gnome tease you, with a wink and a twinkle—that the problem solved itself almost as quickly as it arose. . . . Soon to my surprise I saw him again as the bored Englishman and became often annoyed at his views on music, so much so one time that I brought my fist down on the table at lunch with him and told him rather intensely to listen to music with a

little imagination (the subject was Trautwein's instrument). He and Frau Schwabe were quite surprised at the sudden vehemence.[7]

In her own way Ruth had a streak of toughness in her as well.

So the balance of power between teacher and student shifted as Ruth grew more confident. In a city which held homosexual balls in the winter, she considered herself worldly because she felt less awkward around men in casual society. Charles had advised her to stop spending so much time with women, as she had in Chicago, "to get out there with the men." And so she did in her own small way and made him eat his words.

Such patterns eventually took their toll. In March Ruth felt guilty of the small coquetries in her letters and told him she would stop playing the "*game of love*."[8] Then guilt induced a real crisis about her behavior. Unable to wait the two weeks or so until her letter arrived, an impatient Ruth sent a repentent radiogram in their musical love-code the very next day. Working on the Diaphonic Suite for Oboe (or Viola) and Cello, she wrote:

> Because the oboe discovers it has played thoughtless painful discords to the cello, a dissonant birdsong suffers intensely and begs the cello Monday and Tuesday to sing with the oboe the fleeting but victorious letter, especially last two lines.

The birdsong symbolized the bridge at Arlington, Vermont; the victorious letter, most likely her apology sent by ship.[9]

Other more substantive problems confronted them as they moved closer toward commitment. For by December the thorny question of marriage, that is, divorce and remarriage, had surfaced. Charles did not bring up how Constance had refused his earlier request for a divorce during his affair with Mona—and how relieved he had been. What Ruth knew about her rival (who left New York wishing Charles had died an early death) is unclear. Now he confessed his fears about such a drastic step once more. In what he later called a "horrid letter," he declared that the children "make the formal break with Constance unthinkable."[10]

But Ruth was undeterred. She would not be tempted into premature reproaches:

> [Your letter] did hurt. It had to be said. I am glad you said it. . . . It made me ask myself a number of questions. It made me remind myself that maybe next summer, God forbid, you will find a changed Ruth and (I can scarcely make myself write it), not love me anymore. It made me look into values much more clearly than theorizing ever did.[11]

Even with her own future jeopardized, Ruth could be patient and not press Charles to move faster than he could. Such moderation reassured her indecisive lover that conflict did not necessarily lead to anger—so hard for his Anglo-Saxon temperament to endure. "Dear understanding one," he addressed her in February. In another letter he wrote, "In a way, it is the very sanctum of love—to feel that the beloved grants the fineness that one wants to have but can so rarely be granted by one's self. Dearest idol."[12]

Ruth's charitable integrity only endeared her to him more. She continued to respond generously to Charles, as he began to undo his ties to the mother of his children at his own pace. Even though further vacillations followed, they had broached the forbidden topic without hysteria. That relieved Charles enough to admit rather quickly that he wanted to start over with her. On February 3 Charles sent Ruth a musical love letter—a setting of a sonnet by his Harvard classmate and friend, the poet John Hall Wheelock. "My darling, my beloved one," it ended. That line was added to their repertory of musical signatures. Ruth told him that

> the song you sent me is very lovely. There is a deep simplicity about it. . . . Parts of it come to me often, and it seems strangely, uncannily like your voice—not your physical voice, but something deep in you, silent yet heard. I have sung it a myriad of times, giving myself only the middle C, as you directed. . . . What you say about the sanctum of love has made its way deep into my love for you. . . . And the words about autonomy.[13]

Still, Charles had relapses of anxiety and indecision. In May Ruth received the most desperate letter of the year. Charles "hated to confess" how "helplessly miserable, dragged down and bewildered" he felt since February, because he did not know whether he possessed the resolve to undertake a divorce. On the advice of a friend, Seeger went to see a psychoanalyst and worked himself into a new resolve. He hoped his confession of weakness had killed Ruth's false images of him. In another letter he said, "With the difference in age between us as it is, we must reassure everything that will tend to make us equals, comrades in our chosen work. The most important thing for us is the children—not the music."[14]

In the midst of such turbulence, Ruth offered calmer parallel visions of their life together. She stressed their rare compatibility. She told him how she had "been waiting through the years for this unseparateable mixture of work and love . . . a terribly romantic old-fashioned idea for a modern young woman to have." Although the decision to divorce was his, she reminded him again how the union between work and love could help him as much as her.[15]

Charles answered her in a letter that clarified her true position in his own work life:

> You are perfectly right about my work. I have been very uncomfortable for many years because no concrete results were forthcoming. A year or two in Europe with you would see everything done. . . . There is no doubt that I associate doing things with you. When I speak of you as my inspiration, I mean it very literally as well as in other ways. . . . The plans for my work have been in my mind so long that in the last few years they have actually soured. The use of the word is pardonable when you know, as I think you do, the peculiar nature of my life with Constance and my apparently ineradicable feeling that creative work is not a function of a single individual, but rather of a mating not unlike love. Our work last summer is an example of what I mean.[16]

Thus this motif of work and love sprang from subtly different sources for each of them. To some extent, Charles's view of mutual creativity between husband and wife merged his insecurities with his sense of male entitlement. On the other hand, Ruth's views merged her ambition with her sense of vulnerability as a woman. Perhaps if she were willing to meet his needs, which came easily enough when his needs meant theories of dissonant counterpoint, then she could have both her career and a family. As if his book were not enough proof of how much the teacher thrived with the pupil, she reminded him of his musical composition, "The Letter," which he claimed was "the first time that the joy of writing naturally has ever come to me in the technique you and I admire."[17]

It was only natural that they would raise the subject of having children together. Ruth, who called herself the "October child" and the "February woman" now added a third role of mother:

> The birds were everywhere, making themselves heard, and children and baby-carriages abroad. I asked myself what the career was about anyway, and why I write music. But then I went further, and asked what the children are for anyway, just to grow up and have more children and so on ad libitum. . . . [18]

Could a woman be both composer and mother? As Charles contemplated such a life, his frequent address of Ruth as "my dear child" became:

> Dear Superwoman!
>
> If you knew how my heart warmed at the development of the I into the we and the child into the children—I should have been sad had they not! You have a big problem on your hands, though. . . . The woman with an art is one of the tragedies of our time. . . . I want to see if we cannot so manage that you will not be just one more woman who is neither a good mother or a good artist. Theoretically (and you know how I love theory) it depends on the basis of the theory whether you assume the *possibility* (1) that no woman can become an artist without giving up her womanhood (2) that any woman can be both a mother and an artist. . . . You know my first concern for you was the artist in you. The later concern for the woman has not ousted the first. My very heart is now in the problem of you. . . .
>
> Don't be too hard on yourself when it comes to the fears of not being able to feel, to compose, to be loved. Every civilized person has them and the more sensitive and worthwhile one is the more the fears bother one. To recognize them at all is half the victory! Just know that a fear is usually a conflict in values and with the one you love most, those values can be placed side by side and lived into until they are reconciled or one predominates. You have this to comfort you. You can write better music than any other woman in this country and one you love loves you. There is no obstacle to the loving that enough loving (feeling) cannot overcome. So what happens is best.[19]

Charles could not make up his own mind about his role in the "tragedy of a woman with an art." The little theoretical interlude in this letter of March 11, when the logical opposites are staked out as no-woman versus all-woman, reveal his habits of framing issues as dichotomies. Was Ruth's dilemma rooted in Woman's Nature?

Was Ruth-the-composer less of a woman? On one occasion Charles talked lightly of "the little woman soul of you that you keep so repressed in being this most manful of artists—the musician." On another he teased Ruth about her "presumptuous nose," the outward sign of the "man element in you that makes you want to write music." His pride in Ruth did not totally quell competitiveness. She answered forcefully. If her nose was masculine, she answered, then she was glad it was so prominent in her face, to remind her of the "feminine weakness" she overcame. If she had to have "man elements" to write music, then vanity fell before creativity. She did not analyze Charles's questions or retaliate with a discussion of his "feminine" side.[20]

Charles shifted between his own needs to reconstruct a family and his recognition of Ruth's gifts. A letter from March 17, 1931 contains both, acknowledging how "composition is very deeply ingrained in you," while asserting that "the most important thing for us is the children . . . not the music." Even amidst so much empathy, his Victorian construction of a separate sphere for the woman/composer, albeit in new psychological rhetoric, insured the isolation of her solution. On May 18 he asked her which she would choose—the "life of a mother or a composerin."

Ruth had been working through just these issues for months. She ignored his proclamation of the "tragedy of the woman with an art." Not only did she refuse to choose between work and love, but she explained their relationship as the means through which she might avoid such self-destruction. He himself—her teacher-lover—was the solution:

> If the career and the children find it possible to be built side by side, it will have been because you made it possible, not only through your love but through your understanding and realization of the difficulties and your *confidence* that, with the right attitude, they can be overcome. . . . I feel now a confidence which I never felt before, that the music could still continue in the midst of life. . . . But Charlie, it is only through that the vision of mother and music-maker have been so very simply united. I believe they could be realized though naturally it would not be easy.[21]

Plans for their reunion were made and then changed. Just before Charles was to sail in early June, his oldest son became dangerously ill with pneumonia. He could not leave as scheduled, so Ruth went on to Paris without him, arriving by June 7. She spent the first week finishing the quartet, completing one movement in a few days. On June 13, she sent off the score to the Guggenheim Foundation, still tenaciously pursuing a renewal of her fellowship. Apparently, there was still a chance: Charles had sent Ruth a radiogram in May with that bit of news.

After that Crawford began to enjoy the sights and city life, beginning a vacation of sorts by sharing an important event with friends from home. On June 6 she attended a historic concert of American orchestral music in Paris—the first one in the European tour sponsored by the Pan American Association of American Composers. The "sudden awakening of interest in American art-music in Europe," as Cowell described it, made 1931 a banner year for the ultra-moderns. Cowell would later report that "up to then there had never

been an important orchestra concert of American works in Europe," dismissing his rivals and moderate colleagues in one blow. Now his circle had its
chance to show all those condescending Europeans what American radical
composers had to say. The concert, underwritten by Ives, included *Three
Places in New England; Synchrony* by Cowell; *Intégrales* by Varèse; *American
Life* by Weiss; and *Men and Mountains* by Carl Ruggles, conducted by Nicolas
Slonimsky. Promoted by Varèse, who was in Paris at the time, the event became a happening—"it turned out that I had a brilliant audience," Slonimsky later wrote. "Honegger, Prokofiev . . . all the futurist musicians . . . all the
top critics . . . and we believed that this was the beginning of a new era." Ruth
wrote to Charles that it "went quite well. Henry really sounded surprisingly
good—some of his color combinations I like immensely, tho of course the
work is very impressionistic. Ives was well received, Weiss not so unusually,
tho played very well." She, along with Weiss and Varèse, sent a jointly signed
postcard of congratulations to Carl Ruggles on June 6, 1931. "*Men and Mountains* sounded fine, strong." To Carl Sandburg she wrote of Slonimsky's "phenomenal success," hoping that he could repeat it, for, as she said, he "expressed a great liking for the Rat ["Rat Riddles"] and wants to take the
youngster along together with the Bee ["In Tall Grass"] on next year's tour,
Havana, New York, Boston, probably Paris and other points."[22]

After the concert they went to Varèse's favorite cafe, "where painters etc.
gather, drink wine and play billiards," Ruth wrote Charles. They talked music,
Crawford defending Seeger against Varèse's (undescribed) critique. Apparently, at the time she had applied for the Guggenheim, she had asked Varèse
about studying with him, and he was willing to give her lessons free of charge.
But Charles questioned her intent, saying, "You can write better music than
Varèse, and you must take him as an equal." He told her how to manage this if
she insisted on lessons anyhow. The "whips" she could use to tame him were
"counterpoint—of which he knows little, and your excellent ear—better
than his." Therefore, Varèse could be helpful with instrumentation as opposed
to orchestration.[23]

Charles need not have armed her so fiercely, for she decided against the
plan for the moment and now had to explain her way out. (Although their
personal relationship always remained casual, Varèse did not forget Crawford's
music: many years later, when he was preparing a course on contemporary
music, he included her in his syllabus, and, through his request for her own
analysis, precipitated the lengthiest document that Crawford ever produced
about her own work.)

Toward the end of the month, Charles arrived at long last. The two took
rooms in a pension on Ile St. Louis. It was an idyllic time. Charles would later
say that he "met an entirely different person . . . who had grown at a tremendous rate" than the Ruth who had left ten months earlier. Only the ISCM festival at Oxford interrupted them. Ruth did not attend, probably because of the
risk of their relationship being exposed to other colleagues from New York.[24]

Worried about his job at the institute, Charles insisted on a certain
amount of secrecy. Ruth reassured him that she understood and, most impor-

tant, had stopped obsessing about it. Letters to Madame Crawford-Seeger arrived in his absence.

For all their talk about work, they did little that summer. This made them both somewhat fretful, for they invested so much in fostering mutual productivity. In the future, Ruth assured herself as well as him, "We will work, won't we? Our trouble this summer—wasn't it most that we weren't working together?"25

Charles had brought over the "Neumes," Ruth's nickname for the "Manual of Dissonant Counterpoint," for which he planned to write musical examples; this he did not do. Ruth wrote orchestral ostinati for "Rat Riddles" that summer for Slonimsky's concerts scheduled for Berlin in 1932, but she did not finish the orchestral piece. Instead they strolled along the Paris boulevards, made love, ate croissants at little cafes on the Ile St. Louis, and took pictures of the apartment where they lived together for the first time. If Charles would later bluntly admit, "that summer knocked her out, knocked me out too," he meant that the release from so much anxiety, so much separation, and so much emotional foreplay in letters, made them lovers first and musicians second. That summer he began to draft his essay about Crawford for Cowell's anthology *American Composers on American Music,* filling it with the usual comments about her being an exceptional woman composer, to be sure, but also with praise for her "absence of pretense," and the "increase in sureness of what she is about and a resourcefulness in going about it that are most gratifying."26

In August Ruth learned that the Guggenheim Fellowship would not be renewed. Charles comforted her, recalling the moment years later:

> As we walked by the wall of the Opéra the tears ran down and she said, "What's going to happen to me?" So I put my arm around her and took her across the street to the Café de Paris where we had a nice little alcove in the wall and ordered some refreshments, and I told her what was going to happen to her was that we were going to get married and that we would have some lovely children, but I can imagine the passersby seeing the older man—I was fourteen years older than she—with a weeping young woman and all the thoughts they would have and, of course, was delighted with the picture. We spent that night—I think we walked until sunrise around the streets of Paris, talking about how our future life would be together. And I finally decided that the best thing to do would be for her to stay a little longer in Paris and that I would hurry back to begin my work.27

At the time it was not quite so easy for him. In April 1931 he had commented on her plans to stay another year:

> For your sake, because you want it, I hope this is so. Yet in a way, I dread it because it means our continued separation, if only for a few months next fall. (I think they might let you return in January.) . . . And if you don't get another stipendium, would you not come back with me? My dear love, as long as we love each other, things will be all right won't they?28

Charles left for New York on September 21, resolved on divorce and eager to find an apartment where they could both live. The summer together sealed

Figure 10-1 Ruth's musical signature,
May 18, 1931, with initials as clef and
the last line from Charles's song, "The
Letter": "My darling, my beloved one."

their future. They signed their letters that fall with their initials placed on a staff or intertwined in little models of serial permutations, retrograding and inverting them (Fig. 10-1). Ruth stayed on in order to meet French composers and to show her work around, to satisfy herself that she had "done one's best under the circumstances." When would she ever be back? After a few black days, Ruth recovered—"I'm calm, and working. But I'm calm because we'll be together soon," she told Charles.[29]

She was at peace with the prospects for her future. After Charles left, she had a confirming dream about her vision of mother and music-maker, which involved a character from her Chicago past:

> In the other dream, Stella Roberts (sister of Marion Roberts who was killed here), and who (Stella) kissed me on both cheeks to my utter surprise (for she had always been very distant) after my violin sonata had been played at the I.S.C.M. in Chicago, and with memories of her sister begged me not to get "other things" entangled with my music! . . . Stella came to call. It was as though she knew nothing of you and me. We were talking in the hall, when you, not knowing she was there, came in. I can see you so clearly and feel again as I did in my dream myself full of love for you as I saw you there. I introduced you. Then later it was as tho Stella was very tired and we put her to bed and lay down ourselves.

Some days later, in response to Seeger's interpretation of the dream as fears of sexual infidelity, Crawford clarified its meaning for her as

> a silencing of my 'career vs. love and children' battle. Stella . . . had met you hostilely—and had utterly capitulated, allowing herself to be put to sleep like a child in the room where you and I would ourselves sleep.[30]

Seeger's paternal involvement in her work allayed her fears because she regarded composition as another form of joint offspring, finishing the letter with a clear statement of creative mutuality:

> How much you are part of all this best music I show to people—the best music starting from the suites only. It is us I show. . . .

Ruth had found a new peace and wholeness within herself and lent Charles some of her resolve: "My dearest, I know you have found courage. We *will* have to have it this year," she wrote to him.[31]

Then she threw herself into the musical and social swim of Paris, enjoying the same rush of excitement and "upper-crust life style" that she found in New

York in 1929, as she kept pace with appointments, concerts, even practicing an hour a day and copying music. She saw as many composers as possible. Time with the Hungarian composer Tibor Harsanyi was spent in an "amiable fight" discussing dissonant counterpoint. She told him that she and Seeger were looking for the same thing he was: "line—one of our main searches," and she added that "this principle is the one underlying an orchestral work which I am writing right now." Naturally she sneered quietly at the music of some neoclassicists, but tried to see Madame Nadia Boulanger. She was allotted ten minutes. "She says she's terribly sorry she can't see me longer or look at my music, since she is in the country and only in town one day. She knows already my preludes from New Music and asked me to send her anything I want after it is printed." There was however time enough for Boulanger to discuss "the bad effect of teaching the masses music."[32]

Others paid more attention. Albert Roussel

> looked at the quartet (the slow movement, which I had decided to dare showing him). He compared it to *von Webern*!! The Suite for 2 clarinets, I played some songs because I thought they might please his taste, and the piano preludes, and he also looked at The Rat.

Smart enough to see through composer etiquette, she realized that

> he was very nice, though it isn't his kind of music. A few of his adjectives were fluid, original, radical you have your own style, not like anyone else's and he was very polite and simple. . . . Did you know that Varèse is a pupil of his, had counterpoint with him?[33]

Ruth's meeting with Honegger went much better. Extremely impressed by the "enlarged rat," as she called the new version with ostinati, Honegger suggested ways to arrange some performances of her music. If she wanted to revisit Madame Boulanger with this work, he would lend her his name as further reference. Apparently Crawford did leave some manuscripts with her.[34]

Crawford also promoted her music in other ways, although she occasionally questioned the value of the enterprise and disparaged the artificial publicity in the musical press. "When I turned the pages of the [*Musical*] *Leader* and *Courier* for the first time in nine months, [I] asked myself in horror what it is all about and why the Americans do it that way, when the Europeans steer clear of it." Once she embarked upon the task of making contacts, some of her natural amiability and ambition fueled her onward for a while; then she would retreat. Honest enough to admit that shyness or "fear" of rejection played its part here as well, she talked herself into covering every base possible. The publisher Senart told her that composers themselves were financing the printing of their music in part, at least until a first edition had been sold out. The editor Henry Prunières said times were hard, even with his journal *La Revue Musicale*, backed by Otto Kahn's money. (Why did Henry seem to need to conceal Blanche Walton's assistance with the *New Music Quarterly*, Ruth asked Charles.)[35]

By October the charm of Europe had worn off, partly because she was tired of snobbery about American music:

> It isn't the people themselves individually who make me feel we're wise to be "at home." I suppose to be frank, it's partly a reaction to their combined attitude toward Americans and American music, which is almost nowhere complimentary (either concealed well or badly). And too, Peter's belief that it is foolish to be where you're not at home with yourself. It's a curious thing that you and I could probably live in a foreign country yet feel at home with ourselves and with others anywhere *except* in our own milieu of music.[36]

Such assumptions of cultural superiority angered her. She resented how American patrons reinforced this by supporting European composers more than their own countrymen. Her comments about Elizabeth Sprague Coolidge were unusually pointed: "She has been given the *Legion of Honor*!! Du lieber Gott! She is touring Russia and all Europe with concerts of music 'dedicated' to her (so the print says) and programs of all but American music."[37]

Thus Crawford's later assessments of the work she accomplished abroad were qualified to reflect the distinctions between personal freedom and cultural identity. When her colleague Nicolas Slonimsky, writing articles about music for a Boston newspaper, asked her for biographical information in 1933, she told him that she was "sure that the work [done abroad] was by far the best"—"a fact attributable not to Europe itself . . . as to the financial freedom to work, and to the natural course of her growth."[38]

Crawford made plans to leave, trying to find the most economical way to get home. Her debts were real, although somewhat self-induced by her taking some of the Guggenheim money to invest in one of her brother's real estate plans. She had watched money very carefully in Berlin, moving three or four times to cheaper pensions. By the time she got to Paris, there were stretches when she had lived on bread and tomatoes and onions and little else. After much discussion of options, she decided on a date and point of departure. Ruth scrambled to make her final arrangements, borrowing money from Djane Herz and writing to her brother for another loan.

In September, supporting her young friend Vivian Fine's decision to move to New York, Crawford reflected on her own situation. Teacher and pupil shared this common plight: they would both come to New York "empty-handed." That glorious year at 1 West 68th Street had been an oasis of privilege. Whatever the future would bring, it could not be like that, when her protected carefree existence in 1929 "had nothing to do with rooms, meals or menage." The responsibility of providing for herself awaited her, "with all its worries."[39]

But Charles awaited her as well. Their letters had shifted into quiet intimacy and more protectiveness. The strain of separation made him visit the possibility of losing her with uncharacteristic drama: "If I am ever conscious of a last breath, it will carry your name upon it. . . . Of the three loves in my life the love between us is the best and most beautiful. . . . Keep me in your dear heart, love men, and write fine music for me, for yourself, for us."[40]

At the end of October, Crawford took a train and ferry to London. She wrote Charles more letters and made some last-minute visits to London publishers. The year that she called the most productive of her life was approaching its final cadence. Ruth returned to Cherbourg on November 1 to board a Belgian ship, the *Red Star*, for the eight-day voyage home.

Part V

n
e
w

y
o
r
k

1 9 3 2 – 1 9 3 6

h o m e c o m i n g

I am racing after you," Crawford wrote to Seeger on the train to London, October 27, 1931. She and her new friend, Margaret Valiant, waited as the *Red Star* pulled into port on the clear, cold morning of November 10. Charles was there, and Margaret watched "these two people [who] saw only each other" be reunited: Ruth, the "most completely natural person I ever met," and an older gentleman in a dark coat and derby, wearing a pair of pince-nez glasses attached to his person by a thin black ribbon. He did not strike her as a "totally romantic figure in the popular eye."[1]

They faced a hard period as their private relationship now became public, "butting society," as Charles said, by living together. As usual, Ruth optimistically reprised her faith that love and work insured their security: "it is remarkable—that we have no *doubts* about our future together . . . coming to each other out of the dream of Paris . . . [and] for the first time connecting our combined selves with others." She had been the stronger of the two in Europe, believing in the happy ending of the "fairytale" of their relationship. After his panic in May, Seeger felt just the same.

> It is very peculiar, this love of ours. Such diversity of background, I with my pampered upbringing, you with your hard young life, oh what's the use of even cataloguing what we know so well? We can be blissful together, though no one else can understand or even guess it.[2]

Few people actually did. Their age difference, the fact that Charles was married to someone else, that Ruth was going to live with this legal adulterer "out of wedlock," as one said then, caused comment among Crawford's friends and Seeger's family. Carl Sandburg, according to Pete Seeger, was "a little suspicious of Father—who is this older man taking advantage of this younger woman?" Pete himself was surprised: "[It] never occurred to me they would get married." In spite of the *de facto* separation that had existed since 1927, Constance cast Ruth in the role of the "other woman" who stole her husband away. She initially said she would contest the divorce that, at the least, would eject her from the New York Social Register. At a low moment she asked her oldest son if he might testify against his father in court; he refused. Charles's parents were outraged at the shame of a divorce in their family and said that Ruth was not welcome at their home, causing a rift only superficially healed in subsequent years.[3]

Even Blanche Walton harbored grievances. She had watched the romance take root right under her nose. With her doubts about Charles's capacity for love (mentioned several times to Ruth) and her concern for Ruth's independence, once, when Charles called her "argumentative," Blanche had countered with this: "it won't be long before you'll be with Ruth and she will just let you dictate what she will think." But these were small ruffles in the sea of their otherwise strong friendship.[4]

"How much have you told Blanche?" Ruth had asked Charles from Berlin.

> Does she love us both again? I often thought that if either of us lost her it would be I, for taking you away in her thought. Or was she angry with you for treating me badly? Have you told her about our nocturnal and deliciously secret and too few and so delicately "friendly" beach indulgences? Does she know how very good and how very proper we were—in actions—and does she know that it really was the cupboard door falling and not me stealing in at dawn a week before we left Westport? And that we really did not stay out all night . . . but that we wanted to . . . Ruth ain't say nothin' being so far, but vielleicht Charlie do say much, and have to, being so near.[5]

Charles had "left Blanche to draw her own conclusions." He had said little, less worried about Ruth's reputation than Blanche's jealousy. When Ruth was abroad, Charlie had taken over the guest room at 1 West 68th Street, and Blanche enjoyed Charles's companionship more readily than ever. Unconsciously, she grew possessive as she fell "very much in love" with him. Maintaining a delicate balance between "platonics and passions" over the year, he told Ruth that "I have done some extraordinary things to make that relationship what it is and to keep it what it should be." In the winter of 1931 Blanche had written a letter to Ruth, alluding to "difficulties ahead since he has ties and obligations he can not ignore"; the "grave decision" through which Ruth would be "ennobled"; and her own experience of forty years of widowhood, which as one of "renunciation not fulfillment [was] made none the less beautiful or enduring." Perhaps she expected the younger woman to follow suit. She did not expect them to live together. The following April (1932) Blanche confessed to Carl Ruggles that she and Charles rarely saw each other. Although the letter lacks details, a sense of betrayal lurk beneath these words: "though I miss him terribly, it's just painful and strained to be together. In my long and eventful life this is one of the outstanding sorrows and shocks. But it's all part of living, I guess."[6]

Ruth moved in with Charles at 204½ West 13th Street. The apartment, which once served as quarters for either slaves or stable boys, was entered through a tunnel underneath the two main town houses in front. The block was good, the location convenient, with the Seventh Avenue subway on the corner. She tried to affect the mores of emancipated women in the 1920s and failed. Although she could on rare occasion discuss theoretical "unpossessiveness" (or "free love") as an option to marital fidelity, she and Charles were "reprehensibly old fashioned." So she repeated voguish rationalizations among intellectuals, justifying extramarital affairs as a "way to keep our love for each other loverlike" and diminishing marriage as a "formality one goes through." And then she wondered, "perhaps I'm wrong." In fact, the "formality" meant so much that they both would later dissemble about the legalities. Charles introduced Ruth as his wife, and they predated their marriage from the start as November 10, 1931 (the day Ruth returned from Europe), instead of 1932.[7]

In the fall of 1932 the two renegades decided to legalize their union. Turning their trip into a holiday, Ruth and Charles tented out cross-country, visiting Lake Tahoe and Carmel before settling into Winnemucca, Nevada, for the obligatory six weeks of residence. After Charles got his divorce, they were married by a justice of the peace on October 3, 1932. When they returned to New York, they acted as if nothing significant had happened, since they had considered themselves ethically married earlier. Conflicting memories obscure the event, which was, in any event, underplayed. "You realize," Pete Seeger once said, "Father and Ruth married and they never told us. It was a terrible shock."[8]

Crawford had not really sensed that she would leave a German depression only to encounter one at home. In Berlin she lived with the false comfort of the strong dollar against the declining deutschmark. She did not know how things had changed. Between March 1930 and March 1932 the numbers of unemployed had doubled from four to eight million. Although *Musical America* churned out optimism about the forthcoming season—"it will be an active one . . . despite the familiar rumors of depression"—in New York four-fifths of the American Federation of Musicians were unemployed. The following year Cowell reported "vast numbers of unemployed professional orchestra players, more than ever before in the world's history."[9]

"People were taking the depression very seriously," Charles had warned Ruth on September 30, 1931, three days after he had returned home from Paris. The market was still dropping and his own income stream slowed to a trickle. That fall he was teaching part-time as usual at the Institute for Musical Art and also at the New School for Social Research. What would she do? One of his last letters proposed a concert of music by women composers, like that scheduled in Hamburg for December; women's clubs would finance it, and the program might include her suites and quartet plus works of Vivian Fine and Marion Bauer. He also hoped that Djane Herz might refer some private students. Since he was teaching at the New School, perhaps Ruth could teach a course in harmony or help manage the elementary classes in musicianship and theory. Or perhaps not: she ought "better keep out of the teaching mill as much as possible" for the sake of composing. Unfinished sketches for two orchestral movements had returned with her from Paris, as did plans for ostinati for the two new Sandburg songs.[10]

So Crawford stayed home, partly because Seeger wished it and partly because there was so little work to be had. It was "hard to jump into the 'game,' with all its craziness and imperfection," she had written from Paris. Ruth watched her friend Marion Bauer find security in the music department of New York University. The Guggenheim year remained a private experience; had she been interested, Crawford might have turned her year abroad into talks for both a general and professional audience, in the manner of Henry Cowell or Marc Blitzstein, both spending time on lecture circuits to keep themselves financially afloat. That was not her nature. Besides, anything that hinted at making profit from the "appreciation racket," or what Seeger called the *"Musical Courier* disease on the great tree of music," deterred her. "These business men and women 'professionals' are pests, blights, worms—I refuse to take them seriously," Charles said.[11]

In spite of Seeger's later claim that he was "earning enough for the two of us to get along on," they sank into poverty, barely sustaining a veneer of intellectual gentility. Had she been in Chicago, where she was known, things would have been different, as her American Conservatory friend Martha Beck Carragan pointed out.

> I asked her why she and Charles didn't return to Chicago. "Ruth, you could get any amount of money back at the American Conservatory if you wanted, if you and Charles wanted to move out." She said, "My God." She wouldn't think of it. She would rather starve in New York than to go back to Chicago.[12]

Crawford continued some professional involvements as before. She attended the third season of meetings of the New York Musicological Society held at Blanche Walton's apartment in the fall. On November 30 she heard Seeger, recapitulating ideas from his book, speak on "A Modern Neume Theory" as the basis for musical logic, and Nicolas Slonimsky, on December 28, discussing "Consonant Counterpoint in Mutually Exclusive Tonal Systems."[13]

One small performance of a Crawford piece abroad brightened the year's end. The reception of the Diaphonic Suite for Viola and Cello, which was played on December 8 in Hamburg for the northern chapter of the ISCM concert of "Frauen als Komponisten," redeemed its premiere in Berlin. A German newspaper critic dealt with Crawford and Fine jointly. Their "black and white" miniatures were shaped with "draughtsmanlike" "rhythmically bold" inventiveness, having "a fairly intellectual effect" in the profiles of the line. He discussed male and female spheres within music, stressing the congeniality of female composers with "more intimate" forms: "So long as she doesn't try to write 'mannliche Musik,' Woman will have something to contribute to dialogue about the problems of the day."[14]

Crawford had a backlog of music that had never been heard in New York, and through Henry Cowell, much of it was played, published, and even recorded between 1932 and 1933. As the head of the music department since 1929, Cowell had established a beachhead for radical music at the New School for Social Research. Already in the late 1920s the New School had attracted Aaron Copland and Paul Rosenfeld to its faculty. Now with its new building opened in 1931—one of the most glamorous and thoroughly modernist pieces of new urban architecture in the city—it had emerged in the 1930s as a center for modernist expression in the arts in the United States. Through courses that were run as "meet-the-composer" sessions or new-music concerts, Cowell made the New School one of the "few places where the 'advanced' composer [could be] so cheerfully heard." The composer Arthur Berger, who was writing music criticism for the *New York Daily Mirror* at the time, remembers how Cowell's concerts were attended by ten or fifteen people, "but they were the right people for avant-garde work—mostly composers. . . ."[15]

At the concert inaugurating the New School's splendid auditorium on January 6, 1931, the Swiss pianist Oscar Ziegler played one of Crawford's piano preludes in his recital. She also got exposure through radio. In 1933 Vivian Fine played the "Study in Mixed Accents" for a radio series called the "University of the Air" on WEVD, which sponsored concerts of music by the Pan American Association of Composers under the direction of Arthur Berger. As he describes it, Radio WEVD was a "socialist Yiddish [radio] station, the initials standing for Eugene V. Debs . . . a small operation." Crawford packed so much intensity into this one-minute work—a kind of modernist's minute waltz, as it were—that like a flash of lightning, it made a vivid aural impression at its few performances. At its premiere the *New York Daily Mirror* called it "an intriguing mood picture."[16]

About two weeks later Radiana Pazmor, by now an old hand at performing "Rat Riddles," sang it again, this time adding its partner "The Bee" (later to be retitled Sandburg's original "In Tall Grass") at the New School on February 16, with Georgia Kober at the piano, and Adolph Weiss conducting, in a concert sponsored by the Pan American Association of Composers. Accounts in newspapers were cursory, but *Musical America's* critic said "The Bee" had a "marked poetic beauty." It is not clear whether the new "superimposed" orchestral ostinati were played at this time, but they definitely traveled to Berlin in March with the conductor Nicolas Slonimsky on his second European tour. The "Chrisopher Columbus" of American music—as a French critic had dubbed him—hoped to repeat his earlier success in July 1931. Crawford had shown Slonimsky the songs in Paris and he had liked them.[17]

The Berlin concerts on March 5 and 10, 1932, occurred in the volatile atmosphere of Hitler's rise to power. (The following year Arnold Schoenberg, Kurt Weill, and many other Jewish musicians would flee the city, their music banned as "decadent.") Nazi demonstrators against American "Kulturbolshevismus" blew whistles to drown out the music. Cowell later wrote about the "boos, hisses, and catcalls from the opposition and loud applause from the ones who were pleased."[18]

Although the first concert of orchestral music raised more of a storm, and fewer critics attended the second evening, the concert with Crawford's songs played by the Chamber Orchestra of Michael Taube held its own. Slonimsky cabled Crawford two days later: "Your songs great success. Ratriddles repeated in response to quite thunderous applause." A second letter from Slonimsky detailed the performances, the "delicious Ratriddles repeated with sneezing and all, and the competent German singer (Frau Ottlie Metzger-Laterman) who "sang them very well in English." But the reviews were generally unsympathetic to the quintessentially American texts (one playing with transcendental humor, the other a mystical vision of an American prairie), sung in English at the composer's insistence. ("This is important," she wrote in a set of notes for the pieces.) Just as they labeled Crawford's songs "distorted" and "bizarre," other composers on the program—Riegger, Harris, Chavez, Caturla, and Sanjuan—fared similarly. (Slonimsky would later purloin the choicest bits of critical wrath for his *Lexicon of Musical Invective*.) Trying to maximize the chances of Slonimsky repeating the songs in other cities, Crawford gave him the names of potential performers in Budapest, but to no avail.[19]

Crawford continued revising the last song of the Sandburg set in 1932, and by November she finished "Prayers of Steel," including its orchestral ostinato. Seeger, who had "ruled the paper for her," believed them to be "quite remarkable things." She was so pleased with the Three Songs as a whole that she entered them into the prestigious competition to represent the United States at the 1933 festival of the ISCM, to be held in Amsterdam.[20]

December 1932 was spent copying scores and making parts for the ISCM jury and also for Cowell's special publication series of orchestral works. In a letter to Charles Ives asking for help with funding, Cowell wrote:

> Crawford's three songs with orchestra, which I have just published as the first of the 1933 orchestra series, has been accepted to represent America in April—I am delighted for her. The songs are really fine, I think.[21]

The inclusion of the Three Songs for the ISCM festival marked a high point of public recognition in Crawford's career and a singular achievement for a female composer, for she was the first American woman to be so honored. She was spared knowledge of how the only American composer on the jury, Roger Sessions, who most likely attended Slonimsky's Berlin concerts in March, had opposed her work. As he explained to Nadia Boulanger and Aaron Copland at the time, he felt that the "cause of American music (if one can speak of a 'cause') would be hurt" by this choice. At the time Sessions vehemently spurned the "esoteric theoretical devices" of Schoenberg and Berg and believed that Crawford's music suffered from the same faults. Ironically, Copland, whose Piano Variations were also accepted for this festival, would be tarred with the same brush of "hermetic cerebralism" by other European critics. Sessions was outvoted by other jury members, including Edward Dent, Malipiero and the Dutch composer, Wilhem Pijper, who rated Crawford his "overwhelming choice."[22]

The three Sandburg songs were duly performed on June 14. This time no

Nazi whistle-blowers came, for having banned the German chapter of the ISCM earlier that year, the Reich boycotted the festival as part of an international anti-Germany conspiracy. A few days later Jacobi wrote Crawford of her success: "The songs went simply excellently and were one of the only things which seemed to interest and amuse an otherwise apathetic public at an otherwise pretty lousy concert." He regretted her absence, for the performances were "carefully and skillfully given." European critics were not so kind, calling the style dated, "grotesque," or, as the worst would have it, "moving between Chantantmusik, Negro songs, and the acoustic emissions of a dieselmotor." Writing for *Modern Music*, Jacobi affirmed that despite the disappointing quality of the festival as a whole, both American entries—the Copland and the Crawford—"seemed to have made an excellent impression."23

At home the reception of their publication in *New Music Quarterly*'s orchestra series was mixed; one reviewer denounced them as "extreme Left wing" in a style that had no future; others found them "remarkable" and as the work of "the very young and highly gifted Ruth Crawford, notable for their personal charm, taste and orchestral skill."24

After the premiere of "Prayers of Steel" in Amsterdam, only one work composed in Europe remained unheard—the string quartet. Crawford was "extremely anxious to hear it." As usual, Cowell took action, programming it for an "All North-American Concert" of the Pan American Association of Composers. She made parts for the New World String Quartet and coached them for the premiere at the New School on November 13, 1933. The last work on a long program, which included works by Ives, Ruggles, Weiss, John Becker, and Walter Piston, the String Quartet was an unqualified success, the work as a whole pronounced "original and arresting," its Andante third movement singled out as "remarkable"—heralding its singular role in Crawford's career as her most enduring and important work.25

Within a month the Andante transported Crawford into the new technology of the period. It became side A of the first record produced through another visionary project of Henry Cowell—the New Music Society Recording Series. Ruth's old friend from Chicago, Martha Beck, was involved at an early stage of the project, pressed into service as its treasurer; Crawford served on the executive committee, along with John Becker and Wallingford Riegger; and the final member of the executive committee, Blanche Walton, was recruited for office work. Charles Ives was asked for funds.

Ives responded cautiously. In November he had questioned both the financial soundness of the venture and the repertory. Cowell had proposed music by Ruggles, Riegger, Weiss, Brant, and Crawford; Ives wanted the first recording to feature music by the first two composers and questioned the reputation of the last: was their music "mansize"? Cowell responded that he "would rather hear [Crawford's Andante] than almost anything I can think of . . . I would like to make the record, if only to have you hear it!" Cowell's enthusiasm for the work was boundless. He repeated to Ives the high praise he had written for his annual article in the *Americana Encyclopedia of Current*

Events. The movement was "perhaps the best thing for quartet ever written in this country. This is my unqualified opinion, and it shared by many of my confreres who are not wildly enthusiastic over Crawford's works as a whole!"[26]

In the end Ives funded the project and on December 1, 1933, the New World Quartet recorded the Andante on a twelve-inch shellac disc at the Capital Sound Studios, where six hundred records were pressed. Cowell advertised it as a work that "illustrates the use of tone clusters as applied to strings." By January 15, a grand total of twenty people had subscribed— among them Crawford's friend Alfred Frankenstein. Review copies were also sent to critics, who paid some attention to the significance of the series as a whole, since in 1934 hardly any recordings of contemporary American music were available. As the critic Irving Kolodin noted in *Modern Music*, the New Music Society series and the simultaneous issue of Roy Harris's String Quartet on Columbia Records were landmarks.[27]

In came more glowing reviews of Crawford's Andante movement. To Harrison Kerr, writing in *Trend*, "The Crawford piece is to me the outstanding example of her creative work to date—as far, of course, as I am acquainted with her music. It is an homogenous, expressive movement written with seeming fluency and with deep emotion." Did she realize that this piece might secure her place in American music history, even if at the time she criticized the slow tempo of the performance? Acknowledging how difficult the internal line was to project, she made an arrangement for orchestra, to impose a conductor's discipline on the score. The *New York Post* ran a long feature article on Crawford before the quartet's premiere in the Style section next to "Southern Recipes for Waffle Breakfasts." The article, "A Woman Composer Considers 'Modern' Music," with two columns subtitled "New Works Are Difficult to Elucidate" and "Ruth Crawford Believes Music Should Be Heard, Not Seen" gave Ruth more New York publicity than she had received since the Copland-Sessions concert in 1927. Unfortunately, the reporter from the women's section painted her as uncooperative:

> "I don't believe in talking about music first and hearing it afterward," began Miss Crawford unhelpfully. "It is quite impossible to discuss so-called modern music without hearing it. It is even unfair to use the tag 'modern.' There is always a normal process of change in music, as in the arts and letters. Wagner shocked his generation; so have Brahms and Debussy. Now in recent years have come along Stravinsky, Schoenberg, Honegger and others in Europe, Ives and Ruggles and the rest over here, to lead in the 'modern' movement in composition. But there are so many pathways being followed in 'modern' music it is difficult to generalize upon it. You simply must hear it, that's all."[28]

But Crawford's "all" wasn't enough, so Seeger jumped in to fill the spaces between her lines in what the grumpy reporter labeled a "composite interview" where her "husband . . . [who was] happily more articulate . . . came to her aid." He described Crawford's music as "eclectic in tradition but experimental in tendency," to which she added that her own compositions were not out of the American scene, but derive from the older traditions. As an abstract modernist, she dissociated herself from the "American scene" movement, as it was understood in painting (where it implied regional vernacular themes). Her music, the reporter quoted, "cannot be considered nationalistic. Her work is still experimental. Most modern music is experimental, for that matter, she says." Seeger used the chance to overview the historical moment: "We are at the end of an era," he said. "The romantic music of Beethoven and Mozart has more or less reached the end of its course." And striking out at his hated neoclassical rivals, he added that "the composers who are stumped by the present situation are turning back to those idioms." Then Seeger spoke of the connections between music and "social conditions." He historicized American radical expression by linking it to European utopian modernism:

> Modern music had become very revolutionary in intent up to the war, up to 1914, beginning with Schoenberg and Stravinsky. The European composers suddenly realized its social implications and the movement stopped for lack of impetus. We in America are trying to revitalize it.[29]

The question was how.

" m u s i c   a s   a   w e a p o n
i n   t h e   c l a s s
s t r u g g l e "

I came home from school," Pete Seeger recalled, "and I found Father and Ruth up to their ears in radical politics. They were both enthusiastic members of the Pierre Degeyter Club, and they worked hard." One of twenty-odd left-wing musicians' groups in the Workers Music League, organized in 1931 within the labor federations of the American Communist Party, the Pierre Degeyter Club was devoted to the creation of proletarian culture. Henry Cowell invited Charles to deliver a lecture to the group and Ruth went to that meeting in 1932. The next year they took Pete around, and together they sang Degeyter's most famous song, the Communist anthem "L'Internationale." "There was nothing sissy about this music," Pete said. "'Arise friends and workers, we're ready for battle, Advance Proletarians to conquer the world.'" Armed with the Communist slogan, "Music as a Weapon in the Class Struggle," the Workers Music League logo of a hammer and sickle backdropped against a musical staff symbolizes the political milieu for these reconstructed modernists from 1932 through 1935.[1]

Ruth's path toward the left can be mapped mostly mostly in Charles's words, for no diaries or political writings of hers survive from this period. Charles described Ruth as his partner in the classic journey of many intellectuals and artists in the early 1930s, who became political by witnessing the Depression at firsthand: the homeless men and women in the streets selling apples, rain and snow falling on the heating grates crowded with bodies, the Rolls Royces that still went up and down the streets of New York. The scope and pervasiveness of suffering was staggering. Charles said he and Ruth were shocked, "completely knocked over."[2]

During that fearful New York winter of 1931–32, they reevaluated their purpose and direction as artists and intellectuals. For most of the 1920s their small group of ultra-moderns had been convinced of its historical relevance. Ruth had more than once indicated her readiness to do battle for the precious cause of "dissonant music." Now what meaning did that have? A new battle took its place, as Charles Seeger and Ruth Crawford became what he described as "very loyal fringe members of the Communist front."[3]

To some extent Crawford's experiences in Berlin had forecast her political direction. The Soviet Union was still considered a haven for the avant-garde in the early 1930s, and she planned to go there in the spring of 1931. Furthermore, her friend Imre Weisshaus was an ardent Communist. Witnessing his hard times, she once wrote Seeger that she "may become a Communist yet!" Now she was swept up in the drama of his activism, for Seeger reacted to the historical moment as if the curtain had just been raised on a new act of his life.[4]

"That glorious Depression!" he later said in his old age. If the literary critic Edmund Wilson wrote in 1932 that "Marxism was the only vital political and cultural movement in the West," it was, as Richard Pells explains, not because he agreed with its social ideas but because it represented a new vision of humane life "just coming to maturity" with its "immense creative work" yet to be done, in dramatic contrast to the world of capitalism "dying at the end of its blind alley."[5]

With axioms like "national in form, proletarian in content" emerging from party rhetoricians, Crawford Seeger joined other radical artists trying out new ways to internalize political imperatives. These imperatives needed to be framed as questions that allowed them to build bridges between their social conscience and their musical identity. How could they reach workers with music written in modernist idioms?[6]

Here Henry Cowell's example helped point the way. In the early 1930s Cowell predicted an allegiance between revolutionary art and revolutionary politics. He wrote six political songs and a march during this period, including "Working Men Unite" and "We Can Win Together." The young composer Arthur Berger remembers "Cowell telling us one night that we had to put dissonances in our music for the people—this was at a Pierre Degeyter Club meeting." In a lecture at the club in the fall of 1932, Cowell was reported to have said, "my music corresponds to the proletarian class which is now in the ascendancy." Although this was received with some skepticism, a critic surveyed other American composers from this point of view:

> Among the bourgeois musicians struggling for a place in the musical world, men such as Henry Hadley and Charles Wakefield Cadman have been entirely ineffectual. Gershwin and Carpenter, clever manipulators of musical forms, have nothing much to say, despite their efforts to emulate Stravinsky in the American idiom. Among the composers who though revolutionary in form but as yet take a neutral stand in the class struggle are Charles Ives, Carl Ruggles and Roy Harris. Charles Ives in his "Boston Commons" memorializing black soldiers who fought with the North in the Civil War sees and feels the revolutionary

struggle of the colonies for independence, but cannot see the link of Sacco and Vanzetti and the Boston Commons.[7]

In contrast, Cowell's "fostering of new musical forms, his ruggedness and freshness, are healthy indications of the progress to be made by proletarian music in America." After his piano recital on November 17, 1933, at the Pierre Degeyter Club, the *Daily Worker* critic said, "Here is music that is definitely revolutionary." For a few short years such opinions offered the hope of rapprochement between modernist style and Marxist politics. If one could retheorize dissonance as radical social content rather than individualism or spiritual metaphysics, then modernism could be harnessed to the cause of militant art. Only one small note portended trouble ahead. The *Daily Worker* critic also reported Cowell's rebuke of traditional workers' music, which "combined revolutionary lyrics with traditional music—music which by no means can be termed revolutionary." (The real revolution in the people's music was yet to come. Pete Seeger was fourteen years old at the time.)[8]

Earlier that year, in February 1933, Seeger and Cowell gave a seminar in "Historical and Theoretical Bases for Worker's Music" at the Pierre Degeyter Club. A December 1932 editorial from the *Worker Musician* made them models for the cause:

> American musicians . . . composers, theorists and performers, we call upon you to take the road of Theodore Dreiser, Sherwood Anderson, Henry Cowell, Charles Seeger, John Dos Passos, Lincoln Steffens, and thousands of other intellectuals and professionals, who see in capitalist society, decadence, stagnation, and in the proletarian revolution, a new culture, a new great, creative force. Musicians . . . Turn Left.
> FOR PROLETARIAN MUSIC
> FOR THE DEFENSE OF THE SOVIET UNION
> FOR A SOVIET AMERICA.[9]

Even if Ruth Crawford never appeared so prominently in the radical press, she nevertheless became a politically committed artist—and, as Seeger would later describe it, "deeply involved in the problems of the day." That cozy circle of modernism centered at 1 West 68th Street no longer satisfied her. In the 1920s, as Aaron Copland acknowledged, "Our works were largely self-engendered: no-one asked for them; we simply wrote them out of our own need." In the midst of the Depression, that need could be seen as adolescent and self-indulgent or, at the least, old-fashioned. By the 1930s Marxist polemicists redefined the politics of modernism for radical artists. They turned the critical buzzwords of the 1920s into slogans of reproach, recasting individualism and subjectivity as variations on the theme of bourgeois irresponsibility and selfishness. The new reigning ideal was collective action and militancy. For many, whether on the extreme or moderate left, the issue had ethical as well as aesthetic implications. The language Seeger would later use is typical of the period: it became "somehow or other almost immoral to closet oneself in one's comfortable room and compose music for her own delight and those at least of our immediate acquaintances." The conscience of a minister's daughter prodded Crawford out of that privileged refuge into the streets.[10]

When in 1932 Crawford received a commission for songs from the Society of Contemporary Music in Philadelphia, the quiet revolutionary seized her opportunity to express her new political consciousness. Two songs, "Sacco, Vanzetti" and "Chinaman, Laundryman" were the result. The subjects could not have been more topical. As the notorious trial and execution of two Italian anarchists became a symbol of capitalist evil in the left revival of the 1930s, Crawford's "Sacco, Vanzetti" was only one among many artistic tributes. Perhaps she attended the controversial exhibit of Ben Shahn's epic cycle of paintings, "The Passion of Sacco and Vanzetti," exhibited in New York in April 1932; her friend the composer Marc Blitzstein had started an opera on this theme around this time. Similarly, "Chinaman, Laundryman" reflected the interest in the Chinese Revolution as well as the exploitation of immigrant labor; both causes were discussed routinely in left-wing publications like the *New Masses* or the *Daily Worker*. "Read Agnes Smedley," Crawford reminded herself on a scrapnote that survives from this period, in a reference to the author of *Daughters of the Earth*.[11]

Crawford chose to set two long militant poems written by a young Chinese dissident, H. T. Tsiang (at Columbia University in 1928), and published in his now forgotten collection *Poems of the Chinese Revolution*. Tsiang's work, which was highly praised in the Communist press, conforms to the literary canons of the Communist Party in its ideologically intense Third Period from 1927 through 1935. Then, as Richard Reuss describes it, "Communist artists were not only to portray the contemporary revolutionary struggle . . . but to awaken class-conscious feelings in the uncommitted masses."[12]

Tsiang's poems illustrate the genre that the Communist critic Mike Gold called "a worker's recitation . . . shaped like a solo cantata with the same operatic profusion of literary detail." (Gold's recitation, "Strange Funeral in Braddock," was later set by Elie Siegmeister in 1934 with great success.) They were filled with rhetorical devices such as exclamatory commands, exhortations to characters in the ballad's narrative, and addresses to the reader as well. Brief examples illustrate the technique.[13]

[from "Sacco, Vanzetti"]:

. . . Oh martyrs!
Dead! Dead!
You are dead!
But your human tree and your human root are budding, blooming, growing!
Listen to the war cries of your living brothers!
This is the incense we are burning to you!

[from "Chinaman, Laundryman"]:

. . . Wash! Wash!
Why can I wash away the dirt of others' clothes but not the hatred of my heart?
Iron! Iron!
How can I smooth away the wrinkle of others' dresses but not the miseries of my
    heart?

Dry! Dry!
Why do clothes dry, but not my tears?

. . .

Here is the brush made of study.
Here is the soap made of action.
Let us all wash with the brush!
Let us all press with the iron!

In proletarian literature like this, Crawford found new sermons that corresponded in form if not content to the sounds of her youth. Perhaps in "Chinaman, Laundryman" the woman responded as well. Here was a new weapon:
the iron instead of the hammer. Typically, the symbol of proletarian struggle—a muscular heavily veined arm with the clenched fist raised high in the
air—implied masculinity. If Meridel Le Sueur published "Women on the
Breadlines" in the *New Masses* earlier in 1932 to counter the impression that
poverty was singularly male, then Ruth Crawford might have addressed the
issue that oppression could be female, composing music for a female singer
about symbolic women's work through a poem that placed a public version of
it on center stage. "Wash! Brush! Dry! Iron! Then we shall have a clean
world!"[14]

Nothing subtle or distinguished here. That a composer who previously had
chosen fine poems by Sandburg would be drawn in by this pedestrian verbiage
testifies to Crawford's political militancy at this stage in her life. Still, the freedom and passion of proletarian recitations appealed to her experimental approach to vocal writing. Some of the techniques that she used in the brilliant
Three Songs (on poems of Carl Sandburg), being revised at this time, reappear
in these settings as well, including the classic modernist technique of "Sprechstimme." Charles said that for the political songs, "the singer should stand
about where a lecturer would stand. The piano well behind her. . . . These are
songs for the *diseuse*, or cabaret singer." Crawford's anti-lyricism insured that
angry oratory would dominate a stage that had become a soapbox.[15]

Several schemes for organizing the instrumental accompaniment through
serial procedures have programmatic significance. Good proletarian artists incorporated structural elements of class relationships (as opposed to their own
psychological subjectivity) into the very fabric of their radical art; otherwise
the idea of music being a "weapon in the class struggle" would be reduced to
words, not sound. Crawford solved this issue in her ricercari through the
medium of heterophonic texture. By creating such profound opposition between voice and piano—at one point Charles Seeger claimed they need only
begin and end together—Crawford embodied class conflict into the music itself. In "Sacco, Vanzetti" the conflict between voice and piano correlates with
profound political injustice. Similarly, the "remorseless" patter of the piano
part in "Chinaman, Laundryman" transmits the pervasive oppression of the
capitalist boss on an exploited worker and the inhumanity of his underpaid
manual labor.[16]

Thus Crawford's political songs/ricercare had two parents, one the world of
modernist art and other proletarian culture, shifting names as they moved

from one kind of audience to another at performances in the spring of 1933. New music loyals heard the premiere of "Sacco, Vanzetti" at a concert of the Pan American Composers at Carnegie Chapter Hall on March 6, 1933, where they shared the program with the world premiere of Edgard Varèse's landmark piece, "Ionisation."[17] Although listed on the program, the soprano Judith Litante refused to sing the songs because they were too radical, so Ruth was at the piano in a rare public performance, accompanying her old friend Radiana Pazmor, who "did a beautiful job," according to Charles. Ruth was "very disgusted" with Litante's defection, according to Martha Beck, who attended the concert. Despite the poor audience turnout, Beck remembered how some "very important people were there. . . . It was a powerful work with a social conscience." The critic for the *New York Herald Tribune* described the work as a "conscientious essay to set a text hardly grateful for musical treatment."[18]

"Sacco, Vanzetti" was repeated with the premiere of "Chinaman, Laundryman" at "A Program of Modern American Music" at the MacDowell Club on March 12 in a concert that included works by Marion Bauer, Ruggles, Copland, Ives, Wallingford Riegger, and Henry Cowell. At the end of the month both songs were performed at the Mellon Gallery in Philadelphia for the Society of Contemporary Music (March 27, 1933), which had commissioned them. They were performed by the soprano Irene Williams, with the pianist Arthur Hice. One reviewer called them "fearful, wonderful creations." But after this performance the ricercari disappeared from the concert stage for the rest of the composer's lifetime. For her "program of modern songs" in San Francisco a few months later, on September 26, at which Pazmor gave the world premiere of Ives's masterpiece "General William Booth Enters into Heaven," the contralto returned instead to Crawford's earlier Sandburg songs, "White Moon" and "Sunsets."[19]

The songs had another chance to live when on May 21, 1933, "Sacco, Vanzetti" and "Chinaman, Laundryman" were performed for a mass audience of leftist workers. The "First American Workers Music Olympiad"—the "big shindig," as Siegmeister called it—was sponsored by the Workers Music League and held at City College Auditorium. It lasted "a whole day . . . with various groups and choruses and different soloists and so forth . . . ." Timed to build on enthusiasm generated by the May Day parade, which in 1933 was almost twice as big as the previous year, the Olympiad offered a "counter-demonstration to the bourgeois National Music Week." Similar festivals were scheduled in Europe, including one in Moscow around the same time, and another in June in Strasbourg, which included a performance of a cantata by Crawford's old friend Imre Weisshaus (now known as Paul Arma).[20]

In the 4:15 afternoon session on Saturday Radiana Pazmor again sang Crawford's "new American revolutionary songs"—as they were described in an advertisement in the *Daily Worker*, May 20, 1933, this time with Jerome Moross at the piano. The songs were programmed between Jacob Schaeffer's Freiheit Mandolin Orchestra and the Pierre Degeyter Club Orchestra, New York chapter. Russian translations beneath the English text, found in holographs for both songs, may have been made with this Olympiad in mind.

"Opgeshmissn (overthrow) a Kapitalist!" wrote Jacob Schaeffer in a song for his Yiddish-speaking chorus, the Freiheit Gesang Farein (Freedom Song Society)—perhaps the best-known group on the program. A young Pete Seeger attending the Olympiad returned to the Kent School to write an English theme of his impressions of this stirring music. Most of the many workers' choruses sang in their native languages. At that time English was a second language in the American Communist Party, spoken by only one-seventh of the 20,000 Communist Party members in the early 1930s. The program for the Workers Music Olympiad demonstrates the consequences of this fact for cultural radicalism, as its performing groups mapped out the old country with new politics: the Yiddish "schules" of children's choruses of the IWO; the Lithuanian Workers Chorus "Sietynas," from Newark, New Jersey; the Jugoslav Workers Chorus "Radnik," New York; Finnish Workers Chorus, New York; Italian Workers Chorus, New York; Leontovich (Ukrainian) Workers Chorus, New York; the Pierre Degeyter Club Orchestra, New York; the Freiheit Mandolin Orchestra; the Daily Workers Chorus, New York; the Balalaika Orchestra from the Soviet Union; and the Combined Sections of Jewish Workers Clubs. A "mass chorus of 1000 voices in a Grand Finale of popular revolutionary songs" requested the audience to join in the mass singing. Judging from the program, Crawford contributed new work in the minority language of English. How her songs were received is not known.[21]

They remain period pieces to this day, saddled by texts that Charles Seeger would later describe as "naive" political "verbiage." Few contemporary singers can muster the social outrage their successful interpretation demands. Neither Ruth nor Charles harbored qualms about making propagandistic art at this time. "Music is propaganda—always propaganda—and of the most powerful sort," Charles declared in one of his *Daily Worker* columns, pitting Marxist analysis against the bourgeois concept of autonomous art. Were not many "old masterpieces . . . full of the poisonous propaganda of church, state, salon, barracks, and school room"? To the end of his life, Charles expressed more enthusiasm for Crawford's "extraordinary," "magnificent" declamations than he did for the String Quartet 1931.[22]

As music critic for the *Daily Worker* in 1934 and 1935, Seeger adopted the pseudonym of "Carl Sands" to thwart political harassment—fears that turned out to have more justification later than in the 1930s. A thinly veiled cover for Seeger, the name "Carl Sands" recalls the name of Ruth's Chicago mentor, Carl Sandburg, already popularized as a "people's poet." Perhaps Carl Sands, who disapproved of the poet's socialist politics, hoped that proletarian music might achieve the cultural stature of Sandburg's poetry.

Without doubt the whole idea of a workers' culture to "offset the poisons of capitalist culture," as Mike Gold described it, touched deep strains of musical idealism, for at the same time that it satisfied Marxist goals for working-class participation, it also invested the intelligentsia with a new sense of importance. As the historian Richard Pells has written, "the search for personal freedom and an abstract international culture was giving way to a spirit of commitment. No longer must the writer [or artist] be a pariah in his native land. The Depression gave him a chance to re-establish communication, sink roots, find an outlet for his talents, join a movement larger than himself. Above all, he might gain a sense of belonging—the greatest gift the 1930s could bestow." The pleasures of opposition galvanized Charles, and from his pen flowed articles ranging from scholarly disquisitions on "The Dictatorship of the Linguistic," for the short-lived Communist-funded *Music Vanguard*, to music criticism for the *Daily Worker*, and even one mainstream article, "On Proletarian Music," for *Modern Music*, asked for directly by its editor, Minna Lederman.[23]

Between 1934 and 1935, Ruth Crawford found herself married to a leading spokesman for proletarian music, as Charles Seeger's radical perspective on music history and contemporary countercultural life became prominent among New York dissident musicians. Seeger's thirty-odd columns for the *Daily Worker* set the tone of disengagement from modernism as he and Crawford understood it. Never so doctrinaire that he rejected the present, still championing new work (Copland and Shostakovich), and still sympathetic to dissonant music, Seeger, nevertheless, transferred his intellectual passion elsewhere. The outlet for his work was a group called the Composers' Collective, which he and Cowell had helped start in 1932–33. Among the stalwarts were some whom Crawford counted as old friends—Wallingford Riegger came often, Cowell was there some of the time—and more as new—Lahn Adomian, who founded the Daily Workers Chorus and the New Singers; Elie Siegmeister; Marc Blitzstein, whose brilliant musical *The Cradle Will Rock* had its genesis in the collective; and several others, including Jacob Schaeffer, Herbert Haufrecht, Henry Leland Clarke, Earl Robinson, and, very occasionally, Aaron Copland.[24]

They tried to give agency to music as a weapon in the class struggle. "Songs are as necessary to the fighting movement as bread," Mike Gold said often in his columns in the *Daily Worker*, further suggesting the form they might take: "From ego-poet to mass-poet is the usual path of the proletarian writer. . . . Mass is strength, mass is clarity and courage." Between 1933 and 1936 the members of the Composers' Collective worked to develop the "mass song," in a progressive American idiom different from "Broadway, or commercial music tied to the Capitalist economic machine" of Tin Pan Alley. They set militant protest lyrics with accompaniments modeled after the German school of workers' songs in which musically sophisticated elements (like irregular rhythms and dissonance) gave a special character to an otherwise popular-based style. Inspirations for this kind of protest music came from the Soviet Union and Germany, with the "lehrstucke" (didactic pieces) of Bertolt Brecht and Hanns Eisler regarded as models.[25]

For the two volumes of *Workers Song Books* that the collective published in 1934 and 1935, Charles Seeger composed more music in two years than he had written in the previous decade—three songs, including "Lenin! Who's That Guy" (its text drawn from H. T. Tsiang's novel *China Red*), "Mount the Barricades," and "Song of the Builders." Even though Seeger would later minimize the influence of the collective, historicized by contemporary scholars out of proportion to its influence at the time, back then he was completely involved.[26]

Crawford, on the other hand, remained the quiet revolutionary at home. Although she sympathized with the collective's goals, its minutes record her attendance at only two meetings. Perhaps the style of the collective did not appeal to her, based as it was on the Marxist practice of group criticism. "Everybody was always tearing everybody else apart . . . in a comradely fashion," Siegmeister said. For Seeger, who loved to split hairs, it was perfect. Crawford stayed away. Elie drew this portrait of Ruth during this period:

> Ruth was always a little reticent and a little withdrawn. We'd sit around talking and she didn't say that much. It wasn't male chauvinism or anything, I mean, you know, we were I hope beyond that stage. But Ruth was just a little quieter than Charlie—we were big talkers anyway. She deferred a great deal to Charlie. . . . I don't think that Charlie was in any way as I said, chauvinistic or the dominant male or anything like that. But you see, he had a gift of gab and she was very lovely and sweet and a little withdrawn. My impression was that Ruth was not essentially an intellectual. That's a hell of a thing to say about a composer, but I always felt that she was a lovely person who wasn't particularly interested in all these intellectual discussions and arguments.[27]

Perhaps the atmosphere did not suit other women either, for few seem to have been part of the collective's history. Was this group, like so many others in the radical movement of the 1930s, a "male preserve" if only by default?[28]

She, the composer, wrote less music than her husband, the musicologist—producing virtually nothing after the proletarian ricercari except two short political rounds for three-part chorus, only one of which survives—the sum total of her work between 1932 and 1936. Charles recalled their genesis as a musical moment *chez* Seeger. One evening they read some satirical limericks by Fred Rolland in the *New Masses* about the pirate "captains of industry," among them Rockefeller and Morgan:

> Joy to the World, to live and see the day,
> When Rockefeller Senior, shall up to me and say:
> "Comrade, can you spare a dime?"

"The moment we read that doggerel, we began a hilarious evening. I made three rounds, and she two," Seeger remembered. The his-and-hers compositions were titled "When, Not If" and "Not If, But When." Crawford's setting, for a women's chorus of two sopranos and an alto, begins with a musical quotation from "Joy to the World." She wrote the more dissonant setting of the two; using minor seconds and a sudden change in rhythmic pattern in the last line, she placed "Comrade, can you spare a dime?" up high in a chromatic whine, and rubbing salt in the wounds of his condition, made poor Rockefeller repeat the repugnant address not just once, but four times. It was beautiful, Seeger said.[29]

"Oh, it was very cute for them to do the same one," Siegmeister recalled many years later. But this was no happy accident, as if the genre just invented itself. As a form of 1930s American Gebrauchsmusik "for the masses," he, not

Seeger, invented the agitprop genre. All those lessons with Madame Nadia Boulanger in Paris paid off, for she had shown him medieval English rounds written with the voice-exchange techniques German musicologists called "Stimmtausch"—which Siegmeister now appropriated (scandalizing his former teacher's name). He and Charlie deserved a "juicy footnote" in the annals of musicology on "how the proletarians" were regaled "with this medieval technique, . . . cast in saucy, jazzy rhythms—of which we two were the principal exponents. That's one thing they shouldn't forget!" Crawford's piece never saw the light of day, although both Siegmeister and Seeger published their rounds in the *Workers Song Book* and arranged for performances through the Composers' Collective and Adomian's Communist-supported chamber chorus, the New Singers.[30]

This was only one of many musical and artistic opportunities available to radical composers through the American Communist Party movement. Its cultural community sponsored all kinds of events, from a "proletarian cabaret" to a New Masses costume ball, with two ballrooms and two orchestras (both advertised in the *Daily Worker*). The Pierre Degeyter Club alone sponsored an orchestra and a chorus and had a concert series at which composers from the collective often had works performed.

Charles Seeger as Carl Sands flourished; Ruth Crawford did not. In 1934 she contributed nothing to the second American Workers Music Olympiad. That spring in 1934 the *New Masses* ran a contest for composers to write a vocal setting of a poem by a leading proletarian poet, Alfred Hayes: "Into the Streets May First." Along with Aaron Copland and Marc Blitzstein, Seeger entered the competition; Crawford wrote a song but did not hand it in, and it has not survived.[31]

When Hanns Eisler came to New York in 1934, Charles helped in planning a festschrift for him, arranging lectures for his course on composing mass songs at the New School, and organizing a reception. Crawford was supposed to contribute to the festschrift, as her name is in the table of contents. But there is no composition listed beside her name. A photograph of the Eislers and Seegers in New York testifies to their friendship with a composer later celebrated during the Cold War as an authentic Marxist artist-hero. Perhaps Eisler and Crawford discussed her Berlin days, for she had been there for the premiere of one of his most controversial works, *Die Massnahme* ("The Measures Taken"). Eisler was the man of the hour. No matter that Arnold Schoenberg had arrived in New York the year before, feted by a reception at Blanche Walton's after his lecture at the New School, which Cowell had arranged. To the left, he was irrelevant. (Copland wrote in *Music Vanguard*, "Let the young people say to themselves once and for all, "No more Schoenberg.")[32]

Carl Sands indicted modern music:

> Cliques of only a few thousand hear it. In these immunization wards, "modern" music has been slowly starving to death. In a semi-vacuum, removed from the actualities of life, its composers . . . feel frustration and futility.[33]

His interest in modernist composition diminished, even that written by his former protégée, his wife. As he described it, he had "less and less to do with the compositional end of things."[34]

Crawford lost her muse. She saw her future shrink as subjective modernism went on the defensive. Even if her husband would never deny that modernist music had its place, she could no longer rely on his involvement in her work and did not seem to find the proletarian culture movement an adequate alternative to the musical intimacy of the early years of their relationship. For all of Seeger's descriptions of his wife as a comrade-in-arms, she did not flourish through Marxist cultural ideology. Occasional references to politics surface in contexts from which one infers both Crawford's ease with and distance from the movement, her irreverence suggesting ambivalence. "Thank God, Lenin, Stalin and the planets all that you belong to me," she wrote her husband on July 28, 1935—her trilogy of deities not exactly in accordance with Marxist doctrine. If she called herself "Krawford the Kommunist," the German K's mocked her sobriety.[35]

As for the cause of "dissonant music," she and Charles believed that by 1933, it was virtually dead. Seeger told his Harvard classmates in an alumni report that "it was apparent to all but the most isolated observers that the conflict within the vanguard of 20th-century music between the traditionalists ('neo-classicists') and the experimentalists ('dissonant writers') had been practically settled in favor of the former." He and Ruth still claimed to be "diehards of the defeated faction," but he cared less. He devoted most of his time to proletarian music, writing little scholarship between 1933 and 1938. The book over which he and Ruth labored and loved in the summer of 1930 was revised but never published—and never finished to his satisfaction. Even though he had attempted a third revision of *Tradition and Experiment in Modern Composition*, and was "anxious to bring the work out quickly, if only to mark a grave," he never did. He continued to teach at the New School and support new projects, getting Blanche Walton to underwrite the American Library of Musicology, through which he published the theory of an old modernist (Yasser) and the scholarship of a pioneering "comparative musicologist" (Helen Roberts). The arrival of the famous German scholar Erich von Hornbostel at the New School for Social Research in 1933, where he gave courses on the "music of primitive people," made Seeger's own interest in what would later be called ethnomusicology more focused, and Seeger helped form that discipline's earliest professional group, the American Society for Comparative Musicology.[36]

Crawford stayed loyal to modernism as ideology if not as practice through it all, but with little engagement in the present. She "practically never saw any of the people she knew" in that old world of 1 West 68th Street. As Vivian Fine remembers it, she "remained in contact with Ruth for the first couple of years, 1931–33, and then the whole avant-garde disappeared. The tiny enclave that it was then collapsed."[37]

Hard times cemented resentments into bitterness. Crawford took comfort in the occasional small victory. Her reaction to a review of Howard Hanson's concert of conservative American music in Berlin in 1932 shows the persistence of her Berlin malice toward neoclassicism. She told Slonimsky about a clipping that Cowell had shown her in which Stuckenschmidt reproached Hanson for playing "neither Ives nor Ruggles, Antheil nor Varèse, Cowell nor—I've forgotten the rest," she added in a postscript to a letter on January 29, 1933, but what she remembered was "delightfully biting." Persevering in spite of this, Cowell kept up his work at the New School and also through the New Music Society in San Francisco.[38]

Although Crawford did not have any New York performances of her music in 1934 and 1935, the New Music Society gave her three small performances in 1934. The *Study in Mixed Accents* garnered excellent notices after Douglas Thompson played it on January 11, 1934. An "overflowing audience" heard a piece that one critic described as "virile and highly entertaining" and another as "beautiful through its virility" and its natural accessibility rarely found in atonal writing. On April 9 Carrie Teal revived two preludes. Again San Francisco critics proved receptive to Crawford's idiom, Fisher praising their "human quality." The Andante from the String Quartet 1931, now recorded, was choreographed by Betty Horst and premiered on May 28 at a gala affair that featured Varèse's "Ionisation." Amidst all the publicity for that piece, Crawford's Andante was squeezed into a review by one critic, praised for its "beauty and eloquence."[39]

Crawford was hardly alone in her diaspora from modernism. Ruggles left music for painting; Rudhyar left music for astrology and transcendental communes in New Mexico. And Crawford left important work hanging in the limbo of good intentions. Even though she was no longer bound by the terms of her Guggenheim Fellowship to write a symphony, Crawford nevertheless had returned home with plans to finish the two orchestral movements, even propelling herself toward the summit of the Great American Symbol of cultural emancipation from Europe by announcing the two movements as work in progress in a fairly public way, as if hoping that a public promise would thwart her procrastination. "Two Pieces for Orchestra in preparation" appeared on the works list of Crawford's entry in the second edition of Claire Reis's *American Composers: A Record of Works Written Between 1912 and 1932.*[40]

In addition, she sent Nicolas Slonimsky a letter in January 1933, where she foresaw a return to work now that the Three Songs and a "long siege of copying" were finished. Were these New Year's resolutions? If so, she did not keep them. Seeger's long description of the Paris sketches in his sketch on Crawford written for Cowell's anthology *American Composers on American Music* stands as the only vestige of their existence: a "first movement in three voices —a kind of Toccata-Allegro, with broad lines to the very independent parts, and the second, another experiment in passacaglia form, but this time of a chordal, rather than a melodic unit."[41]

Seeger used the essay he wrote for Cowell's anthology to challenge the uncompromisingly radical composer he admired so deeply; could she move beyond "the rather narrow but recherché field in which she had hitherto moved and had her being, or whether, following her bid for orchestral laurels . . . enter into the already brisk competition among men in the larger fields"?[42]

But the symphonic sketches remained just that. Ruth had expected in Paris that with Charles near, "our symphonic child will grow." Its stagnation left Seeger puzzled. "She tried to finish them but she couldn't." Many years later he said that "the only thing she couldn't do was the great span. . . . I could have given her any number of ideas for a symphony. I dreamed up plans for a symphony by the dozens. Anyone of them she could have taken." Did he offer? Did she refuse? If this extraordinary exception could not finish two orchestral pieces, then what woman could? He would later tell his children "women can't compose symphonies." Crawford's work in this genre meant a great deal, perhaps too much for them both.[43]

The fate of the symphonic sketches point to some serious problems of confidence and productivity. Sometime around 1932 Crawford lost her psychic equilibrium. The symptom was an unprecedented and singular act of self-destruction, hard to fathom even now, for she burned the score of her Sonata for Violin and Piano (1926). It was a work haunted by memories and dreams. Memories of its glowing success at its debut evening in Chicago; of Stella Roberts appearing afterward, reminding Ruth of her sister's brutal murder; of a dream in Paris when both sisters came to call once again; of optimistic expectations for love and work aroused in Ruth when she stood at the threshold of marriage. In a confession written many years later, Crawford camouflaged the significance of the deed by introducing it with an off-hand reminiscence about poetry and childhood:

> I remember deciding, when I was 7, to be a poet. By the time I was sixteen I had filled two books with over two hundred poems, one of them in 800 rhymed couplets. Fifteen years later I burned most of them, together with a violin sonata which had been played in New York at a League of Composers concert and in Chicago at the Cliff Dwellers, with Frederick Stock present.[44]

Nothing more was said—as if the rhymed couplets of a young girl were the equivalent of a major score; as if the only explanation of this act was a rejection of juvenilia (although even here she could not resist mentioning Stock). In 1932 she continued to ignore her Chicago music by excluding these works from her updated entry for Claire Reis's second catalogue of works by American composers. Yet the symbolic importance of the sonata looms too large for us to accept Crawford's account at face value. Her dreams of a union between mother and music-maker that propelled her into marriage faded in the wake of a terrible inner crisis about which no further information survives.[45]

"a thread unwinding"

music, 1930–1932

> *No two rugs are exactly alike. . . . Eschewing measuring devices,
> drawing sportingly like a calligrapher, alternating colors like Mustafa
> on his box, the weaver sets a symmetrical concept against a spontaneous
> technique, and room remains for her spirit to rise through the work.*
>
> —Henry Glassie,
> *Turkish Traditional Art Today*[1]

Even if Crawford too hastily decided that her Chicago past had no mucial fu-ture, today her reputation rests primarily on the music she composed between 1930 and 1932—her second distinctive style period. New metaphors for her style, which emerge in various documents from the period, suggest her shifting priorities. In the 1920s she called her music "trees of sound and color," capturing the vertical impulse behind dense sonorities. In the 1930s she talked about the horizontal impulses in her music. She spoke frequently of her "longing for line" as one of her "main searches" in the new polyphony. She embellished it through metaphors of "thread unwinding"; of "string to lead me out of the mass of root-less treeless leaves." She embedded in her forms rich patterns of symmetry which she compared to the complex designs woven into Persian rugs.[2]

Today the consensus about Crawford's music from this period has been constructed around her systematic approaches to form. She has been hon-ored as a forerunner to integral serialism, a prophetic link between emer-gent modernism here and abroad. To be sure, the affinities are real. Never-theless, her own language complicates that position. Crawford defined her second-style period as the expression of "modern American dissonant music"—a phrase that does not fit the theoretical discourse of the last few decades. Did Schoenberg annul the distinction between consonance and dis-sonance? Not for her. That opposition was crucial to her strategy of explo-ration. Although it remains for others to explore the legacy of dissonant counterpoint on which she founded her second style, it already seems clear that its differences from European serialism are as important as its affinities. Without surveying in detail all of the music from this dense period of activity, we begin where she began: with what one of the heirs to her legacy has called "moving linear exploration."

Crawford clarified the values of modern American dissonant music long after she had composed the music they shpaed. She listed the following principles as "points" about which she "felt strongly," and saved the most important for last:

> Clarity of melodic line
> Avoidance of rhythmic stickiness
> Rhythmic independence between parts
> Feeling of tonal and rhythmic center
> Experiment with various means of obtaining at the same time, organic unity and various sorts of dissonance.

These values reflect her work with Charles Seeger and the course of study which became the book *Tradition and Experiment in the New Music*. In effect, Crawford took what Seeger described as a "discipline" and turned it into what she called a "medium"—a complete aesthetic environment for her mature work.[3]

In his recent study of Crawford's music, Joseph Straus explicates the relationship between discipline and medium by using Seeger's "compositional categories" as the analytic categories for his discussion of the elements of Crawford's style. He begins with one that has until now been relatively ignored in discussions of her work—melody:

> In response to what they perceived as the over-reliance of nineteenth-century romantic music on vertically conceived chordal harmony, Seeger urged her, and Crawford sought to write music that consisted of one or more independent self-contained melodies. Such melodies, carefully structured to avoid triadic references, as Seeger recommended, and to project original compelling designs, in ways that Crawford discovered on her own, are the essential building blocks of Crawford's mature music.[4]

The path to Crawford's inventive melodic idiom began with Seeger's concept of the "neume," a term borrowed from medieval chant theory to name the "smallest melodic unit" to result in a significant musical gesture. Even though this brief summary cannot do justice to the scope of Seeger's work, it suffices to say here that he distinguished neume from motive; created binary (three-pitch) and ternary (four-pitch) groups; and organized neumes by contour into "line" (movement all in the same direction) and "twist" (combinations of up-and-down motion and in compound combinations of both). Most important, he used his theory of "neume conversion" to state his real goal: "any neume can be transformed into any other neume . . . a process that may be made use of in composition." Thus through neume theory he analyzed melodic logic in *tonal* music, providing one example of metamorphosis by taking eight steps to transform the first theme of Schubert's Seventh Symphony into the main theme of Strauss's "Till Eulenspiegel's Merry Pranks."[5]

Crawford went through such excercises very quickly, spending some initial lessons on what Seeger later recalled as analysis of "several of the Beethoven symphonies, all of the Brahms, and odds and ends of other things to show how real the thing [neumes as core melodic units] is." Her allusion to the second and fourth symphonies of Brahms as "full of short choppy motives" comes out of this work. She mastered neume conversion very quickly. (Seeger once recalled Ruth's cleverness in "changing 'Frankie and Johnnie' into the 'Internationale.' . . . It took her about twelve steps," he said, also savoring the memory of shocking some of their Communist friends.) [6]

These feats had a serious compositional point primarily because principles of coherence in tonal music could then be manipulated to produce the ideal oppositional melos. The internalization of neumes as germinal material rather than abstract ideas comes through a passing comment in one of Crawford's letters, where she recalled how they "sang the neumes and continuants" in the summer of 1930. Seeger coined the term "continuant" to mean the development of the melodic germ that realized the "definite implications" contained within the neume itself. He described this part of his work with Crawford informally some years later:

> This concept of a continuant, or the technical means of keeping a melody going without coming to a fall, intrigued Ruth, and so a large part of the first lesson was spent in my outlining various ways of keeping a melody from falling, with the idea that if you were able to take a single melodic line and keep it going for ten minutes without its falling, you would be a heaven-storming composer. [7]

As she distilled the essence from Seeger's methods, Crawford evolved a highly original approach to melody. The neumatic principle acts as an understructure to infuse the lines with chromaticism; one neume—the twist of a half and whole step—becomes a fingerprint in her writing. As Straus further notes,

> most of her melodies play a rapid game of leap-frog, with some new notes balancing old ones around constantly shifting pivots. . . . [They] often give the impression of living organisms, like amoebas that change shape as they move. They expand and contract, surge forward and hold back, twist and turn, move forward and shrink back, and all the while their intervallic identity shifts and changes. Inevitably, then, whatever coherence they may be heard to possess derives not from their content, which is constantly in flux, as from the process of melodic formation. [8]

The idea of process as a defining element in Crawford's compositional identity could be applied to other musical functions as well, especially since the "various kind of dissonance" she mentioned as part of her credo refer to Seeger's strategy of turning that word itself into a metaphor applicable to other musical elements. Thus Crawford began with his concept of inclusive dissonance, which embraced such innovations as "dissonant rhythm," "dissonant dynamics," and "dissonant accents." Seeger described his sound-ideal as "heterophony," perhaps borrowing the term from Plato, to mean a deliberate cultivation of profound difference which he described as "sounding together while sounding apart." Each one of his idealized dissonant functions is treated at length, with more rules to thwart the subconscious mapping of old ways of hearing onto new music.[9]

Again, a few of Seeger's general recommendations will have to stand for the whole. With respect to rhythm, he suggested the following: not using more than three consecutive groups of couplets or two groups of triplets; applying syncopation liberally; avoiding sequentiality; and incorporating unusual meters and uneven divisions of measure and beat, and so on. Comments on Crawford's autograph score for the Diaphonic Suite for Two Clarinets explain metric dissonance as "changing meters." Although time signatures were added only in 1952, when she readied this suite for publication, embedded in the line was "dissonant metric structure" pitting "consonant" meters of 2, 3, 4, 6 against "dissonant meters" of 5, 7, 9. She notated shifting time signatures 43 times in 51 measures.

Another powerful influence on linear applications of dissonant counterpoint came from Seeger's interest in the relationship between music and language. Freely redrawn principles of poetic prosody and metric scansion underlay his three central ideas: "modeling," "phrase balance," and "verse form." He explained how music "can be given what may be called 'verse-form,'" notated through single and double bars that correspond to phrases and sentences. If a precompositional plan analogous to verse is adopted through one of several possibilities ("the number of beats or the number of measures in a phrase, or the number of phrases in a section"), then

> many devices of musical assonance and rhythm can be combined. For instance, a repeated tone, a characteristic interval, some particular neume or rhythmical figure, a distinctive slurring or dotting, can recur at symmetrical intervals at the beginning, middle, or ending of each phrase.

He further explained "modeling the line" as the "proper distribution of primary, secondary, and tertiary accents, breathing-spaces, dynamics, and rubato." These ideas shape his two surviving compositions from the 1920s, which he described as "monody . . . the kind of music which moves me more than nearly any other." Again archaic terminology reconnects old and new music for a musicologist-composer.[10]

Seeger's composition for solo voice, "The Letter" (Ex. 13-1), whose text was written by his friend and Harvard classmate John Hall Wheelock, follows Wheelock's sonnet plan of 8 plus 6 lines, while the melody "follows the speech rhythm absolutely" to project rhyme and phrase length. His own analysis of the merits of this piece suggest why its dissonant counterpoint is handled with what David Nicholls describes as "so much freedom . . . [where] the norm of dissonance is being tempered to a greater or lesser extent by the consonance of reiteration." He explained how intervals followed rhyme scheme (i.e., going down on the first line of the couplet, and up on the second); how rests corresponded to punctuation marks; and, most important, how he justified the deviations from rules regarding repeating pitches, as in

> line 7 [where] the dissonance is perfect in spite of and actually gained by the repetition of the D in the octave. The G flat and F sharp in line 8 do not bother me. The tonal center (C, that is middle C), was absolutely unplanned.[11]

Example 13-1 "The Letter" by Charles Seeger, lines 1–8. © 1958, New Music Edition. Used by permission of Theodore Presser Co.

Many years later he returned to this point, describing "The Letter" as "a play in the extension of the tonality of C major. It ends on the leading tone. The first part ends on C and the second begins with high E's and a G, but the outline of the perfect triad is dissonated by the F♯-E♭-F and the succeeding skip of the E on the syllable 'dark' by a C♯." Such was the mediation of tonal and atonal at this time by a musician who "deplored the increasing tendency of the day [1931] to forbid such long-standing and nearly universal traditional structures," and delighted in his intuitive defiance of the "perfectionism" and "preciosity" of his book.[12]

Crawford's response to Seeger's piece give us further insight into the fine intervallic sensitivity that crafted her own settings of poetry:

> A while ago I hummed your lovely sonnet—hummed it very softly with the words. Those fifths—how that they lift and yet calm. And the ninth at the beginning. And the contrast of the "flings" in the third line with the sliding-down fourth line. But that quiet comforting couplet of perfect fifths—And the whole molds into one.[13]

In her own vocal music she worked out these principles with great finesse, particularly in her setting of Carl Sandburg's poem "Rat Riddles," completed by March 1930. Sandburg's free verse, shaped by assonance and alliteration and the repetition of phrases rather than rhyme, is carefully modeled in Crawford's setting. In Example 13-2, where the melody has been extracted from its instrumental setting and arranged by line to parallel Sandburg's poem, her techniques come into focus. Note, for example, the repetition of A flat, from "gray" (line 1) to "green" in lines 2, 6, 7; the larger repetitions of complete lines 6 and 11; the rhyming interval of a fourth (tritone and perfect) at "the rats" in lines 5 and 10; and the rhyming phrases of lines 1, 6, and 10. Sandburg's repetition of "blinked at me" from line 6 to line 7 is duly imitated by Crawford as well. Her only deviation from the poem is the insertion of the word "rat" in line 8, through which she emphasized its relationship to line 3, that is, "Come again, [rat]" is modeled after the earlier line, "hello, rat." She restructured the text into four sections, each framed by an orchestral accompaniment for oboe, piano, and small battery of percussion instruments, who behave somewhat like a traditional ritornello in a Baroque strophic aria.

The Diaphonic Suite for Solo Flute or Oboe, a work in four movements, applies verse form to textless music in a kind of modernist version of Renaissance "musique mesurée." Various autographs for the verse-form movements rely even more overtly on graphic parallels between musical and poetic lines. In one for the first movement, an empty stave separates the first four lines from the last five. In holograph fragments for the second movement, some musical lines are indented, as if they were Sandburg's blank verse (Fig. 13-1). It seems quite possible that real literary models existed for these movements, such as, as Seeger once suggested, Japanese poetry, whose phrases of five and seven syllables may have been equated here with Crawford's one-beat measures.[14]

With respect to the much analyzed third movement of this suite, Crawford described it privately as a "triple passacaglia perpetuum mobile," the triple re-

Example 13-2　"Rat Riddles," vocal line for first twelve lines of the poem and the process of "modeling."

line 1　There was　a　gray　rat　looked　at　me

l. 2　With　green　eyes　out of a　rat-hole.

l. 3　"Hel - lo,　rat,"　I　said,

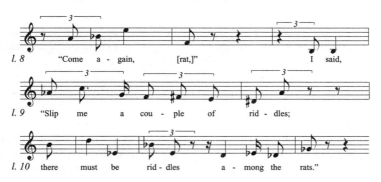

l. 4　"Is　there　an - y　chance　for　me

l. 5　to　get　on - to　the　lan - guage　of　the　rats?"

l. 6　And the green　eyes　blinked　at　me,

l. 7　blinked　from　a　gray　rat's　rat - hole.

l. 8　"Come　a - gain,　[rat,]"　I　said,

l. 9　"Slip　me　a　cou - ple　of　rid - dles;

l. 10　there　must　be　rid - dles　a - mong the　rats."

l. 11　And　the　green　eyes　blinked　at　me

l. 12　and　a　whis - per　came　from the gray　rat - hole:

Figure 13-1   Autograph for Diaphonic Suite for Solo Flute or Oboe, second movement.

ferring to the controlling number 7. One "7" refers to the meter 7/8; the second "7" refers to the seven-pitch set that generates all the rest of the melodic material, initially through rotational permutation, one set per measure/ seven measures per phrase; the third "7" refers to the use of seven other transpositions of the row in the rest of the piece, which begin on each of the seven pitches of the first set (Fig. 13-2). Just like Renaissance and early Baroque passacaglias, this movement uses a single phrase through which to construct a continuous variation form. As usual, there are loose threads in the design, namely the extra bars at the end of the first two phrases.[15]

The value of Crawford's description "triple passacaglia" is to remind us how

meter: 7/8	1	2	3	4	5	6	7	
ostinato original:	G	A	G#	B	C	F	C#	P (prime)
1. m. 9	A							P
2. m. 17	G#							R
3. m. 24	B							R
4. m. 31	C							I
5. m. 38	F							I
6. m. 45	C#							RI
7. m. 52	G							RI

7/4 Coda with P starting on second note to return to G, the center.

P = prime
R = retrograde
I = inversion

Figure 13-2   The plan for the Diaphonic Suite for Solo Oboe or Flute, third movement as a "triple passacaglia" on 7.

often her precompositional schemes involved a kind of number centricity, or the projection of a single number in different musical domains. In the last movement of the String Quartet 1931 (discussed later in more detail), the operative number is ten. In "Chinaman! Laundryman!" the operative number is nine. While the voice declaims its theatrical arioso, the piano accompaniment, with a metronome marking of quarter-note = 99, generates the ostinato scheme contained as a single line doubled in octaves. There are nine half-steps in the set, nine pitches make a measure, nine measures make a phrase, nine phrases make a cycle of row permutations in rotation. The opening of the piece sets out the row, its rhythmic modes, and the transposition plan.

In "Prayers of Steel," the third of the Three Songs, which has been described more than once as the most totally heterophonic of Crawford's works, we encounter two controlling numbers of five and seven. Befitting a text whose theme is the divine plan of construction, the organization of the instrumental parts reaches a pinnacle of intricacy, even though the two stanzas are set to the same music, and even though they are divided by a surprisingly long measure of silence, as if a lunch whistle had blown, and stopped the men at work. Crawford's setting evokes a construction site: (1) an oboe drills away at the foundation with its seven-pitch row in rotational permutation; its pitch content will be adopted by the strings in a vertical pattern. (2) The percussion forges ahead in 5/4, while the piano hammers quintuplet patterns played in octaves. (3) The wind ostinati use accent groups that increase from 1 to 7 pitches, while corresponding rest patterns decrease in length from 7 to 1 (Ex. 13-3).

That such experimentation with symmetry and precompositional schemes for order reflected the preoccupations of the moment was quite clear to Crawford, whose sympathies for the musicological discoveries of early music led her to recommend Riemann's *Geschichte der Musiktheorie* (History of Music Theory) to Seeger, noting his lengthy discussion of "Consonance and Dissonance

Example 13-3   Design Elements of "5" and "7" in "Prayers of Steel." (1) "Prayers of Steel," oboe part, mm. 1–2. (2) "Prayers of Steel," reduction of rhythmic patterns in percussion, oboe, and piano as diagrammed by Charles Seeger in Henry Cowell's anthology *American Composers on American Music.* (3) "Prayers of Steel," accent grouping in the woodwind ostinato.

(1)

(2)

Example 13-3   (*continued*)

(3)

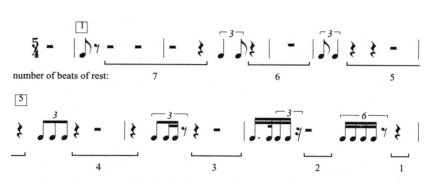

in the Thirteenth Century." Her own appropriation of such terminology as ostinato, ricercar, passacaglia, and monody, as well as her adaptation of isorhythmic techniques to her own ends, reflects the historical sympathies between early modernism and "archaic" music, which she shared with many modernists (both European and American) in the period. Besides, she had learned dissonant counterpoint from a musicologist extremely interested in such affinities. As Cowell wrote, "[a]way back, Seeger insisted on being enthusiastic about very ancient music; no one could see what possible musical value it had. Seeger also pointed out that it has similarity with modern music. . . . Today, nearly all modernists have developed an interest in very old music, and the relationship between the very old and the very new is recognized." Seeger found much early music theory useful, borrowing such terminology as "novum organum," "cantus firmus," and "diaphonic" from old music theory (he most likely used the *Oxford History of Music*, which he would later mention in his own memoirs).[16]

She sent back reports of her encounters with compatible European musicians to Seeger during her year abroad, her description of the music of Imré Weisshaus supplying further clues to her own work:

> It is almost uncanny how he has been seeking out in some ways almost identical paths with many principles of dissonant counterpoint. He showed me a suite for solo instruments which I think would interest you tremendously: great co-ordination and economy of material, and a fine big gross-line. One movement had f as a tonal center: tonal center by avoidance, for it was intimated at, hinted at, expected, you were made to want it, but it was not heard until the end. I remember well your speaking of this. In another, there were many crabbings and conversions, but one thing which especially interested me was that the last page repeated exactly the first page in tone and rhythm, yet was entirely different because the rhythm was preceded by two added beats: thus [Ex. 13-4] (this is not his melody: his has, I think, more interest. I suppose this is not so unusual: but has it ever been applied to an entire long section before?)[17]

Example 13-4   Ruth Crawford's illustration of a melody in which a rhythmic shift alters a pitch canon, in the manner of Imre Weisshaus.

becomes

Crawford essays just this technique of dividing pitch and rhythm in the context of canonic imitation in the first movement of the Diaphonic Suite for Viola (or Oboe) and Cello. In April she reworked the preliminary sketch, with "only the first nine notes remaining" as a "much disguised canon." More important, the Piano Study in Mixed Accents, completed in December 1930, skews pitch-class and rhythm with more complexity. "Mixed accents" (another variation on the theme of mixed meters) shape what Mark Nelson describes as a "steady sinuous stream of irregularly accented sixteenth notes." He clarifies the structure as a "double palindrome" whose "axis of symmetry is an odd segment of eighteen notes which is not symmetrical and is presented in a manner which fundamentally alters the relation of pitch class to accent in the second half of the work."[18]

A ll of these various aspects of her style—dissonated melody, number centricity, the establishment of formal symmetries and their confoundment—came together as resources for the composition of her most important work, the String Quartet 1931, written between February and June 1931. The first two movements handle dissonant counterpoint with greater elasticity and imagination than ever before.

Thematic multiplicity rules the first movement from the beginning, as the "solo" line in Violin I is partnered by a melodic line that characteristically moves from a low to high range in a scale-like fashion. Its opening section began life as a spin-off from verse-form, in another analogy Crawford called "metric" form, undoubtedly referring to poetic rather than musical meter. Principles of phrase modeling shape the two A sections that frame the movement (mm. 1–15; 64–78), where "punctuation marks" of commas and double bars prevail again as in similar movements of the Diaphonic Suite for Flute.

Although she abandons the rigid equation between beats and syllables that governed the diaphonic suite, the phrase structure is clear, the opening fifteen measures of its first movement falling into the pattern: AB/AB as 5 + 2 + 5 + 3. The rising seventh functions as an end rhyme, forming a cadence at the fifth measure, which is reinforced by doubling and is also repeated at the closure of phrase B. Similarly, the falling seventh is used to begin both phrases, and additional repetitions within act as internal rhymes as well.

Once the poem has been heard, Crawford proceeds to weave the themes into a polyphonic fabric built of permutations upon them. This process is laid out by the composer in a key document, an autograph draft for the first movement. In most respects it is similar to the final version, but its great value lies in the composer's annotations, which explicate the understructure of the movement. In the draft she assigns Roman numerals to each theme and names the contrapuntal procedure applied to the material at hand. The themes are subjected to any number of standard contrapuntal operations: con. for conversion or inversion; crab, or retrograde; and basic transposition at various intervals (Fig. 13-3 lists her annotations by measure).

These themes are not ersatz Schoenbergian rows with immutable pitch contents; instead they are modified throughout by "interval stretches," a term coined by Seeger to signify the deliberate alteration of one or two intervals within a fairly literal repeat. The cello, which has the solo line, is based on "III major 3 higher interval stretches"; it begins on middle C and more or less follows the original III with some interval expansion in m. 36 and interval inversion in m. 37. The regimen gives way, however, after four measures, where she continues the cello line freely for the next six measures in rhythmic patterns more like theme IV. In the second violin, she presents theme "IV con" in pitch content only. The first violin "IIA con" begins on C, a major third higher than the original IIA on its second measure. This too moves into free writing after four measures. Using four themes in a relatively short movement presented a challenge. On the one hand, it ensured the heterophony or lack of interrelationship that was Crawford's goal. On the other hand, it raised the specter of disintegration. Crawford handled this problem in a number of ways. She consistently reduced the texture by keeping one voice quiet or giving it sustained tones. In addition, internal relationships among the themes unite them both motivically and tonally. Sevenths are prominent, as mentioned previously in the lines of the metric form sections. But they come into play among the four themes as well. Note for example the opening of theme IV, with its midpoint leap of a seventh and a series of sevenths at the close. Another unifying device in the movement is the use of triplets in three of the four themes.

Paramount also is the projection of the "leading line," or continuous curve. In the autograph draft, the solo lines are indicated as such, a device Crawford retained in the published score, where she indicates as well that "the melodic line as indicated by 'solo' in each part must be heard continuing throughout the movement." Crawford distinguished the solo line by using only two of the four themes, nos. I and III, as its components. As the solo moved from one in-

Linear Organization in the First Movement

section	measure nos.	violin 1	violin 2	viola	cello
A	1–15 ("monody")	S/I	[Ia]		[II, IIa
B	16–20	S/III		IV	IIa
(16–24)	20		S/III		
	22	IV crab			var. IIa
A₁	25	S/I con.		II	
(25–34)	28		IV trans.		
	30		IIa		
	31				S/I crab from m. 5 sempre solo
C	35	IIa con.	IV con		[S]III maj 3 higher with int. stretches
(35–43)					
D	44		S/III crab from m. 25	II [crab and con]	
(44–63)	49	S/III con. with stretches			
	50				cont. of II
	55	ad			
A	64 to end		"monody" returns with rhythm and pitch switched between Ib and Ia.		

Figure 13-3 String Quartet 1931, first movement, notations from autograph draft by the composer, indicating thematic alterations.

strument to another, she coordinated thematic shifts in the other parts as well. By controlling the entrance of the solo themes, she established a balance among the parts. Each solo section takes up roughly the same space, nine or ten measures. In essence, she wrote an instrumental motet in which the solos behaved like quasi cantus firmi, surrounded by nonimitative secondary lines.

Crawford described the last two movements through the categories of dissonant counterpoint or dissonant modern music as she practiced it in the most extended remarks she ever made about her own work (see Appendix A). The underlying plan of the third movement—its "heterophony of dynamics"—was based on the noncongruence of crescendi and diminuendi coordinated with changing meters. The effect of massed pitch evokes her earlier interest in the "complex veil of sound" used in the third Chant for Women's Chorus as well as the ostinato added to the second Sandburg song, "In Tall Grass"; there she explained that "the rhythmic pattern made by their crescendi and diminuendi must be distinguishable as unified pulsating masses of sound." In the quartet movement, she supplied another solo line, only this time she built it into the fabric of the pulsating mass itself. Her example of 5/4 (which can only refer to mm. 39–48) shows the plan that groups these measures into two units of five as well. The "melodic line [which] grows out of this continuous increase and decrease" is indicated as well through a diagram that implies but does not totally expose their canonic treatment. If this is extended, the organization becomes clear.

Since this analysis was written in response to a request from Edgard Varèse, she sent along a score as well, adding her own markings—connecting lines drawn from one sostenuto tone to the other. The history of past performances led her to this because she was so frustrated by how little this line seemed to be coming through in performance. In 1941, when the score was printed, she had hoped that the solo tones might be printed in red to emphasize the point more clearly. At the least, she increased the tempo from 80 to 116 because she blamed the lack of linear clarity on the slow tempo used for the recording. The melodic line, extracted from the movement, has its own irregular phrase structure, although some "tonalitous" factors account for the prominence of C/C♯ at the beginning, at the climax of the piece, and at its end.

With all of the control, this technical description does not do justice to the intense, even tragic power of this movement, which breaks free from all schemes at the climax between mm. 68 and 76 (Ex. 13-5). Accumulating tension like a spring that is stretched ever tauter, when the upper climax is reached, and the texture releases into a welcome homophony of articulation, what follows is a rebounding explosive energy. Thus between mm. 68 and 75, the texture thickens: instead of single tones, there are double stops and finally chords for everyone. In m. 71 the sixth F-D♯ is added, to intensify the A-G♯-D♯ sonority. Even more unusual is the sudden burst of rhythmic energy in mm. 75–76, the only place in the movement where there is any subdivision of the beat.

Here is a section of the work that sounds both spontaneous and inevitable and seems so totally necessary to its success. And yet it was written seven years later. For at the time that Crawford readied the score for publication in 1938, she revised the climax. Although no original score for the movement exists (all manuscript copies for the piece date no earlier than 1938), the old version has been preserved on the recording of the Andante issued by the New Music Society's series. The recording diverges at the crucial juncture of the climax at mm. 68–77: that brilliant gesture of unexpected eighth notes tumbling into a chord, releasing the tension created by the overlapping of single-pitch entries and exits, was not there in the first version of the movement. The original arrival at measure 68 simply sustained one chord for four measures, as a transcription (Ex. 13-6) shows. In effect, the climax and the turning point were one and the same chord—the four-note cluster in m. 76. In a letter to one of the members of the Galimir Quartet in 1948, she discussed her dissatisfaction with the initial recording and referred to the revision as a "major change." Even after the score was printed, Crawford returned to that moment in the movement once again. On one of her printed scores she reworked the spacings, shifting around the double stops to make them easier to

Example 13-5   String Quartet 1931, third movement, mm. 61–76. © 1941, New Music Edition. Used by permission of Theodore Presser Co.

play.[19] The fourth movement has its own very different appeal, a myriad of intricacies shaped through various plans in pitch, rhythm, dynamics, and articulation. Describing the tonal material of the upper voice, or Voice 1, as "free," Crawford explains Voice 2 through serial organization. As illustrated in her own words (in Appendix A), its generating number is 10. She weaves the thread of its rotational permutations across the diagonal of her diagram, showing it in motion, as it were—a symbolic reflection of her interest in organic metamorphosis. The axis of symmetry, E, is the turning tone, not part of the thematic material at m. 58, locating the "crab of foregoing material 1/2 step

Example 13-5 (*continued*)

higher" in m. 62. Measure 93 contained a "defect in Persian rug! The 'f' is absent, making 9 tones in this series."

The overall form, as Crawford describes it, which obeys simple rules of addition and subtraction, is easily audible—and very satisfying. Voice 1, which starts out with a single tone, increases in pitch count with each succeeding entry, while Voice 2, which begins at 20, decreases correspondingly. Just when the rhythmic metamorphosis between the parts concludes, we arrive at the tonal turning point as well. The impulse for a plan of this sort may have been

Example 13-6   String Quartet 1931, third movement, mm. 66–76, as played on the recording of Andante, New Music Recordings series, 1934. Transcribed by Elizabeth Vercoe.

suggested in music by Imre Weisshaus. While in Berlin, in the fall of 1930, she had described Weisshaus's quartet as a work in progress that was "similar to Carl's [Ruggles] Sun Treader in that it will turn backwards. Not only crab, but inverted; and not only that, but the composition as a whole inverted: cello part to the 1st violin, etc. And still another added intricacy I haven't time to explain!"[20]

Perhaps the other "added intricacy" can be found in Weisshaus's Petite Suite pour Solo Clarinette, a work which Crawford saw in November 1930 and later heard in April 1931 at the Novembergruppe concert where her own Diaphonic Suite was played. Its third movement is constructed from the total chromatic, which, while hardly as inventive as Crawford's melody, nevertheless, presents itself with one new note each time, behaving similarly to

Example 13-7   Imre Weisshaus, Petite Suite pour Solo Clarinette, third movement. © 1967. Used by permission of Editions Henry Lamoine Co., 24 rue Pigalle, 95009 Paris.

Voice I in the fourth movement of Crawford's string quartet. In addition Weisshaus's clarinet piece retrogrades at its conclusion, collapsing into a mini-palindrome (Ex. 13-7), constructed from the last notes of each previous phrase group. Even if Crawford's plan outdoes Weisshaus in complexity, this little Clarinet Suite reminds us of formal interrogations going on at the time.

In the fourth movement of the string quartet she controlled still another aspect of interactive metamorphosis between the two voices by organizing the time of entry in a systematic and highly original manner as well. The plan was

Pitch Content

	1	2	3	4	5	6	7	8	9	10	
m. 1	D	E	F	E♭	F♯	A	A♭	G	D♭	C	P rotated x 10
m. 21	E										P2 rotated × 10
m. 47	D										P alone
m. 58	E										turning point of "foreign tone"

palindrome up a half step starts here:

m. 63	C♯	R1 alone
m. 71	D♯	R3 rotated × 10
m. 96	D	R1 rotated × 10

Lengths of rests between entries

1. 𝄻 𝄻
2. 𝄼 𝄻
3. 𝄾 𝄼 𝄼 𝄽
4. 𝄻 𝄽
5. 𝄾 𝄼 𝄽
6. 𝄽 𝄼
7. 𝄾 𝄼 𝄽
8. 𝄼 𝄽
9. 𝄾 𝄼
10. 𝄼

m. 31 as midway point 𝄾 𝄽

Second set from m. 33

1. 𝄼 𝄼
2. 𝄽 𝄼 𝄼
3. 𝄻 𝄼
4. 𝄽 𝄻 𝄼
5. 𝄼 𝄻 𝄼
6. 𝄾 𝄽 𝄼 𝄻 𝄽
7. 𝄽 𝄻 𝄻
8. 𝄾 𝄼 𝄻 𝄼 𝄽
9. 𝄻 𝄻 𝄼
10. 𝄾 𝄽 𝄼 𝄻 𝄻

Figure 13-4 Plan for the String Quartet 1931, fourth movement, as a projection of the number 10 in pitch and rhythm.

increase and decrease, and in Voice 2 these projected the number 10 as well, as summed up by Seeger's description of the movement as "(10-10) + (10-10)' + to followed by a cancrizans, one half-tone higher" (see Fig. 13-4). Crawford's diagram of the rotational permutation of her ten-note set ten times loops lines on the diagonal rather than in a static grid, threading the rows together (Appendix A). Other aspects of the work involve systematic increase and decrease as well. As she indicates, her plan for dynamics (not unlike that found in the Piano Study in Mixed Accents) makes one part get systematically louder, while the other reverses that process.[21]

Other details in Crawford's analysis are worth noting as well. Tempering the severity of this plan are subtleties she calls "rhythmic fluidity." These recall the more basic rules of rhythmic dissonance that yielded the prolix lines of earlier Diaphonic Suites. On the copy of the printed score she sent to Varèse she changed the tempo mark from "Allegro possibile" to "Allegro quasi recitative" with a tempo mark of half-note equals 100. To highlight the contrast of "mood" she added "energico" to the top part and "tranquillo" to the bottom, with complementary crescendi and descrescendi. Everything was designed to contribute to "dissonance of mood."

Crawford pointed out a "defect" in the fourth movement to indicate an inconsistency, that is to say, the addition of a non-set pitch as a turning point for the retrograde, as well as other small discrepancies in the presentation of a pitch set. That statement suggests how her own attitude toward order and form has affinities with the Persian weaver, whose design formulas deliberately contain small asymmetries and irregularities; it was a comparison that Charles Seeger used as well in just the same context, when he described how "she had a way of taking my prescriptions . . . my assignments for the following week, but always putting in a quirk of her own that gave the piece a character distinctly hers. It would be like the departure from the design in a Persian rug, which was always necessary in order that men should never pretend to be perfect. Only the Gods could be perfect." Thus from the beginning of her study with Charles Seeger, she resisted total systematization of her music, attempting to reconcile fluidity and organic flow with heterophony. Beyond that, she used the image of a "Persian rug" to resist demeaning images of female creativity so common in musical discourse. Old oppositions charging formal power with masculinity and detail with femininity had surfaced in her own self-deprecations of her ability in the 1920s, when she called herself a "dressmaker, more worried about sewing on buttons" than a composer crafting a musical totality. When Schoenberg spoke of form as a kind of vision, he too gendered the ability to conceive compositional structure as a "masculine way of thinking"; his remarks echo in Crawford's own words as well as Charles Seeger's claims about giving her form.[22]

Crawford overcame such debilitating rhetoric by creating her own solutions to the dichotomies and contradictions that alternately plagued and gratified her teacher-philosopher. As a composer, she delighted in reconciling Seeger's oppositions and was able to achieve what he only speculated was possible. As Joseph Straus remarks, her music "revels in the instability of oppositional categories, playfully breaking down the barriers between them." The difference between these two people reflects in part the fifteen-year difference in their ages. On some level, Seeger suffered the displacement of the post-Victorian rebel, belonging to a generation "fated to dwell in a kind of no-man's land," according to the historian Daniel Singal. Even if he managed brilliantly to turn this fate into a source of prolix speculation, it occasionally induced a kind of paralysis. Crawford's generation, on the other hand, had an easier time riding out the waves of the Modernist revolution. More distant from the European past, she was less encumbered by it and did not suffer Seeger's sense of loss. Her mediation of his heterophonic ideals reflects the more mature stage of Modernism that has been described as "a dissolving, a blending, a merging of things previously held to be forever mutually exclusive." Their mantra "sounding apart while sounding together" is echoed in this contemporary explanation of the period: "The defining thing in the Modernist mode is not so much that things fall apart, but that they fall together." Thus Crawford's style may have changed, but the same impulse toward synthesis that led her to describe herself as a "message carrier between two worlds" continued to shape her musical identity as a composer in the 1930s. "Spiritual in spite of method," Adolph Weiss said, bestowing his highest praise on the String Quartet 1931. In Crawford's own interpretation of the Persian rug metaphor, spirit unites with order, weaving together spontaneity and clarity —heart and head into her new style. As she wrote to Vivian Fine in 1931, "Music must flow. It must be a thread unwinding, a thread from no one knows just where. It must not be a problem in mathematics, writing music."[23]

"c o m p o s i n g   b a b i e s"

Family. Home. Such magic words for Ruth Crawford, who had waited so long to have children. As a thirteen-year old girl, she had envisioned herself sitting on the porch of a Florida bungalow, singing to her children. At twenty, she joked about having thirty-five children to send to the American Conservatory of Music. At twenty-nine she was in Berlin, and like many women who stand at the threshold of motherhood after years of deferring, she let herself see what had been there all along: a world of baby carriages. On her thirtieth birthday in Paris, she was with the man she hoped would be the father of her children. In December 1932, one month after she married Charles Seeger, she became pregnant. An elated Crawford wrote Nicolas Slonimsky (responding to his request for biographical information) in a postscript about her new life: "and of course—my marriage. That is more important than all these two pages [of career data] put together." Five years later, she was the mother of three children. Looking back on this period in her life, Crawford acknowledged the time and energy mothering demanded, and said that she was "composing babies."[1]

In 1933 Crawford launched herself into the process of motherhood as if she were breaking a champagne bottle over the prow of a transatlantic liner in a public ceremony that the circumstances of her Nevada marriage had denied her. Flushed with baby fever, she asked Margaret Valiant to make maternity clothes that would "exhibit rather than conceal" her pregnancy. Her ship-board friend, who was designing clothes for some New York department stores, "did several dresses for her—one with some fringes, and another with ruffles all around the area of pregnancy . . . we had a lot of fun. That was

Ruth's approach to pregnancy, something to be very proud of because she was so proud of the father."[2]

Michael was born on August 15, 1933, two months before the Seegers' first anniversary. For much of the two-week "lying-in" period that was standard hospital routine in those days, Ruth was alone in New York, while Charles was in Patterson taking care of his other children. "Baby Michael is such a delicious little mystery . . . the dearest little piece of you," Ruth wrote to Charles from the Sloane Hospital for Women.[3]

Within eight days Crawford was talking about resuming her pre-baby life with the naive optimism that shelters new parents. When Vivian Fine told her that Doris Humphreys returned to the stage only five weeks after her baby was born, Ruth was "made very happy." "How about my going to Yaddo?" she asked Charles, as Copland's second festival of Contemporary American Music was planned for the end of September. As for their separation, Charles's work came first even at this precious moment; Ruth was stoically willing to sacrifice his visiting her at the hospital if he felt pressured (he was revising *Tradition and Experiment in Modern Music*).

Within ten days Mrs. Seeger was given permission to leave, the $2.75 savings per day an added incentive for early discharge. However, she stayed longer because she had no place to go: "Charlie dearest, as far as health is concerned, I could leave tomorrow: there are two drawbacks: where shall we go, and could we buy the things I'll need in time for us to leave on Monday?" Regarding the second issue, she asked Charles if he would be "embarrassed to buy such things as diapers?" If so, Vivian Fine could be pressed into service.[4]

As for their temporary homelessness, which other women would have treated as a crisis, Crawford reacted with what her friend Margaret Valiant praised as an "innate grace of Mother Nature—granite." The problem arose because the Seegers had given up their Village apartment, not wanting to pay rent over the summer when they could live at Patterson. Ruth telephoned Marion Bauer, who was at the MacDowell Colony and would thereby have an empty apartment (she was unreachable); she also had Margaret send an emergency cable to friends.[5]

They eventually found shelter in the apartment of Esther Spitzer, an erstwhile member of the Composers' Collective and a well-off student of Wallingford Riegger. The Seegers—mother, father, and newborn—slept on a living-room floor for two weeks. (An extroverted young woman, Esther found Ruth "withdrawn . . . she came a stranger and left a stranger.") At some point in the fall of 1933, the Seegers moved to 111 East 87th Street, a building that seems to have been owned by the New School, where they lived through 1935. Their "railroad" flat was sunless and airless, the only "window" in one room looking into another.[6]

Charles was scrambling to make a living. He held on to his part-time courses at the New School, but after fifteen years of successful teaching, he lost his job at the Institute of Musical Art (by then known as the Juilliard School). Frank Damrosch had fired him, perhaps happy to get rid of this musical radical on his staff, especially one who had divorced a friend of his family. Few of Charles's private students had the money to pay his fees. "He went out lecturing," Pete remembers. His children, whose sensitivities were honed by the contrast between their father's situation and their boarding-school world of privilege, remember how "very very broke" Ruth and Charles were, "living hand to mouth." They were helped along "through gifts from friends and handouts during the Depression while they were living in New York, and an occasional small job that would bring them in a little cash." "They were hard up—My God—they were hard up. I always felt embarrassed to eat any food in their house where it was in such short supply," recalled Charles's oldest son. Pete also remembers coming home from school vacation and lending his father $5 to get milk for Michael. But "Father didn't ever complain, ever. He kept his savoir faire through it all."[7]

Charles's discipline sustained him. And Ruth supported him totally. Particularly because of the Depression, there was no question of whose work came first. She fluctuated between deference and vigilance as the wife of an older man. "My blessing on the article," Ruth wrote to Charles one winter. Another note reads, "I wanted to phone you at the Collective to remind you to eat." The novice mother gave way to the household manager, making "urgent lists" of chores. Sometimes Ruth substituted a musical phrase for her signature, notating the pitches of the first line of Charlie's song, "The Letter," which began "My darling, my beloved one."[8]

That the Seegers fell into conventional division of labor within their household was typical of the times. Even if they had been inclined to consider more egalitarian patterns, the Depression had made these options moot. The "pessimistic shift in the ideological climate" for feminism in the 1930s, as noted by the historian Carl Degler, pervaded the counter-culture of the left as well as the mainstream bourgeoisie. The Communist Party's view of oppression did not distinguish two varieties—his and hers: class, not gender, determined political destiny, and the model had women fighting "side by side" or "shoulder to shoulder" against capitalism. All that earlier feminist ferment seemed like yet another version of modernist hyperindividualism or "bourgeois diversion." Crawford was not working outside the home, and there was no way that she could see her work as entitling her to deprive the breadwinner of time for his.[9]

For all of the hardship, the Seegers had an active social life, nourished from different yet overlapping worlds. The painter Tom Benton (Seeger's colleague at the New School) and his wife Rita invited them to musical evenings on Saturday nights at their Greenwich Village home. Margaret Valiant replaced Marion Bauer and Blanche Walton as Ruth's closest woman friend. Composers from the collective dropped by to talk. The memory of Ruth as one half of "a love match . . . a very very happy marriage" is preserved by both Elie and Hannah Siegmeister. Hannah paints this portrait of the couple:

> Ruth was, first of all, a ruddy rosy person . . . very hearty-looking person who looked as if she had just come down from the Ozark mountains . . . a farm girl. . . . She had the robust full cheeks, rosy complexion, bright eyes, bouncing, full of vitality. My mother said, "Oh what a beautiful wholesome creature she is." . . .

Of course she wasn't as unsophisticated as that although it was always a wonder to us the wide difference in age between Ruth and Charlie. He was elegant and aristocratic in such a take-it-for-granted kind of way. . . . He acted and spoke as if he was not aware that he had these manners. So Charlie who sparkled and this nice rosy girl—that made a good match.[10]

This new stage of life suited Ruth. Looking back on her youth, she rejected the outer signs of her upbringing, becoming fiercely anti-religious. Armed with Freud, she could label her father as someone who "repressed" her mother, who denied the essential physical needs of people to touch and kiss each other. Her own childhood looked drabber than perhaps it really was, partly because her marriage was so different from her mother's. That counted for much in Ruth's life at this time.[11]

Wrapped up in politics and in a myriad of professional activities, Charles lived an active life outside the home. His own work for various left-wing music groups required traveling to start composers' collectives in other cities (Boston and Philadelphia). Other times he sought out colleagues in musical and scholarly circles in a pattern of intellectual fraternization that was simply part of his being.

Occasional fissures in the granite rock of Ruth's optimism and devotion came from bouts of "blueness," probably caused by loneliness and exhaustion. The little opening phrase of Seeger's worker's song, "Lenin! Who's That Guy?" was parodied by Ruth as "Charlie, Where's that guy?" in some letters. Other undated notes refer to conflicts—none of which seems unduly serious—for which Ruth is usually apologizing. "Please do love me and forgive me for breaking out. And please get well soon—a great deal of my blueness is the feeling that you are not like yourself." Another time she pined for their one vacation two years earlier, writing Charles, "Tonight I'm not a red revolutionist that's out to save the world. I'm a blue one and I wouldn't mind trading New York for Nevada— or Paris."[12] There were only rare hints of deeper malaise. One note reads:

> I've felt badly since you left about the way in which I let you leave. I'm all mixed up—I feel as though I'm in the middle of things which I can't tie together. I just can't make the ends meet. . . . I wanted to run after you and put my arms around you. Please love me and forgive me. I *am* worried and I feel so helpless not being able to do anything. Therefore I scold *you*, even though I understand (I really do). Please be patient (you are) with my restlessness. You are tremendously patient with me. And please love me as you always have—as much if not more than when I could get into the lovely white evening dress and not be weary at the end of the evening.[13]

How much did her own neglected career contribute to such restlessness? Even though her works weren't played much, "she knew they were good and had no doubts about it," Charles said. "She knew that Quartet was good. And she knew the songs and the Diaphonic Suites were good." Not surprisingly, she expressed ambivalence about choices not made and commitments left unmet. Was it simply the demands of motherhood that derailed her? Not necessarily, for "[b]eing a composer is an ideal occupation for a woman who's home," Vivian Fine once said. But to Charles, Michael "took up a good deal of her time so that she gave up composition."[14]

Even as traditional roles for women supplied her with the social grammar of retreat, Crawford's words complicate that judgment. Ambivalence surfaces in the qualifying clauses that pit art against motherhood and in the marital camouflage of her own abilities. In one casual note Ruth equated the dedication needed to become an "all engrossed composerin" (adding a gendered German ending from "Komponistin" to English) with the dedication of the "all-sacrificing communistin," in order to reject both identities: she "took far too much pleasure in such trivial things as baby's shoes looking spiff. . . . Guess I'll have to be satisfied to go halfway toward either goal, and let Charlie and the ten babies be the other . . . nine-tenths." Another time, Ruth wrote: "Instead of making you something useful, like a shirt, or me something useful like a skirt, or something really useless, like a quartet, I iron baby dresses and eat 'em up." The year that her string quartet was premiered, she left a note to her husband, asking him to change the baby and then added, "I wondered if Bach's wife left such mundane requests. . . . "[15]

Nevertheless, Crawford took on some professional responsibilities during these years. She gave lessons in dissonant counterpoint to Johanna Beyer (1888–1944), who was both pupil of and devoted friend to Henry Cowell. Beyer had translated Carl Sandburg's poems for the Universal Edition of Crawford's Three Songs.[16]

Slowly, Ruth Crawford, composer, became, in the words of the composer Arthur Berger, a "personage," someone whose reputation rested on hearsay. "I should have assigned her a profile in *Modern Music*," Minna Lederman, its editor, lamented many years later. "It's one of my big regrets, but she just wasn't around much."[17]

When Michael was eighteen months old, a second child was conceived, and Charles's wish for a daughter was gratified on June 17, 1935, when Ruth gave birth to a girl they named Margaret. Ruth indulged her husband's wish to name his first daughter after a childhood sweetheart.

That summer proved to be the nadir of their poverty in New York. Charles and two-year old Michael were already at Patterson. Close to fifty years of age, Charles was forced to do seasonal farm labor, picking blueberries on A. B. Hamel's farm near his parents' home. Trying to keep desperation at bay, Ruth masked worry with girlish pluck: "I think we are going to have a summer with much fun in it, even though it isn't just what we could choose." "Don't let Hamel ride you too much," she advised, worried about his stamina.[18]

Ruth delayed her own arrival at Hamel's farm. At times, Charles had no choice but to ask for help from his parents—who "thought they were crazy to have a second child." Once when Michael was sick, Elsie Seeger hired a nurse to take care of him. On July 25 she wrote to Ruth that "I hope you will approve of what we have done." Keeping the door to her mansion closed, Mrs. Seeger urged her daughter-in-law to come as soon as possible. "Charlie has had a hard month, he looked terribly[;] how he did it without going to pieces" she did not know. "When you can get up here and have the nice glorious air on the Ridge, and do your part caring for the children, he will be able to do his part, and not look too badly." The implication that Ruth was shirking her duty lay just beneath the surface of this cold letter, but for once Ruth balked. Even though she told Charles that "it's just dead and reasonless without you here," she said that Michael was better off with him than with her. She was physically spent; she "longed for just staying put, being quiet, not walking, moving, doing. . . . The thought of physical activity just necessary to moving fills my none-too-frisky body with dismay, say nothing of the activity of the life primitive." Was she supposed to pick berries too? she asked her husband. "Hamel does understand I'm still not good for much? . . . I dread the activity, I can't tell you. Will Mike and Peggy both sleep in the house and we in the trailer? Will Peggy keep Hamel awake? You've probably worked it all out."[19]

Justifying the delay, Ruth gave full accounts of her "queer busy days." Errands and visits to the doctor and dentist followed by meals followed by washing dishes in the endless cycle of housework: all were detailed in obsessive accounts that acted as her defense. By August Ruth had moved up to the farm, and all the Seegers were living in the trailer on the ridge. Pete remembers how

> at times Ruth went frantic, trying to take care of two babies with no running water. She couldn't relax and let something go to pot. . . . Yet she was determined. All of a sudden she was a mother. She gave up everything in life to be a good mother. . . . Once, there were one too many dirty diapers; I remember seeing her shriek and seeing the diapers go up in the air. The Seeger wives in general had this problem: their husbands would ask them to do more than human beings could do.[20]

The Seegers returned to New York in the fall of 1935 at a low point in their lives. Charles's own career and political commitments were in transition as well. Having lost a good deal of income from stocks and investments because of the Depression, Blanche Walton could no longer finance Seeger's project, the American Library of Musicology, which folded after two publications in 1935. When the New York Musicological Society also repudiated Seeger's commitment to systematic musicology, and instead moved toward historical scholarship, Seeger withdrew from that group as well. "I had so alienated all the historical musicologists that they thought that I was just a devil, a Diabolus in musica!" he joked years later.[21]

As "Carl Sands," Seeger was having an equally difficult time. In 1935 he still believed in the German worker model of proletarian music as the ideal: where was the American composer who could match Hanns Eisler's "Peat-Bog Soldiers," reverentially reprinted in the first issue of the journal *Music Vanguard*? Seeger accepted Eisler's pronouncements on how "folk culture is dying off in the United States"; he would later recall a party sometime around the later 1930s or early '40s, where Eisler charged up to Alan Lomax to denounce him as an "evil influence in the world now, encouraging this interest in this terrible American folk music."[22] But trends both inside and outside the group foretold different directions. In his columns for the *Daily Worker*, the writer Mike Gold blasted the collective's songs as "splintered and tortuous things evolved by cerebralists." Anxious to get folk music approved by the Party as the official musical protest idiom of the proletariat, Gold hardened his opposition to Eisler, Seeger (as Carl Sands), and the collective even more after 1934. His views on the elitist nature of the enterprise would be echoed decades later by historians attracted to the collective's politics at the same time that they lacked sympathy for its modernist aspirations—even if, as Seeger would later claim, "most of the songs contributed to the Collective could be managed by the average church-goer and musical show-goer." (As Carol J. Oja has argued, the legacy of the collective would extend from Marc Blitzstein's *The Cradle Will Rock* through Leonard Bernstein, and perhaps even to Stephen Sondheim.) In the mid-1930s the collective could not compete with the emerging recognition of folk music as the proper medium to carry the message of the Party; protest music based on traditional melodies carried the imprimatur of the people. Now, even within his own circles, Seeger's fears about the socio-political irrelevance of composed music seemed to be coming true. "The battle was one that none of us understood," Charles later said; "but it was really a very heartfelt battle."[23]

Within the collective itself Seeger felt equally stymied. Even the presence of the master himself—Eisler was teaching a course in "mass song writing" at the New School for Social Research from 1935 through 1938—did not galvanize the collective in the direction of a new synthesis that could retain some modernist traits and still appeal to the masses. Seeger's frustrations had reached a breaking point in May 1935 when Aaron Copland's setting of "Into the Streets, May First!" won a music competition sponsored by *New Masses*. Despite its beauty, Charles protested that it could not be sung on a picket line or at a protest march. In a sense he found himself on the horns of another dichotomy, with politics on one side and art on the other. What he admired could not be used; what could be used, he did not admire. That summer he began to disengage himself from what a joint member of the party and the collective would later call a "left-wing fool's paradise."[24]

As for their financial situation, the Seegers were facing the worst winter of their lives. Charles applied for a Guggenheim Fellowship, which did not come through. "I managed to find the rent of the apartment and enough money for suppers but not much else. It was a very dim prospect at the height of the Depression." He was "wondering how I was going to get through the winter . . . we could manage it, but it would be tough." And then a federally funded deus ex machina intervened to change their lives.[25]

About a month ago out of the blue descended on us from Washington a job," Ruth wrote in January 1936, still reeling from the miracle. "Heaven knows how long it will last." In early November 1935 Charles Seeger had received a call about a full-time job in a new federal relief agency called the Resettlement Administration; he was asked to train and place professional musicians in communities of displaced and homeless people then living on government-run homesteads throughout the South. Recommended by a casual acquaintance, the artist Charles Pollock, whom he had met through Pollock's teacher, Thomas Hart Benton, Charles "jumped at the job."[26]

And so did Ruth, who called it "our job." Like so many American women, during the Depression she was his "partner in the struggle for survival in a way that the culture had not acknowledged for well over a century." By the time that the *New York Times* ran a front-page story on November 17 citing how Seeger's boss, Rexford Tugwell, "has staff of 12,089 to create 5,012 Relief Jobs," her husband had moved to Washington to become a technical advisor in music, leaving her and the children in New York. Old allegiances vied with new practical realities. When Seeger received a letter from a disgruntled Communist composer from Boston, complaining about his treatment by the New York Composers' Collective, Crawford sent it on, only to worry about whether it would be intercepted and used to fire her husband even before she got there. "I ought never to have enclosed that—if it should go astray and be opened . . . !!!"[27]

The specter of the loss of the job was too horrible to consider. She kept up appearances better a few months later when she recalled that moment when "we were in an amusing position of having a job and being utterly unable to get ourselves to it—so had to borrow again in order to reach that enviable state of being able to repay past borrowings." Then things did not look quite so amusing. Ruth wrote to one prospective borrower about accepting her diamond ring as collateral for a $100 loan. She also asked her brother Carl for a loan on it as well, and he sent them $200. Two other friends offered to lend money for a down payment on a used car.[28]

In late November, when Charles was already in Washington, Ruth repeatedly insisted that he find them a place to live, even if he had to take some time off. Here was one task she could not do. He had to put aside "his incurable desk complex"—one of the few criticisms she ever made of her husband still on the record—and take this seriously. She enlisted Margaret Valiant to come and stay with her and the children, while they packed up the apartment, full of books and papers and "two years of *New Masses*." Margaret planned to go with them in the hopes of getting a job in Charles's office. At the end of the month, Charles returned to drive the family down to Washington. They said goodbye to New York City, home to Charles for twelve years and Ruth, for five, and headed down to Roosevelt's Washington.[29]

Part VI

w
a
s
h
i
n
g
t
o
n

1936 – 1953

d i s c o v e r i n g
" u n m u s i c a l "
a m e r i c a

The Seegers arrived in Washington at the end of 1935, as Roosevelt's third year in office was drawing to a close. The move to Washington promised a new start on many fronts, not the least of which was the end of their hand-to-mouth existence. As soon as a regular salary started coming in, Ruth began to pay back their New York debts, including a milk bill for the last six months and one from the pediatrician. After subsisting for a few weeks in Spartan living quarters, she wrote him that they had found a small brick house at 3007 Pershing Street in Clarendon, Virginia (now part of Arlington), quite close to the district. She was so relieved that her unusually expansive letter voiced enough optimism to mention hopes for her own professional future: "Our house thank God has sunshine and light (shades of New York apartments!) a new stove and a frigidaire (smile at the housewife) and a comfortable desk room (the composer hopes to be able to work again)."[1]

How much substance rested in this hope? The absence of a piano in the Seeger home for their first two years in Washington symbolizes the paucity of support. No ultra-modern kindred-soul composers lived in this city she had last visited in 1929. Then Ruth Crawford had met one of Washington's prime movers in classical music circles, Mary Howe, who had helped found the National Symphony in 1931. Howe's conservative music and social contacts meant little to her now. In the absence of any evidence to the contrary, it seems unlikely that Crawford reached out to the Washington Composers Club or submitted music for the annual spring festivals devoted to women composers sponsored by the National League of American Pen Women. Besides, it went against her own history. Moreover, she acted desultory about the few performances of her music that others arranged. On March 2, 1936, Marion Bauer wrote her a disgruntled letter about an upcoming performance on April 24 of "White Moon" and "Sunsets" (from the five Sandburg Songs, 1929) by a rising young singer, Helen Traubel, who stood at the threshold of a major operatic career. Why hadn't Ruth written to Marion with a new address? She complained, "I have wanted to get in touch with you for weeks. . . . I suppose it will take you another month to answer this. I know you! You're no piker! But please drop me a card from somewhere." Other scattered performances of Crawford's music took place as well. A new-music group in Buenos Aires performed the String Quartet 1931 on August 22, 1937. Radiana Pazmor performed "White Moon" on March 14, 1938, at a concert sponsored by the Los Angeles chapter of Pro Musica. "Well, after all that," Pazmor wrote, referring to her efforts to program the more complicated set of three Sandburg songs (1930–32), "I ended up singing 'White Moon.' I do love it." By that time Crawford had mounted a guitar and Appalachian dulcimer on the living room walls of her new home.[2]

R oosevelt's State of the Union address on January 4, 1935, had set in motion the forces that unmoored the Seegers from New York City. He had then proposed twin programs for emergency public employment—one for the indigent in cities, which established the most famous New Deal agency of his administration, the WPA (Works Progress Administration), and the other for those in rural areas, which resulted in the lesser-known and shorter-lived RA—the Resettlement Administration, Charles's new place of work.[3]

Even if the RA's past has left few traces on our collective memory of the New Deal, its idealistic invocation of "community" would prove valuable to Ruth and Charles Seeger in their understanding of the relationship between music and social experience. The policy aspirations of "resettlement," which moved destitute sharecroppers and unemployed miners into ersatz colonies, were to transform Depression refugee camps into communities of rehabilitated homesteaders. Such goals might have daunted a less idealistic politician than the head of RA, Rexford Tugwell. Just a few months before Seeger got his job, Tugwell declared that "a community does not consist of houses, and it does not consist of houses, schools and roads and water systems and sewers either. . . . There is something else to a community besides that. We are trying to find out what it is if we can, and if we can bring it into being, to make it come alive." That imperative opened the door to a new stage of cultural interventions. Tugwell formed a "Special Skills" Division to hire professional artists who in turn would create recreation programs of various sorts "to keep up morale and to carry the homesteaders through the present pioneer period." Its head, the painter Adrian Dornbush (a close friend of Eleanor Roosevelt, who enthusiastically supported RA projects), hired Charles to set up music recreation programs in various RA colonies. As a former critic for the *Daily Worker*, Charles made the public transition from revolution to liberal reform just around the time that the Communist Party had proclaimed its new policy of a "Popular Front" in 1935, supporting alliances with bourgeois institutions to fight the growing threat of fascism in Europe. As a government employee in one of these institutions, if he differed with prevailing policies, he kept quiet about it, shifting his model for the paradigmatic worker from New York City streets to Appalachian hamlets.[4]

Ruth found friends among Charles's colleagues and their wives. Among them were several people who would have distinguished careers as social artists: the painter Ben Shahn, who worked for RA as a documentary photographer, and his wife, Bernarda, who was also a painter and former organizer of the Unemployed Artists Group, a radicalized quasi-collective in New York; the radio producer Nicholas Ray, who later directed the classic *Rebel Without a Cause*, and his wife, Jean, a writer and editor. Their sense of purpose endeared them to one another. Bernarda Shahn described Ruth and Charles Seeger as "both very very enthusiastic New Dealers," and Jean Ray remembered Ruth as "warm and ebullient . . . a decent liberal human being who was a very caring person." They all grasped the cultural as well as political implications of their work. In his annual message to Congress in 1938, Roosevelt spoke with sociological irony of the revelation of the Other that was American—of "discovering that vast numbers of the farming population live in a poverty more abject than that of many of the farmers of Europe whom we are wont to call peasants." As Bernarda Shahn says, "Roosevelt had opened up the world in a certain way; he had discovered [poor people], he made them important." New Deal workers would photograph their faces and their homes, record their music, celebrate their crafts, and in so doing, themselves create a body of art, which still serves as a primary historical medium through which we see and hear the Depression.[5]

What distinguishes Crawford's experience in the history of the musical aspects of this movement is the sensibility of the composer she brought to the process of discovery. To some extent she and Charles already had some prior encounters with folk music that prepared their way. From a few bits of evidence emerges a sense of continuous if peripheral involvement started in the early 1930s. Ruth had introduced Charles to *The American Songbag*. In the early 1930s, she also visited his music history classes at Juilliard to talk about folk music. The publication of George Pullen Jackson's *White Spirituals in the Southern Uplands* in 1934 proved even more crucial for their growing folk consciousness, as they responded to the beauty of such now standard folk hymns as "Wondrous Love" and "Wayfarin' Stranger" as hidden treasures from a rich mine of vernacular art. Ruth and Charles had also spent late hours at Tom and Rita Benton's loft down on New York's Eighth Street at their famous "Saturday nights." There Benton, a painter famous for his patriotic murals and regional genre paintings, played "Cindy" and "Old Joe Clark" with his students, Jackson and Charlie Pollock; with friends from the "hillbilly" recording industry; and with composers Carl Ruggles and Henry Cowell. The Seegers often came with their baby Michael in tow, and occasionally with Pete, who one evening heard "John Henry" for the first time. When Benton's mural *America Today*, commissioned by the New School for Social Research, was unveiled in January 1931, Charles played in the small pickup band of singers at the reception party.[6]

As good left-wingers, Ruth and Charles also heard the folk musicians who made their way to New York audiences through radical politics, among these the great guitarist and folk singer Huddie "Leadbelly" Ledbetter and the labor organizer Aunt Molly Jackson, who appeared in benefits for the Harlan County Miners. Here their interlocuter was a very young Alan Lomax, son of the famous collector John A. Lomax and, in his early twenties, already an experienced collector in his own right. In 1933 or 1934, Charles and Henry Cowell had reviewed the Lomaxes' first book *American Ballads and Folk Songs* for the publisher (Macmillan), and they had been "tremendously enthusiastic."[7]

Initially wary of musicians from the alien world of classical music, Alan slowly started a friendship with the Seegers based on proletarian culture politics. He would later say that "Charlie was the first person who gave me the feeling that there was a real connection between how people lived—social economics—and music." He dropped by their apartment to discuss Workers Music League business or just to talk, as Ruth wrote of one evening, "to swap limericks [of political satire] with me and Margaret til 1:30 in the morning." At some point in 1933 or 1934, Alan brought Aunt Molly Jackson around to a few meetings of the Composers' Collective, perhaps intending to shake them up by confronting them with the flinty sounds of indigenous protest music. Seeger would later tell the story of the collision between two cultures with bemusement. Aunt Molly neither liked nor understood their songs, and eventually she retreated to the corner of the room, far away from the piano around which the stalwarts were trying out their latest round or march. Seeger said he nevertheless sensed the future, telling her that it was all right—"You're on the right track and we're on the wrong track" in finding "the people's idiom."[8]

Yet with all of this, the Seegers arrived in Washington with the parochial belief that "traditional music had practically died out by 1900." How two such sophisticated musicians could entertain this idea in 1936 speaks volumes about the cultural boundaries between modernists and traditionalists of the period. Apparently the Seegers compartmentalized their prior musical experiences though their ignorance of cultural context. Hence the country music that they heard through Benton's records was made by professionals, not by the folk; the white spirituals from Jackson represented archaic oddities; the message of Leadbelly was infiltrated with stage mannerisms. American vestigial legacies reflected debasements of the Old World rather than any indigenous vernacular with its own identity. Nothing had dissuaded them from the widespread Eurocentric view of America as lacking "enough material that could be called folk song," as a Harvard music professor wrote in 1926. Bruno Nettl's concise summary offers some theoretical perspective on this view:

> In the distant past everyone was "the folk." . . . The folk were the majority of the population, and thus, when an intellectual and economic elite developed, it was

logical that folk music should be regarded as something low, uninteresting, un-creative, unimaginative. This attitude is still reflected in the twentieth-century theory that the members of the folk community are unable to create something new; they only take over what is created by the elite in the cities and at the courts, and while using it, simplify and debase it.[9]

Within months the Seegers realized their mistake, their own confessions resonating with the values of modernity that mattered most. America was not "un-musical." As Ruth explained, "we had been here only a couple of months when Charlie began to get his fingers on the pulse of some of this very live-and-kicking music of 'unmusical' America." Charles said he was surprised and delighted to find that "the traditional music is alive and flour-ishing among millions of people who still introduce fresh variants and new material in the old idiom." Seeger revamped RA orientation procedures to teach urban workers traditional music; he would soon justify field recordings as training tools.[10]

In the winter of 1936, when Mike Gold launched a personal attack on the elitist music of Carl Sands and the Composers' Collective in New York, Charles Seeger was visiting federal homesteads and camps in Pennsylvania, Tennessee, West Virginia, Arkansas (where Johnny Cash grew up at the Dyess Colony), and Florida, where he had just hired Margaret Valiant at Cherry Lake Farms. He entreated others from New York to join him (Herbert Haufrecht, a collective member, also served, but Marc Blitzstein refused). Seeger planned to make field recordings to use in training sessions for music workers, and his request for a Presto sound recording machine, which plowed channels in aluminum discs, was reviewed all the way up the line in the ad-ministration to the President. Seeger also hired Sidney Robertson (who later married Henry Cowell) for this project. A stalwart pioneer in federal field col-lecting, Sidney would prove to be one of the Seegers' most loyal friends.[11]

Ruth waited impatiently to join her husband on some of his field trips. He came home describing places she had never been and sounds she had yet to hear. In a letter to him she called Charles her

> minister preaching the gospel to the forsaken in the wilds of Cumberland, much too far from Clarendon, Virginia. How terrible it would be if you travelled like this steadily and we were always living in the future or the past, with only a scat-tered day here and there in the actual present. One of our chief pleasures has always been the extent to which we live and appreciate the minute we are liv-ing in as we live it.[12]

He missed Ruth just as much. If she were there, "everything would be vibrat-ing with heightened interest and vitality."[13]

In March 1936 Ruth finally got out of Washington. She met Charles in Montgomery, Alabama, with visits planned to Black Mountain College in North Carolina and the Campbell Folk School, where John Jacob Niles worked. But when her first precious trip was cut short by ten days, she reacted with uncharacteristic tenacity. The hired housekeeper had deserted the fam-ily, and although their boarder could watch Mike, somehow Peggy had landed in a hospital ward as a "patient." The makeshift arrangements appalled Judy Tobie, Charles's music office assistant, who wired Ruth to come home.[14]

She returned home with "a bitter sense of frustration" but still would not give up so easily. After working out a rash scheme to transfer Peggy from the hospital ward to a local nursing home, Crawford said that she had "never been in such a muddle in my life—stubbornly determined to rejoin you and making all the arrangements so I could do so, getting Peggy settled in the nursing home at $1 a day, seeing Michael happy and wonderfully improving, also $1 a day . . . yet all the time wavering back and forth til I was almost dizzy with indecision." She rationalized that leaving the children was "the only thing I could afford to do: that I could leave the young ones here on credit and not have to pay til later, whereas I had not enough to keep them fed if I stayed." For two days she tried to find solutions. "It must have been Charlie's doing," Sidney Robertson Cowell sniffed years later. But in fact, Ruth was more determined than he was, and her sense of frustration vented itself in long letters describing her "superactivities" in great detail. She wrote that she could "barely read his letters or . . . sing the songs we sang." They had planned a "scab-song" duet for Cumberland. "Am I foolish?" she asked Charles in a thirteen-page letter, answering herself in the next phrase: "Perhaps, but I do be I."[15]

When Ruth's "weepful letter" greeted Charles in Little Rock, he strategically detailed his itinerary, just in case, and then reminded her of how much there was to do at home. They planned to move from their Virginia apartment to a small house at 2441 P Street, Northwest, in the District of Columbia. Charles urged her to ride herd on Old Man Gasch (their new landlord) to get their new place ready. Perhaps she could start on the packing. He exempted himself from the crush, for when he returned, he would "not be much use—such a lot of work to do at the office!"[16]

A few signs of discontent lingered. "Sorry to say the weepful period is not yet over, as your dear letter from Little Rock hoped," Ruth replied. "Your letters don't make me sad, they make me mad—not at you, but on account of the missed experiences (together) to which I looked forward so long—Ho so 'long." And then finally, she let go, parodying Charles: " 'Ruthie, enough of the sob stuff.' Righto, Charlie m'dear." Her small rebellion over, she returned to routine. And the precious trip deteriorated into drudgery for Charles as well: "I'm tired of colonies, folk music and business," Charles wrote her from Cumberland Homesteads. "If you were here, it would be different. I just want to get home quick." Occasional nostalgic encounters with their New York pasts made him even lonelier. When he discussed "young American composers" with the conductor of the Little Rock Symphony, he answered a question about Ives: Did he know him? And then enthusiastically, " 'And there's Ruth Crawford—do you know her?' Did I!"[17]

In the summer of 1936 Crawford finally got a chance to travel a bit in the South. She and Charles, along with her seventeen-year-old stepson Pete (on vacation and planning to go to Harvard in the fall) and Sidney Robertson, went to some well-known regional festivals of traditional music. They headed for the oldest of the four that had been founded between 1928 and 1934—Bascom Lunsford's Mountain Dance and Folk Festival in North Carolina. As they made their way through the hill country to Asheville, a small town nestled between the Great Smoky Mountains to the west and the Blue Ridge Mountains to the northeast, Pete described it as like "visiting a foreign country. We wound down through the narrow valleys with so many turns in the road that I got seasick. We passed wretched little cabins with half-naked children peering out the door; we passed exhibits of patchwork quilts and other handicrafts which often were the main source of income." The Seegers had entered the world of the rural underclass, with its confounding mixtures of oppression and cultural vitality.[18]

Lunsford's festival took place in a canvas-topped baseball field, whose stands held about five thousand people. The Seegers watched square-dance teams from Bear Wallow, Happy Hollow, Cane Creek, Spooks Branch, Cheoah Valley, Bull Creek, and Soco Gap; heard the legendary five-string banjo player Samantha Bumgarner; and family string bands, including a group of Indians from the Cherokee reservation who played string instruments and sang ballads. They wandered among the crowds who camped out at the edge of the field, hearing music being made there as well. As Lunsford's daughter would later recall, those country people

> held the riches that Dad had discovered. They could sing, fiddle, pick the banjos, and guitars with traditional grace and style found nowhere else but deep in the mountains. I can still hear those haunting melodies drift over the ball park.[19]

It was a conversion experience for Ruth and especially for Pete, who was hearing the five-string banjo for the first time—the instrument he would later master and popularize as a folk-revival musician. Ruth took it all in, not quite sure of where it might lead her. As Pete said later, they were both "busy learning this idiom" as fast as they could.[20]

Bascom Lunsford proved especially important to the Seegers at this time. By profession a lawyer, he too identified himself as a discoverer of the riches of the "natural people." In hindsight his work reflects the dynamic that spiraled traditional music across class and cultural divides. Now Lunsford in turn became the object of discovery himself by urban outsiders: for Charles, who hired him for RA projects at Skyline Farms; for Pete, who learned some banjo technique from Lunsford; and for Ruth, who used tunes from his *30 and 1 Folk Songs from the Southern Mountains* (1929) in her own subsequent projects.[21]

In Washington that fall the Seegers waited for the 1936 election to be over. "Since Roosevelt's been re-elected, we'll not be neglected, We've got Franklin D. Roosevelt back again," sang a rural singer on a recording cut just one week after Roosevelt's big victory. Yet an unsettling decline in the economy during spring 1937 left the president vulnerable. The right wing targeted "Rex the Red" Tugwell, whose rag-tag constituency of tenant farmer, sharecropper, and migrant worker could do little to save him, and he and the Resettlement Administration were declared defunct in September 1937.[22]

The Seeger family stayed on. Charles's job survived as the Special Skills Division regrouped in the newly formed Farm Security Administration, which rose from the ashes of RA. By November the FSA merged with the Department of Agriculture. Seeger ran their music programs, which included an inhouse seventy piece orchestra and a choral society.[23]

One program can serve as guide to the Seegers' evolution at this time. On November 17, 1937, Charles organized "An Evening of American Music in Conjunction with the Exhibition of Rural Arts," celebrating the 75th anniversary of the Department of Agriculture. In a program note he wrote, "The American people possess one of the most distinctive and beautiful folk musics in the world. . . . and the most vigorous of all our rural arts. It has been most sadly neglected by our musical leadership." The concert included three of his arrangements of American folk songs for soloist and orchestra: the classic African American ballad "John Henry," the shape-note spiritual "Wayfarin' Stranger," and the Anglo-American ballad "John Riley."

Although absent as a composer, Crawford appeared on the program as a member of the "Resettlement Folk Singers," a pick-up group of workers (including Tugwell's daughter Tannis) from Special Skills who performed "rural American music." On the scratchy tape that preserves their enthusiastic voices, the trained soprano of Margaret Valiant, back in Washington after six months as a "residential music worker," floats over the rest of the group; Seeger would later tout her experiences as an R.A. success story. Adrian Dornbush sang along in "Careless Love": "How I wish that train would come, to take me back where I come from." In the second song, urbane accents inflect the lyrics of "Cindy": "Get along home, Cindy, Cindy. . . . I'll marry you someday," and the erstwhile folk singers get the quirky rhythms of that last line just right. They sing verses as solos. First up is Charles, his aristocratic New England dialect bending "door" and "floor" into "dohr" and "flohr"; Ruth, third to last, in a "rather nondescript center American" voice, sings: "Cindy is a pretty girl, Cindy is a peach, She'd throw her arms around me and hung on *like a leech*." Emphasizing the alliteration and humor of the last three words, she sounds happy and comfortable.[24]

Both Ruth and Charles had reached a second stage in the development of their urban folk consciousness, from the initial encounter with American traditional music as living culture to a shift in focus at the center of the discourse, away from the rural communities, or the "field" itself, to their own elite class of formally trained musicians. "Back Where I Come From" for the Seegers meant the conservatory. The more they discovered rural traditions, the more the Seegers bridled at the indifference of the urban musical establishment from which they came. Crawford's historical grievances about snobbish dismissals of American music, which she had harbored as a modernist composer, now energized her new mission to build bridges between her two worlds. Both class consciousness and musical conscience inflect this definition of the "folk song revival" offered by the folklorist Norm Cohen: "the 'discovery' by sophisticated culture-conscious urban artists of traditional, generally American folk music, and its presentation by those artists to audiences of similar social background." If, as Sidney Cowell later wrote, Charles Seeger "led the first effective attack on the barriers that separated sophisticated musicians from the music of the American oral tradition," then Ruth Crawford marched with him in the front lines.[25]

This perspective informs the context of their work in the late 1930s. In Special Skills, Seeger had overseen a publication project of nine "Resettlement Song Sheets" in a "series of American songs rarely found in popular collections" (melody only). Who were they really for? asked Sidney Robertson Cowell skeptically, fifty years later when she contributed two copies to the Library of Congress. Not for the people in the RA communities: "a lot of them couldn't read and they were darned if they were going to read!" In point of fact, Seeger's song sheets were "passports" for city musicians traveling in the foreign country of vernacular music, and several would be reprinted years later in Benjamin Botkin's best-selling *A Treasury of American Folklore*.[26]

In the fall of 1937 Crawford composed her own "passports" by arranging "Twenty-two American Folk Tunes" as piano compositions intended for the elementary student. Although seemingly readied for publication in 1938 in a meticulous autograph (with multi-stanza texts for all the songs), if she showed the work to publishers at the time, no records remain. Of the original twenty-two, only nineteen survive, published for the first time in 1995. She chose tunes from four anthologies of folk music—Carl Sandburg's *The American Songbag*, Cecil Sharp's *English Folksongs from the Southern Appalachians*, Bascom Lunsford's *30 and 1 Songs*, and John and Alan Lomax's *American Ballads and Folk Songs*, including a cross-section of repertory: indigenous songs like "Sweet Betsy from Pike," "Billy Boy," and the perennial Seeger favorite, "Cindy"; Child ballads such as "Lord Thomas" and "Darby's Ram"; two African American tunes, "Boll Weevil" and "Gray Goose"; children's songs, such as the lullaby "Mammy Loves" or "London's Bridge"; and Ruth's affectionate tribute to her husband, the song "Charlie's Sweet."

She prefaced her first new music in five years with a short manifesto, explaining that her purpose was

> to acquaint the piano student with at least a small part of the traditional (i.e., "folk") music of *his own country*, and to give this to him in a form which can be used at the same time for piano practice. . . . The melodies around which these pieces have been built are traditional American melodies. There are thousands more, just as good and just as alive. It is the belief of this composer that, just as the child becomes acquainted with his own home environment before experiencing the more varied contacts of school and community, so should the music student be given the rich musical heritage of his own country as a basis upon which to build his experience of the folk and art music of other countries.

In her phrase "there are thousands more, just as good and just as alive," resonating with the fervor of the convert, Crawford was echoing sentiments voiced by other American composers and artists during a period of awakening to tradition. However, her second goal broke fresh ground by suggesting a stylistic resolution between modernism and the past:

(2) to present this music in an idiom savoring as much as possible of the contemporary, preferring a bareness rather than a richness of style, and accustoming the student's ear to a freer use of the fifth, fourth, seventh, and second intervals so abundantly used in most contemporary music.

Here is where a modernist consciousness toward tradition begins to take shape in Crawford's work. Unlike composers such as John Powell, who emphasized the model of the nineteenth-century Romantic Dvořák for precedents in using folk music as the "basis of a fresh and lovely art music, with almost infinite variety and truly our own," radical modernists like Crawford found inspiration in the work of the Hungarian composer Béla Bartók. He would serve as a model for her new work from this point onward for several different reasons. First, he too emphasized the oppositional qualities of folk music, stressing the potential of Hungarian peasant music to counter the "excesses of Romanticists," and he emphasized affinities between folk and contemporary musics as well because he recognized that Eastern European peasant music did not conform to classical functional tonality. The composer Mark Nelson summarizes Bartók's approach in terms that are equally relevant for Crawford:

> His belief that the essence of folk music, and the highest goal of art music influenced by folk music, is the expression of an ineffable spirit embodying a system of values resistant to verbal articulation. According to Bartók, one cannot possibly capture that spirit through the mere lifting of peasant tunes from their rural context and the facile insertion or adaptation of them in a "higher art" composition: such a procedure, like simple transcription of these tunes, "cannot possibly render . . . all the pulsing life of peasant music."

Now Crawford stood at the beginning of the path that would lead her into the same attempts at integration, the same scientific approach to transcription, the same dissatisfaction with facile thematic appropriations. Like Bartók, she celebrated the subversive harmonies of early American hymnody as evidence for her stylistic logic. Recalling the shape-note idiom in George Pullen Jackson's *White Spirituals in the Southern Uplands* (1933), she noted that,

> curiously enough, there is part-singing widespread throughout the southeastern states, and has been for the past hundred years, which revels in these characteristics of "modern music."

This crucial assertion of commonality between contemporary composition and oral tradition would recur frequently in her work as a foundation for the integration of folk and art musics (Charles Seeger would later comment on ties between white spirituals and dissonant counterpoint in his pioneering study of this "extraordinary" repertory). In discovering vernacular idioms at home, Crawford found roots for her own musical difference. At a period of re-emerging folk consciousness among American composers, when the ideology of folk simplicity would guide the course of most "Americanist" composition, she endowed the vernacular as a new kind of dissonant music. She planned to act on this insight within an incipient urban folk song revival movement.[27]

Example 15-1   "Sweet Betsy from Pike," mm. 1–8, from *Nineteen American Folk Tunes for Piano*, © 1994. Used by permission of G. Schirmer.

In her collection *Nineteen American Folk Tunes*, accompaniments thrive on her treasured "bareness and spareness" aesthetic. Seconds, sevenths, and open fifths dominate the left-hand patterns; linear countermelodies and gapped scales supersede the conventional diet of sweet thirds and rich triads. Surprises delight us in the best of the group. "Sweet Betsy from Pike" has a melody in 3/4 accompanied by a bass line pattern in 2/4 tripping over unexpected flats (Ex. 15-1). The "three old crows sit on a tree" of double parallel fifths, reminiscent of shape-note harmony. "The Babes in the Wood" sing their tune in D major, are accompanied by a pattern in B minor, and refuse to resolve the dilemma by ending on G major (Ex. 15-2). Peggy Seeger's comments about this piece and the collection as a whole from her introduction to the new edition bear repeating:

> "Babes in the Wood" coasts along on a soft, almost menacing series of unresolved cadences, as restless and implacable as the forest itself, waiting for the babes to die. . . . This is all so intriguing that the player wants to go back and play the whole thing again, just for that magical bar, that quixotic cadence, that tangled arpeggio—and there are many such moments in these pieces.[28]

During the years 1937–40 Crawford began but did not complete other projects intended for a general trade readership. In 1937–38, she and Jean Ray planned a children's book, for which Ray "would write little stories," as she remembers, "and Ruth, whom I knew of as a good composer, would write arrangements of folktunes." Ruth got as far as transcribing eight or nine "Dusenbury songs," referring to a group of field recordings made of a famous

Example 15-2   "The Babes in the Wood," mm. 1–8, from *Nineteen American Folk Tunes for Piano,* © 1994. Used by permission of G. Schirmer.

Arkansas singer, among them "John Henry," "Barbara Allen," "Bought Me a Cat," and "Cindy." "Of course we want to pay Dusenbury," she told Charles.[29]

The topic of payment touched on problems that were just beginning to surface among urban revivalists, as they moved oral tradition further into the realm of popular media. When in the late 1930s the Seegers also thought about a frankly popular collection of folk songs with keyboard arrangements for city people based on music collected by RA and FSA field workers, that plan was foiled because Charles himself, along with Sidney Robertson and Harold Spivacke, had set a policy prohibiting commercial profits to be made from nonprofit federal collecting. Sidney herself later admitted, "[T]his meant that a lot of good songs could not receive the circulation that they might have had." They stood just at its cusp, when it was easier to envision cultural work that was shared without being commercialized. Controversies over questions of ownership, expressed through marketplace practices of royalties, copyright and creative attributions, that would plague the movement in the 1940s and '50s, are foreshadowed in this moment.[30]

New technology in sound production was also changing the nature of folk-song scholarship itself. As the historian Archie Green has noted, "Because sound technology was perfected well after folklore became an established discipline in Europe, the notion that a recording might be a useful tool was slow in reaching folklorists." By the late 1930s folk-song scholarship in the United States stood at a crossroads in its history. The "field recording had given the collector a tool and the transcriber a source." It forced a conservative discipline, so long engaged primarily with text, to confront music. Some caviled at the "many musicians [who] have burst into the field without proper humility or willingness to familiarize themselves with the background of a subject of distinguished scholarly tradition . . . without preparation, without reverence for the scholarly past of a subject." Arthur Kyle Davis's lament surfaced in 1937, as he called for a new hybrid—a "rare and delicate amphibian"—the musicologist, "the musical scholar or the scholarly musician" to work within folklore, something few of them were doing. In 1938 the Archive of American Folk Song at the Library of Congress acknowledged the opportunities of the moment by establishing a recording laboratory headed by Jerome Weisner, and Harold Spivacke secured a grant from the Carnegie Foundation to produce Library of Congress recordings on a nonprofit basis. As a leading figure in the field, George Herzog admitted, the "musician is at the moment indispensable."[31]

Crawford became one of those "indispensable musicians" in the summer of 1937 when John Lomax asked her to work on a new anthology of American folk songs that would draw on his latest collecting trips. At the time, it seemed like a fairly straightforward task: she would transcribe recordings made on electronic portable sound equipment in the field into written music notation. Alan Lomax once stated simply that "choosing Ruth for the job evolved naturally from their constant association" which began in New York. His father had met Charles Seeger, whom he had described to his wife as "the head of the Resettlement Recreation man, famous musician and collector," when Harold Spivacke, the chief of the music division at the Library of Congress, introduced them at lunch in May 1936. Invitations to dinner at the Seegers soon followed. At the apex of his brilliant career, John Lomax had donated his collection of field recordings to the Archive of American Folk Song. By then the Lomaxes had deposited over 700 aluminum and acetate disks, which totaled 2,800 items, the first portion of a legacy that would eventually number more than 10,000 recordings.[32]

Even though the first Lomax anthology had been a commercial success, they suffered "a musical denunciation" in a review by the founder of the archive, Carl Engel. Eventually Alan realized that the transcriptions were "a disaster." For their next book the Lomaxes swung to the other extreme. They hired George Herzog, a Hungarian musicologist-émigré working at Columbia University, to meet the challenge of African American oral tradition in a book about Leadbelly. As an acknowledged leader in the young field of comparative musicology, Herzog had been trained by Hornbostel in Berlin to produce scientifically accurate transcriptions. Inevitably, Herzog's complex notations (with plus and minus symbols to indicate quarter-tone deviations from standard pitch) detracted from the popular appeal of the book. Alan later said, "We sold twenty-five copies. Nobody could use the book in any way."[33]

In 1937 Harold Spivacke advised John Lomax to find a transcriber with a "fresh point of view." He turned to the Seegers. According to Charles, he was asked first—he "hadn't time," but suggested that Ruth might be interested. And it was work his wife could do at home if necessary—a major consideration, since just that month—on May 4, 1937—Ruth had given birth to her third child in five years, a girl they named Barbara Mona. (Ruth acceded once again to Charles—Mona was her former rival in New York.)[34]

Crawford considered the offer from many points of view. The family could use the income, that was clear. The project seemed fairly straightforward. No one imagined that the process would thrust her into the front ranks of composer-transcribers in the twentieth century, or that it would initiate a collaboration between two families which would eventually involve three generations of urban folk-revival musicians. So in the summer of 1937, Crawford began working on the second Lomax "family book."[35]

l o m a x   c o u n t r y

With the "family book" came the family. Alan Lomax, who had been living in Washington since late 1936, was temporarily employed by his father to work with Lomax materials at the Archive of American Folk Song. In September 1937, John Lomax, his wife Ruby Terrill, and his fifteen-year old daughter Bess came up from Texas to work on the project, hoping to get it off the ground in the next few months.[1]

"What songs are we going to teach America?" The question that Alan Lomax would pose many years later as the mission of the project captures not only his family's enormous pride and ambition, but also its sense of responsibility. Crawford and the Lomaxes spent the hot Washington fall of 1937 in one of the stuffy attics in the archive, gathering around the phonograph to answer that question so characteristic of 1930s cultural optimism. As Alan recalls, "we listened and listened and listened and listened and listened to the stock of recordings we had been making."[2]

The music came from one side of the American continent to the other, and even occasionally beyond it. Even a small selection of place names conveys the breadth of the whole: from such legendary music sites as Livingston, Alabama; the Georgia Sea Islands; Murrells Inlet, South Carolina; and Galax, Virginia; from cities that surprise us, like New York; and from cities that don't, like New Orleans; from Arkansas, Ohio, Texas, Kentucky, California, and even the Bahamas. The variety was extraordinary. If today we understand the cultural contradictions embedded in the term "American tradition," it is partly because of the diversity documented across 16,000 miles of collecting: spirituals, work songs, hollers, dance tunes, game songs, lullabies, whopper ballads, courting songs, hollers and blues, gang songs, Cajun tunes, breakdowns, fiddle tunes, and play-party songs from a "staggering inventory of song types and traditions" of indigenous material.[3]

A repertory that would endure through the next several decades of the urban folk revival began to take shape. A small selection of titles captures its vitality: "Little Bird, Go Through My Window," "Cotton Eye Joe," "The Ram of Darby," "East Virginia," "John Henry," "Darling Corey," "Take This Hammer," "Pauline," "Look Down That Lonesome Road," "Hush, Li'l Baby," "Lynchburg Town," "The Rising Sun Blues," "Jennie Jenkins," "Old Blue," and "Sally Go Round the Sunshine."

At seventy, John Lomax could be as prickly as a Texas cactus about the value of the music he had so arduously collected. He had scrambled his way up—"left parentless in the prairie," his daughter described it—and like any orphan, he loved his own children all the more fiercely for it. Because his children were his field recordings, he waited to see if a classical musician like Ruth Crawford Seeger would welcome them properly. She immediately bonded with the Lomax material. As Bess Lomax explains,

> She was completely excited by the coherence and elegance of the different musical systems that Father and Alan had recorded, by the complexity of American folk music. She was really aesthetically very moved by this.[4]

The family "deliberately set out to talk about the United States as a place with enormous musical creativity," and "deliberately picked out a lot of esoteric songs" to demonstrate the complexity of oral traditions. "Ruth encouraged this," Bess said, "by helping them pick out the most exotic and esoteric of the tunes." Crawford later pointed them out in her music preface to the book:

> a work song in 5/4 meter, a Cajun tune consistently in 10/8 throughout, a Ravel-like banjo accompaniment, a ballad of archaic tonal texture, a Bahaman part-song of contrapuntal bareness.[5]

For Crawford, the musical implications of the Lomax material made the project take on a whole new meaning. As Bess explains,

> She was [also] very concerned about her career as a professional woman . . . and she let you know that. She regarded the work she was doing for Father—the transcription of the music (A) as an interesting job but (B) she was very concerned with it as it contributed to her increasing sophistication as a musician. And I don't think she would have done it if it hadn't had that quality for her.[6]

John Lomax and his wife and daughter left for Europe in February 1938, in effect ceding responsibility for the new anthology to Alan and Ruth. The alliance between Alan Lomax, a collector deeply committed to tradition as living culture, fanatic about his mission to get the "American sound to the American people," and Ruth Crawford Seeger, a modernist composer who "regarded this as a very very interesting music literature that she needed to master," grew stronger as the book progressed over the next two years. Very quickly, Ruth earned the trust of a young man known for his brilliance and volatility:

> She was the fairest person I ever met. The most non-prejudicial, the most balanced. She never went overboard in any way. She was always trying for the best result. She really didn't care about anything but what would be the best result for the whole, for the project.[7]

The implications of their work far exceeded the project at hand. The more they documented folk-song style and culture, the more they shifted the paradigm of traditional music away from Romanticism to modernity. What they challenged was the older ideology that characterized the essence of folk song as "simplicity," a view that continued to find believers among many musicians in the United States in the 1930s. They implicitly undermined the social counterpart of this idea, summed up in the odd phrase, "childhood of the race." That common expression reflected Social Darwinist views of cultural evolution; it placed the "folk" and "primitive" people at the bottom of the cultural food chain because they were supposedly less evolved specimens of civilization. Even John Lomax himself, although "the first to argue for the sound of the singer, the sound of the authentic," as his son once said, still occasionally cleaved to such vestigial grumblings. In his introduction to *American Ballads and Folk Songs*, he repeats the belief that "traditional songs are interesting for breathing the mind of the ignorant" as "a voice from secret places, silent places and old times long dead." But now, under the leadership of Alan and Ruth, the new project left that rhetoric in the dust. No more quaintness, no more ghosts: instead, a reinterpretation of tradition as vital practice in a dialogue with modernity.[8]

"Alan and Ruth were a very tight team, a wonderful team," Pete Seeger once said. He watched them at work during the winter of 1938–39, when employed as Alan's assistant at the archive. "Alan would say, 'there is some wonderful new material, you must hear it.' So we would get copies of it and play it at home. . . . Father and Ruth had all of its [the archive's] facilities right at their disposal."[9]

"Gateways to magic." Peggy Seeger's phrase captures the impact that Crawford's work on the Lomax project had on the entire family. The "gateways" were the field recordings played over and over during the transcription process, so that "the house resounded with music morning, noon and night." The job was perfect for a mother with three children under the age of five. If Ruth was "house-tied" by a delinquent babysitter, no matter: Alan made duplicate disks that were transported to and from Silver Spring by Bess. The Seeger home became a satellite field station for the archive, turning rural singers and their songs into family members. For Charles, it was a crucial turning point, and he would later discuss how Ruth had much more contact with folk music than he had, that this Lomax project brought him closer to it. What pleasure Crawford must have felt hearing her five-year-old son Michael say, "It feels as though the sounds are coming from *inside* me, Dio!" ("Dio" was her family nickname, acquired from Mike's mimicking of his father's New England drawled "dear."). He heard the surprisingly lucid sound of aluminum records, played on a primitive turntable. The records degraded after 50 uses, and Michael was allowed to "sharpen the cactus needle every side." (Much of that repertoire would later surface in his own *New Lost City Rambler's Songbook* in the 1950s.)[10]

The perfection and pleasure of the musical experience for the Seeger family screened out harder truths. Transcribing, however engrossing, was nevertheless someone else's work — work Crawford needed to do. Her careful negotiations over fees with John Lomax early on in the project, which would end in considerable acrimony some time later, make the financial pressures clear. If she expected John Lomax to provide relief from money worries, she was mistaken. (Sidney Cowell once remarked that the Seeger "saw John Lomax as their financial savior through the books, but that wasn't going to make them any money if John could avoid it.") At the very beginning of the project, in August 1937, Crawford proposed a down payment of a dollar per song, to be taken out of her royalties, which she suggested might be a third of 10 percent. "We could discuss later whether this third would pertain also to the subsequent fifteen per cent after the first two thousand books are sold," she wrote to John Lomax. In an oblique reference to the possibility of her husband's losing his job at the FSA, she stated that "we do not know what may be happening after that."[11]

During the first six months of 1938, Seeger suffered a furlough without pay from the FSA. Finally, in June he was hired as the Washington assistant in the Federal Music Project headed by Nicholas Sokoloff, who assigned him the task of overseeing and developing projects in traditional music. Until "we get a job again," Ruth wrote in 1939, they endured several months of dire financial stress. Once when Charles was pressed by a son from his first marriage to help out Pete a bit more, Ruth exploded: "[John] couldn't realize what our near half year of joblessness meant with three young ones. What does a family of five do for five months without a job? Pay for it for the next 25 months?"[12]

In spite of it all, within three months of Charles new job, the Seegers moved from P Street in the District to a house in Silver Spring, Maryland. They defrayed some of the monthly costs by renting out rooms to a single mother and her young son. The Tudor-style stucco house at 9609 Fairway Ave. (later renamed 10001 Dallas Avenue) was fairly close to a streetcar line that came up Georgia Avenue — an imperative for Dio, who never learned to drive a car. "Dallas Avenue was a real neighborhood. [The street] was one block long at that time, unpaved with about five or seven houses on it, then it petered away into woods and brambles. A bit ramshackle, with a big wooden porch on the back that you always got splinters on, the house had more character inside than out." A beautiful mission-style staircase led to the two small eaved-roof bedrooms upstairs. A central thirty-foot living room with a cathedral ceiling and exposed half-timbered beams had as its focal point an oversized fireplace. As Bernarda Shahn remembers, Charles "built up a rug about eight inches deep in front of it, deep as a cushion on a chair. . . . It was his way of wanting people to be relaxed and informal."[13]

The Seeger home was a sea of "calm, a haven where extremely complicated, tension-filled prejudice-filled questions could be looked at with pleasure and calm and love and consideration," Alan Lomax said many years later. A dialogue begun in the Composers' Collective moved to Washington with them, as they explored issues around culture and art. (The symbiotic relationship between social and musical expression that engrossed Charles Seeger would later manifest itself in Lomax's study of folk-song style and culture.) And Ruth was a vital part of the scene, so "charming and alive and fun" to Alan Lomax, "so attractive as a woman . . . you had to be half-way in love with her. She knew what the story was, socially, politically."[14]

That "story" for her was both an old and a new one for American composers. "Getting folk music and the so-called art music connected" ranked as "the thing we talked about all the time," Charles said later. "We didn't know how it could be done." If this issue seemed so problematic, it was partly a question of memory and partly a question of style. How much they knew of the efforts of earlier American composers to integrate folk materials into fine-art music is open to question; that they cared little about it is not. Crawford came of age in the 1920s, a period summed up by H. Wiley Hitchcock as "years when youthful composers could afford to spurn the achievements of the generation that preceded them, and did." The "long American reach of Dvořák," who had inspired earlier generations of American composers to acknowledge Indian and African American melodies as vernacular legacies, had never gripped them because from Crawford's standpoint no great music had been written through his influence: at least none that modernists like herself deigned to respect. Now a new model for the alliance between tradition and fine-art music appeared promising: If there were going to be a "New American Music," as Lomax called it, then classically trained American composers had to immerse themselves in a new language to an unprecedented degree and get out into the field.[15]

Around the same time that Benjamin Botkin advocated the ideal of "creative reciprocity" between the individual writer and the folk, Charles wrote the article "Grass Roots for American Composers" with a similar message. He proposed a radical course of instruction: the American composer should return to rural America, bring a recording phonograph to do field work and leave behind forms derived "from more rarefied regions above." The rehabilitated modernist would then be "ready to forge the link . . . he has finally learned a new language." For his Harvard Class Alumni Report in 1938 he added that such training was necessary for the sanity and health of "'high art.' . . . If successful, the composer . . . can touch millions . . . who will recognize themselves singing through him. He will be their voice, not a freak individual, catering to a specialized minority."[16]

Looking back on his old loyalties, Seeger published an article on Charles Ives and Carl Ruggles with revisionist judgments: "Either [Ives or Ruggles] could have commanded a wide following" had they been willing to temper their "extremely dissonant texture, the whimsical if not haphazard form and the very great difficulty of performance" and replace their idioms with materials bearing a closer relationship to the musical vernacular of plain, everyday America—"the idioms of our folk and popular music."[17]

By 1939 Charles may have been preaching to the converted. Even if few American composers wished to follow him into the field, by the end of the 1930s the practice of quoting, borrowing, or emulating Anglo-American folk music in a composed concert work was widespread. According to the music historian Barbara Zuck, "[I]t seems as if nearly every composer born between 1895 and 1910 produced at least one piece drawing on American traditional sources" in the late 1930s and early '40s, among them some of the most famous concert works in the repertory today: Copland's "Billy the Kid" (1938), "Rodeo" (1942), and "Appalachian Spring" (1943–44), and Virgil Thomson's "The Plow That Broke the Plain" (1936). Hand in hand with the nationalist appropriation of folk materials was a vaunted return to the ethos of "simplicity," or accessibility, articulated most directly at the time by Copland in many now-famous pronouncements, among them his oft-quoted injunction to simplify musical language as much as possible. Nobody wanted to be what Charles Seeger had disparaged as a "freak individual." Ruth Crawford could hardly have missed the double imperative to find a new style and bridge the gap between ideology and practice. Her problems came from the new simplicity and its conservative assumptions.[18]

The fragility of her position surfaced publicly in 1938 in the reception of her music at a concert sponsored by the Composers Forum-Laboratory concert series at the W.P.A. Federal Music Theater in New York City. On April 6, 1938, Crawford was a guest composer for the first half of the evening, where she heard a performance of the String Quartet 1931; Three Songs for Contralto, Piano, Oboe and Percussion; the Four Preludes for Piano; and the Study in Mixed Accents.[19]

Sharing the evening with Hanns Eisler, Crawford received no reviews in local newspapers except for a brief mention in the *Daily Worker*. The performances displeased her, but even worse than that, the reactions of the audience opened old modernist battle scars.[20]

During intermission she confronted an audience who typically put "Composers on the Grill," an ordeal preserved in government records. As a government-sponsored series, these sessions were transcribed, preserving "these tussles between the prosecuting listener and the helpless defendant composer, who needed a tough hide and a sense of humor," a *New York Times* writer said.[21]

Composer-defendant Ruth Crawford answered eighteen questions and dodged a few barbs, as the transcript shows:

QUESTION: Did you try hard to be original? Did you succeed?

CRAWFORD: Doesn't need answering.

QUESTION: Precisely *what* did you have in mind in that last selection (with voice)?

CRAWFORD: Doesn't need to be answered.

As the questions grew more insulting, Crawford defended herself.

QUESTION: Do you really believe that your music is the future music of America? If so, then I pray for its deliverance.

CRAWFORD: No, I do not. I believe for one thing that the music of the future will have more content than this music has. But I do believe that this sort of work has very great value. New techniques must be worked out, experimented with, for a long time before . . . what can be called a true American music can arise.

So Crawford did not retreat into self-repudiation by denouncing modernism, held fast to her ideal of a national art that expressed the essence of an American identity, and vacillated between commitment to simplicity and nostalgia for the past:

> I have become convinced during the past two years that my next music will be simpler to play and to understand. At the same time we should not forget that it is also important to write music for the few. I regret that I could not follow out more completely the direction indicated in the works performed tonight.

That regret tinged one question about her current productivity. She responded how she had been "composing babies in the past five years," mentioned the *Twenty-two American Folk Tunes*, and then admitted her hopes that "some larger plans" would be carried out in the next year.

Perhaps those plans had been set in motion by this concert. Readying the string quartet for performance, and revising the slow movement at this time—and then claiming historical significance for herself and the work by depositing the score at the Library of Congress—were acts that retrieved her old identity. She also joined the recently founded American Composers Alliance around this time as well.[22]

Most important, she made time to compose. Back in Washington, Lomax transcriptions awaited her. In the summer of 1938 Alan told her that he and his father wanted to move on to other projects, making it "all the more important that we get our functional songbook published as soon as possible." Yet, instead of transcriptions, Ruth began to work feverishly on a new string quartet, for which no sketches have survived. Ruth wrote about it in a few letters written to Charles in 1938. While he was away on business, she arranged to "work in town" at Margaret Valiant's apartment during the day. Although asserting how much she needed him "to get the burrs out of her work," it was "better to finish something even if it needs to be done over or put aside than to sit back wondering."[23]

But the children disrupted her plans. They were ill, the baby "dangerously so," with the flu, ear infections, and croup. The baby sitters ran a "combination drug store and hospital ward," but on this rare occasion, composing came first. Ruth endowed her new quartet with maternal entitlement, calling it "Baby number 4, Opus Number ?" Receiving telephone bulletins about temperatures rising and falling, she stayed overnight twice at Margaret's.[24]

"Pretty much of a bedlam situation," one pediatrician wrote of the household. He told Ruth that "something ought to be done . . . that the place needs more of a manager." He "talked again about Washington's extremely high rate of 'motherless' families." When relaying this to her husband, Ruth denied his charges—"perhaps the doctor was underestimating how capable the house-keeper was"—as well as his implicit censure of her behavior. "How nice it was for him to take such an interest." Even though Charles penned a rare re-proach, Ruth did not retreat: "It was my first week of working in town, and well, I just did. . . . I was not away two nights in succession." Later, a chastened Ruth admitted that she should have stayed home.[25]

All that remains today of this quartet are written descriptions and com-ments that expose the conflicts between two ideologies—dissonant music and the new simplicity. Alluding to Marc Blitzstein and his Marxist ap-proach, Ruth wondered why she was bothering to write an elitist quartet at all. She told Charles that she was planning "to combine my two desires: to make use of the old technique [dissonant counterpoint], but to make use also of folk material." But how? "Just introducing dissonance into the actual folk material seems superficial; using it as it is, is out of the question (why not just play a record?)" She chose a fiddle tune called the "Flop-Eared Mule," feeling that "its eighth note prevalence would less interfere with the runs which are built according to my old ostinato favorite with a cumulative rhythmic hitch." She worried about technical balance and accessibility above all: "It may be too strenuous, though there is plenty of simplicity in it. In fact, it is a combination of simplicity and complexity. There is even tonic and domi-nant in it, horrors."[26]

And then she tripped into herself again.

> The quartet went well yesterday, one "piece" is almost finished. It is a terribly strenuous piece of music, I think. I'll call them Etudes for String Quartet—then there won't be so much fuss about their being difficult. Maybe the next section will be easier. Will I ever write really simple music?[27]

Because her music had developed along the trajectory of dissonance and formal complexity, she had more to sacrifice on the altar of accessibility than, for example, a composer like Aaron Copland, who when using cowboy songs for the ballet "Billy the Kid" was inspired rather than hindered by ideals of simplicity. Copland "walked the true path of plainness," Leonard Bernstein later said. In contrast, Ruth Crawford craved experimentation and complex-ity for their own sake. In the end she did not finish this piece, and a year later, when asked to supply music for a "skit club" to which she belonged, she balked again. If her friends didn't like her music, she would "feel like bristling hedge-hog hairs." Self-doubt plagued her: "I'm wondering if I ought not to tackle something; I'm scared stiff and work so slowly, and am so self-conscious now about my whole composition approach."[28]

As if those reasons were not sufficient, she found others. Projects like the Lomax book hung over her "like an ogre." Then there were her children: "I love them more and more," she said. "Alas for Ruthie the composer."[29]

Her regrets yielded to more pressing external demands. Charles's salary barely covered their needs, and they struggled to make ends meet. Her husband's attitudes towards making and spending money were shaded with idiosyncrasies from his privileged upbringing. Occasionally what Sidney Robertson Cowell called his "attacks of luxury" came on in unpredictable ways: she remembered an expensive set of white leather luggage he purchased for himself during his Resettlement days. On the other hand, he had trouble asking for a raise, Ruth felt, and his insecurities over his current job distressed her. Even with sharing the Silver Spring house with a single mother and her son, Ruth (as Sidney remembered it) "realized it was going to be desirable to make some money." In addition to the Lomax job, she went out to homes to give piano lessons to children, and even took on a private theory student occasionally. At a crucial moment in the evolution of the new string quartet she took a temporary job at an art gallery on Saturdays for a few weeks.[30]

Throughout 1939 Crawford worked intensively on the Lomax book. "More songs to transcribe, probably fifty, which means more cash, hopefully." By September of that year she had completed about 300 transcriptions, "some real beauties," she told the composer John Becker.[31]

Ruth's work on the Lomax book dovetailed nicely with Charles's work in the Federal Music Project. Some 2,000 songs—from folk melodies of the Kentucky hills and Creole bayou chants to Negro spirituals and cowboy ballads—were collected on phonograph records. While never officially hired by a federal agency (although a 1938 application to the WPA exists in her papers), she continued to play an active role in her husband's work life, or "their job," as she called it.[32]

As part of a group of people active in government-related projects, they and other New Dealers developed an intellectual approach to their work that moved the process of documentation into the genre of documentary. In William Stott's insightful analysis of the "documentary impulse" so central to '30s America, and so formative for Crawford and Seeger, the New Deal Federal Arts projects laid the "raw cultural material" before the American public, letting it speak for itself as objective primary source. At the same time, project workers gave it a human context, using folk art to cross the divides of class and race. The historian Warren Susman has explained, "the whole idea of documentary—not with words alone, but with sight and sound—makes it possible to see, know, and feel the details of life, to feel oneself part of some other's experience." That captures the agenda of the New Deal urban folk music revival at this stage of its evolution in the late 1930s and early '40s. In 1941 Alan Lomax wrote in *Modern Music* how folk song expressed the "reality of people's lives." Ruth Crawford Seeger would later write how folk song "has crossed and recrossed many sorts of boundaries, and is still crossing and recrossing them . . . giving a glimpse of ways of life and thought" different from our own, her writing style warmed by the social agency imparted to musical process.[33]

An advocacy project called "We Come by It Natural" that she conceived of around 1939–40 shows its political agenda as well. Her book proposal explained the format as a combination of photographs and music (perhaps motivated by the success of Archibald MacLeish's *Land of the Free* and Erskine Caldwell and Margaret Bourke-White's *You Have Seen Their Faces*). Some 40 or 50 American folk songs transcribed from field recordings and fitted "with piano accompaniments simple enough for practical amateur performance yet not banal or hackneyed" would be paired with photographs made by the now legendary FSA staff photographers (Ben Shahn, Dorothea Lange, and Walker Evans). Her purpose was to show that "America sings throughout the whole range of its present-day social experience . . . to dispel stereotypical images of the sordid and tragic side of American rural life by beginning with the prosperous and ideal type of picture and only gradually carrying it . . . to the tragic."

Such a proposal—which came to naught—reflected the "functionalist" approach through which she and her colleagues theorized their work. (The historian D.K. Wilgus would later explain that sociological term as stressing the "meaning of the material and its use in and to the community.") The Seegers' close friend, Benjamin Botkin, who in 1938 was national folklore editor of the Federal Writers' Project, spoke eloquently for a perspective that emphasized "living lore." Named by the American historian Jerrold Hirsch as "one of the first American folklorists who did not view the modern world as a threat to the existence of folklore," Botkin, in such articles as "The Folkness of the Folk" (1937), argued how in the functionalist approach, "folklore becomes germinal rather than vestigial, the "germ plasm" rather than the "fossils" of culture, and "the study of folklore becomes a study in acculturation—the process by which the folk group adapts to its environment and to change, assimilating new experience and generating fresh forms."[34]

Ruth and Ben spent many hours together discussing how folk music is "functional now and how to collect etc." She would later make her search for multiple variants of one folk song a testament of their fidelity to Botkin's concept of "living lore."[35]

Botkin chaired a Joint Committee on Folk Arts in December 1938, which included Charles Seeger as vice chair and Nicholas Ray, with Alan Lomax and Sidney Robertson hired as assistants. Herbert Halpert, who directed the musical efforts of the Folksong and Folklore Department of the Music Division of the National Service Bureau in the Federal Theater Project, served as primary field worker. In letters to Charles from 1938 to 1939, Ruth referred often to the Joint Committee, learning from its various publications by George Herzog and Robert Winslow Gordon.[36]

The Seegers, Alan Lomax, Ben Botkin, and others sustained themselves though their projects in federal agencies. Even if they felt themselves very much "the black sheep and the irregulars" among academics, the black sheep grazed in the green pastures of government support as never before. Alan Lomax would later write how "everybody in Washington from the Roosevelts on down was interested in folk music." He spent an occasional evening at the White House, entertaining the president in private at Eleanor's request. Lomax stated that the Roosevelts were "the first prominent Americans ever to take a position about it in public consistently and the first Washingtonians ever to spend any money on it."[37]

One need not live in Washington to appreciate how much weight White House approval carried. A high point came when Eleanor Roosevelt arranged for folk music to be included in the highly publicized concert arranged for the King and Queen of England during a state visit in May 1939 (they were the first British sovereigns to visit the United States). Charles was directly involved in programming the segment of traditional music, and therefore Ruth was involved as well.[38]

"Do you want to direct the Star Spangled Banner for Majesty?" Ruth wrote him. He was away on a FMP field trip in the South when Eleanor Roosevelt and Adrian Dornbush were planning the event. Ruth wanted him visible at this extraordinary occasion.

> Just talked to Adrian [Dornbush] again. You will have heard from him by the time this letter arrives. When he spoke of your leading the singing of the Star Spangled Banner, I wasn't sure whether it was what you should and would want to do. What he is trying to do, of course, is to get you in on the actual show (as he said himself). To which, the excuse for bringing you back with Morris's ok has arrived![39]

Such letters characterize Crawford's participation in Seeger's work, partly driven by her need to share his life and partly motivated by worries about his latest job. At a time when the right-wing Dies committee (the House Committee on Un-American Activities) successfully liquidated the Federal Theater Project as subversive and decreased funding for other "Federal One" projects, rumors of the decentralization of the Federal Music Project abounded. Ruth wanted Charles to stay abreast of developments and in touch with the line of command.[40]

Even if Charles Seeger did not lead the singing of the national anthem, he played a major role in shaping the June program. Marian Anderson, Kate Smith, and Lawrence Tibbett sang classical and light popular music; Alan Lomax sang cowboy songs; the Coon Creek Girls from Kentucky played and sang southern mountain music; and the Soco Gap Square Dance Team led by Sam Queen (and brought to the White House via Nick Ray and Bascom Lunsford) did clog dancing. It was a singular moment of glory for the Washington New Deal folklorists.

Other letters from 1938 to 1939 reveal the Seegers' working partnership. Ruth often acted as his surrogate with his associates: relaying messages from Ben Botkin that urged him to attend the Federal Arts Conference and the Writers Congress in York in 1938, bulletins from Harold Spivacke about deals being brokered at the archive, dispelling the dark clouds that Alan Lomax often saw on the horizon. She often tried to temper her husband's "discouragements and doubts." She hoped for a time that he might work at the archive, despite the fact that their "temperaments aren't the same" as Alan's. She wrote him:

I am such a chameleon—when you feel you've done a good job, of writing or administrating or composing or whatever, I'm on top of the wave; and when you are sad because you haven't gone over the top (or think you haven't) I'm no where at all.[41]

She added one more tune to her repertory of musical signatures in her letters. Parodies of "Lenin! Who's That Guy?" yielded to a melodic fragment imitating a work song: "Do I miss him, uh-HUH!" Such moments—and there were many—reveal the vitality of their original bond. "It is still a dead old world without you, in spite of the dribbling angels," Ruth wrote.[42]

While the Roosevelt White House provided the political clout to make folk music fashionable, the Washington activist musicians and intellectuals toiled for its recognition among the academic establishment. Herbert Halpert remembered how "Charlie had courage, he was fighting the whole music group, trying to get folksong accepted." Ruth was particularly interested in the reactions of other American composers, hoping that they would hear the same musical fineness in the repertory as she.[43]

In September 1939 she proudly recounted a triumph for her cause. At meetings of the International Congress of Musicology, being held in the United States for the first time (from September 11 to 16 in New York), the "emergence into full view of the American folk song, if not the main musical event of the present [was] its main American musical one." So wrote the critic Paul Rosenfeld, maintaining that the "inclusiveness" of the meetings could not have happened even just a few years earlier, and singling out a concert by Alan Lomax, Aunt Molly Jackson, and three wizened 'pinies' from southern New Jersey. In addition, a concert by George Pullen Jackson's Nashville Old Harp Singers in "An Evening of Early American Folk-and-Art-Music" and a paper session on "Primitive and Folk Music in North America" contributed to what an exultant Ruth called a "day's orgy in American folk music" in a letter to John Becker: "even though they were conspicuous by their absence from the technical-historical meetings, quite a few composers turned out with high enthusiasm for the day's orgy in American folk music. The excitement with which some of them greet this music is in itself exciting to us. . . ."[44]

The impending world war heightened the drama of the event as well. Many of the European participants were stranded by Hitler's invasion of Poland and Austria in late August and the subsequent declaration of war by England and France against Germany. With American neutrality growing less likely each day, the atmosphere in Washington already took on elements of mobilization, even before 1941. In the next few years, folk music, as an expression of "national character," carried a greater symbolic responsibility, straddling propaganda and myth in its representation of American identity in the war effort.

Just as the war spearheaded an economic recovery from the Depression, it created a "boom" that turned what *Time* magazine called "regional curiosities" into a national legacy. The relatively contained language of the 1930s that exhorted Americans to discover and document American folk stuff gave way to rhetoric about political identity. Roosevelt's image of the "forgotten man" had inspired or at least rationalized the first stage of New Deal field work and preservation. Now the forgotten man metamorphosed into the "common man," cousin to the "unknown soldier" who wore anonymity as a badge of honor. From the perspective of the federal government, the documentary impulse which initially gave voice to the culture of marginal classes became supplanted by broader functions of social control, and it supported folk music as a way to mobilize a nation in the war against fascism. In 1941 Alan Lomax, Woody Guthrie, Josh White, and the Golden Gate Quartet were invited to the White House by Mrs. Roosevelt in an "Evening of Songs for American Soldiers."[45]

Old ironies and new opportunities were not lost on the Seegers in the years when the composer Roy Harris could write about "Folksong—American Big Business." Politics continued to play an important role in shaping professional directions within their own family. In Washington the Seegers defined themselves as Roosevelt liberals publicly, while Charles continued to belong to a Marxist cultural study group. In New York, his son Pete Seeger maintained the proletarian cultural values he had learned from his father and Ruth during the years of the Composers' Collective, identifying himself publicly with the Communist Party; by 1940 he had formed the Almanac Singers to perform labor songs and, when the party announced detente with the Soviet Union, antiwar songs; even after a musical about-face, the group disbanded in less than two years because of political animosities surrounding their prior stance. Pete's radical politics would worry Charles Seeger throughout the '40s, and neither he nor Ruth had much sense about the leadership role his son would play in the future of the folk-revival movement at this time. Even so, Pete already belonged to what the folklorist Norm Cohen describes as a "nucleus of folk song activity in New York, which included singers like Josh White, Burl Ives, Leadbelly, Aunt Molly Jackson and Woody Guthrie."[46]

As always, Alan Lomax was at the hub of East Coast action, bringing the Seegers and other Washington liberals into contact with New York trends. Often the musicians Alan brought down to the Library of Congress to make recordings for the archive visited Ruth and Charles at their Silver Spring home. Peggy Seeger recalls the "imposing presence" of Leadbelly, as well as the "slight amiable man, Woody Guthrie, nearly my size, who carried his guitar in a bag carried over his shoulder." After a night of jamming, the musicians would fall asleep in front of the fireplace, and the children would wake up in the morning and see a tangle of bodies stretched out on the floor below.[47]

Alan Lomax included the Seegers in some of his new opportunities in the media as well. His expansive personality suited radio and he produced a new advocacy program, "The Wellsprings of America," which was broadcast on the CBS Radio Network from 1939 to 1942. Crawford eagerly completed her first new composition in several years for this program. "It was supposed to be good for school children to hear American ballads, to remind them of an American past and make them feel the quality of people building and working and singing at the same time," Lomax said ten years later. He brought live performers into the station, among them Burl Ives, Aunt Molly Jackson, the Golden Gate Quartet, Leadbelly, and Woody Guthrie. As part of the educational mission, CBS underwrote twelve commissions for American composers to write orchestral arrangements of folk songs under four and a half minutes (the length of a 78 rpm disc) for a high-school audience. At Alan's special urging, both Ruth and Charles received commissions joining a group that included Copland, Henry Brant, and Ross Lee Finney. The program format paired original field recordings of folk songs with on-air premieres of the commissioned arrangements by the CBS Radio Orchestra. Ideally, the music would be fresh and uncommercial, offering alternatives to the "gussied-up" folk arrangements that André Kostelanetz broadcast on commercial programs.[48]

An excited composer set to work enthusiastically on her first commission in seven years. "She worked hard as hell," Pete Seeger said. "$400 for months and months of hard work." By the end of 1939, Crawford had finished an orchestral fantasy, "Rissolty, Rossolty," which was premiered in New York on Alan Lomax's radio program on January 23, 1940. With Charles at work on his commission (setting "John Hardy"), the process revived old patterns of dependency and competition between a former-student wife and her former-teacher husband, which surfaced in letters and in the conflicting memories of their family. One letter from Ruth to Charles evokes the Berlin years, as she asks for criticism and closes with an ironic farewell from a self-anointed subject:

> Damn it, I wish you were here! Yet of course, it's good for me to go ahead and make decisions on my own. I've decided not to try and send you anything. I need it all here. *Can you give me Thursday and Friday?* That will be very important. We could tear the thing to pieces and I could still have time to mend it and copy it, if the tearing weren't too complete. . . . "Bye—Czarl—the czar of composition."[49]

Competitive sparks flew at the dinner table. As Mike remembers, "I think Charlie said, 'Well, mine came out best.' They sparred a little bit about it, which I thought was humorous. I always thought that they handled it pretty well." Pete offered another perspective, which complicates this memory further. "Ruth did a first-rate job. Father's was nice, but he knew it didn't measure up to hers."[50]

"Rissolty, Rossolty," a three-minute work for high-school orchestra, is an attractive and ambitious work. A piece of some complexity, it exceeds the limits of the genre of orchestral arrangement by combining three tunes in one work: the fiddle tune "The Last of Callahan" and two folk songs, whose texts comment on marriage from humorous contrasting points of view. "Rissolty, Rossolty" sings of the hapless husband burdened by a lazy wife (who "swept the floor but once a year," "churns her milk in her dad's old boot," and "combs her hair but once a week.") The blame shifts to the husband in the second borrowed folk song, "Phoebe" (also known as "The Old Grumbler" or "Equinoctial"). What is a wife worth? asks Phoebe's husband, who arrogantly claimed "he could do more work in a day than his wife could in three." The wife asks him to trade places. And sure enough, he does nothing right. Sweet revenge finishes the tune: "And presently little Phoebe came and saw him looking sad, She clapped her hands upon her sides and said that she was glad."

How the composer came to these texts is not clear, but perhaps her status as a female composer inspired the choice. As Alan Lomax later recalled, it was "quite a departure to even raise these themes or the relevance of music to women's problems." On the radio premiere Aunt Molly Jackson, whom Lomax called a "cantankerous feminist," sang the title tune and talked about the "function such songs played in the lives of mountain women." In contrast to the rest of the composers in the CBS commissions, celebrating male heroes ("John Henry," "John Hardy") and male work (sea shanties), the only female composer among the CBS commissions had written the only work touching on women's lives.[51]

As the one completed effort of Crawford's ideal of new American music, "Rissolty, Rossolty" is enlivened by her modernist approach to tradition. Although the commission specified an amateur level of difficulty, she could not resist exceeding it. Rather than presenting the borrowed melodies as audible themes, she fragments and recombines elements from them in a sophisticated polyphony. The playful repeated-note figure that opens the piece comes from the title tune. Soon lilting pairs of triplets (derived from the inner section of the tune) act as the mainstay-accompaniment (Ex. 16-1). "Phoebe," also in triple meter, emerges briefly in a solo flute section and then as countermelody in string pizzicato, and later in the horns.

A third tune, "The Death of Callahan," appears in the third section of the piece. It was not a song, but a "real stumper" of a fiddle tune that she had just transcribed for *Our Singing Country*. As "Callahan" is overtaken by fragments from "Phoebe" and "Rissolty, Rossolty," the meter (which began in 6/8 and shifts to 2/4) forges ahead to a "one beat per measure" at the climax. Here Crawford juggles three tunes at once. "Callahan" dominates winds and high strings; the brass oppose that double-time with "Rissolty, Rossolty"; and the low strings echo the leading idea of "Phoebe." It is a moment that recalls the spirit of Charles Ives.

In fact, this may be more than coincidental, for Ives had mailed several scores to Charles Seeger in 1939 for the *Magazine of Art* article. Ruth, who typed the paper for Charles, thanked Mrs. Ives: "It has been always one of our strong regrets that though having such close bonds to Charles Ives both in music trends and friends, our paths have never crossed." "Music trends" united their sympathetic response to vernacular sound as heard by modernist ears.[52]

Both of them shared an approach to musical borrowing that penetrated culture as well as musical style. For Ives, the idealized sincerity of amateur hymn-singing at camp meetings inspired experimental textures and simulated out-of-tuneness. Crawford endowed several compositional elements in her piece with parallel kinds of symbolism. By using more than one version of the title tune, which she transcribed from different field recordings, she honored the dynamic nature of oral tradition. If there was no one fixed tune in com-

Example 16-1   (*continued*)

mon practice, then her piece would use two variants. Similarly, the unusual meter of 1/4, which marks the climax of the piece, asserted the irrelevance of the norm of strong and weak beats that define meter in the classical sense. Her unusual, indeed exceptional ending for the work abstracted a quality she cherished most in tradition: an unselfconscious approach to music-making which symbolized being in life rather than on a stage.

"Rissolty, Rossolty" does not really "end"—it shuts down abruptly as the three tunes mix it up. And then, from nowhere we hear the opening moment of the work as a whole. Why this extraordinary whimsy? My end is my beginning, the composer tells us. As a fleeting recall of lilting triplets leaves our ears suspended in time and harmony, the composer pays homage to the way traditional singers and players did not really come to an applause-seeking cadence (as she perceived it), but stopped in readiness to start again. She described this quality of performance practice as "keeping the tune going"; its matter-of-factness seemed different from concert "airs," as she called them. Here again was a point of contact between the very old and the very new, as oral tradition opposed the emotional excesses of Romanticism. This brief gesture simultaneously satisfies her insight into the essence of folk music and her desire to resist conventional tonal closure. She got little feedback at the time from the press. When Colin McPhee reviewed the series for *Modern Music*, he ignored her work, praising Frederick Converse's sea chantey as "effective in spite of being Brahmsian, [because] the theme was always easy to follow. . . . an important point in a program designed for teaching purposes in the school." Perhaps the complexity of Crawford's arrangement displeased him: "Wait til you see what I have to say about Ruth Crawford," he wrote to Henry Cowell, forgetting their relationship. But nothing appeared in print.[53]

"Rissolty, Rossolty" is Crawford's only composed music between 1932 and 1951. She never repeated her experiment with symphonic arrangements. According to Pete, who regretted this, "she and Father kind of sloughed it off, felt that it wasn't important. I don't know why."[54]

Instead of working out the implications of the folk revival in compositional terms, she responded to the source itself. The process of transcribing became her vehicle of self-expression, as she completely immersed herself in the problems of documenting an idiom. Her perfectionist sense of responsibility to the musical material became family legend. Pete recalls how, as he "got more into music in 1938 and 1939—you know, I was working with Alan Lomax and watching Ruth transcribe—I got to appreciate her fantastic determination. She was just going to do the absolute best job possible, whatever it required."[55]

Ruth Seeger "had read Bartók and she had taken it very seriously, as she should," Alan Lomax said. "And she had read Herzog, and she set out to make music look that way . . . and we went with her." As she grew more involved with transcription method, a project that was supposed to take two months stretched into four years. She struggled to "really represent the tunes, to paint them somehow with notes. . . . I was witness to that struggle," Alan Lomax told Mike Seeger several decades later, the "struggle of the conservatory-trained musician"—a "musico-intellectual lambkin gambolling in the lion's jaws" of oral tradition. It was a memory to relish. "We had given her the chance, and she, in total youthful wonderful confidence, set out to take the terrible European notational system and to do it, to make it communicate the ultimate originality of a living tradition."[56]

The "lambkin" could turn "bulldog" if necessary. As they worked intensively on the book in the winter of 1939, there were inevitable disagreements —"we fought over every note," Alan once said. But Ruth held her own in what she called an "eternal fencing match."[57]

While she tolerated "considerable argument" over musical decisions, occasionally she counterattacked with a "glare" at Bess, the messenger bearing bad news. "I have listened to this song 83 times," she told Bess indignantly one time. "Has your brother listened to it 83 times?" Shuttling records and disputes between the archive office and Silver Spring, Bess could see Ruth's tally marks in the notebook next to the turntable and the small speaker wired to the black earphones on Ruth's desk. The turntable had no fixed rpms, but was variable from a little below 33 rpm to 80 rpm. When stuck, Ruth could slow down the speed, and even though the pitch would change, the relationships between pitches remained constant. She called the Ansley turntable a "godsend," her "new toy":

> I'm checking all the songs through on it. Am very much gratified to see in some of the faster songs that I was nearly always correct on touchy little fast-disappearing notes. I'd like sometimes to see if blue notes aren't always accompanied by a 1/2 step grace note from below—if perhaps that helps to produce the uncertainty of pitch. It has been true in several I've tried.[58]

As Pete recalls:

> I remember once she was transcribing some Afro-American work songs. Everybody came to her house, she would ask, "Is that a B or B flat? . . . plus the guy's slurring, only a machine could have drawn a picture of his voice if it went from A up to C and passed through B and B flat along the way. . . . And we'd listen to it and she knew she had to put down one or the other and you know, "what to do?" "What would be the best thing?" What an extraordinary intense concentration on things.

Pete watched her "agonize days, weeks over a little musical decision. You would think, decide one way or another; it doesn't matter that much." Yet it did to a composer, for whom the choice of every note involves an act of will.[59]

Her commitment extended beyond transcription into production. She had worked out a way to have the visual design support aural design by placing each line of the song, whether beginning with part of a measure or not, as a separate printed line. She insisted on full documentation of sources, a headnote before each transcription listing the singer's name and place and date of recording, as well as the references to other versions of the tune already in print (concordances) in other collections. In all, she transcribed about three hundred tunes, of which 190 were published. In 1940, as the project stretched into its third year, she was blamed for delays by Macmillian's executive editor,

Jim Putnam, Ruth's old acquaintance from New York (he was married to Blanche Walton's daughter). He transferred the disagreeable task of confronting her to a colleague, and a redoubtable "Miss Prink" issued an ultimatum of January 1940 to Mrs. Seeger. When that date passed, Putnam wrote an anxious John Lomax that Ruth had missed yet another deadline. A round of reproaches followed.[60]

In June, John Lomax lost patience with her as well. Lomax sent her a "scolding letter," as she phrased it, but while she bowed under the criticism as if she had received a fatherly reproach, she yielded not one inch. Part of the problem lay with her study of transcription methodology—an appendix that was growing longer daily, which she eventually titled "The Music of American Folk Songs." As the music editor, she corrected music proof, much of which in its first stages she found unacceptable.[61]

Faced with inferior musical examples set in poor type, Ruth sent several single-spaced letters of corrections to the publisher. In June 1940, after receiving the first seven pages of music proof, she dropped Michael off at Manumit Camp in upstate New York, where he had a two-month scholarship, and went to New York to speak directly to Macmillan's printer and the formidable Miss Prink. There she discovered that the first proof had been done with an old and dirty font, and that a "re-ordering was the only way out." But Miss Prink would not yield to Ruth's demand that the music be engraved.[62]

The duel continued. "I am asking nothing unusual," she wrote an exasperated John Lomax on July 30, 1940. "I am simply insisting that the music job be as professional as possible from the standpoint of customary fine-art-music publishing practices." Perhaps she recalled how John and Alan had dubbed Leadbelly's version of "Frankie and Albert" his "Ninth Symphony."[63]

In August 1940 Crawford took the entire manuscript back from New York to Washington for "a long-desired drawing-together which I had never been able to give it, since it had not been in my hands as a whole for any length of time, and gave the first proof a final going-over." A newly made "Check-List of Recorded Songs" in the Archive of American Folk Song, a project supervised by Charles for the Federal Music Project, allowed access by title to records. Ruth heard every record over again. Worse yet, she pronounced the second proof "though improved, bad work, and unprofessional. Not acceptable." A few days later in August, a letter of surrender arrived from Miss Prink, announcing that Macmillan had agreed to switch to an engraving process. Ruth had won. Although "the engraver is careless," she wrote Lomax on October 7, 1940, "the job is professional in the way that a piece of music from Schirmer's looks professional, and any musician looking at the book will feel at home."[64]

On a trip to Washington that November Lomax overheard Mrs. Seeger at the archive desk

> ask for copies of five or six records for examination in her home as backing for one footnote in the Appendix. (Some of these records may have to be cut from master records, requiring delay and expense.) I suppose you know that she is asking for *third* proofs on about twenty-five percent of the second proofs in her

hand. Seriously, unless you can get these proofs from her finally, I think she will come down from nervous prostration."[65]

Several months later Lomax took his last stand. He wrote the president of Macmillan that "the changes that Mrs. Seeger has made be charged to her. It is understood, of course, that you will take care of the entire charges and make any adjustments direct with her or through royalty assignment to us."[66]

Whether Lomax took this route is not known. But he did not soften when the book went to press. "I am glad that you are pleased with the appearance of *Our Singing Country*, he wrote Jim Putnam on November 12, 1941. "I wasn't but didn't say." He thought Crawford obsessive, even "fanatical" and later wrote so in print. Backed up by the publishers, he understandably refused to publish her lengthy monograph on singing style and transcription. So consumed by the musical challenges of transcribing, Ruth had lost touch with the real audience for *Our Singing Country*. She had hoped her eighty-page study, "The Music of American Folk Songs," would be published as an appendix to a popular book.

But, as Pete remembers it, "the publisher put his foot down [and said,] 'people are not interested in buying a thesis.' Then the Lomaxes asked her, 'Ruth, why can't you be satisfied with a ten-page introduction?'" Very "proud of her work," as Pete said, she refused to surrender. "It is unique as a musical treatment of American folk music," she wrote Miss Prink. "It must go through uncut." The Lomaxes and the publisher said no and stood firm. Ruth suffered "one of the biggest disappointments of the last ten years of her life," according to her stepson. "It just killed her. . . . She was trying to analyze the whole style and problem of performing this music. I hope some day that it can be published." The eventual compromise condensed her work into ten pages of print, matching the general preface in length. In acknowledgment of her crucial role, her name went on the book's cover and title page—a tribute also to the new status of transcription within the field.[67]

The Lomaxes expected great things for *Our Singing Country*, being released as the first real wave of popularity for traditional music crested on rising tides of nationalism. They enlisted Archibald MacLeish, who then headed the Library of Congress, to write a stirring prologue eulogizing a "body of words and of music which tells almost as much about the American people as the marks they have made upon the earth itself." If the first Lomax anthology, *American Ballads and Folk Songs*, had been so successful in 1934, they anticipated far greater rewards for its sequel, into which they had put so much hard work and care. Now the Lomaxes and the Seegers awaited glory and royalty checks.

"the breath of
the singer"

transcriptions

B ut *Our Singing Country* did not live up to their high hopes. Initially, its suc-cess appeared likely as generous reviews in the popular press marked its re-ception. One critic spared no superlatives: the "poetry is superb, the music, virtually all of it previously unpublished. The musical notation is impeccable. The scholarly apparatus is complete. The literary presentation of each num-ber is a gem. . . . A profoundly exciting book that cuts deep into America and its music." Even occasional dissenting grumbles from academic folklorists, re-sisting the Lomax emphasis on African Americans or the white underclass — too much emphasis on "Niggah convicts and white bums," Carl Engel had said of *American Ballads and Folk Songs* in 1934; "loose rambling lyrics of the 'un-derdog classes,'" Louise Pound wrote of *Our Singing Country* — seemed incon-sequential amidst so much praise. If only critical acclaim had been reflected in sales figures. While Alan Lomax resented Pound's review forty years later, he far more bitterly recalled the "terrible blow" he suffered at the time. *Our Singing Country* was a failure, going out of print in just a few years.[1]

If he did so at the time, no record stands, but Alan ultimately held Ruth re-sponsible. He came to believe her transcriptions were "too detailed to be used because the notation was so complex. . . . No one could handle it."[2]

In fact, nothing could have prevented the commercial debacle of *Our Singing Country* because of a serious miscalculation about its audience. By de-signing a book of single melodies without accompaniment, the Lomaxes side-stepped the primary needs of a middle-class urban audience who craved piano-vocal arrangements of folk tunes first and foremost. Just as nineteenth-century Americans simplified opera arias and gave them parlor piano accompaniments for home entertainment, so would mid-twentieth-century Americans press the same treatment on its folk musics. The *Treasury of American Folksong*, edited by Olin Downes with piano-vocal arrangements by Elie Siegmeister—whose alleged ignorance of the "complexity and richness of the songs as they actually exist on the lips of folksingers" spawned arrangements which Alan Lomax reviewed as "pretentious, quaint, funny, cute"—took hold as the "best-balanced" best-selling anthology of American folk songs in the early 1940s.[3]

Eventually time settled the indisputable stature of the still unduly neglected *Our Singing Country*. Bess Lomax believed it to be the finest of the family books. In his classic study *Anglo-American Folksong Scholarship Since 1898*, D. K. Wilgus pronounced it a "superior volume" to the first Lomax anthology, singling out its transcriptions as "better than those in many books of pure scholarship . . . despite the popular aim." In a finely argued sympathetic literary critique, the writer Gene Bluestein called it a "catalogue worthy of [Walt Whitman's] *Leaves of Grass*."[4]

Ruth Crawford Seeger had a personal triumph by receiving a rave review in *Modern Music*, which reached her fellow composers. The reviewer—her friend Marc Blitzstein—heard rather than read *Our Singing Country*, responding to its "high level of musical beauty" and "high level of the poetry." Directing his remarks to the mission of the Seegers within the urban folk revival, Blitzstein wrote, "This is what we have been all talking about, when we said that the 'folk art must stimulate and fertilize the fine art,' and these transcriptions marked the first great step towards that musical utopia." With insight no other reviewer ever matched, he described her achievement from a composer's point of view:

> Mrs. Seeger hears with extraordinary precision and love. In particular, she hears a pause as a pause, not as a tied-over note or as an aimless wait until the next line: some of the rests, as in "God Don't Like It" are really thrilling in the way they evoke the singer's breathing apparatus and niceness of phrasing. Five-fours, six-eight-plus-three fours etc. hold no terrors for her; if it was sung like that, that's the way it gets notated, and no nonsense. It is true that no folksong was ever sung twice, even by the same voice, in exactly the same way; still, by recording and transcribing one single performance with complete painstaking fidelity, the Lomaxes and Mrs. Seeger have let us in on an *alive* musical moment, from which we . . . can reconstruct the variations and the possibilities. These tunes spring from the page in the same way they leapt from the throat. I think I understand better (now that I have been through this collection) the humility with which such true stuff should be approached.[5]

We need discuss only a few examples to confirm Blitzstein's reaction. In one spiritual, "God Don't Like It," recorded in Columbia, South Carolina, in 1937 (Ex. 17-1), the rests breathe the pace of the group (the Pearson Funeral Home Choir) responding to the pace of their (unnamed) leader. In the even more visually stunning "Trouble, Trouble" (Ex. 17-2), the transcription of an African American holler (as sung by James Hale in Atmore, Alabama, in 1937) documents a moment in the life of a mule-driver as powerfully as a Dorothea

Example 17-1 "God Don't Like It," from *Our Singing Country,* © 1941. Used by permission of the Macmillan Company.

* The group sings in parts.

Lange photograph. Tracking the singer by changing meters—moving him through 3/4, 4/4, 5/4, 6/4, and 7/4—the score invokes spontaneous virtuosity. The small "x" symbols from the modernist convention of "Sprechstimme" as well as invented symbols (such as wavy lines) convey the flexible timbres along the speech-song continuum as Mr. Hale prods his mules along with "Giddaps" and "Whoa deres" in between verses. Words, whoops, half-sung and half-talked pitches, bluesy slides: all of this crazy-quilt vocal artistry gets frozen in print.

The transcription of a fiddle tune (a first for a Lomax book), "Bonyparte," recorded in Kentucky in 1937 (Ex. 17-3) focused attention on a tradition which, as Judith McCulloh has written, "has been notoriously neglected by folklorists, at least in their printed publications." W. M. Stepp's performance

Example 17-2 "Trouble, Trouble" (a) first stanza; (b) alternative transcriptions for the last line. From *Our Singing Country*, © 1941. Used by permission of the Macmillan Company.

Example 17-3   Excerpt from "Bonyparte," from *Our Singing Country*, © 1941. Used by permission of the Macmillan Company.

of "Bonyparte," sometimes known as "Bonyparte's Retreat Across the Rocky Mountains," is a novelty piece—a "fiddle-picture" imitating marching troops, howling winds, bagpipes or fife, and the general chaos of battle (not dissimilar in intent to that nineteenth-century piano favorite, "The Battle of Prague"). It became a signature tune for an American sound after Aaron Copland swallowed it whole for the "Hoedown" movement in the ballet suite *Rodeo* a few years later, and Agnes de Mille's dancers moved to the upbeat triplet figures and the double-stop drones so assiduously notated by Crawford.[6]

Perhaps because music in its visual form still retains so much authority for the Western-trained musician, these transcriptions still communicate the reality of a style with surprising vividness. Even with all our access to field recordings, notation triggers our intellectual responses to the material in a different way. In the Anglo-American sailor song "Peter Gray" (Ex. 17-4), the unusual triplet rhythms, the key signature hovering between two and three flats, the lyrical melismas in the refrain—even the unusual ritardando at the end of the song—all these visual devices prepare the ear to hear details that might otherwise elude our perception of the familiar.

Example 17-4 "Peter Gray," from *Our Singing Country,* © 1941. Used by permission of the Macmillan Company.

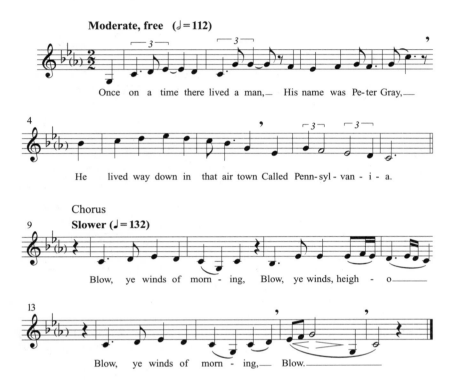

Thus, somewhat ironically, Crawford's profound response to the Lomax field recordings has its roots in her own classical training. As Bruno Nettl explains, "Western urban society has a special view of music. . . . We think of a piece of music as existing in its truest form on a piece of paper." Trained in a Western conservatory, she had been raised in that print tradition and felt the pressures of mediation all the more powerfully for it. Both the printed music preface and the unpublished monograph "The Music of American Folk Songs" benefit from her insight and authority about this process.[7]

The musical preface offers up personal testimony to convince the reader of the depth of the musical problems involved. She confessed the ambiguities of her position as a "mere composer," a humble novice, loath to cast votes about songs, wishing to postpone her evaluations until she had mastered the repertory. Although on occasion the "authenticity" of a spiritual or a work song appeared "unmistakeable," most of the time she "gained a reputation for thinking it over—for wishing to postpone decision [before] attempting to pass judgment" on what constituted common practice. If a mere composer learned to appreciate the nice and common as much as the esoteric, then the reader could surely appreciate "Little Willie's My Darlin'," a beautiful example of

Example 17-5   Excerpt from "Little Willie's My Darlin'," from *Our Singing Country*,
© 1941. Used by permission of the Macmillan Company.

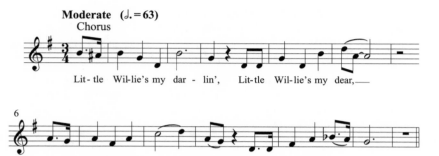

black lyrical song with "more charm than any other version we have heard."
Its sentimentality dissolved when sung "more or less in the manner which the
folk musician sings it, particularly in this unusually fine variant." She notated
the ornamented half cadence in the first line and the blue note in the second
and then wrote how she "found her taste expanding" (Ex. 17-5).

A deceptively simple section in the music preface called "Suggestions for
Singing the Songs in This Book" amplifies that crucial "manner of singing" to
defend vernacular music against the intrusive imposition of classical and popular habits in performance; they disrupted the fundamental ethos she called
"keeping the song going." She wrote:

> It is often to be noticed that the city person, unacquainted with folk idioms, will
> endow a folk song with the manners of fine-art or popular performance which
> are foreign to it, and will tend to sentimentalize or to dramatize that which the
> folk performer presents in a simple, straightforward way. I have heard "Careless
> Love" sung by a considerable number of folk musicians, but not once "dreamily,"
> "with expression," "patetico," "con amore." Some sing it moderately fast, some
> fast.

Even if the lines were not so consistently drawn between the urban singer and
her rural cousin as Crawford contended, the legacy of this aesthetic has endured. The contrast between urban egotism and rural humility sets up a dichotomy between traditional style as a positive norm and popular and concert
style as negative which persists, as Archie Green has noted, in the way we
"continue to use related terms for class and culture: pure, authentic, field versus slick, exhibitory and commercial."[8]

For Crawford, the dichotomy between rural and urban had its roots in aesthetics as much as cultural politics. By emphasizing the mutual antagonism
towards the Romantic ethos shared by both modernism and tradition, she
linked her past to her present. Referring to folk music, Pete Seeger once remarked how "Father and Ruth didn't like the Romantic aesthetic. Once you

started off with one rhythm, you held it to the end. And if a song was in a certain key, you didn't suddenly make it louder in one place and softer in another. A typical Romantic trick."[9]

The absence of such "tricks" marked meeting points between "high" contemporary musics and "low" oral singing style. "The Music of American Folk Songs" amplifies this point in language that heroicizes difference:

> such omissions [of expression or changes of tempo and dynamics] may come to take on for the [fine-art] listener positive rather than negative value. He may begin to see in them signs of strength rather than of weakness. He may even discover that he likes this music for these very omissions—and may find himself singing along with it . . . and perhaps come to recognize its "epic quality."(p. 9)

This is only one of many critical strategies that allowed Crawford to conceptualize traditional music as oppositional to European classical music, as she analyzed the Lomax repertory in detail. In "The Music of American Folk Songs," she continued to note affinities between modernism and tradition, as she did in her piano arrangements, *Nineteen American Folk Songs*. Perhaps occasionally she stretched the point, once observing, for example, that rural out-of-tuneness in singing could be linked to Joseph Yasser's theories of evolving tonality—both liberating music from the "fetters of tonality." Still, she set a course for integration between two cultural worlds that sustained her own identity as a modernist, as her work documented the musical style of American vernacular tradition on an unprecedented scale.

"The Music of American Folk Songs" contains brilliant technical culture-specific analysis. With separate sections devoted first to "Remarks on Transcription" and second to "Notes on the Songs and On Manners of Singing," the table of contents (Fig. 17-1) displays the scientific detail of the argument. One example from the voluminous documentation suffices to illustrate the nature of her work. In the published transcription of the spiritual "Choose You a Seat 'n' Set Down," a small metric shift from 2/4 to 3/4 in the chorus notates an irregular rhythm as something other than a conventional syncopation. Such a small moment, but so alive. One need only compare the version she rejected with her elegantly nuanced solution (Fig. 17-2) to see the importance of the detail. She explained the issue at length:

> It might be of interest in presenting one further example (taken from the chorus of "Choose You a Seat 'n' Set Down") to include two types of transcription. Type B was chosen in publication. The pattern of metrical alternation is maintained almost without change through the four recurrences which comprise each singing of the chorus, as well as throughout all the repetitions of the chorus. [This] notation can be said to represent more or less accurately the individual metric norm felt to have been established in this particular singing of this particular song as a whole.

She treated other aspects of performance practice with the same kind of technical zeal, making observations about singing style that have held up over the decades: about off-beat rhythms, vocal timbre, invariance of dynamics, tempo, metric irregularities, and non-diatonic intonation.

TABLE OF CONTENTS

I

REMARKS ON TRANSCRIPTION

1. The singer and the song
2. Phonographic recording of the song
3. Transcription of the song from phonographic recording
   a. Transcription from phonograph recording versus dictation direct from folk singer, player or intermediary
   b. Transcription through graph notation
4. The reader and the song
5. Music notation as a bridge
6. Three basic types of transcription illustrated
7. Song-norm
8. Majority usage
9. Underlimits of amount of detail shown in notation, especially with regard to the simpler singing-styles
10. The model tune as representative of the song as a whole
11. The initial tune as a model tune
12. The composite tune
13. The transcriber and a changing oral tradition

II

NOTES ON THE SONGS AND ON MANNERS OF SINGING

14. Adherence to a dynamic level thoughout the song as a whole
15. Adherence to a dramatic level throughout the song as a whole
16. Adherence to the tempo set at the beginning of the song
   a. Infrequency of long ritardandos from the beginning to the end of the song as a whole
   b. Infrequency of short stereotyped ritardandos at ends of phrases and stanzas
17. Strict time and free singing-styles
18. Pulse and count
19. Anticipation and delay of beat
20. Simple and compound meter
21. Metrical irregularities—prolongation and contraction of measure
   a. Contraction of measure
   b. Prolongation of measure—the extended tone and the extended or inserted rest
   c. Underlimit of metrical irregularity shown in notation, especially with regard to extension of tone and extension and insertion of rest
   d. Manners of notating the extended tone and the extended or inserted rest
22. Metrical irregularities—divisions of beat and measure
23. Rests
24. Phrase patterns
   a. Number of measures to the phrase
   b. Number of phrases to the song
25. Interstanzaic variation
26. Manners of accommodating extra syllables of succeeding stanzas
27. Tone attack and release
28. Intonation
29. Scale and mode
30. Accompaniment

Figure 17-1 Table of Contents for "The Music of American Folk Songs"

(a)

(b)

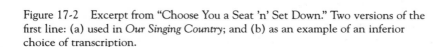

Figure 17-2   Excerpt from "Choose You a Seat 'n' Set Down." Two versions of the first line: (a) used in *Our Singing Country*; and (b) as an example of an inferior choice of transcription.

Such observations immediately led to method theory about the process of representation or, to put this another way, the problem of the one and the many: What was the relationship of one field recording to the many versions of the tune that existed in tradition? Was the shift in "Choose You a Seat" a "commonly possessed metrical norm" or an idiosyncratic event? Might not a skeptic maintain that complex variants were exceptions to the rule? Several theoretical terms help her tackle solutions to these thorny issues: the "model tune"—"*the tune of one single stanza of one song as sung in one performance*"; "song-norm," which referred to the "basic tune pattern" of an individual piece, which could then serve as a guide to understanding the contributions of individual singers in shaping variants; and "majority usage," which referred to a particular "variation being representative, within that musical function and at that point in the tune of the song in its entirety."[10]

As she reflected on the project as a whole, Crawford portrayed transcription as mediation on two levels, one between two kinds of singers and the other between two kinds of analysis. She wrote of a bridge between peoples, over which a "vital heritage of culture can pass." She described how such a bridge might be built:

> The manner of its building must be determined, for the most part, by the specific use to which the notations will be put. If they are to be used for strictly scientific study rather than for singing, the transcriber will wish to include in them all details—rhythmic, tonal, and formal—perceptible to him. If they are to be published in song books for school or community use, he will no doubt feel constrained to indicate only the outline, the bare skeleton of the song. It has been the aim, in transcribing this collection of songs, to follow a course *midway between these extremes: to catch a just balance which will convey as much as possible of*

the rich complexity of the folk singer's art, yet in simple enough terms to allow ready grasp by the interested amateur. (emphasis in original)

This process was made manifest in examples giving several versions of the same tune in varying degrees of complexity, from precise to "skeletal," to use her term: what was lost, what was gained—the reader witnessed scholarly judgment at work by watching foreground details slowly yield to alternative versions (Fig. 17-2b).

Crawford drew on her research for *Our Singing Country* throughout her work as transcriber and later as an editor and arranger in her own books. And so did Charles, his role in "The Music of American Folk Songs" acknowledged by Ruth: "The Appendix has bloomed, been pruned, added to, pruned again, tightened up and filled in, til even Charlie (who has had to have it talked at him, read to him, and thought out to him, with plenty of suggestions from him and ideas and new angles resulting) thinks it is pretty good." Thus he contributed the terms "song norm" and "model tune" to theory, although "majority usage" was hers. His handwritten notes on one of the manuscript drafts suggest his involvement in the charts demonstrating various levels of complexity in transcription. It seems clear as well that she followed his advice in quoting mechanical transcriptions of "Swing Low, Sweet Chariot" on graph from Metfessel's early work on phonophotography, for Charles preferred mechanical methods of transcription as an ethnomusicological tool and would argue that position throughout his life with little success. He himself had not yet attempted scholarly transcribing, calling his federal music work "repopularizing," which he believed could be subverted by "fancy transcriptions." (Better to give people a kind of "norm" of the song in the simplest terms possible, and then "let them make the inevitable variants when they make it their own.")[11]

Charles called *Our Singing Country* a "turning point" in his own work. He relied on its repertory in a few articles, reprinted the transcription of "The Death of Callahan" for an encyclopedia entry on "Folk Music: USA" some years later, and most important, reworked Ruth's technical observations on various musical functions of pitch, rhythm, dynamics, and tempo many times over.[12]

"The Music of American Folk Songs" also proved formative for Charles's theories about American folk music in the context of the larger problems of speech and music; at its core, transcription is a kind of linguistic problem. Thus Crawford's analytic focus on the function of a transcription as a bridge-building enterprise articulated the dichotomy in his article "Prescriptive and Descriptive Music Writing," which Bruno Nettl calls one of the "most influential pieces of writing" about transcription in the ethnomusicological literature." Ruth and Charles discussed these ideas at the time, for Pete, who read parts of Ruth's "thesis" in 1940–41, recalls her using the term "descriptive music writing" then.[13]

When a husband and wife "think like a team" (to borrow Pete's often-repeated phrase about Ruth and Charles), pitching and catching ideas between them, it is hard to freeze the process in motion. As Charles later said, "I learned a lot from her experience." Yet, when the memory of this reciprocity might have been given more weight and more public credit, her husband often let the moment pass. There were important differences between them, captured not only in the nature of their work, but in their approach to problematizing it. Given his propensity for dichotomies, Seeger tended to exaggerate polarities. As Bruno Nettl has remarked, "The difference between descriptive and prescriptive notation, insightful as it appears, is not always as clear as Seeger implies." More adept at integrating theory and practice, Crawford flourished in the middle ground, operating in her familiar stance as the straddler, the bridge-builder. She gave the process of transcription a life of its own by connecting it to the agency of both the singer and the song, dignifying the mediating process into a discipline all its own.[14]

Despite its limited sales, *Our Singing Country* established Ruth Crawford Seeger's reputation among folklorists, and she continued to work as a freelance transcriber the rest of her life. In 1943 she completed one exceptional transcription of an African-American surge song built on "Amazing Grace" for George Pullen Jackson's book *White and Negro Spirituals*. For her friend Ben Botkin, Ruth transcribed "Take This Hammer" as sung by the Almanac Singers (Pete Seeger's group) in his *A Treasury of American Folklore*; later (with some help from Peggy) she did all the transcriptions for *A Treasury of Western Folklore*. George Korson paid $5 per song for his classic collection of mining lore and industrial folk songs, *Coal Dust on the Fiddle*, which in those days of excitement about vernacular culture, received numerous reviews in the trade press. "I am the slowest evaluator, in words that satisfy me, of anyone on earth," she wrote to Korson, adding that "Michael and I find the 'Harlan County Blues' is a family favorite, but to buttress that up with reasons properly couched is something else again." Michael heard "Harlan County Blues" on a paper transcription disk supplied by Korson during the summer of 1942, as she transcribed thirteen songs. It would inspire and reappear in his own recording of industrial songs many years later.[15]

Her experience transcribing Lomax field recordings changed the way she approached the material for the rest of her life. In the future, she relied on field recordings whenever possible, combing through the archives for variants, transcribing many versions of the same tune to find just the one she wanted. And even when one variant satisfied her musically, alternatives tempted her just for the sake of representing possibility. A letter written some years later captures the flow of this experience in her own words: "I would so much as always, rather have the breath of the singer as close to my books as possible."[16]

american folk songs
go to school

The ordeal of finishing *Our Singing Country* had taken a toll on the entire family, particularly on Michael:

> Dio is very nice. She loves us too. She used to sit up all night working on that old book and when I woke up in the morning she was still there. So then she would come out and get our breakfast and make my sandwiches for lunch. When she doesn't drink coffee at night and goes to bed at night she is different. Sort of quiet and comfortable and mends our clothes and lets us sew and even teaches Peggy to crochet. I hope when I marry, my wife won't want to write a book.[1]

That summer of 1940 had been a low point, when a bout of colds spread from one to another of her three children and then finally to her as well, just at the time when Lomax, Prink and company pressured her the most. She vented her frustrations in a real-life "Letter to Miss Prink" later turned into a formal essay, "Mother Writes Her Editor." Her "instruction manual" in the perils of "perfectionism, in treating of children and in making of books" offered the demands of her own life as an antidote to the "three-ring circus" of *Our Singing Country*. Crawford's musical metaphors describe the "countless interruptions which increase in tempo each day and whose doing is spun out through the counterpoint of work and love." The texture of her marriage had stayed constant throughout the years; the dizzy juxtapositions of mundane chores, children's needs, and deadlines made her prose heterophonic. She advised Miss Prink to "stay cheerful" while doing housework, not to forget to be grateful that the children weren't whining or crying, to try to relax, to remember to rest during the day so she could stay up at night to transcribe songs. "So hurry up, hurry up, shut your eyes and rest," she told her. The tone sounds close to that of a contemporary women's magazine sold at a supermarket, blending the themes of women's domestic humor—self-irony, guilt, tenderness—into apology and defense. Omitting the many projects that had sidetracked her— other book proposals, composing "Rissolty, Rossolty," and a second uncompleted string quartet, Crawford countered the unfair expectation that a mother working at home should be able to function with the efficiency of a man at the office. Miss Prink must wait her turn, just as the children do. And stop fussing.[2]

The idealized "mother," whose frustrations and anger were always tempered by humor, was a favorite persona used by such writers as Shirley Jackson and Betty MacDonald in the 1940s and early '50s. But Ruth more candidly acknowledged her work as a magnet pulling her with equal force. Since in the early 1940s, few middle-class women with small children worked (even during wartime), this theme would find its audience somewhat later. On the surface "Mother Writes Her Editor" is "hilarious," as Ruth's daughter Peggy once said. "But underneath it has the seriousness of all good humor."[3]

Peggy spoke from her own experience of her mother's frustrations. When a grand piano ceremoniously arrived in 1941—"she had worked and saved for it for years," Peggy recalled —Peggy defaced it by scratching her brother's name on the new black surface next to the signature "Steinway." Her mother lost her temper:

> She virtually kicked me around the house. She spanked me in every room of the house. She dragged me from one room to the next crying—I was six. I remember in the middle of this spanking somebody came to the door. She answered the door, got rid of them, and then came back to me. I'll never forget it. And I was six, for God's sake. I have a feeling that there were a lot of frustrations in that woman that we never ever saw. . . . She really loved being a mother. But there must have come some point when she remembered who Ruth Crawford was and that possibly could have been it.

The arrival of the grand piano coincided with the end of work for the Lomax book. In its aftermath Crawford considered "going back to her own music." Her younger daughter, Barbara, could go to a newly formed cooperative nursery school in Silver Spring in the fall. She would be obliged to participate one morning a week as a teacher's aide, help with the administrative tasks, and pay a small tuition of $4.50 a month. In turn, other mornings would be free and the house quiet. The decision precipitated several days of doubt.

Could she consider spending $4.50 a month for tuition? She fretted about this even though Charles had just been appointed to an impressive post at the Pan American Union, where he directed their Inter-American Music Center and was chief of the Music and Visual Arts Division, with an impressive annual salary of $4,600 as well.[5]

She wrote about her quandary by again retreating to domestic humor, eventually grouping several diary fragments from August 18 through August

29, 1941, into a quasi-literary piece she called "Diary of a Cooperating Mother" or "Mother Has Improved Since She Went to Nursery School."[6]

> How can anyone with three children and no maid, and a few ideas for books and compositions on the side, expect to cooperate with anything except her own inter-tangled can-do's and can-not-do's. On the other hand, it would help both Barbara and me (and I might be able to get back to my own music every morning at least) if Barbara could be in school.

She also wondered if she could work comfortably with other mothers: "I can't quite see myself . . . cooperating with a lot of women. I've always avoided women like the plague. And clubs and organizations." When she challenged Miss Prink, Ruth donned the mantle of frazzled mother-at-work. This time she dropped the persona for her professional self, rejecting ordinary womanliness as "charming voices, with smiles Polyannaing briskly about" and too much hypocritical niceness or, as she stated, "sisterhood of man." Then she changed her mind:

> It will probably be good for me, though I'm not sure it won't bore me. It is a tenet of these cooperative nursery schools that the child and the mother benefit by doing things together at the school. It sounds logical, and I can improve plenty as a mother, heaven knows. But I hate to give up the time. I wanted it for my music, here at home.

Charles recalled the first morning that Ruth began a music program in September 1941. "She was in a panic," he wrote.

> Wringing her hands and walking up and down and asking me "What can I do? . . . I have never done anything except teach piano and I certainly don't want to do that. . . . You know, I don't think I can dare go." . . . I said, "Why, just walk in, smile at the children not too broadly, sit down on the floor and do just what you do with our children." . . . You should have seen her when I got back. She was radiant about the morning's work. She had sung about the clothes that each of the children were wearing, using a tune of the pretty little song "Mary Was a Red Bird":

> Mary Wore Her Red Dress,
> Red Dress, Red Dress,
> Mary Wore Her Red Dress,
> All Day Long.[7]

By November the minutes for the Silver Spring Cooperative Nursery School noted a discussion of a "music booklet that Mrs. Seeger is preparing"; a few weeks later the "booklet" had become a "book."[8]

Ruth asked John Lomax if he would give her permission to reproduce some of the transcriptions she had made for *Our Singing Country*, adding details of her new project. Purple dittos of single song sheets in the format of English broadsides contained a transcribed melody with a piano accompaniment, several stanzas of text and documentary attributions to field recording sources at the Archive of American Folk Song, Library of Congress. She had begun making "simple piano arrangements so that the mothers would learn the songs and practice them," and then "not only the musicians but all the mothers may co-operate in bringing the songs to the children."[9]

By March she had collated "American Songs for American Children," Volume I, reproducing copies to circulate in the school. In April 1942 she wrote her first request for permission to use a folk tune to Harvard University, using a new title for the project—"American Songs Before Six."

Thus Crawford's year at the Silver Spring Cooperative Nursery School proved to be the beginning of a new focus for her work in folklore that engrossed her for the next ten years. The book, eventually titled *American Folk Songs for Children* when published in 1948, made her nationally famous; the classic is still in print today. The cooperative nursery school launched her career as a music consultant in early education; eventually hired by several private schools in the Washington area, she worked at the Foxhall Nursery Group (1943–45), the Whitehall Country School in Bethesda, Maryland (1945–47), the Green Acres School, and the Potomac School.

The most significant innovation of her work came in the "experimental" (as she termed it) exclusive use of American folk song. The principle that children's first musical experience should start with the music of their own country was already practiced in Germany and would later become the cornerstone of the Hungarian reform movement of Kodály. However, its use in the United States represented a major departure for music education in the 1940s.

The development of commitment to national traditions that characterized much of the 1930s had yet to alter the conservative habits of the compilers of public school music books. Surveying "The Utilization of Folk Music in Public School Education" for the Music Teachers National Association, a music teacher concluded in 1941 that most of the folk songs in the music books of the last fifty years came from Europe. The widely used *Concord Series of Educational Music* exemplified the state of things. In *140 Folk-Tunes with Piano Accompaniment for Use in School and Home* (1921), the editors identified only two songs as American (Stephen Foster's "Old Folks at Home" and "My Old Kentucky Home"). They borrowed whole selections from nineteenth-century German anthologies such as Engelbert Humperdinck's *Sang und Klang fürs Kinderherz* and Ludwig Erk's multivolumed *Deutscher Liederschatz* without acknowledging their sources. Even a song about Independence Day has a tune imported from Germany. "Some of these tunes were quite nice," said Pete Seeger, "and I even play a Bavarian tune on my banjo." Yet the imbalance of musical trade, flowing so often in one direction, symbolized a colonial mentality toward indigenous American culture, which was often rationalized through appeals to aesthetic ideals of universalism.[10]

New Deal folk-revival activists reproached, explained, and promoted indigenous traditions as alternatives. As the head of the archive, Harold Spivacke, wrote that in the 1920s materials for the dissemination of American traditions "had not been readily available." Now, in the early 1940s, the work of the Archive of American Folk Song, which he headed, could remedy that "sad neglect" through its new multivolumed catalogue, the "Check-List of Recorded Songs" and the new recording duplication services.[11]

Crawford reinforced this approach, typically sensitive to the snobbery that hid behind appeals to musical universalism. "How little our American material has been known in our schools, by our teachers and by the parents. Not only have they not been known, but people have looked down their noses at them," she wrote some years later. Now, in the wake of *Our Singing Country*, Ben Botkin heard about Ruth's nursery school project, as she played him the songs and discussed the philosophy behind this functional use of the material. And now she and Charles redefined their mission together. Even though her accounts of the nursery school book sounded like so much happenstance, once again her course paralleled that of her husband.[12]

At the Pan American Union, Seeger promoted cultural dialogue between the United States and its Latin American neighbors at a time when cooperation was crucial to mobilization in World War II. "The object was to keep German airplanes off of Colombian airfields so that they wouldn't bomb the Panama Canal," Charles said later; at the same time, he argued for "good neighborliness" at home by suggesting that Latin American music and folk music be included in American schools. To further these goals, he aligned himself with large, powerful national organizations for music educators in the early 1940s, among them the Music Educators National Conference (MENC) and the Music Teachers National Association. With a substantial national membership base of some three thousand that included many of America's major composers, the MENC counted as an influential lobby group in the 1940s; it had just replaced the Department of Music Education within the Washington-based office of the National Educational Association. "Father and Ruth were trying to help folk music enter the lives of working people," Pete said. "That's why Father wanted to work through the public school system." Charles later said that his work "sort of just dovetailed [with Ruth's], but we were doing the same thing and we learned from each other. . . . I was working at it more in the supervisory capacity. . . . Ruth approached the work with actual American children in the concrete. . . . It was a nice piece of cooperation." Crawford researched the literature thoroughly. After she had surveyed about two hundred physical education, nursery, kindergarten and children's books, she told Carl Sandburg that "it looks as though we are doing a job worth doing."[13]

Crawford's "American Songs for American Children" was recycled as a project for the MENC. Vanett Lawler, the executive secretary of MENC, was also working for Seeger on Pan American Union projects. Indispensable to his success, she paved the way for Charles's various projects, including this early attempt at reform. Ruth, Charles, Ben Botkin, and Alan Lomax compiled a sample songbook which was brought to the 1942 MENC convention in Milwaukee that March, for which she did transcriptions and final copy; Charles wrote the foreword; and Alan wrote headnotes for the ten songs, among them "Cindy," "Jenny Jenkins," "John Henry," "The Wabash Cannonball," and Woody Guthrie's "So Long, It's Been Good to Know You," described as a "contemporary folk song." Vanett Lawler arranged for live performance at the convention by hiring Alan Lomax and Pete Seeger to give a folk concert.

"They asked me to come and sing for the teachers, as inexperienced as I was," Pete remembers.

Not all school supervisors and music teachers wanted to switch their loyalties from classical music to Woody Guthrie. In a hallway a teacher accosted Alan, shaking his fist: "Mr. Lomax, you are tearing down everything we are trying to build up." This music teacher was trying to build up the great music of Europe. He said [to Alan and me] we were teaching the kids trash." The so-called culture wars of our own time have precedents in the early stages of the urban folk revival movement.[14]

Riding the wave of patriotism engulfing the country in the crisis of the war, the Seegers helped change policy at the convention. (Their language suggests how the war, declared officially only that December, touched every kind of activity, shaping public life into a series of "efforts," "drives," and "fronts.") In his own words, Charles mounted several "offensives" in a "military operation" to advance the cause of American folk music on several fronts. The MENC convention of 1942 remained a watershed for him in the history of the urban folk revival, marking what its president Lilla Belle Pitts called "official recognition by music educators of the American folk song. Music educators individually and collectively, are directly responsible for the furtherance of the American Songs for American Children program, and as an outgrowth of that, indirectly, for the general dissemination of knowledge and appreciation of the indigenous songs of the American people." From this endorsement sprang the revisions of music textbooks during these years.[15]

Even though popularity inevitably brought acculturation in its wake, the Seegers persisted in their original music values. As Pete said, "Father and Ruth were trying to get these songs 'done right.'" "Done right" meant "authentically" or as close as possible to original tradition in musical style and in spirit. Crawford's credo, stated simply, was to give people a taste for "the thing itself." That "thing" meant all of the musical values she had so painstakingly analyzed for *Our Singing Country*. "Father and Ruth did not want to repeat the mistakes of the German folklorists," Pete recalls. In this respect their views paralleled those of Hanns Eisler, who criticized Erk's anthologies "because the publisher cut out all politically unsuitable and all morally obnoxious songs," with the "bourgeoisie expunging" the most valuable folk songs and rendering them "unknown to the broad mass of the working class." Pete stated American goals: "This is magnificent music, it can be recreated."[16]

Crawford criticized American publishers for their "sanitized" texts and their pasteurized music. She persuaded the Silver Burdett Company, who hired her as a consultant for a new series, to include folk materials in their textbook *New Music Horizons* (1944). Out went "If I a Bird Could Be" and in came "Old Molly Hare":

Old Molly Hare,
What you doing there?
Sitting in my fireplace
A-smoking my cigar.

Such a small step forward in Ruth's eyes, and even here the text bureaucrats could only take tiny steps toward her view of musical vigor. She indignantly exposed them: "they will not dare to publish this stanza":

> Old Molly Hare
> What you doing there?
> Sitting on a butter-plate
> A-picking out a hair.

Her own children, as Charles once noted with both pride and amusement, could sing "My Father Is a Drunkard," "Three Nights Drunk," and "Careless Love" (a morality tale about an unwed mother), "unexpurgated and unaccompanied"—and unadulterated.[17]

According to Pete, "Father and Ruth felt strongly that when folk music was toned down by upper middle class people and turned into something quaint, it becomes a rather trivial thing compared to what it was out in the countryside. . . . I think that they felt it was a debasement of the original art."[18]

"If my mother called something 'sweet,' she did not intend this as a compliment," Peggy once said. In preparation for her work at the Silver Spring Nursery School, Crawford explained how she "was disturbed by the sweetness and lack of backbone in nursery songs." Just as the composer in Berlin had decried the "sweetness" of neoclassicism, so did the urban revivalist decry the "sweetness" of popular taste. And the feminist rejected the "sweetness" of conventional feminine roles, shrinking from the "honey smiles of mothers laid on thicker than the honey that Charlie put on my home-baked bread." How ironic that women at the Silver Spring Nursery School proved to be her greatest support in her new work in the 1940s. In the end she embraced them as friends, coworkers, and her new audience for the children's books of American folk songs that made her famous. She called them her "music mothers."[19]

From 1941 through 1943 Crawford plunged into the life of the nursery school. She made new friends among the other co-op mothers, finding them more serious and more political than she had expected. Many of them had already worked together in the Montgomery County League of Women Voters. As Roosevelt liberals, they tried to make the school more diverse, its early charter stipulating, for example, that the "religious backgrounds of the children be divided equally between Jew and Gentile" to combat social anti-Semitism. (Another charter member, Esther Peterson, later became assistant secretary of labor in the Kennedy administration.) As one of the charter co-op mothers, Fran Irving said, "We were a very enthusiastic bunch of people . . . a great bunch of women. . . . It took a progressive woman to want to belong to the co-op."[20]

The "folk movement" of mothers' cooperatives (ostensibly parent cooperatives), as the historian Katherine Taylor explains, responded to a "new psychological emphasis on the importance of early child care and also from the wish to allow women a little free time (a reason often guardedly offered amidst much psychological concern for 'the child')." Just at the time Ruth Seeger joined, the cooperatives grew in size and visibility, as women went into the labor force in record numbers because of mobilization for the war. The Silver Spring Cooperative Nursery School, one of three in the metropolitan area of Washington, D.C., in 1941, counted as one of 65 by 1947. This growth created a market for literature about and for the preschool child. Within a few years the Silver Spring school received national recognition, featured in an article in *Parents' Magazine* by one of its teachers. Today the school is one of the oldest, most prestigious cooperatives in the country.[21]

Cooperative process fit the historical mood of the early 1940s, when wartime need for a socially cohesive society "demonstrated the absolute necessity of sublimating the self to the larger whole, of melding the individual into the life of the group." From a woman "who avoided other women like the plague," Crawford found that she could accept a prerequisite of the cooperative movement, and, as a *Parents' Magazine* writer put it, come to "like women and believe in their ability to accomplish things in a group."[22]

And they believed in her. Even though some co-op mothers "had a strong opinion that *American Folk Songs for Children* was already in the back of Ruth Seeger's mind when she started out with us," others credited Glenore Horne, a founder and leader in the school, who became one of Ruth's closest friends in the 1940s. "Glenore said to Ruth, 'You must, you *must* get this published.' [She] was the one that got Ruth into it. I think the book was in her mind, but . . . if it had been left just to Ruth, it might not have gotten done." Ruth described Glenore as her "most enthusiastic backer at the school."[23]

In January 1942 Crawford asked several women to participate in a course that combined music with progressive education and child development, taught by the preschool music educator Laura McCarteney at the National Child Research Center in Washington, D.C. The Silver Spring Cooperative Nursery school board agreed to pay her tuition as well. McCarteney had written *Songs for the Nursery School* (1937), which applied theories of the pioneering progressive educator Lucy Sprague Mitchell (founder of the Bank Street School) to classroom music. This book influenced Crawford's own work greatly in several ways.[24]

McCarteney emphasized the importance of "here and now" lyrics, using Mitchell's apt phrase for materials that treated the "kind of experiences which nearly every child has before he is six." Borrowing tunes from the Concord Series and other standard collections, McCarteney replaced their archaic texts with vernacular American English. She also suggested how children might "dramatize the rhythm and the story of the song" through what she called "tone-play." Crawford in turn influenced McCarteney, who by June was using traditional American songs in her own experimental nursery school at the National Child Research Center.[25]

Ruth's four-year-old daughter Barbara and her classmates learned to sing at school, and at home the Seeger children got dressed, combed their hair, and went to bed accompanied by what Mike called "suggestion songs," or "hints"

that meant "you had to do something"—as children in a classroom. Peggy described it:

> [Dio] didn't say go to bed. She'd go to the piano and she'd play "Cindy" and that
> meant "up you go." Or she'd sing, "Such a gittin' upstairs I never did see, Such
> a gittin' up stairs, it don't suit me. Some love coffee, some love tea, I love a lit-
> tle girl that smiles at me." It was done so nicely you didn't have to be nagged.[26]

Crawford worked so well with progressive educators like McCarteney and
others in the Washington area—a historic stronghold of the movement—because the values of progressive education meshed with those of the urban folk
revival movement. John Dewey's axiom "learning through doing" emphasized
participatory experience in a newly democratized classroom; sharing or *bringing* learning experiences to the child, rather than *teaching* him. She easily cast
her goals into Deweyian rhetoric, writing about "helping mothers bring songs
to children" rather than teaching folk songs. Some years later, she glossed
over her leadership role by writing how "we mothers decided to use American
folk song," investing her decision with the authority of the collective. That
one did not "teach" folk song became a point of honor maintained by both
Ruth and later Charles. Thus progressive education implicitly supported the
values of the urban folk revival at the same time that it supplied Crawford
with sophisticated pedagogy.[27]

That would not have been the case in earlier decades, when "child-centered"
progressive schools focused on each student as a creative artist in the making.
Then, individual creativity was the byword of the moment, and the height of
success was to produce "composers," exemplified by Satis Coleman's grade-
school students in her book *A Children's Symphony* (1931). "Self-expression"
had governed most progressive arts education in the 1920s, with the "production of individuality more than the socialization of the child into the group" as
its goal.[28]

But the Depression and then the war changed the trajectory of progressive
education in the arts away from individual creativity toward group participation. In the 1940s, Crawford behaved not only like a good revivalist, but also
as a politically sophisticated Deweyite when she made her three- and four-
year-old pupils into a folk music collective. When they sang, they were "making a sort of musical composition together, in which one song experience grew
out of another, and out of that another, and so on." Such pronouncements
echoed the ideas of the musical psychologist, Carl Seashore, who often
charmed mothers with descriptions of how "the child composes by performing" with composition, performance, appreciation, and body response forming
interlocking steps.[29]

The Silver Spring nursery school functioned as a laboratory for the collec-
tion *American Folk Songs for Children*. Crawford used Anglo-American and
African American musics already in print in scholarly monographs along with
twenty new transcriptions from field recordings. She used material from New
Deal collectors like the Lomaxes, Sidney Robertson, Herbert Halpert, Bascom
Lunsford, Ben Botkin, and Fletcher Collins; and songs associated with famous

archive informants, such as Emma Dusenbury, Rebecca Tarwater, Alec Dun-
ford, and the Gant Family. Play-party songs, nonsense songs, children's chants,
spirituals, cowboy tunes, drinking songs, and classic Anglo-American ballads
eventually filled its pages. In its own way, *American Folk Songs for Children* was a
brilliantly transformed children's version of *Our Singing Country*. Along with
"Old Molly Hare" came scores of other fresh American folk songs that had
never before been deemed suitable for young children:

> Old Aunt Kate she bake a cake,
> She bake it 'hind the garden gate,
> She sift the meal, she gimme the dust
> She bake the bread, she gimme the crust
> She eat the meat, she gimme the skin,
> And that's the way she took me in.

The question of text loomed large. If the original folk song seemed too gruesome or bizarre, compromise sometimes extracted one or two stanzas from a
ballad, giving it the title of its first line, preserving original language. Peggy
Seeger, making her way though traditional repertory later in her life, found
bits and pieces of songs from her childhood, among them "Lord Daniel's
Wife," which she knew as "Down Came a Lady"; "The Two Brothers," as
"Monday Morning Go to School"; Leadbelly's "Poor Howard," as "Pretty Little Girl with the Red Dress On"; and the Gant Family's "Yaddle, Laddle," as
"How Old Are You?" The Child ballad "Sir Hugh" ("In an Old Jew's Gar-
den"), a bloody tale about a murder, was represented through one stanza only,
"It rained a mist." This one stayed behind:

> And then she called for her butcher knife
> To stab his little heart in, in, in
> To stab his little heart in.[30]

"Juba this and Juba that, Juba killed a yellow cat," ran the lyrics to what
Ruth called an "Old Patting Song" (leaving out its African American prove-
nance). The music mothers "had a long discussion about Juba, about the right-
ness of the word killing in the lyrics. I can't remember what we did . . . we
tried various ways to work it out," Mrs. Irving said. In *American Folk Songs for
Children*, the cat stayed killed.

Carefully, Crawford made her way through the land mines of educational
platitudes and sentimentalizing. Her celebrated prefatory essay written for
American Folk Songs for Children included yet another variation on a familiar
revival motif: "Why American Folk Music for Our Children?" Familiar
themes of democracy and cultural legacy seemed fresh because she gave so
much agency to music.

> It knows and tells what people have thought about the ways of living. It bears
> many fingermarks. It has been handled roughly and gently. It has been used . . .
> It is not "finished" or crystallized—it invites improvisation and creative alive-
> ness. . . . It invites participation.

The preface to *American Folk Songs for Children* offered advice for mothers, encouraging them to behave like the folk: "The using of pieces of songs you know—small motives, or half phrases or phrases—is an excellent springboard toward the making of your own songs." And similarly, "feel free to use tidbits of songs you know." The sins were "artificiality," the imposition of adult self-consciousness and cuteness on the material. Through such values Crawford wrote what Robert Cantwell has recently called "one of the master texts of the expanding folk revival." "My mother's greatest gift to me was the sense of music as a part of everyday life," Peggy Seeger once said, and a section of *American Folk Songs for Children* called "Using the Songs at Home" glows with the spirit that also graced the lives of the lucky children at the Silver Spring Cooperative Nursery School:

> A fast crisp tune of the old minstrel song "Buffalo Girls" lays Penelope's head quiet on the pillow to hear Peggy and Barbara improvise questions and answers on any or all of the day's happenings, from dancing by the light of the sun to milk-drinking to tooth-brushing to looking at the stars and on, until the song sends them one by one away to bed.[31]

Thus that first morning when Crawford changed "Mary Was A Red Bird" into "Mary Wore Her Red Dress," she launched a process she eventually called "text improvisation." On one level it looked serendipitous. But on another level, it became the basis for theorizing middle-class city children into a new "folk" community, aided by the "music mothers." Drawing on Ben Botkin's concepts of "contemporary folk expression" as a "modern dynamic conception of the folk as part of urban society," she viewed the children as a folk community who created fresh variants of classic tunes in oral tradition.[32]

She regarded her ability to convince the music mothers of the vitality of folk song as a triumph which she typically articulated in domestic metaphors. She wrote how they told her: "These songs are fresh. We like them. At first we thought some of them a little queer, but now we feel at home with them. And we like them."

Crawford paid tribute to musical bonds through this personal accolade of "at homeness" that resonated with so much psychic as well as artistic meaning for her since her early childhood. While others glorified the male folk hero and his exploits out in the field or mine, she centered the revival into the world of women and women's work. Her sense of space looked inward, as she wrote about "bringing the song into the room"—a musical interior which crossed generations and forged intimate bonds. Even if she had adopted the world of vernacular tradition as "home," it was all the more loved because it was chosen. She reprises the theme at the very end of the introduction to *American Folk Songs for Children*, when she quotes a song about another homely creature perhaps to explain herself to herself: "the boll weevil cannot be frozen by ice nor burned by fire." No matter what, it survives: "Here I are, here I are, this'll be my home."

d i o ' s   c i r c u s

I am running a four-ring circus—school teaching, private teaching, books, and four children of my own," Ruth wrote in 1946. This was what she wanted, for she meant what she said to Peggy over and over—that she always wanted children. In 1943 when she was forty-two and Charles was fifty-seven, they had their fourth child. Her friends at the archive, who saw her frequently with one to three of the other children in tow, were surprised. "She's pregnant again?" Harold Spivacke asked Rae Korson at the Archive of American Folk Song. "She can't be. She's too old." But the baby was wanted, perhaps more by Ruth than Charles. This time she chose her third daughter's name, balking at any more reminders of her husband's previous girlfriends.[1]

The cycle of new-baby care for Penelope, born on December 24, started around the same time that the Seegers moved from Silver Spring, Maryland. Their landlord had sold their quirky Dallas Avenue house, turning the spring of 1943 into what Ruth described to John Lomax as a "six-months' enforced house hunt" that "occupied all the Seeger time, thought and energy until last August":

> I looked at hundreds of houses . . . most of them depressing has-beens. . . . And of course had to buy—nothing is for rent. Three weeks from moving time we were rewarded. . . . We found almost a perfect house for our family and for my teaching, took it in twelve hours, and have been settling ever since. Forty years old, but roomy and in good condition and with what we had none of on the prairies of Silver Spring—great towering trees.[2]

In the fall of 1943 the Seegers moved to 7 West Kirke Street in Chevy Chase, an older, flossier suburb directly adjacent to Washington. Their new community lay closer to town, and their street bordered the main thoroughfare of Connecticut Avenue, only two blocks from the district line, which ended at Chevy Chase Circle. Crawford, who never learned to drive a car, appreciated her access to a major bus line, which could take her to the Archive of American Folk Song in under an hour. In addition, she benefited from the greater supply of piano students to be found in a wealthier community. But she missed "Silver Spring, still the liveliest place to live . . . much more so than conservative Chevy Chase," where she was never quite at home in the same way. As Pete recalled, "they asked the real estate agent what kind of people live here? He answered, 'elderly, conservative people like you.' Ruth was laughing as hard as anyone at that."[3]

"Ruth Seeger was never fancy," one of her friends later said, "but the house [in Chevy Chase] . . . was definitely a big step up." Briefly dubbed "Seeger's Barn" by Ruth, the splendid white-clapboard, three-story Victorian was anything but. It stood on a substantial corner lot, with lots of land on the side that allowed for a play area and a garden. Light hit in all directions and streamed in through the big windows. Space abounded, with four bedrooms on the second floor and three more on the third floor. Downstairs, fireplaces warmed up the living room and the adjacent spacious room which served as Crawford's teaching studio. There she put two grand pianos side by side on a bare floor. As Peggy said, "that's civilization and plenty of room to rattle around in. I can see why they wanted it, I would want it."[4]

Charles liked the idea of a larger home and a more prestigious address. As a former daughter-in-law observed, the move restored him to his upper-class roots and the "old, stable, secure world of Grandfather and Grandmother Seeger." Here "Father set the tone," Penny said. "He ordered calling cards from Tiffany," and Ruth's read "Mrs. Charles Seeger." He had a call bell installed underneath the dining room table to ring for the maid. Peggy said, "I think if it had been left to Dio, she would not have done that, but because he wanted it, it was done."[5]

Ruth added the role of diplomat's wife to her roster of responsibilities. As chief of the music and visual arts division at the Pan American Union, Charles frequently entertained foreign dignitaries, particularly during the tense years of the war when good relations between the United States and South America were more vital than ever. Visitors came in ever-increasing numbers to West Kirke Street, turning the Seeger home into an extension of Charles's professional workplace. Ruth supervised a formidable social life. "We'd throw parties, great big fantastic dress parties," Barbara recalled. "And my mother would arrange for them . . . and us kids would go around with our eyes wide open [listening to] all these people talking these strange languages." "My God, the entertaining that went on in that house!" son John recalled.

> Father was not a person that didn't have friends. . . . People were always coming by, coming to dinner, coming to weekend luncheon and spending the whole day, and the whole house was a part of his ethos. Someone would come in from

Brazil and they'd just be charmed. They'd all be invited to Thanksgiving dinner, for instance, because they would not have seen an American family at Thanksgiving. And here was an American family at Thanksgiving with children dancing to songs around the table. Here was a whole way of life.[6]

As hostess to a musical diplomat of sorts, Ruth impressed her friend Sydney Robertson Cowell with her efforts and success. Sidney later paid tribute to the Seeger home as "an unforgettable center of warmth and hospitality," which was described "over and over again by foreign visitors as their most important musical experience in the United States."[7]

Like most men in conventional marriages in the 1940s, Charles left the daily running of the house to his wife. "Father had inputs . . . but in the daily operation, compared to what Dio did, there was never much there. He'd come home and he would spend time with the children one way or another, but then he would be spending time at his desk and he carried on business at home as much as in the office. And Dio was a high-pressure person who was aware of what had to be done." "She had to keep the 'great manor house' going the way he wanted it," one of her daughters-in-law said years later. "I think they sacrificed a lot for that house," Peggy said.[8]

Crawford sacrificed time, as their house-poor financial straits set her on a course of work that surpassed even the frenzied period of *Our Singing Country*. Was it the right decision? A down payment had barely been scraped together with a few hundred dollars borrowed from Ruth's brother, Carl. Her son Mike would later question the rationale, "Buy the big house—to get the piano to teach—to buy the big house." But few could resist the American dream of owning your own home, especially with a family of four children.[9]

And Crawford could not resist the siren call of books. A letter to her brother in 1945 captures the "allegro possibile" tempo of her life.

One of my problems is of course to find time even to shop for the children's necessary school clothing. This summer has been so full of many things and many decisions. Even before my last week of teaching, I went up to New York to talk to publishers about the nursery school book and various others. Saw about fifteen publishers, carried 20 or 30 pounds of manuscript all around New York during a bus strike. Had a marvelous time of course, but worked like a dog having it. Saw many old friends after working hours. . . . I came back from New York with interest on the part of publishers in a number of books, if I could just find the time to do them. . . . All during the housecleaning I was thinking of the books I might be working on. Even more I was thinking of the consultancy I ought to be working on. A textbook house had engaged me a few months before to hunt up a hundred American folksongs for use in children's books and I had scarcely begun work on that. In addition, I have been trying to decide whether to accept an additional job for next year (i.e. this fall) with a private school. It will completely fill my teaching week. I have already two mornings at nursery school and every afternoon and most of Saturday at private teaching. I finally decided, a week ago, to accept it so that I can help increase the initial payment on the house—we were given an extra year to add a certain amount which will substantially decrease not only the very large monthly payments but also the interest rate. So this will be by far the busiest year I have ever spent.[10]

After years of listening to his sister describe her workload, Carl Crawford resented Charles Seeger ever more. To their clash in political values (for Carl voted Republican) was added an underlying note of disapproval about a head of household who did not provide.[11]

But even this schedule did not extinguish Ruth's desire to have child number five in her mid 40s. Charles acceded, wanting her to be happy, and retreated from a clash of wills over a decision he knew would affect her more than him. Yet the time came when he inadvertently communicated his own wish. One of the few times that her daughter Peggy remembers her mother "having a good weep over anything" occurred when she realized Penny would be her last child. Charles had put up a small fence to mark off a toddler's playing area. When Penny reached four or perhaps five years old (1947–48), he took it down, and Dio "exploded; she felt that taking down the fence was a sign that she wasn't going to have any more children. She went upstairs and cried in her room. We had dinner without her."[12]

In 1943 Crawford wrote to John Lomax that she "more or less accidentally returned to piano teaching and was enjoying the work very much." By 1945 she had developed a full-scale practice, handling between 20 and 30 private students each week in order to help support her large family. When the teaching income stopped, as it did each summer, sometimes the Seegers borrowed money to make it through.[13]

Pupils came after school from 3 to 6 o'clock five days a week and from 8 to 6 on Saturday, waiting their turn in a small room outside the double doors to the studio on which a posted sign warned: "Do not disturb. Mother Working." Very much in demand, Mrs. Seeger—as she was known to her students—had waiting lists of pupils from the well-to-do Maryland suburbs adjacent to the district—from senators' wives to the problem student referred by a local child psychologist. She had her failures but more typically successes and occasional "spectacular turn-arounds." Her pupils "were a community," said Peggy, sharing what one called a "house of music." "Everybody wanted to have music lessons with her," according to Sylvia Parmalee, who, along with her two daughters, studied piano in the late 1940s. And, as long as there was room in Crawford's day, everybody could. As Peggy describes it: "She'd take whoever came to her for piano lessons. She never had anything bad to say about anybody. She could teach people with a sense of optimism, compassion, a sense of communication."[14]

Crawford drew on every part of her musical being to make her piano teaching vital. Some students learned dissonant couterpoint, others analysis, still others the fine art of transcription. Marion Sibley heard field recordings and was encouraged to transcribe them. Routine discussions of "how the composer did things" and memories of how "Mrs. Seeger liked to take apart things and dissect them" from one student (Elsa Borman) and of her interest in contemporary music from another (Marion Sibley) suggest how much creative energy was channeled into this sphere. Contemporary composers (Bartók, Shosta-kovich, David Diamond, Marion Bauer) balanced out the traditional reper-tory of European old masters. A resurrected method of dissonant counterpoint taught Chuck Miller about neumes and continuants. Most important, impro-visation using American folk material functioned as the core of her teaching. Miller (who began lessons in 1945, at ten years old) remembers how he ar-rived at 7:30 a.m. on Saturday morning, and while waiting for his teacher, who was having coffee in the kitchen nearby, improvised at the piano. After a while,

> Mrs. Seeger would . . . sit down at the piano and then we would improvise with the two pianos together. And we carried on that conversation with the two pi-anos that way. [This] is certainly the most important thing about her teaching. Basically, the improvisation was contrapuntal, but sometimes it was drawn from folk music, but not only folk music.[15]

Excerpts from programs printed up for the "jam sessions" that constituted the annual spring recitals record an eclectic mix of traditional repertory, mod-ernist practice, and folk-revival materials—all used to encourage keyboard improvisatory composition.

> Spot improvisation on the strings of the piano. Experiment with sound effects [shades of Cowell]; Square dance tune "learned from recordings and chorded" by the student; Leopold Mozart piece (a) played as written, (b) tune upside down in the right hand, tune as written in left hand, transposed to C, (c) back-wards. American folksongs, one "played as a three-part canon," two pianos used in one case; tune backward, tune upside down, backward and upside down, left hand contrary to right; traditional songs played rightside up and upside down (contrary), in several modes, upside down starting on the fifth tone of the scale, upside down in right hand, left hand a 6th below in parallel motion; a song played in "7 old modes and a new one."[16]

In retrospect, one sees the composer rather than the performer at work here. The guiding spirit was imbued with what Chuck Miller so finely calls "democratic professionalism: the work with children is not what she did (or anyone should do) because of inattention or lack of skills to deal with 'real' students; it was rather exactly focused where a musical soul is formed."[17]

Given Crawford's work at various local private schools, her involvement as a parent in the Silver Spring cooperative, and her large teaching prac-tice, she knew many people in the community. Often, their social life was based on music making. On some Saturday nights (perhaps once a month) the Seegers turned the living room and dining room into a square dance area. Friends like Alice Powell, a progressive educator who ran the Green Acres School, and pupils like Chuck Miller and the Parmalees came over to sing and dance to American traditional music.

With the publication of *Our Singing Country*, Crawford was linked with the field collecting and folk materials of the Lomaxes, who in turn were associated with the Library of Congress and its Archive of American Folk Song. As she continued to draw on the archive's resources for her nursery school book, it became her de facto office, so familiar was she to its staff and so sought out by other visitors. "She was a celebrity in the Archives," Rae Korson once said, "and people came and asked about her, wanted to meet her and to talk to her."[18]

Even though *American Folk Songs for Children* was not published until 1948, Crawford promoted her theories of folk music and pre-school children's education among folklorists. In 1946 she participated in a panel at the Second Folklore Institute held at Indiana University, which for several weeks, from June 19 to August 16, 1946, brought experts in the field together, including Wayland Hand, Samuel Bayard, Thelma James, John Jacob Niles, John and Alan Lomax, Richard Dorson, and Stith Thompson.[19]

Introducing herself as a composer of "dissonant modern music," Crawford spoke on "The Use of Folklore for Nursery Schools." Also invited as a guest lecturer, Charles, acting as a respondent, proudly heralded her work as the "basis for reorientation in music education." In addition, she and Charles delivered papers at meetings of local chapters of various musicological societies. Bill Lichtenwanger, a music librarian at the Library of Congress, recalls hearing them both in the mid-1940s, at the southeastern chapter of the American Musicological Society in February or March 1945. "I have no memory of what either of them talked about, only that the language was about as abstrusely technical as one could find. They were regarded as a good match for each other." All of this activity paralleled Ruth's desire to do independent folk music projects of one sort or another. In between thirty pupils and various school jobs, she doggedly pursued various book projects, large and small, her drive to produce them explained partially by Charles as work that "paid something which the 'art' compositions never did." And by Ruth, as a magnet that pulled her away from the family.[20]

A long letter to a friend exlained the cycle:

> I sometimes wonder if my friends wouldn't be excellent barometers as to whether I'm working on a book or not. It might run something like this: If she answers a letter in a week, she was in "normal condition," keeping house, tending children; in a month, she is restless, planning a book; in two months, she has a growing folder of material marked "book"; in three months, she is classifying a mass of manuscript, which she fingers much too often just because she likes the feel of it; in four months, she is making a table of contents to show a publisher; in five months, she has been refused by two publishers, has no housekeeper, can't get to New York, puts the manuscript in a drawer and makes cookies and Spanish cream; in six months, she has a housekeeper and a publisher, but the book doesn't please her: she is re-doing it; in seven months, she is writing the publisher many letters, promising in each that the manuscript will reach him next week; in eight months, has met the publisher's final deadline, and is sleeping off a month of all-night coffee-orgies; in nine months, is correcting first proof, rewriting the book again as she corrects; in ten months, eleven months, twelve months, the second proof comes, the third proof comes, the final pasted

dummy comes and has to be completely rearranged. During the entire process, so much material has had to be cut out, by publisher's expense-orders, that there is enough material left to start another book.[21]

Its tone similar to the earlier essay, "Mother Writes Her Editor," this letter could have been titled "Mother Plans a New Book." Crawford's deeply in-grained writer's trait of constructing her life as literature made her impose order on the behavior of mother-as-book-maker—even if she had not lived her "normal condition" for many years. The precision and loving care lav-ished on these books was remarkable. Book-making meant "a lot more than making money," Pete Seeger remarked. Indeed, it was essential to her life in the 1940s.[22]

No sooner did she finish one project than she generated others. In 1943 she, along with her husband and Pete, contributed some transcripts to Ben-jamin Botkin's *Treasury of American Folklore*. Ruth transcribed "John Henry" and "Take This Hammer" as sung by the Almanac Singers; Charles, "The Young Man Who Wouldn't Hoe Corn," "The Dodger," "The Farmer Comes to Town," and "Gray Goose"; and Pete, "The Midnight Special" (as sung by Leadbelly). Although Botkin moved away moved from Washington about a year later, his values continued to influence Crawford's approach to her work—as did his success. Watching Botkin's *Treasury* climb onto the best-seller charts and go through twenty editions fueled her entrepreneurial side. When in the early 1940s the nursery school book claimed most of her atten-tion, she asked Carl Sandburg to recommend her to the publishers of *The American Songbag*. After he praised her editing job for *Our Singing Country*, as "topping everything in the field," she thanked him for his grand letter, but then still delayed "peddling the [nursery school] book" as of June 1942, be-cause, as she told Sandburg, "it needs its hair trimmed in a few places before meeting a publisher's eye," closing her note with a tribute to the inspiring in-troduction to folk music he had given her in the Elmhurst days. By 1943 her book had received provisional acceptance from a publisher, but "with such a bad contract that the agent advised looking further," Ruth wrote to John Lomax that fall. With war-induced paper shortages, she recognized the wis-dom of avoiding additional delays, but she could not help it. Only three years later did she sign a firm contract with Doubleday. During the early rounds of negotiations with the editor, Crawford had proposed additional projects as well, working up "dummies" for two children's books series in the fall of 1945. These included "a large inclusive book and a series of small books for children themselves, taking one song from the large book and illustrating on separate pages each stanza of the song" and also "a second series of song-story se-quences, including several songs worked into story material, the age level being about 3 to 7 or 8." The picture-music books included "Let's Build a Rail-road," "Mary Wore Her Red Dress," and "Bought Me a Cat."[23]

Despite the frictions over *Our Singing Country*, Crawford also cultivated a relationship with John Lomax, hoping to collaborate again. In 1944 she wrote a disarming letter, intermingling family news with a proposal for a children's book of folk songs, a collection "from all the Lomax books which would be good for children" for which she could "make very easy accompaniments." She distinguished it from the nursery school book because of its age limit. "I think we could really do it quickly," she wrote, humbling herself further by assuring him that she "would have none of the perfectionist attitude I had toward the other book. I turn out such arrangements fairly quickly. . . . Don't you think we both might make quite a little bit of money out of such a book?"[24]

But Lomax had other plans in mind. He answered that Mrs. Lomax had planned a children's folk-song book as well. At the apex of his fame, with an article in the *Reader's Digest* of October 1945 celebrating "John Lomax and His Ten Thousand Songs," the grand old man of ballad hunting signed a contract with Thomas Y. Crowell for a book tentatively titled *44 Best Ballads* several months later. Within a year he had recruited Crawford as his music editor for the project that eventually became *Folk Song U.S.A.*[25] But she had not been John Lomax's first choice for this new book. When, in September 1945, he considered using other music editors in her stead, his publisher Thomas Crowell and editor Arthur Wang offered some alternatives (none of them with any reputation), which, notwithstanding, Lomax verged on accepting. In the end it came down to money, for Crowell's choice would have cost him $500 and Lomax, a "hard bargainer who always wanted top dollar," knew Crawford would sign for less. In October 1945 Lomax offered her half that amount as arranger, suggesting his usual piece-work approach of $5 per song, and if completed in thirty days, $6 per song. When he informed the publisher of his deed, Crowell agreed and asked Lomax to work out details outside of their contract negotiations with him.[26]

On October 18 Ruth responded that she would be "delighted to have my name linked with yours again," and, incredibly enough, even contemplated his "challenge" of meeting a thirty-day deadline for a bonus—this, in spite of a hectic schedule that included "teaching . . . 'ribald songs' to 100 children (grades 2 to 8) in a private school; teaching nursery music twice a week; and teaching private pupils every afternoon . . . and all day Saturday."[27]

Lomax settled the matter, admonishing her not to "overwork" by suggesting from the onset that she "bring in Mr. Seeger" if necessary. He asked her to "hold to [her] resolve to keep the arrangements simple," and teased her by recalling her tenacity about *Our Singing Country*: "whatever you wish to have done will be done, as you well know, whether I want it done that way or not!"[28]

In November she received ballad material from Crowell for 52 songs, which included music as well as words. Among them were "Home on the Range," "Cotton-Eye Joe," "Going Down the Road Feeling Bad," "Another Man Done Gone," "Poor Wayfaring Stranger," "Shenandoah," "Sweet Betsy from Pike," "Deep River," and "John Henry." Shortly after that, the publishers proposed doubling the size of the book to 99 songs.[29]

By January 1946 Ruth and Charles had made 45 piano arrangements that Charles duly mailed to Lomax while Ruth visited New York for a few days. He asked Lomax for advice on "how to manage our relationships with Alan in regard to this job."[30]

Officially acting as literary editor, Alan Lomax decided music policy as well. He resolved to avoid the mistakes of *Our Singing Country* because "the old method of complex transcription from field recordings" did not work. "I resang all the tunes. I translated the whole thing," Alan later told Mike Seeger. "They learned [the tunes] directly from me." Furthermore, by compiling "composite tunes," he protected his financial hold over the material as well, since he could justify copyrighting each individual song. According to Harold Spivacke, a "compository" might be considered an arrangement and therefore "a newly delimited artifact"; at least that was the context for the controversial issue as it was understood then. From Alan's point of view, copyright staked his claim to years of work and he was entitled. The ethical and musical ambiguities of his position lingered for decades. ("I know your generation finds these versions stale," Alan said to Mike Seeger forty years later.)"[31]

For the sake of the larger project at hand, the Seegers accepted his editorial policy, initially adopting a posture of detachment, not participating in choice of tunes or the making of versions. They argued more as the project went on. (Charles deemed Alan's version of "Grey Goose," as sung by Alan on a visit to the Seegers in May 1946, as "garbled.") With respect to copyright, after winning a concession from Alan to acknowledge singer-informants with credit lines, Ruth followed a strict code in her subsequent independently produced books of arrangements in which permissions gleaned from original sources were scrupulously obtained; copyright of any part of the music except for the arrangement itself was eschewed; and full acknowledgments of singer-informants were included as a matter of course.[32]

Inevitably, as the Seegers' involvement grew, so did their dissatisfaction with the original contract. Some time in early 1946 Ruth suggested to John Lomax that they become "partners" on a royalty percentage basis. But when in July Lomax offered them one-third of the royalties, they procrastinated for six weeks because of qualms about editorial policy and then signed a new contract. Charles told John Lomax how "a large part of the actual page coverage in the book represents our creative contribution. . . . [In the] tussle between the head and the heart, . . . the heart has won out. So we shall accept, provided the offer is still open." Lomax replied he was "delighted . . . and if Alan . . . has not changed his mind, you may consider the matter settled. . . . I'm sorry you didn't help select the songs." Ruth later wrote that "we are very happy to think of the new book as partly ours."[33]

The alliance between the Lomaxes and the Seegers had inherent strains, as each of the players struggled with somewhat different goals. John Lomax had ridden his populist impulses to a severely conservative politics at the end of his life, as the Seegers well knew. This book was his last chance to consolidate his legacy. His son, Alan, radicalized by the 1930s, continued to frame traditional music in opposition to mainstream bourgeois culture, and in some ways shared more politically with Pete than with Ruth or Charles, whose academic values tried his patience. He also worried about maintaining the Lomax pre-eminence in a much more crowded field of folklore popularizers. Charles Seeger stayed moored in scholarship; his own intellectual ambitions would later make him disavow the label "folk musicologist" rather fiercely in favor of a more abstract affiliation with comparative musicology as a discipline, re-garding the American vernacular as only one case in point. Ruth Crawford Seeger had her own vantage point that did not wholly mesh with the others. Even though she found Alan easier to work with than did her husband (as Peggy once said, the two men were "cocks of the walk," used to taking center stage), as a composer she knew her inevitable engagement with the musical material would exceed her own good intentions to be pragmatic. Bess Lomax summed it up: "Ruth was pure. She took it on as pure as you could get." Her "outlook towards the songs [was] very very traditionally oriented."[34]

That they all sustained their working friendship over so much time speaks to the tenacity of their convictions about the importance of their larger mis-sion and their insight into their mutual strengths. The Seegers recognized the Lomax genius for pushing the parameters of vernacular repertory for-ward, even into the domain of commercial recordings. (A young Pete Seeger had helped Alan cull treasures from early "hillbilly" catalogues in the win-ter of 1938–39, bringing home new finds to Charles and Ruth.) By 1940 Alan had prepared a "List of American Folk Songs on Commercial Records," reaching across lines of class and status that would be drawn ever sharper in the ensuing years of the urban folk revival. Both Lomaxes issued retrospec-tive records of classic string band performances from the 1920s and 1930s (now called "old-time") between 1945 and 1947. Many of these tunes found their way into *Folk Song U.S.A.*, reinforcing the impact of an extraordinary instrumental tradition of indigenous fiddle and banjo playing.[35]

Alan Lomax, in turn, recognized the musical integrity of the Seegers. As Pete recalls, Charles and Ruth "were really quite interested with that job. There were very strict standards that they had, you know, the accompaniments must be simple and the melody must be clearly defined. They worked over their accompaniments, and they did some unusually good things." She and Charles jointly wrote an elegant musical foreword to the book, covering the kinds of is-sues first raised by Ruth in *Our Singing Country*. They discussed performance practice for the urban singer, confronting ambiguities of mediation in a direct and honest way. Anticipating opposition from the folk artist who might regard piano arrangements as a "perversion" and the composer of concert music who "may consider it beneath notice or banal," they defined their reader as an "av-erage person who accepts piano arrangements of folk stuff without question as a normal procedure." They extended tolerance to the hybrid styles that accul-turation inevitably produces, including a "concert spiritual" because that "par-ticular license" was "almost of itself a tradition." Even the old-fashioned "com-munity song book setting" applied to "Home on the Range" was validated by being theorized as common practice; privately they made fun of it (according to Ruth's friend Sylvia Parmalee), publicly, they stood by it. The great American living room had space enough for everything.[36]

Folk Song U.S.A. ranged far and wide over the field at large, including work from other collectors (Hudson, Botkin, Colcord) and tunes associated with other revival singers (John Jacob Niles and Burl Ives)—even a tune from Pete Seeger's controversial Almanac Singers. Alongside such venerable spirituals as "Sometimes I Feel like a Motherless Child" are Harry McClintock's "Big Rock Candy Mountain," composed in the mid-1920s and later popularized by Burl Ives, and then Peter, Paul and Mary; the banjo breakdown "Old Joe Clark," directly followed by the Almanac Singers' parody, "Round and Round Hitler's Grave"; the mountain murder ballad "Tom Dooley," which landed the Kingston Trio on the Hit Parade in 1959; Leadbelly's "Midnight Special"; the venerable "Springfield Mountain"; "Rock About My Saro Jane," which paid tribute to the banjo playing of Uncle Dave Macon; a World War I popular song, "Mademoiselle from Armentières"; Woody Guthrie's "900 Miles"; and John Lomax's signature tune, "Home on the Range."[37]

Folk Song U.S.A., which was published on April 2, 1947, proved to be the success that the Lomaxes hoped for—a volume of standards from which future generations of folk-revival singers learned repertory that satisfied the professional field and the public as well. Rave reviews came rolling in from popular commentators and the academic press. Richard Waterman, writing in the *Journal of American Folklore*, praised the Seegers for "achieving that almost impossible end" of arranging folk songs for piano in a way that did not "falsify" the material, and predicted that the Lomaxes' "composite" versions would some day "come to be recognized as standard." George Pullen Jackson wrote that even if Alan Lomax "overemphasized Negroes' racial contribution, the songs are without doubt among the best if not the best we have. . . . The names of Charles and Ruth Seeger on the title page as music editors is all that is needed to assure one that the very important musical portion of this collection is 100% adequate." Acclaim appeared in many newspapers, with some songs singled out routinely, among them "Another Man Done Gone," which the folk singer Odetta would make famous in the 1950s. This time sales followed suit. The Seegers' first royalty statement listed 7,047 copies sold between April and November 1948, then about 3,600 copies between May 1948 and May 1950. After the initial flush of sales, producing about $2,000 in royalties, the Seegers received more modest amounts of about $1,000 a year.[38]

Ever the political radical idealist in an increasingly cold war climate, Woody Guthrie inscribed a jacket cover with a private tribute:

april 10, 1948
Dear lomaxes and dear seegers,

"Your book very plainly shows, at least, just what spunkfire it had to stop its reaching, your nose to smell things that aren't there, and your mouth to stop its tasting and its yelling and cussing." This music was "not bought and paid for." Well you lomaxes, you seegers, you banjers, you kid bringers, you payfaring fare-payingfolks, all of you make such a good team that I'd say America's wakingup, shakingup, looking up folksongs and ballads.

On the heels of this book Crawford began another more ambitious project, this time collaborating with Duncan Emrich, the new director of the archive. Succeeding Benjamin Botkin in 1945, Emrich set a new tone responsive to the postwar climate by ending the New Deal policy of field collecting and cultivating ties with the emerging professional establishment in the American Folklore Society. Yet at the same time he followed the old models of large-scale treasuries and encyclopedic publications designed to reach the public at large. When Dial Press offered him a contract to compile what Crawford called a "mammoth inclusive book of American folk songs that was conceived on top of a success wave," he asked Charles Seeger to serve as music editor. Ruth collaborated from the start, setting aside two days a week by the fall of 1946 "to help Charlie with his compendious volume." "If only the success of [*Folk Song U.S.A.*] could be multiplied by 10!" So Ruth and Charles signed on to produce the encyclopedic *American Ballad Book or 1001 American Folk Songs*. Without piano arrangements, they persuaded themselves that the task seemed manageable.[39]

And even then, the Ruth Seeger work-machine did not miss a beat. Just as she agreed to the Emrich project, she pitched another proposal to Carl Sandburg. She had not one, but two "inclusive" books in mind, for while the Emrich project targeted the adult audience, one for children could follow suit.

> A bright idea hit me a few months ago, and the more Charlie and I think about it, the better it sounds. The times are ripe for a big encyclopedic book of American traditional songs especially gotten together for children's use—and why shouldn't it be a CHILDREN'S AMERICAN SONGBAG?

She envisioned a volume of three or four hundred songs as a sequel to her nursery school book with simple but honest arrangements. Knowing the value of the Sandburg name, whatever contractual terms or business arrangements he suggested would be all right with her. She wrote that they could stop by the Sandburgs' Connemara Farm in North Carolina on their planned vacation to Asheville and Bascom Lunsford's Folk Festival in August.[40]

Sandburg rejected the idea of a children's version of the *American Songbag*, and a visit proved impossible that summer in any case, as the Seeger family—Ruth and Charles recruiting Mike and Peggy to type texts and copy transcriptions—worked frantically to meet an August 1 deadline extension for the Emrich project. Back rooms at the archive turned into a factory.

To her friend Rose Gregg, Ruth described the craziness of those months—the "most intensive book experience we have had yet." Some days she supervised "four copyists copying songs—all to be overseen for we had certain ways of copying according to phrases." She feared leaving out some "obscure but folkloristically important song," so they "combed the archive, including journals year by year, for material, trying to match up text with tune." She transcribed 400 or 500 songs from recordings, and Charles, who was too hard of hearing at that time to transcribe easily, pored over journals and books for additional material. From Mike's perspective, the mission of *1001 American Folk*

Songs was to reach a popular audience, and that perhaps explained a few tunes that seemed out of place, "such as 'Abdul Ameer,' a nineteenth-century popular tune hanging on in college song nostalgia collections."[41]

Any notion of purity had yielded to the awesome challenge of living up to their title. But for the most part, the Seegers drew on their long expertise in the field, the typically full citations documenting their intimacy with archival resources and their own New Deal experiences. Ruth wrote to Rose Gregg how "that summer of finding a thousand songs toward an August deadline is something neither we nor the children will forget."[42]

When the manuscript was delivered to Dial Press in September, "everybody was joyful." But, sadly enough, all that work came to naught. Dial canceled the contract a few months later, citing inflated production costs. Repeated attempts to market segments from this book in the next few years also met with failure. Several large loose-leaf volumes of transcribed tunes and texts are relics of the effort. As Mike saw it, "eventually Alan Lomax, in *Folk Songs of North America*, did what this book was supposed to do."[43]

All the while Crawford anxiously watched for progress in the publication of her own nursery school book, *American Folk Songs for Children*. In 1945 she asked her old friend Ben Botkin to write letters of entrée to various editors. Finding the "delay and silence too abysmal" from Crown Publishers, she told Botkin that "she had to do something" and accepted the offer from Doubleday without negotiating a signed contract. Two years later the book still languished on the desk of Margaret Lesser, the children's book editor. In spring 1947 Ruth hired Alan Collins, a literary agent at Curtis, Brown, to negotiate a contract. Retaining Collins for all subsequent books and related projects for the rest of her life, she signed a contract on August 28, 1947. During the next several months Crawford sent out permission letters and oversaw details of music printing.[44]

In addition, she told a friend that she was "quite scared" about the prospect of adding illustrations to her work, a new component that Lesser considered crucial to the marketing of the book. She worried that insensitive illustrations would exploit the folk as a source of quaintness and cuteness; as her friends knew, she often "made fun of the pictures in the *Fireside Book of Folk Songs*," whose illustrations for the labor movement anthem "Joe Hill" shows a Joe as a smiling angel carrying a placard "unfair" like a cherub holding up a wreath of Venus.[45]

Lesser hired the illustrator Barbara Cooney (at the beginning of a distinguished career), arranging for both to meet her in New York. That was "unusual," Cooney later recalled. "We sat at Peggy Lesser's desk at Doubleday and Ruth sang to us the folksongs she had gathered together for *American Folk Songs for Children*. A great collection and wonderful arrangements." Ruth and her Silver Spring co-op friends "waited breathlessly to see if anyone else could really catch these songs as we knew them," as Glenore Horne later told Cooney. "It would be so easy and so fatal if they got someone who would be precious or cute or gaunt or ludicrous or too rustic or stylized beyond the understanding of children, or just generally inadequate." Cooney later recalled how she "kept an accordion beside my drawing table (no piano or other instrument in the house where I was) and all one long winter in Maine I lived in those songs." Cooney triumphed with remarkable illustrations that pleased Crawford. "Their being so comfortable and not-too-pretty was a grand surprise."[46]

Peggy Lesser produced another surprise by initially approving equal billing for Cooney on the design of the dust jacket. Breaking business protocol, a furious Ruth telephoned Lesser at home to protest. "I am not a fighting person, and I think I am not unduly selfish but I have seldom felt so right about anything. . . . It seems to me that our relative parts in this book, author and illustrator, are quite clear, and should be made clear in the name sizes."[47]

Ruth prevailed and met the August 1 deadline for second proof. Book work filled the late hours of the evening, often until 2 or 3 in the morning, and Ruth drank "gallons, absolutely gallons of coffee" to meet her deadlines and to keep all the various other book ideas moving along their tracks. When *American Folk Songs for Children* was finished she allowed herself a moment to reflect on her habits. An unusually weary letter to her brother and his wife found her making resolutions "never again to run a schedule like last year (or the year before that and that) which was ten hours of teaching every day but Monday, only five on that day, and including weekends."[48]

They celebrated the end of the book with their second vacation in thirteen years. On their first vacation in August 1945, they had rented a cottage in Chilmark, Martha's Vineyard, about a mile from their old friends Tom and Rita Benton. Charles wrote to a friend, "We used to go in swimming—lunch on the beach (no clothes of course), and mixed light and dark rum at the Bentons' afterward." This time, in August 1948, the Seeger family went to Vermont. Being together as opposed to "doing together"—which usually centered around music-making—was a rare event.[49]

The way Crawford united mother with music-maker had helped foster a family who regarded traditional songs as their personal legacy. In many respects it was an enviable way of life. At dinner she talked over work with her family, her books discussed so often at the table that Peggy regarded them as virtual "members of the family." After dinner they sat around and sang, just as Charles and his sons used to do on summer evenings at Patterson. Sometimes Peggy and her mother would play "double piano." Few families had television sets then; the Seegers did not even own a radio. For Saturday night family sings, the used *Our Singing Country* or *Folk Song U.S.A.* or even some of the mimeographed song sheets from RA days. On the special occasions when Pete visited, Ruth announced school holidays. She and the children sat around the living room singing with Pete, accompanied by the piano in early days, and later on, by banjo and guitar. Pete recalls, "I'd be teaching newer songs that I learned from somewhere. African songs, Indonesian songs, and they would be trying out some new ones on me." Ruth treated Peggy in particular as an apprentice, teaching her how to transcribe and giving her piano lessons for a time.[50]

Yet music could only do so much family work. Even though Crawford "attached a kind of transcendental importance to her home and her family and to being the mother of children," the image of harmony implied by a singing family did not consistently reflect the texture of Seeger family life. She worked too hard, routinely putting in fourteen-hour work days. That she made or did music either with her children or for them served to justify her consuming work habits.[51]

From her point of view, enough pressing financial needs reminded her how crucial her second income was. To some of her friends and other members of her family, it seemed as if "a great deal of the financial responsibility was on her shoulders."

Charles's oldest son from his first family found Ruth's workload "appalling," increasing as "Charlie's deafness got worse." Teaching provided a steady cash flow; book royalties allowed some spending beyond the ordinary. When in early adolescence, first Mike and then Peggy spent some high-school years at boarding school, royalty checks financed it. Occasional requests from Ruth to her agent Alan Collins for advances suggest the pressures. On August 5, 1949, she wrote, "I thought we could sweat the summer out without asking, but can't quite make it. I need $1,000. I shall need it no later than Monday, August 14, and sooner would be better. I'll watch the morning mails for your letter."[52]

After a book manuscript was finally sent off to the publisher and she wanted to restore some semblance of normalcy to her days, Ruth had spells of domestic energy. But the relatively more peaceful and conventional mothering that had shaped the lives of her two older children in Silver Spring dissolved in the pressures of a new, more expensive lifestyle in Chevy Chase.

Given her teaching schedule and her habit of working until late hours in the morning night after night, Crawford lived in her own rhythms. She slept in most mornings, and from the time Mike was seven or eight years old, he and then Peggy made their breakfasts and lunches and went off to school. When they returned, she was already at work. A lesson could be interrupted for a moment, so when the children came in from school, "we just said 'hello, I'm home'"; Peggy might bring her mother a cup of coffee. They read the notes of instructions left for them in the kitchen. Although housekeepers did most of the heavy work around the house, Ruth asked her children to get supper on the table. From the time Peggy was eleven or twelve, she "had the menu written out for me, I had to shop for it. I had money in my pocket. . . . We had a day of housework we had to do." She would "run the whole thing like a battle," Peggy said, "with little 'sweet notes,' we used to call them. Saying, 'Peggy, go down and get two chickens, Mike you're making the dinner tonight so you're peeling the onions. . . . We'll have chicken cacciatore. It's in *The Joy of Cooking*, p. 225.' She'd teach often right up until dinner time. Most of the time she'd join us for dinner."[53]

In effect, the younger children, Barbara and Penny, had a different kind of mothering from Mike and Peggy, who were raised by a mother who baked her own bread for several years, who possessed the "eagle eye which saw when your hair wasn't combed, . . . who always had time for us, except when she started teaching." For the two younger children, in particular, that was a big "except." Consequently, there were some in the extended family of Seegers who watched Ruth's coordination falter as the juggling act of home and books and teaching outran her best intentions. Perhaps Charles's oldest son and his wife Inez noticed most. Inez has said that "somewhere in the back of her head, she was always busy with something else. She never looked like a housewife. She never behaved like a housewife." And as the next generation is wont to do, she and her husband judged both Charles's and Ruth's parenting sometimes lacking. To Barbara, who did not share the Seeger musicality and wanted nothing more than to be a conventional American teenager in a household where that wish approached heresy, Dio was the kind of mother who "did not want to take care of children all day, who should probably not have had so many children." Yet Barbara felt that Dio managed to give her enough love to compensate for her absence. Barbara suffered far more from her father's disinterest in her— he once heaped scorn on her by saying she "must have come from Dio's side of the family"—shades of his "Don Carlito" superiority complex at its worst. Penny, the youngest, missed her mother's presence the most. "Dio had this tear between her work and her family, and as the youngest, I always felt that—coming home and having a sign on the door—'Do not disturb—I'm working.' She was very driven, she had this tremendous drive to get things done."[54]

By the mid-1940s, Crawford hired housekeepers more or less full-time. The patterns shifted according to book deadlines: some years she did without; other years, she had help in seven days a week. Like so many middle-class women in Washington, she relied on the cheap and desperate labor pool of African American women. They came and went, some acknowledged in Crawford's books, others remembered fondly by the children. But one in particular was thrust into prominence within the folk revival world initially because of her association with the family. Elizabeth or "Libba" Cotten (so nicknamed by Penny) often told of her serendipitous encounter with "a fine looking lady" in 1948. Working in a department store where black customers could not go beyond the first floor, she returned a lost Penny Seeger to her mother and in turn received an invitation to work in the Seeger home. Cotten was a gifted instrumentalist. Her story—success through the universal appeal of her song, "Freight Train"; the widespread imitation of the "Cotten" left-handed style of guitar playing; her prominence as a folk artist—all that happened after Crawford's death. But the musical sympathies between them were captured on a family-made tape, ca. 1950. An eager documentor tries to persuade her tired maid to talk about her folkways. They sit on the floor and pat rhythms. "Get the banjo out more, remember some of those things again," Ruth says plaintively. "Oh, Libba, sing me—just before you go—the one you were doing out in the kitchen . . . and I said, now we have to get it." Libba sings "Snake Bake a Hoecake" and "Old Cow Died," both used in *Animal Folk Songs for Children*. Ruth is in her element, doing field work in her own house.

"Yes, ma'am, we used to have fun, didn't we have fun!" a tired Libba says, negotiating roles of informant and domestic, not entirely comfortable with the demands of either.[55]

Charles took responsibility for maintaining the house itself. His skills at carpentry came in handy. At his woodworking bench in the basement, he made amenities for the house, such as doorstops and railings, and once even painted the outside of the entire house. Still, he was expected to do very little in the daily operations of child rearing, and exercising the privilege of his sex by accepting that division of labor as equitable, he did not work as hard as Ruth. He also made sure that his various "particular" needs were met as often as possible by others, if not his wife, then his daughters or a maid. Even his adored Peggy—the first girl in either of his two families—did not fail to note that her father "had the common male failing of wanting things done for him. He came home and somebody would fix him a glass of fresh orange juice. His cafe au lait had to be made just so; his coddled egg just so. If left alone, he could produce these things for himself; if someone else was there, it was to be done for him." In such situations, Peggy observed, echoing generations of female accommodation, "if the man is set in his ways, all you do is create unpleasantness without teaching anything. . . . I really wouldn't venture to say beyond that. I know that he was a selfish man."[56]

Remembering a visit to the Seeger household in the late 1930s, a very old Virgil Thomson snapped out a disparaging domestic epitaph on the Seeger marriage: "he worked her too hard and she cooked too much." Yet to others in the family, Charles did not "work her at all" in that crude sense of patriarchal ownership, but "just sat back and accepted what she did" and counted himself lucky that he had found such harmony with a woman who was his creative partner.[57]

The patterns of deference established in the early years of the marriage seem to have become more deeply ingrained over time. As Peggy observed, "the tempo of the relationship was set up when they were teacher and pupil, and I think it would have been in his interest to keep it that way." Certainly Charles's comments about other women suggest that although he appreciated achievement in the opposite sex, he admired most those strong women who nevertheless behaved within the boundaries of traditional roles, which men of his age expected. Not for him the "career women" he encountered in New Deal agencies; he once said that they supervised "subservient" men. Some of this rigidity was relieved by a sense of irony about his own sex as well that made the daily fray between men and women amusing on occasion. He cited his own assistant, the devoted Vanett Lawler, as a case in point. Miss Lawler conveyed her superior expertise to "eighteen music men . . . trying to make music serve the war effort" by waiting until last to speak, thanking those who mentioned her contributions, and "perhaps expand[ing] a bit [on their comments], not *too* much, so as not to show that she knew more than they did, and an ordinary career woman might have spread herself to show how she really did know more than all the rest of them." Lawler, Charles's secretary at the Pan American Union, who had the proverbial crush on her boss, was also

Ruth's "best friend, and they used to stay on the phone for hours." Like Vanett, Ruth did not behave like an "ordinary career woman" but rather with old-fashioned discretion. The cooperating wife kept shady, but the pace took its toll.[58]

Although Ruth was fairly even tempered, she sometimes got "peppy"—the family word for irritable. Mike sensed that "she was really extending herself for the family," "to keep that middle class life style afloat. . . . At some point decisions were made and they wanted to live that way. . . . She could have composed." Every marriage has its contradictions and its checks and balances. At the most important level of emotional and sexual fulfillment the Seeger marriage worked because, as many around them could see, they were "kindred souls," Rae Korson said. "Charlie didn't know anyone else existed. The only one who knew a part of him was Ruth. They just adored each other." Even so, others sensed Ruth's lack of confidence, perhaps because her shyness seemed all the more noticeable in comparison with the dazzling conversation that flowed so effortlessly from Charles's erudition. To some of her intimates Ruth projected a "sense of personal unworth," seen in part as a consequence of "years of comparing yourself to Charlie." Just as his "mega-intellect" could intimidate and did inspire admiration among his colleagues and students, his wife never fully transcended the limits of the subordinate role of former student. More than one intimate noted how she "worshipped Charlie." Sylvia Parmalee said, "she felt he had so much more ability in music than she. You have no idea of the reverence in which she held Charlie." At the same time, she had the deep satisfaction of being needed. For she knew him at his weakest moments, insecure and frayed by worries in a state perhaps seen only by a few close friends and intimates, and she bolstered him up with her own faith in his ability.[59]

If Ruth resented the unequal division of labor, she never showed it directly. Ruth told her oldest daughter repeatedly that "I didn't really enjoy life until I met your father." And Pete believed she "held her own pretty well considering that Father was 15 years older. She stuck up for her rights in many small ways. But undoubtedly it was not easy for her. He loved her and all, but at times he was impossibly superior. He patted her hand, 'nice Ruthie,' he said."[60]

Ruth reciprocated, assuaging his own irritabilities at mealtimes, for example, when a man who had been a child in the 1890s faced four children in the 1940s. His deteriorating hearing, which hampered communication, occasionally buffered him from too much tumult: when the noise got too much, off would go the hearing aid. "If Ruth had let him, every meal would have been a constant lesson in behavior from one child to the next." "Nice Charlie," Ruthie said, patting his hand.[61]

So she had married a man who was worthy of her love at the same time that she changed in a marriage which, as he would later admit, "was better for him than for her." "She glowed with health," Peggy said, but any trace of the young woman who discussed clothes so avidly with her mother disappeared, replaced by the no-nonsense workaholic, who wore the same dress in different colors as a teaching uniform. Peggy regarded her mother as "old-fashioned" and indifferent to conventional standards of beauty. "Charlie put her feet into men's shoes and she blessed them. She didn't do the things other mothers did, they had their hair permed, wore earrings and lipstick, and they didn't wear the same dress day after day after day the way my mother did." To be sure, she fretted about her weight, taking a good whiff of the mashed potatoes as she passed them on by.[62]

At the Library of Congress, Harold Spivacke despaired over Ruth in a mixture of affection and male exasperation. When prestigious visitors were expected, he asked Rae Korson to take matters in hand and call Libba to see if Ruth might be persuaded to take a few more pains with herself. The young woman who had daringly bobbed her hair at twenty-five aged into a matronly woman who wore her hair in double braids, a style that her husband preferred. "It took hours to do" Barbara said, who instead admired the pictures of a young Ruth Crawford, rarely seen around the home. To her children, Ruth was what the French call "jolie laide," paradoxically beautiful. In Peggy's description, "Her own color was very high. She was almost like a peasant woman in appearance. I don't ever remember thinking she was pretty, but she had a homely kind of a beauty." In contrast to her husband, whose considerable personal style and charm graced him even into old age, Ruth "had no sense of personal vanity at all. She had no sense of ego." "She was only too conscious of her deficiencies," said Pete. "There Father was, tall and charming and she felt herself to be a homely person. But there was a lovely softness about her, an unconventional look."[63]

a fork in the road

Finally, after surmounting so many obstacles like Doubleday's "incredible" and "unforgivable" delay and wartime paper shortages, Crawford reached a milestone in her life when *American Folk Songs for Children* appeared on November 4, 1948. Margaret Lesser sent a telegram—"Folk Songs Officially Published Today with an advance order of more than 2000. Three Cheers for you and the book." Doubleday launched the book with a splash, taking photographs and collecting blurbs from Carl Sandburg, who gave the book "sweeping and unqualified endorsement" for their press packets.[1]

With "Children's Book Week" in the Washington area taking place in mid-November, and with Christmas at hand, a happy author began a round of local book signings and promotions, often bringing some of her children along with her. A few accounts convey her activity. On November 12, a publicity photo of "Mrs. Ruth Crawford Seeger singing some of the songs that are featured in her current book . . . with a group of youngsters at the Silver Spring Cooperative Nursery School" appeared in the *Maryland News*. Two days later she and Peggy sang and conducted folk songs at Miller and Rhoads, a department store in Richmond, and visited a local elementary school as well. The Seeger family sang at a benefit for the Green Acres School on December 11.

The book was welcomed with rave reviews from around the country in newspapers from California to New York, literary magazines, and academic journals for teachers, professional musicians, and folklorists. Everybody from the *Daily Worker* and *People's Songs* to the *Nebraska Farmer*, *Parents' Magazine*, the *New Yorker*, and the *Campfire Girls Newsletter* paid tribute. The *Journal of American Folklore* called *American Folk Songs for Children* "one of the finest contributions to the field of children's folksongs that has appeared in a long time" Music librarians were told, "You will love this book from the minute you open it. When you read its first words, 'These songs were sung around home,' you sense its special quality and realize that here is something you have been waiting for." In May 1949 the Children's Library endorsed it as one of the outstanding books of the year, generating more reviews, more promotional appearances, and more "gift book" endorsements. Even a few serious composers took note. Ruth's old friend Marion Bauer wrote, "The collection has one great advantage! It is the work of a musician and a composer so that the piano parts are well done, are musically full of charm and yet have unusual simplicity." Within months Virgil Thomson, already respectful of Ruth Crawford as an "advanced composer in her own right," gave the book its most important endorsement in his syndicated column for the *New York Herald Tribune*: "It is a dream of a book for both children and parents. It is full of joy and jokes and beauty and human variety. The songs are impeccable; the accompaniments offered are of the simplest and most ingeniously apt. . . . So jolly a collection of ditties presented in awareness of all the artistic and pedagogic angles involved has not previously come to my happy notice."[2]

What a relief to have a project which started in 1941 get out into the world! Ruth felt free; she was "out of exile—book and teaching exile," she wrote her brother Carl in August 1948, just after she sent off second proof. She added a familiar refrain: "I am hoping to get back into composition, unless I am lured into another book."[3]

Even though Carl and others had heard this before, she meant it more seriously. That winter in the midst of the final publication process for *American Folk Songs for Children*, Ruth received a letter from Edgard Varèse. In preparing a series of lectures for a course on twentieth-century music scheduled for the 1948 summer session at Columbia University, Varèse had written to many composers, asking them to choose their "most representative" recorded work and to send him a copy of that score with their own analysis, as well as a statement of their musical "credo." His letter either coincided with or triggered a new bout of creative restlessness. Crawford took several months to reply. Finally, on May 28, she answered him.[4]

Reciting her litany of jobs to apologize for the delay, she plunged into a question he had not asked: why had she been silent as a composer? Because, as she described it, composing took place in the "stratosphere," the elitist air above the fray. Representing herself as a bird—that classic image of female musicality—she recounted a descent from rarefied atmosphere to the "solid well-traveled highway" of folk music. Expanding the image, she described herself as gently grounded: she had "folded her wings" and "breathed good friendly dust as she traveled in and out of the thousands of fine traditional folk tunes which she had been hearing and singing and transcribing from field recordings, for books and for pleasure." She had listened to nothing else but traditional music, and for years the only instruments in the house were a guitar, a mountain dulcimer, and a special slow-speed phonograph for transcription of folk recordings. Her narrative omitted any facts that might have tarnished this portrait of the convert: her efforts to write another string quartet in 1938, the rewriting of the slow movement of the String Quartet 1931 around that time, the two grand pianos in the music room at Chevy Chase purchased for a time-consuming teaching practice, the concerts of the National Symphony Orchestra which she often attended with scores in hand, the contemporary music she assigned her pupils.

Now she acknowledged the consequences for her own music. Dust, however "friendly," had clogged her composerly lungs. Crawford told Varèse she had "felt somewhat like a ghost when my compositions were spoken of"; that she answered no letters pertaining to her former life; and that "requests for scores or biographical data were stuck in drawers." Even though there were "occasional periods" of return (she mentioned "Rissolty, Rossolty"), if she intended to paint her composer-silence as a choice, the stark image of a "ghost" suggested her pain and the depersonalizing of her earlier achievements.

Now Crawford candidly confessed that she found it a "little hard" to produce a compositional "credo" because she was in the midst of a crisis precipitated by this question:

> [Was] the road I have been following the last dozen years a main road or a detour. . . . I had felt so at home among this (to me) new found music that I thought maybe this is what I wanted most. Whether I ever unfold the wings and make a start toward the stratosphere again, and how much of the dust of the road will still cling to me, is an interesting question, at least to me. If I do, I will probably pull the road up with me.

Such musical restlessness may have precipitated the emotional problems that surfaced for her around this time as well. Although the exact reasons as well as the length of treatment are unknown, that year Crawford had some sessions with a psychiatrist, perhaps because old conflicts about a "career or life" had reappeared once again. Now in this remission from work she had time to think about her choices. Was she "straining at the leash" of marital responsibilities just at a time when the "bitter antifeminism of the immediate postwar years" made it harder than ever for educated middle-class women to meet new and onerous standards for family roles and responsibilities? The two older children recall external "tensions with Charlie" and internal tensions within Ruth. As Mike has said, "Any creative person, I think, makes these choices between family and their work. Dio did, as well. And I know that she felt a good deal of conflict in her choices." But this time the spirit of Ruth Crawford, composer, did not retire to the shadows of her consciousness, although the possibility of being "lured into another book" did in fact turn into a new contract a few months later.[5]

That process accumulated momentum in the next year, aided in part by the shift in attitudes toward contemporary music that marked the postwar years. As nationalist sensibility fomented in part by wartime receded, populism began to look dated, and perhaps turned into a reminder of the Depression and the war—just what everybody wanted to forget as fast as possible. Now neoclassic styles, which had prevailed in the interwar years, competed with renewed interest in avant-garde and serial techniques for contemporary classical music. A new generation of modernists began to shape a very different compositional climate, which inevitably benefited earlier pioneers of atonality and serialism. Some attention trickled down to the earlier generation of American composers as well. Ultra-modern American "dissonant music" rose from the ashes of populism in time to give Ruth Crawford's music a second chance at life.[6]

For most of the 1940s, within or outside of Washington, few performances of her compositions had taken place. Among those were a lecture-recital by Marion Bauer that included an unspecified piano prelude at a Washington concert in 1941, and a recital by Radiana Pazmor, who sang "White Moon" at the Phillips Gallery in 1944. When the String Quartet 1931 appeared in a separate score in January 1941, its proud composer alluded to a performance about which little else is known. Now the time was right, and within a year of her letter to Varèse, the reception that accompanied new performances of the String Quartet 1931 fueled her new resolve.[7]

Its performance at a concert in the fifth Annual Festival of Contemporary Music (the Alice M. Ditson chamber series) at Columbia University, New York, on March 15, 1949, won a rave review from Virgil Thomson. He described the work as "thoroughly absorbing. It is in every way a distinguished, a noble piece of work. It is also a daring one and completely successful." Thomson's review marked the work as a modernist classic.[8]

Whether Crawford went to New York to hear this performance is not known. Yet a harbinger of her new sense of entitlement occurred a few months later, when she decided on a trip to New York just for the purpose of attending two concerts—one, the International Society for Contemporary Music concert honoring Arnold Schoenberg on his seventy-fifth birthday held at the Museum of Modern Art on November 23, 1949, and the other, a premiere of Carl Ruggles's orchestral work *Organum* by the New York Philharmonic Orchestra, conducted by Leopold Stokowski the following evening.[9]

"It took me four changings of my mind to justify to myself, financially, my final decision to go up to New York for the sole purpose of hearing two concerts: yours and the Schoenberg the night before," she wrote Carl and Charlotte Ruggles. "It involved calling off a day and a half of pupils—and I'm so glad I did it." Sitting in the balcony, she had not been able to get down to the main floor to see Carl, although she "presumed he would not stay through the uninspiring remainder of the program"—the "awfulness" of Prokofiev's Sixth Symphony being given its American premiere, and the "surface cleverness" of Benjamin Britten's Piano Concerto.[10]

That same fall of 1949 Crawford learned from her old friend Wallingford Riegger that the ISCM had programmed the String Quartet 1931 for a concert in spring 1950. "How very especially nice," she wrote him. "You people will have me bridging the gap yet."[11]

She returned to New York in April 1950 for that performance, this time played by the Galimir String Quartet at Columbia University. According to Felix Galimir, the first violinist, she came to a rehearsal in the morning. "She did not like the way we played the slow movement. It was very unusual, a very nice idea, this slow movement, but it was very difficult to stay together, to perform it. She said that it was too clear where we made the little accents and she suggested that we not do that." That evening Crawford heard the work in concert with an enthusiastic audience, among them her old friend Marion Bauer and a young composer, George Perle, who would later champion the piece in the 1960s. According to Galimir, she loved the performance. In light of her long period of isolation, it must have been especially sweet for her to read that "although nearly twenty years old, Miss Crawford's Quartet still seems advanced in style."[12]

Late at night Crawford spent hours improvising on the piano and working through ideas for pieces still in embryonic stages. "All of a sudden," Peggy recalled, "when I was about 14 [1949], she started composing in the evening." In bed at night Peggy could hear her mother in the piano room directly below. The music, different from the idiom that Peggy knew intimately, "disturbed" her because she could not "understand it." Yet she remembers her mother radiating a "sense of delight" that she was working again.[13]

Family and friends heard more about plans to return to composition. Her stepson Charles even had the impression that she had "kept notes about some things she wanted to explore," but "she didn't complain but just treated it as a fact of the universe that other things had gotten in the way." According to Charles's first wife Inez, "she either told or wrote us while we were in Leiden that she had fixed up a room over the garage for a workroom for herself and she was composing again, and the last time I saw her, she had done it." Crawford showed one of her pupils her old scores and talked about plans for new work.[14]

Still she produced no new music in 1949 or the next year as well. It seems unlikely that she went to New Orleans to hear the New Orleans Symphony Orchestra perform "Rissolty, Rossolty" on February 2, 1950. She did not manage to take time from her book projects to make room for composing. Instead, she was "trying to live a few too many lives," she told her agent, Alan Collins: "four children, thirty pupils, an orchestral composition to correct, score and parts, a house to superintend":[15]

> My teaching schedule is heavier than it ever has been; whether this is wise is a question. I have a wonderful time at it, and I am tired after it. Also we are still being Spartan about permanent help. . . . Meanwhile a composer friend here, just down from New York, is scolding me high and wide for not doing more writing of music.[16]

Finally, in 1952 a new work was finished. Probably under the influence of her friend Esther Williamson Ballou, a composer on the faculty of American University in Washington, D.C., Crawford joined the local chapter of the National Association for American Composers and Conductors. When the chapter announced a competition for a chamber work with a prize of both a performance and publication by Edwin Kalmus, she took the plunge. Working furiously for six weeks in the middle of her teaching season in 1952, she produced the Suite for Wind Quintet by the deadline.[17]

Her daughter Peggy remembers the "vigor" with which she "attacked" the writing of the wind quintet. She was "almost like a new person; it was almost like a new life." In a letter to Benjamin Botkin, Crawford described the experience as a period of grace. Since composing the wind quintet had delayed a set of transcriptions expected by Botkin for his new *Treasury of Western Folklore* to be completed just at this time, she apologized and then moved quickly to explain her still tentative sense of rebirth.

> I'm sorry. This week has been such a precious thing. I have done a rare thing: turned off the feeling of weight and conscience about letters and deadline, and spent two solid days, parts of others, just writing music. I don't know whether I'm a lost soul or a found one . . . I think I'll work much better for this orgy of vocal silence and pianistic noise.[18]

On June 8, 1952 the *Sunday Washington Star* ran the announcement by the Washington chapter of the National Association for American Composers and Conductors (NAACC) that Ruth Crawford Seeger had won the contest, with its prize a promised publication of the score. Charles was proud of her, later saying, "She wrote very easily, and she had no trouble winning the prize." Crawford was more than delighted by her success. According to Peggy, Ruth was "absolutely flabbergasted. . . . She was so pleased as to be almost frightened by the fact that something she had done had been recognized by someone else."[19]

Copies of the clipping went off to friends outside Washington. With Carl and Charlotte Ruggles, an exultant Ruth rejoiced in the implications of the prize:

> It's not the winning of the contest—or the name of the Association—that counts. It's the fact that, by gosh, I have for the first time since 1934 finished a thing of some length. It has been a most wonderful feeling. I used the contest deadline as a dare: finished the piece in six weeks in the midst of a busy teaching season. My best critic, Charles Seeger, seems also to have respect for the work. I believe I'm going to work again—more. If I live to be 99 as my grandfather did, that gives me 48 more years.[20]

The great value of the Suite for Wind Quintet lay in its symbolic representation of her reemergence as a composer. Renewed self-confidence overcame her usual habits of passive resistance; she began to piece together her professional life. "The Wind Quintet has catapulted me into a number of things I should be doing," she wrote Wallingford Riegger when she applied for reinstatement in the American Composers Alliance. Crawford had been one of its earliest members, but then bowed out. "Henry has been scolding me gently for years," she told Riegger. Similarly, in July she resurrected a composition from her Chicago years. A letter to her old musical sorority Sigma Alpha Iota asks if there is any hope of getting "Tom Thumb" published. She "took out this piece a year or so ago to become reacquainted, and even Charlie thinks it's nice."[21]

On December 2, 1952, the Suite for Wind Quintet was premiered at a concert at American University sponsored jointly by its Department of Music and the NAACC. Wearing a red blouse bought for the occasion and a black taffeta skirt made by Peggy, Ruth had a moment in the sun. Peggy watched her walk on stage, "holding her head almost as if she didn't know whether to look at the audience. She didn't make a bow. She didn't scurry off. She held herself very well. But she took her prize and couldn't get off that stage quick enough, almost as if the pleasure had been more in the writing of the thing than in accepting any particular recognition for having done it."[22]

The Suite for Wind Quintet, a work in three movements that lasts about ten minutes, reveals a composer returning to her craft by reclaiming familiar techniques and even borrowing from her previous work in a deliberate act of self-resurrection. As Charles would later tell a colleague, the suite reverted to her Chicago style in her pre-Seeger days (and he did not like it much). In fact, Crawford began the first movement with an ostinato that is almost identical to one she had used in the second movement of the Sonata for Violin and Piano in 1926 (see Ex. 5-3). Supposedly, she had neither seen nor heard that work since she burned the autograph twenty years earlier. Apparently, her musical subconscious recalled the theme because of special autobiographical connotations surrounding this particular piece. It was linked to the incident involving an American Conservatory colleague, Stella Roberts, who after its Chicago premiere in 1928 had told her "not to let other things interfere with her music." At the time the gruesome murder of Stella's sister (Marion Roberts) had made these words seem like an omen rather than advice. Then a vulnerable young Ruth Crawford had taken it so to heart that messenger and message were inextricably bound up with this musical work. In 1931 Ruth had written a letter to Charles about a dream where Stella came to call, and upon meeting him, retreated peacefully to another room. The outcome satisfied Crawford that she had resolved her conflicts about having what she called a career or a life. At least so a woman in love with her teacher had believed. Now at the threshold of a return to that former self, Crawford unconsciously recapitulated the autobiographical leitmotif from the sonata in her first new composition in ten years (Ex. 20-1).[23]

Ruth leaned heavily on past material to recharge herself and to expedite a piece for a deadline. In addition to the ostinato in the first movement, the third movement's twelve-tone row is quite similar to material in the fourth movement of the String Quartet 1931. The second movement completely recycles the unpublished Chant for Women's Chorus once titled "To an Unkind God" by rearranging it for winds. Described by an influential Washington critic as a "dirge" formed by the "sonorous blending of instruments in the neo-Schoenberg" manner, the chant arrangement offers much more harmonic interest than the outer movements, which could be called "diaphonic suites," so closely aligned are they to that set of compositions Ruth wrote in 1930–31.[24]

Crawford's manipulation of serial material in the third movement is simpler, identifying the twelve-tone series as a theme that shapes the refrain section of a well-defined rondo. Like the fourth movement of the String Quartet 1931 or the third movement of the Diaphonic Suite for Solo Flute, the set

Example 20-1   Suite for Wind Quintet, first movement, mm. 1–6. Used by permission of the Seeger estate.

runs through rotational permutation (Ex. 20-2). The dance-like rhythms of the fourth episode behave enough like traditional fiddle tunes to raise the possibility that this movement uses material from her unfinished string quartet of 1938 and represents transformations of the standard "Flop Eared Mule" (Ex. 20-3). Crisp single lines dominate the texture. Shifting accents in different rhythmic groups, the unexpected stop, and the introduction of dance rhythms and small repeated notes lend a folksy, whimsical character to some of its phrases. She begins with even sixteenths in octaves and slowly adds different

Example 20-2   Suite for Wind Quintet, third movement, mm. 101–5. Used by permission of the Seeger estate.

Example 20-3   "Flop Eared Mule," from Marion Thede, *The Fiddle Book* (New York, 1967).

combinations of eighths until we approach the rhythmic character of a fiddle tune, with octave displacements producing great skips and leaps that suggest a frenetic fiddle tune or hornpipe. For the first two sections the only note values are eighths and sixteenths, shaping phrases that do not stop, but rather run into a wall, as if rhythmic current is suddenly turned off to produce a rest. Duets between clarinet and bassoon that act as transitions between refrain and episode are particularly attractive.

Was she "bringing the road up with her," as she suggested to Varèse in 1948? Opinions among her own family members vary. Although Seeger at one time speculated that "Negro syncopations" of two and three might have influenced the first movement, at other times he acknowledged that she had simply gone back to her old style. Somewhat dated in approach, the work still garnered some favorable reviews. While hardly a match for the String Quartet 1931, the Suite for Wind Quintet was a credible reentry into composition.

For all of the talk about integrating two idioms, Crawford rejected solutions worked out by Henry Cowell in his symphonic work in the 1940s (dubbed his "second style" by Charles) or by Aaron Copland. How much awareness she or Seeger had of Copland's work is difficult to know for sure. When did she hear *Appalachian Spring*, for example? Charles said he first heard it in the late 1940s, played by a Chicago high-school orchestra. A surprising sense of distance between Washington revivalists and New York composers echoes in his statement that "Copland got the idea, entirely independently of me, that he should weave folk music into concert music." The model of Bartók, whom Ruth and Charles so admired, remained an elusive goal. Crawford was equally removed from the newer postwar activity.[25]

Only Henry Cowell transmitted news of the latest trends. He and his wife Sidney stayed close to the Seegers throughout the 1940s. The Seegers had attended their wedding in 1941, and they continued to visit off and on, especially when new works of Henry's were premiered at the National Symphony. As Sidney recalls, "we stayed with the Seegers for the [Cowell's] fifth symphony and we all went. . . . Charlie couldn't hear very well, but we all went." Mike, in particular, cherished these visits. Visits from the Cowells "were the ones I looked forward to, we'd romp and we'd have music and . . . really good conversation. One time [Henry] talked about one of the composers, who was determining his compositions by pick-up-sticks. . . ."[26]

During 1951–52 Crawford was also readying all four Diaphonic Suites for publication in the *New Music Quarterly*. In 1951, its editor, Vladimir Ussachevsky, had suggested that both she and Charles contribute music for the twenty-fifth anniversary issue of the magazine. In November 1951, Ruth answered that the idea pleased them, but the "problem is pulling the stuff out of our hands. Henry [Cowell] tried to when he was here a few weeks ago. Perhaps a deadline is what I need. Would you care to suggest one?"[27]

With other editorial responsibilities weighing on him, Ussachevsky dallied until several months later. By that time her letter in June suggested that "perhaps the completing of my wind quintet—the first work of any length which I have finished in ten years—will encourage me to release the older ones."

And in a burst of energy she recopied the four Diaphonic Suites and sent them off. A postscript informed Ussachevsky that although she had written the Diaphonic Suites as Ruth Crawford, she wanted them to be published under the recently adopted hyphenated signature "Crawford-Seeger," a moniker erratically maintained until her death. Happy that the matter had been resolved, Ussachevsky assembled performers in New York to read through the music. A three-page letter of suggestions went off to her soon after.[28]

Now Ruth wavered, withholding her final consent. The sticking point was not her music, but her husband's, for she waited on Charles's indecision. Even though she tried to expedite matters, in August she gave up, explaining the chain of events to Ussachevsky: "Charlie's song is almost ready. But he does not wish to include the violin pieces because they were published in the South American Bulletin and he does not, for various reasons, wish to ask permission. I myself shall have to ask permission (and immediately for the flute piece). I have also urged him on the inclusion of the little piano pieces, but not successfully. (I may be successful with a second song.)" Since the onerous permission letters could obviously not be secured in time for the anniversary issue, she withdrew from the project. In her view she should not be included unless he was as well, and then too, the amount of music each contributed had to be equalized. "For this reason, I am somewhat regretful that the plans to include us as part of the Anniversary issue are being laid aside. He with so little and I with so much, I don't like." Lost in the moment was the opportunity for three of the four Diaphonic Suites to be published for the first time. The issue that appeared after the special anniversary edition included two compositions by Charles and only one by Ruth, her previously published Diaphonic Suite for Flute.[29]

This incident affords a rare glimpse into the dynamics of the Seeger marriage, the phrase "He with so little and I with so much, I don't like" summoning up one strategy she believed necessary to maintain marital equilibrium. Just when she had galvanized her creative power, she retreated from the opportunity to get music into print in order to maintain the fiction that Charles's work as a composer paralleled hers. Such self-effacement reflected the ideals of subordinating womanhood that prevailed in the society at large, the backlash of antifeminism of the postwar years and the "concern about the threat to men's masculinity that competition with women posed." Crawford's containment of her own gifts may have been her sensitivity to the threat it posed to her husband; that in spite of the extent to which "he gloried in her independence"—and so it seemed to Peggy—his own frustrations over his abandoned musical career blunted the pleasure he took in her achievements. Like Peggy, Mike believed his father to be "proud and respectful of her music." On the other hand, Barbara once said her father could be "jealous." Other comments from Mike acknowledge the latent tensions buried deep in the marital partnership: "Charlie was ambivalent about her excellence in a way. His attitude towards her work was a mixture of love and fear."[30]

Even so, it is overstating the case to maintain that Charles deliberately deflected Ruth from composition or told her not to compose. That would have been almost too personal, too invasive for a man of his temperament and un-ethical for a man of his character. Sidney Cowell, one of Charles's sternest critics, said, "I don't think Charlie had the slightest idea of diverting her, ex-cept that she went along, she liked to share his enthusiasms. That would have been wrong." Still, it would have been equally wrong from his point of view for Ruth to place music before her family responsibilities.[31]

Henry Cowell watched the artist he knew as Ruth Crawford recede into the background, growing smaller as husband and children claimed the fore-ground of her life. The woman whose exceptional originality he praised so ful-somely in the 1920s turned into a dependent companion of a marital team, a husband and wife who Cowell said "composed together." Once, he said, no woman composed music like her; twenty years later, she couldn't compose without her husband. As years passed and Cowell's importunings about her own composition had little effect, he became disappointed and ultimately a bit disillusioned with her.[32]

And in turn Charles Seeger struggled not to be disillusioned with Cowell as well, never quite getting over the way he was unacknowledged in Cowell's landmark volume, *New Musical Resources.* Seeger had every right to resent how he "was edited right out" of this book, as he once told Cowell's wife, who naturally disagreed. The degree to which this justly rankled Seeger rankled her. The warrior in Sidney Cowell once retaliated by saying that "if an idea crossed his [Seeger's] mind once, and then 15 years later somebody did some-thing like this, he was sure it had come from him." Who among us is immune to the pride of ownership that often blunts our best intentions about creative altruism? Cowell may have called his former teacher the "greatest explorer in intellectual fields which America has ever produced," but a part of Charles Seeger wanted to own every bit of the territory he had explored in theory, even if he had never homesteaded it through art.[33]

And Ruth Crawford knew this about him. She did not tamper with his proprietary feelings about her work because she believed they lay so close to love. (His attitudes would later lead others to flinch at the way he "felt re-sponsible for Ruth Crawford's creative life.") Perhaps she adopted the hy-phenated form of her name (Crawford-Seeger) at this point in her career to preserve the equilibrium in her marriage and to reaffirm the vows of creative partnership on which it was founded. She never lost her sense of obligation to her former teacher. The social gender codes for American women at this time reinforced her priorities. The "model girl" she had written about when she was thirteen years old occasionally behaved like the 1950s version of a "model wife."[34]

Throughout these years Crawford continued to find pleasure and purpose in traditional music. In October 1949 her agent Alan Collins began ne-gotiations with Doubleday for her second book, *Animal Folk Songs for Chil-dren.* Unexpectedly, they became protracted and unpleasant. Although the Doubleday editor, Peggy Lesser, was "quite keen" to do the book, she proposed some harsh changes in the format, wanting to cut the book by half in order to make room for larger, more abundant illustrations. Hence, she proposed that the author's royalties of 10 percent should now be split between writer and illustrator, with Crawford at 7 percent and the artist Barbara Cooney receiving 3 percent instead of a flat rate. Despite the wide acclaim for *American Folk Songs for Children*, "from her experience with book stores," Lesser believed that "illustrations in a music book were of vast importance in selling it."[35]

Crawford wrote her agent that she was "deflated." Although the "wonderful" pictures were an "integral part of the success of the first book," why should the author rather than the publisher absorb the cost of paying Cooney more? She defended herself by enumerating her contributions: "gathering and choosing the songs from hundreds of possible choices in the Archive [of American Folk Song]; combing the Checklist of 10,000 titles; having and paying for duplicate recordings made at the archive; transcribing, making arrangements, acquiring permissions." Vacillating between pragmatic retreat and defiance, she suggested that Collins demand a firm publication date. "Or perhaps they should contemplate changing publishers?" she asked.[36]

Rejoinders came swiftly. *Animal Folk Songs for Children* would be "even more dependent on illustrations than the first one," Margaret Lesser wrote. "And when pictures assume such importance, writers must absorb the cost." She reproached her for "changing her mind about material so much that the publication costs had almost doubled, changing the final estimate of the book from a get-out of about 14,000 copies to the actual get-out of 27,025." They had not charged Mrs. Seeger full penalty for her changes, but "under no circumstances would we set a publication date without Mrs. Seeger's assurances" that this would not happen again.[37]

Crawford acceded. "So far as I can see, Doubleday holds the cards," she wrote Collins, as her original collection of 96 songs shrunk to 43. However, she salvaged her dignity with another letter to Lesser. "Because, unfortunately or not, I have to believe there is a friendly mutual feeling existent between myself and people I work with," she had to clarify two points. Yes, she would accept Lesser's "exasperated accusations" for delays caused by author's proof revisions, but Lesser had procrastinated for two years before that. Lest Cooney think her greedy or insensitive, she reiterated praise for the illustrator. As for the deadline, she asked Lesser to "give me as much time as you can, and I will be adult enough to consider a final deadline as final." Observing client/agent protocol, Ruth sent this letter to Collins; he may not have dispatched it. Besides, she needed or wanted income too badly to delay this book or to nurse grievances. Just before she signed the contract in mid-January 1950, she asked Collins to press Doubleday for not only the usual advance ("as close to a thousand as can be had") but also to query the obdurate Doubleday editor about reviving two old series ideas, one for "single-song picture-books," with two dummies, including "Mary Wore Her Red Dress" and "Bought Me a Cat," and the other for "song-story sequence" books, with the prototype "Let's Build a Railroad." They had been sent to Lesser in 1945; perhaps now they could get off the ground. Here too a peremptory Lesser rubbed salt in the wound, telling Crawford that one "picture book per author per year was quite enough."[38]

Her disappointment and resentment tinged letters to colleagues for months afterward. She told one friend that her book "got cut in half because it was bigger than Doubleday wanted—and that fish, birds and small things were omitted sadly. Some of my most favorite songs (like the whale, and the flea) are therefore awaiting another book." She met her March deadline, but more disappointment awaited her. Doubleday did not get the book out in time for Children's Book Week in November; nor did they spend much money for promotion. In a plaintive letter to Alan Collins, Ruth found the neglect "a little hard to understand." The real issue was the changing consumer habits of the postwar baby-boomer generation. Just at the time when Crawford put more energy in making the book meet the standards of folk-song scholarship, the book was marketed less as a music anthology and more as a specialty picture book for young children—a growing market in the early 1950s.[39]

In spite of the diminished space for her work, Crawford tenaciously clung to her standards. Echoing the spirit of Benjamin Botkin's work, she explained to a friend, "I was trying to straddle and talk to folklorists and also ordinary human beings (help the humans see how a folklore book is made, help the folklorists to see how a book can be a really true folklore book and yet be made for humans)." That spirit belonged more to the 1940s than it did to the 1950s, with the increasing concern for professional academic validation pervading the field. Nevertheless, she sustained her usual standards of excellence, taking "three times longer than expected" to write the introduction. As usual, her friends had rallied around her. Glenore Horne dispensed "comfort and assistance . . . staying up with me til 3 a.m. one memorable morning," as Crawford described it, while she cut and "lightened up" its language at Doubleday's insistence.[40]

The opening paragraph of another exceptional introduction in *Animal Folk Songs for Children* immediately bonded children, animals and music in the "accumulated affection which generations of singers have felt for child, animal, and song." This elegiac view of folk-singing as life process was reinforced by the illustration at the top of the page. Rather than showing sentimental child faces, a mother, four children, and a cat have their backs to the reader, as they look off the page. The small cat stares intently, undifferentiated in pose from the children, effectively capturing the spirit of Crawford's prose, for the animals have agency in these songs:

> Like a friendly visiting uncle. . . they feel free to observe, tease, comfort, give advice, scold a little, make wishes, jest loud or delicately, tell stories true or nonsensical—and make up monstrously unbelievable lies.

This vernacular wisdom was dispensed along with acute analyses of folk-song performance practice. Ten years after she had written the ill-fated appendix for *Our Singing Country*, she managed to integrate its values into this introduction, urging her readers to listen to field recordings. She praised the music's "epic objectivity, its refusal to act chameleon to word meanings or moods, its rough vitality, its monotony."

Editorial neglect at Doubleday continued to plague the book. Its late publication date of November 22 caused the publishers to withhold Christmas
season promotion. Downcast and "quite aggravated," Crawford told Botkin
she "was quite lonesome for a few nice words dribbling in." Some did in the
New York Times, Saturday Review, and a variety of big and small trade journals.
Could Ben help in getting the book reviewed in the *Washington Post,* as Rae
Korson suggested? "I haven't yet acquired ease and worldly knowledge in the
book process after it's published and done," she told him. But the book mer-
ited her intervention. "We like it. . . . It has some music mistakes due to my
not having a chance to see final proof. But even Charlie is pleased with the
book as a whole." A spot on the *New York Herald Tribune's* lucrative Christmas
list, 100 Gift Books for Young People, of December 3, 1951, and that of the
Child Study Association's Books of the Year supported sales, although these
never matched that of her first collection.[41]

Animal Folk Songs for Children was a highwire act of cultural mediation.
Could Crawford balance her standards of professional folklore against the
thematic focus on animals and a target market of mothers and children without falling on the floor of sentimentality? (One can almost hear those genteel
Victorian voices from her youth saying "how dear" and "how cunning.") An
unusually candid reviewer (W. Edison Richmond writing in *Hoosier Folklore*)
confessed his initial skepticism: "Even my tremendous respect and admiration for its editor, her knowledge, and her ability, boggled somewhat at a collection of folk song based upon so arbitrary a thing as subject matter." But
this editor was a composer, who suspected sweetness in any form and passionately loved the folk in the field who unwittingly thwarted it. Richmond
candidly admitted

> I was wrong. Nowhere else is the spirit of folksingers so completely and effec-
> tively characterized. As a consequence, this book . . . has a double value—chil-
> dren will pore through it eagerly for the delightfulness of the songs which it
> contains and folklorists will prize it for its explicit and lucid descriptions of what
> a folksong is and how a folksinger sings.[42]

But even he missed the musical mission of her work. In contrast to *American Folk Songs for Children,* where most of the melodies came from printed
sources, this book came from "fresh notations" from field recordings which
other reviewers understood. The research value of Crawford's work lay in the
aesthetic quality of the variants she had unearthed in her "field"—the Archive.
Thus she called *Animal Folk Songs for Children* both a "family and children's
song book" and a "sort of folklore source book as well."[43]

Returning to the musical methods of *Our Singing Country,* she mined the
Archive for the nuggets of musical gold to show off the fineness and freshness
of the material and then crafted her arrangements to match their gleam. "This
book does have some gems in it," Crawford told Herbert Halpert, whose wife
Letty supplied her with one of them, a beautiful version of "Little Lap Dog."
"All but five are off recordings or personally notated by me. It really is a folklore book: I have done very little compositing." In painstaking detail she
tracked down her quarry, writing countless letters to settle questions of details.

"I have 'done nutty things,'" Ruth confessed to Alan Lomax. She had listened to a dozen versions of "Ground Hog" (transcribing all of them) before choosing one, settling on Austin Harmon's version that had been collected by Herbert Halpert in 1939. Now she was retranscribing a tune from *Our Singing Country*. She ordered

> six versions of "Boll Weevil" out of the check list, spending $50 on 16-inchers, and after listening to a half dozen other crawdads—coming back to our favorite in *Our Singing Country*, but ordering a recording of it so I could transcribe the exact music of the first stanza I expect to use—so I could feel I am giving people another of the several ways he sings the many stanzas of that one song.

Could Alan also help her locate the original singers so she could get the words right for the song "Old Bell Ewe and The Little Speckled Wether?"[44]

All of this grated on Alan Lomax's professional nerves. He initially refused permission for another variant of "Old Bell Ewe" to be circulated in print because he had copyrighted all transcriptions that Ruth had done for *Our Singing Country*, and her letter would deprive him of income from permissions fees. When Ruth did not give in, insisting on making new transcriptions from field recordings, he attacked her whole way of working as a kind of appropriation of the labor of others who had actually been out in the field. He asked her to consider these factors: What had she added of her own—arrangements? A new and creative presentation? Or was she using the work of others as her own scholarly work which her commercial books supported? Rather theatrically, he posed his letter as an existential challenge that she had to face, the sooner the better.

In the midst of polishing the introduction to *Animal Folk Songs for Children*, Ruth wrote three different responses of retaliatory thrusts and parries, although it is unclear which, if any, were ever sent. Since Alan's letter was prompted by her queries about new transcriptions for songs, she denied any resentments against paying permission fees. She analyzed his motivations as projected guilt. Since he had been accused of "commercialism"—a serious sin for a former radical as well as professional folklorist—now he accused her. Not only that, he had never admitted that knowing her had aided his work, never acknowledged her in print. She defended the integrity of her original work through her accompaniments, lovingly crafted with "affection for the amateurs that used her books."[45]

Lomax's timing could not have been more inappropriate or ironic, considering the "permission agony" Crawford incurred in the making of all of her books—all the months of fretting over sources and details of text. Her policy of working from field recordings had hardened, not softened over time. Had she not delayed Edna Boggs's collection of children's folklore of Santo Domingo for just such a reason? She finished transcribing about 100 songs from field recordings, with help from Charles on the Spanish, a few months later and explained to a disappointed Edna Boggs that the book exemplified her slow careful way of working: "I am sure that all the various jobs I have done, on my own books and others—all of which I have laid away awhile and then come back to—have been better because I didn't do them too much in a hurry. (That is nice rationalizing for procrastination; but it is 50 percent true)."[46]

Ruth and Alan patched up their quarrel by the summer when they met at the Midcentury International Folklore Conference at Indiana University, July 21 to August 4, 1950. The conference was a "landmark event" for American folk music. Organized by Stith Thompson at Indiana University, "a number of world-class scholars . . . as well as nearly fifty of the most prominent American folklorists" were there, as Bruno Nettl, then a young student of George Herzog, has recalled: Albert Lord, Samuel Bayard, Bertrand Bronson, George Herzog, George Pullen Jackson, and Maud Karpeles. Ruth, Charles, and Alan all participated in the afternoon session of the third symposium on "Making Folklore Available." In her remarks Crawford summed up her work within the urban folk revival with some of the most profound and moving statements she ever made about the process of cultural mediation. She spoke about aesthetics and the beauty of field recordings with the empathy of a modernist: "I think we should remember that ugliness is also a very beautiful thing, that is, things that many other people might consider ugly. I like what some people call ugliness of tone quality in some singer." Then she built the bridge between city people and their rural peers, as a minister's daughter reiterated the mission that had shaped her books:

> giving children the real or the authentic or the old or the original, or whatever we want to call it . . . but also giving them the feeling that they can use it. . . . Somehow let them have a taste of the thing itself. . . . Though we have love for the folk, we also have love for the people we are giving it to, and we must make it as usable by them as possible. And it often requires the hearing of twenty versions before you find the one which fits both these ideals.[47]

Yet for all of the idealism, financial pressures also drove her work. Even though its quality never faltered—if anything, she became more oriented toward folklore scholarship rather than less—she grew increasingly sensitive to the needs of the trade-book marketplace because she had found a particular niche within it. Thirty years later Alan Lomax reiterated his charges once again, this time to her son Mike. "The American system makes us all careerists and Ruth became a careerist in a sense about working in the Archive and mining it as far as children's books were concerned. And that changed her a little bit. She became a little bit opportunistic and it lowered her valance for me."[48]

In the early 1950s, after finishing *Animal Folk Songs*, she let the publisher decide which of several projects had the most market potential: a collection based on songs of love, courtship, and marriage that excerpted material from *1001 Folk Songs*, for which Carl Sandburg had agreed to write headnotes (but she would rather have left as was); the remaindered material from *Animal Folk Songs*, possibly titled *Birds, Fish and Small Things*; or a book of folk songs for Christmas.[49]

Collins wrote Crawford the diappointing news that Lesser "wasn't very keen about either a second big book or a book consisting of the rest of the animal folk songs." The Christmas idea "sounded best," but Lesser stalled on an official decision for several months. Finally, on August 25, 1951, Doubleday contracted with Ruth for a new collection of arrangements, with the understanding that publication be scheduled for 1953. Ruth's new deadline was September 15, 1952.[50]

This book became *American Folk Songs for Christmas*. Ruth had some material at hand because she had organized Christmas music programs while working at the Whitehall Country School in Bethesda, Maryland, from 1945 to 1947. By 1948 she began assembling a collection of that material with a prospective book in mind. Following the school tradition of telling the Christmas story through verse and song, the book balanced music for "holiday" and "holy day" in three parts: a "prelude of stars, shepherds, and sheep," a central section on "Mary and the baby," and a postlude of "praise, worship and festivity." That strategy admitted many songs that would not ordinarily be considered seasonal. Pete, working on a small Christmas book of his own at the time, admired how she "reached out to material that wasn't literally about Christmas"; she remembered the African American lullaby "Oh, Watch the Stars, See How They Run" because "she'd heard Carl Sandburg do it thirty years before" in the *American Songbag*. The book exemplified the excellence, the "creative job" which "could be done in this whole field of acculturation," Pete believed.[51]

Again, Crawford shaped a rather complex context of cultural mediation for this deceptively simple book. No doubt, with Barbara Cooney's illustrations larger than ever, the book looked like a children's book and was marketed as such. However, it succeeded in bringing the best possible folklore scholarship to the attention of the American public. Reviewed in the trade press, newspapers, children's education magazines, and folklore journals, it was deemed a "family book," a "teacher's book," and a "folklorist's book."

In comparison to the premise of her two previous books, the editorial tone shifted from parent advisor to folklore advocate. No longer intended for mothers of preschool children, the introductory essay reviewed folklore of the past and living folkways of the present. Her prose style evoked the scholarly warmth of Constance Rourke and Benjamin Botkin. Echoing themes writ large in Benjamin Botkin's work, she conflated the "everyday people" of rural America with the people of the cities by writing that she was "giving back to the people songs that belong to them." Her 1930s revival posture of declaring cultural autonomy resurfaced in her observation that "in this country our modern Christmas has been celebrated to a large extent with songs gathered from other countries" and that we have not been aware of our own traditions: "They have been hidden away, hard to find, or crowded out by the more easily available published collections around us." To Herbert Halpert she wrote that she deliberately excluded commercial songs about Santa. "Someone wanted her to include 'Santa Claus Is Coming to Town,' which children are always asking for and which is not in any Christmas songbooks, but that someone is not a folklorist."[52]

Crawford managed to pull off the feat of producing a Christmas book for children without mentioning Santa Claus. As one reviewer wrote, the songs "are rooted deep in our past, in a time before America knew the Christmas tree and the Santa Claus on every corner." In offering alternatives to cherished European carols and to commercial Christmas music, she used tradition as an implicit critique of mass culture and simultaneously offered up a musical rainbow. Not only were her Christmas songs more "American" than "Anglo," they were also more black than white.[53]

Black church singing, including spirituals and gospel tunes, outnumbered the white shape-note tunes by half, giving the book a special richness and depth of tone. Crawford knew this repertory very well and had in fact written a review of John N. Work's *American Negro Songs for Mixed Voices.* She had come to treasure African American music as a mainstay of the national canon of oral tradition. Considering the large number of African American tunes contained in *American Folk Songs for Christmas,* Crawford requested that the illustrator Barbara Cooney draw some "brown faces" among the white children. The publishers refused. The Supreme Court decision against school segregation lay two years away.[54]

Professional scholarly values, emerging from her purist approach to applied folklore, continued to inform her work. Of 55 songs and one fiddle tune, 13 came from recordings in the archive, the others from often obscure anthologies from the early 1900s. As usual, she was "very conscientious, trying to credit everybody that should be credited," Pete remembers. Working on a little paperback of Christmas songs around this time, Pete once suggested that she slough off her scruples about using a John Jacob Niles tune. "She was shocked at my cavalier attitude towards copyright." Three permission requests searched out the collectors of "Oh That Lamb, Sing a Lam" from an obscure pamphlet on *Ole Time Religion* (copyright El Karubah Temple in Shreveport, Louisiana). She delighted in its "exact likeness" to the rhythm of the work song "Black Betty" from the Lomax book *American Folksongs and Ballads.* Such details confirmed her authority over a vast repertory.[55]

The nature of the musical arrangements changed for this book, partly because many tunes came from choral rather than solo song. One of her first loves—shape-note hymnody, which she had discovered in the early 1930s—led her to include several tunes from William Walker's *Southern Harmony.* Here the piano condensations highlighted the open fourths and fifths which had originally attracted her so many years earlier, while more counterpoint and more modal harmonies shaped other piano accompaniments as well. Shifting the musical audience away from very small children to the upper elementary grades, she allowed herself more composerly choices. She even included a fiddle tune adaptation as "prelude and interlude" for her version of "The Cherry Tree Carol." The complexity of this arrangement, with its shifting meters and alternate melodic variants, echoes the old days of transcribing for *Our Singing Country.*

The search among sources of "older oral tradition" led her to exceptional material, a few songs later emerging among folk revival singers in the 1950s, among them "Bright Morning Star" and "Virgin Mary." One of the few traditional carols to make its way into the book, the "Twelve Days of Christmas," counted "Twelve studs a-squealin, eleven bulls a-bellerin, ten hares a-runnin." That gem came from Jean Ritchie, just starting her career as a dulcimer player and singer. Crawford's unceasing quest for new variants to those already in print enriched a tune's history, as "Go to Sleepy" appeared for the third time in her books in a third version. As she wrote Jean, "I feel so strongly about not crystallizing any one version."[56]

Reviews were excellent, covering the usual wide spectrum from the *New Yorker* and the *New York Times*, which named it one of the ten best books for juveniles in 1953, to scholarly journals like *Western Folklore*. A "brilliant essay on Christmas life," said that reviewer, while D. K. Wilgus, in the *Journal of American Folklore*, praised the "taste and care which governed the selection and the editing of the material [which] scarcely could have been bettered." Ruth's friend Ben Botkin noted how "there is more folklore in this book than in either of its predecessors." He believed it to be her "best book" because she "lavished on it all the love (of music, people, and children) and all the labor of love of which she was capable." Privately, he wrote her that "there is so much of you in the book and so much of Christmas—the lore as well as the song—that it is hard to tell where one (you) begins and the other (Christmas) leaves off."[57]

In a way this book, like the others, was a family book. She filled the Christmas book with hymns even though she was "rabidly anti-religious," because that was tradition and tradition meant family. Christmas brought out her playful side, allowed her to relax her usual worries about money and buy all sorts of presents for the children. She made rituals about dressing up the tree, then dramatically paraded the children through a darkened house to the spectacle of lights and gifts. "They made a great deal of Christmas," Ruth's friend Sylvia Parmalee noted. "Penny's birthday was right around then, so they would celebrate her birthday and they had a Christmas tree in the living room that they never would take down until about May."[58]

"keep the song going"

folk-song arrangements

Throughout the 1940s Ruth Crawford Seeger channeled much of her compositional gift into her anthologies, publishing about 200 arrangements of folk tunes for solo voice and piano. Despite the disclaimers in her books that folk songs do not need any instrumental support, she took pride in her craftsmanship. She had a definite sense of their value, as her family and colleagues knew. Her daughter Peggy would later state that "her accompaniments of folk music, to me anyway, mean more to me than her work as a composer."[1]

But of course a composer did them both. At her best Crawford produced miniatures of exceptional quality, gaining inspiration from the same sensibility that loved order and line and experiment in the 1930s. Because this body of work is published in anthologies designated as song books, its potential as piano literature for beginners has been overlooked. Perhaps because her own attraction to dissonance was incorporated into her arrangements of traditional music, she reimagined essential aspects of vernacular practice in her own compositional terms to produce a body of work unmatched by any other American composer of the period.

From a technical point of view, Crawford wrote "settings" as opposed to "accompaniments," the former distinguished by the original melody functioning as the solo line in the right hand of the keyboard. Other print sources supplied most of the melodies in her first book, *American Folk Songs for Children*. After that, she adopted the policy of transcribing tunes from field recordings, taking more control in order to present the material in "its most vigorous form." Sounding very much like Charles Ives in her ability to invest the vernacular with modernist idealism, she opposed turning a tune into "something

Example 21-1 "Little Bird," from *American Folk Songs for Children,* © 1948. Used by permission of Doubleday & Co.

that has had all the corners rounded off so that it is very smooth" in search of false beauty. In comes "Little Bird, Little Bird" through a window of alternating duple and triple meters (Ex. 21-1); in the refrain of "Jim Crack Corn," syncopation over the bar line makes the accented down-beat on "don't" sound fresh and impudent.[2]

The musical values of her unpublished monograph for *Our Singing Country* stayed with her throughout her life. "Keeping going, the insistent moving on, the maintaining of pulse and pace and mood unbroken through the singing of a song" acted as emblematic values, representing an essential difference between two types of music-making:

> Professional music isn't like that; it always tells you where it is going to end. Vigor is an overused word, but it certainly is there. . . . In making accompaniments for this book, this "keep-goingness" or "never-endingness" has been a thing cherished.

In *Animal Folk Songs for Children,* "Keep-goingness" (coined like a German noun) symbolized an existential stance which was amplified through documentary bonding music and daily life:

> Songs are sung as though they might continue off into space. This singing and playing is a close accompaniment to living: to working, to playing games, to dancing all night, to doing nothing, to doing anything a long time, to jogging down a night road behind the unhurried clop-clop of the old mare's hoofs, or riding along in a car or truck with miles rolling away underneath.[3]

She aimed at left-hand musical material that could "give the feeling of the idiom and not just the feeling of the beauty of the song itself." By comparing her work with that of two other composers, we see her point. In "Drunken Sailor" or "Rose, Rose, Up She Rises" (Ex. 21-2), Cecil Sharp's pianistic conception of four-part harmony and art song phrasing sounds prim. Elie Siegmeister's closed-position triads suffocate the line. Crawford neatly conceives the left hand intervallically in two-part counterpoint rather than four-part harmony: open fourths control key moments at the ends of all three phrases; the leap to the climactic open fifth on "she rises" flouts the rules of classical

Example 21-2   Three arrangements of the chorus from "Drunken Sailor": (a)
"Drunken Sailor," chorus refrain, transcribed by Cecil J. Sharp, *English Folk-Chanteys*.
(b) "What Shall We Do with the Drunken Sailor?" chorus arranged by Elie
Siegmeister, *Work and Sing*. (c) "Rose, Rose, Up She Rises," arranged by Ruth
Crawford Seeger, *American Folk Songs for Children*.

Example 21-3   "A Squirrel Is a Pretty Thing," from *Animal Folk Songs for Children*,
© 1992. Used by permission of The Shoestring Press.

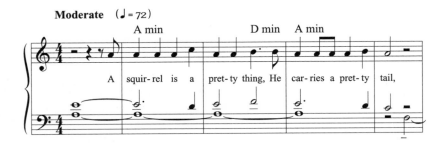

counterpoint and support the meaning of the words in a small but telling detail. "I have found that almost all children have immediate and strong affection for 'The Drunken Sailor,'" Ruth told Joanna Colcord, a compiler of sea-
songs and chanteys. They "play it with great gusto at piano lessons, with left
hand 'chording' in shockingly un-chantey-like manner but with what I am
sure is chantey-like vigor."[4]

She found other ways to emulate tradition in her arrangements. One key
strategy contested norms of musical closure. In *Animal Folk Songs for Children*,
Crawford wrote how "the last measure of a song has often been left up in the
air, with no final home chord (tonic) tempting the player to ritard or to stop
and pay homage to the double bar." She wanted to "pull the player past the
double bar and on back to the beginning without loss of the song's speed or
pulse." Sometimes she ended on the dominant, implying a continuous succession of verses rather than a suspension of the music in time. (Exaggerating the
universality of this principle, Crawford chose to ignore the occasional exception to the rule, for in the field recording of "Old Bell'd Yoe," the fiddle player
in fact finished off his last variation with two double stops to underscore an
end.) Her setting of "A Squirrel Is a Pretty Thing" (Ex. 21-3) enhances a
somewhat limited tune by making a virtue of the bare bones of the melody
and keeping it open-ended through the lack of final chord and the single resonating pitch. Frequently her arrangements flouted classical symmetry and
perodicity. "Much of the 'reality' of vernacular music lies in its departure from

four-square metrical structure," she and Charles wrote in their musical preface for *Folk Song U.S.A.* Singers often introduced a triple measure into a duple structure, or shortened a four-beat measure by one or two counts, a matter discussed at length in her unpublished treatise to *Our Singing Country*. In very simple tunes with undistinguished lyrics, she reflects this by adding the extra bar between the end of the line and the end of the tune. In "Yonder She Comes," eight bars plus one are followed by six bars plus one.

Another source of arrangement technique came from the instruments that legitimately accompanied singing among rural people — banjo, fiddle, and guitar. Piano figures come directly from figures and patterns associated with these instruments. As Ruth herself stated, and as her friend Sidney Cowell underscored, she wanted to "make the piano sound as nearly like the country instruments as possible that would have been used with those songs." Many "banjo-songs" or "fiddle-songs," among them "Old Joe Clarke," "Lynchburg Town," "The Old Hen Cackled and the Rooster Laid an Egg," and "Hop Up, My Ladies," found their way into her anthologies of folk songs. Described by the pioneering folk-song scholar Robert Gordon as "American products, not importations," they "filled a different need," Gordon wrote, and "had a different technique":

> Music is all important, words are secondary. The stanzas used are quite unlike those of the ballad. They are brief and incisive; they lack dignity of musical appeal; most of them are decidedly humorous in tone. And each is complete in itself. . . . But in many cases it is the instrument alone and not the voice that furnishes the musical background, the neutral repetition from which at intervals the stanzas leap out with startling vividness.[5]

Capturing this "startling vividness" became Crawford's ideal, as fiddle and banjo breakdowns inflected her musical syntax increasingly throughout the 1940s. Her work for *Folk Song U.S.A.* marks the stage of imitation, where original sources are disclosed in its musical preface: how the blues piano accompaniment for "Po' Laz'us" emulates African American improvisation; how the left hand in "Sourwood Mountain" evoked the "continuous wall of sound" made by the Appalachian dulcimer. (And for "a more traditional sound, the player could stick to one chord, as did so many rural performers and ignoring all harmonic implications of the tune, layer on a single triad throughout, playing light and fast.") Transcribed banjo patterns from Uncle Dave Macon provided "Rock About My Saro Jane" with a coda. One hears the echoes of other famous commercial artists in some other settings as well: the Carter Family in Ruth's setting of "John Hardy" with its unusual separate bass line and the strumming in the right hand intended to imitate Maybelle Carter's guitar; and perhaps Dock Boggs's banjo in the setting of "Pretty Polly."

Since the arrangements were shared by both Ruth and Charles, exactly who did which arrangement remains somewhat obscure. However, both Mike and Peggy have described Ruth's arrangements as "sparse and punchy" and Charles's as more elaborate. A sketch of "Skip to My Lou" survives in his hand, and he later claimed "Red River Valley," with its elaborate nineteenth-

Example 21-4   "The Juniper Tree," from *American Folk Songs for Children*, © 1948.
Used by permission of Doubleday & Co.

century chords, as characteristic of his style. "Sometimes I Feel like a Moth-erless Child" and "Another Man Done Gone" typify Ruth's spare approach.[6]

A more complex compositional process manifests itself in other musical habits, including approaches to harmony and tonality, and a preference for lin-ear texture rather than harmonic chording. Rarely did she employ four-part har-mony, avoiding "sweet thirds" as much as possible, voicing pitches to emphasize and expose open fourths and fifths, major seconds and sevenths. In "The Ju-niper Tree" (Ex. 21-4), exposed fourths, emphasized even further through oc-tave displacements, vie with exposed seconds to pressure the conventional tonic-dominant harmony of the tune to the sidelines. "We sat UNDer" on a tri-tone followed by a half-cadence on "Juniper TREE" with its fourth starts the rout; the unusual melodic skips in the tune when poised against a ninth and yet another fourth compensate for conventional classical phrase symmetry.

What she described as her "conversation with the song tune" produced superb and increasingly idiosyncratic arrangements in *Animal Folk Songs for Children*. Its introduction (written in 1948–49) explains how keyboard accompaniments had "bass lines shaped by banjo or guitar and should be played with a staccato or semi-staccato tone . . . 'picked' but not dainty": a tone she described as "popcorn" touch and illustrated on family-made tapes. She acknowledged how "melodic reminders of banjo or guitar figures" have been integrated into the lines and should be heard as counterpoint: "Cross-eyed Gopher" has banjo figures for an interlude; "Old Bell'd Yoe" has fiddle figures for piano playing; "Wolves A-Howling" has "interwoven song tune and fiddle tune."

This latter choice fiddle song, sung by John Hatcher from field collecting by Herbert Halpert, worked itself into an unusual transcription for which Seeger wrote a rare three-stave score. A separate vocal line accommodates her transcription of the fiddle tune, supplying a descant to the vocal line. Capturing the vagaries of fiddle song, the meter switches from duple to triple for one measure to accommodate the "wolves" that howl for an extra beat in the second measure. The stanza is equally challenging with its three-bar phrases and instrumental rhythms in the vocal line. And it is fast (quarter note = 116), the tempo taken directly from the field recordings, as was her practice (Ex. 21-5).

Even when not explicitly acknowledged, instrumental accompaniments on field recordings played an implicit role in Seeger's settings. For example, the pointed syncopations in "Muskrat" and "Old Ground Hog" most likely originated in the banjo playing of Austin Harmon, whose field recording is cited as a source. By steeping herself in the style, she gave such settings an indelible vitality. Field recordings could inspire and confound. From the point of view of a field worker, Sidney noted occasional lapses of judgment in which Ruth supplied accompaniments to "some things that would never have been sung with any instrument. . . . Because again that was a matter of knowing the community. You couldn't sit in Washington and know which songs were unaccompanied and which weren't." But as a mediator rather than a field worker, Ruth let that point go. Even when the original field recording did not provide a model, the accompaniment did not violate tradition; it imparted some of its spirit, and at its best made the setting a miniature with its own identity.[7]

The challenge of capturing the sense of improvisation and spontaneity, so important to the integrity of tradition, loomed large. By filling her settings with a variety of figures and frequent small, surprising details that refute consistency on many levels, Crawford reinforced the value of variant vitality in understated ways. One case in point is her setting of "Little Brown Dog" sung by Mrs. Birmah Hill Crissom from Saltille, Mississippi, collected by Halpert on a field trip in 1939. She wrote Halpert how much she appreciated the song. "Charlie too is fond of it. I hope you will like the accompaniment it drew from me."[8]

Since the field recording is without accompaniment, she worked out the implied harmonies (Ex. 21-6). The dissonant leap of the seventh in the me-

Example 21-5   "Wolves A-Howling," refrain, from *Animal Folk Songs for Children,* ©
1992. Used by permission of The Shoestring Press.

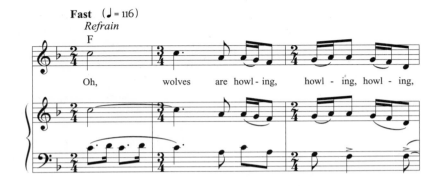

lody is perfectly echoed in the harmony one beat later, adding bite to the accompaniment, which at that point produces a mini-tone cluster with the
voice. Most important, the frisky syncopated figure in the left hand is alive,
and when it shifts to a more regular pattern at the text "ride," momentum
starts up, shifts again a measure later, and returns to the original syncopated
figure for a deft turn-around bar in B minor, for a song notated in D major.

Example 21-6   "Little Brown Dog," *Animal Folk Songs for Children*, © 1992. Used by permission of The Shoestring Press.

Her settings of lullabies, traditionally sung as melodies, further exemplify the general direction of her stylistic development. "Hush 'n' Bye" (also titled "All the Pretty Little Ponies"), appears first in *American Folk Songs for Children* in a somewhat elaborate "fine-art" setting, written in 4/4, with a melody engaged by a countermelody in the tenor range of the three-part polyphony. Another variant, "All the Pretty Little Horses," appears in *Folk Song U.S.A.*, this time in 2/4, with a carefully crafted single counterline in the left hand in steady eighth notes that lull in the background. "Go to Sleep," a related lullaby in *Animal Folk Songs for Children*, moves more leisurely at 2/2 (Ex. 21-7).

"Go to Sleep" is a triumph of simplicity. A single-line descant establishes octaves, fourths, fifths, and dissonant sevenths and seconds as the norm, with

Example 21-6 (continued)

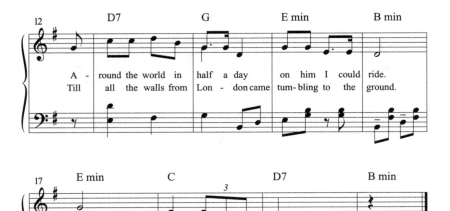

the careful withholding of the third except for the very first sound and the last sung syllable. If the background is dissonant and spare, then the third has a natural lightness that suddenly appears fresh. The line rocks and moves regularly for two measures, then is unpredictable for a third measure. As the voice shifts down in range for the second part of the tune, the piano returns to the beginning, confounding the vocal repetition but remaining true to the function of the song. With the deceptive ease of the master, Crawford makes a sequence of parallel octaves, a fourth, and a major ninth sound just right, as if the old aesthetic of dissonant counterpoint guided choices to create a context in which consonance sounds fresh. Particularly artful is the evocation of nontonal practice by careful control of linear motion and vertical intervals.

Accompaniments such as these illustrate Crawford's achievement, as the settings transcend their frame of a children's book format to serve as a unique kind of pedagogical literature, perhaps closer to Bartók's work than might first appear. Throughout these years the Hungarian composer's achievement at synthesizing tradition and modernism continued to command her profound admiration. He captured the "essence of the music," she told her friend and piano student, Sylvia Parmalee, who even remembers how her teacher shed tears over Bartók's fate, his poverty, his lack of public recognition, and his untimely death. Watching the folk music book boom going on around her in the 1940s, she believed some important musical canons of stylistic ethics were being violated in casually assembled popular anthologies. When others treated

Example 21-7   "Go to Sleep," from *Animal Folk Songs for Children*, 1992. Used by permission of The Shoestring Press.

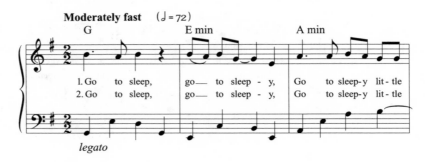

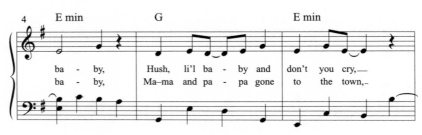

folk music as commercialized nostalgia, it aroused her anger and contempt. She targeted *The Fireside Book of Folksongs* for special censure. "What she said about those accompaniments isn't fit to be printed," Sylvia Parmalee said. "She said [they] weren't any good . . . she said there was just no life to them, she was quite scornful of them." Her own close identification with the material produced settings with integrity, where the limits of simplicity that had so troubled her as a composer of concert music empowered a unique mediation of tradition and modernism for a new urban audience.[9]

" w a d i n g   i n   g r a c e "

So farre as you walk in the waters,
so far are you healed

—John Cotton, "Wading in Grace,"
The Way of Life, 1641

At the height of her career in the early 1950s, Crawford witnessed her experimental idea of using American traditional songs in music education
become accepted as a part of the "American heritage" that shaped postwar
culture. If, as Michael Kammen has written, that phrase became a "virtual
cliché" in the years following World War II in a period when "traditionalism
kept pace with modernism at least in the realm of national taste," then the
range of requests to use material from her books gives ample evidence of the
breadth of the consensus toward a musical past. She answered letters granting
permission to reproduce folk songs from such groups and individuals as the
Lutheran Church Missouri Synod, the Board of Christian Education and Publication, the public-school music textbook company Silver Burdett, the publishers of the fourteen-volume series called *Childcraft*, an educational motion-
picture production company making a film for Los Angeles County public
schools, a teacher planning to make a record for preschool hard-of-hearing
children, and the Bank Street School music specialist Beatrice Landeck. "Old
Molly Hare" and the "Boll Weevil" had found their homes.[1]

More projects, taking advantage of the postwar baby boom in early childhood education and the proliferation of "young people's" record companies,
surface among her papers from the early 1950s. To the composer Vincent Persichetti, then a music editor for Elkan-Vogal Company, she relayed intentions
to compose folk-song arrangements for elementary piano. Letters to Alan
Collins discuss a joint venture with Burl Ives, to be called the "Burl Ives–Ruth
Seeger Piano Songbook" (this project faltered and then was abandoned by her
after Ives cooperated with the House Un-American Activities Committee).

He had recorded some tunes from *Animal Folk Songs for Children*, and apparently they worked together (their pictures were taken together in a radio studio). Locally, she did book signings and appeared at PTA panels on "child development and the arts." She accepted an offer to appear on the television show "Mothers, Inc.," whose producers invited her to sing folk songs on the air and then balked at her counterproposal to bring "real children" into the studio. She said, "Well, I'll not do it unless I have children," agreeing to "vouch for their behavior." Peggy watched the program, remembering that the children were "marvelous, and she was marvelous. The children couldn't have cared less where they were."[2]

The live demonstration with "real children" became her tour de force between 1950 and 1952, accounts of her work in front of mammoth audiences of musicians and teachers confirming a master teacher at the height of her powers. As always, she received hosts of letters from enthusiastic teachers afterward. "You are even better than your reputation says," wrote Marguerite Hood, the president of the Music Educators' National Conference. "I saw a big group of teachers taking notes, then enjoying themselves so much that they forgot that task." Ruth's old friend and power at Columbia Teachers College, Lilla Belle Pitts, praised her lavishly: "You are as perfect a teacher as I fully expected you to be. I fairly hugged myself with pride and satisfaction while watching you work with those two groups of youngsters. The four-year-olds did just what that age would do, when unmolested. And the five-year-olds were so exactly their five-year-old selves that it was funny." She enclosed another letter from one of her students who witnessed the demonstration as well. "Wasn't Mrs. Seeger a dear? [Her] shyness and utter modesty [were] very touching."[3]

At one of several MENC demonstrations, this one in Philadelphia in 1952, arranged by Vanett Lawler, Crawford worked with several children in a "classroom" that was the basketball court of the school gymnasium, set up for spectators on three sides—about 1,200 music educators from across the country. Charles was there, watching an audience watch Ruth; they were "absolutely fascinated" because "they had never seen that kind of teaching before. . . . On the way out, I heard two music teachers talking. One said, 'Well if they want us to do that sort of thing, children won't take anything else.'" Her technique was "extraordinary."[4]

Ruth's teaching looked as effortless as a gymnast's routine, technically varied, seamlessly moving from one experience to another. Sidney Cowell described its spontaneity:

> She gave as few verbal directions as possible, letting the music itself chart the movement, as she improvised marching, skipping, jumping patterns on the piano. "Put on wings," she said and every arm would go up and wings would wave . . . big circles with their arms for fast and slow, strong and weak beats, dictated by sound. "Bring your wings down and sit near me." . . . And before they had all settled, she started to sing a traditional tune with the kind of text that the children could vary themselves. Once they had learned the refrain, she let the children vary the verses, until a perfectly strange song had been taught in

such a way that the children were conducting it themselves, she pointing to one child, then another to take a turn. Then through clapping or tapping or variations on the theme of "patting Juba" she built up several patterns at once, forming a small percussion orchestra. And from that she would go perfectly smoothly into another song. There were climaxes, there were quiet moments, as if she had choreographed the whole thing, all achieved through powerful concentration on the music. It was so successful for the children . . . you could see them almost visibly enlarging their sense of life from one end of the period to another. It was a marvelous thing that she did.[5]

Details of the process appeared in Crawford's article, "Keep the Song Going," in the *National Educators' Association Journal.* Concentrating on "text improvisation," she recycled ideas from *American Folk Songs for Children* in this classroom anecdote:

We had been singing a song and improvising stanzas about Libby and color and things to wear. We kept the song going from one newly made stanza to another, with no pausing between stanzas except for some suggestions from Libby. . . . When at last the song stopped, she said, "Now I'm all clothed with a song." Maybe Libby expressed the satisfaction children feel as they take hold of a song, sing anywhere from one to a dozen of its traditional stanzas, and then make up a dozen more of their own.

However, she sounded a note of caution that had not appeared in her earlier work:

We must remember that both the old and the new are essential to a folk song's staying alive—that although the song grows and spreads partly through its ability to gather fresh experiences from whatever is happening around it, it will lose its identity if these new elements crowd out or obliterate the old.

Crawford's concern for "loss of identity" came from ambivalence about the state of the urban folk revival in the early 1950s, which had reached an unprecedented national audience through the success of a member of her own family, Pete Seeger, as part of the now legendary group, the Weavers. Norm Cohen describes the consequences of their successful cover of Leadbelly's song "Goodnight, Irene" in December 1950 as "ushering in an era of two decades of folk music on the pop music charts." She and Charles watched it all with a mixture of loyalty, pride, and some reservation. Since most folk-revival singers did not concern themselves with the musical recreation of traditional singing style, musical values she had lived by for fifteen years were endangered by "commercialism" that inevitably followed in the wake of popular success.[6]

New models for the varieties of folk-music consciousness that mark the history of the revival in the second half of this century were still evolving. As much as Crawford altered texts with children in her classrooms, she still maintained traditional musical values in her books. The occasional conflicts over style and authenticity within her family and the disparate views between two generations of Seeger musicians mirror the change between New Deal documentary values and the postwar development of the folk-pop genre. She expressed disapproval if her children Mike and Peggy, who were becoming professional musicians during these years as well, compromised her standards at all. Peggy said that "[the one which] I chose I now admit was the less handsome tune and the much inferior text, but the one that was more easily accompanied on the banjo, my mother was very distressed, unusually so. I had changed one or two of the lines and she knew how it went because she had put the accompaniment to it in *Folk Song U.S.A.*, and she was quite upset." When Ruth took Mike to buy a guitar, he watched her "explode when the salesman said, 'Oh, wouldn't you like this nice steel string Martin guitar, it's just like the one Burl Ives has.' And that was just what he shouldn't have said. . . . Dio told him, 'We don't want one of those commercial guitars.' I had never quite seen her like that."[7]

Like Mike and Peggy, Pete felt some censure from the older generation. As he changed in response to his newer audience, his musical orientation shifted away from the emulation of rural singers toward a more personal style. Parental displeasure over stage mannerisms were typical because "Father and Ruth frowned on what they called 'platform graces.' I remember once I ended a song on a high note, and they both frowned and said, 'Shame on you.'" Even so, "because it was Pete, Dio and Charlie were less censorious than they might have been," Mike once remarked; and in fact, Charles went on public record praising the musical quality of his son's work within the folk-pop genre at the same time that he argued for its intellectual relevance to ethnomusicology.[8]

Ruth's musical bonds with Pete were sustained throughout the 1940s by their mutual involvement in music education, each so charismatic in different ways for young children that they recognized this gift in the other. Pete remembers how "it was Ruth who said to me, 'Pete, I think something you're especially good at which not everybody is good at, is getting a lot of people to sing with you. And you ought not to forget this.'" He had been there at a crucial moment in 1942, when he and Alan Lomax sang folk songs for the MENC convention. He watched Ruth struggle with transcriptions for the Lomax books; he knew how instrumental traditions—particularly his own instrument, the five-string banjo—informed her piano arrangements. When in 1946 he founded People's Songs, Inc., as a venue for writing new songs and disseminating old ones, he included children's songs in the mix. After *American Folk Songs for Children* was published, Pete suggested that the *People's Songs Bulletin* (which went out to about 2,000 subscribers) feature a different children's song in each issue. "I said I'd do a little border of dancing figures and said each month we could put a different children's song in that special border." Even when working for Henry Wallace's presidential campaign in 1948, Pete reached out to children through his stepmother's work. And she took his musical advice very seriously. A letter from Ruth to a Doubleday editor in 1948 sent off a song for *American Folk Songs for Children* that "Pete Seeger urged us to include, after singing with numerous groups of children on this three-month tour from Hollywood to here. Said it was asked for again and again."[9]

Ruth trusted his musical judgment and tried to generate projects for her own books that involved Pete as well. In 1948 she suggested to Decca Records a project involving Pete and a recording of American folk songs for children. The Weavers' success seemed like a golden opportunity for her own work. In 1951 she told her agent Alan Collins that "Pete Seeger and the Weavers (now with Decca and quite successful) may record the book, 'Let's Build a Railroad,'" a project floating around since 1941. At the national MENC Philadelphia conference, where Ruth presented a live demonstration to 1,200 educators, she approached Moe Asch, the head of Folkways Records, about the possibility of Pete's recording an album based on *American Folk Songs for Children.* Asch had just released an album called *Songs to Grow On,* which was coordinated with Beatrice Landeck's book of the same title—a collection that relied heavily on Ruth's model as well as several of her songs. Although it seemed like a fairly natural next step for Ruth to suggest an album with Pete, she preferred that Moe Asch approach him with the idea. It seemed a fairly straightforward project, particularly because Pete had already recorded some songs from her books. Asch told Crawford that he would try to collate the cuts and issue them as a unit.[10]

Unfortunately, she was not consulted much about the project and was not awarded any royalties. Much to her dismay, the record appeared in 1953 with extensive citations from her book, pairing songs with suggestions for activities, even though Asch had not asked Crawford for permission to quote directly from the text. Ruth, who was so meticulous, indeed obsessive about such matters, wrote a rare angry letter to Pete, asking him to take the record off the market.

Moe Asch's interceding letter was intended to hurt. He told her that her book was nowhere to be seen at any of the seven conventions on music education that he had attended that year; Pete had just received a fine review in the *New York Herald Tribune* and the album was now on the recommended list for the Association for Childhood Education. If she wished, he would excise all direct quotes from the book and all suggested activites:

> The only sorrowful thing about this is that Pete thought he was giving you joy and instead of writing to me you made him feel that I utilized him to do you harm. As is often the case, the best of good will often turns sour.[11]

Perhaps this moment also exposed some resentment of the older pioneering revivalists at the success of the younger generation. Ruth complained to Sidney Cowell that she had been entitled to make the arrangements with the record company because she held the rights to the title and concept of the collection. "She had been planning to do it, and now it was done." Rarely did Ruth admit quite so baldly that her work in folklore had such a strong financial motive. Rarely did she allow herself to get so publicly angry. "I was surprised to hear her talk so about income," Sidney said. Few people knew just how entrepreneurial Crawford could be, how tenaciously she tried to recycle projects, some ten years old. Ruth's anger was "uncharacteristic," said Sidney.[12]

With all of that, 1953 began well. The different parts of her career seemed to be integrated more fully than ever before. Her old arrangement of "Rissolty,

Rossolty" was performed by the National Symphony Orchestra, with Hans Kindler conducting, on January 8 at Constitution Hall. Sponsored by radio station WGMS, the concert was taped, and the announcer, who condescended a bit to the folk songs (texts printed in the program), noted that the composer was in the audience. However, the performance was "sloppy," and one of Ruth's friends thought she was "not pleased, though she didn't say so." That month the International Music Council and UNESCO invited her to participate in the International Conference on the Role and the Place of Music in the education of young people and adults, scheduled for Brussels that summer. As suited her habits, she was "buried in work" on the Christmas book, she told Felix Greissle. Sounding contented and on course, she enumerated her "full teaching schedule, plus composition activities, plus a very satisfactory family all home this year."[13]

And other projects loomed on the horizon. On February 4, 1953, Crawford queried her agent about yet another reincarnation of old work, excerpting a large section of *1001 American Folk Songs* into "Love Songs of the American People: Folksongs of Love, Courtship and Marriage." Greissle also had suggested that she make her song arrangements available to other teachers in a piano teaching format. He told her that "I am very happy to hear that you are now composing again and I hope that the period of silence is now over definitely."[14]

But within the month the specter of a more ominous silence haunted her. All that previous year she had been feeling not quite herself and in fact had undergone a series of medical tests. Although the doctors found nothing wrong initially—as Charles would bitterly recall—in early February Ruth was diagnosed with intestinal cancer. "She was the picture of health when the diagnosis was made, bright eyes and pink cheeks and a confident carriage." In an era when taboos against discussing the disease were fierce, Ruth candidly spoke of it. "She told me that she had cancer. . . . She just said it as a matter of course," an acquaintance recalled.[15]

That devastating blow was followed by another threat to her family's security. The cold war persecution of leftists had escalated in the early 1950s, and for various reasons the Seeger family was particularly vulnerable. To some extent, Charles's sense of political vulnerability and caution had strained his relationship with Pete in the mid-1940s, when, employed by the Pan American Union, he did not want to be too closely associated with his son's radical politics. They identified themselves as progressive liberals rather than Marxist radicals, watching the persecution of the Old Left start in earnest in Washington as early as 1946. Now the black-listing of the Weavers at the height of their success in 1951 accelerated the FBI's investigation of Charles himself.

This possibility had been trailing him for many years; FBI surveillance had started in the 1940s. Charles's relationships with other suspected Communist "sympathizers" and New Deal progressives, who were subsequently charged and found guilty of Communist associations, also propelled his dossier forward. Several documents in his file linked his name with that of the composer Hanns Eisler, who had been deported from the country in 1947 after testimony before the House Committee on Un-American Activities. A favorable review of Ruth's book *American Folk Songs for Children* that appeared in the Communist newspaper the *Daily Worker* was also duly noted. Other "facts" implied a relationship with people named by others associated with the spy trial of Nathan Silvermaster. Portents of trouble had already surfaced in 1951 when Charles lost his diplomatic passport privileges. Then, in 1952, his passport was downgraded to permit travel abroad for official reasons only.[16]

In 1953 the pace of investigation quickened. On February 9 Charles appeared before the Passport Division. The file stated that the "subject" admitted that at one time he had been a member of a study group in Washington and New York connected in some way with the Communists, but he did not know whether or not he had been a member of the Communist Party. The "subject" claimed his relations terminated with these study groups in the early 1940s. Charles survived the ordeal with his integrity intact, "unwilling to furnish any information concerning fellow members of the groups or to discuss the political beliefs of any persons whose names were mentioned to him." On February 16, the Passport Division notified Seeger that his application for a passport was disapproved tentatively on the ground of Sedition 51.135, Title 22, "Limitation on the Issuance of Passports to Persons Supporting Communist Movements." Under siege in that dark period of McCarthyism, Seeger resigned from the Pan American Union, taking retirement at age sixty-seven.

In the meantime, Ruth tried to cope with her illness. Perhaps the shadow of death propelled her into more projects that might produce future income for the family. On February 4 she offered Collins *Love Songs of the American People*, a collection of 250 songs from the ill-fated Duncan Emrich project, an attempt to salvage some material from the wreck of the *1001 American Folk Songs* project from 1946. She reviewed its history and ended with this uncharacteristic hard sell: "Honestly, with the American folk music boom booming stronger, and adolescents singing hillbilly and busy with guitars and banjos, I can't see anything but a bright and possibly lucrative future for such a book." Eleven days later she used leftovers from the Christmas book to propose a literary piece to be co-authored with Charles, titled *Christmas Old and New in the United States*. Two weeks after, around the time that Charles formally resigned from the Pan American Union, out of mothballs came her old skit "Mother Writes her Editor" from 1941. "Might it be placed somewhere?" she asked Collins.[17]

Despite her illness, Crawford maintained her routines as much as possible. She attended the Washington premiere of "Rissolty, Rossolty" on May 2. She refused to stop teaching. One student told her mother that she couldn't believe what Ruth "looked like, that she was just wasting away." Some thirty-two private pupils participated in a recital on June 7, 1953. Some played the standard classics: others, music by Bartók, Honegger, Roger Sessions, and Marion Bauer; still others, the Weavers' "If I Had a Hammer," the signature song for Pete Seeger and People's Songs, still defiantly committed to the Left. "Why was it controversial?" Pete would later reflect. "In 1949 only Commies used words like 'peace' and 'freedom.'"[18]

Throughout most of the summer of 1953 Ruth marched onward through work, keeping up the illusions of normal life as much as possible. She sent a cheery letter in August to Lillian Bragdon, an editor at Aladdin Books, about how July was "swallowed whole" by the final proof of the Christmas book and by the family—that, plus the heat, and a plunge into housework. "The messier the desk, the more attractive the kitchen, with its making of the cakes I have no time to concoct in winter months." Bragdon had finally agreed to publish *Let's Build a Railroad*, in the works for twelve years.[19]

Simultaneously, Ruth called her agent, Alan Collins, to propose several new book and recording projects. In a burst of efficiency, she planned to write an "itemized resumé" for him: "There were so many that I felt it would help me, and maybe you, to lay them out one and two and three." In addition, she had sketched out plans for a children's record in which talk and singing were combined, she to be the speaker. Alan Collins answered her on September 29 that Columbia was interested, but they wanted to use Tom Glaser instead of her or any woman because "women's voices on children's records are not good commercially." That August Ruth and Charles brought fifteen-year-old Barbara and ten-year-old Penny to stay with Pete and his wife Toshi in Beacon, New York. Despite years of strife between Constance and Charles, Ruth strove to effect a peace treaty between them, arranging a meeting at Pete's. "The intent was doomed to fail," said Sidney, who learned of Ruth's illness at that time.[20]

Crawford's illness moved rapidly into its terminal stages. On August 16 she went into the hospital for abdominal surgery to remove several malignant growths, rebounding fast enough to revive her hopes for a full recovery. In the midst of it all, Ben Botkin came and spent a month as a house guest while he finished up a manuscript for a book. As the ever cordial hostess, she wrote him a comic letter of recommendation, certifying him as a duly proper "ideal guest . . . with the exception of his predilection for making a pun upon any occasion," and he in turn answered with a limerick that lightly turned on her illness, whose seriousness he could not acknowledge.[21]

By the end of September Ruth felt sick again, and daily experimental radiation therapy did little to slow her decline. In October Charles was told there was no hope. "No one has told her this," Charles wrote to Carl Crawford, and "we are all agreed that no one should. We are positive she knows, deep in her heart, but holds the realization off from the increasingly arduous—now almost 24-hours-a-day—attention to bodily pain and discomfort."[22]

Charles kept Ruth at home: "to send her to a hospital would be the end of us," he told Carl. Ruth allowed a few close friends—Glenore Horne, Vanett Lawler—to attend to her, but more often she called friends to talk. Sarah Miller, the mother of one of her best students, received a phone call because she too had been sick and Ruth wanted to know how she had "managed them" during her illness: how had Sarah stayed at home without letting her family get too upset about it? Sarah thought this a strange question. She had not thought of "managing the family" while she was sick and replied, "probably the same way you do." Ruth said, "Well, I wish I could do *that*. You don't mind my asking, do you?"[23]

Ruth also called Sidney Cowell fairly often. "Imagine me in bed," she said, "not working. I never thought I would ever feel that all I wanted to do was lie in bed." She blamed herself for her illness, telling Sidney in one of those last telephone conversations that, of course, "I did this to myself because my mother died of cancer of the stomach and I knew with the family history that I should keep track and have regular tests, and I didn't do it." To Sidney she also confided her worries about Charles and the children. Would he be able to support them? How would they manage? Sidney had few answers.[24]

Her final project was seeing the long delayed story sequence picture book, *Let's Build A Railroad*, on its way to publication. Ignorant of the nature of her illness, Alan Collins reported on the book's progress, coloring his dry news with humor: "Why is it juvenile editors are harder to get to talk business than the Communist negotiators in Korea?" On October 8 Ruth sent back the contracts, anticipating Collins's reaction. "Don't faint," she told him, but years of dealing with Margaret Lesser had made her wary enough to worry that they might have given away recording rights in the phrase "recorded readings." He gave her his absolute assurance on October 20 that this was not the case. At the same time she asked him in a separate letter about a $145 discrepancy in royalty statements.[25]

Even in the midst of her illness, Crawford continued to look after her music. That August she sent off her new Suite for Wind Quintet to Robert Russell Bennett to try to arrange for a New York performance through his chapter of the National Association for American Composers and Conductors, of which he was president. By mid-October she had heard of its acceptance: "one of the last things that Ruth did before she died was to make some small corrections" in the parts.[26]

But it was too little, too late. The forty-six years of composing that she had so optimistically prophesied in her triumphant letter to Carl and Charlotte Ruggles evaporated. "I'm sure it was a bitter disappointment to her," Pete told Mike. "She didn't go gently at all." To Pete as well as Sidney, Ruth revealed her deepest regrets. "It isn't fair," she told them. "I am just getting back into composing." Years later Pete recalled a scene that had reminded him of that unmet need. About his "last memory of Ruth" was the year before, at Thanksgiving, when they happened to listen to a recording of Japanese koto music late at night. "She was leaning against the door jamb, just entranced by this artist and this ancient music, and I remember both of us just listening and marveling at the skill of this musician and how he could say so much with a piece of silence."[27]

In one of her last conversations with Sidney Cowell, Crawford started the process of relinquishing her life by playing through her memories, weighing achievements against regrets. She took some small measure of comfort in recognizing the composer she once had been and knew she still was, as she summoned up that self in its essence. She said to Sidney, "I had been thinking about writing some music that had nothing to do with folk song. I have thought about some things and Ruth Crawford is still there."[28]

Charles tried to comfort Ruth through their usual habits of work. That fall he acted as her secretary and assistant, answering letters and taking dictation, playing music for her on the piano that she could hear upstairs, writing letters that hid the truth from strangers, forestalling the sympathy that he could not bear. He finally told Alan Collins on November 15 that his Ruth was "gravely ill and cannot think of going to New York. She has asked to acknowledge receipt of your letter of November 9 and to enquire whether Caedmon is thinking of rushing though recordings for this Christmas or whether he is such an early bird as to be getting ready for Christmas 1954. If it is this Christmas, any question of her singing is out." In his anxiety over their impending finances he clutched at straws: "Other members of the family or someone outside whom she would approve of might be put to work in a week."[29]

In the last days of her life, Crawford dictated three letters concerning *Let's Build a Railroad*. One letter contained suggestions for illustrations and several points about the format of words and music to ensure the right balance between narrative intended to be heard and narrative intended as action. On November 11 Charles typed the original copy of *Let's Build A Railroad*, assembled the dummy, and wrote the music notations, later remarking to Lillian Bragdon that Ruth had been "as keenly concentrated as ever on the job, though a little tired." On November 14 she sent off her preference for "John Henry's" text, "the one without the 'Lord, Lord' at the ends of the fourth line of every stanza. I leave to your staff the easy job of striking out the nine appearances of the offending items, together with the commas preceding them." Worried that Bragdon would use the first variant instead of the second, she asked her to send back the original music of the song, "less likely to confuse someone along the line. And I'll be reassured, too."[30]

Earlier that month Charles called Peggy to come home from Radcliffe. "During that week and a half Dio never complained, she never moaned, she never gave me any recognition that she knew she was dying. She would wake up every now and then for a drink and would ask for something but never petulant, never complaining of the pain, not even saying goodbye."[31]

Ruth Crawford Seeger died in a coma at Wednesday noon on November 18, 1953. With her were Charles and Peggy. Vanett Lawler, who had done so much for the family at this time, was downstairs. On that day Mike and Peggy were at the Children's Book Fair held at the Washington Post Building in order to promote *American Folk Songs for Christmas*, just published with a back order of 4,000 copies. A newspaper feature highlighted the "special thrill that the 20-year-old Michael felt on the occasion" because he was singing songs from his mother's new book.[32]

Henry Cowell learned about Crawford's death when he was in Baltimore, teaching his composition course at Peabody Conservatory:

> He went someplace for breakfast and a man at a neighboring table had a newspaper that was opened to the obituary page and he saw a picture of Ruth. And he said he went back to his room and closed the door and finally, he said, "I had never had an experience like that—of feeling a loss like that." And he had lost

two other people close to him—his mother and the girl he was engaged to in the early '20s. And he said, "I had to telephone Peabody and say that I was ill and couldn't come in to teach." And I'm sure [that] had never happened to him before because he was the last word in professionalism in doing what he had undertaken to do.[33]

In the days after Ruth's death, Charles consoled himself by carrying out her responsibilities. When proofs of *Let's Build a Railroad* arrived in the mail, he replied immediately: "I hasten to answer it and enclose the galleys with the only comments I have made in green pencil, just as Ruth would have wished." He complimented the editor, Lillian Bragdon, on the quality of the proof, making only a few changes of his own on a book he had finished as a tribute to his wife. Then he turned the routine business letter into a declaration of survival of his family:

> The making of this book—as of all others—has really been a family affair. Our daughter Peggy and our son Michael, as well as I, have participated in every step. Both of the children have successfully done work with children, following closely Ruth's methods, and more than a few times I have pinch-hitted for her with groups of mothers, once conducting a whole school Christmas program, when she was ill. Did you, by any chance audit Peggy's and Michael's session at the Washington Book Fair, in which they filled in for their mother? We hear it was successful.[34]

That duty to Ruth's work met, Charles retreated to his room for several days. Emotional confusion blanketed the family, as one housekeeper left "in hysterics," Peggy said, leaving Elizabeth Cotten in charge. "It was a tribute to her friendship with my mother that Libba would put up with the depression the household sank into," Peggy said. Vanett Lawler tried to help, although in the face of their father's grief and uncharacteristic collapse, the children more or less fended for themselves; it was not clear to ten-year-old Penny that her mother was not in a hospital until some days later. Peggy wrote an obituary the next day, which she sent to Nicolas Slonimsky. Plans were made for a private service, and Charles called Pete and asked him to come to her cremation. Accompanied by Peggy and Mike as well, Charles carried out the final steps of the ceremony by himself, eschewing a formal burial, commemorative headstone, or any kind of memorial service at all. Later, Henry and Sidney Cowell came down for a visit. "The life was gone out of the household when she died," Peggy said. "It just vanished." Within one year, Charles had sold the house and dispersed the children, who never again lived together under one roof. When he died, he said, he wanted his ashes mixed with Ruth's and scattered in the countryside.[35]

epilogue

The trouble with you Seegers is all you care about is music.

Alan Lomax[1]

After Ruth Crawford Seeger's death, her family carried on her work, each of them in somewhat different ways. Her legacy flowed into their many streams of activity in the amalgamation of different styles that fly under the banner of contemporary folk music today. The Seeger name became attached to a "family of musicians," rather than any one individual.[2]

The documentary traits in his mother's professional character were inherited by Mike Seeger, who, as Bruno Nettl has written, "tries to maintain the oldest ways of singing the oldest songs he can find." Even though he had resisted formal musical training as a child, by the early '50s he was already playing guitar for publicity spots promoting his mother's books. He soon learned fiddle, jew's harp, and most important, five-string banjo. In 1958 he cofounded the New Lost City Ramblers, a trio specializing in southern traditional music, or "old-time," and this group played an important role in the revival of string band and bluegrass in the 1960s. The sense of discovery and reclamation, so vital for the New Deal "functional" folk activists, comes through in other ways as well. His work with George Wein's Newport Folk Festivals made it possible for classic old-time performers like Dock Boggs and Bill Monroe to mix with a new generation of urban folk singers like Joan Baez and Bob Dylan, black freedom singers, antiwar activists, and the next generation of middle-class college students. Mike has called that mix a "coalition" that provided a springboard for the 1960s' fabled cultural vitality. In addition, he carried Elizabeth Cotten into his world by shepherding her career at this time as well.[3]

Politics has played a more formative role in Peggy Seeger's musical life,

353

whose career as a folk-revival musician has been focused in England, where she lived between 1957 and 1994. In 1956 Peggy met the singer-songwriter Ewan MacColl, forming a love-and-work relationship with this towering figure in the British folk music revival of the 1960s. In a sense she recreated a partnership she had seen in her own family. Starting in 1957, Peggy began to pay homage to her mother's work through recordings of the repertory in her books, which occasionally included her own piano playing of some of the original arrangements themselves and liner notes full of memories and reflections on Dio. Mike and Peggy continue to be active performers through the 1990s, repeatedly returning to their mother's repertory in recordings based on her books.

Pete Seeger is now regarded by many as the most important folk song revival performer of our time. Throughout his career—so intimately intertwining with protest and politics—he continued to make children's records. *American Folk Songs for Children* (1953), initially conceived as a tribute to Ruth Crawford Seeger's work, is one of his thirteen albums in the Folkways catalogue. If, as one historian has recently written, his real place within the folk revival is "his stature as a music educator," reaching generations of children who later supported the folk revival of the 1960s, then Ruth Crawford Seeger's spirit lives on in his work.[4]

Charles Seeger turned definitively to ethnomusicology, a profession which now holds him in considerable esteem as a patriarchal figure. Although he wrote important articles about Anglo-American folk music, music education, and even "world music" in the classroom long before multiculturalism became a buzzword, mainly he returned to his first love of philosophy and systematic musicology, revisiting old themes of music and language. Speculative and difficult though his philosophical work may be, it nevertheless continues to command respect and attention from contemporary scholars.

Ruth Crawford Seeger's work in folk music is sustained by her books, the first remaining in print to this day and the second recently reissued. Even if the academic folklore community knows her primarily through transcriptions in the Lomax books, music educators continue to use the repertory of folk music for children that she pioneered. When the music education methods of Zoltán Kodály eventually migrated to the United States, her books found another outlet. Since Kodály's method used indigenous folk songs as the primary source material for teaching, a young generation of American Kodály teachers relied on them as repertory for young children. It seems fitting that a composer who so admired Bartók should become a resource for a movement inspired by a fellow Hungarian compatriot. To this day, however, the unique quality of her piano arrangements has not been fully appreciated.[5]

Although Crawford's achievement in composition has taken longer to establish, it is secure. To be sure, among composers sympathetic to the American experimental tradition, her work remained alive. John Cage, Elliott Carter, Lou Harrison, Gordon Mumma, James Tenney, and Christian Wolff have all acknowledged her influence in different ways. When in 1960 George Perle published the first analysis of the last two movements of the String Quartet 1931, he not only paid tribute to his own roots, but launched that work into the historical literature as well. By the time Gilbert Chase wrote a second edition of his landmark survey, *America's Music*, he confidently established Ruth Crawford as an important innovator.[6]

Other factors contributed to the process of recognition, which gathered momentum in the 1970s through the rise of interest in women's history and the growth of women's studies in general. After a new recording of the String Quartet 1931 appeared in 1973, the work received extraordinary praise from respected critics in the national press. In 1975 the Performers' Committee for Twentieth-Century Music, under the direction of Joel Sachs and Cheryl Seltzer, presented the first major retrospective concert in New York. That same year Sarah Caldwell conducted the New York Philharmonic Orchestra in an evening of works devoted to compositions by women, and included the Andante movement in its string orchestra arrangement. Today, Crawford's place in music history is being secured through the most powerful tools in higher education—textbooks and their accompanying anthologies. Her music has received even more attention from theorists in the last few years, as a postmodern tolerance for diversity within the modernist canon has challenged the rigid Eurocentric approaches of the 1960s. Similarly, more recent scholarship is drawing on newer critical approaches of feminist musicology to explore the controversial issues of gender and female identity in Crawford's music.[7]

To some degree this attention has changed the way the Seeger children regard their mother's composition. Knowing virtually nothing of her original music during her lifetime, they struggled with its style and its emotional implications. Near the beginning of this process, Peggy said, "I don't understand how the woman that I knew as a mother created something like the 1931 string quartet. It is like someone crying; it is like someone beating on the walls . . . and I don't want to think about this as regarding my mother because my mother always seemed to me to have it all together, to have gotten a life that pleased her." In 1979 Mike and Penny Seeger contributed the bulk of the Seeger estate to the Library of Congress, which issued a microfilm of Crawford's holograph manuscripts in 1982.[8]

By default Charles became the chief documentor of Ruth's life as interest in "women composers" grew from the 1970s onward. He himself had helped sustain her reputation as a composer by actively collaborating with CBS Records to produce the first complete recording of the String Quartet 1931 in 1960. At that time he deliberately kept his influence on her work in the background. Indeed, when his friend Gilbert Chase wrote about the string quartet in 1955 in *America's Music*, Charles Seeger's name was not even mentioned. Beginning in the 1970s, curious scholars and journalists asked him to explain the silence of Ruth Crawford, composer. He had his answers, ranging from family responsibilities to politics. He lived long enough to see the sexual polarities he had learned in his Victorian youth begin to shift. Occasionally he sounded too proprietary about her creative accomplishments to his friends and somewhat chary about the attention paid to her original composition at the expense of the work with traditional music. He told one researcher: "Ruth was quite as much absorbed by her work in folklore as by her composition, but still retained of course, the fascination of her 'artistic' composition as all of us do who have made a few successful works of our own." Still, the man who could wear a tie clip that read "MCP" (standing for the 1970s epithet "male chauvinist pig") as a joke also talked about music and gender as a credible area of scholarly inquiry to his female graduate students at a time when few considered this a plausible option.[9]

Charles died in 1979, some years before Wilfrid Mellers wrote that his wife had been a "composer of genius" who had misguidedly devoted herself to her husband's political causes; Mellers heard a woman's protest in the dissonances of the String Quartet 1931. "She has been elevated to the position of a modern classic," Nicolas Slonimsky said, "something that no one would have predicted back then." Least of all the composer herself, who knew that "Ruth Crawford was still there" at the end of her life, but would not have suspected how much interest would eventually be taken in her fate.[10]

Perhaps what has happened to "Ruth Crawford" will finally happen to "Ruth Seeger" as well. Perhaps we will be less hampered by the oppositions she inherited and struggled with so heroically. As we look back on the first half of this century, through her life and work, we can see ever more clearly how the dynamic relationship between tradition and modernity has shaped our culture in ways we are just beginning to understand through art we are still learning to accept. Ruth Crawford Seeger's profound approach to cultural mediation belongs not just to her past, but to our own present—the effort we expend on her goals, one of the hallmarks of our own historical moment.

appendix a

Analysis by Ruth Crawford Seeger of the Third and Fourth Movements of the String Quartet 1931, including Facsimile Reproductions of Her Musical Examples and Diagrams

Third Movement

The underlying plan is heterophony of dynamics—a sort of counterpoint of crescendi and diminuendi. The crescendo and diminuendo in each instrument occurs in definite rhythmic patterns, which change from time to time as the movement proceeds. The crescendos are intended to be precisely timed; the high point is indicated to occur at some specific beat of the measure. A few sample patterns and meters are:

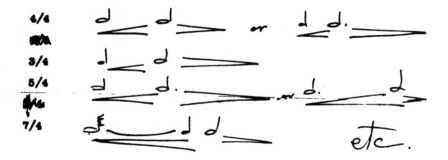

No high point in the crescendo in any one instrument coincides with the high point in any other instrument. For example:

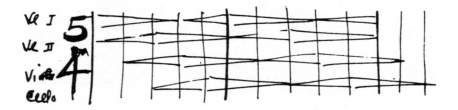

The melodic line grows out of this continuous increase and decrease; it is given, one tone at a time, to different instruments, and each new melodic tone is brought in at the high point in a crescendo. (Melodic tones are always indicated by a tenuto mark.) The melodic line of measures 13, 14, and 15, for example, is:

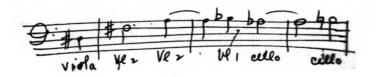

Fourth Movement

Form

The movement is written in two voices. Voice I is played by Violin I, Voice 2 by the three other instruments. Voice I begins with a single tone; at each succeeding entry one more tone is added until, at measures 52, 3 and 4, and again at measures 55–57, there are 20 tones in the group or entry. Voice II begins with 20 tones, decreasing to one tone at measure 57. At the Turning Point in measure 57 and 58, both voices settle on a single tone, and the two processes are then reversed.

Tone

The thematic material of Voice 2 consists of a 10-tone row, given 10 appearances, each repetition beginning with a successive tone of the row, as follows:

occurrence is completed, and at measure 47 the 10-tone row appears at its original pitch, once. At measure 57, count 3, a single foreign tone is introduced as a turning-tone (E, tied through 2 measures and a half). From measure 60 the entire foregoing material proceeds in crab-form, transposed 1/2 step higher. [Some text is obviously missing from Crawford's typescript. It probably would have noted that a new set of rotations of the 10-tone row begin in the middle of m. 21. At measure 46, the tenth occurrence is completed.]

There is a loose thread in the persian rug: in measure 24 the 10th tone of the 2nd occurrence of the transposed 10-rone row is omitted (f-sharp), making only 9 tones in that occurrence. Correspondingly, in measure 93, one tone is absent.

The tonal material of Voice I is free. At measure 60 it proceeds, like Voice 2, in crab-form.

Dynamics

The two voices are written to be independent of each other dynamically. Voice 1 begins its single tone fortissimo and, with increase in number of tones in each entry, it decreases in dynamics to pianissimo at measure 55. Oppositely, Voice 2 begins its greatest number of tones at measure 3 with pianissimo, and increases in tone to fortissimo as the number of tones in each entry decrease. There is therefore a sort of dissonance within each voice between volume in dynamics and number of tones, and also a sort of dissonance between the two voices, in volume and number. [In the margins Crawford wrote this note by hand: "Also count. of mood/   pp = laxity   ff=tenseness]

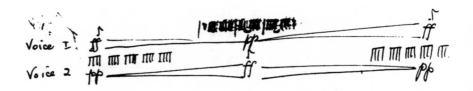

Rhythm

Rhythmic fluidity is sought in Voice 1 through use of varied divisions of the half-measure—groups of 3 and 5 alternating with 4+2. In Voice 2 the 8th note is constant, but irregular rhythmic patterns are obtained through bowing:

As to length of rest between entries: in Voice 2 the rest-length between entries decreases gradually as the number of tones decrease, to a midway point at measure 33

At measure 33 an increase in rest-length begins (the number of tones continuing to decrease) and continues gradually to measures 60,61,62:

Similarly in Voice 1 to measure 36: to ; from then on there is a graduated but slight increase in rest-length, then decrease again to measure 60, where there is no rest at all.

a p p e n d i x   b

Chronological Checklist of Works

Original Compositions

Undated works (1924–29), mostly student compositions or teaching pieces
  Fugue in Four Voices for String Quartet
  "Caprice," for piano
  "Little Lullaby," for piano
  "A Russian Lullaby," for mezzo soprano and piano (with Louis Untermeyer)
  "Whirligig," for piano

1922
  "Little Waltz," for piano

1923
  Theme and Variations for piano
  Sonata for piano (first movement only)
  Nocturne for Violin and Piano
  Untitled piece for violin and piano
  Three Songs to Poems by Sara Teasdale for soprano and piano
    "To One Away"
    "Return"
    "Joy"
  "To Night," for soprano and piano (with Louise Moulton)

1924

Five Canons for Piano

"Kaleidoscopic Changes on an Original Theme, Ending with a Fugue," for piano (6 min.)

Preludes for Piano, nos. 1, 2 (2 min.). Prelude no. 2 in *Historical Anthology of Music by Women Composers*. Ed. James Briscoe. Bloomington: Indiana Univ. Press, 1987. *Preludes for Piano 1–5*. Ed. Rosemary Platt. Bryn Mawr, Penn.: Casia Publishing, 1993.

    no. 1: Andante

    no. 2: With subtle sparkling humor

1925

"Adventures of Tom Thumb," for piano and narrator (6 min.)

Preludes for Piano, nos. 3–5 (4 min.). *Preludes for Piano 1-5*. Ed. Rosemary Platt, Bryn Mawr, Penn: Casia Publishing, 1993.

    no. 3: Simply, wistfully

    no. 4: Grave, mesto

    no. 5: Adagio

1926

Music for Small Orchestra (flute, clarinet, bassoon, violins, cellos, and piano). (8 min.). *Two Chamber Compositions by Ruth Crawford*. Ed. Judith Tick and Wayne Schneider. Music of the United States, vol. 1. Ann Arbor, Mich.: A-R Editions, 1993.

    1. Slow, pensive

    2. Fast

Sonata for Violin and Piano (15 min.). Bryn Mawr, Penn.: Merion Music, 1984.

    1. Agitated-vibrant-andante lusingando

    2. Buoyant

    3. Mystic-intense

    4. Fast with bold energy

1927–28

Preludes nos. 6–9 (9 min.). *New Music Quarterly*, vol. 2 (Oct. 1928). Reissued. Bryn Mawr, Penn.: Theodore Presser, 1984.

    no. 6: Andante mystico

    no. 7: Intensivo

    no. 8: Leggiero

    no. 9: Tranquillo

Suite no. 1 for Five Wind Instruments and Piano (flute, oboe, clarinet, bassoon, horn) (rev. 1929) (11 min.)

    Introduction, Adagio religioso

    1. Giocoso, allegro non troppo

    2. Andante tristo

    3. Allegro con brio, brillante, andante religioso

"Mr. Crow and Miss Wren Go for a Walk" ("A Little Study in Short Trills"), for piano [before 1928]

"Jumping the Rope," for piano

1929

Five Songs to Poems by Carl Sandburg (11 min.). *Five Songs to Poems by Carl Sandburg*. Ed. Judith Tick. New York: C. F. Peters, 1990.
"Home Thoughts"
"White Moon"
"Joy"
"Loam"
"Sunsets"

Suite no. 2 for Four Strings and Piano (10 min.). *Two Chamber Compositions by Ruth Crawford*. Ed. Judith Tick and Wayne Schneider. *Music of the United States*, vol. 1. Ann Arbor, Mich.: A-R Editions, 1993.
1. Lento
2. Leggiero
3. Allegro energico

"Lollipop-a-Papa," for mezzo soprano and piano (words and music by Fred Karlan, pseudonym for Ruth Crawford) (n.d.)

1930

Diaphonic Suite No. 2 for Bassoon and Cello (4 min.). New York: Continuo Press, 1972.
1. Freely
2. Andante cantando
3. Con brio

Diaphonic Suite No. 3 for Two Clarinets (3 1/2 min.). New York: Continuo Press, 1972.
1. Tranquillo
2. Giocoso
3. Moderato

Diaphonic Suite No. 1 for Solo Oboe or Flute (5 min.). Montevideo, *Boletín Latinoamericano de Musica*, vol. 1, 1941; *New Music*, vol. 26 (April 1953); New York: Continuo Press, 1972.
1. Scherzando
2. Andante
3. Allegro
4. Moderato, ritmico

Three Chants for Women's Chorus (3 min.). "To an Angel" as "Chant 1930." New York: Alexander Broude, 1971, in SATB arrangement with soprano solo.
"To an Unkind God"
"To an Angel"
"To a Kind God"

Piano Study in Mixed Accents (1 1/2 min.). *New Music*, vol. 6 (Oct. 1932).
  Reissued: Bryn Mawr: Theodore Presser, 1984.

1931

Diaphonic Suite No. 4 for Oboe (or Viola) and Cello (6 min.). New York:
  Continuo Press, 1972.
  1. Moderato
  2. Andante cantando
  3. Scherzando ritmico
String Quartet 1931 (11 min.). New York: *New Music*, vol. 14 (Jan. 1941).
  Reprint: New York: Merion Music, 1941.
  1. Rubato assai
  2. Leggiero
  3. Andante
  4. Allegro possibile

1930–32

Three Songs to Poems by Carl Sandburg for Contralto, Oboe, Piano and
  Percussion with Optional Orchestral Ostinati for Strings and Winds (9
  min.). New York: New Music, Orchestra Series, 1933.
  "Rat Riddles" (March 1930)
  "In Tall Grass" (1931)
  "Prayers of Steel" (1932)
  optional ostinati (1931–32)
Two Ricercare for Mezzo Soprano and Piano. Santa Fe, New Mexico: Sound-
  ings Press, 1973; Bryn Mawr: Merion Music, 1973.
  (with H. T. Tsiang) "Sacco, Vanzetti" (5 min.)
  "Chinaman, Laundryman" (3 min.)

1933

"When, Not If," unaccompanied three-part round

1936–38

Twenty-two American Folk Tunes arranged for piano, elementary grades.
  Published as *Nineteen American Folk Tunes* arranged for piano, elemen-
  tary grades. With a new introduction by Peggy Seeger. New York: G.
  Schirmer, 1995. (13 min.).

"The Babes in the Wood"	"Ground Hog"
"Billy Boy"	"The Higher Up the Cherry
"The Boll Weevil"	Tree"
"Charlie's Sweet"	"I Ride an Old Paint"
"Cindy"	"London's Bridge"
"Darby's Ram"	"Lord Thomas"
"Frog Went A-Courtin'"	"Mammy Loves"
"The Gray Goose"	"The Old Gray Mare"

"Sweet Betsy from Pike"   "Turtle Dove"
"The Three Ravens"   "What'll We Do with the Baby?"

1939

"Rissolty, Rossolty"—An American Fantasy for Orchestra (flute, oboe, two clarinets, bassoon, two horns, trumpets, trombone, tympani, strings) (4 min.)

1952

Suite for Wind Quintet: (11 min.). New York: Continuo Music Press, 1969.
  1. Allegretto
  2. Lento rubato
  3. Alle-gro possibile

Transcriptions

1941

Our Singing Country. Ed. John A. and Alan Lomax. New York: Macmillan. 205 transcriptions.

1943

Coal Dust on the Fiddle. Ed. George Korson. Philadelphia: Univ. of Pennsylvania Press. 13 transcriptions.

Jackson, George Pullen. *White and Negro Spirituals: Their Life Span and Kinship.* New York: J.J. Augustin. One transcription of a surge song ("Amazing Grace").

[1947]

1001 Songs, co-edited with Charles Seeger and Duncan Emrich. Words and melodies only in manuscript.

1951

Treasury of Western Folklore. Ed. Benjamin A. Botkin. New York: Crown. 32 transcriptions.

1955

Folklore Infantil de Santo Domingo. Ed. Edna Garrido Boggs. Madrid: Ediciones Cultura Hispanica.

Arrangements

1927

American Songbag. Ed. Carl Sandburg. New York: Harcourt, Brace. 4 arrangements.
  "Lonesome Road"

"Ten Thousand Miles Away from Home"
"There Was an Old Soldier"
"Those Gambler's Blues"

1947

Folk Song U.S.A.: The 111 Best American Ballads. Ed. John A. and Alan Lomax. New York: Duell, Sloan and Pearce. 111 settings for voice and piano, with Charles Seeger.

"Ain't No Mo' Cane on Dis Brazis"
"All the Pretty Little Horses"
"Almost Done"
"Amazing Grace"
"Another Man Done Gone"
"The Big Rock Candy Mountains"
"The Bigler"
"Black Is the Color"
"Black-eyed Susie"
"Blow Ye Winds in the Morning"
"Blue Mountain Lake"
"The Boll Weevil"
"Bound for the Promised Land"
"Brave Wolfe"
"Buckeye Jim"
"Buffalo Gals"
"The Buffalo Skinners"
"Bury Me Not on the Lone Prairie"
"Can'cha Line 'Em"
"Careless Love"
"Casey Jones" (two versions)
"Cindy"
"Coffee Grows on White Oak Trees"
"Come All You Fair and Tender Ladies"
"The Cowboy's Dream"
"Darlin' Corey"
"The Days of '49"
"Dink's Song"
"Down, Down, Down"
"Down in the Valley"

"Down in the Willow Garden"
"The Durant Jail"
"Easy Rider"
"The E-R-I-E"
"Frankie and Albert"
"Gee, But I Want To Go Home"
"Git Along Little Dogies"
"Go Down, Moses"
"Go Tell Aunt Nancy"
"Goin Down the Road Feelin' Bad"
"Great Gittin' Up Mornin'"
"The Grey Goose"
"Ground Hog"
"Home on the Range"
"I Was Born about Ten Thousand Years Ago"
"The Jam on Gerry's Rocks"
"Jennie Jenkins"
"Jesse James"
"John Brown's Body"
"John Hardy"
"John Henry" (two versions)
"Johnny Has Gone for a Soldier"
"Joshua Fit the Battle of Jericho"
"Keep Your Hand on the Plow"
"Leatherwing Bat"
"Lolly-Too-Dum"
"Lonesome Valley"
"Lowlands"
"The Lumberman in Town"
"Mademoiselle from Armentières,"
"The Midnight Special"
"Mister Rabbit"
"Never Said a Mumblin' Word"

"Nine Hundred Miles"
"O Freedom"
"O, Lula!"
"Old Blue"
"The Old Chisholm Trail" (two versions)
"Old Dan Tucker"
"Old Joe Clark"
"Old Paint" (two versions)
"The Old Settler's Song"
"Old Smoky"
"Once More A-Lumb'ring Go"
"Paddy Works on the Erie"
"Pick a Bale of Cotton"
"Po' Laz'us"
"Po' Lil Jesus"
"Pretty Polly"
"Raise a Rukus"
"Red River Valley"
"Rock About my Saro Jane"
"Rye Whiskey"
"Sacramento"
"Sam Bass"
"Santy Anno"
"Set Down, Servant"
"Shenandoah"
"Shoot the Buffalo"

"Shorty George"
"Skip to My Lou"
"Sometimes I Feel like a Motherless Child"
"Soon One Mornin'"
"Sourwood Mountain"
"The Sporting Bachelors"
"Springfield Mountain"
"Starving to Death on a Government Claim"
"The State of Arkansas"
"The Streets of Laredo"
"Sweet Betsy from Pike"
"Sweet Thing"
"Take a Whiff on Me"
"Take This Hammer"
"Tom Dooley"
"Wayfaring Stranger"
"When I Was Single" (two versions)
"When My Blood Runs Chilly an' Col"
"When You Go A-Courtin'"
"Whoa Buck"
"Wond'rous Love"
"The Young Man Who Wouldn't Hoe Corn"

1948

American Folk Songs for Children. Garden City, N.Y.: Doubleday. 95 arrangements (with titles of original sources according to the author).

"Adam Had Seven Sons"
"All Around the Kitchen" ("Cocky Doodle Doo")
"As I Walked Out One Holiday" ("The Jew's Garden")
"Baby Dear"
"Big Old Owl" ("Jim Crack Corn")
"Billy Barlow"
"Blow, Boys, Blow"
"Bought Me a Cat"
"Buffalo Girls"
"Built My Lady a Fine Brick House"
"By'm Bye" ("Stars Shining")

"The Cherry Tree Carol"
"Clap Your Hands"
"The Closet Key"
"Did You Go to the Barney?"
"Do, Do Pity My Case"
"Dog Tick"
"Down by the Greenwood Sidey-o"
"Down Came a Lady" ("Lord Daniel's Wife")
"Ducks in the Millpond"
"Eency Weency Spider"
"Every Monday Morning" ("John Henry")
"Fire Down Below"

"Free Little Bird"

"Frog Went A-Courtin'"

"Getting Upstairs"

"Go to Sleepy"

"Going Down to Town" ("Lynchburg Town")

"Goodbye, Julie" ("Miss Julie Ann Johnson")

"Goodbye, Old Paint"

"Hanging Out the Linen Clothes"

"Have a Little Dog" ("Toll-a-Winker")

"Here Sits a Monkey" ("Here Sits a Lady")

"Hop, Old Squirrel"

"How Old Are You?" ("Yaddle Daddle")

"Hush, Little Baby"

"Hush 'n' Bye" ("All the Pretty Little Horses")

"I Got a Letter This Morning"

"I'm Goin to Join the Army"

"It Rained a Mist"

"Jesus Borned in Bethlea"

"Jim Along Josie"

"Jimmy Rose He Went to Town"

"Jingle at the Windows" ("Tideo")

"John Henry"

"Johnny Get Your Hair Cut" ("Hey Betty Martin")

"Juba"

"The Juniper Tree"

"Little Bird, Little Bird"

"The Little Black Train"

"The Little Pig" ("Tale of a Little Pig")

"Lula Gal" ("Tie My Shoe")

"Mary Had a Baby"

"Mary Wore Her Red Dress"

"Monday Morning Go to School" ("The Two Brothers")

"My Horses Ain't Hungry"

"Oh, John the Rabbit"

"Oh, Oh, the Sunshine" ("Oh, Oh, You Can't Shine")

"Old Aunt Kate"

"Old Joe Clarke"

"Old Mister Rabbit"

"Old Molly Hare"

"One Cold and Frosty Morning" ("Old Jessie")

"Pick a Bale of Cotton"

"Poor Old Crow" ("The Three Ravens")

"Pretty Little Girl with the Red Dress On" ("Poor Howard")

"Rain, Come Wet Me"

"Rain or Shine" ("Doney Gal")

"Riding in the Buggy, Miss Mary Jane"

"Roll That Brown Jug Down to Town"

"Rose, Rose, and Up She Rises"

"Run, Chillen, Run" ("Run, Nigger, Run")

"Sailing in the Boat"

"Sally Go Round the Sunshine" ("Sally Go Round the Moon")

"Scraping Up Sand in the Bottom of the Sea" ("Shiloh")

"Skip-a to My Lou"

"Such a Getting Upstairs"

"Sweet Water Rolling"

"There Was a Man and He Was Mad"

"This Lady She Wears a Dark Green Shawl"

"This Old Hammer"

"This Old Man"

"Toodala"

"The Train Is A-Coming"

"Turtle Dove"

"Walk Along, John"

"What Did You Have for Supper?" ("Jimmy Randall, My Son")

"What Shall We Do When We All Go Out?"

"What'll We Do with the
Baby?"
"When I Was a Young Maid"
"When the Train Comes
Along"
"Where Oh Where Is Pretty
Little Susie?" ("Pawpaw
Patch")

"The Wind Blow East"
"Who Built the Ark? Noah,
Noah"
"Who's That Tapping at the
Window?"
"Yonder She Comes"

1950

Animal Folk Songs for Children. Garden City, N.Y.: Doubleday. Reprint.
Hamden, Conn.: Shoe String Press, 1993. 43 piano arrangements.

"And We Hunted and We
Hunted" ("Three Jolly
Welshmen")
"Animal Song"
"The Big Sheep" ("The Ram of
Darby")
"Black Sheep, Black Sheep"
"Crocodile Song"
"Cross-eyed Gopher"
"Daddy Shot a Bear"
"The Deer Song" ("Sally Buck")
"Go On, Old 'Gator"
"Go to Sleep" ("Buy a Pretty
Pony")
"The Gray Goose"
"Hop Up, My Ladies"
"Jack, Can I Ride?" ("See the
Elephant Jump the Fence")
"The Kicking Mule"
"The Little Black Bull"
("Hoosen Johnny")
"Little Brown Dog"
"Little Dog Named Right"
"Little Lap-Dog Lullaby"
("Come Up, Horsey")
"Little Pig"
"Mister Rabbit"
"Mole in the Ground"

"Muskrat"
"My Old Hen's a Good Old
Hen" ("Cluck Old Hen")
"Of All the Beast-es"
"Oh, Blue"
"Old Bell'd Yoe"
"The Old Cow Died" ("Sail
Away")
"Old Fox"
"Old Ground Hog"
"The Old Hen Cackled and the
Rooster Laid an Egg"
"Old Lady Goose"
"The Old Sow"
"Peep Squirrel"
"Raccoon and Possum"
"Riding Round the Cattle"
("The Old Chisholm Trail")
"Shake That Little Foot,
Dinah-O"
"Snake Baked a Hoecake"
"A Squirrel Is a Pretty Thing"
"Stewball"
"There Was an Old Frog"
"Turkey Song"
"Whoa, Mule! Can't Get the
Saddle On"
"Wolves A-Howling"

1953

American Folk Songs for Christmas. Garden City, N.Y.: Doubleday. 56 piano
arrangements.

"Ain't That A Rocking All
    Night"
"Almost Day" ("Looka Day")
"The Angel Band"
"Awake"
"Babe of Bethlehem"
"Baby Born Today" ("Mother
    Mary, What Is the Matter?")
"The Blessings of Mary"
"Bright Morning Stars Are
    Rising"
"Bye and Bye"
"Child of God"
"Children of the Heavenly
    King"
"Christmas Day in the
    Morning"
"Cradle Hymn"
"Don't You Hear the Lambs
    A-Crying?"
"Exultation"
"Found My Lost Sheep"
"Go Tell It on the Mountain"
"Great Big Stars" ("Shine,
    Shine")
"Heard from Heaven Today"
"Heaven Bell Ring"
"Holy Babe"
"How Many Miles to
    Bethlehem?"
"January, February" ("The Last
    Month of the Year")
"Jehovah Hallelujah"
"Jesus Borned in Bethlea"
"Joseph and Mary" ("The
    Cherry Tree Carol")
"Little Bitty Baby"

"The Little Cradle Rocks
    Tonight in Glory"
"Look Away to Bethlehem"
"Mariner's Hymn"
"Mary Had a Baby"
"Mary, What Are You Going to
    Name That Pretty Little
    Baby?"
"A Mince Pie or a Pudding"
"The New-Born Baby"
"O Mary, Where Is Your Baby?"
"Oh, Mary and the Baby, Sweet
    Lamb"
"Oh, Watch the Stars"
"Old Christmas" (fiddle tune)
"Poor Little Jesus"
"Rejoice My Friends"
"Rise Up, Shepherd and
    Follow"
"Shepherd, Shepherd"
"Shepherds in Judea"
"Shepherds, Rejoice"
"Shine like a Star in the
    Morning"
"Sing Hallelu"
"Sing-a-Lamb"
"Singing in the Land"
"Star in the East"
"Sweep, Sweep, and Cleanse
    Your Floor"
"'Twas a Wonder in Heaven"
"The Twelve Apostles"
"The Twelve Days of
    Christmas"
"Virgin Most Pure"
"Wasn't That a Mighty Day"
"Yonder Comes Sister Mary"

1954

Let's Build a Railroad. New York: Aladdin Books. 6 arrangements.
    "Hammer Ring"
    "John Henry"
    "The Little Black Train"
    "This Old Hammer"
    "Tie Tamping Song"
    "Train Is A-Coming"

Other Published Writings

1948

Review of John N. Work, *American Negro Songs for Mixed Voices* in *Notes* (Dec. 1948): 172–73.

1951

"Keep the Song Going," *National Education Association Journal* (Feb. 1951): 93–95.

1953

Remarks on "Making Folklore Available." In *Four Symposia on Folklore*. Ed. Stith Thompson. Bloomington: Indiana Univ. Press. Reprint. Westport, Conn.: Greenwood Press, 1976.

notes

PS   Pete Seeger
PgS   Peggy Seeger
PnS   Penny Seeger
RC   Ruth Crawford
RCS   Ruth Crawford Seeger
RCd   Diary of Ruth Crawford
SRC   Sidney Robertson Cowell
UI   University of Illinois, Carl Sandburg Collection
UN   University of Nebraska, Botkin Collection
UT   University of Texas at Austin
VF   Vivian Fine
Yale Beinecke Library

1. A Minister's Daughter

1. "How does one": interview with Martha Beck Carragan, July 13, 1983; "moderns" and "to represent": Paul Rosenfeld, *An Hour with American Music* (Philadelphia: J.B. Lippincott, 1929), 126-27.

2. "members": "American Youth to Have Its Fling in League Concert," *Musical America* (Feb. 12, 1927): 27; "most masculine": unsigned review, "Music by Six Young Americans Is Heard by a Large Audience," *New York Herald Tribune*, Feb. 14, 1927, p. 10; "boldly energetic": R.C.B.B., "League of Composers Gives a Recital of New Music," *Musical America* 45 (Feb. 19, 1927): 4.

3. "sling dissonances": Edward Moore, "Modern Music Society Offers Its First Bill," *Chicago Daily Tribune*, Feb. 9, 1928, p. 13; "intrepid": Karleton Hackett, "Contemporary Music in Its First Concert," *Chicago Evening Post*, Feb. 9, 1928, p. 6.

4. "came to my seat": RCd, Feb. 9, 1928. The program included Milhaud's String Quartet no. 6, op. 77; Stravinsky's Serenade in A for piano; Castelnuovo-Tedesco's *Alt Wien*, op. 30, for two pianos; and Louis Gruenberg's "Four Indiscretions," op. 20.

5. "Four new compositions": letter from ClC to CaC, Feb. 24, 1928, CWH.

6. "On my sixth birthday": RCS, autobiographical sketch, ca. 1947.

7. On growth of Methodism: Frederick A. Norwood, *The Story of American Methodism* (Nashville, Tenn.: Abingdon Press, 1924), 259; on Mary Graves: "Extract from the Memoirs of the Minutes of the Forty-Eighth Annual Session of the Central Illinois Conference of the Methodist Episcopal Church held at Monmouth, Illinois, September 1903," CWH; "web of preaching": Sidney E. Ahlstrom, *A Religious History of the American People* (New Haven: Yale Univ. Press, 1973), 436.

8. "candlelit drama": Corra Harris, "The Circuit-Rider's Wife," cited in Edwin Mims, "The Southern Woman: Past and Present," *Bulletin of Randolph-Macon Woman's College* (Lynchburg, Va., 1915), p. 6; "totally insipid": ClG, diary, May 1898, CWH.

9. "Grandmother": RCS, autobiographical sketch, ca. 1947; information about Northwestern: letter from ClC to RC, Oct. 23, 1922, CWH.

10. "piano girl": James Huneker, *Overtones* (New York: Charles Scribner's Sons, 1904), 286.

11. "kept away": ClG, diary, March, 1877; "When will we": ClG, diary, April 10, 1879, CWH.

12. "many variations": ClG diary, Aug. 24, 1876, CWH; "to wait": ClC diary, March 1, 1876; "womanly manifestations": interview with PgS, Aug. 14, 1985.

13. "heard about": letter from RC to ClC, May 25, 1922, BS.

14. Information about women in the labor force: Lois W. Banner, *Women in Mod-*

ern America: A Brief History (New York: Harcourt Brace Jovanovich, 1974), 6. Banner notes that the percentages grew from 15 to 20 percent from 1870 to 1900. See also Sara M. Evans, *Born for Liberty: A History of Women in America* (New York: Free Press, 1989), 133–37. "One of those": RCS, autobiographical sketch, ca. 1947.

15. Charlotte Perkins Gilman, "On Women's Evolution from Economic Dependence," *Women and Economics* (1898), reprinted in *Root of Bitterness: Documents of the Social History of American Women*, ed. Nancy F. Cott (New York: E.P. Dutton, 1972), 367; "very hard": ClG to Will Graves, June 5, 1886, CWH.

16. Information about the piano and bedtime music from RCS, autobiographical sketch, ca. 1947.

17. "I am only": unidentified relative to ClG, April 22, 1894, CWH; "very much" to "his work in life": letter from ClG to Will Graves, May 6, 1894, CWH.

18. Clark Crawford's sermons are in family papers of CWH; On East Liverpool, see William C. Gates, Jr., *The City of Hills & Kilns: Life and Work in East Liverpool, Ohio* (East Liverpool Historical Society, 1984), 182, 279.

19. "father used to": RCS, autobiographical sketch, ca. 1947.

20. On Muncie, see Robert and Helen Lynd, *Middletown* (New York: Harcourt Brace Jovanovich, 1956); "very happy": RCS, autobiographical sketch, ca. 1947; details about the High Street Church come from "A Souvenir Booklet of Muncie, Indiana" (Muncie: Muncie Commercial Club, 1910), and Margaret Shepard Jackson, *A Tower on High: A History of High Street United Methodist Church* (Muncie, Indiana: High Street United Methodist Church, 1986), 18–19.

21. "pink hair ribbons": RCS, autobiographical sketch, ca. 1947.

22. "playing games": RCS, autobiographical sketch, ca. 1947; "the pastor's family": RC, autobiographical sketch, May 17, 1916, BS; "she danced": RCd, April 25, 1919, BS.

23. "She would": RC, autobiographical sketch, May 17, 1916, BS; "You told": letter from RC to CkC, July 29, 1912, CWH.

24. "put more to it": letter from RC to CkC, July 31, 1912, CWH.

25. *History of the Snyder Memorial Methodist Church from 1870 to 1944, Published in Connection with the Centennial Celebration of the Florida Annual Conference of the Methodist Church* (Jacksonville, Florida, 1944), 25, 35. Death certificate for Clark Crawford, March 5, 1914, State Board of Health of Florida.

26. "would be displeased": RC, essay on "Time," in "Poems, Stories and Such, 1909–1918," typescript edited by BS, 1971; "And listen": RCd, Aug. 21, 1917.

27. "fairly normal": RC, autobiographical sketch, ca. 1947; "Mrs. Crawford": interview of CaC with MG, March 18, 1968; "transcendental": interview of SRC, Dec. 14, 1982.

28. T. F. Davis, *A History of Jacksonville, Florida and Vicinity, 1513–1924* (Gainesville: Univ. of Florida Press, 1964), 246, 251, 500.

29. "I wore": RCd, April 18, 1917, BS.

30. "I will": RCd, Jan. 14, 1915; RC later rewrote portions of this diary and omitted the "ugly"; Carl's recollections from an interview with CaC by MG; "Yes, Ruth": RCd, Sept. 23, 1917, BS.

31. "Mama's Advice": RCd, [ca. March], 1915, BS.

32. "a sort of burning" to "mend your ways": RCd, Aug. 21, 1917, BS; "to keep everything out": RC, essay for Duval High School, ca. 1916, BS.

33. "filled two books": RC, autobiographical sketch, ca. 1947; "Now I will": RCd, Jan. 14, 1915.

34. "Fireside Fancies," ca. 1914, BS; "the world of women": Jessie Taft, quoted in

Rosalind Rosenberg, *Beyond Separate Spheres: Intellectual Roots of Modern Feminism* (New Haven: Yale Univ. Press, 1982), xix.

35. "high school": RC, autobiographical sketch, ca. 1947; all other quotations from *The Oracle* graduation issue, June 1918, BS.

2. An "American Woman Pianist"

1. Harriette Brower, "American Women Pianists: Their Views and Achievements," *Musical America* 26 (Oct. 28, 1918): 18–19.

2. Foster's fee: RCd, June 1917; Trumbull: RCd, June 28, 1918; eleven pupils, RCd, Aug. 28, 1918; "Hurrah": RCd, Feb. 11, 1919, BS.

3. For statistics, see Henry J. Harris, "The Occupation of Musician in the United States," *Musical Quarterly* 1 (April 1915): 301; census statistics in Tick, "Passed Away Is the Piano Girl," *Women Making Music: The Western Art Tradition 1150–1950* (Urbana: Univ. of Illinois Press, 1986), 326–27; "feminized": Sophonisba Breckenridge, *Women in the Twentieth Century* (New York: McGraw-Hill, 1933), 190.

4. Harris, "The Occupation of Musician," 303.

5. Bertha Foster's certificate of death, Feb. 29, 1968, Florida; on the Florida Female College: Ella Scoble Opperman, *Annals of the School of Music of Florida State University, 1911–1944* (Tallahassee: Florida State Univ., n.d.), 13; on women as organists: Mary Chappell Fischer, "Women as Concert Organists," *Etude* 19 (Sept. 1901): 332.

6. See Grier Moffat Williams, "A History of Music in Jacksonville, Florida, from 1822 to 1922" (Ph.D dissertation, Florida State University, 1961), 167, 220, 237, 254; also Ann Hyman, "A Musical Riviera—Jacksonville in the 1880s," Program Booklet of the 24th Annual Delius Festival, March 7–10, 1984, Jacksonville, Florida, p. 12; concert listings are in "History of the Ladies Friday Musicale," undated [ca. 1915], typed pamphlet, Jacksonville Public Library.

7. Catalogues of the School of Musical Art, 1912–13, 1916–17, Jacksonville Public Library.

8. Information about Damrosch from Williams, "A History of Music in Jacksonville," 241; clippings in RC, scrapbook, BS; information about *Musical America* from MG-RCS, p. 15; "way back": interview with PS by MS, Dec. 8, 1982.

9. "Miss Foster": RCd, [Aug.] 1917, BS.

10. "warm-hearted": RCd, [Aug.] 1917; "with open": RCd, Oct. 11, 1917, BS.

11. "She said" to "came home": RCd, Oct. 16, 1917, BS; "pours a torrent": RC, 1917, BS; "very fine": letter from RC to Nicolas Slonimsky, Jan. 29, 1933.

12. "trash, bash": from RC's story about Mary Marshall, BS; biographical information from catalogue of the School of Musical Art, 1912–13 and 1916–17.

13. Repertory listed in RCd, Dec. 18, 1917, BS; "Gallic eau sucrée": James Huneker, *Chopin: The Man and His Music* (New York: Charles Scribner's Sons, 1901), 311.

14. "Am scared": RCd, June 18, 1917; "large and most": George Hoyt Smith, "Students Were Heard in Fine Musical Program," *Florida Times-Union*, June 21, 1918; "somewhat of a": CaC, note in RC's scrapbook, "The Girl Graduate"; "Recital over": RCd, June 19, 1918, BS.

15. RCd, Nov. 17, 1918: "Began a story this p.m.—Mary Marshall and Mme. Zielinsky."

16. "tales of": letter from RC to Alice Burrow, July 13, 1929.

17. Doris Allen, "Women's Contributions to Modern Piano Pedagogy," in *The Musical Woman: An International Perspective*, ed. Judith Lang Zaimont (New York: Greenwood Press, 1984), 411–44.

18. Linda Kerber, "Separate Spheres, Female Worlds, Woman's Place: The Rhetoric of Women's History," *Journal of American History* 75 (Summer 1988): 17.

19. William S. B. Matthews, "The Young Woman Pianist and Her Business Prospects," *Etude* 24 (Feb. 1906): 64; James M. Tracey, "Some of the World's Greatest Pianists," *Etude* 25 (Dec. 1907): 773–74; Harriette Brower, "Are Women Men's Equals as Pianists?" *Musical America* (Dec. 16, 1916): 19; Brower, "American Women Pianists: Their Views and Achievements," *Musical America* (Oct. 28, 1918): 18–19.

20. "the commercial monopolists": Charles Ives, *Memos*, ed. John Kirkpatrick (New York: W. W. Norton, 1972), cited and discussed by Judith Tick, "Charles Ives and Gender Ideology," in *Musicology and Difference*, ed. Ruth Solie (Berkeley: Univ. of California Press, 1993), 85, 104; "Please see": CS-UCLA, p. 96.

21. *Etude* ran issues on "Women's Work in Music" in 1901, 1909, 1918, and 1929.

22. "played piano": RCd, July 7, 1918; "Just missed": RCd, Jan. 3, 1919, BS.

23. RC, autobiographical sketch, ca. 1947. Paderewski appeared under the sponsorship of the Ladies Friday Musicale on Jan. 27, 1917; Leopold Godowsky on March 30, 1916; Mischa Elman played at the Duval Theater on March 3, 1919.

24. "Song Without Words": RCd, Dec. 1917; "great piece": RCd, Sept. 26, 1917; "Just to think": RCd, Sept. 28, 1917, BS.

25. RCd, Sept. 9, 1918, BS.

26. "four dry lessons": letter from RC to Nicolas Slonimsky, Jan. 29, 1933; "real cunning" to "gave her": RCd, Dec. 28, 1918, BS; "certain perfection": letter from RC to ClC, Feb. 5, 1922, BS; "few little bits": letter from RC to Nicolas Slonimsky, Jan. 29, 1933.

27. "Carl is home": RCd, Dec. 7, 1918; "perfectly wonderful": RCd, April 22, 1919; Foster's plans written up in "Notes from Jacksonville," *Musical America* (Sept. 3, 1921): 20.

28. "ability" to "considerable sacrifice": interview with CaC by MG, March 28, 1968.

29. Amy Fay, *Music Study in Germany* (Chicago: A. C. McClurg, 1880); "how lessons": letter from ClC to RC, May 1922, BS.

30. "get a big price": RCd, Oct. 21, 1918; information about Levy: letter from RC to ClC, Sept. 9, 1921, and Jan. 23, 1923, BS.

31. "achieved:" RC to Nicolas Slonimsky, Jan. 29, 1933.

32. "humiliated": letter from RC to ClC, Sept. 19, 1921, BS.

33. "beautiful": letter from ClC to RC, March 31, 1922; "charming to watch": letter from ClC to RC, May 1922, BS.

34. "different": letter from ClC to RC, June 1922, BS.

3. The "Wonder City"

1. "Metropolis of the West": *Bulletin of the American Conservatory of Music*, 1922–23.

2. Information about the Kimball building from the Bulletin of the American Conservatory, 1922–23, pp. 8–9; "It was so": letter from RC to ClC, Sept. 19, 1921, BS.

3. "it smelled": Margaret Anderson, *My Thirty Years War* (New York: Covici, Friede, 1930), 20; Cather used Chicago as a setting for two novels about female musicians, *The Song of the Lark* and *Lucy Gayheart*; "so nice": letter from RC to ClC, Sept. 13, 1921, BS.

4. Statistics from Harold Randolph, "The Feminization of Music," in *Studies in Musical Education, History and Aesthetics* 17 (Hartford, Conn.: Music Teachers National

Association, 1923), 194–200; "the consensus": letter from RC to ClC, Sept. 18, 1921; "Sometimes": letter from RC to ClC, Oct. 23, 1921, BS.

5. Claudia Cassidy, "The Years of Splendor," *Chicago History* 2 (Spring 1972): 8; for a review of Chicago critics, see "Behind the Guns of Chicago's Critical Battery" *Musical America* (Sept. 24, 1921): 9.

6. "travelling chamber": RCS, autobiographical sketch, ca. 1947; Cassidy, "The Years of Splendor," 8; see also Ronald L. Davis, *Opera in Chicago* (New York: Appleton-Century, 1966), 127ff., and Edward Moore, *Forty Years of Opera in Chicago* (New York, H. Liveright, 1930), 232ff. on the 1921–22 season; "they were both": letter from RC to ClC, Dec. 4 and 18, 1921, BS.

7. "the great center": Dena Epstein, "Frederick Stock and American Music," *American Music* 10 (Spring 1992): 21; "longed to hear": letter from RC to ClC, Nov. 8, 1922, BS.

8. Interview with Grace Welsh by MG, Nov. 18, 1983. Welsh studied at the American Conservatory of Music in the 1920s; for a list of Stock's American repertory, see Epstein, "Frederick Stock," 35–47.

9. Information on pianists performing in Chicago from MG-RCS, p. 20; "one of the most": interview with Alfred Frankenstein by Rita Mead, Nov. 7, 1975; Annette Essipoff was an associate and the wife of Theodore Leschitizky, the preeminent piano teacher of the period.

10. "finger[s] like velvet": letter from RC to ClC, Nov. 8, 1922, BS; "Ossssssip": Charles Ives, *Memos*, ed. John Kirkpatrick (New York: W. W. Norton, 1972), 43–44, 135.

11. "up to the middle": Bulletin of the American Conservatory, 1922–23, pp. 9–10.

12. Levy's background is described in the Bulletin of the American Conservatory of Music, 1922–23, p. 21. Levy studied composition as well, working with Max Bruch and winning composition contests in Warsaw and Paris; the Chicago Symphony played Levy's "Twenty-Four Variations on an Original Theme" in 1942. "He was": interview with Otto Luening; "excellent teacher": letter from Radie Britain to the author, Jan. 25, 1986.

13. Information about requirements from catalogues of the American Conservatory of Music; "dear darling Ruth": Christmas card from Valborg Collett to RC, 1921, BS.

14. "shake all over": letter from RC to ClC, March 6, 1922; "I cannot practice": letter from RC to ClC, BS; "fatal thing": interview with Martha Beck Carragan, July 13, 1983.

15. "killer": interview with Edith Borroff, April 16, 1988; "Mr. Levy's": letter from RC to ClC, ca. March or April 1923, BS.

16. "I am the only": letter from RC to ClC, May 18, 1922; "A week ago": letter from RC to ClC, May 22, 1922, BS.

17. "it seems": letter from RC to ClC, Dec. 11, 1921, BS.

18. "at some new": ibid.

19. "You will": letter from ClC to RC, Nov. 2, 1921, BS.

20. "You *do*": letter from RC to ClC, Jan. 30, 1922; "Push yourself": letter from ClC to RC, April 17, 1922, BS.

21. Information about Crawford's degrees from the program of Thirty-sixth Annual Commencement Exercises and Concert, American Conservatory of Music, June 20, 1922; Levy recommendation: letter from RC to ClC, May 24, 1922, BS; "rode an hour": RC, autobiographical sketch, ca. 1947.

22. "He is so amusing": undated fragment, probably 1922–23, BS; "it often": letter from RC to ClC, Nov. 8, 1922; "I do not know": undated fragment, but probably ca. 1922–23, BS.

23. "I am full": undated fragment on back of theater bill for *The Hindu,* BS.

24. "most prominent": interview with Grace Welsh by MG, Nov., 18, 1983; "real standing": interview with Jean Anderson Wentworth, Dec. 5, 1992; "big name": interview with Edith Borroff, April 16, 1988; information about Storm Bull from a letter to the author, Aug. 13, 1986; "never marry": letter from RC to ClC, Nov. 20, 1921, BS.

25. "apprenticeship": letter from RC to ClC, ca. Feb. 9, 1923; "incredible": interview with Edith Borroff, April 16, 1988.

26. "What am I": letter from RC to ClC, Nov. 18, 1922; "The knowledge": letter from RC to ClC, Jan. 3, 1923; "I think and think": letter from RC to ClC, Feb. 9, 1923; "Again and again": letter from RC to ClC, Nov. 18, 1922, BS.

27. For biographical information about Adolf Weidig, see the *Dictionary of American Biography,* 1936, p. 606, and the obituary by Florence French, "Adolf Weidig," *Musical Leader* (Oct. 1, 1931): 13; on Brahms and Weidig: interview with Edith Borroff, April 16, 1988.

28. "He must": letter from RC to ClC, Dec. 18, 1921; "extremely tactless" and "Just because": letter from Storm Bull to the author, Aug. 13, 1986; "go all out": interview with Grace Welsh by MG, Nov. 18, 1983.

29. "definite" to "gold in the rough": letter from RC to ClC, Feb. 20, 1923, BS.

30. "Every time": letter from RC to ClC, March 8, 1923; "Can they": letter from RC to ClC, March 1923, BS.

31. "I had always": letter from RC to ClC, Jan. 3, 1923; "I have written": letter from RC to ClC, March 29, 1923, CWH; "trite": letter from RC to ClC, Dec. 13, 1922, BS.

32. "Why can't": letter from RC to ClC, Jan. 3, 1923; "I think and think": letter from RC to ClC, Feb 9, 1923; "If I am" to "it would be": letter from RC to ClC, April 16, 1923, BS.

33. RC to ClC, Nov. 18, 1922, and Jan. 3, 1923. "Robert had become": ClC to RC, spring 1923, BS.

34. "You certainly": letter from ClC to RC, March 18, 1923, BS.

35. "brilliant future": letter from RC to ClC, May 9, 1923; "You speak": letter from ClC to RC, May 13, 1923.

36. "You speak": letter from RC to ClC, May 16, 1923, BS.

37. "If I could": letter from RC to ClC, May 23, 1923, CWH; "Chicago is": letter from ClC to RC, May 25, 1923, BS.

38. "So you have": letter from CaC to RC, Dec. 30, 1923, BS; "as for": letter from RC to CS, Jan. 18, 1931, MS.

39. "poses" to "It is not": letter from RC to ClC, Jan. 3, 1923, BS.

40. "was hoping": letter from RC to ClC, Dec. 4, 1922, CWH.

41. "Whole-tone harmonies": Adolf Weidig, *Harmonic Materials and Their Uses* (Chicago: Clayton F. Summy, 1923), 318; "Weidig chord": Horace Miller, *New Harmonic Devices: A Treatise on Modern Harmonic Practices* (Boston: Oliver Ditson, 1930), 151.

42. The assessment of Teasdale is by Ellen Williams, *Harriet Monroe and the Poetry Renaissance* (Urbana: Univ. of Illinois Press, 1977), 277; "restless movement": letter from RC to ClC, May 2, 1923, BS.

43. "What do you think": RC on program for "New Compositions Written by Members of Mr. Weidig's Class," May 31, 1924, BS.

44. Information about the concert in "A Second Program of New Compositions Written by Members of Mr. Weidig's Class." A brief report appeared as "Weidig's Composition Concert," *Musical Leader* (June 19, 1924): 597. Ruth was mentioned as follows: "Misses Thorkelson, Marion Roberts, Crawford, Markman, Coryell, were all heard in their own instrumental works, of interesting content for the most part, well constructed and agreeable." "An event": letter from RC to ClC, April 25, 1923, BS.

45. "I don't": letter from ClC to CaC, June 18, 1924, BS.

46. "Ruth was a little": telephone interview with Helen Watson, fall 1991; "bring out": interview with Martha Beck Carragan; "somewhat baffled": interview with Stella Roberts in MG-RC, pp. 34–35.

47. "Ruth's improvement": letter from ClC to CaC, June 18, 1924, BS.

4. New Ways of Knowing

1. "best teacher": letter from ClC to CaC, June 18, 1924, BS; "greatest interpreter": "Contemporary American Musicians," *Musical America* (Jan. 10, 1925): 23, which also gives the dates of Gradova's recitals as Nov. 23, 1923, and Jan. 28, 1924. The comments are from various undated reviews quoted in a publicity sheet, including H. T. Parker, "In Gradova Darts the Flame," *Boston Transcript*, Dec. 8, 1924.

2. "Djane Lavoie Herz," *Musical Canada* 9 (Nov. 1914): 159. See also the entry "Lavoie-Herz" in *The Encyclopedia of Music in Canada* (Toronto: Univ. of Toronto Press, 1981), 532. Lavoie Herz's son, Tristan Hearst, supplied her birthdate of Oct. 15, 1888, and death date of March 2, 1982, in an interview with Nancy Reich for the author, Sept. 7, 1985; "initiated in": Djane Lavoie Herz, "Scriabine's Prometheus," *Musical Canada* 10 (May 1915): 3–7.

3. Details on Theosophy from Bruce F. Campbell, *Ancient Wisdom Revived: A History of the Theosophical Movement* (Berkeley: Univ. of California Press, 1980), 78; see also Sydney E. Ahlstrom, *A Religious History of the American People* (New Haven: Yale Univ. Press, 1972), 1041; "missionary movement": Claude Bragdon, *Old Lamps for New: The Ancient Wisdom in the Modern World* (New York: Alfred Knopf, 1925), 31; information about the 1926 convention is in "News Summary," *Chicago Daily Tribune,* Aug. 30, 1926 and *The Theosophist* 47 (Nov. 1926): 120–21.

4. Scriabin's *Divine Poem* was programmed annually with the exception of 1926, 1929, and 1932. *Prometheus* was performed in 1914, 1930, and 1937.

5. Siegfried Lavoie-Herz, "The Art of Alexander Nikolaievetch Skriabin," *Etude,* May 1926—reprint courtesy of Tristan Hearst; Nietzsche club: letter from Tristan Hearst to the author, Nov. 10, 1988; "redolent": interview with VF, April 18, 1989; "knew everybody": interview with Tristan Hearst by Nancy Reich, Sept. 7, 1985.

6. "soul experience" and "music of": "Gradova Discusses Modern Music," *Musical Leader* (Oct. 2, 1924): 330; "the greatest spirits": RCd, Aug. [26], 1927; *The Secret Doctrine* in RCd, Nov. 2, 1927; "especially interested": RCd, Oct. 29, 1928.

7. The *Bhagavad Gita* in RCd, Oct. 29, 1928; "That man": R. B. Blakney, *The Way of Life, Lao Tzu* (New York, 1955), 46; "knowledge of philosophy": RCd, [Aug. 26], 1927; "distinction between": RCd, Oct. 29, 1928.

8. "made a study": E. French, "Around the Chicago Studios: Djane Lavoie Herz's Interesting Career," *Musical Leader* (Dec. 13, 1923): 562; details about Djane Herz from an interview with VF, April 18, 1989, and an interview with Ann Scott, Jan. 26, 1986. Scott studied with Djane Lavoie Herz from 1943 to 1950 in New York; "typical": letter from DR to the author, Oct. 5, 1984.

9. "nature that responds": RCd, [Nov. 2, 1927].

10. "any others" and "I always feel": RCd, [Sept.] 1927.

11. "idol [that] gripped": letter from RC to CS, Jan. 18, 1931, MS; "sexual suppression": interview with VF, April 18, 1989; "rousing the flame": DR, "The Regeneration of Piano Teaching: Djane Lavoie-Herz and Her Work," *Musical Observer* (1926), reprint supplied by Tristan Hearst; "spoke universes": RCd, [Nov. 6], 1927. When the preludes were published, the dedication appeared only on no. 6, but an autograph score of the set has the dedication inscribed on the title page of the group. "Shades of Dead Planets" and "Creator": RCS, unpublished poems.

12. All quotations by Gradova from an interview with Gitta Gradova Cottle, Sept. 8, 1984; Gradova's obituary appeared in the *Chicago Tribune*, April 28, 1985.

13. "Ruth Crawford": "Gitta Gradova to Play Compositions by Cowell, Rudhyar and Ruth Crawford," *Musical America* (Nov. 28, 1925); "several preludes": interview with Gitta Gradova, *Musical Courier* (Dec. 17, 1925); "charming": "Weidig Composition Class Presents Remarkable Program . . . Several Young Composers Well Known in Chicago and a Few Throughout the Country," *Musical Leader* (May 14, 1925); "sensational": "Gitta Gradova Displays Rare Talent at Piano. Scarcely 20, Her Aeolian Hall Recital Is Made Noticeable by Individual Qualities," *New York Herald Tribune*, Dec. 14, 1925, p. 14; "most daringly modern": "Gitta Gradova Delights," *Musical Leader* (Dec. 2, 1926): 16.

14. "the six and a half": interview with VF by Andrea Olmstead, April 29, 1978, for ISAM.

15. "saving": letter to author, Oct. 5, 1984; visit with Herz: interview of DR by Vivian Perlis, March 18, 1970.

16. "magical force" and "record": Rita Mead, *Henry Cowell's New Music 1925–1935: The Society, the Music Editions and the Recordings* (Ann Arbor: UMI Editions, 1981), 47.

17. "regeneration": DR, "Djane Lavoie-Herz and Her Work," *Musical Observer* (1926), undated clipping from Tristan Hearst; "as a[n] homage" and "composed the first": interview with DR by Sorrel Hays for the author, March 19, 1984; on Herz's underwriting: letter from DR to Edgard Varèse, March 7 [1928] in the Department of Special Collections and University Archives, Stanford University Libraries.

18. "idol": letter from RC to CS, Jan. 18, 1931, MS; "immersed": letter from RC to CS, April 21, 1931, MS; "to feel his beauty": RCd, Nov. 9, 1928; "suddenly realized": RCd, [Nov. 15], 1927.

19. "blends all": RCd, Nov. 11, 1928; for his views see DR, "The Dissonant in Art," in *Art as Release of Power* (Carmel, Calif.: Hamsa Publications, 1930), 1-22. *The Rebirth of Hindu Music* (1928; rpt., New York: Samuel Weiser, 1979), 75, discusses "tonalism as musical feudalism."

20. "scorned": letter from RC to CS, Jan. 18, 1931, MS; "ossified": Robert Morgan, "Secret Languages: The Roots of Musical Modernism," *Critical Inquiry* (March 1984): 449.

21. "The mind" and "bit of": letter from Martha Beck Carragan to MG, Sept. 5, 1983.

22. "I like": RCd, July 26, 1929; "contact with": interview with Martha Beck Carragan by Rita H. Mead, May 22, 1975.

23. Mead, *Henry Cowell's New Music*, 88.

24. "pale young man": "Elbows and Knuckles—Otherwise Conventional," *Musical Leader* (March 6, 1924): 233; on Hart, Schaeffner and Marx: interview with Gitta Gradova Cottle, Sept. 8, 1984.

25. "Goossens": Dora Hagemeyer, "Modern Music Discussed by a Modern Composer," *Carmel Cymbal* Nov. 17, 1926, p. 6.

26. "completely natural": quoted by SRC in an interview, Dec. 14, 1982; "vital": Henry Cowell, "Music," *The Americana Annual: An Encyclopedia of Current Events*, ed. A.H. McDannald (New York: Americana Corp., 1928), 543–44; "Her work": Henry Cowell, "Compositores Modernos de Los Estados Unidos," *Musicalia* 1 (Nov.–Dec. 1928): 124–27.

27. A list of world premieres and American premieres is in the commemorative catalogue *Chicago Symphony Orchestra Celebrates Ninety Years, 1891–1980* (Chicago: Chicago Symphony Orchestra, 1980), 20, 23.

28. "I discovered": letter from RCS to Nicolas Slonimsky, Jan. 29, 1933.

29. "These recordings": interview with Alfred Frankenstein by MG, March 16, 1968.

30. "myopically local," "in four," and "anyone": Alfred Frankenstein, *Syncopating Saxophones* (Chicago: Robert R. Ballou, 1925), 81, 90, 37.

31. "a little jazz dance": RCd, [Sept. 11], 1927; "shimmy": RCd, [Sept. 3], 1927; letter [undated] from Alfred Frankenstein to RC discusses the Diaphonic Suite.

32. "liked Alfred": RCd, July 24, 1929; "repressed": letter from RC to Alice Burrow, RCd, July 13, 1929; "little reserve": interview of Alfred Frankenstein by MG, March 16, 1968.

33. On Frankenstein: Rita Mead, "A Conversation with Alfred Frankenstein about Henry Cowell's New Music," in *A Celebration of American Music: Words and Music in Honor of H. Wiley Hitchcock*, ed. Richard Crawford, R. Allen Lott, and Carol J. Oja (Ann Arbor: Univ. of Mich. Press, 1990), 320.

34. "The skill": letter to the author from Helga Sandburg, Nov. 21, 1984; "we all loved": telephone interview with Margaret Sandburg, Dec. 3, 1988; "boisterous" and "Mrs. Sandburg's": letter from RC to VF, Sept. 27, 1930, VF; "ethereal": RCd, [Sept. 9], 1927; "he comes": RCd, Dec. 15, 1927.

35. "sort of added": letter from Carl Sandburg to Tom Stokes, Dec. 26, 1947, in *The Letters of Carl Sandburg*, ed. Herbert Mitgang (New York: Harcourt, Brace and World, 1968), 465; "spontaneity" and "ran like": letter from RC to CS, Nov. 10, 1930, MS; "see this Amazon": interview with PS by Penny McJunkin Niven for the Carl Sandburg Oral History Project, March 18, 1983; "Chinese face": interview of Alfred Frankenstein with MG, March 16, 1968.

36. "My first appreciation": letter from RCS to Carl Sandburg, June 25, 1942; "You get me started": letter from RCS to Carl Sandburg, July 1947.

37. "steadily increasing interest": Edmund Wilson, quoted in Michael Kammen, *Mystic Chords of Memory: The Transformation of Tradition in American Culture* (New York: Alfred A. Knopf, 1991), 429; "constructive memory" and "Who in hell": Niven, *Carl Sandburg* (New York: Charles Scribner's Sons, 1991), 449.

38. "there in the lamplight": RCd, Dec. 11, 1927.

39. The "Russian Lullaby" is not dated, but the poem by Untermeyer appeared in his collection *Burning Bush* (New York: Harcourt, Brace, 1928), 109.

40. "having set them" and "my mind wasn't": interview with SRC, Dec. 1, 1987; "the emotional discovery": Kammen, *Mystic Chords of Memory*, 299; "ragbag of strips": Carl Sandburg, *The American Songbag*, vii; "landmark": interview of PS by Penny McJunkin Niven, March 18, 1983; "were always singing": Carol J. Oja, "Composer with a Conscience: Elie Siegmeister in Profile," *American Music* 6 (1988): 169.

41. Arnold Rampersad, *The Life of Langston Hughes*, vol. 1: *1902–1941: I, Too, Sing America* (New York: Oxford Univ. Press, 1986), 29; "right to search": RCd, [Sept. 11], 1927.

42. The poems were titled "Lightly Sprinting," winter 1928; and "Ever So Lightly Leaning," 1927.

43. "I pick": RCd, [Sept. 28], 1927; "His constant": RCd, Aug. 26, 1927.

44. "One can draw": RCd, [Sept. 2], 1927; "seem to have": RCd, [Sept. 3], 1927; "Last spring": RCd, Sept. 11, 1927.

45. "dreaming, feeling": "Filling the Lake," undated poem from the 1920s; "Earth will": RCd, Sept. 29, 1929.

46. "Sandburg": RCd, July 26, 1929.

47. "I am very": letter from CrC to ClC and RC, Jan. 4, 1925, CWH; catalogue of the American Conservatory of Music, 1925–26, pp. 29–30; "The teaching": RCS, autobiographical sketch, ca. 1947; twenty pupils: RCd, Nov. [11], 1927.

48. the crowd: interview with VF, April 18, 1989; "with pride" and "disgusted": RCd, Oct. 26, 1927; "compelled": letter from RC to GF, Nov. 19, 1929; "at night": RC, autobiographical sketch, 1933.

49. "selfish": RCd, Sept. 1, 1927; "extremely modest": interview with Alfred Frankenstein by MG, March 16, 1968; "annoyed": RCd, Nov. 9, 1928.

50. "One day": interview with VF by Elizabeth Wood and Ruth Julius, May 1977.

51. "their profuseness" and "how very late": RCd, [Sept. 9], 1927.

52. Composers' Night concert, Pan Pipes (SAI newsletter), May 1926; information supplied to author by Ethel M. Bullard, Director, SAI Memorial Library, Oak Park, Illinois, June 24, 1986; annual recital: "Weidig's Composition Class Produces Works of Merit," *Musical Leader* (May 27, 1926): 19.

53. "the percussion": RCS, autobiographical sketch, 1933. Chicago Allied Arts was founded as a music and dance collaborative for new work in 1924 by the dancers Adolph Bolm and Ruth Page and the composer John Alden Carpenter. A program for a concert on Oct. 24, 1926, by Chicago Allied Arts describes the event as "New Ballets and Music for Small Orchestra." This program is located in papers for Chicago Allied Arts and Eric De Lamarter at the Newberry Library.

54. "bitter": RCd, [Aug. 26], 1927; letter from CrC to RC, Sept. 1, 1925, discusses an operation that he hopes will "correct the trouble with your arms," CWH; "depression": RCd, [Nov. 2], 1927.

55. Letter from CaC to ClC, Oct. 2, 1927, CWH.

56. "sunny": interview with Martha Beck Carragan, July 13, 1983; "children": RCd, [Sept. 25], 1927; "the thin": RCd, [Sept. 20], 1927.

57. "younger friends": letter from Storm Bull (Elwind's son) to the author, Aug. 13, 1986; "imbued": interview with VF, April 18, 1989; Burrow (1889–1960) was described as a "singer, reader and writer of plays" in "A Versatile Artist's Activities," *Musical Leader* (Oct. 1, 1931): 14.

58. "ability": RCd, [Sept. 20], 1927; Darrow and Hecht are mentioned in RCd, [Nov. 26], 1927.

59. For details on the Chicago Arts Club, see Howard Pollack, *Skyscraper Lullaby: The Life and Music of John Alden Carpenter* (Washington, D.C.: Smithsonian Press, 1995), 383–87.

60. "sponsored": "Leading Musicians of Chicago Plan to Encourage Contemporary Composers," *Musical Courier* (Jan. 5, 1928): 44; "There is": Edward Moore, "Modern Music Society Offers Its First Bill," *Chicago Herald Tribune*, Feb. 9, 1928, p. 18. See also Eugene Sticker, "With the Musicians . . . New Music," *Chicago Daily Journal*, Feb. 9, 1928, p. 14.

61. "already widely": *Musical Leader* (June 6, 1929): 67; "very talented": interview

with VF, April 18, 1989; Carol J. Oja, "The Copland-Sessions Concerts," *Musical Quarterly* 65 (April 1979): 213.

62. Aaron Copland and Vivian Perlis, *Copland: 1900 through 1942* (New York: St. Martin's Press, 1984), 146. Other works included Copland's Two Pieces for String Quartet, Robert Delaney's Violin and Piano Sonata, and a Quintet for Piano and Strings by Quincy Porter.

63. "Buhlig": letter from Copland to Sessions, April 15, 1928, in *Correspondence of Roger Sessions*, ed. Andrea Olmstead (Boston: Northeastern Univ. Press, 1991), 104; "anarchist": Aaron Copland, Notes for "Lectures: Masterpieces of Modern Music," Lecture VIII: "Prometheus (Mysticism of Scriabine), listing 'Detractors, Many' and Admirers, Dane Rudhyar, Ruth Crawford etc." Copland Collection, Library of Congress; on the choice of preludes, the program does not list them by number; however, the tempo markings as given in a review of the concert by Nicolas Slonimsky suggests this. I thank Carol Oja for the information on Copland.

64. "very charming": Rita Mead, *Henry Cowell's New Music*, 24; "composer's pianist": "Richard Buhlig Backs Modernism . . . Delves into It with Soulful Glee . . . Finds a Real Tune in Cowell Work," *Musical Courier* (Jan. 12, 1928) in clippings file on Buhlig at NYPL; "landmarks": Nancy Wolbert, "Richard Buhlig, a Concert Pianist: His Career and Influence in the Twentieth Century" (M.A. thesis, California State University, 1978), 111–12.

65. "individuality": *Musical Leader* (May 17, 1928); "strange sonorities": Winthrop Tryon, "Music of the Hour," *Christian Science Monitor*, May 10, 1928, p. 10; "running a race": Charles Isaacson, *New York Telegraph*, quoted in Nancy Wolbert, "Richard Buhlig," p. 90; "naked and ashamed": W. J. Henderson, "American Works Presented," *New York Sun*, May 7, 1928, p. 19, quoted in Rita Mead, *Henry Cowell's New Music*, p. 103. For comparisons to Chopin and Debussy, see B.F., "Music, Modern Style," *Musical America* (May 19, 1928): 29; for comparisons to Scriabin and Schoenberg, see Edward Burlinghame Hill, "The Young Composer's Movement," *Modern Music* 5 (May–June 1928): 32–34; for other reviews see Olin Downes, "More New Music," *New York Times*, May 8, 1928.

66. Nicolas Slonimsky, "Young Modernists Hoe Their Own Row," *Boston Evening Transcript* (May 11, 1928).

67. "How much": RCd, [Sept. 8], 1927; "Do I know": RCd, Nov. 1, 1927.

68. "What an inconceivably": RCd, [Nov. 11], 1927.

5. *"Trees of Sound and Color": Music, 1924–1929*

1. "eclectic tendency": Paul Rosenfeld, *An Hour with American Music* (Philadelphia: J.B. Lippincott, 1929), 100; "International Composers Guild": Louise Varèse, *Varèse: A Looking-Glass Diary*, vol. I: *1883–1928* (New York: W. W. Norton, 1972), 167; for a discussion of Crawford's music from this period, see David Nicholls, "The Music of Ruth Crawford Seeger: A Study in Advanced Compositional Techniques" (Ph.D. dissertation, St. John's College, 1982).

2. "tonal centricity": letter from RCS to Edgard Varèse, May 29, 1948; "profundity": Henry Cowell, "Compositores Modernos de Los Estados Unidos," *Musicalia* 1 (Nov.–Dec. 1928): 124–27; "sublime, strident dissonances": letter from RC to Alice Burrow, Oct. 23, 1929, quoted in RCd.

3. "I heard much": RCd, May 3, 1930, MS; "we wrote": interview with VF, Nov. 29, 1984; "must have read": letter from DR to the author, Oct. 5, 1984.

4. DR, *Rebirth of Hindu Music*, 18. See also "The Mystic's Living Tone," *Modern Music* 7 (1929–30): 32–36.

5. Nicholls, "The Music of Ruth Crawford Seeger," 7.

6. "light, all light": RCd, July 23, 1929.

7. "beautifully made" to "Ivesian": Alfred Frankenstein, "A Remarkable New New-Music Group," *High Fidelity* 26 (Jan. 1976): 80; "I would": telephone interview with VF, Jan. 21, 1989. For CS's remarks, see Ray Wilding-White, "Remembering Ruth Crawford Seeger: An Interview with Charles and Peggy Seeger," *American Music* 6 (1988): 445.

8. Eugene Flemm, "The Preludes for Piano of Ruth Crawford Seeger" (Ph.D. dissertation, University of Cincinnati, 1987); "blending chords": DR, *Moments*, preface.

9. "it was very" and "if that is": RCd, Oct. 20, 1928.

10. "scorner of titles": letter from RC to CS, Oct. 17, 1930, MS; "personal element" and "too material": RCd, Sept. [2], 1927.

11. "Ives is": RCd, New York, Feb. 1930.

12. "eternal reversion": *The Wisdom of Laotse*, trans. and ed. Lin Yutang (New York: Modern Library, 1948), 108–10.

13. "awe": RCd, Nov. 25, 1927.

14. "asked her": interview with Martha Beck Carragan, July 11, 1983.

15. thematic development: RCd, Sept. 13, 1927. "I read the first act of Honegger's King David and feel that one of my difficulties, that of developing my themes, is also a weakness of his. . . . But isn't this typical of most modern music?"

16. "literally fell": RCd, Nov. 1, 1927; species counterpoint: RCd, Sept. 19, 1927. In this entry, Crawford discusses a visit with Guy Maier, "who speaks at length of counterpoint and the slovenliness of American composition."

17. "dissonant counterpoint" described generally in Marion Bauer, *Twentieth-Century Music* (New York: G. P. Putnam's, 1923), 13, 118–19.

18. Letter from RC to Alice Burrow, Oct. 23, 1929, quoted in RCd.

19. RC to VF, Nov. 7, 1929, VF.

6. "A Career or Life?"

1. "feminization": Deems Taylor, "Music," in Harold E. Stearns, ed., *Civilization in the United States: An Inquiry by Thirty Americans* (New York: Harcourt, Brace & Co., 1922), 205; "distinguishing virility": Irving Weill, "The American Scene Changes," *Modern Music* 6 (1929): 7–8; "emotional life": R. M. Knerr, "Noted Feminist Defends Women's Place in Music," *Musical America* (Jan. 21, 1922): 5.

2. "attitude": letter from Edith Borroff to the author, Nov. 24, 1991; on the poses, see Chapter 3; on the Prix de Rome: *Musical Leader* (Nov. 22, 1922): 484. Leo Sowerby won the prize in 1922.

3. "We didn't": interview with VF, Nov. 12, 1982; "very thick-skinned": interview with Arthur Berger, May 2, 1990; "I don't": interview with Martha Beck Carragan, July 13, 1983.

4. "ardent feminist": interview with CS by Ray Wilding-White, Sept. 17, 1976. (This is the source of but not identical to the published review in *American Music*.)

5. On the ambivalence of the "modern young woman": see Dorothy Dunbar Bromley, "Feminism, New Style," *Harpers Magazine* 155 (Oct. 1927), discussed by Sara Evans in *Born For Liberty: A History of Women in America* (New York: Free Press, 1989), 155.

6. Adrienne Fried Block and Carol Neuls-Bates, *Women in American Music: A Bibliography of Music and Literature* (Westport, Conn.: Greenwood Press, 1979), xxv.

7. Ruth Klauber Friedman, *History of the Musicians Club of Women* (Chicago, 1975), 28–29; "it would": letter from Martha Beck Carragan to the author, Dec. 19, 1988; "first woman": Carol Neuls-Bates, "Women's Orchestras in the U.S., 1925–1945," in *Women Making Music*, ed. Jane Bowers and Judith Tick (Urbana: Univ. of Illinois Press, 1986), 350–51, 357.

8. "vented" to "mysterious": RCd, Aug. [26], 1927.

9. "to work" to "for all": RCd, Aug. 1927.

10. "thought her": letter from RC to CS, Oct. 10, 1931, MS; "trivial news": RCd, Aug. [26], 1927; "inspired" to "truly remarkable": RCd, Aug 30, 1927.

11. "female": Linda Gordon, "What's New in Women's History," in Teresa De Lauretis, ed., *Feminist Studies, Critical Studies* (Bloomington: Indiana Univ. Press, 1986), 30.

12. "Stella, the dignified": RCd, Feb. 8, 1928; "on the threshold": "Couple Found Slain in Car Near Paris, Both Americans," *New York Times*, April 24, 1927, p. 1, 5; in addition to the previous article, see also "Meredith Shooting Laid to Quarrel" and "Paris Tragedy Laid to Broken Troth," *New York Times*, April 25 and 26, 1927; "Kills Chicago Girl and Self in Paris Tryst," *Chicago Sunday Tribune*, April 24, 1927, p. 1; Roberts engagement: telephone interview with Edith Borroff, Nov. 9, 1991.

13. "sensed at once" and "She said": RCd, Feb. 8, 1928.

14. "gripped" and "what great": RCd, Feb. 8, 1928.

15. "Count Von B": interview with VF, Nov. 29, 1984.

16. "incredible" to "Such a thing": RCd, March 11, 1928; "Any man": RCd, March 25, 1928.

17. Herz letter: RCd, March [14], 1928; "longed for": RCd, March 25, 1928.

18. "received in": interview with VF, April 18, 1989; Djane coming to dinner: interview with CaC and Catherine Crawford by MG, March 18, 1968.

19. Date of operation: letter from ClC to VF, June 8, 1928, CWH.

20. "to read": RCd, July 14, 1928; "Tonight": RCd, Aug. 1, 1928.

21. "I find": RCd, Aug. 1928.

22. "I am getting": RCd, Nov. 7, 1928.

23. Undated performances by Corelli, Rudhyar, and Weisshaus in a performances list among her biographical papers; Weidig recital: "Weidig's Composition Class Gives Program," *Musical Leader* (June 6, 1929): 67.

24. "lack of skillful": RCd, Sept. 5, 1927; "great limitations" and "dressmaker": RCd, Aug. [27], 1927.

25. "great musicianship": letter from RC to VF, Sept. 27, 1930, VF.

26. Opinions of Cowell and Frankenstein: interview with SRC, Dec. 14, 1982; Cowell and Seeger: CS-UCLA, p. 99.

27. "[W]hen an offer": RC, autobiographical sketch, ca. 1947; "feeling of owning": letter from RC to CS, Sept. 7, 1930, MS; Sandburg vacation: letter from RC to VF, June 24, 1929, VF.

28. date of arrival: register for summer 1929 from the papers of the MacDowell Colony, LC; "Mrs. MacDowell": RCd, July 7, 1929.

29. "studio": RCd, July 2, 1929; "Tom Thumb": RCd, July 11, 1929.

30. RC to VF, Sept. 15, 1929.

31. List of artists in residence the summer of 1929: letter to the author from the administrative offices of the MacDowell Colony, Inc., Dec. 5, 1988.

32. Peter Hugh Reed, "The Sutro Sisters Come to Town," *Musical America* (Dec. 1, 1928): 15; "sewing-machine sisters": RCd, July 25, 1929.

33. "first work": RCd, July 1, 1929; "glorious": RCd, July 2, 1929; "more power":

RCd, July 12, 1929; "worked with": RCd, July 13, 1929; "the best" and "most genuine": RCd, July 23, 1929.

34. "The entire setting" and "It hurts": RCd, July 23, 1929.

35. "had no intention": Edward Dahlberg, *The Confessions of Edward Dahlberg* (New York: George Braziller, 1971), 238–39.

36. "The environment": letter from RC to Alice Burrow, July 23, 1929, quoted in RCd.

37. "He was mad": interview with VF, Nov. 29, 1984; "liked him": RCd, July 16, 1929.

38. "The dear": RCd, July 7, 1929; "nice": telephone interview with Gene Shuford, Feb. 2, 1984; "She didn't": interview with Martha Beck Carragan, July 13, 1983.

39. "Always": letter from RC to Alice Burrow, July 23, 1929, quoted in RCd.

40. "dear Gene": letter from RC to Alice Burrow, July 23, 1929.

41. On attitudes toward premarital sex: Banner, *Women in Modern America*, 150–51; "puritanical": RCd, July 26, 1929; "I cannot": RCd, July 27, 1929.

42. "second self": RCd, July 31, 1929.

43. "if I shall": RCd, Aug. 12, 1929.

44. "sex act": Banner, *Women in Modern America*, 144–45; conversation between Bauer and RC from RCd, Aug. 16, 1929.

45. "abusing" and "Sublimation": RCd, Aug. 16, 1929; "You have": RCd, Aug. 21, 1929.

46. RCd, excerpt from letter to Gene Shuford, Aug. 12, 1929.

47. See, for example, the cover portrait of Bauer for the *Musical Leader*, May 12, 1927.

48. "early aspiration": quoted in Christine Ammer, *Unsung: A History of Women in American Music* (Westport, Conn.: Greenwood Press, 1980), 127; statistics from Marion Bauer and Claire Reis, "Twenty-five Years with the League of Composers," *Musical Quarterly* 34 (Jan. 1948): 1–14; "this does not": Henderson quoted in Irving Bazelon, "Woman with a Symphony," *Baton of Phi Beta Fraternity* 30 (March 1951): 6; details about Bauer from Ammer, *Unsung*, 286.

49. *Toccata in Four Piano Pieces*, op. 21, Nos. 1–4 (New York: Cos Cob Press, 1930); "affinities" and "She draws": RCd, Aug. 16, 1929.

50. "final week": RCd, Aug. 1927; "Courage": RCd, Aug. 16, 1929.

51. "such relief" to "I am writing": RCd, Aug. 16, 1929.

52. "worry about" to "It is a question": RCd, Aug. 1, 1929.

53. Lorine Pruette and Iva Lowther Peters, eds., *Women Workers Through the Depression* (New York: Macmillan, 1934), 4; Lois Scharf, *To Work and to Wed: Female Employment, Feminism, and the Great Depression* (Westport, Conn.: Greenwood Press, 1980), 22, 27, 41.

54. Copland and Perlis, *Aaron Copland*, I: 164 and 380n.

55. "the 1920s": Laurine Elkins-Marlow, "American Women as Orchestral Composers, 1890–1960," typescript monograph quoted with permission of the author.

56. "All the poetic": RCd, July 1929; "I do believe": letter dated Aug. 12, quoted in RCd, Aug. 1929.

57. "New England" to "white sails": letter from RC to VF, Sept. 15, 1929, VF; "I am the gull": RCd, Sept. 29, 1929.

7. One West 68th Street

1. Details of the view: letter from RC to Carl Sandburg, March 8, 1920, UI; On Steinway B: tape made by CS for MG, July 28, 1967.

2. "undoubtedly": Oliver Daniel, *Stokowski: A Counterpoint of View* (New York: Dodd, Mead, 1982), 300; on the league: *The League of Composers: A Record of Performances and a Survey of General Activities from 1923 to 1935* (New York, 1935).

3. Edmund Wilson, "The Problem of Higher Jazz," Jan. 13, 1926, reprinted in *The American Earthquake: A Documentary of the Twenties and Thirties* (New York: Farrar, Straus and Giroux, 1980), 112–15; Otto Ortman, "What Is Wrong with Modern Music?" *The American Mercury* 19 (March 1930): 372–76; "an American music": Paul Rosenfeld, *An Hour with American Music* (1929; rpt. ed. Westport Conn: Hyperion Press, 1979), 26.

4. "get into" and "wasting time": interview with CS by Andrea Olmstead, July 7, 1977.

5. "cool tombs": letter from RC to Carl Sandburg, March 10, 1930; "awed by" to "startlingly impressionistic": letter from RC to VF and Rose Neistein, Sept. 15, 1929, VF.

6. "disappointing" to "Alice": letter quoted in RCd, Oct. 1929.

7. Concert information from Program of Elizabeth Sprague Coolidge Festival of Music, Coolidge Collection, Library of Congress; "spiritual singing" to "even the shade": letter to Alice Burrow quoted in RCd, Oct. 1929.

8. "influentials" to "are plastered": letter to Alice Burrow quoted in RCd, Oct. 1929.

9. "My dear": RCd, Oct. 17, 1929; "like mad" to "Lesbian subject": letter from RC to CS, Feb. [14], 1931, MS; "I am Marion's": RCd, Feb. 1930; "I constantly": RCd, Oct. 1929.

10. "In the fourteen" to "It would": RCd, Oct. 1929.

11. "We walk" to "carried away": RCd, Oct. 17, 1929.

12. Information about Blanche Walton from an interview with Marion Walton, Feb. 24, 1984, and an obituary, *New York Times*, July 19, 1963.

13. "she played": interview with Marion Walton, Feb. 24, 1984.

14. "Gala evening" to "dear European": letter to Alice [Burrow] in RCd, Nov. 22, 1929; "dear European" and "Ara stands": RCd, Oct. 1929.

15. "she was tired": interview with Marion Walton, Feb. 24, 1984; "they could forgather": CS-UCLA, p. 168.

16. "The one": BW, "Only a Sketch," typescript memoir in the Blanche Walton collection, NYPL.

17. "greying" to "Mother looked": interview with Marion Walton, Feb. 24, 1984.

18. "young woman": BW, "Only a Sketch," 4; "I told": RCd, Oct. 1929.

19. "without knowing": interview with DR by Sorrel Hays, March 19, 1984, for the author.

20. "major" to "begun work": RC, application for a Guggenheim Fellowship, Nov. 14, 1929, p. 5.

21. "to make" and "some valuable": RCd, Nov. 1929.

22. "short": RCd, Oct. 1929.

23. "tried very hard": Marilyn Ziffrin, *Carl Ruggles: Composer, Painter, and Storyteller* (Urbana: Univ. of Illinois Press, 1984), 3; "Yankee Blues": MacDonald Smith Moore, *Yankee Blues* (Bloomington: Indiana Univ. Press, 1985); "You are American": RCd, Dec. 5, 1929.

24. "could bob": "Orchestra Posts Opened to Women . . . Conductorless Symphony Group Will Offer Them Vacancies in the Strings," *New York Times*, Aug. 23, 1929, p. 11.

25. "an astounding": letter from RC to VF, Feb. 12, 1930, VF.

26. "Too many": RCd, Dec. 7, 1929.

27. "grandly glorious": letter to Alice Burrow quoted in RCd, Oct. 1929.

28. "belated" to "terribly depressed": RCd, Dec. 1929.

29. "How I": letter from Marian MacDowell to BW, Dec. 20, 1929, NYPL; "The crowd": letter from BW to RC, Jan. 7, 1931, NYPL.

30. "the entire" to "Observers": RCd, Dec. 1929.

31. "very receptive": CS, audio tape of "Recollections" made for MG, July 28, 1967; "there's one thing": interview of CS by Judith Rosen, Jan. 18, 1972.

32. Marion Bauer, "Ruth Crawford's Compositions Heard," *Musical Leader* (Dec. 19, 1929): 10.

33. "The reception": RCd, Dec. 1929.

34. "ever-growing": "Women Composers Heard. Women's University Glee Club Gives Recital at Engineering Hall," *New York Times*, Dec. 17, 1929, p. 29; See also "Women's Glee Club Heard," *New York Herald Tribune*, Dec. 17, 1929, p. 23; "Doria with Women's Glee Club," *Musical Leader* (Dec. 26,1929): 15.

35. Malcolm Cowley, *Exile's Return* (New York: Viking Press, 1951), 301.

36. "grand" and "busy on counterpoint": letter quoted in RCd, Dec. 1929; "only God": RCd, Dec. 1929.

37. "is tall": RCd, Oct. 1929; "the quintessential": Ann Pescatello, *Charles Seeger: A Life in American Music* (Pittsburgh: Univ. of Pittsburgh Press, 1992), 3.

38. "German": Pescatello, *Charles Seeger*, 23; "amusing": interview with Marion Walton, Feb. 24, 1984.

39. "hyperidealism": CS-UCLA, p. 54; "Endymion" from *Seven Songs* is recorded on *Music of Charles Seeger* (Berkeley: 1750 Arch Records S-1801, 1984).

40. On Seeger's place in musicology: Claude V. Palisca, "The Scope of American Musicology," in Frank Harrison, Mantle Hood, and Claude Palisca, eds., *Musicology* (Englewood Cliffs, N.J.: Prentice-Hall, 1963), 96.

41. "purify the style": tape made by CS for MG, March 16, 1968.

42. "I reached": Pescatello, *Charles Seeger*, 77; "tendency to view": Daniel Singal, "Towards a Definition of American Modernism," *American Quarterly* 39 (Spring 1987): 9.

43. "musical Tower of Babel": CS, "Style and Manner in Modern Composition," 424.

44. On this period see CS-UCLA, p. 173; "depths": interview with Andrea Olmstead, July 7, 1977 for ISAM; emotional breakdown: Pescatello, *Charles Seeger*, 79–80; information about teaching from catalogues for the Institute for Musical Art, 1921–29.

45. "literary work": Harvard Class of 1908, Quindecennial Report (1923), p. 482; "Music is": CS, "Music in the American University," *Educational Review* 66 (September 1923): 97.

46. "new more systematic": David Nicholls, *American Experimental Music, 1890-1940* (Cambridge: Cambridge Univ. Press, 1990), 95-96; Cowell on Seeger as explorer: "Charles Seeger," in Henry Cowell, ed., *American Composers on American Music: A Symposium* (1933; rpt., New York: Frederick Ungar, 1962).

47. "not-very-high" and "based mostly": tape made on CS for MG, July 28, 1967.

48. "Henry said" and "that's what": interview of CS by Rita Mead, Nov. 15, 1974.

49. arrangement of lessons: CS-UCLA, p. 169. The letter from CS to RC is no longer extant but is referred to by RC, letter to VF, Sept. 26, 1929, VF; "After your": RC to CS, Sept. 26, 1930, MS; "was so furious": interview of PS by MS, Dec. 8, 1982.

50. Information about foyer: letter from RC to CS, Oct. 9, 1930; "buxom": CS-UCLA, p. 169.

51. "would appear" to "You were": letter from RC to CS, Oct. 9, 1930, MS.

52. "genteel": CS-UCLA, p. 169.

53. "critique": MG-RCS, p. 64; "too diffuse": CS, tape made for MG, July 28, 1967; on Suite no. 1, "came to him": interview of CS by Karen Cardullo, June 11, 1978.

54. "Henry" and "almost any composer": Pescatello, *Charles Seeger*, 78; "they didn't particularly": Vivian Perlis, ed., *Charles Ives Remembered* (New York: W. W. Norton, 1976), 146; "very poor" to "he was a flop": letter from CS to Barbara Krader, Nov. 12, 1960; "almost hopelessly" and "Sinfonietta": interview of CS with Rita Mead, Nov. 15, 1974, NYPL.

55. "freer": RCd, Oct. 29, 1928; "pattern": RCd, July 13, 1929.

56. "bits" to "Would you not": letter from RC to VF, Nov. 7, 1929, VF.

57. "breath of": letter from CS to RC, March 1, 1931, MS.

58. "off-accents": letter from RC to VF, Feb. 7, 1930, VF.

59. On Schoenberg's Quartet no. 3: RCd, [mid-]Aug. 1929; on *Pierrot lunaire* in 1928: letter from RC to Carl Sandburg, March 8, 1930; IU; Crawford's attendance: letter from RC to CS, Jan. 30, 1931, MS; "had the distinction": Oscar Thompson, "Variations and the Season's New Music," *Modern Music* 6 (1929–30): 28–31; "small motives": RCd, Feb. 14, 1930.

60. "We discover": RCd, Feb. 1930; "grown too many": letter from RC to VF, Feb. 7, 1930, VF.

61. CS's comments about Weiss's paper and the assessment of Schoenberg are in a letter from CS to RC, April 30, 1931, MS.

62. "assignments" and "showed my point": video interview of CS by Vivian Perlis, July 19, 1977, Yale; "departing from" to "musical character": interview of CS by MG, July 28, 1967.

63. "Charles Seeger's": letter to VF, Feb. 7, 1930, VF; "airplane" and "Sitting there": letter from RC to CS, Sept. 26, 1930, MS.

64. "five feet": Ugo Ara quoted in RCd, Oct. 23, 1929; "cold almost": letter from RC to VF, Feb. 7, 1930, VF; "Anyone who can": RCd, Feb. 1930.

65. "one of the most exciting": CS-UCLA, p. 174; "could almost say": CS-UCLA, p. 187.

66. "she never": tape made by CS for MG, March 19, 1968; "imitator": interview of CS by Rita Mead, Nov. 15, 1974; "she had studied": interview of CS by MG, July 28, 1967; "There is no": interview with VF, Nov. 29, 1984.

67. "turning point": letter from RC to Nicolas Slonimsky, Jan. 29, 1933.

68. "this young immigrant": interview of CS by MG, July 28, 1967; "You told me": letter from RC to CS, Nov. 11, 1930, MS.

69. Details of attendees: New York Musicological Society Bulletin No. 1, Nov. 1931; on the four treatises: Daniel Schuyler Augustine, "Four Theories of Music in the United States, 1900–1950: Cowell, Yasser, Partch, Schillinger" (Ph.D. dissertation, University of Texas, 1979).

70. "because only women's clubs": CS-UCLA, p.191; "we live in a world": Linda Kerber, "Separate Spheres, Female Worlds, Woman's Place: The Rhetoric of Women's History," *Journal of American History* 75 (1988): 39; "expert stenographer": CS-UCLA, p. 190.

71. "irate" and "I turn": RCd, Feb. 22, 1930.

72. "might as well" to "Ruth hasn't": RCd, Feb. 22, 1930; "your integrity compelled": letter from CS to RC, Oct. 23, 1930, MS "Charlie should have": RCd, Feb. 22, 1930.

73. on the admission of women: CS-UCLA, p. 191; "plan seemed": letter from RC to VF, March 15, 1930, VF; "thrills me": RCd, Feb. 22, 1930.

74. On the distance between RC and CS after this incident: letter from CS to RC, April 21, 1931, MS; "very charming": CS-UCLA, p. 175; "All my life": letter from CS to RC, Oct. 23, 1930, MS; "marriage": video interview of CS by Vivian Perlis, July 10, 1979, Yale; request for divorce: Pescatello, *Charles Seeger*, p. 89.

75. Account of rehearsals and RC's reactions: RCd, Feb. 17, 1930; "fat, filthy": letter from Carl Ruggles to Adolph Weiss, May 31, 1930, included in William George, "Adolph Weiss" (Ph.D. dissertation, University of Iowa, 1971), 171; "Ives is": RCd, Feb. 1930.

76. On the reception: RCd, Feb. 1930. For details on Pazmor, see Mead, *Henry Cowell's New Music Society*, 242–46.

77. "swallowing opinions whole": RCd, Feb. 1930; "Have you heard": letter from RC to VF, Feb. 12, 1930, VF. The concert featured music by Jeffrey Mark, Robert Russell Bennett, Vladimir Dukelsky, Nino Rota, Henry Brant, and Robert Delany. Details are in Carol J. Oja, "The Copland-Sessions Concerts and Their Reception in the Contemporary Press," *Musical Quarterly* 65 (1979): 223.

78. "a season of distress" and "loves the instrument": RCd, April 1930.

79. "beautiful Guggenheim letter" to "for helping": letter from RC to Carl Sandburg, March 8, 1930, UI.

80. "It was attractive": Pro Musica, *Musical Courier* (March 15, 1930): 24; "Philharmonic Presents Beethoven and Pro Musica Does Not," *New York Evening Post*, March 10, 1930, p. 15. The concert also included Rudhyar's "Pentagram" for two pianos, Riegger's Study in Sonority arranged for ten violins, songs by Otto Luening, and Adolph Weiss's third string quartet.

81. "entirely tuneless": "A," in *Musical America* 50 (April 25, 1930): 32; "I do": letter from Radiana Pazmor to RC, March 16, 1935.

82. Accompanying Pazmor were D. Desarno on oboe; Stephanie Schehatowitsch and Imre Weisshaus, both pianists, were listed as well. Which of them played percussion is not clear.

83. On request for no applause: "Pan American Association of Composers," *Musical Courier* (May 3, 1930): 22; for concert programs, see Deane L. Root, "The Pan American Association of Composers (1928–1934)," *Yearbook for Inter-American Research* 7 (1972): 49–70. Works performed at this concert included Chavez, sonatina for violin and piano; Cowell, solo for violin; Weisshaus, piano suite; Fine, solo for oboe; Ives, Three Songs ("The New River," "Indians," "Ann Street"); Antheil, second piano sonata; Weiss, prelude. Other reviews include: "Pan American Association," *Musical America* 50 (May 10, 1930): 46; "Pan Americans Heard: Works of North and Central American Composers are Given," *New York Herald Tribune*, April 22, 1930. On Weisshaus: Ruth was sufficiently impressed by his performance to write a grotesquerie of the work—"It hypnotizes. It drugs. A slimy worm"—which later appeared in *The Carmelite* (Carmel, California), Aug. 7, 1930; "very extreme": "Pan American Association of Composers," *Musical Courier* (May 3, 1930): 22.

84. "Of course": letter from RC to VF, April 23, 1930, VF.

85. "playing the game": RCd, Feb. 17, 1930; "triple" to "was not": RCd, May 3, 1930.

86. "It was": interview of DR by Sorrel Hays for the author, March 19, 1984.

87. "Ruth Crawford, Winner of Guggenheim Award, to Make European Visit," *Musical America* 49 (May 10, 1929): 41.

88. "very brilliant": and "dictating": CS, tape of recollections for MG, July 28, 1967; "teaching of Ruth": CS-UCLA, p. 187; "very tentatively": interview of CS with

MG, Oct. 7, 1974; see CS, "On Dissonant Counterpoint," *Modern Music* 7 (June–July 1930): 25–31; *Tradition and Experiment in the New Music*, in *Studies in Musicology II: 1929–1979*, ed. Ann M. Pescatello (Berkeley: Univ. of California, 1994), 39–275. On summer schedule: letter from RC to VF, March 26, 1930, VF.

Chapter 8. *"The Curves in Our Friendship"*

1. Memoirs of Charles Louis Seeger, Sr., 1928–38, vol. III, pp. 576–77. This is an unpublished typescript, owned by members of the Seeger family.

2. Ancestors: CS-UCLA, p. 9; nickname: Memoirs of Charles Louis Seeger, Sr., vol. I, p. 249.

3. "general feeling": CS-UCLA, p. 13.

4. "marked by": Pescatello, *Charles Seeger*, 86; "since [1921]": Harvard Class of 1908, Twenty-fifth Anniversary Report, 1933, p. 629; "cooked for": CS-UCLA, p. 458; general background: Pescatello, *Charles Seeger*, 86–87. Charles III went to Loomis; John went to the Kent School; and Peter went to the Spring Hill School—their tuitions paid for in part by family friends.

5. "just one": interview with CS3, June 30, 1989; "as a friend": interview with PS by MS, Dec. 8, 1982.

6. Description of barn: interview of John Seeger by MS, Dec. 16, 1982.

7. "four hours straight": interview with PS by MS; "she put her": interview of CS by MG, Oct. 7, 1974.

8. Reference to Schillinger: letter from CS to RC, March 1, 1931, MS.

9. "our magnum opus": letter from CS to RC, Sept. 14, 1930; "including my name" and "Before another word": letter from RC to CS, Sept. 21, 1930, MS; "creative energy": interview of CS with MG, Oct. 7, 1974; "book that": interview of CS with MG, Oct. 7–8, 1974; "gave him enough": letter from CS to RC, Dec. 8, 1930, MS.

10. "You have": letter from BW to RC, summer 1930.

11. "She and Charlie": interview of Alfred Frankenstein with MG, March 16, 1968.

12. "Are you giving": letter from BW to RC, [summer 1930], MS.

13. "I remember": telephone interview with PS, March 12, 1983; "compositions" and "earnest, very straight": interview with John Seeger by MS, Dec. 16, 1982; "She'd joined a family": telephone interview with PS, June 25, 1983.

14. "we would open": interview with John Seeger by MS, Dec. 16, 1982.

15. "Such a lovely two months" and "You do give": letter from RC to CS, Jan. 7, 1931; "one of the boys": letter from RC to CS, Jan. 5, 1931; "natural kind": letter from RC to CS, Jan. 7, 1931, MS.

16. The continuation of work: interview of CS by MG, July 28, 1967; "During those four months": letter from RC to VF, Sept. 27, 1930, VF.

17. "two foot-sore": undated letter, ca. late July 1930 from BW to RC, Yale.

18. "You knew": letter from BW to RC, Oct. 3, 1930, MS; on the Walton-Seeger-Crawford triangle: letter from BW to RC, Oct. 3, 1930, MS; "Ruth let": interview of CS by MG, Oct. 7, 1974.

19. "We stopped": interview of CS with MG, Oct. 7, 1974.

20. "Do you know": letter from CS to RC, April 21,1931, MS.

21. "couldn't face": interview of CS with MG, Oct. 7, 1974; "it seemed": letter from RC to CS, Aug. 23, 1930, MS.

22. "first woman": interview of CS3, June 30, 1989; "[O]ur intellects": letter from CS to RC, Jan. 5, 1931, MS.

23. "crazy child" and "proud to look": letter from RC to CS, Jan. 18, 1931; "unique experience": letter from RC to CS, Nov. 11, 1930; "so deeply thankful": letter from RC to CS, Oct. 30, 1930, MS.

24. "you and I": letter from RC to CS, Nov. 2, 1930, MS.

25. "During past": letter from RC to CS, Nov. 2, 1930, MS.

26. "my fundamental": letter from CS to RC, Aug. 22, 1930; "end in itself": letter from CS to RC, Sept. 3, 1930; "thought of that": letter from CS to RC, Sept. 14, 1930; MS.

27. "the long curve": letter from CS to RC, Aug. 27, 1930, MS.

28. "Do you" to "between two": letter from CS to RC, Oct. 18, 1930, MS; "kind of hopelessly": conversation with Helen described in letter from CS to RC, Aug. 24, 1930, MS.

29. "O Charlie dear": letter from RC to CS, Oct. 9, 1930, MS.

30. "Ruth, dear child": letter from CS to RC, [ca. Aug. 19], 1930, MS.

31. "comparatively calm": letter from RC to CS, May 18, 1931; "partly in": letter from RC to CS, May 5, 1931; "a selfish" and "the new circus": letter from RC to CS, Feb. 14, 1931, MS.

Chapter 9. *"In Europe One Can Work!"*

1. "stepped heavily": letter from RC to CS, Feb. 14 or 15, 1931, MS.

2. "exquisite songs" to "consisted of a series": letter from RC to CS, Sept. 6, 1930, MS.

3. "fiasco": Hans Gutman, "The Festivals as Music Barometers," *Modern Music* 8 (Nov.-Dec. 1930): 32; "one of the poorest": Henry Cowell, "Music," *Americana Annual* (1931): 513.

4. "of trends": letter from RC to Henry Allen Moe, Jan. 22, 1931, GF. The American premiere of *Wozzeck* occurred on March 19, 1931, in Philadelphia, under the direction of Leopold Stokowski. "deeply felt": letter from RC to CS, Sept. 6, 1930, MS.

5. On Bartók: letter from RC to CS, Sept. 10, 1930, MS.

6. "Breathless": letter from RC to CS, Sept. 25, 1930, MS; "overflowing": Josef Rufer, "Letter from Berlin," *Pro Musica Quarterly* (May–June 1929): 51.

7. "carnival": Lillian Mowrer, *Journalist's Wife* (New York: William Morrow, 1937), 242.

8. On the 1930 election, see John Willett, *Art and Politics in the Weimar Period: The New Sobriety, 1917–1933* (New York: Pantheon, 1978), 202; "Feuermann": Bruno Walter, quoted in Otto Friedrich, *Before the Deluge: A Portrait of Berlin in the 1920s* (New York: Harper and Row, 1972), 323; "the great days": Otto Klemperer, *Minor Recollections* (London: Dobson Books, 1964), 44.

9. "dear inevitable flowers": letter from RC to CS, Sept. 26, 1930; "sunshine and": letter from RC to CS, Oct. 17, 1930; "Is there any place" and "lead in me": letter from RC to CS, Oct. 29, 1930, MS.

10. Avoiding Schoenberg and Boulanger: CS in "Remembering Ruth Crawford Seeger," 447; "anxious": CS-UCLA, p. 201; "the United States": interview of CS by MG, Oct. 7, 1974.

11. On composers in Berlin, see Hans W. Heinsheimer, *Best Regards to Aida: The Defeats and Victories of a Music Man on Two Continents* (Alfred A. Knopf, 1968), 18; "At present": letter from RC to CS, Nov. 11, 1930, MS.

12. "ideas": letter from RC to Henry Moe, Jan. 22, 1931, GF.

13. On the chants: letter from RC to CS, Oct. 9, 26, 1930; Holst performance: for details see Judith Tick, "Ruth Crawford's 'Spiritual Concept,'" 246; "a help": letter

from RC to Gerald Reynolds, Oct. 11, 1930, NYPL; "extremely Oriental": RCd, Oct. 1929; "another world" and "a few things": RCd, Feb. 27,1930; "newly discovered": catalogue for the New School for Social Research, spring 1930. Holst's prayers to Hindu deities (e.g., "To Varuna," "To Agni") may also have prodded her into titles.

14. "had wanted": letter from RC to Gerald Reynolds, Oct. 13, 1930, NYPL.

15. "what you will think": letter from RC to CS, Oct. 9, 1930; "there are many": letter from RC to CS, Oct. 11, 1930, MS.

16. "between an objective view": letter from RC to CS, Oct. 26, 1930, MS.

17. "Each voice": letter from CS to RC, Oct. 17, 1930, MS.

18. "kind of new": letter from RC to Gerald Reynolds, Nov. 10, 1930, NYPL; "nothing else": Nicholls, *American Experimental Music*, 114, 130.

19. "chanting done": RC to Gerald Reynolds, Nov. 10, 1930, NYPL; "I may be": letter from RC to CS, Nov. 11, 1930, MS; "how much easier": letter from RC to CS, Oct. 17, 1930, MS.

20. "Please give me": letter from RC to CS, Oct. 26, 1930, MS.

21. "You know": letter from RC to CS, Nov. 11, 1930, MS.

22. "So often": letter from RC to CS, Nov. 11, 1930, MS.

23. "My dear dear": letter from BW to RC, Dec. 26, 1930, MS.

24. On dates of work: letter from RC to Henry Allen Moe, Jan. 22, 1931, GF; letter from RC to CS, Jan. 31, 1931, MS. The exact date of the beginnings of the two of the Three Songs for Voice, Contralto, Oboe and Percussion are unclear. In information given to Claire Reis for early editions of *American Composers Today* (1930 and 1932), Crawford dated the manuscript of Three Songs as 1930. "'In Tall Grass'": letter from RC to Carl Sandburg, Jan 26, 1931, UI; "tremendously impressed": letter from CS to RC, Jan. 7, 1931, MS.

25. "like his Variations": letter from RC to CS, Jan. 30, 1931, MS.

26. "the spiritual force" and "solitary": Hans Gutman, "Young Germany, 1930" *Modern Music* 7 (Feb.–March 1930): 4; "dangerous subjectivity": Hans Mersmann, Hans Schultze-Ritter, Heinrich Strobel, "Die Situation in Deutschland," *Melos* 8 (Aug.–Sept. 1930): 348–49; "abstruse": Hans Mersmann, cited by Stephen Hintin in *The Idea of Gebrauchsmusik: A Study of Musical Aesthetics in the Weimar Republic (1919–1933) with Particular Reference to the Works of Paul Hindemith* (New York and London: Garland, 1989), 102; "the unanimity": Schoenberg quoted in Glenn Watkins, *Soundings: Music in the 20th Century* (New York: Schirmer Books, 1988), 182.

27. "fresh air": *Conversations with Klemperer*, comp. and ed. Peter Heyworth, rev. ed. (London and Boston: Faber and Faber, 1985), 76.

28. "a sophisticated" to "go to America": letter from RC to CS, Oct. 17, 1930, MS.

29. On protests: Peter Heyworth, *Otto Klemperer: His Life and Times*, Vol. 1, 1885–1933 (New York: Cambridge Univ. Press, 1983), 349.

30. "Imagine a kind": letter from RC to CS, Nov. 18, 1930, MS.

31. Susan Cook, *Opera for a New Republic* (Ann Arbor, Mich.: UMI Press, 1988), 17–18; "Someone said": undated note among letters from RC to CS, probably Nov. 1930. No reviews of this concert have yet been found.

32. "Perhaps sometime": letter from RC to CS, Dec. 21, 1930, MS.

33. On Stravinsky: letter from RC to CS, Feb. 23, 1931, MS.

34. "the numbers": Hans Mersmann, Hans Schultze-Ritter, Heinrich Strobel, "Die Situation in Deutschland," *Melos* 8 (Aug.–Sept. 1930): 348–49.

35. "He is a droll": letter from RC to VF, Sept. 1931, VF.

36. "his interest": letter from RC to CS, Dec. 22, 1930; "the poor": letter from RC to CS, Jan. 5, 1931; "As to the future": letter from CS to RC, Jan. 7, 1931, MS.

37. "Life over" to "At the end": letter from Imre Weisshaus to VF, Nov. 14, 1930, VF; on Crawford and politics: interview with Paul Arma by Peter Bloom and James Tick, Sept. 27, 1984.

38. "The Europeans" to "Though it is": letter from RC to VF, Jan. 26, 1931, VF.

39. "always in touch": letter from RC to CS, Nov. 13, 1930; "It is the most": letter from RC to CS, April 20, 1931, MS.

40. "come out of" and "make some of the": letter from RC to CS, Jan. 15, 1931, MS; "So far I have" letter from RC to Adolph Weiss, Jan. 15, 1931, printed in George, "Adolph Weiss," 193.

41. "tremendously excited": letter from RC to CS, Feb. 23, 1931; application for a second year: letter from CS to RC, Nov. 1, 1930, MS.

42. "consolidate her winter's": letter from CS to Henry Moe, Feb. 7, 1931; "forgive the": letter from CS to RC, Feb. 7?, 1931, MS.

43. "Henry says": letter from CS to RC, March 11, 1931, MS; a letter from SRC to CS, Dec. 11, 1978, refers to this concert and to a letter from RC to HC complaining about the lack of organization of the concert.

44. "false impression": Mead, *Henry Cowell's New Music*, 158; "Negro Music": Henry Cowell, "Bericht aus Amerika: Amerikanische Musik" *Melos* 9 (Aug.–Sept. 1930): 364; "might have succumbed": letter from CS to SRC, March 6, 1977; on anti-Semitism and attitudes toward the Jewish influence in jazz, see MacDonald Smith Moore, *Yankee Blues* (Bloomington: Indiana Univ. Press, 1985), 144.

45. "Uriah Heep": letter from RC to CS, Oct. 14?, 1931, MS.

46. Cowell, "Bericht aus Amerika: Die kleineren Komponisten," *Melos* 9 (Dec. 1930): 527.

47. On her return to composing: letter from RC to Henry Allen Moe, Jan. 22, 1931, GF; "a little lazy in seeking": letter from RC to CS, Nov. 11, 1930, MS.

48. "Am I not": letter from RC to CS, Jan. 29(?), 1931, MS.

49. "appropriate all": letter from CS to RC, Feb. 7, 1931, MS.

50. "the finest, dearest": letter from RC to CS, Feb. 22, 1930, MS.

51. "suggestion": letter from CS to RC, March 1, 1931, MS.

52. "in spite of" "haunts," and "That morning": letter from RC to CS, Feb. 22, 1931, MS.

53. "I went to the piano": letter from RC to CS, Feb. 22, 1931, MS.

54. "Dear . . . your idea": letter from RC to CS, March 16, 1931, MS.

55. "It was strange": letter from RC to CS, March 16, 1931, MS.

56. "one movement": letter from RC to Henry Allen Moe, June 13, 1931, GF.

57. "I am so glad": letter from CS to RC, April 7, 1931, MS.

58. "I have told": letter from CS to RC, Feb. 1, 1931, MS; McPhee's "disfavor of female composers" is mentioned in a letter to Henry Cowell in 1936: Carol J. Oja, *Colin McPhee, Composer in Two Worlds* (Washington D.C.: Smithsonian Institution Press, 1990), 96; "calm and enigmatic": "The League of Composers, Feb. 4, March 1," *Modern Music* 9 (March–April 1931): 44. The reviews include Albert Goldberg, "Mina Hager Shows What Song Recital Should Be," *Chicago Herald and Examiner*, March 11, 1931; Edward Moore, "Praise Given Mina Hager After Recital," *Chicago Tribune*, March 10, 1931—"There were songs by Debussy. . . . She likes to sing unmusical songs. Ruth Crawford, one of Chicago's harmonic and melodic insurgents, contributed one. . . ."

59. On grants: letter from CS to RC, March 29, 1931, MS.

60. On Vogel: letter from CS to RC, Feb. 1, 1931, MS.

61. On how Stuckenschmidt helped Antheil in the early 1920s: *George Antheil: Bad Boy of Music* (Garden City, N.Y.: Country Life Press, 1945), 24; "it was a rather": letter from RC to Weiss, Jan. 15, 1931; "He whipped the pages": letter from RC to CS, April 4, 1931, MS.

62. On concert and its "unpleasantnesses": letter from RC to CS, April 13, 1931, MS.

63. "passably well" and "quite a number": letter from RC to CS, April 13, 1931, MS. Other works included a violin sonata by Paul Hoffer and Sonata no. 3 for Violin and Piano, op. 22 by Alexander Jemnitz.

64. "asked me why": letter from RC to CS, May 18, 1931; "what made me": letter from CS to RC, April 21, 1931, MS.

65. "really glad": letter from RC to CS, May 18, 1931, MS; "very sweet": interview of Paul Arma [Imre Weisshaus] with Peter Bloom and James Tick for the author, Sept. 27, 1984.

66. "The work of a lady": unsigned review in a column entitled "Neue Werke," *Morgen Post*, April 14, 1931; "Antheil's": Edgar Mowrer, *Chicago Daily News*, April 9, 1931.

67. "It was interesting": letter from RC to VF, Sept. 1931, VF.

68. On ISCM concert: letter from RC to CS, March 30, 1931, MS; on reaction to Webern: Heyworth, *Otto Klemperer*, 369.

69. "Through my own": letter from RC to CS, April 13, 1931; "Only accidentally": letter from RC to CS, May 18, 1931, MS.

70. "frightfully rude": letter from RC to CS, April 20, 1931; "book should": letter from RC to CS, Jan. 29, 1931, MS.

71. "cocksure": letter from RC to CS, April 15, 1931; on Hindemith's concerto: letter from RC to CS, May 19, 1931, MS.

72. "incomprehensibility": George Antheil, *Bad Boy of Music*, 23. "Germans": letter from RC to CS, May 19, 1931, MS.

73. On Roger Sessions and Klemperer, *Conversations with Roger Sessions*, ed. Andrea Olmstead (Boston: Northeastern Univ. Press, 1987), 160; on RC meeting Copland: letter from RC to Henry Allen Moe, May 15, 1931, GF.

74. "It is strange" and "had gone through": letter from RC to CS, April 24, 1931, MS.

75. "hiding in my shell": letter from RC to CS, Oct. 18, 1931, MS.

76. "I walked along": letter from RC to CS, April 5, 1931, MS.

77. "She should": CS in Wilding-White, "Remembering Ruth Crawford Seeger," 442; "pleasant kind person": letter from RC to CS, May 6, 1931, MS.

78. Conversation with Hertzka: letter from RC to CS, May 6, 1931, MS.

79. "He opened": letter from RC to CS, May 8, 1931, MS.

80. "direction" to "which has crabs": letter from RC to CS, May 14, 1931, MS.

81. "Neo-Romanticism" to "towering personality": letter from RC to CS, May 14, 1931, MS.

82. "He has been": letter from RC to CS, May [4?], 1931, MS; "unity" to "tonalitous": letter from RC to CS, May 8, 1931, MS.

83. "he was very" and "Childlike": letter from RC to CS, May 19, 1931, MS.

84. "It is a lovely": letter from CS to RC, May 9, 1931, MS.

85. "long coda" to "I didn't dream": letter from RC to CS, May 18, 1931, MS.

10. *"Dear Superwoman"*

1. "we have 4000": letter from RC to CS, Nov. 2, 1930, MS.

2. "I don't : letter from CS to RC, Aug. 1930; "Even if": letter from CS to RC, Aug. 27, 1930, MS.

3. "it will be": undated fragment, probably 1922, BS; "Last night": letter from RC to CS, Nov. 2, 1930, MS.

4. "possessiveness" and "save": letter from CS to RC, Nov. 11, 1930, MS.

5. "Like an ache": letter from CS to RC, Nov. 17, 1930, MS.

6. "I have": letter from CS to RC, Nov. 17, 1930, MS.

7. "Shall I be": letter from RC to CS, Dec. 22, 1930, MS.

8. "game of love": letter from RC to CS, March 6, 1931.

9. "Because the oboe": telegram from RC to CS, March 7, 1931, MS.

10. On Mona: letter from Mona Dunlop to CS, Oct. 7, 1930; "horrid": letter from CS to RC, Feb. 25, 1931; "make the formal": letter from CS to RC, Dec. 1, 1930, MS.

11. "[Your letter]": letter from RC to CS, Jan. 5, 1931, MS.

12. "In a way": letter from CS to RC, Feb. 5, 1931, MS.

13. "the song": letter from RC to CS, Feb. 23, 1931, MS.

14. "hated to confess": letter from CS to RC, May 18, 1931, MS; "With the difference": letter from CS to RC, March 17, 1931.

15. "been waiting": letter from RC to CS, Nov. 2, 1930, MS.

16. "You are perfectly": letter from CS to RC, Jan. 20, 1931, MS.

17. "the first": letter from CS to RC, Feb. 3, 1931.

18. "The birds": letter from RC to CS, April 4, 1931, MS.

19. "Dear superwoman": letter from CS to RC, March 11, 1931, MS.

20. "the little woman": letter from CS to RC, Jan. 20, 1931; "presumptuous nose": letter from CS to RC, Nov. 11, 1930, MS.

21. "If the career": letter from RC to CS, May 18, 1931, MS.

22. "sudden awakening" and "up to then": Henry Cowell, "Music," *The Americana Annual* (New York: Americana Corp., 1932), 486; "it turned out that I": Nicolas Slonimsky, "Muses and Lexicons," interview with Thomas E. Bertonneau, U.C.L.A., 1979, p. 116; "it went quite well": letter from RC to CS, June 7, 1931; "phenomenal success": letter from RC to Carl Sandburg, July 23, 1931, UI.

23. "where painters": letter from RC to CS, June 7, 1931, MS; "You can write": letter from CS to RC June [22–28], 1931, MS.

24. "met an entirely": interview of CS by MG, July 28, 1967.

25. "We will work," letter from RC to CS, Oct. 1931, MS.

26. CS on RC in *American Composers on American Music*, 116; "that summer": interview of CS by MG, Oct. 8, 1974.

27. "As we walked": interview of CS by MG, July 28, 1967.

28. "For your sake": letter from CS to RC, April 1931, MS.

29. "done one's best": letter from RC to CS, Oct. 11, 1931, MS; "I'm calm": letter from RC to CS, Oct. 6, 1931.

30. "a silencing of my career": letter from RC to CS, Sept. 24, 1931, MS.

31. "How much" to "My dearest": letter from RC to CS, Oct. 8, 1931, MS.

32. "amiable fight": letter from RC to CS, Oct. 9, 1931; meeting with Boulanger: letter from RC to CS, Oct. 8, 1931, MS.

33. "looked at" to "he was": letter from RC to CS, Oct. 7, 1931, MS.

34. Meeting with Honegger: letter from RC to CS, Oct. 18, 1931, MS.

35. "When I turned": letter from RC to CS, Oct. 7, 1931, MS; "fear" discussed in

letter from RC to CS, Oct. 11, 1931; "Why did Henry": letter from RC to CS, Oct. 30, 1931, MS.

36. "It isn't": letter from RC to CS, Oct. 10, 1931, MS.

37. "She has been": letter from RC to CS, Oct. 10, 1931, MS.

38. "sure that": letter from RC to Nicolas Slonimsky, Jan. 29, 1933.

39. "empty-handed": letter from RC to VF, Sept. 27, 1931, MS.

40. "If I am ever": letter from CS to RC, Oct. 23, 1931, MS.

11. Homecoming

1. The *Red Star*'s arrival is mentioned in the *New York Times*, Nov. 10, 1931; "these two people": interview with Margaret Valiant by MG, May 29, 1980.

2. "butting society": letter from CS to RC, Oct. 4, 1931; "it is remarkable": letter from RC to CS, Oct. 31, 1931; "fairytale": letter from RC to CS, May 18, 1931; "It is very peculiar": letter from CS to RC, Oct. 4, 1931, MS.

3. "a little suspicious": interview of PS by MS, Dec. 8, 1982; "[It] never occurred": telephone interview with PS, June 25, 1983; Constance's reaction: interview with Toshi Seeger, June 3, 1990; *The New York Social Register*, vol. 46, no. 2, for the year 1931, published in 1932, p. 716, lists Mr. and Mrs. Charles L. Seeger, Jr., and their two older sons; they are not in the 1934 edition published in 1933. On being separated since 1927, and on testifying in court: interview with CS3 by MS, April 19, 1983; on the reaction of Charles's parents: interview with PgS, Aug. 14, 1985.

4. "it won't be long": BW quoted in letter from CS to RC, April 30, 1931, MS.

5. "How much" and "Does she": letter from RC to CS, Oct. 1, 1931, MS

6. "left Blanche": interview of CS by MG, Oct. 7, 1974. On living at 1 West 68th: CS-UCLA, p. 176; "very much in love": interview with SRC by MS, Dec. 14, 1982; "platonics" and "I have done": letter from CS to RC, Feb. 1931, MS; "difficulties ahead" to "renunciation": letter from BW to RC, Feb. 16, 1931; "though I miss": un-dated letter from BW to Carl Ruggles, mentioning a performance of Schoenberg's *Gurrelieder*, which received its American premiere with Stokowski and the Philadelphia Orchestra on April 8, 1932, Yale.

7. Interview on the apartment from David K. Dunaway, "Charles Seeger and Carl Sands: The Composers' Collective Years," *Ethnomusicology* 24 (May 1980): 160; stable boys: interview with CS by Andrea Olmstead, July 7, 1977, ISAM; "way to keep" and "formality": letter from RC to CS, Oct. 1931, MS. Charles gave the false date for his alumnus class report in 1933 in the "Harvard College Class of 1908, Twenty-Fifth Anniversary Report, 1933," p. 628. Ruth did likewise in a letter to Nicolas Slonimsky, Jun. 29, 1933.

8. "You realize": telephone interview of PS, March 16, 1988. However, in an interview with Karen Cardullo, June 8, 1979, Pete said that the family was told.

9. Statistics on the unemployed from Arthur M. Schlesinger, Jr., *The Crisis of the Old Order* (Boston: Houghton Mifflin, 1973), 171; "it will be an active one": "Light Cast by Coming Events," *Musical America* 51 (Aug. 1931): 16. On unemployed musicians in New York: Barbara Zuck, *A History of Musical Americanism* (Ann Arbor, Mich.: UMI Research Press, 1980), 156. "Vast numbers": Henry Cowell, "Music," in *The Americana Annual: An Encyclopedia of Current Events* (New York: Americana Corp., 1933), 514.

10. Concert of women composers: letter from CS to RC, Sept. 25, 1931; possibility of Ruth teaching at New School: letter from CS to RC, Sept. 30, 1931; "better keep": letter from CS to RC, Oct. 16, 1931, MS.

11. "hard to jump": letter from RC to CS, Oct. 8, 1931; "*Musical Courier*": letter from CS to RC, Oct. 19, 1931, MS.

12. "earning enough": tape made by CS for MG, July 16, 1967; "I asked": interview with Martha Beck Carragan by Rita Mead, May 22, 1975.

13. The New York Musicological Society, Bulletin no. 2, Nov. 1932.

14. M. Br.-Sch., "Frauen als Komponisten. III Konzert der Ortsgruppe der Internationalen Gesellschaft für Neue Musik," *Hamburger Fremdenblatt*, Dec. 10, 1931. Other works included pieces by Ilse Fromm-Michaels, Natalie Prawossudowitsch, Trude Ritmann, Gertrud Schweizer, Germaine Tailleferre, and Vera Winograda.

15. Peter M. Rutkoff and William B. Scott, *New School: A History of the New School for Social Research* (New York: Free Press, 1986), 55; "few places": Harrison Kerr, "Creative Music and the New School," *Trend* (March–April 1934): 89; "but they were": interview with Arthur Berger, May 2, 1990.

16. "Oscar Ziegler Heard: Swiss Pianist Inaugurates New Concert Hall," *New York Herald Tribune*, Jan. 7, 1931; information on Cowell's course: catalogue of the New School for Social Research, spring 1932; "socialist": interview with Arthur Berger, May 2, 1990; "an intriguing mood picture": untitled review, *New York Daily Mirror*, Jan. 28, 1932.

17. The program of Feb. 16 also included (in order) two songs by Broqua, a string quartet by Roy Harris, the Concerto Arabesque by John Becker, Set for Theater Orchestra by Ives, and "Energia" by Carlos Chavez. "Marked poetic": "Pan American Program at New School," *Musical America* (Feb. 25, 1932): 38. See also the *New York Times* and the *New York Herald Tribune*, Feb. 17, 1932. "Christopher Columbus": Nicolas Slonimsky, *Perfect Pitch: A Life Story* (New York: Oxford Univ. Press, 1988), 123; on the three songs: letter from RC to Carl Sandburg, July 23, 1931, UI.

18. "boos, hisses": Henry Cowell, "Music," *Americana Annual* 1933, p. 516.

19. "Your songs": letter from Nicolas Slonimsky to RC, March 12, 1932; on the second concert, see Deane Root, "The Pan American Association of Composers (1928-1934)," *Yearbook for Inter-American Research* 7 (1972): 58; "delicious": letter from Nicolas Slonimsky to RC, March 16, 1932; "distorted" and "bizarre": *Deutsche Allgemeine Zeitung* (Berlin), March 18, 1932; both reviews cited in Mead, *Henry Cowell's New Music 1925–1936*, 222. On Slonimsky's *Lexicon*, see Slonimsky, "Muses and Lexicons," interviewed by Thomas F. Bertonneau (Los Angeles: Univ. of California, 1979), 180. The program included Pedro Sanjuan's "Sones de Castilla," Roy Harris's "Andante," Carlos Chavez's "Energia," and Alejandro Caturla's "Bembe."

20. On the completion of "Prayers of Steel": letter from RC to Carl Sandburg, Jan. 26, 1931, MS; "ruled the paper" and "quite remarkable": interview with CS by Rita H. Mead, Nov. 15, 1974.

21. "Crawford's three songs": letter from HC to Charles Ives, Dec. 30, 1932, Yale.

22. On the ISCM festival: Anton Haefli, *Die Internationale Gesellschaft für Neue Musik: Ihre Geschichte von 1922 bis zur Gegenwart* (Zurich: Atlantis Musikbuch Vereng, 1982); "cause of": letter from Roger Sessions to Nadia Boulanger, Dec. 27, 1932. In a letter of Jan. 13, 1933, Sessions told Copland, "I certainly make no stand against it, but wish America were represented by something better for its second work; I don't find the Crawford songs good or even particularly 'interesting.'": *The Correspondence of Roger Sessions*, ed. Andrea Olmstead (Boston: Northeastern University Press, 1992), 204; "Esoteric": Roger Sessions, "Music in Crisis," *Modern Music* 10 (1933): 63–78, reprinted in *Roger Sessions on Music*, 37; "hermetic": R. Aloys Mooser, *Regards sur la Musique Contemporaine 1921–1946* (Lausanne: Librairie F. Rouge, 1947), 196; ISCM jury members: June 4, 1933, clipping from *New York Herald Tribune* located in ISCM clippings file at BPL.

23. Other works included the Sonatina for flute and clarinet by Juan Carlos Paz, Clarinet Sonatina by Hungarian Isa Krejci, three songs op. 71 by Ernst Krenek, and a wind quintet by Ljubica Maric; "carefully and skillfully": letter from Frederick Jacobi to RC, June 15, 1933; Henry Prunières called the style dated: "Le XIe Festival de la S.I.M.C.," *La Revue Musicale* 14 (July–Aug. 1933): 141–46; Crawford's music called "grotesque": Karl Holl, "Das internationale Musikfest 1933," *Melos* 7 (July 1933): 250–52; "moving between": Erich Steinhard, *Die Auftakt* 13 (1933): 102–4; "seemed to have": Frederick Jacobi, "Festival Impressions—Amsterdam, 1933," *Modern Music* 11 (Nov.–Dec. 1933): 30–33.

24. "Ruth Crawford's Settings of Sandburg Poems Issued by New Music," *Musical America* (May 25, 1933): 53; "New Music, San Francisco," *Musical Digest* (March 1933): 23.

25. "extremely anxious": letter from RC to Nicolas Slonimsky, Jan. 29, 1933, NS-LC. The following handwritten note was added to Slonimsky's copy of the letter: "Thanks for the suggestion about a new work for percussion and string quartet! I'd have done it if I hadn't this one which I am extremely anxious to hear. Cordially, Ruth Crawford." The members of the New World String Quartet were Ivor Karman, first violin; Lucien Baran, second violin; Lotta Karman, viola; and David Freed, cello. The program included Becker's Soundpiece for String Quartet and Piano; Four Songs for String Quartet and Voice by Richard Donovan; Piston's String Quartet (no. 1); Weiss's seven songs for String Quartet and Voice; Seven Songs by Ives; and "Toys," a song by Ruggles. For reviews, see "New American Compositions Heard," *Musical Leader* (Nov. 30, 1933): 2; "All North American Program is Heard," *Musical America* (Nov. 25, 1933): 27.

26. "would rather hear": letter from HC to Charles Ives, Nov. 14, 1933, Ives Collection, Yale University, quoted in Mead, *Henry Cowell's New Music, 1925–1936*, 257; "perhaps the best": Henry Cowell, "Music," in *The Americana Annual: An Encyclopedia of Current Events* (New York: Americana Corporation, 1934), 392.

27. "illustrates": advertising flyer from June 1934; reproduced in Mead, *Henry Cowell's New Music*, 268, more details on 262–65; Irving Kolodin, "American Composers and the Phonograph," *Modern Music* 11 (March–April 1934): 128. Kolodin did not praise the music, however.

28. "The Crawford piece": Harrison Kerr, review of RC's Andante and Adolph Weiss, Three Songs for Piano and String Quartet, *Trend*, March 1934 [n.p.], RC papers; Howard Cushman, "A Woman Composer Considers 'Modern' Music," *New York Post*, Nov. 13, 1933, p. 23.

29. CS quoted in Cushman, "A Woman Composer," p. 23.

12. "Music as a Weapon in the Class Struggle"

1. "I came home" and "There was nothing": interview with PS by MS, Dec. 8, 1982.

2. "completely knocked over": Ray Wilding-White, "Remembering Ruth Crawford Seeger: An Interview with Charles and Peggy Seeger," *American Music* 6 (Winter 1988): 452.

3. "very loyal": CS-UCLA, p. 215.

4. On the Soviet cultural campaign in the 1920s, see David Caute, *The Fellow-Travelers: A Postscript to the Enlightenment* (London: Weidenfeld and Nicolson, 1973), 53; "may become": letter from RC to CS, March 1, 1931, MS.

5. "Marxism was": Richard H. Pells, *Radical Visions and American Dreams: Cultural and Social Thought in the Depression* (Middletown, Conn.: Wesleyan Univ. Press, 1973), 98.

6. "national in": "Platform of the Workers Music League," *Worker Musician* (Dec. 1932): 6.

7. "Working Men": William Lichtenwanger, *The Music of Henry Cowell: A Descriptive Catalog* (Brooklyn: Institute for Studies in American Music, 1986), 140–41; "Cowell telling us": interview with Arthur Berger, May 2, 1990; "my music corresponds" and "Among the bourgeois": editorial, "15 Years," *Worker Musician* 1 (Dec. 1932): 4.

8. "fostering": *Worker Musician* 1 (Dec. 1932): 4; "Here is music": A.L., "Cowell Performers Own Compositions in Piano Recital," *Daily Worker*, Nov. 21, 1933.

9. "American musicians": "Fifteen Years: A Survey of American and Soviet Music," *The Worker Musician*, Dec. 1932, p. 5. For information on the seminar, see Carol Oja, *Colin McPhee*, 447.

10. "deeply involved": letter from CS to MG, March 13, 1974; "Our works were": "Aaron Copland, Composer from Brooklyn," *The New Music* (New York: W. W. Norton, 1968), 161–62; "somehow or other": interview tape made by CS for Judith Rosen, Jan. 18, 1972.

11. "Sacco, Vanzetti" and "Chinaman! Laundryman!" are described in a program of March 27, 1933, as "music written for the Society of Contemporary Music by Miss Crawford." The program is in the Free Library, Philadelphia. On Blitzstein, see Eric Gordon, *Mark the Music: The Life and Work of Marc Blitzstein* (New York: St. Martin's Press, 1989), 71; "Read Agnes": RC papers, undated fragment, ca. early 1930s.

12. H. T. Tsiang, *Poems of the Chinese Revolution*, English edition with an introduction by Upton Sinclair (New York, 1929); "Communist artists": Reuss, "American Folklore, and Left-Wing Politics: 1927–1957" (Ph.D. dissertation, Indiana University, 1971), 53.

13. "a worker's recitation": Mike Gold, *120 Million*, 184–90.

14. Meridel Le Sueur, "Women on the Breadlines," *New Masses* (Jan. 7, 1932), discussed in Charlotte Nekola and Paula Rabinowitz, eds., *Writing Red: An Anthology of American Women Writers, 1930–1940* (New York: Feminist Press, 1987), 2–3.

15. "the singer": letter from CS to MS, Dec. 23, 1976.

16. Seeger's claim and "remorseless": CS in "Remembering Ruth Crawford Seeger," 451.

17. The program also included works by Carlos Chavez, Gerald Strang, Carlos Pedrell, William Grant Still, Adolph Weiss, Amadeo Roldan, Heitor Villa-Lobos, John Becker, and William Russell.

18. "very disgusted": letter from Martha Beck to the author, Dec. 19, 1988; also telephone interview, July 6, 1983; "conscientious essay": F.D.P., "Pan-American Concert Offers Unusual Works," *New York Herald Tribune*, March 7, 1933.

19. On Pazmor's participation: interview tape made by CS for Judith Rosen, Jan. 18, 1972; "fearful, wonderful": "Modernistic Airs Feature Concert/Works of New Authors Given on Contemporary Music Group Program," *Philadelphia Ledger*, March 28, 1933.

20. Advertisements for the Music Olympiad appeared in the *Daily Worker* and in the *New York Herald Tribune*, May 21, 1933, [n.p.], clipping in New York Scrapbooks, NYPL; "a whole day": interview with Elie Siegmeister, Dec. 18, 1985. The simultaneous festival in Moscow is mentioned in "Worker's Music League, Its Role and Activities," from Program Booklet of First American Workers Olympiad-1933; the First International European Olympiad of Workers' Music and Song is described in "Notes," *Music Vanguard* 1, p. 93.

21. On PS attending the festival: interview with PS by Karen Cardullo, June 8, 1979; on the languages of the Communist Party, see Reuss, "American Folklore," 9.

22. "naive": CS in Wilding-White, "Remembering Ruth Crawford Seeger," 451; "extraordinary": letter from CS to Barbara Krader, May 16, 1968; "magnificent": interview with CS by Karen Cardullo, June 11, 1978; "Music is": *Daily Worker*, Feb. 23, 1935.

23. "the search": Pells, *Radical Visions*, 158-59, 178; CS, "On Proletarian Music," *Modern Music* 11 (March–April 1934): 121-27; see also Barbara A. Zuck, *A History of Musical Americanism* (Ann Arbor: UMI Research Press, 1980), 121–25.

24. Richard Reuss lists Seeger's contributions to the *Daily Worker* in "Folk Music and Social Conscience: The Musical Odyssey of Charles Seeger," *California Folklore Society* 38 (Oct. 1979): 221–38; on the Composers' Collective membership, see Carol J. Oja, "Marc Blitzstein's *The Cradle Will Rock* and Mass-Song Style of the 1930s," *Musical Quarterly* 73 (1989): 447.

25. "Songs are as necessary": Mike Gold, quoted in Zuck, *A History of Musical Americanism*, 114; "From ego-poet": Gold, *120 Million*; "Broadway, or commercial music": interview with CS, quoted in David Dunaway, "Charles Seeger and Carl Sands," *Ethnomusicology* 24 (1980): 164.

26. "Lenin! Who's That Guy," reprinted in Zuck, *A History of Musical Americanism*, 128.

27. "Everybody" to "Ruth was always": interview with Elie Siegmeister, Dec. 18, 1985. The minutes of the Collective list RCS as a member in 1935, Blitzstein Collection.

28. "male preserve": Elinor Langer, *Josephine Herbst: The Story She Could Never Tell* (New York: Warner Books, 1983), 132. The other women in the Composers' Collective were Janet Barnes (Jeannette Barnett) and Esther Spitzer.

29. "The moment we": letter from CS to MG, March 13, 1974.

30. "Oh, it was very cute" to "with this": interview with Siegmeister, Dec. 18, 1985; on "Stimmtausch": letter from Siegmeister to CS, Aug. 19, 1977.

31. The Music Vanguard sponsored a concert at the New School for Social Research on May 12, 1935, which featured the work of the collective, including "Charlie Schwab" and "Not If, But When" by Carl Sands and "The Three Brothers" by Siegmeister. CS's mention of RCS's song: interview of CS by MG, July 28, 1967.

32. "Let the young people": Aaron Copland, "A Note to Young Composers," *Music Vanguard* 1 (March–April 1935), 14.

33. Carl Sands, "The Workers Music League–Its Tasks," program for Second Workers Music Olympiad, 1934, 1.

34. "less and less": CS-UCLA, p. 221.

35. "Thank God": letter from RCS to CS, July 28, 1935; "Krawford the Komunist": letter from RCS to CS, June 14, 1934, MS.

36. "it was apparent" to "anxious to bring": Harvard Class report of 1938, p. 121.

37. "practically never": interview of CS with Karen Cardullo, June 11, 1978; "remained in contact": interview of VF with Ruth Julius and Elizabeth Wood, May 1977.

38. "neither Ives": this material is not in the Crawford letter to Slonimsky of Jan. 29, 1933, in Ruth's file, where it had been excised, but it is in the Nicolas Slonimsky Collection at LC.

39. "overflowing" and "virile and highly": Marjory Fisher, quoted in Mead, *Henry Cowell's New Music*, 277; "beautiful through": Johanne Salinger, review in *Courier du Pacifique*, Jan. 16, 1934; on the preludes: Marjory M. Fisher, "Modern Songs Heard by New Music Society," *San Francisco News*, April 10, 1924, wrote that "Ruth Crawford's two Preludes bespoke a rich human quality in the composer's use of modern idioms, and there was an irresistible touch of humor in the finale of the second"; Alexander

Fried, "Taste for Modernism Satisfied in New Music Society Recital," *San Francisco Chronicle*, April 10, 1934, less enthusiastically wrote that Crawford's "impressionistic dissonances" were "colorful and plausible"; "beauty and eloquence": Redfern Mason, quoted in Mead, *Henry Cowell's New Music*, 288.

40. Claire Reis, comp., *American Composers: A Record of Works Written Between 1912 and 1932*, 2nd ed. (New York: International Society for Contemporary Music, U.S. Section, 1932), 35–36.

41. "long siege": letter from RCS to Nicolas Slonimsky, Jan. 1933; "first movement": CS in Henry Cowell, ed., *American Composers on American Music: A Symposium*, (1933; 2nd ed. New York: Frederick Ungar Pub. Co., 1961), 116.

42. CS in Cowell, *American Composers on American Music*, 118.

43. "our symphonic": letter from RC to CS, May 6, 1931, MS; "the only thing": interview with CS by Karen Cardullo, June 11, 1978.

44. "I remember deciding": RCS, autobiographical sketch, ca. 1947.

45. Reis, *American Composers: A Record*, (p. 35), lists the Three Songs, Two—not three—Chants for Women's Voices, the String Quartet, and Four Diaphonic Suites.

13. "A Thread Unwinding": Music, 1930-1932

1. Henry Glassie, *Turkish Traditional Art Today* (Bloomington: Indiana Univ. Press, 1993), 185.

2. "one of our": letter from RC to CS, Sept. 23, 1931; "string": letter from RC to CS, January 30, 1931; "moving linear": interview with Lou Harrison, July 13, 1990.

3. For *Tradition and Experiment in the New Music*, see CS, *Studies in Musicology II: 1929–1979*, ed. Ann M. Pescatello (Berkeley: University of California Press, 1994); "modern dissonant music": in archival materials of the Folklore Institute of America, Indiana University, with "Informal Notes on Transactions and Lectures" Second Session, Mrs. Charles Seeger, "Use of Folklore in Nursery Schools," June 19–Aug. 16, 1946; "credo": letter from RC to Edgard Varèse, May 19, 1948; "medium": letter from RC to VF, Jan. 26, 1931, VF.

4. "In response to what": Joseph Straus, *The Music of Ruth Crawford* (Cambridge: Cambridge Univ. Press, 1995), 4.

5. "smallest melodic unit" and "any neume can be": *Tradition and Experiment*, 138, ibid., 149.

6. "several of the Beethoven": tape made by CS for MG, July 28, 1967; "full of short": RCd, Feb. 1930; "changing 'Frankie and Johnnie'": interview of CS by MG, March 19, 1968.

7. "This concept": tape made by CS for MG, July 28, 1967.

8. "most of her melodies": Straus, *Music of Ruth Crawford*, 41–42.

9. Willi Apel translates the relevant quotation from Plato in *the Harvard Dictionary of Music*, 2nd ed. (Cambridge: Harvard Univ. Press, 1969), 383, as "the heterophony and diversity of the lyre, with the tune of the chords being different from the poet's melody. . . . "

10. "can be given" to "many devices": *Tradition and Experiment*, 196; "modeling the line": Charles Seeger, "Ruth Crawford," *American Composers on American Music*, 115; "monody . . . the kind" letter from CS to RC, Feb. 3, 1931, MS.

11. "follows the speech" to "line 7": letter from CS to RC, Feb. 3, 1931, MS; "so much freedom": David Nicholls, *American Experimental Music*, 93–94.

12. "a play in": letter from CS to Steven E. Gilbert, July 9, 1969; "perfectionism" and "preciosity": letter from CS to RC, Feb. 3, 1931, MS.

13. "A while ago": letter from RC to CS, Oct. 2, 1931. The fifths probably refer to line six, "while the evening brings."

14. Seeger recalls the five- and seven-syllable source as "a pattern of syllabic arrangement of a Japanese poem which we'd run across" in CS, tape made for MG, July 28, 1967.

15. "triple passacaglia": RCd, May 1930; the 7-7-7: Charles Seeger, "Ruth Crawford," 113.

16. RC's comments on Riemann: letter from RC to CS, Jan. 11, 1931; "[a]way back": Henry Cowell, "Charles Seeger," in H. Cowell, ed., *American Composers on American Music* (New York, 1933); rpt. ed. (1961), 123. That Seeger knew Wooldridge's work is confirmed by the musical excerpts taken from the *Oxford History of Music* for *Tradition and Experiment in the New Music*, 167.

17. "It is almost": letter from RC to CS, Nov. 18, 1931, MS.

18. Mark Nelson, "In Pursuit of Charles Seeger's Heterophonic Ideal," *Musical Quarterly* 72 (1986): 458–75.

19. "major change": letter from RC to Seymour Barab, Feb. 28, 1950.

20. "similar to Carl's": letter from RC to CS, Nov. 13, 1930, MS.

21. Seeger's number description: Charles Seeger, "Ruth Crawford," *American Composers on American Music*, 113.

22. On order as a masculine value, see Jenny Anger and David A. Brenneman, "Music and the Aesthetic of Masculine Order, as Proposed by A. J. Eddy and W. H. Wright," in *Over Here: Modernism, The First Exile*, catalogue for exhibit at Brown University, April 15–May 29, 1993 (Providence, R.I.: Brown University, 1989): 78–89; "masculine way of thinking": Arnold Schoenberg, *Style and Idea: Selected Writings of Arnold Schoenberg*, ed. Leonard Stein (Berkeley: Univ. of California Press, 1975), 385.

23. "revels in the instability": Straus, "The Music of Ruth Crawford," 224; "fated to dwell": Daniel Singal, "Towards a Definition of American Modernism," *American Quarterly* 39 (summer 1987): 10; "revels in the instability": Straus, "The Music of Ruth Crawford," 224; "a dissolving" and "The defining thing": James McFarlane, quoted by Daniel Singal, "Towards a Definition," 10; "Music must flow": letter from RC to VF, Feb. 7, 1930, VF.

14. "Composing Babies"

1. "And of course": letter from RCS to Nicolas Slonimsky, Jan. 29, 1933; "composing babies": RCS, transcript of Composers Forum/Laboratory Concert.

2. Interview with Margaret Valiant by MG, May 29, 1980.

3. "Baby Michael": letter from RCS to CS, Aug. 17, 1933.

4. "Charlie dearest": letter from RCS to CS, Aug. 20, 1933, MS.

5. "innate grace": interview with Margaret Valiant by MG, May 29, 1980.

6. Interview of Hannah Siegmeister, Dec. 18, 1985.

7. On firing by Damrosch: CS-UCLA, p. 202; "He went out": interview with PS by MS, Dec. 8, 1982; "They were hard up": interview with CS3 by MS, April 19, 1983; "Father didn't ever complain": interview of PS by Karen Cardullo, June 8, 1979.

8. "I wanted": note from RCS to CS, Dec, 21, 1934, MS; "urgent lists" from undated papers, ca. early 1930s; note from RCS to CS, June 14, 1934, or 1935, MS.

9. Carl N. Degler, *Women and the Family in America from the Revolution to the Present* (New York: Oxford Univ. Press, 1980), 413; "bourgeois diversion": Robert Schaffer, "Women and the Communist Party, USA, 1930–1940," *Socialist Review* 9 (May–June 1979): 79.

10. Interview of Hannah Siegmeister, Dec. 18, 1985.

11. Details about RCS, religion and father: tape made by PgS for MG, April 1976.

12. "Please do love me": letter from RCS to CS, April 7, 1934; "Tonight I'm not": letter from RCS to CS, April 18, 1934, MS.

13. "I've felt badly": RCS, undated note, probably spring 1934, MS.

14. "she knew they": interview with CS by MG, Oct. 8, 1974; "[b]eing a composer": telephone interview with VF, June 3, 1990; "took up a good": interview with CS by MG, Oct. 8, 1974.

15. "Instead of making": letter from RCS to CS, April 18, 1934; "Bach's wife": note from RCS to CS, Dec. 21 [1934], MS.

16. Charles Amirkhanian, "Johanna Beyer," [Radio Station] KPFA Program Guide, March 1990/Folio, p. 5.

17. "personage": interview with Arthur Berger, May 2, 1990; "I should have": interview with Minna Lederman, Oct. 23, 1990.

18. "I think: letter from RCS to CS, July 21, 1935; "Don't let": letter from RCS to CS, July 25, 1935, MS.

19. "I hope you will": letter from Elsie Seeger to RCS, July 25, 1935, MS; "it's just dead": letter from RCS to CS, July 28, 1935, MS.

20. "at times": telephone interview with PS, June 25, 1983.

21. "I had so alienated": interview of CS by MG, Oct. 8, 1974.

22. "evil influence": interview of CS by Karen Cardullo, June 11, 1978.

23. "splintered and tortuous": Mike Gold, "Change the World," *Daily Worker*, June 13, 1934, quoted in Zuck, *A History of Musical Americanism*, 5; for critical contemporary assessments of the Composers' Collective, see Robbie Lieberman, "*My Song Is My Weapon*": *People's Songs, American Communism, and the Politics of Culture, 1930–1950* (Urbana: Univ. of Illinois Press, 1989), 39; David K. Dunaway, "Unsung Songs of Protest: The Composers' Collective of New York," *New York Folklore* 5 (Summer 1979): 1–19; "most of the songs": letter from CS to David K. Dunaway, Oct. 28, 1977; Oja, "Marc Blitzstein's *The Cradle Will Rock*," 459; "The battle was one": interview of CS with Karen Cardullo, June 11, 1978.

24. On CS's opinion of Copland: CS-UCLA, pp. 477–78; "left-wing fool's paradise": letter from Lahn Adomian to CS, ca. 1975.

25. "I managed": interview of CS with PnS, April 22, 1977; "wondering how": interview of CS and PgS by Ray Wilding-White, Sept. 17, 1976.

26. "About a month": letter from RCS to Dr. McCandlish, Jan. 2, 1936, MS; "jumped at": CS-UCLA, 260.

27. "partner": Sara Evans, *Born for Liberty*, 7; "I ought": letter from RCS to CS, Nov. 23, 1935, MS.

28. "we were in": letter from RCS to Dr. McCandlish, Jan. 2, 1936, MS.

29. "incurable desk complex": letter from RCS to CS, Nov. 12, 1935, MS.

15. *Discovering "Unmusical" America*

1. Overdue milk bill: interview of John Seeger and Ellie Seeger by MS, Dec. 16, 1982; "Our house": letter from RC to Dr. McCandlish, Jan. 2, 1936, MS.

2. On absence of piano: letter from RCS to Edgard Varèse, May 22, 1948; for reviews of Traubel's concert, see "Helen Traubel Gives Program," *New York Herald Tribune*, April 25, 1936. The program included three songs by John Kessler; Bauer's Four Poems, op. 16; three songs by Marguerite Fischel; Roger Sessions's "On the Beach at Fontana"; and

Ives's "Serenity" and "Walking." The Brazilian group was the Agrupacion nueva musica. "Well, after all": letter from Radiana Pazmor to RCS, March 16, 1938, MS.

3. On the WPA and RA beginnings: Roosevelt, "Annual Message to the Congress," Jan. 4, 1935, in *The Public Papers and Addresses of Franklin D. Roosevelt* (New York: Random House, 1938), 4: 21.

4. "a community": Joseph P. Lash, *Eleanor and Franklin* (New York: W.W. Norton, 1971), 410; "to keep up": memo from Katherine Kellock to CS, Nov. 15, 1935, in Records, Music Unit, U.S. Farm Security Administration, Special Skills Division, Music Unit Miscellaneous, LC.

5. On the Unemployed Artists Group, see Richard D. McKinsie, *The New Deal for Artists* (Princeton: Princeton Univ. Press, 1973), 14; "both very" and "Roosevelt had": interview with Bernarda Shahn, Sept. 6, 1987; "warm and ebullient": interview of Jean Ray Evans, Aug. 4, 1990; "discovering": Roosevelt, "Annual Message to the Congress," Jan. 3, 1938.

6. On CS learning about Sandburg through RC: letter from CS to David Dunaway, Oct. 28, 1977; RCS acknowledges the Bentons in *American Folk Songs for Children*; on RC visiting CS's classes: interview with Minuetta Kessler, June 26, 1992; see also Tom Benton, "Our Saturday Night," record jacket notes to the album *Saturday Night at Tom Benton's*, Decca A-311, 1941.

7. "tremendously enthusiastic": CS-UCLA, p. 243.

8. "Charlie was": interview with AL by MS, Jan. 5, 1983; "to swap": letter from RCS to CS, Nov. 23, 1935, MS; "You're on the right": interview of CS by Vivian Perlis, March 16, 1970.

9. "traditional music": Jannelle Warren-Findley, "Passports to Change: The Resettlement Administration's Folk Song Sheet Program, 1936–1937," *Prospects*, ed. Jack Salzman (New York: Cambridge Univ. Press, 1985), 203; "enough material": Archibald Davison, *Music Education in America: What Is Wrong with It? What Shall We Do About It?* (New York: Harper and Brothers, 1926), 48; "In the distant past": Bruno Nettl, "'Words and Music': English Folksong in the United States," in *Contemporary Music and Music Cultures*, ed. Charles Hamm, Bruno Nettl, and Ronald Byrnside (Englewood Cliffs, N.J.: Prentice-Hall, 1975), 219.

10. "we had been here": letter from RCS to John Becker, Sept. 22, 1939; "the traditional": letter from CS to Mrs. Edith Barker, March 31, 1937.

11. On the Presto equipment: CS-UCLA, p. 244.

12. "minister preaching": letter from RCS to CS, Jan. 2, 1936, MS.

13. "everything": letter from CS to RC, Jan. 1, 1936, MS.

14. On Peggy in hospital: letter from RCS to CS, April 9, 1936, MS; on Tobie: interview with SRC, Dec. 8, 1982.

15. "a bitter": letter from RCS to CS, April 3, 1936; "never been": letter from RCS to CS, April 6, 1936, MS; "It must have": telephone interview of SRC, Jan. 15, 1988; "barely read": letter from RCS to CS, April 9, 1936, MS.

16. "weepful letter": letter from CS to RCS, April 7, 1936, MS.

17. "Sorry to say": letter from RCS to CS, April 9, 1936; "Ruthie": letter from RCS to CS, April 10, 1936; "I'm tired": letter from CS to RCS, spring 1936; "And there's": letter from CS to RCS, undated, April 1936, MS.

18. "visiting": interview of PS by Karen Cardullo, June 8, 1979; for the chronology of early folk festivals, see David Whisnant, *All That Is Native and Fine: The Politics of Culture in an American Region* (Chapel Hill: Univ. of North Carolina Press, 1983), 185.

19. "held the riches": Loyal Jones, *Minstrel of the Appalachians: The Story of Bascom Lamar Lunsford* (Boone, N.C.: Appalachian Consortium Press, 1984), 106.

20. About performers: Bascom Lamar Lunsford Collection, Memorial Library, Mars Hill College, Mars Hill, N.C.; "busy learning": interview of PS by Karen Cardullo, June 13, 1979.

21. "natural people": Jones, *Minstrel*, 1; on Lunsford and RA, p. 67; on Lunsford and PS, p. 134; quoting PS's liner notes for Lunsford's record, *Smoky Mountain Ballads*, Folkways FA 2040, 1953. RCS acknowledged Lunsford in *American Folk Songs for Children* and *Animal Folk Songs for Children*.

22. "Since Roosevelt": *The New Lost City Ramblers Song Book*, ed. John Cohen and Mike Seeger, musical transcriptions by Hally Wood (New York: Oak Publications, 1964), 246; "Rex the Red": *Franklin D. Roosevelt: His Life and Times*, ed. Otis L. Graham, Jr., and Meghan Robinson Wander (Boston: G. K. Hall, 1985), 430.

23. Dept. of Agriculture music: WPA guide to Washington, D.C., p. 152. Other agencies with orchestras were the Bureau of Engraving and Printing, the Procurement Division of the Treasury, Federal Housing, and the Government Printing Office.

24. "Resettlement Folk Singers": Archive of American Folk Song, AAFS tape 1618, described as "sung by the Resettlement Folk Singers at the Department of Agriculture," "An Evening of American Music," Nov. 17, 1937; on Valiant, see Margaret Valiant and Charles Seeger, "Journal of a Field Representative," *Ethnomusicology* 24 (May 1980): 169-210; "rather nondescript": interview of BLH by Karen Cardullo, Aug. 18, 1978.

25. "the 'discovery'": Norm Cohen, "The History of The Folk Song Revival," in *Folk Song America: A 20th Century Revival* (Washington, D.C.: Smithsonian Collection of Recordings, 1991); "led the first": SRC, "Charles Seeger (1886-1979)," *Musical Quarterly* 65 (April 1979): 305–7.

26. "a lot of them": memo by SRC to the Library of Congress, Feb. 18, 1986; "passports": Archie Green, quoted in Jannelle Warren-Findley, "Passports to Change," 197; Benjamin A. Botkin, *A Treasury of American Folklore* (New York: Crown, 1944), includes "A Farmer Comes to Town," "Wayfarin' Stranger," and "The Dodger."

27. All quotations from RCS are from the preface to *Nineteen American Folk Tunes* (New York: G. Schirmer, 1995); "basis of a fresh": John Powell, quoted in Kammen, *Mystic Chords of Memory*, 430; "excesses of Romanticists": Béla Bartók, "The Influence of Peasant Music on Modern Music," 1931, reprinted in *Essays*, ed. Benjamin Suchoff (New York: St. Martin's Press, 1976), 340–44; "His belief that": quoted by Mark Nelson, "Folk Music and the 'Free and Equal Treatment of the Twelve Tones': Aspects of Béla Bartók's Synthetic Methods," *College Music Symposium* 27 (1987): 61; CS, "Contrapuntal Style in the Three-Voice Shape-Note Hymns," *Musical Quarterly* 26 (Oct. 1940): 245.

28. "Babes in the Woods": foreword by PgS to *Nineteen American Folk Tunes*.

29. "would write": telephone interview with Jean Ray Evans, Aug. 4, 1990; "Dusenbury songs": letter from RCS to CS, Oct. 28, 1938; "Of course": letter from RCS to CS, Nov. 5, 1938, MS.

30. Popular collection: letter from RCS to CS, Jan. 29, 1938; details about memo: Archie Green, "A Resettlement Song Sheet," *Bulletin of the John Edwards Memorial Foundation* 11 (1975): 83-84; "[T]his meant": telephone interview with SRC, Jan. 15, 1988.

31. "Because sound": Archie Green, *Only a Miner*, 407; "field recording": Karen Cardullo, "Ruth Crawford Seeger, Preserver of American Folk Music" (Master's thesis, George Washington University, 1980); "many musicians" and "rare and delicate": Arthur Kyle Davis, Jr., "Some Recent Trends in the Field of Folksong," *Southern Folklore Quarterly* 1 (June 1937): 19–23; George Herzog, "Observations and Suggestions

[on Research in Primitive and Folk Music in the United States]," *Southern Folklore Quarterly* 1 (June 1937): 25–27.

32. "choosing Ruth": interview of AL by Karen Cardullo, July 27, 1979; "the head": letter from JL to Ruby Lomax, May 23, 1936, UT; Peter T. Bartis, "A History of the Archive of Folk Song at the Library of Congress: The First Fifty Years" (Ph.D. dissertation, University of Pennsylvania, 1982), 63.

33. "a musical denunciation": telephone conversation with Edward Waters; Engel review cited in D. K. Wilgus, *Anglo-American Folksong Scholarship Since 1898* (New Brunswick, N.J.: Rutgers Univ. Press, 1959), 217; "a disaster": interview of AL with MS, Jan. 5, 1983.

34. "hadn't time": interview of CS with Karen Cardullo, June 11, 1978.

35. "family book": interview with BLH, July 13, 1984.

16. Lomax Country

1. Nolan Porterfield, *Last Cavalier: The Life and Times of John A. Lomax* (Urbana: University of Illinois Press, 1996), 397, 407.

2. "What songs" and "we listened": interview with AL by MS, Jan. 5, 1983.

3. "staggering inventory": interview with BLH, July 13, 1984.

4. "left parentless": interview with BLH, March 8, 1994; "She was completely ex-cited": interview with BLH, July 13, 1984.

5. RCS, Music preface, *Our Singing Country* (New York: Macmillan and Co., 1941), xviii.

6. "She was [also]": interview with BLH, July 13, 1984.

7. Nolan Porterfield, *Last Cavalier*, 408; "American sound" and "She was the fairest": interview with AL by MS, Jan. 5, 1983; "regarded this as a very": interview with BLH, July 13, 1984.

8. On simplicity as the essence of folk song, see Hazel G. Kinscella, *Music on the Air* (New York: Viking Press, 1934), 15; "childhood of the race": T. Jackson Lears, *No Place of Grace: Anti-Modernism and the Transformation of American Culture* (New York: Pantheon, 1981), 529; SRC also used this term in an interview with MS, Dec. 14, 1982; "traditional songs": anonymous source cited in JL and AL, *American Ballads and Folk Songs* (New York: Macmillan, 1934), xxvi.

9. "Alan and Ruth were": interview with PS, March 16, 1988; "Father and Ruth had all": interview with PS by Penny McJunkin Niven, March 18, 1983; on the copies from the archive: letter from AL to RCS, July 12, 23, 1938.

10. "Gateways to magic": interview with PgS, Aug. 14, 1985; "house-tied": letter from RCS to CS, May 28, 1937; "the house resounded": Irwin Silber, "Peggy Seeger— The Voice of America in Folksong," *Sing Out* 12 (Summer 1962): 5; CS's acknowledgment of RCS: interview with Ed Kahn, Nov. 9, 1991; "It feels": letter from RCS to CS, Feb. 11, 1938; on the recording equipment: John A. Lomax, "Field Experiences with Recording Machines," *Southern Folklore Quarterly* 1 (1937): 60.

11. "Saw John": SRC, quoted by Porterfield, *Last Cavalier*, 441; "We could discuss": letter from RCS to JL, Aug. 18, 1937, UT.

12. Charles's furlough is confirmed not only by correspondence between RCS and CS, but also in a memo of Sept. 30, 1952, in CS's FBI file; on Nicolas Sokoloff and the Federal Music Project, see Cornelius B. Canon, "The Federal Music Project of the Works Project Administration: Music in a Democracy" (Ph.D. dissertation, University of Minnesota, 1963), 250; "we got a job": letter from RCS to CS, Jan. 31, 1939, MS; "[John] couldn't": letter from RCS to CS, Feb 7, 1939, MS.

13. "Dallas Avenue": interview with Ray Turner, April 19, 1991; "built up": telephone interview with Bernarda Shahn, Sept. 6, 1987.

14. "calm, a haven" to "so attractive": interview with AL by MS, Jan. 5, 1983.

15. "Getting folk music": tape made by CS for MG, July 1967; "years when youthful": H. Wiley Hitchcock, *Music in the United States. A Historical Introduction*, 3rd ed. (Englewood Cliffs, N.J.: Prentice-Hall, 1988), 189; "long American": Adrienne Fried Block, "Dvorak's Long American Reach," *Dvorak in America, 1892–1895*, ed. John C. Tibbetts (Portland, Ore.: Amadeus Press, 1993), 157–81.

16. "creative reciprocity": B. A. Botkin, "The Folk and the Individual: Their Creative Reciprocity," *English Journal* 27 (1938): 121–35; Charles Seeger, "Grass Roots for American Composers," *Modern Music* 16 (March–April 1939): 143–49; "high art": Harvard, Class of 1908, Thirtieth Anniversary Report, June 1938, p. 123.

17. "Either [Ives]": Charles Seeger, "Charles Ives and Carl Ruggles," *Magazine of Art* 27 (July 1939): 435–37.

18. "[I]t seems as if ": Barbara Zuck, *A History of Musical Americanism* (Ann Arbor, Mich.: UMI Press, 1980), 149.

19. On the Composers Forum series see: Ashley Pettis, "The WPA and the American Composer," *Musical Quarterly* 36 (Jan. 1940): 101–12; Zuck, *A History of Musical Americanism*, 168–82, and Lehman Engel, "New Laboratories and Gebrauchsmusik," *Modern Music* 13 (March–April 1936): 50–52.

20. Martin McCall, "Works of Foremost Composers Heard on W.P.A. Forum," *Daily Worker*, April 12, 1938, p. 7.

21. "these tussles": "Composers on the Grill," *New York Times*, Feb. 13, 1938.

22. A note on the holograph score of the String Quartet 1931 at LC reads: "Gift of the composer, 9 March 1938"; on RCS joining the ACA: letter from Rosalie Calabrese to the author, May 4, 1992.

23. "all the more important": letter from AL to RCS, July 23, 1938; "work in town" to "better to finish": letter from RCS to CS, Nov. 1, 1938, MS.

24. "dangerously so": letter from RCS to CS, Nov. 4, 1938, MS.

25. "Pretty much" to "It was my": letter from RCS to CS, Nov. 4, 1938, MS.

26. "to combine": letter from RCS to CS, Nov. 9, 1938; "It may be": letter from RCS to CS, Nov. 4, 1938, MS.

27. "The quartet": letter from RCS to CS, Nov. 5, 1938, MS.

28. On Copland, see Copland and Perlis, *Copland*, I: 317; "I'm wondering": letter from RCS to CS, Feb. 3, 1939, MS.

29. "like an ogre" to "Alas": letter from RCS to CS, Feb. 3, 1939, MS.

30. "attacks of luxury" and "realized": interview with SRC by MS, Dec. 14, 1982; on teaching piano and theory, letter from RCS to CS, Oct. 25, 1938, MS.

31. "More songs": letter from RCS to CS, Jan. 26, 1939; "some real": letter from RCS to John Becker, Sept. 22, 1939, MS.

32. "their job": letter from RCS to CS, Jan. 31, 1939, MS.

33. "raw cultural material": William Stott, *Documentary Expression and Thirties America* (Chicago: Univ. of Chicago Press, 1986),109; "the whole idea": Warren Susman, quoted in Stott, *Documentary Expression*, 8; "reality": Alan Lomax, "Songs of the American Folk," *Modern Music* 18 (Jan.–Feb. 1941): 138; "has crossed": RCS, preface to *American Folk Songs for Children*.

34. "functionalist": Benjamin Botkin, *A Treasury of American Folklore* (New York: Crown, 1944), 818; "meaning": D. K. Wilgus, *Anglo-American Folksong Scholarship Since 1898* (New Brunswick, N.J.: Rutgers Univ. Press, 1959), 343; "one of the first":

Jerrold Hirsch, "Folklore in the Making, B. A. Botkin," *Journal of American Folklore* 100 (1987): 3.

35. On their discussions: letter from RCS to CS, Jan. 26, 1939, MS.

36. The committee's first meeting is documented in CLS correspondence, box 30, and mimeographed account of the meeting on Dec. 23, 1938; "Federal One" is the short name for the executive order establishing the various projects for the WPA. The publications of the joint committee are George Herzog, ed., *Folk Tunes from Mississippi*, collected by Arthur Palmer Hudson (New York: National Play Bureau, 1937), and Robert Winslow Gordon, *Folksongs of America* (New York: National Service Bureau, 1938).

37. "the black sheep": CS-UCLA, p. 278; "everybody in Washington": AL, "Folk Music in the Roosevelt Era," in *Folk Music in the Roosevelt White House: An Evening of Song, Recollections, and Dance, January 31, 1982*, Program Booklet for the Commemorative Program Presented by the Office of Folklife Programs at the National Museum of American History, January 31, 1982 (Washington: Smithsonian Institution, 1982), 15.

38. On the visit of the king and queen, see Elise K. Kirk, *Music at the White House: A History of the American Spirit* (Urbana and Chicago: Univ. of Illinois Press, 1986), 242–45.

39. "Just talked": letter from RCS to CS, May 21, 1939, MS.

40. Cornelius B. Canon, "The Federal Music Project of the Works Project Administration: Music in a Democracy" (Ph.D. dissertation, University of Minnesota, 1963), 66ff.

41. "discouragements": letter from RCS to CS, fall 1938; "temperaments": letter from RCS to CS, Jan. 27, 1939; "I am such": letter from RCS to CS, Oct. 28, 1938, MS.

42. "Do I miss": and "It is still": letter from RCS to CS, Jan. 25, 1939, MS.

43. "Charlie had courage": telephone interview with Herbert Halpert, Sept. 26, 1989.

44. "emergence into full view": Paul Rosenfeld, "Folksong and Culture-Politics," *Modern Music* 17 (Oct.–Nov. 1939): 21; "day's orgy" and "even though": letter from RCS to John Becker, Sept. 22, 1939, MS; *Papers Read at the International Congress of Musicology*, ed. Arthur Mendel, Gustave Reese, and Gilbert Chase (New York: MENC, 1944).

45. "regional": "Songs for the U.S.," *Time* (May 22, 1939): 46; "Mrs. Roosevelt's Evening of Songs," *Time* (March 3, 1941): 57.

46. Roy Harris, "Folksong—American Big Business," cited in Norm Cohen, *Folk Song America: A 20th Century Revival* (Washington, D.C., Smithsonian Collection of Recordings, 1990), 34; "nucleus of folk": ibid., 26.

47. "imposing presence" and "slight amiable": interview with PgS, Aug. 14, 1985.

48. On Lomax's role: telephone interview of AL, April 27, 1990; on the CBS commissions: Barbara Zuck, *A History of Musical Americanism*, p. 149; "gussied up": AL, "American Folk Music in Radio Broadcasts," *Music Teachers National Association Proceedings* 36 (1941): 60.

49. "She worked hard as hell": interview with PS by Karen Cardullo, June 8, 1979; "Damn it, I wish": letter from RCS to CS, Jan. 6, 1940, MS; date for first performance of "Rissolty, Rossolty" is aircheck tape, Jan. 23, 1940, MS; PS recorded this folk song on *Darling Corey* FA 2003.

50. "I think Charlie": MS talking to PS in an interview of PS by MS, Dec. 8, 1982; "Ruth did a first-rate job": interview with PS, June 3, 1990.

51. "quite a departure": telephone interview with AL, April 27, 1992.

52. "It has been": letter from RCS to Harmony Ives, May 30, 1940, MS.

53. "effective in spite of": Colin McPhee, "Over the Air," *Modern Music* 17 (Jan.–Feb. 1940): 115–16; "Wait til you": letter cited in Carol J. Oja, *Colin McPhee* (Washington: Smithsonian Press, 1990), 321, n.71.

54. "she and Father kind of sloughed it off": interview with PS by MS, Dec. 8, 1982.

55. "got more and more": interview with PS by MS, Dec. 8, 1982.

56. "had read Bartók" to "really represent the tunes": interview with AL by MS, Jan. 6, 1983; "musico-intellectual lambkin": letter from AL to RCS, July 12, 1938; "We had given": interview with AL by MS, Jan. 6, 1983.

57. "we fought": conversation with AL, Oct. 28, 1994; "eternal fencing match": letter from RCS to CS, Jan. 26, 1939, MS.

58. "considerable argument": interview of BLH by Karen Cardullo, Aug. 18, 1978; on tally marks: interview with MS, Dec. 1, 1987; "I'm checking": letter from RCS to CS, Nov. 8, 1939, MS.

59. "I remember once": interview with PS by MS, Dec. 8, 1982.

60. Missed due date: letter from James Putnam to JL, April 4, 1940, UT.

61. "scolding letter": letter from RCS to JL, July 30, 1940, UT.

62. On first proof: letter from RCS to JL, June 30, 1940, UT.

63. *Negro Folk Songs as Sung by Lead Belly*, transcribed, selected and edited by John A. Lomax and Alan Lomax (New York: Macmillan, 1936), 192.

64. "a long-desired" and "though improved" letter from RCS to JL, Oct. 7, 1940, UT.

65. "ask for copies": letter from JL to James Putnam, Nov. 19, 1940, UT.

66. "the changes": letter from JL to Macmillan, June 16, 1941, UT.

67. "the publisher": interview of PS by Karen Cardullo, June 8, 1979; "proud of her work": telephone interview of PS, May 21, 1990; "It just killed": interview of PS by MS, Dec. 8, 1982.

17. *"The Breath of the Singer": Transcriptions*

1. "poetry is superb": Lewis Gannett, "For Lovers of America's Poetry, Song and Soil," *New York Herald Tribune*, Dec. 28, 1941; "Niggah convicts": Carl Engel, in "Views and Reviews," *Musical Quarterly* 21 (1935): 108–9; "loose rambling": Louise Pound, review of *Our Singing Country*, *Journal of American Folklore* (Jan.–March 1943): 79–80; "terrible blow": interview with AL by MS, Jan. 5, 1983.

2. "too detailed": interview with AL by MS, Jan. 5, 1983.

3. "complexity and richness": Alan Lomax, "Songs of the American Folk," *Modern Music* 18 (Jan.–Feb. 1941): 139; "best-balanced": Horace Reynolds, *New York Times Book Review*, Nov. 17, 1940.

4. Finest of the family books: interview with BLH, Jan. 24, 1992; "superior volume": Wilgus, *Anglo-American Folksong Scholarship*, 219; Gene Bluestein, *The Voice of the Folk* (Amherst: Univ. of Massachusetts Press, 1972), 107.

5. "This is what" to "Mrs. Seeger": Marc Blitzstein, "Singing Country," *Modern Music* 19 (Jan.–Feb. 1942): 139–40.

6. "Bonyparte" is the theme of the fourth movement; "has been notoriously neglected": Judith McCulloh, introduction to the reprint edition of Ira W. Ford, *Traditional Music of America* (1940; rpt., New York: Da Capo Press, 1978), viii; "fiddle-picture": ibid., "Bonaparte's Retreat," 129; for a contemporary reissue of Stepp's performance on cassette tape, see "American Fiddle Tunes," ed. Alan Jabbour (Washington, D.C.: Library of Congress, Archive of Folk Culture, AFS L 62), which includes Stepp's performance of "Bonyparte."

7. "Western urban": Bruno Nettl, *The Study of Ethnomusicology: Twenty-nine Issues and Concepts* (Urbana and Chicago: Univ. of Illinois Press, 1983), 64–68.

8. "continue": telephone interview with Archie Green, Feb. 5, 1990.

9. "Father and Ruth": interview of PS, June 3, 1990.

10. She amplified the "question of relationship between this individual metrical norm and the individual metrical norms established by other singers in the singing of this tune and of related tunes within the same tune-family, existent over a specific period of time and within a coherent cultural unit."

11. "The Appendix": letter from RCS to JL, July 7, 1940; "majority usage": letter from CS to Judith McCulloh, Feb. 8, 1970: "The term 'majority usage' was, to best of my knowledge, an invention of my wife Ruth's when she was working on the transcriptions of *Our Singing Country*; but maybe Cecil Sharp or even Percy Grainger used it. . . ."; "repopularizing" to "let them make": letter from CS to George Korson, May 17, 1937.

12. "turning point": interview of CS with Ed Kahn, Nov. 9, 1991; on the repertory from OSC being used by CS, see "Contrapuntal Style in Three-Voice Shape-Note Hymns," 1940, reprinted in CS, *Studies in Musicology 1935–1975*, 250; "Callahan" appears in "Folk Music: USA," in *Grove's Dictionary of Music and Musicians*, 5th ed. (New York: St. Martin's Press, 1955), 387–98. One set of excerpts from RCS's "The Music of American Folk Songs" and CS's articles demonstrates my point. She writes:

> *Adherence to a dramatic level throughout the song as a whole*: With few exceptions, the singer sets the dramatic mood at the beginning of the song and maintains that mood throughout. Dramatization in the conventional style of fine-art performance, with emphasis on fluctuation of mood, is scarcely ever heard on these disks. The singer does not try to make the song mean more, or less, than it does. No special emphasis is given to words or details which the sophisticated singer would tend to point up. The strong dramatic conviction with which the singer begins his song underlies each stanza from first to last; the gay stanza, or the comic, is sung in precisely the same manner of musical expression as the tragic and the dignified. The tune makes no compromises, is no slower nor faster, no softer nor louder. There is no climax—the song "just stops."

And further:

> *Adherence of dynamic level set at the beginning of the song*: With few exceptions, the singers of these songs maintain approximately the same level of loudness or softness from phrase to phrase and from stanza to stanza throughout the song. The calculated gradations of broad dynamic levels so characteristic of fine-art performance, with emphasis on climax and morendo, is not typical of folk singing recorded on these disks.

The following appears in CS's "Versions and Variants of 'Barbara Allen,'" 1966, reprinted in *Studies in Musicology*, 284:

> Loudness is comparatively unorganized. It is customarily regarded as a characteristic of the way a whole piece or substantial part of it is performed. . . . Even by the elite, the professional or fine art musician, loudness is not articulated beyond the somewhat vague steps of *pp, p, mp, mf, f, ff*, and so on. None of these has any significance in traditional ballad singing. Thus, while continual variance in loudness is the rule in twentieth-century concert music (and in the singing of folk songs by professional or professionally influenced performers), in the folk art the tendency is to invariance.

And further, in his article "Singing Style" (1958, reprinted in his *Studies in Musicology*, vol. II: *1929–1979*, 403):

> While examples of fairly free or vacillating tempo can be found—as for example, in the field holler—I hazard the proposition that the tradition normally maintains a steady tempo. The unit is the sung syllable, not the counted measure of the professional or fine art. Once established, the tempo is not changed. Gross retardations and accelerations are entirely foreign to the style.

The sentence beginning with "I hazard" suggests that his speculations are fairly recent—and entirely his own.

13. "most influential": Nettl, *Study of Ethnomusicology*, 69; "descriptive music writing": interview with PS, March 16, 1988.

14. "I learned a lot": interview of CS with Karen Cardullo, June 11, 1978; "The difference": Nettl, *The Study of Musicology*, 70.

15. Jackson, *White and Negro Spirituals*, 250; "Take This Hammer": Botkin, *A Treasury of American Folklore*, 913; the fee received from Korson is mentioned in a letter from RCS to AL, June 15, 1949; "I am the": letter from RCS to George Korson, Jan. 1, 1943; on Michael hearing "Harlan County Blues": liner notes for the recording "Tipple, Loom and Rail," *Folkways* FH 5273.

16. "I would so much": letter from RCS to Jean Ritchie, July 31, 1952.

18. American Folk Songs Go to School

1. "Dio is very nice": MS, Oct. 1940

2. RCS, "Mother Writes Her Editor," Aug. 4, 1940. In 1977 CS had an "exact copy made of Ruth's typed original essay, adding her corrections by hand. No editing." Sections reprinted in MG-RCS, pp. 208–12.

3. On domestic comedy, see Nancy Walker and Zita Dresner, *Redressing the Balance: American Women's Literary Humor from Colonial Times to the 1980s* (Jackson, Miss., and London: Univ. Press of Mississippi, 1988), 108; on working women, see Lynn Weiner, *From Working Girl to Working Mother: The Female Labor Force in the United States, 1820-1920* (Chapel Hill: Univ. of North Carolina Press, 1985), 135; "hilarious": interview with PgS by MG, July 22, 1977.

4. "she had worked" to "She virtually": interview of PgS, Aug. 14, 1985.

5. On PAU and salary: Pescatello, *Charles Seeger*, 173.

6. RCS, "Diary of a Corporating [sic] Mother," typescript made by CS for Karen Cardullo, Aug. 11, 1978. "Corporating" is a typo for "Co-operating."

7. "She was in" and "Wringing": interview of CS by Karen Cardullo, Aug. 21, 1978.

8. "music booklet": minutes of Nov. 25, 1941, in Archives of the Silver Spring Cooperative Nursery School.

9. "simple piano": letter from RCS to JL, Nov. 11, 1941.

10. Lorrain E. Waters, "The Utilization of Folk Music in Public School Education," *Music Teachers National Association Proceedings* (Pittsburgh: MTNA, 1941), 52–57; Humperdinck, *Sang und Klang fürs Kinderherz* (Berlin: Neufeld & Henius, 1909); Erk, *Deutscher Liederschatz* (Leipzig: C. F. Peters, 1893–94); "Some of these tunes": interview with PS, June 3, 1990.

11. "had not been": Harold Spivacke, "Archive of American Folk Song," *Music Educators Journal* (Sept.–Oct. 1942): 29–31.

12. "How little": RCS in Stith Thompson, ed., *Four Symposia on Folklore* (Bloomington: Indiana Univ. Press, 1953), 192–93; on Ben Botkin: interview with Gertrude Botkin, June 28, 1989.

13. "Father and Ruth": interview with PS by MS, Dec. 8, 1982; "sort of just": interview with CS by MG, Oct. 8, 1974; "it looks": letter from RCS to Carl Sandburg, June 15, 1942.

14. "Indispensable to": Pescatello, *Charles Seeger*, 175; "They asked me" to "Mr. Lomax": interview with PS and Toshi Seeger, June 3, 1990.

15. "military operation": CS-UCLA, p. 309; "official recognition": Lilla Belle Pitts, "Music Education Advances to a New Front," *Music Educators Journal* 28 (1942): 9. See also James Edward Houlihan, "The Music Educators National Conference in American Education" (Ph.D dissertation, Boston University, 1961), 148ff.

16. "Father and Ruth": interview of PS, June 3, 1990; "because the publisher": "Problems of Working-Class Music," interview with Hanns Eisler, in *Hanns Eisler, a Rebel in Music: Selected Writings*, ed. Manfred Grabs (New York: International Publishers, 1978), 98.

17. Information on Ruth's role as a consultant and on the novelty of including folk music in a textbook from interview with Alan Buechner, Oct. 22, 1982; *New Music Horizons* (New York: Silver Burdett, 1944) acknowledged "Dr. and Mrs. Charles Seeger for research into American folklore and folk song literature" and included one African American song, "Rag Man," arranged by John W. Work, and "Old Molly Hare." "Sanitized": RCS in Stith Thompson, ed., *Four Symposia on Folklore* (Bloomington: Indiana Univ. Press, 1953), 192-93.

18. "Father and Ruth": interview with PS, June 3, 1990.

19. "If my mother": interview with PgS, June 13, 1992; "was disturbed": RCS, "The Use of Folklore for Nursery Schools," transcribed comments from panel at Folklore Institute of America, Indiana University, June 19–Aug. 16, 1946.

20. Information on the link with the League of Women Voters from the Cooperative Nursery School, Silver Spring Nursery School, 1954, p. 45. "We were a very": interview with Fran Irving and Jane Irving Bond, July 13, 1991.

21. Katherine Taylor, *Parent Cooperative Nursery Schools* (New York: Teachers College, Columbia Univ. Press, 1954), 1. The movement is discussed in these articles: "Nursery School," *New York Times*, March 14, 1943, p. 26; Catherine MacKenzie, "Home vs. Nursery Child," *New York Times Sunday Magazine*, June 27, 1943, p. 22, and Nov. 7, 1943, p. 32. The number of cooperatives in the area: letter from RCS to Rose Gregg, [Feb.] 1947; the literature on cooperatives includes: Nathalia Walker, "Twenty Mothers Go to School," *Parents' Magazine* (Sept. 1941): 28–29; Ruth Leigh, "How to Start a Nursery School," *Good Housekeeping* (Dec. 1942): 27; Ann Ross, "What Seven Mothers Did. Mothers Have Time for War Work," *Parents' Magazine* (May 1943): 96–97; Catherine MacKenzie, "Nursery Co-Op," *New York Times Magazine*, April 17, 1949, p. 36; and Margaret Hickey, "Cooperative Play Schools. Communities Find the Answer," *Ladies Home Journal* (May 1950): 23.

22. "who avoided": RCS, "Diary of a Co-operating Mother," ca. 1941; "like women and": Barbara Hubley Finck, *Parents' Magazine* (Aug. 20, 1945): 25.

23. "had a strong": interview with Fran Irving and Jane Irving Bond, July 13, 1991; "Glenore said": Betty Wright quoted in Betty Claire Scott, "Ruth Crawford Seeger Remembered" (Master's thesis, University of Maryland, 1975); "most enthusiastic": letter from RCS to JL, Nov. 11, 1941.

24. On paying the tuition: minutes from the Silver Spring Cooperative; Laura McCarteney, *Songs for the Nursery School* (Cincinnati, Ohio: Willis Music, 1937).

25. "dramatize the rhythm": letter from RCS to Harcourt, Brace and Co., June 6, 1942.

26. "didn't say": tape made by PgS for MG, April 1976.

27. Concerning Washington, D.C., as a progressive stronghold: the Association for the Advancement of Progressive Education was founded there in 1919. See Lawrence A. Cremin, *The Transformation of the School: Progressivism in American Education, 1876-1957* (New York: Alfred A. Knopf, 1962), 240, 278. "Helping mothers": letter from RCS to JL, Nov. 11, 1941; "we mothers": RCS in Thompson, ed., *Four Symposia*, 191–94.

28. "Self-Expression Through Music": Harold Rugg and Ann Shumaker, *The Child-Centered School* (New York: World Book, 1928), 184–203; "production of individuality": Evelyn Weber, *The Kindergarten: Its Encounter with Educational Thought in America* (New York: Teachers College, Columbia Univ. Press, 1969), 162–63.

29. "making a sort": RCS in *American Folk Songs for Children*, 33; "the child composes": Carl E. Seashore, "Music Before Five," *Parents' Magazine* (March 1939): 66.

30. Ballad text from Arthur Kyle Davis, *Traditional Ballads of Virginia* (1929; rpt., Charlottesville: Univ. of Virginia Press, 1969). See texts for "Sir Hugh" or "The Jew's Daughter," which is Child no. 155, pp. 400–415.

31. "My mother's greatest": interview with PgS, Aug. 14, 1985; "one of the master": Robert Cantwell, *When We Were Good: The Folk Revival* (Cambridge: Harvard University Press, 1966), 278.

32. "Mary Was a Red Bird," OSC, p. 98; its discovery mentioned in John A. Lomax, *Adventures of Ballad Hunter* (New York: Macmillan, 1947), 253. Benjamin A. Botkin, "The Folk and the Individual," *English Journal of the National Council of Teachers of English* 27 (1938): 129.

19. Dio's Circus

1. "I am running": letter from RCS to S. Watkins, Dec. 26, 1946; on children: interview with PgS, Aug. 14, 1985; "She's pregnant": Harold Spivacke quoted by Rae Korson in an interview with Rae Korson, Nov. 8, 1983; on wanted baby: interview with PgS, Aug. 14, 1985; on RCS's attitudes toward her daughters' names: interview with BS, June 26, 1989.

2. "six months'" to "I looked at": letter from RCS to JL, Nov. 21, 1944, UT.

3. "Silver Spring": letter to Rose Gregg, Feb. 1947; "they asked": interview with PS, March 16, 1988.

4. "Ruth Seeger was": interview with Ruth Holstein, April 18, 1991: "Seeger's Barn": letter from RCS to JL, Nov. 21, 1944, UT; "that's civilization": interview with PgS, Aug. 14, 1985.

5. "old, stable, secure": interview with Inez Seeger, July 25, 1989; "Father set": interview with PnS, April 22, 1985; "I think if it had": interview with PgS, Aug. 14, 1985.

6. "We'd throw": interview with BS, June 26, 1989; "My God": interview with John and Ellie Seeger by MS, Dec. 8, 1982.

7. "an unforgettable center": SRC, "Ruth Crawford Seeger: 1901–1953," *International Folk Music Journal* 7 (1955): 56.

8. "Father had inputs": interview with CS3 by MS, April 19, 1983; "She had to keep": interview with John and Ellie Seeger by MS, Dec. 8, 1982; "I think they": interview with PgS, Aug. 14, 1985.

9. "Buy the big": interview with MS, July 16, 1986.

10. "One of my problems": letter from RCS to CaC, Aug 31, 1945, BS.

11. Carl Crawford's attitudes: based on interviews with Carl's children, Dan Crawford, June 26, 1989, and Mary Crawford Whitman, June 26, 1989, and his granddaughter, Claudia Whitman Hardin, June 26, 1989.

12. "having a good": tape made by PgS for MG, April 1976.

13. On income, interview with PgS, Aug. 14, 1985.

14. "spectacular turnarounds": interview with MS by Karen Cardullo, June 8, 1979; "were a community," "Everybody wanted," and "she'd take whoever": tape made by PgS for MG, April 1976; "house of music": interview with Ellen Parmalee by Ann E. Feldman, July 24, 1989.

15. Information about lessons from interviews with Marion Sibley Gushee, Oct. 17, 1987, Elsa Borman, Aug. 4, 1990, and Charles Miller, July 11, 1984; "American folk material": letter from RCS to JL, Nov. 13, 1943.

16. "jam sessions": interview with PgS, Aug. 14, 1985. Summary of recital programs prepared by Chuck Miller, Jan. 1984, for the author. Additional information from interview with Sylvia Parmalee by Ann E. Feldman, May 25, 1989.

17. "democratic professionalism": letter from Chuck Miller to the author, Aug. 20, 1984.

18. "She was a celebrity": telephone interview with Rae Korson, Nov. 8, 1983.

19. On Institute: letter from Eric L. Montenyohl to the author, Sept. 1, 1992.

20. "dissonant modern music": "Informal Notes on Transactions and Lectures" from the Second Folklore Institute, Indiana University; "I have no memory": letter from William Lichtenwanger to the author, June 20, 1988; "paid something": letter from CS to Barbara Krader, May 16, 1968.

21. "If she answered": letter from RCS to Ruth Liebes, ca. 1942, PgS.

22. "a lot more than": interview with PS, June 3, 1990.

23. "topping everything" to "it needs": letter from RC to Carl Sandburg, June 25, 1942, UI; "with such a bad contract": letter from RCS to JL, Nov. 13, 1943, UT; on two children's book series: letter from RCS to Alan Collins, June 2, 1947.

24. "from all the Lomax books": letter from RCS to JL, Nov. 21, 1944, UT.

25. Plans for children's song book: letter from JL to RCS, Dec. 16, 1944, UT.

26. "hard bargainer": interview with MS, Oct. 2, 1984; details regarding *Folk Song U.S.A.* from letters between JL and Arthur W. Wang, Sept. 24, 26, Nov. 15, 23, 28, Dec. 11, 1945, and letter from JL to Arthur Crowell, Nov. 1, 1945, UT.

27. "challenge": letter from RCS to JL, Oct. 18, 1945.

28. "overwork": letter from JL to RCS, Oct. 23, 1945, UT.

29. Song titles: letters to JL from Arthur Wang, Nov. 23, 28, 1945, UT.

30. "how to manage": letter from CS to JL, Jan. 3, 1946, UT.

31. "the old method" and "I know your generation": interview with AL by MS, Jan. 5, 1983; Alan Lomax believes he may have sent tapes of his singing; "compository" and "a newly delimited artifact": Harold Spivacke, "Remarks on Copyright for the Conference on the Character and State of Studies in Folklore," *Journal of American Folklore* (1946): 525.

32. "garbled": letter from CS to JL, Aug. 20, 1945, UT.

33. "a large part": letter from CS to JL, Aug. 20, 1946; "delighted": letter from JL to CS, Aug. 27, 1946; "we are very": letter from RCS to JL, Oct. 3, 1946.

34. "cocks of the walk": interview with PgS, Aug. 14, 1985; "Ruth was pure": interview with BLH, Jan. 4, 1992; "outlook towards the songs": interview with MS by Karen Cardullo, Aug. 9, 1978.

35. Archie Green, "Sound Recordings, Use and Challenge," in Richard Dorson, ed., *Handbook of American Folklore* (Bloomington: Indiana Univ. Press, 1983), 435; on

PS and AL, see David King Dunaway, *How Can I Keep From Singing: Pete Seeger* (New York: McGraw-Hill, 1981), 63.

36. "were really quite": interview with PS by MS, Dec. 8, 1982.

37. The reputation of *Folk Song: U.S.A.* declined later. See D.K. Wilgus, *Anglo-American Scholarship Since 1898*, p. 220.

38. "achieving that": Richard A. Waterman, "Folk Song: U.S.A.," along with other books in *Journal of American Folklore* 63 (July–Sept. 1950): 377–78; "overemphasized Negroes": George Pullen Jackson, "Folk Song U.S.A.," *Notes: Quarterly Journal of the Music Library Association* 5 (June 1948): 377. Another review is by William G. Tyrell, "Folk-Song Anthologies," *New York Times*, May 16, 1948.

39. On Emrich and Botkin: John Alexander Williams, "Radicalism and Professionalism in Folklore Studies: A Comparative Perspective," *Journal of the Folklore Institute* 11 (1975): 227; description of project as collaborative: letter from RCS to Alan Collins, Feb. 4, 1953; "to help Charlie": letter from RCS to Ben Botkin, Oct. 3, 1946.

40. "inclusive" to "A bright idea": letter from RCS to Carl Sandburg, April 7, 1947.

41. "most intensive" letter from RCS to Rose Gregg, Feb. 1947. This and all other letters with Rose Gregg are owned by Moira Gregg.

42. "that summer": letter from RCS to Rose Gregg, Feb. 1947.

43. "everybody was joyful": letter from RCS to Rose Gregg, Feb. 1947; "eventually Alan": interview with MS, March 8, 1991.

44. letters of entrée: letter from Benjamin A. Botkin to "Nat," June 11, 1945, UN; "delay and silence": letter from RCS to Ben Botkin, Oct. 3, 1946.

45. "quite scared" to "made fun of": interview with Sylvia Parmalee, with Ann E. Feldman, May 25, 1989; *Fireside Book of Folk Songs*, ed. Margaret Bradford Boni and arranged for piano by Norman Lloyd (New York: Simon and Schuster, 1947).

46. Cooney's recollections: letter from Barbara Cooney to the author, April 4, 1988; "It would be": letter from Glenore Horne to Cooney, Nov. 19, 1948; "Their being so comfortable": letter from RCS to Rose Gregg, Oct. 31, 1948.

47. "I am not": letter from RCS to Peggy Lesser, May 3, 1948.

48. "gallons": interview with PgS by Judith and Ron Rosen, Feb. 21, 1972; "never again": letter from RCS to CaC and Katherine Crawford, Aug. 2, 1948.

49. "We used to": letter from CS to Archie Green, April 29, 1976.

50. "members of our family": interview of PgS with MG, Nov. 7, 1977; absence of radio: tape by PgS for MG, April 1976; "I'd be teaching": interview of PS, June 3, 1990.

51. "attached a kind": tape made by SRC, Jan 1, 1983; fourteen-hour work days: letter from RCS to Benjamin Botkin, Oct. 3, 1946.

52. "Charlie's deafness": interview with CS3, June 30, 1989.

53. On morning ritual: interview with MS by MG, Nov. 7, 1977; "had the menu": interview with PgS by Judith Rosen, Jan. 18, 1972; "run the whole": tape made by PgS for MG, April 1976.

54. "eagle eye": tape made by PgS for MG, April 1976; "somewhere in the back": telephone interview with Inez Seeger, July 25, 1989; "did not want": interview with BS by Judith Rosen for the author, Dec. 15, 1984; "must have come": telephone interview with MS, Mar. 8, 1991; "Dio had this": interview with PnS by MG, Oct. 8, 1974.

55. "Ah, that's a fine": Carol Coy, "Elizabeth Cotten: A Legend Tells Her Story," *Folkscene* 2 (April 1974): 16; Hollie I. West, "Folk Grandma: 'Freight Train's' Libba Cotten Turns 87," *Washington Post*, Jan. 5, 1980.

56. "had the common" to "if the man": interview with PgS, Aug. 14, 1985.

57. "He worked": conversation with Virgil Thomson, spring 1985 or 1986; "work her": interview with Inez Seeger, July 25, 1989.

58. On Vanett Lawler: CS-UCLA, p. 325; "best friend": interview of BS by Judith Rosen, Dec. 15, 1984.

59. "kindred souls": interview with Rae Korson, Nov. 8, 1983; "mega-intellect": interview with PgS, Aug. 14, 1985; "worshipped Charlie": interview with AL by Karen Cardullo, July 27, 1977; "She thought": interview of Sylvia Parmalee by Ann E. Feldman, May 25, 1989.

60. "I didn't": interview of PgS with Judith and Ronald Rosen, Feb. 21, 1972; "held her own": interview of PS by Karen Cardullo, June 8, 1979.

61. "Nice Charlie": tape made by SRC, Jan. 27, 1983.

62. "She glowed": interview with PgS, Aug. 14, 1985.

63. On double braids: interview with BS, June 26, 1989; "her own color": tape by PgS made for MG, April 1976.

20. A Fork in the Road

1. "incredible" and "unforgivable": letter from RCS to Rose Gregg, Feb. 1947; "sweeping": Carl Sandburg, publicity material from Doubleday, 1948.

2. There are too many reviews to list here. A sampling taken from RCS's clippings file includes: William G. Tyrrell, "American Folk Songs for Children," *New York Times*, Dec. 19, 1948; *Nebraska Farmer*, Sept. 3, 1949; *New Yorker*, Dec. 11, 1948, p. 139; *Saturday Review of Literature*, Dec. 11, 1948: 37; *Daily Worker*, Dec. 19, 1948; Beatrice Landeck, *People's Songs Bulletin*, n.d.; *Parents' Magazine* (Dec. 1948); "one of the finest": Marion Emrich, *Journal of American Folklore* 63 (Jan.–March 1950); "You will love this book": unattributed review, *Notes: Quarterly Journal of the Music Library Association* 5 (Dec. 1948): 166; "The collection": Marion Bauer, *The Baton*, Jan. 1949; Virgil Thomson, "Three Collections," *New York Herald Tribune*, Nov. 21, 1948.

3. "out of exile": letter from RCS to CaC and Katherine Crawford, Aug. 2, 1948, MS.

4. "most representative": letter from Edgard Varèse to RCS.

5. Information about psychiatrist: interview with MS, Jan. 5, 1983; "straining at the leash": interview with PgS, Aug. 14, 1985; "bitter antifeminism": Lois Banner, *Women in Modern America: A Brief History* (New York: Harcourt, Brace Jovanovich, 1974), 214–15; "Any creative person": letter from MS to Anne Pescatello, June 28, 1985, cited in Pescatello, *Charles Seeger*, 204; "lured into": interview with PgS, Aug. 14, 1985.

6. On shift in attitudes: Elliott Antokoletz, *Twentieth-Century Music* (Englewood Cliffs: Prentice-Hall, 1992), 369.

7. On Radiana Pazmor: listing of concert on April 9, 1944, in a letter from the Phillips Gallery to the author; RCS, "Letter to Miss Prink" refers to a performance of the String Quartet 1931.

8. "thoroughly absorbing": review, Virgil Thomson, *New York Herald Tribune*, March 16, 1949.

9. On Schoenberg concert: "Full House Hears Schoenberg Music," H.T., *New York Times*, Nov. 24, 1949, p. 46. The concert included the New York premiere of Schoenberg's Serenade, op. 24, and the "Ode to Napoleon," op. 41.

10. "It took me": letter from RCS to Carl and Charlotte Ruggles, Dec. 6, 1949, Yale.

11. Letter from RCS to Wallingford Riegger, Nov. 1949.

12. On Marion Bauer: interview with George Perle, Feb. 15, 1987; "she did not like": telephone interview with Felix Galimir, April 19, 1992; "although nearly": Francis D. Perkins, "Contemporary Music Group," *New York Herald Tribune*, April 13, 1950.

13. "All of a sudden": tape made by PgS for MG, April 1976.

14. "kept notes": interview of CS3 with MS, April 19, 1983; "she either": interview with Inez Seeger, July 25, 1989; on plans for new work: interview with Marion Sibley Gushee, Oct. 17, 1987.

15. On going to New Orleans for performance: RCS obituary, *Washington Post*, Nov. 20, 1953; "four children": letter from RCS to Alan Collins, April 27, 1950.

16. "My teaching schedule": letter from RCS to Benjamin A. Botkin, Dec. 2, 1951, UN.

17. On RCS joining: the 1951–52 National Association for American Composers and Conductors program lists RCS as a member.

18. "vigor" and "almost like": Ray Wilding-White, "Remembering Ruth Crawford Seeger," 454; "I'm sorry": letter from RCS to Benjamin A. Botkin, Dec. 2, 1951, cited in Botkin's review of *American Folk Songs for Christmas*, *New York Folklore Quarterly* (Spring 1954): 74.

19. On contest win: *Sunday Washington Star*, June 8, 1952. The contest was judged by Gordon Smith, Esther Williamson Ballou, Richard Dirksen, and John Yesulaitis; "she wrote": Ray Wilding-White, "Remembering Ruth Crawford Seeger," 454; "absolutely flabbergasted": tape made by PgS for MG, April 1976.

20. "It's not the winning": letter from RCS to Carl and Charlotte Ruggles, June 1952, Yale.

21. "The Wind Quintet": letter from RCS (no date) to Wallingford Riegger while he was at Walden School, 1951–52; "took out this piece": letter from RCS to Miss Rose Marie Grentzer, Oberlin Conservatory, July 3, 1951.

22. "holding her head": tape made by PgS for MG, April 1976.

23. CS's opinion of Suite for Wind Quintet: telephone interview with Alan Stout, March 31, 1985.

24. "dirge": "Remarkable Is the Word for American University Concert," Paul Hume, *Washington Post*, Dec. 3, 1952.

25. On CS hearing *Appalachian Spring*: interview of CS by MG, Oct. 8, 1974; "Copland got": interview of CS by MG, Oct. 8, 1974.

26. On Cowell's new works: Kindler and National Symphony Orchestra gave the world premiere of his "Hymn and Fuging Tune," Dec. 17, 1947; "we stayed": interview of SRC, Jan. 15, 1988; "were the ones": comment by MS in his interview with SRC by MS, Dec. 14, 1982.

27. "problem is pulling": letter from RCS to Vladimir Ussachevsky, Nov. 30, 1951.

28. "perhaps the completing": letter from RCS to Vladimir Ussachevsky, June 17, 1952.

29. On Charles's indecision: interview of SRC by Rita Mead, Dec. 12, 1974; "Charlie's song": letter from RCS to Vladimir Ussachevsky, Aug. 16, 1952.

30. "concern about": Lois Banner, *Women in Modern America: A Brief History* (New York: Harcourt Brace Jovanovich, 1974), 214; "gloried in": tape made by PgS for MG, April 1976; "jealous": interview with BS, June 23, 1989; "proud" and "Charlie was ambivalent": interview with MS, June 14, 1992.

31. "I don't think": interview with SRC by MS, Dec. 14, 1982. Opinions of CS based on family interviews, including telephone interview with MS, June 15, 1994, and telephone interview with Ed Kahn, June 17, 1994.

32. "composed together": Henry Cowell, "Dos Estudios: La Creacion musical en los Estados Unidos," *Boletin Latino Americano de Musica* 5 (Oct. 1941): 108–13; Cowell's view of RCS: telephone interview with Alan Stout, March 31, 1985.

33. "the greatest": Henry Cowell, *American Composers on American Music: A Sym-*

posium (New York: Frederick Ungar, 1962). For Seeger's published remarks on "swiping," see David Nicholls, "Henry Cowell's *New Musical Resources*" in the new edition, Henry Cowell, *New Musical Resources* (1930; New York: Cambridge University Press, 1996), 163–64.

34. "if an idea": interview with SRC by MS, Dec. 12, 1982; "felt responsible": telephone interview with VF, June 3, 1990.

35. On splitting royalties: letter from Alan Collins to RCS, Oct. 21, 1949; "from her experience": letter from Alan Collins to RCS, Nov. 5, 1949.

36. "deflated": letter from RCS to Alan Collins, Oct. 28, 1949.

37. "even more dependent" to "changing her mind": comments from Margaret Lesser, as repeated in a letter from Alan Collins to RCS, Dec. 2, 1949.

38. "So far as I can see": letter from RCS to Naomi Burton, Dec. 7, 1949; "Because, unfortunately or not" to "give me": letter from RCS to Peggy Lesser, Dec. 7, 1949; "as close to a thousand": letter from RCS to Alan Collins, Jan. 15, 1950; ideas for other projects detailed in a letter from RCS to Alan Collins, June 2, 1947; "picture book per author": Lesser quoted in letter from RCS to Alan Collins, Jan. 15, 1950.

39. "got cut in half": letter from RCS to Joanna Colcord, Jan. 23, 1951; "a little hard": letter from RCS to Alan Collins, Feb. 19, 1951.

40. "I was trying to straddle" and "comfort and assistance": letter from RCS to Rose Gregg, Jan. 28, 1951.

41. "quite aggravated": letter from RCS to Benjamin A. Botkin, Jan. 16, 1951, UN; "I haven't yet acquired": letter from RCS to Botkin, Nov. 27, 1950, UN.

42. "Even my tremendous" to "I was wrong": W. Edison Richmond, *Hoosier Folklore* 9 (Dec. 1950): 126–27.

43. "fresh notations": review of *Animal Folk Songs for Children, New York Times,* Jan. 7, 1951.

44. "This book does": letter from RCS to Herbert Halpert, July 18, 1952; "I have done" to "six versions": letter from RCS to AL, March 14, 1950.

45. This is based on a letter from AL to RCS, March 23, 1950; and a letter from RCS to AL, March 29, 1950, MS.

46. "permission agony": letter from RCS to Felix Greissle, Jan. 29, 1953; "I am sure": letter from RCS to Edna Boggs, July 2, 1950 (letter owned by Edna Boggs).

47. "landmark event": interview with Bruno Nettl, Nov. 1990; on Crawford's remarks at conference: Stith Thompson, ed., *Four Symposia on Folklore* (Bloomington: Indiana Univ. Press, 1953), 191–94.

48. "The American system": interview of AL with MS, Jan. 5, 1983.

49. On future projects: letter from RCS to Alan Collins, April 27, 1950.

50. "wasn't very": letter from Alan Collins to RCS, March 13, 1951.

51. On oral tradition and hymnody: letter from RCS to Al Brackman, Aug. 9, 1952; "reached out": interview with PS, May 21, 1990; "commercial setting": Pescatello, *Charles Seeger,* 200–201.

52. On echoing themes: Benjamin A. Botkin, "Folklore as a Neglected Source of Social History," in *The Cultural Approach to History,* ed. Caroline Ware (New York: Columbia Univ. Press, 1940), 315: "In fact, the historian has a real service to render the folklorist by rescuing the folklore from the museum and the archive and from the folklorist himself and giving it back to the people and to history." "Santa Claus": letter from RCS to Herbert Halpert, July 18, 1952.

53. "are rooted deep": Ellen Lewis Buell, "New Christmas Books for Young Readers," *New York Times Book Review,* Dec. 6, 1953, p. 58.

54. "brown faces": interview with PgS, June 14, 1992.

55. Mary Belle McKellar, *Ole Time Religion* (Shreveport, La.: El Karubah Temple, 1927); "She was shocked": interview with PS, June 3, 1990.

56. "I feel so strongly": letter from RCS to Jean Ritchie, July 31, 1952.

57. Brief review in the *New Yorker*, Nov. 28, 1953, p. 202; top ten: *New York Times Book Review*, Dec. 6, 1953; "brilliant essay": Charles Heywood, review in *Western Folklore* (Oct. 1954): 292–93; "there is more": Benjamin Botkin, "Ruth Crawford Seeger," *New York Folklore Quarterly* 10 (Spring 1954): 73–74; D. K. Wilgus, review in *Journal of American Folklore* 67 (Jan.–March 1954): 330–31.

58. "rabidly anti-religious": and Christmas memories: interview with PgS, Aug. 14, 1985; "They made": interview of Sylvia Parmalee with Ann E. Feldman, May 25, 1989.

21. *"Keep the Song Going": Arrangements*

1. "her accompaniments": tape made by PgS for MG, April 1976.

2. "its most vigorous form" and "something that has": RCS in Stith Thomson, ed., *Four Symposia on Folklore* (Bloomington: Indiana Univ. Press, 1953), 243.

3. "Keeping going" and "Professional music" and "Songs are sung": RCS in ibid., 192–94.

4. "give the feeling": RCS, *Four Symposia*, p. 194; *Work and Sing: A Collection of the Songs That Built America*, selected and arranged by Elie Siegmeister (New York: William R. Scott, 1944), 10–11; Cecil Sharp, *English Folk-Chanteys* (New York: H. W. Gray, 1914); "I have found": letter from RCS to Joanna Colcord, Jan. 23, 1951.

5. "make the piano sound": interview with SRC by MS, Dec. 14, 1982; "American products" to "Music is all important": Robert Gordon, *Folk-Songs of America, 1927-1928* (rpt., Washington: W.P.A., 1936), 71.

6. "sparse and punchy": telephone interview with PgS, June 13, 1992.

7. "some things that": telephone interview with SRC, Jan. 15, 1988.

8. On "Little Brown Dog": letter from RCS to Herbert Halpert, March 13, 1950.

9. "essence of the music" to "What she said": interview with Sylvia Parmalee by Ann E. Feldman, May 25, 1989.

22. *"Wading in Grace"*

1. "virtual cliché": Kammen, *Mystic Chords of Memory*, 536-38; Lutheran Church Missouri Synod: letter from William A. Kramer to RCS, Oct. 2,1953; Silver Burdett: letter from Venila B. Colson to RCS, Aug. 26, 1952; *Childcraft*: letter from Joanna Foster to RCS, Oct. 31, 1952; film company: letter from Silas E. Johnson to RCS, April 3, 1952; record for preschool hard-of-hearing children: letter from Kay Fleetwood to RCS, May 11, 1951; on mainstreaming folk music: Beatrice Landeck, *Children and Music: An Informal Guide for Parents and Teachers* (New York: William Sloan, 1952). Landeck adopted *American Folk Songs for Children* as a textbook in music education courses, as did Alan Buechner, teaching at Harvard.

2. On her intentions to compose more folk song arrangements: letter from RCS to Vincent Persichetti, Aug. 12, 1952; the panel on "Child Development and the Arts" took place at the PTA meeting of the Bradley School in Bethesda, Maryland on Feb. 6, 1951; information on the TV show "Mothers, Inc." in letters between RCS and Alan Collins, March 21-March 24, 1949; "real children" to "marvelous, and she was marvelous": PgS, quoted in Ray Wilding-White, "Remembering Ruth Crawford Seeger: An Interview with Charles and Peggy Seeger," *American Music* 6 (1988): 449.

3. On preparing children: The Silver Spring Nursery School newsletter for Dec. 1950–Feb. 1951 mentions "the few weeks that Ruth Crawford Seeger worked with our children" and says a group illustrated Mrs. Seeger's theories at the annual Music Teachers National Convention. "You are even better": letter from Marguerite Hood to RCS, May 18, 1951; "You are as perfect": letter from Lilla Belle Pitts to RCS, Dec. 22, 1951.

4. "absolutely fascinated": Ray Wilding-White, "Remembering Ruth Crawford Seeger," 450.

5. "She gave as few": tape by SRC for the author, Jan. 27, 1983.

6. "We had been singing a song" and "We must remember that both the old and the new": RCS, "Keep the Song Going," *National Education Association Journal* (Feb. 1951): 93; "ushering in an era": Norm Cohen, "*Folk Song America: A 20th Century Revival*" in booklet to accompany CD set, Norm Cohen, ed., *Folk Song America: A 20th Century Revival*" (Washington, D.C.: Smithsonian Collection of Recordings, 1990): 31, 41.

7. "[once when]": tape made by PgS for MG, April 1950; "explode when": tape made by MS for Barbara Jepson, ca. 1977–78.

8. "Father and Ruth frowned": interview of PS, June 3, 1990; "because it was Pete": telephone interview with MS, March 8, 1991; on Charles and Pete: Pescatello, *Charles Seeger*, 226.

9. "it was Ruth": interview with PS and Toshi Seeger, June 3, 1990; "I said I'd do a little border": telephone interview with PS, May 21, 1990; "Pete Seeger urged": letter from RCS to Blanche Van Buren, March 29, 1948.

10. On RCS and Decca Records: letter from RCS to Decca Records, April 20, 1950; on collaborations between RCS and PS: letter from RCS to Alan Collins, March 25, 1951.

11. "The only sorrowful thing": letter from Moe Asch to RCS, April 13, 1953.

12. "She had been planning": interview of SRC by MS, Dec. 14, 1982; that there was "some hostility between the first and second family of Seegers" was suggested to me in an interview with Anne Myers Hirschfang, June 23, 1989.

13. "sloppy" and RCS reaction: interview with Sylvia Parmalee by Ann E. Feldman, May 25, 1989; on IMC and UNESCO: letter from Jack Bornoff to RCS, Jan. 29, 1953; "buried": letter from RCS to Felix Greissle, Jan. 29, 1953.

14. On query: letter from RCS to Alan Collins, Feb. 4, 1953; "I am very happy": letter from Felix Greissle to RCS, Feb. 4, 1953.

15. "She was": Ray Wilding-White, "Remembering Ruth Crawford Seeger," p. 454; "She told me that she had cancer": telephone interview with Gertrude Pinkus, Aug. 4, 1990.

16. The discussion on CS's FBI file is based on documents received from the Department of State under the FOIA.

17. "Honestly, with": letter from RCS to Alan Collins, Feb. 4, 1953; on Christmas book: letter from RCS to Alan Collins, Feb. 15, 1953; "Might it be": letter from RCS to Alan Collins, March 3, 1953.

18. "looked like": interview with Sylvia Parmalee by Ann E. Feldman, May 25, 1989; on June 7 program: courtesy Sylvia Parmalee; "Why was it controversial?": PS quoted in David King Dunaway, *How Can I Keep from Singing: Pete Seeger* (New York: McGraw-Hill, 1981), 157.

19. "swallowed whole": letter from RCS to Lillian Bragdon, Aug. 1, 1953.

20. "There were so" letter from RCS to Alan Collins, Aug. 1, 1953; "The intent was": interview with SRC by MS, Dec. 14, 1982.

21. "ideal guest": letter from RCS and CS to Benjamin Botkin, Sept. 2, 1953.

22. "No one has": letter from CS to CaC, Oct. 31, 1953.

23. "to send her": letter from CS to CaC, Oct. 31, 1953; "managed them" and "managing the family": interview with Sarah Miller, July 11, 1984.

24. "Imagine me in bed": interview with SRC by MS, Dec. 14, 1982.

25. "Why is it": letter from Alan Collins to RCS, Sept. 17, 1953; "Don't faint": letter from RCS to Alan Collins, Oct. 8, 1953.

26. On new Suite: letter from Robert Russell Bennett to RCS, Oct. 9, 1953. Apparently the package was mishandled as it was returned to RCS in October. On acceptance: letter from RCS to Bennett typed by CS, Oct. 19, 1953; "one of": letter from CS to William A. Schroeder, Nov. 24, 1953.

27. "I'm sure it was": interview of PS by MS, Dec. 8, 1982; "It isn't fair": telephone interview with PS, June 25, 1983; "last memory": interview with PS, June 3, 1990; "She was leaning": interview with PS by MS, Dec. 8, 1982.

28. "I had been thinking": RCS quoted by SRC in interview with SRC by MS, Dec. 14, 1982 and repeated in tape made by SRC for the author, Jan. 27, 1983.

29. "gravely ill" to "Other members": letter from CS to Alan Collins, Nov. 15, 1953.

30. "as keenly": letter from CS to Lillian Bragdon, Nov. 20, 1953; "the one without" to "less likely to confuse": letter from RCS to Lillian Bragdon, Nov. 14, 1953.

31. "During that week": tape made by PgS for MG, April 1976.

32. On RCS's death: letter from CS to Lillian Bragdon, Nov. 20, 1953; on back-order of copies: letter from Alan Collins to CS, Nov. 17, 1953; "special thrill": "Christmas Early for Book Fair," *Washington Post*, Nov. 12, 1953.

33. "He went someplace for breakfast": interview with SRC with MS, Dec. 14, 1982.

34. "I hasten" to "The making": letter from CS to Lillian Bragdon, Nov. 20, 1953.

35. "It was a tribute" to "The life was gone": interview with PgS, Aug. 15, 1985.

Epilogue

1. "The trouble": AL quoted by MS, Jan. 7, 1983, at a concert at Folk City, New York.

2. "family of musicians": *The New Grove Dictionary of American Music*, ed. H. Wiley Hitchcock and Stanley Sadie (New York: Macmillan, 1986), vol. 4, 181.

3. "tries to maintain": Bruno Nettl, "Words and Music: English Folksong in the United States," in Charles Hamm, Bruno Nettl, and Ronald Byrnside, eds. *Contemporary Music and Music Cultures* (Englewood Cliffs, N.J.: Prentice-Hall, 1975), 195; "coalition": interview with MS, *Boston Globe*, July 28, 1989.

4. "his stature": James Porter, "Muddying the Crystal Spring: From Idealism and Realism to Marxism in the Study of English and American Folk Song," in *Comparative Musicology and Anthropology of Music*, ed. Bruno Nettl and Philip V. Bohlman (Chicago: Univ. of Chicago Press, 1991), 124.

5. *American Folk Songs for Children* is cited repeatedly in Lois Chosky, *The Kodaly Method: Comprehensive Music Education from Infant to Adult* (Englewood Cliffs, N.J.: Prentice-Hall, 1974).

6. For the influence of Crawford on Harrison and Cage, see Nicholls, *American Experimental Music*, 196, 205. On Mumma, see Richard S. James, "ONCE: Microcosm of the 1960s Musical and Multimedia Avant-Garde," *American Music* 5 (Winter 1987): 372. Wolff has recently titled a new composition "For Ruth Crawford" on hatART CD

6156. On Carter, see David Schiff, *The Music of Elliott Carter* (New York: Da Capo Press, 1986), 69n. For Perle's analysis, see George Perle, "Atonality and the Twelve-Tone System in the United States," *Score* (July 1960): 51–66. Gilbert Chase's assessment is in *America's Music*, rev. 2nd ed. (New York: McGraw-Hill, 1966). Eric Salzman's strong interest in early American modernism, advocated in books and criticism, was also important.

7. Two important reviews of the Fine Arts Quartet's recording are Andrew Porter, "Modern Pleasures," *New Yorker*, Feb. 10, 1973, and John Rockwell, review in *High Fidelity* (July 1973). The retrospective concert by the Performers' Committee for Twentieth-Century Music, now known as Continuum, was on February 19, 1975, at Columbia University. The New York Philharmonic Concert on November 10, 1975, was funded in part by the feminist magazine *Ms*.

8. "I don't understand": interview with PgS, Aug. 15, 1985.

9. "Ruth was quite": CS, letter to Karen Cardullo, Aug. 11, 1978; on "MCP": interview with CS3, June 30, 1989.

10. "composer of genius": Wilfrid Mellers, *Music in the New Found Land*, 2nd ed. (New York: W. W. Norton, 1987), new preface; "She has been": letter from Nicolas Slonimsky to the author, March 4, 1986.

selected bibliography

Manuscript Sources

The Music Division of the Library of Congress holds the papers of the Seeger estate. The collection, Ruth Crawford Seeger Holograph Music Manuscripts and Folk Materials, is available on Microfilm 84/20, 216, Reels 1–5.

A number of people have allowed me access to privately held materials: Paul Arma (Imre Weisshaus): letters and programs; Edna Boggs: letters; Vivian Fine: letters; Moira Gregg: letters; Claudia Whitman Handin: correspondence between Clara Graves Crawford and her family, and diaries and memorabilia from Clara and Clark Crawford; Tristan Hearst: manuscripts, clippings, photographs, and scores relating to Djane Lavoie Herz; Charles Miller: materials from piano lessons with Ruth Crawford Seeger; Steven Spackman: letters of Wallingford Riegger; Barbara Seeger: Ruth Crawford's diaries, childhood writings, high-school scrapbooks, correspondence between Ruth Crawford and Clara and Carl Crawford; Mike Seeger: correspondence between Ruth Crawford Seeger and Charles Seeger; manuscripts of unpublished folk song arrangements and books; photographs; music tapes; Inez Seeger: letters to and from Ruth Crawford Seeger; Jeremy Seeger: memoirs by Charles Louis Seeger; and Peggy Seeger: photographs and letters.

A number of people further contributed to this book by sharing personal correspondence, recollections, and anecdotes: Mildred Baker, Edith Borroff, Radie Britain, Muriel Humphrey Brown, Alan Buechner, Storm Bull, Karen Cardullo, Vivian Fine, Matilda Gaume, Archie Green, Joe Hickerson, Joan Hollander, Fran Irving, Ed Kahn, Mildred Kramer, Charles Miller, Bruno Nettl, Samuel Puner, Alexander Ringer, Alan Stout, Bonnie Wade, Edward Waters, and Marilyn Ziffrin.

Institutional Sources

American Conservatory of Music, Chicago: archives and records
Boston Public Library, Music Division: Nicolas Slonimsky Collection
California State University at Long Beach: materials about Dane Rudhyar
John Simon Guggenheim Memorial Foundation: materials relating to Ruth Crawford
Jacksonville Public Library: materials relating to School of Musical Art; Snyder
    Memorial Church
Mars Hill College, North Carolina: Bascom Lunsford papers
Monterey County Free Libraries, California: clippings and newspapers
Newberry Library, Chicago: materials on Adolf Weidig; Eric De Lamarter; Cliff
    Dwellers Club
New York Public Library, Lincoln Center Research Division: papers of Blanche
    Walton; letters of Gerald Reynolds
Carl Sandburg Home National Historic Site, Flat Rock, N.C.: music manuscripts
Silver Spring Cooperative Nursery School, Silver Spring, Maryland: records, minutes,
    music manuscripts
Stanford University, Department of Special Collections and University Archives: cor-
    respondence of Dane Rudhyar
University of Illinois at Urbana-Champaign, Carl Sandburg Collection: correspon-
    dence; materials relating to the *American Songbag*
University of Miami, Coral Gables, Otto G. Richter Library: clippings file for Bertha
    Foster
University of Nebraska, Lincoln, Archives: Benjamin A. Botkin Collection
Yale University, Beinecke Library: correspondence between Henry Cowell and
    Charles Ives; Carl Ruggles and Blanche Walton

Interviews

Paul Arma (formerly Imre Weisshaus): Interview with Peter Bloom and James Tick,
    Sept. 27, 1984.
Mordecai Baumann, Dec. 3, 1987.
Jane Irving Bond, July 13, 1991.
Harriet and Windsor Booth, March 11, 1985.
Elsa Pinkus Borman, Aug. 4, 1990.
Edith Borroff, April 16, 1988; Nov. 9, 1991.
Gertrude Botkin, June 28, 1989.
Alan Buechner, Oct. 22, 1982.
Arthur Berger, May 2, 1990.
Martha Beck Carragan, July 13, 1983.
Sidney Robertson Cowell: Interview with Mike Seeger, Dec. 14, 1982. Tape made for
    author, Jan. 27, 1983. Interviews with author, Dec. 1, 1987; Jan. 15, 1988; May
    22, 1992.
Gitta Gradova Cottle, Sept. 8, 1984.
Dan Crawford, June 26, 1989.
Jean Ray Evans, Aug. 4, 1990.
Eya Fechin, June 27, 1990.
Vivian Fine, Nov. 29, 1984; April 16, 1989; June 3, 1990; Jan. 21, 1991; Aug. 12,
    1991.
Felix Galimir, April 19, 1992.
Archie Green, Nov. 7, 1990; January 22, 1992.

Marion Sibley Gushee, October 17, 1987.
Herbert Halpert, Sept. 26, 1989.
Claudia Whitman Handin, Nov. 10, 1988; June 26, 1989.
Herbert Haufrecht, March 9, 1991.
Lou Harrison, May 7, 1989; July 13, 1990.
Bess Lomax Hawes, July 13, 1984; January 24, 1992; April 27, 1992.
Tristan Hearst: Interview with Nancy Reich, Sept. 7, 1985.
Ann Myers Hirschfang, June 23, 1989.
Joan Hollander, March 31, 1995.
Ruth Holstein, Apr. 18, 1991.
Fran Irving, July 13, 1991.
Dave and Linda Jessup, April 19, 1991.
Ed Kahn, Nov. 9, 1991; June 17, 1994.
Minuetta Kessler, June 26, 1992.
Rae Korson, Nov. 8, 9, 1983.
Minna Lederman, Oct. 23, 1990.
Alan Lomax: Interview with Mike Seeger, Jan. 5, 1983. With author, April 27, 1992.
Charles Miller, July 11, 1984.
Sarah Miller, July 11, 1984.
George Perle, Feb. 15, 1987.
Gertrude Pinkus, Aug. 4, 1990.
Vivian Rogosa Pollack, Jan. 12, 1991.
Dane Rudhyar: Interview with Sorrel Hays, March 19, 1984.
Margaret Sandburg, Dec. 3, 1988.
Ann Scott, Jan. 26, 1986.
Charles Seeger III, June 30, 1989.
Barbara Seeger, June 23, 1989.
Inez Seeger, July 25, 1989; Aug. 6, 1990.
Mike Seeger, Jan. 5, 1983; Nov. 16, 1985; Dec. 1, 1987; Aug. 3, 1988; June 14, 1992.
Peggy Seeger, Aug. 14, 1985; Tape, June 19, 1992.
Penny Seeger, April 22, 1985.
Pete Seeger, March 12, 1983; June 25, 1983; March 16, 1988; May 21, 1990; June 3, 1990.
Toshi Seeger, June 3, 1990.
Naomi Selbst, May 9, 1990.
Bernarda Shahn, Sept. 6, 1987.
Eugene Shuford, Feb. 22, 1984.
Elie and Hannah Siegmeister, Dec. 18, 1985.
Carleton Sprague Smith, April 15, 1988.
Esther Spitzer, April 20, 1985.
Alan Stout, Nov. 17, 1985.
Marion Walton, Feb. 28, 1984.
Helen Watson, Fall 1991.
Mary Crawford Whitman, June 26, 1989.
Jean Anderson Wentworth, Dec. 5, 1992.
Elizabeth Wright, April 19, 1991.
Henrietta Yurchenko, July 7, 1986.

In addition, I have used publicly available interviews, including Karen Cardullo's interviews with Archie Green, Bess Lomax Hawes, Mike Seeger, and Pete Seeger at the Library of Congress; William Ferris's interview of Charles Seeger at the Center for Southern Research, University of Mississippi; Matilda Gaume's interviews with Dan

Crawford, Alfred Frankenstein, Charles Seeger, Mike Seeger, and Margaret Valiant at the Library of Congress; Penny McJunkin Niven's interview of Pete Seeger at the Carl Sandburg Project, University of Illinois; Andrea Olmstead's interview of Charles Seeger for the Institute for the Study of American Music; Vivian Perlis's interviews of Dane Rudhyar and Charles Seeger for the Oral History/American Music Program, Yale University; Sheila Rayner, Clare Rayner, and Bob Newell's interview of Dane Rudhyar for California State University at Long Beach; Betty Scott's interviews of Fran Irving, Margaret Nolte, and Betty Wright at the University of Maryland; Adelaide Tusker and Ann Briegleb's interview with Charles Seeger, Oral History Program, U.C.L.A.

I have also had access to private sources: Ann Feldman's interviews with Ellen Parmalee and Sylvia Parmalee; Ev Grimes's interview with Vivian Fine; Barbara Jepson's interview of Mike Seeger; Ed Kahn's interviews of Charles Seeger; Rita Mead's interviews of Sidney Cowell, Alfred Frankenstein, and Charles Seeger; Judith and Ron Rosen's interviews of Charles Seeger, Barbara Seeger, and Peggy Seeger; Mike Seeger's interviews of John and Ellie Seeger, Charles Louis Seeger III, and Pete Seeger; Penny Seeger's interview of Charles Seeger; Ray Wilding-White's interview with Charles and Peggy Seeger; and Elizabeth Wood and Ruth Julius's interview of Vivian Fine.

Books

Ammer, Christine. *Unsung: A History of Women in American Music*. Westport, Conn.: Greenwood Press, 1980.

Banner, Lois. *Women in Modern America: A Brief History*. New York: Harcourt Brace Jovanovich, 1974.

Bauer, Marion. *Twentieth-Century Music: How It Developed, How to Listen to It*. New York: G. P. Putnam's, 1933.

Bluestein, Gene. *The Voice of the Folk*. Amherst: Univ. of Massachusetts Press, 1972.

Bradbury, Malcolm and James McFarlane, eds. *Modernism, 1890–1930*. New York: Penguin Books, 1976.

Breckenridge, Sophonisba. *Women in the Twentieth Century*. New York: McGraw-Hill, 1933.

Brown, Dorothy M. *Setting a Course: American Women in the 1920s*. Boston: Twayne, 1987.

Cantwell, Robert. *When We Were Good*. Cambridge: Harvard Univ. Press, 1996.

Carter, Elliott. *The Writings of Elliott Carter*. Ed. Else and Kurt Stone. Bloomington: Univ. of Indiana Press, 1977.

Cohen, John, and Mike Seeger, eds. *The New Lost City Ramblers Song Book*. Musical transcriptions by Hally Wood. New York: Oak Publications, 1964.

Copland, Aaron, and Vivian Perlis. *Copland: 1900 through 1942*. New York: St. Martin's Press, 1984.

Cowell, Henry, ed. *American Composers on American Music: A Symposium*. 1933. Reprint. New York: Frederick Ungar, 1962.

Degler, Carl. *At Odds: Women and the Family in America from the Revolution to the Present*. New York: Oxford Univ. Press, 1980.

Denisoff, R. Serge. *Great Day Coming: Folk Music and the American Left*. Urbana: Univ. of Illinois Press, 1971.

Dorson, Richard, ed. *Handbook of American Folklore*. Bloomington: Indiana Univ. Press, 1983.

Dunaway, David. *How Can I Keep from Singing: Pete Seeger*. New York: McGraw-Hill, 1981.

Eisler, Hanns. *A Rebel in Music: Selected Writings*. Ed. Manfred Grabs. New York: International Publishers, 1978.

Gaume, Matilda. *Ruth Crawford Seeger: Memoirs, Memories, Music*. Metuchen, N.J.: Scarecrow Press, 1986.

Gold, Mike. *A Literary Anthology*. Ed. Michael Folsom. New York: International Publishers, 1972.

Gordon, Eric. *Mark the Music: The Life and Word of Marc Blitzstein*. New York: St. Martin's, 1989.

Hartmann, Susan M. *The Home Front and Beyond: American Women in the 1940s*. Boston: G. K. Hall, 1982.

Huyssen, Andreas. *After the Great Divide*. Bloomington: Indiana Univ. Press, 1986.

Kammen, Michael. *Mystic Chords of Memory: The Transformation of Tradition in American Culture*. New York: Alfred A. Knopf, 1991.

Kirk, Elise K. *Music at the White House: A History of the American Spirit*. Urbana and Chicago: Univ. of Illinois Press, 1986.

Liebermann, Robbie. *"My Song Is My Weapon": People's Songs, American Communism, and the Politics of Culture, 1930–1950*. Urbana: Univ. of Illinois Press, 1989.

Lomax, John A. *Adventures of a Ballad Hunter*. New York: Macmillan, 1947.

Luening, Otto. *The Odyssey of an American Composer*. New York: Charles Scribner's Sons, 1980.

Malone, Bill C. *Country Music, U.S.A.*, rev. ed. Austin: Univ. of Texas Press, 1985.

McDonald, William F. *Federal Relief Administration and the Arts*. Columbus: Ohio State Univ. Press, 1969.

Mead, Rita. *Henry Cowell's New Music 1925–1936: The Society, the Music Editions and the Recordings*. Ann Arbor, Mich.: UMI Editions, 1981.

Mellers, Wilfrid. *Music in the New Found Land*. 2nd ed. New York: W. W. Norton, 1987.

Mintz, Steven, and Susan Kellogg. *Domestic Revolutions: A Social History of American Family Life*. New York: Free Press, 1988.

Nicholls, David. *American Experimental Music, 1890–1940*. Cambridge: Cambridge Univ. Press, 1990.

Niven, Penelope. *Carl Sandburg: A Biography*. New York: Scribner's, 1991.

Pells, Richard H. *Radical Visions and American Dreams: Culture and Social Thought in the Depression*. Middletown: Conn.: Wesleyan Univ. Press, 1973.

Pescatello, Ann M. *Charles Seeger: A Life in American Music*. Pittsburgh: Univ. of Pittsburgh Press, 1992.

Porterfield, Nolan. *Last Cavalier: The Life and Times of John A. Lomax*. Urbana: Univ. of Illinois Press, 1996.

Prince, Sue Ann, ed. *The Old Guard and the Avant-Garde: Modernism in Chicago, 1910–1940*. Chicago: Univ. of Chicago Press, 1990.

Reis, Claire. *American Composers Today*. New York: International Society for Contemporary Music, 1930.

———. *Composers in America*. New York: Macmillan, 1938.

Rosenfeld, Paul. *An Hour with American Music*. Philadelphia: J. P. Lippincott, 1929.

Rudhyar, Dane. *Art as Release of Power*. Carmel, Calif.: Hansa Publication, 1930.

Samson, Jim. *Music in Transition*. New York: W. W. Norton, 1977.

Sandburg, Carl. *The American Songbag*. New York: Harcourt Brace Jovanovich, 1955.

———. *The Letters of Carl Sandburg*. Ed. Herbert Mitgang. New York: Harcourt, Brace and World, 1968.

Salzman, Eric. *Twentieth-Century Music: An Introduction.* 3rd ed. Englewood Cliffs, N.J.: Prentice-Hall, 1988.

Scharf, Lois. *To Work and to Wed: Female Employment, Feminism, and the Great Depression.* Westport, Conn.: Greenwood Press, 1980.

Schiff, David. *The Music of Elliott Carter.* 1983; reprinted New York: Da Capo Press, 1985.

Seeger, Charles. *Studies in Musicology 1935–1975.* Berkeley: Univ. of California Press, 1977.

———. *Studies in Musicology II: 1929–1979.* Ed. Ann M. Pescatello. Berkeley: Univ. of California Press, 1994.

Seeger, Pete. *The Incompleat Folksinger.* Ed. Jo Metcalf Schwartz. New York: Simon and Schuster, 1972.

Sessions, Roger. *Correspondence.* Ed. Andrea Olmstead. Boston: Northeastern Univ. Press, 1992.

Singal Daniel, ed. *Modernism in American Culture.* Belmont, Calif.: Wadsworth Pub. Co., 1991.

Slonimsky, Nicolas. *Perfect Pitch: A Life Story.* New York: Oxford Univ. Press, 1988.

Spackman, Stephen. *Wallingford Riegger: Two Essays in Musical Biography.* Brooklyn: Institute for Studies in American Music, 1982.

Stott, William. *Documentary Expression and Thirties America.* Chicago: Univ. of Chicago Press, 1986.

Straus, Joseph. *The Music of Ruth Crawford Seeger.* Cambridge: Cambridge Univ. Press, 1995.

Susman, Warren. *Culture as History: The Transformation of American Society in the Twentieth Century.* New York: Pantheon Books, 1984.

Tawa, Nicholas E. *Serenading the Reluctant Eagle: American Musical Life, 1925–1945.* New York: Schirmer Books, 1984.

Thomson, Virgil. *American Music Since 1910.* New York: Holt, Rinehart and Winston, 1971.

Tischler, Barbara L. *An American Music: The Search for an American Musical Identity.* New York: Oxford Univ. Press, 1986.

Tuchman, Maurice, ed. *The Spiritual in Art: Abstract Painting 1890–1985.* Exhibition Catalogue, Los Angeles County Museum of Art. New York: Abbeville Press, 1986.

Ware, Susan. *Holding Their Own: American Women in the 1930s.* Boston: Twayne, 1982.

Weiner, Lynn Y. *From Working Girl to Working Mother: The Female Labor Force in the United States, 1820–1980.* Chapel Hill and London: Univ. of North Carolina Press, 1985.

Whisnant, David E. *All That Is Native and Fine: The Politics of Culture in an American Region.* Chapel Hill and London: Univ. of North Carolina Press, 1983.

Wilgus, D. K. *Anglo-American Folksong Scholarship Since 1898.* New Brunswick, N.J.: Rutgers Univ. Press, 1959.

Willett, John. *Art and Politics in the Weimar Period: The New Sobriety, 1917–1933.* New York: Pantheon, 1978.

Wolfe, Charles K. and Kip Lornell. *The Life and Legend of Leadbelly.* New York: Harper-Collins, 1992.

Ziffrin, Marilyn. *Carl Ruggles: Composer, Painter, and Storyteller.* Urbana: Univ. of Illinois Press, 1994.

Zuck, Barbara A. *A History of Musical Americanism*. Ann Arbor, Mich.: UMI Research Press, 1980.

Articles and Dissertations

Augustine, Daniel Schuyler. "Four Theories of Music in the United States, 1900-1950: Cowell, Yasser, Partch, Schillinger." Ph.D. dissertation, University of Texas, Austin, 1979.

Bartis, Peter Thomas. "A History of the Archive of Folk Song at the Library of Congress: The First Fifty Years." Ph.D. dissertation, University of Pennsylvania, 1982.

Botkin, Benjamin A. "The Folk and the Individual: Their Creative Reciprocity," *The English Journal of the National Council of Teachers of English* 27 (1938): 121–135.

Canon, Cornelius B. "The Federal Music Project of the Works Project Administration: Music in a Democracy." Ph.D. dissertation, University of Minnesota, 1963.

Cardullo, Karen. "Ruth Crawford Seeger, Preserver of American Folk Music." Master's thesis, George Washington University, 1980.

Cowell, Henry. "Dos Estudios, La Creacion musical en los Estados Unidos." *Boletín Latino Americano de Musica* 5 (Oct. 1941): 108–13.

———. "Bericht aus Amerika: Die kleineren Komponisten." *Melos* 9 (Dec. 1930): 526–29.

———. "Music." In *The Americana Annual: An Encyclopedia of Current Events*. New York: Americana Corporation, 1927–1934.

Cowell, Sidney Robertson. "Charles Seeger (1886–1979)." *Musical Quarterly* 65 (April 1979): 305–7.

———. "Ruth Crawford Seeger: 1901–1953." *International Folk Music Journal* 7 (1955): 55–56.

Dunaway, David K. "Charles Seeger and Carl Sands: the Composers Collective Years." *Ethnomusicology* 24 (May 1980): 159–68.

———. "Unsung Songs of Protest: The Composers Collective of New York." *New York Folklore* 5 (summer 1979): 1–19.

Epstein, Dena. "Frederick Stock and American Music." *American Music* 10 (Spring 1992): 20–52.

Filene, Benjamin. "'Our Singing Country': John and Alan Lomax, Leadbelly, and the Construction of an American Past." *American Quarterly* 43 (Dec. 1991): 602–24.

Flemm, Eugene. "The Preludes for Piano of Ruth Crawford Seeger." D.M.A. dissertation, University of Cincinnati, 1987.

Gaume, Matilda. "Ruth Crawford Seeger: Her Life and Works." Ph.D. dissertation, Indiana University, 1973.

———. "Ruth Crawford Seeger." In *Women Making Music: The Western Art Tradition 1150-1950*, ed. Jane Bowers and Judith Tick, 370–88. Urbana: Univ. of Illinois Press, 1986.

———. "Ruth Crawford: A Promising Young Composer in New York, 1929–30." *American Music* 5 (Spring 1987): 74–84.

George, William B. "Adolph Weiss." Ph.D. dissertation, University of Iowa, 1971.

Gilbert, Steven E. "The Ultra-Modern Idiom: A Survey of New Music." *Perspectives of New Music* 12 (Fall–Winter 1973): 282–314.

Green, Archie. "Thomas Hart Benton's Folk Musicians." *John Edwards Memorial Foundation Quarterly* 12 (Summer 1976): 74–90.

———. "A Resettlement Song Sheet." *John Edwards Memorial Foundation Quarterly* 11 (1975): 80–84.

————. "Charles Louis Seeger (1886–1979)," Obituary, *Journal of American Folklore* 92 (Oct.–Dec. 1979): 391–99.

————. "Vernacular Music: A Naming Compass," *Musical Quarterly* 77 (Spring 1993): 35–46.

Greer, Taylor. "Critical Commentary on Tradition and Experiment in the New Music." In Charles Seeger, *Studies in Musicology II: 1929–1979,* ed. Ann Pescatello. Berkeley: Univ. of California Press, 1994.

Halpert, Herbert. "Coming into Folklore More Than Fifty Years Ago." *Journal of American Folklore* 105 (Fall 1992): 442–57.

Hawes, Bess Lomax. "Reminiscences and Exhortations: Growing Up in American Folk Music." *Ethnomusicology* 39 (Spring–Summer 1995): 179–92.

Herzog, George. "Observations and Suggestion on Research in Primitive and Folk Music in the United States." *Southern Folklore Quarterly* 1 (June 1937): 25–27.

Hirsch, Jerrold. "Folklore in the Making, B. A. Botkin." *Journal of American Folklore* 100 (1987): 3–38.

Hisama, Ellie. "Gender, Politics, and Modernist Music: Analyses of Five Compositions by Ruth Crawford and Marion Bauer." Ph.D. dissertation, City University of New York, 1996.

————. "The Question of Climax in Ruth Crawford's String Quartet, Movement 3." In *Musical Pluralism: Aspects of Structure and Aesthetic in Music since 1945,* ed. Elizabeth West Marvin and Richard Hermann. Rochester, N.Y.: Univ. of Rochester Press, 1992.

Houlihan, James Edward Jr. "The Music Educators National Conference in American Education." Ph.D. dissertation, Boston University, 1961.

Jepson, Barbara. "Ruth Crawford Seeger: A Study in Mixed Accents." *Feminist Art Journal* (Spring 1977): 13–17.

Karpf, Juanita, "'Pleasure from the very smallest things': Trichordal Transformation in Ruth Crawford's Diaphonic Suites," *Music Review* 53/1 (February 1992): 32–46.

Kerber, Linda. "Separate Spheres, Female Worlds, Woman's Place: The Rhetoric of Women's History." *Journal of American History* 75: (Summer 1988): 9–39.

Lomax, Alan. "Songs of the American Folk." *Modern Music* 18 (Jan.–Feb. 1941): 137–39.

————. "American Folk Music in Radio Broadcasts." *Music Teachers National Association Proceedings* 36 (1941): 58–61.

Lomax, John A. "Field Experiences with Recording Machines." *Southern Folklore Quarterly* (1937): 57–60.

Lott, R. Allen. "'New Music for New Ears': The International Composers' Guild." *Journal of the American Musicological Society* 36 (1983): 266–86.

Meyer, Felix. "'Thoughtful Briklaying': Zu einigen Werker der americanischen Ultramodernisten' Ruth Crawford." In *Festschrift Ernst Lichtenhahn,* ed. Christoph Ballmes and Thomas Gastmann, 167–92. Winterthur: Amadeus, 1994.

Mirchandani, Sharon. "Ruth Crawford Seeger's Five Songs, Suite no. 2, and Three Chants: Representations of America and Explorations of Spirituality," Ph. D. dissertation, Rutgers University, 1997.

Nelson, Mark. "In Pursuit of Charles Seeger's Heterophonic Ideal: Three Palindromic Works by Ruth Crawford." *Musical Quarterly* 72 (1986): 458–75.

Nicholls, David. "The Music of Ruth Crawford Seeger—A Study in Advanced Compositional Techniques." Ph.D. dissertation, St. John's College, 1981.

————. "Ruth Crawford Seeger: An Introduction." *Musical Times* 124 (1983): 421–25.

Oja, Carol. "The Copland-Sessions Concerts and Their Reception in the Contemporary Press." *Musical Quarterly* 65 (April 1979): 212–29.

————. "Composer with a Conscience: Elie Siegmeister in Profile," *American Music* 6/2 (Summer 1988): 158–80.

————. "Marc Blitzstein's *The Cradle Will Rock* and Mass-Song Style of the 1930s," *Musical Quarterly* 73 (1989): 445–475.

————. "Women Patrons and Crusaders for Modernist Music: New York in the 1920s." In *Women Activists in American Music*, ed. Ralph Locke and Cyrilla Barr. Berkeley: Univ. of California Press, 1996.

Perle, George. "Atonality and the Twelve-Tone System in the United States." *Score* (July 1960): 51–66.

Pettis, Ashley. "The WPA and the American Composer." *Musical Quarterly* 26 (Jan. 1940): 101–12.

Reuss, Richard. "American Folklore and Left-Wing Politics: 1927–1957." Ph.D. dissertation, Indiana University, 1971.

————. "Folk Music and Social Conscience: The Musical Odyssey of Charles Seeger." *California Folklore Society* 38 (Oct. 1979): 221–38.

Root, Deane. "The Pan American Association of Composers (1928–1934)." *Yearbook for Inter-American Research* 7 (1972): 49–70.

Rosenfeld, Paul. "Folksong and Culture Politics." *Modern Music* 17/1: (Oct.-Nov. 1939): 18–24.

Scott, Betty Claire. "Ruth Crawford Seeger Remembered." Master's thesis, University of Maryland, 1975.

Seeger, Charles. "Folk Music: USA." In *Grove's Dictionary of Music and Musicians*. 5th ed. London: Macmillan, 1955.

————. "Reminiscences of an American Musicologist." 1972. Oral History Program, University of California, Los Angeles.

————. "On Dissonant Counterpoint," *Modern Music* 7 (1930): 25–31.

————. "On Proletarian Music," *Modern Music* 11 (1934): 121–27.

Silber, Irwin. "Peggy Seeger—The Voice of America in Folksong." *Sing Out* 12 (Summer 1962): 4–8.

Smith, Catherine Parsons. "A 'Distinguishing Virility': On Feminism and Modernism in American Art Music." In *Cecilia Reclaimed: Feminist Perspectives on Gender and Music*, ed. Susan C. Cook and Judy S. Tsou. Urbana: Univ. of Illinois Press, 1994.

Spragg, Deborah. "Time and Intervallic Language in Crawford's Diaphonic Suite No. 3." *Sonus* 3 (Fall 1982): 39–56.

Upton, William Treat. "Aspects of the Modern Art-Song." *Musical Quarterly* 24 (1938): 11–30.

Warren-Findley, Jannelle. "Musicians and Mountaineers: The Resettlement Administration's Music Program in Appalachia, 1935–37." *Appalachian Journal* 7 (Autumn–Winter 1979): 105–23.

————. "Passports to Change: The Resettlement Administration's Folk Song Sheet Program, 1936–1937." In *Prospects*, ed. Jack Salzman, 197–241. New York: Cambridge Univ. Press, 1985.

Widner, Ronna Lee. "Lore for the Folk: Benjamin A. Botkin and the Development of Folklore Scholarship in America." *New York Folklore* 12 (1986): 1–22.

Wilding-White, Ray. "Remembering Ruth Crawford Seeger: An Interview with Charles and Peggy Seeger." *American Music* 6 (1988): 442–54.

Williams, Grier Moffatt. "A History of Music in Jacksonville, Florida, from 1822 to 1922." Ph.D. dissertation, Florida State University, 1961.

Wolbert, Nancy. "Richard Buhlig, a Concert Pianist: His Career and Influence in the Twentieth Century." M.A. thesis, California State University, Long Beach, 1978.

selected discography

Compositions

Ruth Crawford Seeger. Deutsche Gramaphon, DG 449 925-2, 1997. Oliver Knussen, conductor; Reinbert De Leeuw, piano; Lucy Shelton, soprano; members of the Schönberg Ensemble; New London Chamber Choir.
Music for Small Orchestra
Piano Study in Mixed Accents
Three Songs for Voice, Piano, Oboe, Percussion, and String Orchestra
Three Chants for women's chorus (1930)
String Quartet 1931.
Two Ricercare
Andante for Strings
"Rissolty, Rossolty," Fantasia for Orchestra
Suite for Wind Quintet
(also, Charles Seeger, Variations on "John Hardy")

Music for Violin and Piano by American Women. Gasparo GSCD-300, 1995.
Sonata for Violin and Piano. Catherine Tait, violin; Barry Snyder, piano

White Moon. Songs to Morpheus. Dawn Upshaw, soprano. Nonesuch Records 79364-2, 1996.
"White Moon"

Ruth Crawford Seeger: American Visionary. Continuum, Cheryl Seltzer and Joel Sachs, Directors. Musical Heritage Society, 513493M, 1993.
Suite for Five Wind Instruments
Sonata for Violin and Piano

Two Ricercare
Prelude no. 1
Prelude no. 9
Study in Mixed Accents
Diaphonic Suite no. 1 for Flute
Diaphonic Suite no. 2 for Bassoon and Cello
Three Songs for Contralto, Piano, Oboe, Percussion and Orchestral Obligati

Ruth Crawford: American Masters Series. CRI 658, 1993 (remastering of LP recordings
   from CRI Archive)
Sonata for Violin and Piano, Ida Kavafian, violin; Vivian Fine, piano (1985)
Study in Mixed Accents, Joseph Bloch, piano (1968)
Nine Preludes for Piano, Joseph Bloch, piano (1968)
Diaphonic Suite no. 1 for Solo Oboe, Joseph Ostryniec, oboe (1980)
Three Songs to Poems by Carl Sandburg. Patricia Berlin, mezzo-soprano; Paul Hoff-
   man, piano; Dan Armstrong, percussion (1978)
Suite for Wind Quintet, The Lark Quintet (1970)

The American Innovator. Alan Feinberg, piano. Decca 436 925-2, 1993.
Piano Study in Mixed Accents

Arditi String Quartet. Gramavision R 215 79440.
String Quartet 1931

Clarinet Counterpoints. CPO 999 116-2.
Diaphonic Suite for Two Clarinets. B. Zelinsky and D. Smeyers.

Lucille Field Sings Songs by American Women Composers. Cambria 1037, 1990, with
   Harriet Wingreen, piano.
Five Songs on Poems by Carl Sandburg

Premiere Performances. Delos 1012 (remastering of LP 25405, 1975).
Two Movements for Chamber Orchestra (Music for Small Orchestra), Boston Musica Viva, Richard Pittman, conductor

Songs of America. Elektra/Nonesuch, 1988.
"White Moon" and "Joy," Jan De Gaetani, mezzo-soprano; Gilbert Kalish, piano

Selected Noteworthy LP Performances

Ruth Crawford Seeger. Musical Heritage MHS 91229Z, 1986.
   Five Songs. Poems by Carl Sandburg, Ann E. Feldman, mezzo soprano
   Selections from folk song arrangements: "Those Gambler's Blues," "The Squirrel Is
      a Pretty Thing," "What'll We Do with the Baby?" "Sweet Betsy from Pike"
   Diaphonic Suite for Solo Flute
   Diaphonic Suite for Two Clarinets
   Diaphonic Suite for Oboe and Cello

The Composers Quartet. Nonesuch LP H-71280, 1973.
   String Quartet 1931

The Amati String Quartet. Columbia LP, ML 5477, 1960.
   String Quartet 1931

Andante from *String Quartet 1931*. New Music Quarterly Recordings. New World String Quartet, 1934.

Suite no. 2 for Four Strings and Piano. Pulse. Works for Percussion and Strings. The New Music Consort. Recorded Anthology of American Music. New World Records 319, 1984.

Diaphonic Suite No. 2 for Bassoon and Cello. LP Gasparo GS-108CX, 1981.
Otto Eifert, bassoon; Roy Christensen, cello

Four American Women. Northeastern Records NR 204, 1981.
Preludes for Piano, nos. 6-9; Study in Mixed Accents, Virginia Eskin, piano

Music by Women Composers. Volume 2. Coronet LPS 3121.
Nine Preludes for Piano, Rosemary Platt

America Sings (1920–1950). Vox LP SVBX-5353, 1977.
Chant 1930 ("To an Angel"), Gregg Smith Singers

Folk Song Arrangements

Seeger, Mike and Peggy. *American Folk Songs for Children*. Rounder 8001, 1977.
———. *American Folk Songs for Christmas*. Rounder 0268, 1989.
———. *Animal Folk Songs for Children*. Rounder 8023, 1992.
Seeger, Peggy. *Animal Folk Songs for Children*. Smithsonian Folkways, SF 7551, 1958.
Seeger, Pete. *American Folk Songs for Children*. Smithsonian Folkways, SF 45025, 1962.

index

Note: In the index, all subentries mentioning "Crawford" refer to Ruth Crawford Seeger; all subentries mentioning "Seeger" refer to Charles Seeger.

437